Contents

Credits

The publisher would like to thank Mark Shenton for his help and advice on this project.

Picture credits

The publisher would like to thank the following for their kind permission to reproduce their photographs:

(Key: b-bottom; c-centre; l-left; r-right; t-top)

Alamy Images: Alan King 249, Andres Rodriguez 3, Andrey Kekyalyaynen 65, Antony Nettle 69, Art Kowalsky 290, Creativeact-Education Services 105, David J Green 21, Dennis Hallinan 306, Dmitry Erokhin 71, Glenn Murray 263, Imagebroker 303, Jim Holden 11, Juice Images 35, Matthew Richardson 9, Nicola Asuni 123, Office 183, Photostock-Israel 374, Susan E Degginer 307, Trigger Image 241; **Andy Boyce**: 361; **Claudio Bacinello/Photographers Direct**: 72; **Corbis**: Construction Photography 4, Rachel Frank 39; **David Green/ Photographers Direct**: 212, 215; **David Roberts**: 292; **Getty Images**: Chris Ryan / OJO Images 63, Kalim Saliba 156, Reportage 291; **Graham Hare**: 359; **Health & Safety Executive**: 7; **iStockphoto**: Thomas Perkins 54, Paul Prescott 40; **Pearson Education Ltd**: David Sanderson 22tl, 22tr, 22l, 22r, 22bl, 22br, Gareth Boden 107; **Peter Garwood/Photographers Direct**: 368; **Press Association Images**: Larry McDougal / The Canadian Press 230; **Science & Society Picture Library**: 355; **Science Photo Library Ltd**: Andrew Brookes National Physical Laboratory 147, Andrew Lambert Photography 199, 201, 351, Lockheed Martin Corporation / NASA 138, Martyn Chillmaid 188, Maximilian Stock 294, Pasieka 209, Rosenfield Images 347, Sheila Terry 185, 298; **Shutterstock**: Andresr 237, Edyta Pawlowska 305, Jesper Skov 261, Ronen 345, StD 229, Stocklite 227, Hano Uzeirbegovic 44; **Thinkstock**: Brand X Pictures 301, Comstock 37, 265, 349, Creatas 67, Digital Vision 1, 145, Hemera 187, 287, iStockphoto 22cl, 22cr, 103, 225, Pixland 149; **Tomislav Stajduhar/Photographers Direct**: 354; **Warren McConnaughie/Photographers Direct**: Warren McConnaughie 27

Cover images: *Front*: **Corbis**: Bill Varie / Surf
Back: **Science Photo Library Ltd**: Andrew Brookes National Physical Laboratory

All other images © Pearson Education

Every effort has been made to trace the copyright holders and we apologise in advance for any unintentional omissions. We would be pleased to insert the appropriates acknowledgement in any subsequent edition of this publication.

BTEC
Level 3

edexcel
advancing learning, changing lives

ENGINEERING

LEVEL 3

Ernie Cooke | Robert Jones | Bill Mantovani
David Roberts | Bryan Weatherill
Series editor: Andy Boyce

BTEC National

A PEARSON COMPANY

Published by Pearson Education Limited, a company incorporated in England and Wales, having its registered office at Edinburgh Gate, Harlow, Essex, CM20 2JE. Registered company number: 872828

www.pearsonschoolsandfecolleges.co.uk

Edexcel is a registered trademark of Edexcel Limited
Text © Pearson Education Limited 2010

First published 2010

14

10 9 8 7 6 5

British Library Cataloguing in Publication Data
A catalogue record for this book is available from the British Library.

ISBN 978 1 84690 724 1

Development editing by Paul Stirner (DSM Partnership)
Designed by Wooden Ark
Original illustrations © Pearson Education Limited 2010
Illustrated by TechSet and Steve Moulds (DSM Partnership)
Cover design by Visual Philosophy, created by eMC
Cover images Corbis: Bill Varie/Surf
Picture research by Alison Prior and Pearson Education Limited
Index by Indexing Specialists (UK) Ltd
Printed and bound in Malaysia, CTP-PJB

Hotlinks

There are links to relevant websites in this book. In order to ensure that the links are up to date, that the links work, and that the sites are not inadvertently linked to sites that could be considered offensive, we have made the links available on the following website: www.pearsonhotlinks.co.uk. When you access the site, search for either the title BTEC Level 3 National Engineering or the ISBN 978 1 84690 724 1.

Disclaimer

This material has been published on behalf of Edexcel and offers high-quality support for the delivery of Edexcel qualifications. This does not mean that the material is essential to achieve any Edexcel qualification, nor does it mean that it is the only suitable material available to support any Edexcel qualification. Edexcel material will not be used verbatim in setting any Edexcel examination or assessment. Any resource lists produced by Edexcel shall include this and other appropriate resources.

The suggested activities in this book that involve practical work and exposure to hazards must be risk assessed and supervised by a qualified staff member.

Standards are current at the time of publication, unless otherwise indicated, but may be subject to change during the life of the book. Please check with the relevant standards organisations.

Copies of official specifications for all Edexcel qualifications may be found on the Edexcel website: www.edexcel.com

About the authors

Andy Boyce has 30 years of further education experience, teaching, assessing and managing engineering programmes from Level 2 to Level 5. His previous writing experience includes producing material for BTEC in a Box and Pearson Education's materials for the Engineering and Manufacturing Diplomas. He has also written downloadable tutor support material for Edexcel.

For a considerable number of years he has worked as an external verifier and is also a principal moderator. He has provided input to the transition of the engineering programmes from NQF to QCF and now provides training to centres to help them achieve the transition. He is a BTEC standards verifier.

Ernie Cooke has spent all of his working life in the engineering industry, starting with an apprenticeship in the structural steelwork and mining engineering industry. This was followed by employment as a craftsman in the agricultural machinery, commercial vehicle, industrial acoustics and industrial belt manufacture industries. He has taught in further education for 25 years, teaching in engineering disciplines at all levels.

Robert Jones started his career in engineering with a five-year apprenticeship with Frigidaire, during which he attended Hendon College of Technology. He went on to study for a Diploma in Engineering at Middlesex Polytechnic. After finishing his apprenticeship he worked for Frigidaire as a product engineer and later for AC Delco as an experimental engineer.

His teaching career started at Riversdale College of Technology, teaching a wide variety of engineering subjects. He joined the Kenya Polytechnic as a lecturer in mechanical engineering in 1979, later leaving to study for a Master of Science Degree in Mechanical Engineering at the University of Manchester. In 1985 he joined Mombasa Polytechnic as a lecturer, before returning to the to join North Devon College. He was until recently the BTEC programme co-ordinator for the National Engineering courses at the college.

Bill Mantovani has a long association with BTEC and delivering BTEC units but his involvement with electronics stretches back much further. He trained as an electronics engineer and was a founder member of the team that developed the electronic and digital telephone system in use today. Bill joined the team delivering BTEC courses at Wakefield College in the 1980s. He was course tutor at a number of levels, including Higher National, and eventually took on all responsibilities for a number of Higher National Diploma courses run jointly with Sheffield Hallam and Leeds Metropolitan universities. Bill is currently involved with BTEC First and National for Electrical and Electronic Engineering at Leeds City College and continues to write on his favourite subject of electronics and IT.

David Roberts is currently a course tutor for the BTEC Higher National Certificate and Diploma in Fabrication and Welding Engineering, which is taught on behalf of Teesside University at Hartlepool College of Further Education. His academic qualifications include a Batchelor's degree in Engineering along with a Higher National Certificate and Diploma in Fabrication and Welding. David specialises in teaching materials engineering and technology, theoretical and practical metallurgy, and welding metallurgy on both National and Higher National programmes. Prior to entering full-time education and lecturing, David worked as a time served engineering craftsman.

Bryan Weatherill began his career working in manufacturing engineering before completing teacher training at Garnett College and teaching at North Devon College. As an advanced practitioner and curriculum leader he was involved with the introduction of BTEC Engineering courses. As curriculum leader, he selected the teaching team and carried out the training requirements for the BTEC ethos, a new style of teaching and learning for staff and learners. He also created links with college feeder schools in their introduction of BTEC courses. He is a Registered Safety Practitioner and has specialised in the health and safety learning outcomes. He currently works in the UK and abroad as an educational, engineering and health and safety consultant.

About your BTEC Level 3 National in Engineering

Choosing to study for a BTEC Level 3 National Engineering qualification is a great decision to make for lots of reasons. This qualification will help you to build a foundation of knowledge in engineering, leading you into a whole range of professions or further study.

Your BTEC Level 3 National in Engineering is a vocational, or work-related, qualification. This doesn't mean that it will give you *all* the skills you need to do a job, but it does mean that you'll have the opportunity to gain specific knowledge, understanding and skills that are relevant to your future career.

What will you be doing?

The qualification is structured into **mandatory units** (ones that you must do) and **optional units** (ones that you can choose to do). How many units you do and which ones you cover will depend on the type of qualification you are working towards.

Qualifications	Credits from mandatory units	Credits from optional units	Total credits
Edexcel BTEC Level 3 Certificate	10	20	30
Edexcel BTEC Level 3 Subsidiary Diploma	20	40	60
Edexcel BTEC Level 3 Diploma	70	50	120
Edexcel BTEC Level 3 Extended Diploma	70	110	180

Other pathways available are:

- Electrical and Electronic Engineering
- Manufacturing Engineering
- Mechanical Engineering
- Operations and Maintenance Engineering.

For these pathways you will take the following:

Qualifications	Credits from mandatory units	Credits from optional units	Total credits
Edexcel BTEC Level 3 Diploma	60	60	120
Edexcel BTEC Level 3 Extended Diploma	60	120	180

How to use this book

This book is designed to help you through your BTEC Level 3 National Engineering course.

This book contains many features that will help you use your skills and knowledge in work-related situations and assist you in getting the most from your course.

Introduction ●━━━━━━━━

These introductions give you a snapshot of what to expect from each unit – and what you should be aiming for by the time you finish it!

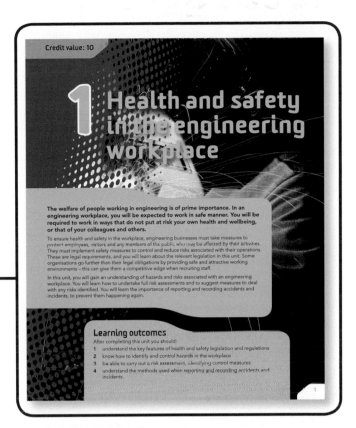

Assessment and grading criteria ●━━━━━━

This table explains what you must do to achieve each of the assessment criteria for each unit. For each assessment criterion, shown by the grade button **P1**, there is an assessment activity.

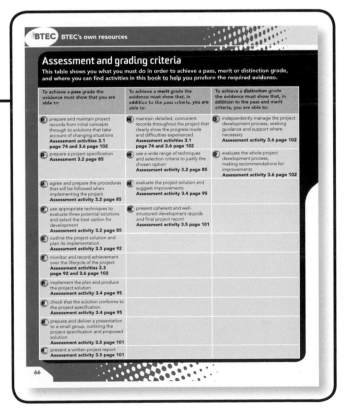

Assessment

Your tutor will set **assignments** throughout your course for you to complete. These may take the form of projects where you research, plan, prepare, make and evaluate a piece of work, sketchbooks, case studies and presentations. The important thing is that you evidence your skills and knowledge to date.

Stuck for ideas? Daunted by your first assignment? These learners have all been through it before...

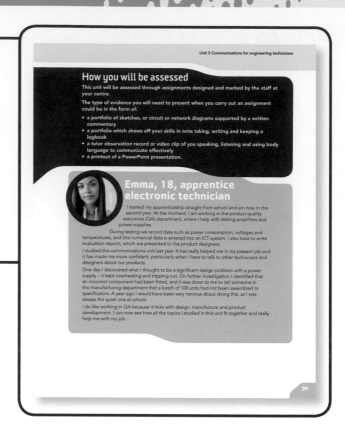

Unit 2 Communications for engineering technicians

How you will be assessed

This unit will be assessed through assignments designed and marked by the staff at your centre.

The type of evidence you will need to present when you carry out an assignment could be in the form of:

- a portfolio of sketches, or circuit or network diagrams supported by a written commentary
- a portfolio which shows off your skills in note taking, writing and keeping a logbook
- a tutor observation record or video clip of you speaking, listening and using body language to communicate effectively
- a printout of a PowerPoint presentation.

Emma, 18, apprentice electronic technician

I started my apprenticeship straight from school and am now in the second year. At the moment, I am working in the product quality assurance (QA) department, where I help with testing amplifiers and power supplies.

During testing we record data such as power consumption, voltages and temperatures, and this numerical data is entered into an ICT system. I also have to write evaluation reports, which are presented to the product designers.

I studied this communications unit last year. It has really helped me in my present job and it has made me more confident, particularly when I have to talk to other technicians and designers about our products.

One day I discovered what I thought to be a significant design problem with a power supply – it kept overheating and tripping out. On further investigation I identified that an incorrect component had been fitted, and it was down to me to tell someone in the manufacturing department that a batch of 100 units had not been assembled to specification. A year ago I would have been very nervous about doing this, as I was always the quiet one at school.

I do like working in QA because it links with design, manufacture and product development. I can now see how all the topics I studied in this unit fit together and really help me with my job.

39

Activities

There are different types of activities for you to do:
Assessment activities are suggestions for tasks that you might do as part of your assignment and will help you develop your knowledge, skills and understanding. **Grading tips** clearly explain what you need to do in order to achieve a pass, merit or distinction grade.

Assessment activity 35.1

P Study the two analogue circuit diagrams supplied (Circuits A and B). Choosing suitable components from the selection supplied, build and test the circuits and ensure they work correctly. Carefully record your observations.

P Record the type of diode used in both circuits, then produce a detailed explanation of the purpose of each diode. Record the type of transistor used and explain its operation in the circuit in Circuit B.

P Study the digital circuit diagram shown in Circuit C. Record the type of transistor used and explain its operation in the circuit.

M Measure the minimum and maximum values for darkness and bright light of the light-dependent resistor (LDR) in Circuit B. Modify the circuit by selecting and changing just one of the components so that it can be made to operate over a range of different light levels.

Grading tips

P **P** There are many basic circuits that use diodes and transistors where, simply put, the function of the device depends on how it is biased or connected into the circuit. By carefully studying the circuits you should be quickly able to identify what they do and the function of the diodes or transistor.

M Because a transistor requires few resistors to establish the bias point, it should be possible to alter when it begins to conduct by only altering the value of one component. Can you identify which one?

There are also suggestions for **activities** that will give you a broader grasp of the industry, stretch your imagination and deepen your skills.

Activity: CAD coordinates

Figure 16.49 shows a dimensioned rectangle whose lower left-hand Cartesian coordinate is (70,50). The position of the circle's centre is half way along the X-axis of the rectangle and half way up the Y-axis of the rectangle.

What are the Cartesian coordinates of (a) the upper right-hand corner of the rectangle and (b) the centre of the circle?

Personal, learning and thinking skills

Throughout your BTEC Level 3 National Engineering course, there are lots of opportunities to develop your personal, learning and thinking skills. Look out for these as you progress.

PLTS

When you were reaching the make-or-buy decision for the given product this should have involved discussion with other people. You may well have used a bit of persuasion to get your case across. In completing this assessment activity you will also show that you able to process and evaluate information when carrying out investigations.

Functional skills

It's important that you have good English, maths and ICT skills – you never know when you'll need them, and employers will be looking for evidence that you've got these skills too.

Functional skills

Carrying out costing calculations and techniques to inform make-or-buy decisions will develop your skills in mathematics (identify the situation or problem and the mathematical methods needed to tackle it).

Key terms

Technical words and phrases are easy to spot. You can also use the glossary at the back of the book.

Key terms

Nominal the stated size of some dimension. In reality, parts cannot be manufactured to a given nominal measurement, so they are produced within some specified tolerance.

WorkSpace

Case studies provide snapshots of real workplace issues, and show how the skills and knowledge you develop during your course can help you in your career.

There are also mini-case studies throughout the book to help you focus on your own projects.

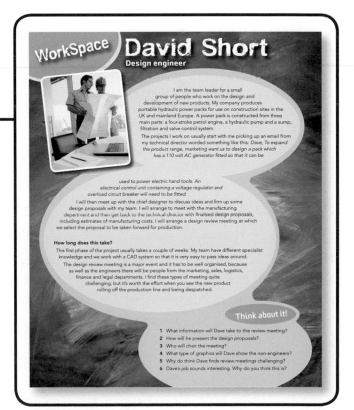

WorkSpace **David Short**
Design engineer

I am the team leader for a small group of people who work on the design and development of new products. My company produces portable hydraulic power packs for use on construction sites in the UK and mainland Europe. A power pack is constructed from three main parts: a four-stroke petrol engine, a hydraulic pump and a sump, filtration and valve control system.

The projects I work on usually start with me picking up an email from my technical director worded something like this: Dave, To expand the product range, marketing want us to design a pack which has a 110 volt AC generator fitted so that it can be used to power electric hand tools. An electrical control unit containing a voltage regulator and overload circuit breaker will need to be fitted.

I will then meet up with the chief designer to discuss ideas and firm up some design proposals with my team. I will arrange to meet with the manufacturing department and then get back to the technical director with finalised design proposals, including estimates of manufacturing costs. I will arrange a design review meeting at which we select the proposal to be taken forward for production.

How long does this take?
This first phase of the project usually takes a couple of weeks. My team have different specialist knowledge and we work with a CAD system so that it is very easy to pass ideas around.
The design review meeting is a major event and it has to be well organised, because as well as the engineers there will be people from the marketing, sales, logistics, finance and legal departments. I find these types of meeting quite challenging, but it's worth the effort when you see the new product rolling off the production line and being despatched.

Think about it!
1 What information will Dave take to the review meeting?
2 How will he present the design proposals?
3 Who will chair the meeting?
4 What type of graphics will Dave show the non-engineers?
5 Why do think Dave finds review meetings challenging?
6 Dave's job sounds interesting. Why do you think this is?

Just checking

When you see this sort of activity, take stock! These quick activities and questions are there to check your knowledge. You can use them to see how much progress you've made or as a revision tool.

Edexcel's assignment tips

At the end of each chapter, you'll find hints and tips to help you get the best mark you can, such as the best websites to go to, checklists to help you remember processes and really useful facts and figures.

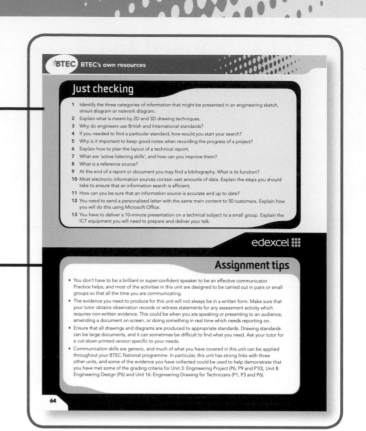

Have you read your **BTEC Level 3 National Engineering Study Skills Guide**? It's full of advice on study skills, putting your assignments together and making the most of being a BTEC Engineering learner.

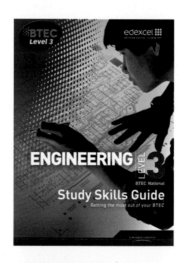

Ask your tutor about extra materials to help you through your course. The **Teaching Resource Pack** which accompanies this book contains interesting videos, activities, presentations and information about the engineering sector.

Your book is just part of the exciting resources from Edexcel to help you succeed in your BTEC course.

Visit:
- www.edexcel.com/BTEC or
- www.pearsonfe.co.uk/BTEC2010

1 Health and safety in the engineering workplace

The welfare of people working in engineering is of prime importance. In an engineering workplace, you will be expected to work in safe manner. You will be required to work in ways that do not put at risk your own health and wellbeing, or that of your colleagues and others.

To ensure health and safety in the workplace, engineering businesses must take measures to protect employees, visitors and any members of the public who may be affected by their activities. They must implement safety measures to control and reduce risks associated with their operations. These are legal requirements, and you will learn about the relevant legislation in this unit. Some organisations go further than their legal obligations by providing safe and attractive working environments – this can give them a competitive edge when recruiting staff.

In this unit, you will gain an understanding of hazards and risks associated with an engineering workplace. You will learn how to undertake full risk assessments and to suggest measures to deal with any risks identified. You will learn the importance of reporting and recording accidents and incidents, to prevent them happening again.

Learning outcomes

After completing this unit you should:

1. understand the key features of health and safety legislation and regulations
2. know how to identify and control hazards in the workplace
3. be able to carry out a risk assessment, identifying control measures
4. understand the methods used when reporting and recording accidents and incidents.

Assessment and grading criteria

This table shows you what you must do in order to achieve a pass, merit or distinction grade, and where you can find activities in this book to help you produce the required evidence.

To achieve a **pass** grade the evidence must show that you are able to:	To achieve a **merit** grade the evidence must show that, in addition to the pass criteria, you are able to:	To achieve a **distinction** grade the evidence must show that, in addition to the pass and merit criteria, you are able to:
P1 explain the key features of relevant regulations on health and safety as applied to a working environment in two selected or given engineering organisations **Assessment activity 1.1 page 17**	**M1** explain the consequences of management not abiding by legislation and regulations and carrying out their roles and responsibilities in a given health and safety situation **Assessment activity 1.1 page 17**	**D1** justify the methods used to deal with hazards in accordance with workplace policies and legal requirements **Assessment activity 1.2 page 30**
P2 describe the roles and responsibilities under current health and safety legislation and regulations, of those involved **Assessment activity 1.1 page 17**	**M2** explain the importance of carrying out all parts of a risk assessment in a suitable manner **Assessment activity 1.2 page 30**	**D2** determine the cost of an accident in the workplace from given data **Assessment activity 1.3 page 34**
P3 describe the methods used to identify hazards in a working environment **Assessment activity 1.2 page 30**	**M3** explain how control measures are used to prevent accidents **Assessment activity 1.2 page 30**	
P4 describe how hazards which become risks can be controlled **Assessment activity 1.2 page 30**		
P5 carry out a risk assessment on a typical item/area of the working environment **Assessment activity 1.2 page 30**		
P6 suggest suitable control measures after a risk assessment has been carried out and state the reasons why they are suitable **Assessment activity 1.2 page 30**		
P7 explain the principles that underpin reporting and recording accidents and incidents **Assessment activity 1.3 page 34**		
P8 describe the procedures used to record and report accidents, dangerous occurrences or near misses **Assessment activity 1.3 page 34**		

How you will be assessed

This unit will be assessed through assignments that will be designed and marked by the tutors at your centre. Assignments are designed to allow you to show your understanding of the unit learning outcomes. These relate to what you should be able to do after completing this unit.

The type of evidence you will need to present when you carry out an assignment could be in the form of:

- practical activities
- tutor observations of your practice in the workshop
- written reports.

Tracy, 18-year-old engineering apprentice

This unit helped me to understand the responsibilities that are placed on people when they are at work. It was interesting to realise that everyone has responsibilities for health and safety.

I enjoyed learning about health and safety law. I learned about the hazards and the risks that arise in everyday work. It surprised me that even a computer or cleaning materials can be hazardous if they are not used correctly. I just took this for granted before. It was important to realise how everybody relies on other people to have the training and experience to do their jobs safely and correctly.

The practical tasks, such as carrying out a workplace inspection, helped me to identify common hazards. This helped me to conduct a risk assessment to show the risk factors. I also now understand why it is important to report and record all health and safety incidents – to prevent the same accidents happening time and again. All this will help me if I achieve my goal to progress into management.

1.1 Understand the key features of health and safety legislation and regulations

Start up

Why does 'health and safety' matter?

Think about the possible hazards in an engineering workshop. In this environment you could be:

- working with heavy tools
- operating machinery
- coming into contact with hazardous substances
- working alongside noisy machinery.

List ten hazards within a typical engineering workshop. Choose a workshop with which you are familiar. For each hazard, consider:

- its possible effects on you
- the training required by people in the workshop to minimise the risk it poses
- any psychological factors.

Discuss your findings in small groups. Compare the hazards you have identified and consider any common issues or problems that you uncovered.

How many hazards can you spot?

An engineering workplace can contain many hazards and pose risks to the health and wellbeing of anyone in the environment. Hazard and risk are key concepts in health and safety, and it is important that you understand these terms. A hazard is something that has the potential to cause harm to you or to someone else. For example, a substance such as acid is a hazard, as it will cause injury if it is handled by someone who is not wearing the correct personal protective equipment. A risk is the likelihood that harm will occur, and a measure of the severity of the harm that the hazard poses.

Safe working is about identifying hazards and minimising risks. There are three good reasons why safe working is important in an engineering workplace:

- cost – accidents can be expensive for employers
- morality – employers should look after their staff
- the law – there is a legal duty on everyone to work safely.

The cost of accidents at work can be very high. Employers can face the costs of accident investigation, machinery repairs and possibly lost production, and compensation payments to injured persons, legal costs and increased cost of insurance.

People's lives and wellbeing can be put at risk at work. Everybody has a moral obligation not to cause harm to others. It is not acceptable to subject people to unnecessary risk through poor health and safety systems. Training is essential – untrained workers are often not aware of the dangers in carrying out work or the risks their action can pose to others.

To reinforce these moral obligations, the law makes health and safety in the workplace a legal responsibility. Health and safety legislation places responsibilities on all persons involved in engineering activities. The legislation sets duties and roles for employers and employees.

Did you know?

You can get information about health and safety legislation on the internet. Put the words 'UK health and safety legislation' into a search engine. Make sure you only access sites that cover requirements under UK law, and always check that the information is up to date.

1.1.1 Key features of legislation and regulations

For this unit, you require an understanding of the roles and responsibilities of everyone involved in engineering. We will consider these later in the unit (see page 14), but let's start by looking at the relevant legislation and, in particular, statute law.

There have been laws on the statute books governing working conditions for over 200 years. The first, in 1802, was designed to prevent the exploitation of child workers in textile factories. Subsequently, Factories Acts were passed that extended the law to other industries and placed responsibilities on employers to maintain health and safety in the workplace. The main legal instrument for ensuring safe workplaces today is the Health and Safety at Work Act 1974.

The Health and Safety at Work Act 1974

The Health and Safety at Work Act (HASAWA) is a United Kingdom Act of Parliament. This means that it has progressed through the parliamentary system. Any person who does not comply with the act is breaking the law. Anyone suspected of breaking the law can be taken before the courts and, if found guilty, faces being fined or even sent to prison.

The Health and Safety at Work Act clearly outlines the health and safety responsibilities of everybody within an engineering business. Section 2 of HASAWA formalises the legal responsibilities of employers in respect of their employees. This means that if you are an employee of an engineering business, you are entitled to:

- safe machinery and systems of work – such as machine guards and safe procedures for operating machines so that you will not be injured
- a safe and healthy workplace – you should be provided with good welfare facilities, adequate lighting, appropriate temperatures and washing facilities at work
- a safe place of work – you will receive instruction on good housekeeping to ensure that all emergency exits are kept clear
- safe methods of storing, transporting, handling, using and disposing of substances and materials – all employees should be instructed in manual handling, the use of oils and greases, and disposing of waste, and this helps to ensure that you are not injured at work or suffer ill health
- competent and properly trained colleagues and supervisors – starting a new job in a strange environment is a challenge, but understanding the hazards that you can face is an even greater challenge, and supervisors and colleagues help you through these challenges.

Other obligations under the Health and Safety at Work Act include that employers should have a written health and safety policy as well as imposing specific responsibilities on employees. These are set out later in this unit (see section 1.1.2 on the roles and responsibilities of those involved, on page 14).

Employers also have more general legal responsibilities towards their employees.

Employment Act (EA) 2002

This legislation sets out an employer's duties and the rights of employees in respect of pay issues and general terms of employment such as Sunday working. The Employment Act also deals with maternity rights and the procedures that have to be followed for the termination of employment, and it offers some protection against unfair dismissal. Under this Act, employees have the right to be paid even if the employer has no work for them – to qualify, employees only have to have been in work for one month.

You need to know your rights when in employment. The Employment Act sets out:

- your right to belong to a trade union
- your right to be allowed reasonable paid time off work to look for another job if you are being made redundant
- your right to be paid for up to 26 weeks if you are unfortunate to be suspended from work on medical grounds
- your right to be given a minimum period of notice based on your length of service if you are being fired – however, if you have been with your employer for less than two years, this only entitles you to one week's notice of termination of employment.

Other employment rights are set out in law. The Employment Equality (Age) Regulations (EEAR) protect employees of any age from age discrimination, including contract workers and anyone in vocational training. All aspects of employment are protected from age discrimination, including recruitment, employment terms and conditions, promotion, transfer to other positions, dismissal and training. There is no statutory upper age limit on the right to receive redundancy payments or to make a claim against an employer for unfair dismissal.

This legislation – and other legislation designed to prevent discrimination at work – needs to be taken into account in a health and safety context. In general, employers cannot bar people from particular jobs because of their age or gender, but they may need to take additional health and safety measures for particular groups of employees. For example, special considerations have to be made for any activity that may adversely affect any female employee who is pregnant, such as activities that involve manual handling, the use of lead, or radiography. Now let's return to specific health and safety legislation.

Regulatory Reform (Fire Safety) Order (RRFSO)

This order imposes a duty on employers to carry out fire risk assessments. The order also places duties on employees. If you work in an engineering business, you need to know what to do if there is a fire. Your duties in the event of a fire or other emergency are:

- to know the emergency routes and exits to a place of safety – you will be informed of these routes during the induction period when you first start work
- to turn your back on the fire and walk away, informing others in the vicinity
- to sound the alarm – this usually involves breaking the glass at a fire point at the point of exit from the building
- to make your way to the designated assembly point.

The Regulatory Reform (Fire Safety) Order (abbreviated RRFSO) requires workplaces to have fire detection and firefighting equipment. Detectors should be placed in each work area to check continuously for the presence of smoke or flames. The detectors are linked to an alarm system, which is activated when smoke or flames are detected. You will notice these detectors, usually fixed to the ceiling. They are white and sometimes display a small flashing red light.

Firefighting equipment includes extinguishers, fire hoses, fire blankets, sprinkler systems and inert gas systems. You can find these in various areas in a workplace, generally placed on emergency exit routes. Employees should not use this equipment unless trained to do so.

All detection and firefighting equipment must be maintained. You should be able to find evidence of maintenance on fire extinguishers. Ask permission to look closely at one or two extinguishers, and examine the label that keeps a record of the maintenance. When you are in an engineering workplace, check that you know the location of all firefighting equipment.

Companies must provide information about what to do in the event of a fire or other emergency to employees and to any visitors to their premises. Employees can expect to receive training on their duties in an emergency situation. This training will start on their first day at work or during induction training.

The fire triangle. You sometimes see a symbol like this displayed in workplaces. It is used as a short visual guide to preventing fires. Make sure you understand what the diagram means. If you are unsure, do some research on the internet by putting the term 'fire triangle' into a search engine.

Other health and safety legislation

There are many regulations that impose obligations on employers in respect of health and safety. Regulations are derived from European directives. The United Kingdom has been a member of the European Union since 1973 and, as it is a member state, European directives have to be implemented into UK law. This is to ensure harmonisation across all EU member states. Regulations are secondary to the Health and Safety at Work Act. However, regulations form part of UK legislation, so any person or company not complying with them is breaking the law. They can then be prosecuted under UK criminal law.

There is some guidance for employers to help them operate within the law. Approved Codes of Practice (ACOPs) provide a recognised interpretation of how an employer may comply with regulations. For example, Regulation 3 of the Management of Health and Safety at Work Regulations – the section that deals with risk assessments – can be difficult to understand due to the legal terminology. The approved codes of practice interpret the regulation in layman's terms. This makes the regulation more understandable and easier for employers to implement in the workplace. Employers

must either meet the requirements set out in ACOPs, or show that they have complied with an equal or better standard.

The Health and Safety Executive (HSE) also issues guidance notes that give advice on how to comply with health and safety legislation. These have no legal standing. You will come across many HSE guidance notes in engineering. They contain more practical advice than that provided in ACOPs. For example, the HSE's guidance on the Manual Handling Regulations gives the recommended maximum weights that men and women respectively can safely hold and carry.

The approved code of practice for the Management of Health and Safety at Work Regulations. These can be obtained from the Health and Safety Executive (HSE).

The Management of Health and Safety at Work Regulations 1999

The Management of Health and Safety at Work Regulations (MHSW) apply to all workplaces, not just those carrying out engineering activities. These regulations state that the employer has the major responsibility for health and safety in the workplace, but further recognise that the employees also have responsibilities.

Regulation 3 requires that employers carry out 'suitable and sufficient' risk assessments for all activities. To lessen the **risk**, precautions have to put into place so that employees are not injured. The aim of risk assessments is to identify **hazards** so that action can be taken to eliminate, reduce or control them, thereby helping to prevent accidents.

Regulation 4 requires that employers integrate health and safety into the management systems of the engineering companies. This ensures that employees are protected by precautionary measures that are properly planned and organised.

Provision and Use of Work Equipment Regulations (PUWER) 1998

Working in engineering involves the extensive use of machinery. The Provision and Use of Work Equipment Regulations define work equipment as any machinery, appliance, hand tool, powered tool or assembly of components.

Table 1.1: Types of work equipment

Type of equipment	Examples
Machinery	Photocopier, bench grinder, lathe, milling machine
Appliance	Car-lifting jack, microwave oven, air compressor
Hand tool	Hammer, screwdriver, spanner, chisel
Powered tool	Circular saw, industrial vacuum cleaner, electric drill
Assembly of components	Excavator, crane, concrete mixer, car assembly plant

To protect everybody who uses equipment at work, the regulations require employers to ensure that:

- all machinery is suitable and fit for purpose
- work equipment is maintained
- work equipment is inspected on a regular basis
- training and instruction is given to anyone who needs to use the equipment
- dangerous parts of work equipment are guarded as far as reasonably practicable
- controls on machinery are clearly marked
- machinery can be isolated from the electrical supply
- warning signs are fixed either on or close to machinery.

Key terms

Hazard something with the potential to cause harm, such as machinery being used by an untrained person.

Risk the combination of the likelihood that the hazard will cause damage or harm and the severity of the resulting injury.

This means businesses must select and purchase work equipment with care, paying attention to size, suitability for use and safety requirements. Engineers should check that the equipment is fit for purpose. This equipment must be properly maintained, ensuring that operatives do not hurt themselves and that machinery works efficiently.

All work equipment must be inspected on a regular basis. If you need to use a tool or carry out work on a machine, give it a check before you start work. So before you use a hammer, carry out a pre-use inspection. Check that the wooden shaft is not split and the striking face is not damaged. Before you use a grinding machine, check that the abrasive wheel is not cracked or broken and that the guards are in place. Before using any work equipment, you must also have received adequate training and instruction. It is wrong to ask someone to use work equipment without the appropriate training. If you are not sure how to use or operate any piece of work equipment, then ask someone who knows.

All machinery should have features to reduce the risk of injury. All dangerous parts of work equipment must be guarded if this is practicable. This ensures that when the machine is used correctly, it is safe. The controls on machinery should be clearly marked. The start control is green and recessed, so you have to push your finger in to switch the machine on. The stop control is red, mushroom shaped and stands proud for easy access. It must be possible to isolate any machinery from the electrical supply. Think of a kettle – it is usually switched off when not in use but not isolated. To isolate the kettle, the plug must be removed from the socket. This called an air gap.

Most machinery has warning signs fixed either on or close to the machine. It is important that you are familiar with these signs and understand what they mean. The signs can be referenced from the Health and Safety (Safety Signs and Signals) Regulations.

Supply of Machinery (Safety) (Amendment) Regulations 2005

You will find that engineering machinery, tools and other work equipment is marked or stamped with a CE mark. This mark denotes that the equipment meets European Union standards for safety. Known as harmonised standards, these are applied to a wide range of industrial equipment used in agriculture, engineering, construction, textiles and other industrial sectors.

A technical file has to be issued with the equipment. This is usually a comprehensive instruction manual, which includes:

- drawings of the machine and circuit diagrams
- technical specifications
- essential health and safety requirements
- methods to be adopted by the user to eliminate hazards when equipment is operated.

These ensure that when you operate work equipment, you are protected from all risks as far as possible.

The standard CE mark shown on work equipment. This denotes that it meets EU safety standards.

Lifting Operations and Lifting Equipment Regulations (LOLER) 1998

Engineering organisations use cranes, hoists and lifting equipment for a wide range of lifting operations. You can see tower cranes being used on construction sites and forklift trucks being used in many workplaces. The Lifting Operations and Lifting Equipment Regulations (LOLER) are not industry specific and apply to most lifting operations. They place duties on employers and all persons using the equipment.

All persons operating lifting equipment must be authorised to do so. This means that they will have received appropriate training and instruction so that they can operate lifting equipment competently. This ensures safe operation, and reduces the risk for anyone working close to the lifting activity.

The lifting equipment must have the strength and stability for the planned lifting operation. Cranes, lifting accessories, forklift trucks and lorry-mounted lifting equipment are used for lifting goods, material and equipment (but not people). All these lifting devices are marked with a safe working load (SWL), and are fitted with overload protection. This sounds an alarm if the load is overweight, and the equipment should not work. All goods-lifting equipment must have a thorough examination by a competent engineer every year.

Lifts and hoists used for transporting persons are also covered by these regulations. Next time you are in a lift, look for a sign indicating the number of persons and the weight that can be carried. This is strictly controlled by an overload protection device. If the lift is overloaded, an alarm will ring and the lift will not move. Lifts are subject to a six-monthly thorough examination by a competent engineer, working on behalf of an insurance company.

When you get the opportunity, look closely at the structure of any lifting equipment and observe the size and strength of the various parts. Always ask permission first and do not approach if the equipment is being operated.

Manual Handling Operations Regulations (MHO) 1992

About a third of all reported injuries at work are the result of people using incorrect **manual handling** methods. Most engineering activities involve some form of manual handling. Working in engineering, you will be instructed and trained in the correct methods of manual handling. This is usually carried out in the first week as part of your **induction programme**.

Employers should ensure that their staff avoid manual handling any items in such a way that could cause them injury. If manual handling cannot be avoided, then a risk assessment must be carried out. This is in four parts, and involves considering:

• the task or activity that needs to be carried out

• the capacity of the individual doing the work

• the load to be moved

• the working environment.

A description of how to carry out a manual handling risk assessment is given later in this unit (see page 27).

Key terms

Manual handling the process of transporting or supporting a load (including lifting, putting down, pushing, pulling, carrying, or moving) by hand or by bodily force.

Induction programme introductory sessions and training that are provided to employees in the first few days of starting at a new place of work.

Control of Noise at Work Regulations 2005

Everybody working in an engineering environment will be exposed to noise. It is the responsibility of the employer to control noise to acceptable levels. The level of noise must be as low as reasonably practicable. Anyone subjected to excessive noise may suffer ill health, including temporary or permanent hearing loss, tinnitus, headaches or fatigue.

The Control of Noise at Work Regulations require employers to eliminate or reduce noise levels. For airborne noise, this can be achieved by installing sound absorbing shields, enclosures or coverings. If you can look under the bonnet of a car, notice the sound absorbing material immediately under the bonnet and against the bulkhead. This material looks like quilting and it is placed there to absorb the sound of the car engine. It is possible to use similar material to suppress the noise from machinery used in engineering.

Engineering organisations can take other steps to suppress noise. In particular, regular maintenance of work equipment and machinery helps to reduce noise. You would be surprised how a small amount of oil or grease applied to the right places can reduce noise.

When employees are exposed to excessive noise they should be allowed to recover in a quieter area. Any employee exposed to 80 dB – this noise level is known as the lower exposure action value – must be supplied with hearing protection. If you are likely to be exposed to this noise level, then your employer must provide you with the appropriate personal protection equipment (PPE). You must be trained in its use, storage, cleaning and replacement. At this noise level, it is your choice whether or not to wear the protective equipment. At noises levels of 85 dB and above – 85 dB is known as the upper exposure action value – employees *must* wear the supplied hearing protection. The work area must be designated a hearing protection zone and the correct signs should be displayed.

Did you know?

The ear senses sound as pressure waves travelling through the air. The ear has three parts: the outer ear, which channels pressure waves to the eardrum; the middle ear, in which eardrum vibrations are transmitted through three small bones to the cochlea; and the inner ear (the cochlea), which is filled with fluid and tiny hairs that respond to the sound and transmit signals via acoustic nerves to the brain.

Sound is measured in decibels (dB), a unit of sound pressure divided by intensity based on the threshold of hearing 0 dB. Table 1.2 shows some typical noise levels for different sound sources.

Table 1.2: Typical noise levels

Source	dB
Threshold of hearing	0
Library	> 30
Television at home	> 65–70
Engineering workshop	> 90
Activated smoke detector	> 100–105
Night club	> 105–115

Personal Protective Equipment at Work Regulations 1992

Personal protective equipment (PPE) must be supplied by an employer to protect workers. For example, if you are asked to sharpen a chisel on a grinding machine, then you must be provided with (and must wear) safety glasses or goggles to avoid eye injuries.

The choice of personal protective equipment is based on the type of hazard that the activity poses. It must be produced from appropriate material. For example, a welder wears a boiler suit made from flameproof material.

The equipment must fit the person it is supplied to, and it should be comfortable to wear. A welder must be issued with a flameproof boiler suit that is neither too small nor too large, and is made from breathable material. All PPE must be supplied free of charge and must be cleaned, repaired or replaced when not fit for use.

As an employee, you have the right under the regulations to have a say in the choice of the PPE and be trained in its correct use.

Can you identify the personal protection equipment being used in this photograph?

Electricity at Work Regulations (EAWR) 1989

Electricity is used to power machinery, lighting and work equipment in engineering. Electricity flows through circuits, which are easily controlled by switches and other electrical apparatus to ensure that machinery and lighting works efficiently and safely. However, electricity can create a hazard. Fires can be caused by sparking or arcing through faulty or overloaded electrical equipment.

Direct contact with electrical conductors can result in an electrical shock. This can cause injury, and severe shocks can be fatal. The victim can suffer electrical burns at point of contact with the electricity and point of exit, usually the hand or arm, through the body to the feet. It is therefore important to ensure that nobody touches a live bare wire.

Electricity cannot be seen or smelt, so it is vital to isolate any electrical equipment before working on it. Think of an electric kettle in a kitchen. Is it switched off or isolated? Switched off means that either the switch on the kettle is off or the switch is off at the socket on the wall. Isolated means that the plug is pulled out of the socket. In engineering terms, this is called an air gap. Electricity cannot flow through the air gap. Make sure that you know which is safer: switched off or isolated?

The Electricity at Work Regulations (EAWR) require employers to maintain all electrical systems and circuits. Inspections must be carried out regularly to look for hazards, broken sockets, loose connections, crushed cables and wires, etc. You are required to report any defects when you notice them. All circuits are required to be thoroughly inspected by a competent electrician every five years.

It is important to assess the strength and capability of circuits, as well as the insulation. Fuses are used as protection devices. Fuses or circuit breakers must be installed to withstand the effects of overloads or faults to earth. Fuses are often referred to as the weak link in a circuit. Carefully inspect the lead and plug of an electrical appliance. You will find that the plastic covering acts as the insulator, so that nobody can come into contact with the copper wires and connections inside. The copper wires inside cables and wires are highly conductive to electrical flow.

Confined Spaces Regulations (CSR) 1997

A confined space is any enclosed space where there is a specified risk of serious injury. Some enclosed spaces are easy to identify, such as deep excavations, storage tanks and poorly ventilated rooms. Other confined spaces might be less obvious, such as silos, furnace combustion chambers and vats.

Risks from working in confined spaces arise from both hazards present in the confined space and those that may flow into the confined space, and they can include loss of consciousness due to asphyxiation.

Entry into confined spaces is hazardous. Work in confined spaces is strictly controlled by risk assessments, safe systems of work and **permits to work**. A permit to work details the work to be done and the safety precautions to be taken. It is only valid for a fixed period of time, usually eight hours.

Workplace (Health, Safety and Welfare) Regulations 1992

The Workplace (Health, Safety and Welfare) Regulations (WHSWR) are concerned with general safety and welfare in engineering workplaces. They ensure that you can enter and exit from any part of the workplace in a safe manner. The regulations also require that:

- all **fixtures and fittings** are maintained and kept clean
- the workplace atmosphere is healthy, receiving an adequate supply of fresh air
- temperatures are maintained at a minimum of 16°C for normal work and 13°C for energetic work
- lighting is the correct level for work being carried out, and there is **emergency lighting** for evacuations
- all work areas are kept clean (this is known as housekeeping)
- measures are taken to prevent falls from height, which are likely to cause injury to employees
- traffic management systems in work areas segregate vehicles and pedestrians
- welfare facilities are provided, including toilets and facilities to wash and dry hands
- fresh drinking water is provided when required.

Control of Substances Hazardous to Health (COSHH) Regulations 2002

COSHH regulations are designed to ensure the safe use and handling of hazardous chemicals in engineering. This reduces the likelihood of anyone

Key terms

Permit to work a document issued to control entry into confined spaces. These are usually issued by a senior engineer for a single activity to a competent engineer, who carries out the work.

Fixtures and fittings items like electrical wiring, lighting, doors, ventilation systems, windows, carpets etc.

Emergency lighting illuminated green and white signs indicating emergency evacuation routes.

First aid treatment for preserving life and minimising consequence of injury or illness until medical help arrives and treatment for minor injuries that do not require professional medical attention.

suffering ill health or injury from coming into contact with any chemicals.

Some chemicals, such as petrol and oils, can be absorbed into the body through your skin and eyes. Others can enter your body through cuts and grazes. Chemicals can also enter your body by accidental or deliberate injection, such as from contaminated needles. Chemicals can also be swallowed. This can occur if you eat or drink while handling or using hazardous chemicals.

Airborne chemicals, such as gases, dusts and fumes, can be breathed in and enter your bloodstream through your lungs. There can also be microscopic particles in some environments, such as asbestos, which when breathed in can stay in the lungs and cause severe disease.

When using or working with chemicals:

- appreciate that some chemicals are more hazardous that others
- understand that some will harm faster than others
- always wash your hands before eating or drinking
- always use the correct type of personal protection equipment (PPE).

Did you know?

To investigate chemical hazards, information can be obtained from the internet and from the labels on chemical containers. You can also obtain information from the relevant material safety data sheets (MSDS) – these contain information on all the safety aspects related to a material, including the risk and safety phrases.

Health and Safety (First Aid) Regulations 1981

Employers have a legal requirement to provide **first aid** in the workplace. Every employer must provide adequate first-aid equipment. When you work in engineering, you must be aware of the location of first-aid boxes and know who are the first-aiders working in your area.

Anybody who works away from the main site must be supplied with a first-aid box. The law requires that first-aid boxes must be kept in delivery lorries and vans, and a travelling salesperson must have one in the car. First-aid boxes must be maintained. This means that the contents have to be topped up on a regular basis – you can check this as a list of contents is supplied with the box.

First-aiders must have a certificate of qualification, obtained by completing a four-day training course run by St John Ambulance or other recognised trainers. The certificate is valid for three years, after which first-aiders must attend a refresher course. First-aiders can give treatment and help until a injured person can receive professional medical help, but they are not allowed to give any form of medicine. You will find that many people are proud of achieving a first-aid qualification. First-aiders in the workplace are often recognised by the wearing of a badge, and they generally receive a small increase in pay for their first-aid duties.

Reporting of Injuries, Diseases and Dangerous Occurrences Regulations (RIDDOR) 1995

All accidents, incidents (near misses) and dangerous occurrences in the workplace must be reported. The reporting procedure should be explained to new employees in their first few days at work.

An employer has a legal duty to report certain types of injuries, diseases, dangerous occurrences and gas releases. The reports are used by the Health and Safety Executive (HSE) to analyse health and safety trends and to compile statistics on the numbers of different types of accidents.

A responsible person, usually a manager, has to report serious accidents and incidents as soon as possible to the HSE, either by telephone or online. This same person has to complete RIDDOR form F2508, and send it to the HSE within 10 days.

An accident must be notified when a person dies or suffers a serious injury at work. Serious injuries include:

- the fracture of any bone, except a finger or toe
- amputation of any part of the body
- dislocation of a shoulder, hip, knee or spine
- permanent or temporary loss of sight
- loss of consciousness resulting from an electrical shock
- any injury requiring a stay in hospital of more than 24 hours
- acute illness or loss of consciousness due to inhalation, ingestion or absorption through the skin of any chemical
- any other injury leading to hypothermia or a heat-related illness.

If someone suffers an injury that causes them to remain off work for more than three days, then this is notifiable to the HSE.

Occupational diseases must also be notified. Diseases that are notifiable if contracted at work include:

- anthrax, which can be caught from animals
- hepatitis, caught from another person's body fluids
- legionellosis, caught from sprayed droplets of contaminated water
- leptospirosis, caught from contact with rat's urine
- tetanus, caught from contaminated soil or animals
- occupational dermatitis, caught from contact with cement dust, oils, waste materials.

Dangerous occurrences that must be notified include:

- the failure of any crane, lift, hoist or derrick
- the failure of a pressurised container, such as a tank on a compressor
- the turning over of a forklift truck.

Working Time Regulations 1998

People make mistakes when they are tired, and working excessive hours can pose safety risks. Under the Working Time Regulations all employees are entitled to regular rest breaks and days off. In most industries (there are exceptions for the armed forces, those who work at sea and some other occupations), no employee can be forced to work more than

48 hours a week on average. Anyone under 18 years of age, should not normally work more than eight hours a day or 40 hours a week.

Employees can choose to work longer hours. However, to comply with the law, there should be a written agreement between the employer and the employee stating that both parties agree to opt out of the provision setting a 48-hour limit on the working week. The Health and Safety Executive is responsible for enforcing the maximum weekly working time limit. It also monitors the provisions in regulations in respect of night work – work that takes place between 11pm and 6am.

Activity: Complying with the law

Ali is a production engineer in a small engineering company that makes racking for warehouses. This involves rolling, piercing and cutting steel to length and then spray painting the resulting steel strips. Ali has been asked to carry out an analysis of health and safety legislation and regulations to ensure that the company is complying with all relevant legislative requirements.

- How would you carry out the analysis?
- Which legislation and regulations would you expect to be applicable to Ali's company?

1.1.2 Roles and responsibilities

You should by now understand that everybody within an engineering business has some health and safety responsibilities. These are clearly outlined in the Health and Safety at Work Act 1974 and the various regulations that we have considered in this unit. More generally, we all have **common law** responsibilities to each other. The responsibility is based on a **duty of care** owed to other persons.

Employers

An employer owes you a duty of care while you are at work. If you have an accident and are injured at work, then you can seek **compensation** if you think your employer is a fault. A civil law case will decide if the accident was the result of **negligence** on the part of your employer. If proven on the **balance of**

probability, you would be entitled to compensation. The level of compensation is an amount that should restore your quality of life to that you enjoyed before the accident.

You will find that all engineering organisations have a health and safety policy. This is a legal requirement. The policy should be in three parts.

- A statement of intent – one page that sets out the organisation's health and safety aims and objectives. It show the management's commitment to safe working, and should be signed and dated by the employer.
- Organisation – a description of how health and safety is organised by showing a structure of responsibility for all employees. This determines accountability and should indicate the lines of communication for health and safety issues. The allocation of responsibilities for health and safety should be given to competent employees. The whole system requires the co-operation of all employees through consultation.
- Arrangements – the nuts and bolts of the policy. This should include the procedures and systems for first aid, risk assessments, welfare requirements and consultation with employees, among others. These are legal requirements, as set out in the various regulations and the Health and Safety at Work Act.

Employees

All persons who work in engineering have roles and responsibilities for health and safety. As engineers progress through their careers, their level of responsibility generally increases. The Health and

Key terms

Common law based on the judgements made in past cases, called precedents.

Duty of care acting towards others in a manner that a reasonable person would adopt.

Compensation an amount of money paid to an injured person by an employer (or the employer's insurance company) in the event that the accident resulted from the employer's negligence.

Negligence tort, or wrong doing, of one person (or organisation) against another.

Balance of probability a less robust standard of proof than in criminal law, where cases must be proved beyond reasonable doubt.

Case study: Mustapha Mohammad

Mustapha, a 17-year-old apprentice engineer, suffered a horrific accident at work while operating a drilling machine. The little finger on his left hand was drawn into the rotating chuck, causing severe lacerations and a broken finger. As a consequence, Mustapha's finger had to be amputated close to his hand.

Mustapha had received no training on the machine – he was just told to go and drill the holes in a metal plate. He was not supervised while using the drilling machine, and an investigation revealed that the machine was running at too high a speed for the size of the drill bit in the chuck.

The engineering company was prosecuted for breaches of the Health and Safety at Work Act and Mustapha eventually received compensation for the loss of his finger.

1 Explain why Mustapha's company faced both criminal proceedings and a civil action in this case.

2 Describe the different levels of proof that are required in criminal and civil proceedings under UK law.

Safety at Work Act requires the involvement of employees and sets out the part that they have to play.

Section 7 of the act formalises these responsibilities. Employees must take reasonable care of their own health and safety and that of others who may be affected by their acts and omissions. This means, for example, that you must wear a hard hat when necessary, you must not obstruct a fire exit, or operate a machine unless authorised. You must cooperate with your employer (and your tutors at your centre when you are in the workshops) so that the organisation can comply with legal requirements. You should report any defects in machinery and attend training sessions when instructed.

These two responsibilities – to take reasonable care and to cooperate with an employer – are reinforced in the other regulations that we considered in the first section of this unit. In general, however, you should follow these rules whenever you are in an engineering environment.

- Be aware of your responsibilities under Section 7 of the Health and Safety at Work Act.
- Be aware of the hazards and the risks from any engineering activity in which you will be engaged.
- Be familiar with the risks assessments that have been made.
- Make sure you know about any relevant regulations. If you don't know which regulations apply to your area of work, then ask somebody who knows.
- Make sure that you know how to use any work equipment. This covers any hand tool to the most complex piece of machinery, from screwdrivers to automated assembly equipment.

- If an accident or incident occurs, report it.
- Ensure that you know the emergency evacuation routes.

The Health and Safety Executive

The Health and Safety Executive (HSE) is the enforcing authority for workplace safety under powers set out in the Health and Safety at Work Act. The HSE appoints inspectors to monitor health and safety in workplaces. These inspectors have wide-ranging powers to ensure that engineering companies comply with legislation. Their role is to ensure that employees and others are protected, to enforce the law and to advise on matters related to health and safety.

The inspectors' role is defined in the Health and Safety at Work Act. They have the power to enter any workplace at any reasonable time during normal opening hours. They can take a police officer with them if they are likely to be obstructed.

They can examine and investigate any part of an employer's premises or machinery. This can involve:

- directing that a part, or the whole, of a workplace be left undisturbed – this could mean shutting down that area of the site
- taking photographs, measurements and details of any piece of work equipment or part of the site
- taking samples of unsafe articles and substances for investigation
- testing, dismantling and examining any work equipment or substance
- interviewing and taking statements from any person.

Employers must give assistance where required. Inspectors have the ultimate power, and they can demand anything within reason.

The powers of HSE inspectors extend to enforcement. They can take a variety of actions depending on the seriousness of the issue. If the issue is relatively minor, they can give advice to employers either verbally or in writing. For example, they might advise employers on how to improve their risk assessment systems.

If there is a breach of health and safety law, inspectors can issue an improvement notice. An improvement notice might be issued if risk assessments have not been carried out in part of the workplace. Employers can appeal against improvement notices, and they can continue operating as before until an appeal is heard.

If in the opinion of the inspector there is, or there is the likelihood of, a risk of serious injury to an employee, an employer would be issued with a prohibition notice. The prohibition notice stops the activity as soon as it is issued. For example, if employees are being exposed to unacceptably high noise levels caused by poorly maintained machinery, then an employer would have to shut down the offending machinery on receipt of the prohibition notice.

Inspectors can also start prosecution against an employer following a accident to a employee.

Other individuals

The focus in this unit has been on the roles and responsibilities of employers and employees, and the enforcement role of the Health and Safety Executive. However, you should note that other people could be affected by engineering activities. These could include visitors to the site, such as a postal worker or salesperson, neighbours (anybody living or working close to the site) and contractors, workers from other organisations that come on to the site to carry out specific work, such as builders, painters and decorators, or caterers.

Health and safety legislation applies to these individuals just as much to as to the organisation's own employees. This means that the employer has a duty of care to all people who visit the site or who might be in the vicinity and affected by its operations. Similarly, anybody visiting the site must take reasonable care and must cooperate with any health and safety requirements.

Activity: Structuring a written health and safety policy

Karen works part time as a health and safety adviser to an agricultural engineering company. She has years of experience in the industry, and she has been employed because the company has been served with an improvement notice by an HSE inspector. The improvement notice has been issued because the company has not got a current health and safety policy. This is a breach of the Health and Safety at Work Act 1974. Karen's first job is to write a company health and safety policy.

If you had to produce a health and safety policy that would be compliant with the Health and Safety at Work Act, what three headings would you use to structure the document? How would you expand on the three headings?

Assessment activity 1.1

To complete this activity, you will need to write a report that covers the features of health and safety legislation as it applies to two workplaces. You will also report on the health and safety responsibilities of those working in each workplace and the management of health and safety in each organisation.

You can select the two separate working environments to write about in your report. An appropriate choice would be to choose one electrical and one mechanical engineering work area. This will allow you to show knowledge and understanding of the health and safety issues in different workplaces. For example, you might consider:

- your place of work (if you are in work, or on an apprenticeship or work placement)
- a training workshop
- a machine shop environment
- a maintenance workshop
- the health and safety issues facing electricians working on a site.

Get some advice from your tutor before making your final decision. Then begin the process of researching and writing your report. It should be in three sections.

P1 In the first section, explain the key features of the relevant legalisation and regulations applicable to each workplace.

P2 In the second section, describe the roles and responsibilities of the employees and others involved at each workplace.

M1 In the third section, explain the management of the health and safety system within one of your selected engineering workplaces.

Grading tips

P1 You should cover at least four appropriate regulations relevant to each chosen workplace. Try to select different regulations for each workplace, as this will enable you to cover a wider range.

P2 In this section of your report, try to relate the roles and responsibilities to the legislation and regulations that are applicable in each workplace.

M1 For this grade, you need to develop your work by looking at the management of health and safety in more depth. To do this, it is not enough to simply describe the various responsibilities; you need to explain the potential consequences of managers not complying with relevant legislation and of failing to meet their responsibilities.

PLTS

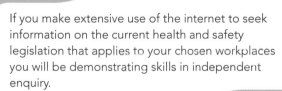

If you make extensive use of the internet to seek information on the current health and safety legislation that applies to your chosen workplaces you will be demonstrating skills in independent enquiry.

1.2 Know how to identify and control hazards in the workplace

In this section we will consider how to identify hazards in engineering environments. Hazards can be broken down into different types:

- mechanical (related to machinery), such as being entangled with moving parts, suffering abrasions on grinding wheels, being crushed between moving parts, and being cut by sharp blades
- electrical, such as contact with bare conductors owing to poor maintenance
- chemical, such as inhalation of exhaust fumes or contact with waste oils and greases
- thermal, such as contact with hot parts of machinery or excessive cold from the rapid use of LPG bottles
- noise, most machinery makes some noise
- vibration, machinery under operating conditions produces vibrations
- radiation, such as heat radiated from a welding operation
- ergonomics, such as injuries or disabilities caused by the poor selection, use and maintenance of work equipment.

We will start by considering how to assess some general hazards within the workplace.

1.2.1 Within the workplace

There are several methods of assessing hazards within an engineering environment. Perhaps the best way is

to analyse a task, and then rank the hazards in order of severity. For simple tasks the hazards are easily identifiable, but for more complex tasks the hazards are not easy to determine.

Table 1.3 shows how this is done for two tasks. You will see that each task has the same basic objective, splitting a corroded nut, but the two tasks employ different methods and equipment. Observe how the hazards increase when undertaking the complex task.

The table shows the different types of hazards associated with each task. All these hazards have an associated risk. You will notice that the table also lists the possible outcomes of each hazard. When you carry out a risk assessment, you will have to analyse all hazards associated with an activity or an environment and assess their associated risks. Note that you need to consider more than the environment and the equipment that will be used; it is also important that you also take into account the *methods* of working.

Use of accident data

All reported workplace accidents and incidents should be investigated to determine their causes. If you can tackle the causes of health and safety incidents, then accident rates can be reduced. Accident investigations help managers learn any lessons to ensure that dangerous practices can be eliminated.

Accident data is used both to direct the need for risk assessments and to determine risk. Because risk is

Table 1.3: Task analysis

Task type	Equipment used	Hazards	Outcomes
Simple	Cold chisel to split nut	Hitting hand with hammer Flying steel particle into eye	Bruise on hand Loss of sight
Complex	Operating pneumatic jack hammer to split nut	Flying particle into eye	Loss of sight
		Noise	Temporary loss of hearing
		Vibration	Vibration white finger
		Compressed air	High pressure air into eye, and/or high pressure air into cut on hand – embolism – could cause death
		Manual handling of equipment	Strains and sprains, or long-term muscular injuries to back

Inspection of: *Mechanical workshop*	Date: *8/10/2010*		Carried out by: *AN Other*
Fire hazards	Acceptable?		Comments
	Yes	No	
Fire extinguishers: Are these the correct type?	✓		*Correct types for fire hazards in area*
Fire extinguishers: Have they been Inspected?	✓		*Records show up-to-date maintenance*
Emergency exits: Are they correctly signed?	✓		*Right safe conditions signs*
Emergency exits: Are they unobstructed?		✓	*Remove obstructions and instruct staff to keep exits clear*
Emergency exits: Do they open?		✓	*One door is very tight to open – it seems to be sticking*

Figure 1.1: Part of a health and safety inspection checklist

a product of the probability that a hazard will cause damage or harm and the severity of the resulting injury, you can use past accident data to estimate these probabilities. For example, if there have been several reports of workers suffering crushed fingers in an engineering department, this would indicate that the probability of this type of accident is quite high and you would know from the reports the extent of the injuries. This data would also highlight the need for a new risk assessment to be carried out to lessen the risk of employees getting their fingers crushed.

Inspections

It is not sufficient to monitor accident data; engineering companies also need to be proactive in monitoring all aspects of health and safety. As well as conducting risk assessments (which we consider later in this unit, see page 24), inspections are carried out on a regular basis in all engineering organisations.

As an engineering employee, you are likely to be involved in these health and safety inspections. A standard form or checklist, which covers all aspects of health and safety in the workplace, is used for consistency. Your job will be to assess each aspect for compliance, tick yes for compliance or no if there is a problem or something lacking. There should be room on the form to add comments and suggestions for corrective action. Figure 1.1 shows part of a typical inspection checklist, covering two aspects of preventing fire hazards (namely the provision of fire

extinguishers and emergency exits). The full inspection form would cover all parts of the workshop (and all relevant health and safety considerations) and would extend to at least two A4 sheets.

1.2.2 Working environments

Now let's look at some specific aspects of the engineering workplace in more detail. Particular situations, such as working in confined spaces and working with mechanical machinery, have the potential to cause harm and can pose hazards that become risks. In seeking to identify and control hazards in the workplace, it is useful to consider these situations individually as each poses specific risks.

Confined spaces

In assessing the risks from working in confined spaces, you need to consider both the hazards already present in the space and those that could flow or be introduced into the space.

One obvious concern is any gases that are present in the confined space – flammable gases could result in a fire or explosion. Dangerous gases could also be introduced into the space, such as fumes when carrying out welding in the confined space. Another hazard is the potential lack of drainage, as water from excessive rain or a broken water main may flow into the confined space and this could lead to a risk of drowning.

All confined spaces must have adequate ventilation. Without proper ventilation, workers could risk losing consciousness as a result of:

- an increase in body temperature – it becomes excessively hot to work and this can be exacerbated by the need to wear personal protective equipment (PPE)

- asphyxiation – gases, fumes and vapours can build up in the confined space and displace the oxygen.

Working at height

Falls from height are a common cause of fatalities and major injuries to employees. The main causes of falls can be attributed to:

- workers and employers not recognising the risk

- a failure to use correct access equipment

- a failure to adopt a safe system of work

- employees' lack of awareness of their own capabilities or that of their equipment.

There are several steps that can be taken to reduce the risks of working at height. First, everyone must understand that all work at height is hazardous. So, if possible, avoid having to work at height by the use of some other method of access.

If working at height is necessary, ensure that the correct type of equipment is used and that safe systems of work are followed.

A safe system of work is a step-by-step procedure to ensure that employees have the appropriate level of training, instruction and supervision, and that they use the correct working methods, access equipment and materials.

Electricity

Electricity is the energy source used to power most machinery, lighting and work equipment in an engineering environment. You will probably already know the basics of electricity: electrical current is the flow of electrons through a conductor and this flow results from electrical differences, known as pressure, measured in volts. In direct current (dc) the electrons flow in one direction, in alternating current (ac) the flow reverses direction 50 times per second. Most electrical systems used in engineering operate on alternating current.

Direct contact with an electrical conductor can result in an electric shock, which can be extremely harmful. The current flowing through the body interferes with muscles and the central nervous system, and can cause internal burns, convulsions, restrictions in the respiratory system and cardiac arrest. In addition, a person can suffer electrical burns – burning marks on the skin at the point of entry and exit – from the heating effect of the current burning body tissue. Electrocution from the mains supply (230 V ac) often results in a fatality.

It is essential therefore to isolate any electrical equipment before working on it. This will ensure that you do not touch a bare wire that is live. Remember, electricity cannot be seen or smelt.

Although electrocution poses the greatest threat, electricity poses other hazards. Fires can be caused by sparking or arcing from faulty or overloaded electrical equipment. Circuit overloading, such as connecting too many appliances into one socket, can also cause overheating of conductors and sockets, which poses a fire hazard.

To control electrical hazards in engineering workplaces, it is necessary to:

- select suitable and adequate electrical equipment

- ensure that circuits are built using the correct materials and installed with good workmanship

- inspect, maintain and test systems regularly

- only use circuits up to designed current loading

- isolate any circuit before maintenance.

There are other steps that can be taken to improve safety. Equipment can come with double insulation. This offers additional protection in portable equipment by providing layers of insulation built around live electrical parts. Look carefully at electrical drills and saws for a double box sign. Equipment should show recognised standard marks for compliance to CE and double insulation requirements.

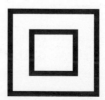

The symbol indicating that equipment comes with double insulation.

Another piece of protection that can be fitted to equipment is a residual current device (RCD). This is a fast-acting electromechanical device that automatically isolates the electrical supply to reduce the effect of a shock. You should use an RCD when working with any portable electrical tool in the garden or garage.

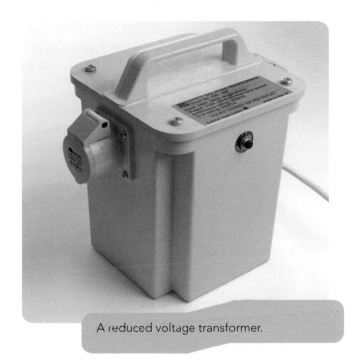

A reduced voltage transformer.

It is important to select the correct fuses for portable appliances. A fuse has only limited usefulness in protecting people from electrocution. Fuses break slowly if the current is just above their rated capacity. If the fuse has too high a rating, then the circuit will remain intact and still drawing power when it is overloaded. This can cause overheating leading to a fire.

As contact with the mains supply is often fatal, reduced voltage systems are used extensively in engineering. These are typically 110 volts, rather than the 230 volts mains supply. Look for equipment that is coloured yellow.

Mechanical

When operating any type of machine that involves mechanical movements, you must be aware of the hazards and you must take appropriate control actions to minimise the risk. Table 1.4 shows a way of categorising mechanical hazards and lists appropriate control actions to deal with each type of hazard.

The most important safety action is training and instruction. Before using any work equipment, employees must have been trained and instructed in

Table 1.4: Mechanical hazards

Hazard	Resulting from (example)	Control and prevention actions
Entanglement	Caught in the rotating chuck and drill of a drilling machine.	Employees must not wear any loose clothing or jewellery when operating machines that rotate.
Cutting	Contact with the sharp edges of a blade on a circular or band saw.	Keep fingers away from the hazardous area; use a push stick for the final part of the cut.
Friction and abrasion	Contact with a grinding wheel.	Always wear eye protection when working on grinding machines and keep fingers clear of the wheel. Abrasive wheels cause nasty injuries.
Ejection	Hit by sparks from a grinding wheel.	Wear eye protection and ensure that there are no combustible articles in the vicinity.
Shearing	Contact with guillotine knife.	Guards must be adjusted so that fingers cannot enter the hazardous area.
Stabbing and puncture	Entry of a rotating drill into hand or incorrect use of nail gun.	Use a telescopic guard to cover the rotating chuck and drill.
Impact	Contact with the moving arm of a robotic device.	Interlocking systems for perimeter fence must be working. Entry only by trained, competent and authorised employees. Sensors used to ensure that the robot arm stops working before person enters hazardous work area.
Drawing in	Caught between a pair of meshing gears.	Must be protected by a fixed guard so that employees cannot gain access to the gears.
Injection	Hit by outflow from a leaking high pressure hydraulic system.	Regular preventative maintenance programme to ensure that hydraulic pipes do not degrade. Inspect equipment before use.

its use. It is wrong and potentially dangerous to ask an untrained employee to use any work equipment. If you are not sure about how to use any equipment in a workshop, then ask someone who knows.

Noise

There are several ill-health effects that can be attributed to working in a noisy environment. Excessive noise over a long time can damage the sensory hairs in the cochlea, which can result in temporary or permanent deafness. It can also bring on (or make worse) tinnitus, a condition also known as ringing in the ear. Excessive noise over a short time can cause headaches and fatigue. A single excessive noise of short frequency can cause dislocation of one of the three ear bones – the hammer, anvil and stirrup – or rupture of the eardrum.

If it is not possible to reduce the noise generated by engineering operations to safe levels, then all workers in the vicinity must wear equipment to protect their ears.

Type of sign	Examples	
Mandatory		
Warning		
Prohibition		
Fire	Fire alarm	
Safe condition	Fire assembly point	

Figure 1.2: Warning and safety signs

Warnings

Throughout engineering environments you will find signs that warn you of potential hazards and tell you of appropriate actions. Figure 1.2 shows different types of signs you will come across. It is important that you know what each of the signs mean. The signs can be referenced from the Health and Safety (Safety Signs and Signals) Regulations.

Activity: Identifying hazards

You have been asked to use an electric drill to drill some holes in pieces of angle iron so that they can be bolted together. Before starting work, your manager has asked you to identify the hazards that would be encountered in drilling the holes. This is because a list of hazards is required so that a risk assessment can be made before you start work.

1 List the hazards that you might encounter in the drilling task. Divide this list into columns: one for mechanical hazards and one for non-mechanical hazards.

2 Suggest measures that could be used to control any risk arising from the hazards that you have identified.

1.2.3 Hazards that become risks

You must be able to distinguish a trivial risk and a significant risk. The reason is that under the Management of Health and Safety at Work Regulations employers have 'to carry out suitable and sufficient risk assessments for all significant hazards'.

A form similar to Figure 1.3 can be used to determine the difference between trivial and significant risk for a given activity. This should be filled in section by section. First list the hazards. Then list all the people likely to be affected by that hazard. Note that this will often include workers who might be in the vicinity, as well as those who are actually carrying out the activity. Then, for each hazard and each group of people that could be affected, score the likelihood that they might be affected on a 1–5 scale (1 = very unlikely, 5 = extremely likely) and the severity of any injury that they might receive also on a 1–5 scale (1 = minor injury, 5 =

Task: *Changing a wheel on a car*		Date: *8/10/2010*		Assessor: *AN Other*		
Hazards	Persons affected	Likelihood	Severity	Risk factor	Trivial or significant	
Collapse of lifting jack	*Mechanic – crushing*	*3*	*3*	*9*	*S*	
	Other employees – crushing	*1*	*3*	*3*	*T*	
Unlocking wheel bolts – strains or injuries from wrench slipping	*Mechanic – strains, sprains, bruises*	*3*	*2*	*6*	*S*	
	Other employees – bruises and cuts	*1*	*1*	*1*	*T*	

Figure 1.3: Part of a form to assess the significance of risks involved in changing a wheel

fatality). Multiply the two scores together to get a risk factor. Risk factors above 4 are considered significant risks. We shall explore these ideas further in the next section of the unit (see page 24).

Potential to cause harm

Many articles, substances and activities in engineering have the potential to cause harm. All need to be subject to risk assessment.

For example, if you use petrol to clean parts of machinery, then the potential hazards are:

- an outbreak of fire – petrol gives off vapours that are highly flammable
- skin damage – petrol will remove the protective layer of your skin and possibly cause dermatitis
- breathing difficulties – if working in a confined space, the petrol vapours will displace oxygen so that your breathing will be affected

- eye damage – in brushing petrol on to a machine, you could splash some into your eye; this stings and although it can be removed with natural lubrication, it leaves the eye very painful and dry.

These are all *foreseeable* hazards with the potential for harm. Measures must be put in place to control these hazards so that the risk is reduced. In this example, appropriate control measures to reduce the risks would include:

- using a non-flammable engine cleaner rather than petrol
- ensuring that you wear non-pervious gloves to protect your hands
- working in a well-ventilated environment
- using goggles to protect your eyes
- ensuring that you have received adequate instruction and training in the correct way to clean machinery.

Remember that all hazardous work must be controlled by health and safety measures.

1.3 Be able to carry out a risk assessment and identify control measures

You will be required to undertake a risk assessment in one of your assignments for this unit. In this section, we will show how this should be done.

1.3.1 Risk assessments

It is a legal requirement for all employers to carry out risk assessments. An employer has to assess risk in relation to:

- the use of any work equipment (under the Management of Health and Safety at Work Regulations)
- the operation of any type of machinery (Management of Health and Safety at Work Regulations)
- any work area (Management of Health and Safety at Work Regulations and the Workplace (Health, Safety and Welfare) Regulations)
- the use of chemicals (Control of Substances Hazardous to Health Regulations)
- manual handling (Manual Handling Operations Regulations)
- use of computers (Display Screen Equipment Regulations).

The Health and Safety Executive suggests a framework for undertaking risk assessments in its leaflet *Five steps to risk assessment* (HSE leaflet INDG163). Most engineering organisations use this as a framework for their risk assessment systems. It is suggested that you adopt these five steps in any activities and assignments that require a risk assessment.

Step 1

First, look for the significant hazards in the work area or activity you are investigating. You should use these methods:

- observe the activity being undertaken (or the work area being considered)
- undertake workplace inspections
- interviewing employees (or those using the area) – ask if there are problems.

Step 2

Decide who might be harmed, and how. You could split those who might be affected by an activity into groups:

- employees who undertake the activity or who work permanently in the area
- other employees who could be affected, such as maintenance workers, other operators and cleaning staff
- non-employees, such as visitors, contractors, agency workers and neighbours
- vulnerable persons, such as young employees, new and inexperienced workers, and expectant or new mothers.

Step 3

Evaluate the risks, and consider whether existing precautions are adequate or if more can be done. Recall that a risk is the likelihood that harm will occur, and a measure of the severity of the harm that the hazard poses. To evaluate the risk posed by any hazard, you must assess the likelihood of that hazard causing harm and the probable severity of that harm.

To help make this assessment, and to calculate a numerical risk factor, many organisations use a five by five matrix (see Figure 1.4). For the hazard being considered, the rows concern the likelihood of that hazard causing harm. Score this on a scale of 1–5 (from extremely unlikely [1] to almost certain [5]), basing your score on your judgement and/or past accident data. The columns concern the severity of the harm that the hazard could cause, again scored on a 1–5 scale (from minor injury [1] to fatality [5]).

The elements of the matrix are the likelihood score multiplied by the severity score. For any given hazard or situation, this is the risk factor. Use the matrix to prioritise actions: any result in the red zone is not acceptable and requires immediate and extra control measures to move your assessment into the yellow or (even better) into the green zone.

Severity

Likelihood			Minor injury (First aid) 1	Moderate injury (Lost time) 2	Serious injury (RIDDOR reportable) 3	Major injury (RIDDOR reportable) 4	Fatality (RIDDOR reportable) 5
Extremely unlikely	1		1	2	3	4	5
Unlikely	2		2	4	6	8	10
Likely	3		3	6	9	12	15
Extremely likely	4		4	8	12	16	20
Almost certain	5		5	10	15	20	25

Figure 1.4: The risk factor matrix

Let's consider some practical examples. What about the risk posed by cables in a classroom? Use reasoned judgement here: for example, you might assess the likelihood of someone tripping over a cable in a classroom as unlikely (2), especially if an inspection revealed no exposed cables connected to computers or other equipment, and you also might assess the severity as 2 – if someone did trip they might sustain a moderate injury. This gives a risk factor of 4 (2 x 2). This is in the green zone, so you might decide that existing precautions are adequate.

Suppose, however, you were inspecting a two-storey workshop and you found an exposed cable at the top of stairs in a dark corridor. The likelihood of someone tripping will certainly be higher (say 4) and the severity of fall down a flight of stairs would also be greater (again, perhaps 4). This gives a risk factor of 16 (4 x 4), which is in the red zone – further actions must be taken to eliminate or reduce this risk.

Additional control measures can be considered using a hierarchy of control (see Table 1.5). Note that this table is set out in order of effectiveness – the actions taken in the lower rows will not reduce or remove the hazard, but will provide some measure of protection This ensures that a standard system is used to determine further actions.

Table 1.5: Hierarchy of control

Action (in order of effectiveness)	Example
Eliminate the hazard	Use water-based rather solvent-based paints. Research would show that most car manufacturers take this precaution.
Reduce the risk	Use electrical tools that operate on reduced voltages, say on 110 V rather than on the 240 V mains supply.
Isolate employees and other persons from the hazard	Notice the two-metre-high fencing that surrounds construction sites. This protects all people near the site by stopping unauthorised access.
Control the extent of exposure or contact with the hazard using engineering means	Using an RCD will limit the exposure to electricity if a portable drill develops a fault.
Personal protective equipment	Staff should wear hard hats when carrying out lifting operations. Note that this would only protect those individuals and not anyone else.
Discipline in working practices	All employees are given instruction, information and training for their work. This also includes appropriate supervision during work.

Step 4

Record the findings of the risk assessment. Figure 1.5 shows an example of a risk assessment form based on a template produced by the Health and Safety Executive. When you carry out the risk assessment, you should complete a form making sure that you record:

- all significant hazards that have been identified
- all affected persons
- the adequacy of the existing control measures
- the **extent of the risk** (possibly by use of the 5 x 5 risk factor matrix)
- any additional control measures that are required.

All employees who carry out any work activity in engineering organisations must have access to the relevant completed risk assessments. This is because they must be aware of all hazards and risks, as well as any control measures to use for the activity.

Step 5

Review the risk assessment. A review date is always entered on a risk assessment form. Risk assessments must be reviewed if there is any change in the recorded details or if they are no longer valid (the review date has passed). Other reasons for undertaking a review include if there is:

- an accident, near miss or dangerous occurrence
- a change in the people carrying out the activity
- the involvement of young people in the activity.

1.3.2 Use of control measures

The hierarchy of control (see Table 1.5) is a useful tool to determine control measures. The steps it suggests – eliminate, reduce, isolate, control, personal protection equipment and discipline – are recognised procedures in engineering organisations. The hierarchy of control can be used for general risk assessments in a workshop. It is also a good procedure for the control of substances as required by the COSHH regulations.

Let's now look at the control measures that are used to reduce the risks of common operations and hazards in engineering.

Key terms

Extent of risk the product of the number of persons likely to be affected by the hazard and the severity of the damage.

Company name:						
What are the harzards?	Who might be harmed and how?	What are you already doing?	What further action is necessary	Action by who?	Action by when?	Done
Slips and trips	Staff and visitors may be injured if they trip over objects or slip on spillages.	• General good housekeeping. • All areas well lit, including stairs. • No trailing leads or cables. • Staff keep work areas clear, e.g. no boxes left in walkways, deliveries stored immediately, offices cleaned each evening	• Better housekeeping in staff kitchen needed, e.g. on spills. • Arrange for loose carpet tile on second floor to be repaired/replaced	All staff, supervisor to monitor Manager	From now on 01/10/10	01/10/10 01/10/10

Figure 1.5: Risk assessment template

Guarding

The reasons for using guards on machines are to:

- prevent people coming into contact with dangerous parts of machinery
- prevent physical harm from both power-driven and manually operated machines
- allow machines to be operated safely without interference to produce completed components.

You should be aware of the different types of guarding. Fixed guards are fitted so that they cannot be removed without special tools. They create a physical barrier and have no moving parts. Interlocked guards are movable, generally hinged and connected via micro-switches to the machine's electrical supply. If the guard is opened, the electricity is switched off. These guards are fitted to domestic microwave cookers found in many kitchens.

Ask permission to inspect some machinery in a workshop and see if you can identify the different types of guards.

Lifting operations

There are several hazards associated with any lifting operation, including:

- overloading
- failure of a load-bearing part
- overturning
- loss of load.

All cranes and lifting accessories have a safe working load (SWL). Care must be taken to ensure that cranes are not overloaded, that the loads being lifted do not exceed the safety limits. Cranes can overturn if they are used outside of their operating capacity. They can lose their loads if they are incorrectly attached to the hook or if there is bad slinging practice.

Failure of a load-bearing part can be caused by placing the crane over a drain, a failure to extend the outriggers or by a failure of an individual part of the crane structure. All cranes must be positioned on ground that can withstand the loads that will be lifted. All cranes require maintenance and there should always be pre-use inspections.

All lifting operations have to be properly planned. If you observe crane operations, you will see that two persons are involved. One is the driver of the crane, the other is the banksman. The banksman is in charge of the lifting operation, guiding the driver throughout the lift. Sometimes a slinger is used, who attaches the loads to the lifting equipment. All persons carrying out lifting operations must be fully trained and competent in their work.

Manual handling

Manual handling is the transporting or supporting of a load (including lifting, putting down, pushing, pulling, carrying or moving) by hand or by bodily force. Employers should ensure that their employees avoid manual handling items that could injury them. If manual handling cannot be avoided, then a risk assessment must be carried out. This is in four parts.

The fixed guards on a belt-driven machine. Can you identify any other control measures in the photograph?

First, consider the task or activity being carried. Imagine that you have to carry out maintenance on a machine. This would involve lifting and moving parts of machinery. Assess the manual handling job that you have been asked to do.

- Does it need to be done?
- Can it be made safer by splitting the machine into smaller parts?

Second, assess the capacity of the individual doing the work.

- Are you fit and healthy?
- Have you any existing back, arm or shoulder problems?
- Have you been trained in manual handling?

Third, consider the load.

- Are parts of the machine greasy, dirty or hot?
- Does it have any sharp edges?
- Can you make the load smaller, lighter or more secure?
- Can you make it easier to move by finding a better grip or using some handles?
- Can you put the load into a container so that it is more stable?

Fourth, and finally, look at the working environment.

- Is there sufficient space to work in?
- Is there enough light?
- Are there any obstructions on the route over which you have to carry or move the load?

- Are there any changes in floor level, such as steps or flights of stairs?
- Are there any spills of water, oil or other substances on the floor?

Completed manual handling assessments must be available to any employee who has to carry out handling activities. Employees must be aware of the hazards, risks and control measures to use when manual handling.

Regular inspection of work equipment

All work equipment that is used in engineering is subject to inspections. When you are working, it is your responsibility is to inspect all tools and machinery before use. Ask for advice if there seem to be problems or faults, or if you are not sure how to use work equipment.

It is employer's responsibility is to ensure that work equipment is fit for use. This responsibility extends to making careful inspections of all equipment on a regular basis. These inspections should be carried out by competent persons. Registers, or lists, should be kept as evidence of the inspections. There could also be evidence of this inspection and testing on work equipment. For example, you should find a white and green sticker attached to a portable electrical tool. This is evidence of Portable Appliance Testing (PAT), and it shows the equipment is electrically safe.

Case study: The raw material stores

You have been asked to take control on a temporary basis of the raw material store of an engineering company. Part of the job involves undertaking manual handling assessments.

The store holds a wide range of raw materials, including sheets of aluminium, steel and plywood, and bars of steel, aluminium and brass. The bars come in various diameters, although no bar is longer than 2 metres. The store has aluminium, nickel and brass castings in various sizes and shapes. It also holds 25 kg sacks of plastic granules for use in the company's plastic injection's moulding machines.

The weights of the raw materials held in the store vary between 0.25 and 30 kg, according to material type and physical size. Materials need to regularly be loaded on to pallets for transfer to the company's production area.

1 An acronym widely used for manual handling assessments is TILE. Find out what these letters stand for in this context.

2 Describe the factors that should be taken into account when conducting a manual handling risk assessment for this store.

Personal protective equipment

Using personal protective equipment (PPE) is a necessary precaution. However, you should always try to eliminate risks rather than just relying on PPE. Remember that PPE is near the bottom of the hierarchy of control, so it is much better to eliminate hazards or reduce the risk.

Table 1.6: Examples of PPE

Part of body protected	Equipment
Eyes	Safety spectacles, goggles, face masks
Head	Safety helmets, hard hats, bump caps
Body or trunk	Flameproof boiler suits, Kevlar trousers, chemical suits
Hands	Thin or thick rubber gloves, leather gloves, chain mail gloves
Ears	Internal earplugs, external earmuffs
Feet	Steel-toe boots, safety shoes, rigger boots, wellington boots

Employers have a responsibility to provide their employees with the correct type of PPE for any work activity. You will be instructed on the selection, use, storing, cleaning and replacement of any PPE issued to you. You have a responsibility to wear PPE when required. Remember, however, that only the person wearing PPE is protected. If you are wearing eye protection when operating a grinding machine, that does not mean that other people who might be in the vicinity will necessarily be protected.

Training and other control measures

When working in engineering, training for all activities is a priority. Training can be anything from a short session on emergency procedures to a longer programme to provide instruction on the operation of a complex machine. Training must be given to all employees in engineering. Employers break the law if employees are asked to do something for which they have not been trained.

Employees also have responsibilities. In an engineering environment, you need to take health and safety seriously. It is important not just for your self preservation, but you have an obligation to others to work in safe and healthy manner. This is a personal responsibility in both criminal and civil law. If you cause an accident resulting in someone being injured, then you could have breached the law.

Your welfare at work is also important – both for you, others and your employer. It is your responsibility to keep clean and tidy. For example, you should wash your hands after contact with any chemicals, and especially before going for a drink or food break.

Assessment activity 1.2

For this activity, you need to identify hazards in two working environments and to produce a written risk assessment of a work activity. Your work should be produced in the form of a written report covering the material required by the numbered tasks. Appropriate working environments could be:

- your place of work
- a training workshop
- a machine-shop environment
- a maintenance workshop
- an environment faced by electricians when working on a site.

P3 Identify a range of hazards in your two working environments. Describe methods you used to identify these hazards.

P4 Describe how the hazards you have identified which pose non-trivial risks can be controlled. Justify your choices.

P5 Produce a written risk assessment on a typical activity in one of your chosen environments. Cover a practical activity, such as a machining operation, electrical assembly and wiring, or welding.

P6 After your risk assessment has been carried out, suggest suitable control measures and state reasons why they are suitable.

M2 Explain the importance of carrying out all parts of a risk assessment in suitable manner.

M3 Explain how control measures are used to prevent accidents.

D1 Justify the methods you have used to deal with hazards and control risks and explain how they are in accordance with workplace policies and legal requirements.

Grading tips

This is a lengthy activity that will require workplace investigation as well as written work. Keeping a task sheet and a logbook or diary will be helpful. Try to base this activity on one electrical and one mechanical work area. This allows you to show knowledge and understanding of identifying health and safety hazards in different workplaces.

P3 It is expected that you identify at least four hazards relevant to each chosen workplace. Select different hazards for each workplace, as this will cover a wider range.

P4 Start this work by assessing which of the hazards you have identified pose non-trivial risks. Try to relate control measures to the relevent regulatory requirements.

P5 It is a good idea to use a standard risk assessment template (see Figure 1.5). When you undertake a similar exercise as part of an assignment for this unit, part of the evidence will be based on your tutor's observations of your work.

P6 It is suggested that you write down your reasons for why the control measures you have suggested are suitable. In an assignment, this evidence could be obtained through a question and answer session with your tutor.

M2, **M3** and **D1** To develop your work for the merit and distinction grades, you are required to be more proactive. You need to show that you have thought about the risk assessment process. This means that you have to think about the consequences of situations and actions, and show that you understand the connection between hazard identification, risk assessment and accident prevention.

PLTS

In carrying out this wide-ranging investigation, you will demonstrate that you are an independent enquirer, a creative thinker, an effective participant and that you can self-manage your work.

Functional skills

Writing your risk assessment and describing and explaining aspects of risk management will help develop your **English** skills.

1.4 Understand the methods used when reporting and recording accidents and incidents

Before considering the methods used to report accidents and incidents, we need to provide some definitions.

An accident is an unplanned or unwanted event that results in a loss of some sort. This loss could be an injury to a person or damage to machinery or buildings.

An incident is an unplanned or unwanted event that has the potential to result in a loss of some sort. An incident does not necessarily cause injury or damage. For example, a piece of material could become unclamped when being worked on, or a forklift truck could lose some of its load while in transit in the workshop.

1.4.1 Principles

There must be a procedure for the reporting of all accidents and incidents within an engineering workplace. You will be informed of the procedure when starting at any place of work as part of the induction process. Employers must keep records of all accidents, incidents and emergencies. Engineering organisations have reporting forms for each of these occurrences.

So why would the organisations need the reporting procedure? First and foremost, it is a legal requirement (see RIDDOR, page 13) to report serious accidents and incidents to the Health and Safety Executive. However, it also directly benefits the employer. A proper reporting system means that every accident and incident gets logged and can be investigated. An investigation will determine the causes of the accident or incident. This is not to put the blame on an individual but to determine why the event happened and to prevent a similar accident or incident occurring again. The investigation will find the causes, and it can be used to draw up an action plan to prevent recurrences.

The Health and Safety Executive can prosecute the engineering organisation following accidents and incidents. The accident and incident reports, together with relevant investigation reports, can be used as a defence in a criminal court. An investigation can also be used in any claim for compensation by an injured person.

Competent persons

When you are working for an engineering organisation, you must be trained for any activity that you would be expected to do. When you have completed an activity several times you will become experienced at that task. This is known as becoming competent at work.

Competence means that someone has been trained to carry out an activity – that the person is able to complete the activity, that they have completed the work before. It can also mean that the person is qualified to do a particular type of work, such as welding. It means that an employer will recognise the employee's competence for a particular type of work.

When you are in an engineering workplace, you rely on the training and competence of others. This competence is necessary so that one person does not put themselves or others in a hazardous situation.

Accident and incident costs

Accidents and incidents cost time and money. The cost to an engineering organisation of implementing health and safety control measures such as risk assessments and machine guarding can easily be calculated. The cost of any health and safety failures are not so easy to calculate and tend to be absorbed into the normal running costs of the organisation. As Table 1.7 shows, the costs of any accident or incident can be split into two broad categories – direct and indirect costs. These costs are not likely to covered in full by insurance.

Table 1.7: Costs to an employer of accident or incident

Direct costs	Indirect costs
Sick pay of injured employees	Internal accident investigation time
Lost working time	Extra time, overtime pay, temporary staff
Clearing the site of any damage	Production delays
Damage to materials and/or products	Loss of business reputation
Legal costs and fines	Loss of contracts
Excess on insurance claims	
Increased insurance premiums	

The Health and Safety Executive has a 'ready reckoner' on its website to help employers calculate the likely costs of accidents and incidents. It may be useful to access this resource when completing assignments covering this section of the unit. To find the resource, type 'HSE ready reckoner' or 'HSE cost calculator' into a search engine.

After an accident at work, an injured employee is usually entitled to compensation in the form of a monetary award. The award amount is based on criteria such as the injured employee's age, their possible earning power in the future, the degree of injury and the time kept away from work by the injury. The purpose of the compensation payment is to restore the injured person to, or as close as possible to, the quality of life that they enjoyed before the accident. Some injuries can be extremely severe, involving loss of limbs or worse. In these circumstances ask yourself, what price is worth the pain and suffering after the accident and into the future?

Accident trends

Accident and incident reporting allows an engineering organisation to spot trends by statistical analysis. Accidents and incidents are reported on standard forms. Statistics can be determined from the data on these forms, and any trends can be investigated. For example, an engineering organisation will want to find out why accidents are increasing in any work areas. If, say, the statistics show an upward trend in crush injuries in the packaging area, then this should investigated.

Worked example: Accident costs

These are some typical costs arising from an accident in a workshop in which a forklift truck ran over a machine operator. The worker suffered a crushed foot. The material (some work-in-progress) being carried on the forklift truck was dislodged and damaged when the driver swerved to try to avoid colliding with the machine operator. The worker received compensation for his injuries, some of which was met under the engineering company's insurance policy. The Health and Safety Executive prosecuted the company following an investigation into the accident.

1: Dealing with the accident
Immediate first aid: £40 per hour
Making the area secure and safe: say £600, but depends on the location
Taking the injured person to hospital: £40 per hour in the ambulance or by car
Informing next of kin: £40 per hour
Immediate cost of down-time because worker has been taken to hospital, plus cost of any other work stopped in the area: £1000–£2000, depending on location

Total: £1720–£2720

2: Investigation
Staff time for investigation and report: £1600
Meetings to discuss accident: £600
Time spent with HSE Inspector: £400
Consultant's fees: £1000

Total: £3600

3: Getting back to business
Assessing work schedules: £200
Recovering work/lost production: £4000
Cleaning and disposal of clinical waste: £50
Product reworking caused by material falling from forklift truck: £200
Hiring forklift truck to cover for the one out of action during investigation: £600

Total: £5050

4: Business costs
Salary of machine operative who is off work for six months: £14,000
Replacement staff: £16,000
Lost work time: £800
Overtime cost: £500
Recruitment of replacement staff: £3000

Total: £34,300

5: Sanctions and penalties
Compensation excess: £2000
Solicitor's fees and legal costs: £5000
Staff time dealing with legal issues: £3000
Fines and costs due to criminal proceedings: £15,000
Annual increase in insurance premiums: £2000

Total: £27,000

As you can see, the total costs arising from this single accident amount to over £70,000. This is not a notional sum. This example is based on an actual accident and uses the Health and Safety Executive's incident costs calculator.

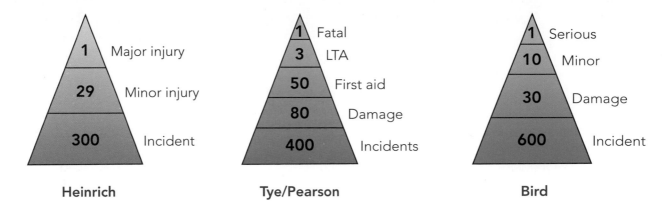

Figure 1.6: Accident triangles (results from statistical studies)

Statistics can also indicate the severity of the accidents, giving the numbers of fatalities, serious and minor injuries for particular types of incidents. Statistics can also classify accidents by parts of the body – eyes, hands, feet, ears etc – that suffer injuries.

Over the last 50 years, several statistical studies have shown that there is a clear relationship between accidents and incidents in the workplace. Accident triangles (see Figure 1.6) clearly show that incidents are the foundation of major injuries. If you look at the Heinrich model in Figure 1.6, you can clearly see that for every major injury there are 29 minor injuries and 300 incidents. We can learn from the triangles. Major injuries and accidents can be reduced through a strong reporting and investigation system that reports incidents and near misses. Any increase in incidents and minor injuries could be a warning that there is growing risk of a major accident.

1.4.2 Recording and reporting procedures

Engineering organisations have standardised forms to complete for accidents and injuries. Generally, there is one type of form for each category of accident, and they are coloured differently. The reason for standardised forms is that it gives consistency in the reporting process.

An accident book must be kept by engineering organisations. This should be used to record the details of every accident. The private details of anyone injured are not recorded to comply with the Data Protection Act.

There must be documented procedures for dealing with accidents, incidents and emergency situations. These procedures should explained during induction programmes for new employees. Some procedures, such as what to do in the case of a fire emergency, should even be explained to visitors to the workplace.

To comply with the law, accidents and incidents that met the RIDDOR criteria (see page 13) must be reported by a responsible person to the Health and Safety Executive by telephone or fax as soon as possible after the event. This must followed up by the completion and submission of Form F2508 within 10 days.

Assessment activity 1.3

 **::BTEC**

This activity requires you to produce a written report in three sections.

P7 Explain the principles behind the reporting of accidents, incidents and near misses. Describe why it is important that engineering organisations have (and adhere to) a health and safety reporting system.

P8 Describe the procedures for reporting accidents, incidents and near misses in an actual engineering workplace. You could choose one or both of the workplaces you investigated for assessment activity 1.2.

D1 In the final section of the report, you need to determine the actual cost of an accident. To do this you need to focus either on an actual accident in an engineering workplace or on a case study or scenario. For example, you could estimate the cost of the accident suffered by Mustapha Mohammad (see page 15).

You may not be able to get full information about some aspects that you will need for your costing, such as the employment costs of any injured employee or the cost per hour of lost production. You will have to make sensible estimates where this information is missing. In your report, you should state any assumptions or estimates that you have made, and list the information sources you have used to produce your costing.

Grading tips

P7 This activity is about whether you are able to relate to the importance of follow-up actions after accidents and incidents. For this grade, you should outline the general principles that inform actions.

P8 This is a more specific task. It requires you to consider the procedures in actual workplaces. An appropriate choice for you would be to focus on one electrical and one mechanical work area. This allows you to show knowledge and understanding of the identification of accidents, incidents and near-misses in differing workplaces.

D1 You need to calculate the costs of a specific accident. In the assignment for this part of the unit, you will be provided with a scenario and some background information. As well as using the information provided, you may need to undertake further research as well as draw on the information you have collected while studying this unit to make a full costing. For this assessment activity, you need to undertake your own research, making extensive use of the internet to seek information on accident rates, incidents and the cost of accidents.

Kevin Longshaw
Production engineer

I am responsible for the production of car seats for a well-known car manufacturer. This means that I have to ensure that the right materials are in the right place for my team to make the individual component parts of the seats. The individual parts are then assembled into the finished product.

My job also covers the heath, safety and welfare issues in the production area. From my first day at work as an apprentice 12 years ago, I have been made aware of my personal responsibility for health and safety. As a production engineer I have to meet targets set by the company – put simply, if the seats are not made to targets then car production could be held up or stopped.

However, this does not mean that I can ignore health and safety. I have to balance the demand for the seats against the legal, moral and financial obligations for the health, safety and welfare of the people under my control.

For my job, I have received extensive training as an engineer. Part of this training included several modules on health and safety. These made me aware of my responsibilities towards myself and other people at work. During my yearly appraisal I asked my senior manager if I could attend a dedicated health and safety course; she agreed and the company paid for this training. This gave me an extra qualification and has made me more confident and knowledgeable about health, safety and welfare issues.

I have to complete risk assessments for all hazardous activities carried out in the workshop. This sounds like a lot of work, but it is made simple by having a set of forms on my computer. When completing a risk assessment, I have a team briefing for all people involved in the activity. This helps implement any control actions, as staff feel ownership of the risk assessment due to their involvement. I also carry out daily inspections of the work area to ensure that all machine guards are in place, that individuals are wearing their PPE and that general housekeeping is being maintained to the required standard.

Think about it!

1 What type of hazards could be present in a works making car seats?

2 Why did Kevin have to know about health, safety and welfare on his first day at work as an apprentice?

3 Why would Kevin hold a team briefing to carry out a risk assessment?

4 Are risk assessments required by law?

Just checking

1 List the main responsibilities of employers under the Health and Safety at Work Act. What responsibilities does the act place on employees?

2 What is a hazard?

3 Explain what is meant by risk.

4 The Workplace (Health, Safety and Welfare) Regulations place requirements on employers. List three things that must be provided to employees under these regulations.

5 Which regulation should be referred to for advice on how to carry out risk assessments? Could you list the relevant regulation number for risk assessments?

6 List the five steps to follow when completing a risk assessment.

7 Explain the importance of carrying out all parts of a risk assessment in a suitable manner.

8 Outline what is meant by manual handling. Describe the main factors that need to be considered in a manual handling risk assessment.

9 Explain how control measures are used to prevent accidents.

10 Engineering organisations must record accidents, incidents and ill-health on standard forms. Define in your own words (a) an accident, (b) an incident and (c) ill-health.

11 Why does the engineering organisation have to keep accident records?

edexcel

Assignment tips

- Keep a diary of the reading and research that you do, as well as evidence of all activities you undertake. This will help when it comes to your assignments and will help you to produce a portfolio of evidence to identify your work against the learning outcomes.

- Try to arrange visits to local engineering companies so that you can see health and safety practices at first hand, and so you can learn about the processes and regulations that underpin safe practice. You can also learn from visiting other workplaces, such as civil engineering operations and garages. Ensure that you obtain permission first.

- You can also learn from the college environment. Look carefully around the woodworking, engineering and chemistry areas of your school or college. Ask permission first – do not enter without. Look for hazards, and precautions to control them.

- In undertaking your assignments, make extensive use of the internet to seek information on risk assessment systems, health and safety law, engineering processes and accident statistics.

- For the risk assessment assignment, choose a practical activity that you are familiar with and one that you can easily observe. You will need to suggest suitable control measures after the risk assessment has been carried out and state the reasons why they are suitable.

2 Communications for engineering technicians

Engineering involves a wide range of activities, so it is important that there is effective communication between the people doing them. This may take a variety of forms, but it must always be done in a way which ensures that data is accurately conveyed. In engineering there is no place for ambiguity because mistakes cost money, and this ultimately affects the profitability of a business.

If a designer prepares a component drawing which has errors or which incorrectly specifies the material to be used, then the product will be manufactured incorrectly. Time and money will have to be spent rectifying the problem. To prevent this happening again, designers need to know that they have made a mistake. Suppose you are an apprentice engineer responsible for machining the component. You would have to tell the designer that there is a problem. What information will you need and what's the best way to present it?

In this unit you will explore the principles and use of visual communication methods, technical report writing and verbal presentation. You will also investigate how information communication technology (ICT) operates in engineering settings.

Learning outcomes

After completing this unit you should:

1 be able to interpret and use engineering sketches/circuit/network diagrams to communicate technical information

2 be able to use verbal and written communication skills in engineering settings

3 be able to obtain and use engineering information

4 be able to use information and communication technology (ICT) to present information in engineering settings.

Assessment and grading criteria

This table shows you what you must do in order to achieve a pass, merit or distinction grade, and where you can find activities in this book to help you produce the required evidence.

To achieve a **pass** grade the evidence must show that you are able to:	To achieve a **merit** grade the evidence must show that, in addition to the pass criteria, you are able to:	To achieve a **distinction** grade the evidence must show that, in addition to the pass and merit criteria, you are able to:
P1 interpret an engineering drawing/circuit/network diagram **Assessment activity 1 page 43**	**M1** evaluate a written communication method and identify ways in which it could be improved **Assessment activity 3 page 53**	**D1** justify your choice of a specific communication method and the reasons for not using a possible alternative **Assessment activity 3 page 53**
P2 produce an engineering sketch/circuit/network diagram **Assessment activity 2 page 47**	**M2** review the information sources obtained to solve an engineering task and explain why some sources have been used but others rejected **Assessment activity 4 page 58**	**D2** evaluate the use of an ICT presentation method and identify an alternative approach **Assessment activity 5 page 62**
P3 use appropriate standards, symbols and conventions in an engineering sketch/circuit/network diagram **Assessment activity 2 page 47**	**M3** evaluate the effectiveness of an ICT software package and its tools for the preparation and presentation of information **Assessment activity 5 page 62**	
P4 communicate information effectively in written work **Assessment activity 3 page 53**		
P5 communicate information effectively using verbal methods **Assessment activity 3 page 53**		
P6 use appropriate information sources to solve an engineering task **Assessment activity 4 page 58**		
P7 use appropriate ICT software packages and hardware devices to present information **Assessment activity 5 page 62**		

How you will be assessed

This unit will be assessed through assignments designed and marked by the staff at your centre.

The type of evidence you will need to present when you carry out an assignment could be in the form of:

- a portfolio of sketches, or circuit or network diagrams supported by a written commentary
- a portfolio which shows off your skills in note taking, writing and keeping a logbook
- a tutor observation record or video clip of you speaking, listening and using body language to communicate effectively
- a printout of a PowerPoint presentation.

Emma, 18, apprentice electronic technician

I started my apprenticeship straight from school and am now in the second year. At the moment, I am working in the product quality assurance (QA) department, where I help with testing amplifiers and power supplies.

During testing we record data such as power consumption, voltages and temperatures, and this numerical data is entered into an ICT system. I also have to write evaluation reports, which are presented to the product designers.

I studied this communications unit last year. It has really helped me in my present job and it has made me more confident, particularly when I have to talk to other technicians and designers about our products.

One day I discovered what I thought to be a significant design problem with a power supply – it kept overheating and tripping out. On further investigation I identified that an incorrect component had been fitted, and it was down to me to tell someone in the manufacturing department that a batch of 100 units had not been assembled to specification. A year ago I would have been very nervous about doing this, as I was always the quiet one at school.

I do like working in QA because it links with design, manufacture and product development. I can now see how all the topics I studied in this unit fit together and really help me with my job.

2.1 Be able to interpret and use engineering sketches/circuit/network diagrams to communicate technical information

Start up

Speaking, listening, interpreting and writing

Get together with three other people from your group and find somewhere quiet to sit. Make sure that each member of the group has a pen and paper to take notes.

Each member of the group should then introduce themselves, talking for a couple of minutes about an interesting activity that they have carried out during the previous week. This could be something at work, a hobby or sport, or it could be about a radio or television programme – anything that will gain the attention of the other members of the group.

The rest of the group should make notes. Then, working individually and using a word-processing package, write a **profile** about each of the other members of the group based on their talks. Each profile should be about 150 words long.

Now regroup, and give the profiles to the relevant person and see if they agree with what you and the rest of the group have written about them.

Your profiles may be completely accurate: why is this?

There may be errors in your profiles: why is this?

Engineers use many different graphical techniques to communicate ideas and information. These include sketches, assembly drawings, **3D** exploded diagrams, electrical circuit diagrams, plant layout diagrams and operating procedures presented as flow charts.

When using graphical techniques it is important to follow accepted codes of practice so that there is no ambiguity about the message being conveyed. Machining metal, installing a fluid power system or assembling components are expensive activities, and it is important that the requirements of the designer are conveyed accurately to people working on the shop floor or at a customer's premises.

Looking at and understanding graphics is a common aspect of everyday life. For example, most people understand the signs used in public places to indicate fire exits or no smoking. It only requires common sense to understand what the graphics mean. Other graphics are more specialised and may be difficult for people to understand unless they have **expert knowledge**.

You should be able to understand graphics even if some of them include words in a foreign language. Can you interpret the signs in this photograph?

Key terms

Profile a short review which contains key facts about a person, object or process.

3D three dimensions; three dimensional.

Symbol something used to represent something else by association; for example ω represents angular velocity, © means copyright.

Expert knowledge specialist knowledge about a subject gained through education and training.

2.1.1 Interpret

When you look at an engineering sketch, circuit diagram or network diagram there will different types of information presented. You need to know which bits are relevant, and you need to be able to interpret what they mean.

The process that you need to carry out is no different to someone reading a page of music or a piece of text written in a foreign language. Beginners might be able to pick out the individual meaning for each of the notes or words, but do they really understand what is being presented when read as a phrase?

To illustrate the problem, access a search engine online (such as Google or a similar site) and look for the translate text option. Type in and translate this sentence into Estonian:

The electrical control unit is fixed to the frame of the power pack using rubber anti-vibration mountings.

Now paste the translation back into the text box and convert it back into English. This is what you might get:

Electrical control unit is attached a frame pack, using a rubber anti-vibration.

Similarly, translating the sentence into Polish and back, you get:

Guards are attached to the frame of the power pack with rubber anti-vibration mountings.

Something has got lost on the way each time, perhaps because the software doesn't have expert knowledge about engineering. This isn't a trivial exercise: many UK companies have manufacturing facilities in Poland and other countries in which English isn't the first language. As accuracy is essential in engineering, clearly they need to use means other than search

engine translators to commnicate information. So how do engineers ensure that there is no confusion about what is written in documents or presented in drawings?

To answer this question, we need to look at the type of information that engineers typically need in their work. There are three types of information to consider and interpret when communicating technical information:

- features which describe a product or system
- instructions for producing a product or system
- graphical information which aids written or verbal communication.

Can you identify the graphic **symbols** presented on this label and interpret what they mean?

Did you know?

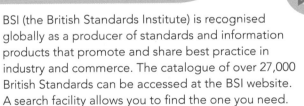

BSI (the British Standards Institute) is recognised globally as a producer of standards and information products that promote and share best practice in industry and commerce. The catalogue of over 27,000 British Standards can be accessed at the BSI website. A search facility allows you to find the one you need.

Features which describe a product or system

At some point in your engineering career you will be asked to manufacture a component using machine and hand tools. Before starting work you need to know about the component's features, and these will usually be presented to you in a drawing or sketch. The starting point will be features relating to the component's physical appearance, such as the lengths of sides, diameters of holes and cylindrical surfaces,

tolerances, **surface finish** and **surface coating**. If the drawing or sketch has been produced to a recognised BS or ISO standard, you should be able to easily unpick the information presented.

Perhaps you are not involved with machining but are more interested in building and testing equipment. For example, you might be fitting together the valves, actuators and power lines of a **pneumatic circuit**. What sort of information do you need? A list of components and a layout diagram would be useful. You might also want to refer to BS2917.

Key terms

Tolerance an allowable deviation from the desired size (no size can be achieved exactly).

Surface finish the roughness and waviness of a surface; also referred to as surface texture.

Surface coating substances applied to a surface after it has been machined, such as paint or chromium plating.

Pneumatic circuit a system that operates using compressed air.

Heat treatment a process that changes the mechanical properties of a metal by using controlled heating and cooling.

Specification technical requirements that a product or service must conform to.

2D two dimensions; two dimensional.

Instructions for producing a product or system

Drawings and sketches are very useful, but unless a product is very simple they will not hold all the information needed to guide someone through the steps necessary for its production. Production refers to activities such as manufacturing by cutting materials, assembly of components, and processes like **heat treatment** and surface coating.

Drawings might be accompanied by documentation such as cutting lists, tool requirements, assembly instructions, operating procedures for testing circuits and anything else which will help someone to produce a product or system to **specification**. This may even include information about the plant layout. Specialist engineers and technicians will produce this type of documentation.

This documentation will be used by the production team. For example, a manufacturing engineer will look at a component drawing and decide on a machining sequence and the tooling requirements. This information is then passed as a paper or electronic document to the person operating the machine tool that will be used to manufacture the component.

Graphical information which aids written or verbal communication

So far we have considered drawings and sketches, and the associated written documentation, used in a production environment. Now think about a different situation. Suppose you are writing a technical report or putting together a PowerPoint presentation. The text is fine, but you are unsure if it will fully get the message across and you decide to include some graphics. What form might these take? These are the most commonly used options.

- Illustrations such as hand-drawn pictures and digital images imported from a camera.

- Technical diagrams showing how components fit together. Good examples can be seen on manufacturers' websites when looking for replacement parts.

- Sketches that, for example, show how to assemble components or how to install a product into a service position.

Activity: Communicating information

Find an everyday object such as a mobile phone or a piece of equipment used in a workshop and produce a 3D freehand sketch of it. Do not use any words on your sketch.

Give the sketch to a colleague and ask them to redraw it as three **2D** views. These drawings should then be passed to a third person, who is asked to turn the 2D views into a 3D sketch. When completed, this sketch is passed back to you.

How accurately does this final drawing compare with the item you initially sketched?

Is there anything missing? Did anything get lost in translation?

Case study: Ryan proposes a better way to do a job

Ryan is a maintenance technician for a company that produces carbon fibre body struts for commercial aircraft. When he services the filament winding machines he follows procedures set out in a service manual. There are 10 machines, each requiring a monthly service.

Ryan has been doing the job for about two years and has come up with an idea that he thinks will reduce the servicing time for each machine by about 4 hours.

Suppose you are Ryan's supervisor. He arranges a meeting with you to discuss his idea.

1 What questions will you be asking him?

2 What evidence do you expect him to present?

3 Ryan will need to clear his suggestions with the manufacturers of the machine. How should this be handled?

Assessment activity 2.1

P1 BTEC

You only need to carry out **one** of these tasks. Choose a task that relates to your area of interest.

P1 Find a drawing of a component that is presented in 2D using orthographic projection and to drawing standard BS8888. From the drawing identify and describe six pieces of technical information that relate to features of the component, such as datum positions, dimensions, tolerances and surface finish.

P1 Find a circuit diagram of a pneumatic system, presented in accordance with BS2917, and identify and describe six pieces of technical information that relate to features of the circuit, such as power source, conditioning device, flow lines, control valves, actuators and sensors.

P1 Find an electronic circuit diagram that is presented in accordance with BS3939. Identify and describe

six pieces of technical information that relate to features of the circuit, such as power source, voltage regulation, connections and output characteristics.

P1 Find an IT network diagram that is presented in accordance with PP7307 and includes a range of hardware items. Identify six pieces of technical information that relate to features of the circuit.

Grading tip

P1 You are looking for technical information that could be used to help you manufacture or test the product.

2.1.2 Engineering sketches/ circuit/network diagrams

People involved with the production of engineering graphics should present their work so that it conforms to relevant British (BS) and international (ISO) standards. This is important because it will prevent any misinterpretation of the information being communicated, but it does assume that the person reading the diagram is also familiar with the standards.

Because of the way that businesses operate globally, components for a product could be manufactured in several different countries and then brought

together for assembly. Think about what happens in car manufacturing where, for example, engines might be designed in the UK, manufactured in Spain and then brought to Germany for vehicle assembly. The drawings and documentation associated with the manufacturing process are moved around electronically and read by many different people.

In Unit 16: Engineering Drawing for Technicians you have the opportunity to develop your sketching and formal drawing skills, and there is considerable overlap with this unit. For now, let's consider three particular aspects of engineering graphics.

Freehand sketching

Why produce a freehand sketch when we have access to CAD software and formal drawing methods? Many famous engineers have claimed that they sketched out their ideas for a new product on the back of an envelope. This may be true, but you would need a very large envelope for something like a wide-body aircraft or a motor vehicle. What they are really implying is that freehand sketching is a quick way to get ideas down on paper and it allows for the free flow of ideas. People can sit round a table, look at what is drawn and then add or take away detail – this is why sketching is the ideal way to start a design project.

Pictorial sketches presented in 3D are a good way to give an overall impression of what a product looks like. If specific detail needs to be shown, it may be better to sketch in 2D with views laid out using **orthographic projection**. Sketches can include calculations and notes, so that they can be passed to the designers responsible for producing detailed component and assembly drawings.

The process of sketching, whether it is totally freehand or done with the aid of a rule and set square, should follow some basic guidelines:

- ensure sizes and shapes are in good proportion
- work off centre lines and lay out views in the same way as for formal drawing
- represent standard features, such as tapped holes, with **conventions** as detailed in the relevant **drawing standard**
- produce work that is neat and easy to read
- provide adequate labels.

Key terms

Orthographic projection the representation of a 3D object by a set of linked 2D views, such as plan, front and side.

Conventions accepted ways of representing the features of an engineering component in a drawing.

Drawing standards a publication that specifies how an engineering drawing should be produced so that there is no ambiguity in its presentation.

Annotations written notes and numerical information added to a drawing.

Pneumatic a system that operates using compressed air.

Hydraulic a system that operates using compressed oil.

Schematic a representation of a component using a graphic symbol.

Unless they are very detailed or relate to extremely simple components, it is not recommended that sketches are used for manufacturing purposes. It is much safer to convert a sketch into a formal engineering drawing, so that it can be properly checked and approved for use.

Activity: Freehand sketching

USB flash drive memory sticks are a popular way of storing data. They are small, reasonably cheap to buy and people often end up with a drawer full of them.

Design a simple desktop caddy that will hold 10 standard-sized memory sticks.

Prepare a freehand sketch with **annotations** of the caddy and discuss your design proposal with a colleague.

Think about a suitable material for the caddy, and consider how it might be manufactured.

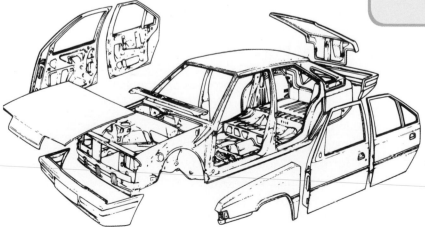

Some design technicians in industry now use CAD systems to sketch out their ideas. Your sketch of the memory stick caddy should be drawn freehand, but it should illustrate some of the details of your design.

Circuit and system diagrams

Circuit and system diagrams show the functional relationship between components and are used for assembly, testing and fault-finding purposes. Typically, they are referred to when working with electrical and electronic circuits, fluid power systems (**pneumatic** and **hydraulic**) and IT networks. Circuit diagrams show how the various components are linked and are usually **schematic**. You should be aware that the position of a component in a circuit diagram does not necessarily indicate its physical position in an assembly.

A circuit diagram is very often accompanied by a parts list, assembly notes and values for test measurements. For an amplifier, these would be the measured voltages at different points in the circuit. In a hydraulic circuit, pressure readings would be made.

System or network diagrams may show how components are linked or can be in the form of block diagrams, which trace through how the system operates. For example, a block diagram may be used to show the sequence of events as a central heating boiler fires up and switches off.

IT networks have varying levels of complexity. Think about the one installed at your college or place of work. If there is a communications problem, the IT technician will need to look at the system diagram and carry out a fault-finding procedure. You can find examples of IT network diagrams on the internet or on electronic databases. Print off an example, and note how the 'boxes' link together. Annotate this diagram with brief notes that explain the functions of the equipment shown in the network.

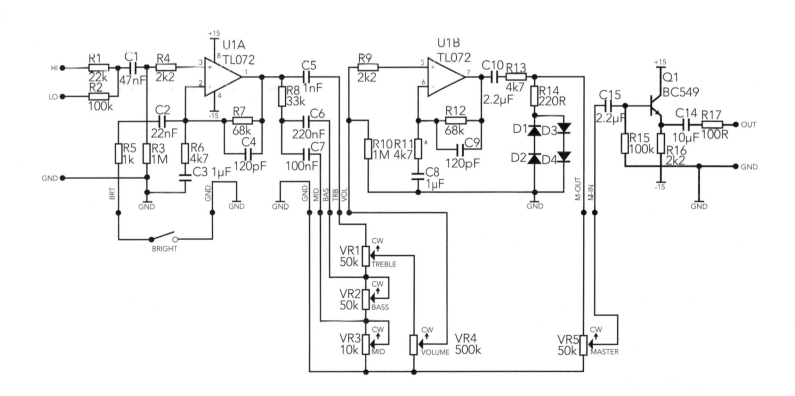

This circuit diagram is for a guitar pre-amplifier. See if you can obtain a circuit diagram for a piece of equipment you have at work or at college. It is useful to compare the circuit diagram with the actual circuit layout in the equipment.

A simpler form of system diagram will be used to provide information to consumers. For example, a telecommunications company might provide a simple system diagram for customers linking up to broadband at home, together with instructions about setting up the router and linking it to a computer. This could be supplemented with more instructions about getting it all to work. There may even be the option of verbal communication, with purchasers invited to ring up customer service if they have problems so that they can be talked through the set-up procedure.

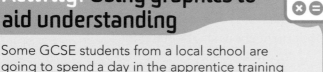

Activity: Using graphics to aid understanding

Some GCSE students from a local school are going to spend a day in the apprentice training workshop of your company. One activity they will be carrying out is drilling a 12 mm diameter hole through a 5 mm thick mild steel plate clamped in a pedestal drilling machine.

The instructor wants to be sure that the students follow the correct sequence of events when drilling holes and asks you to prepare a worksheet.

1   On an A4 sheet of paper draw a flow diagram for producing the hole.

2   Add sketches showing how the plate should be clamped. These can be drawn separately and pasted onto the diagram.

3   Show your work to a non-engineer. Can this person understand what is going on? If there is any ambiguity, modify what you have drawn and sketched.

Conventions and standards

It is important to use the correct graphical representations and drawing standards when producing sketches and diagrams. This prevents confusion and ambiguity.

The starting point is to decide on the layout of your sketch or diagram. If you are sketching a component, then you need to decide if it is to be in 3D or if you are going to present it in an orthographic projection using one or more views. This will depend on your intended

audience: 3D is good if you are trying to sell an idea and you want to give an overall impression of your product, but an orthographic projection may be better if you are passing your idea on to a detail designer.

Circuit and network diagrams are usually drawn in 2D but it is still important to think about how you want them to look on paper, so you need to think about the correct positioning and leave room for notes.

Sketching components will involve using lines and cross-hatching and applying dimensions and tolerances, all of which should be done in accordance with the appropriate British Standard or International Standard. If there are specific requirements about the surface quality of an object, and you know what type of manufacturing process is to be used, then you can specify the surface finish using the 'tick' symbol.

An assembly drawing will always be accompanied by a parts list. There are recommended standardised ways of setting these out, so that if a product is modified the parts list can be easily updated.

When producing circuit diagrams it is important to use the correct component and connection symbols. For example, if you are drawing a hydraulic circuit then the filters, pressure regulators, valves and actuators will be shown using symbols. Connecting pipework, high pressure supply and low pressure return connections will also be shown using drawing conventions.

The conventions and standards for different types of drawings are set out in separate British Standards. Engineers producing and interpreting engineering graphics must be familiar with the British Standards (BS) and International Standards (ISO) that apply in their industry. You should find out which type of drawing each of these British Standards relates to:

- BS8888
- BS4500
- BS3939
- BS2917
- BS4058.

Key term

Hard copy a physical (not electronic) version of a document.

Case study: Ali solves a networking problem

Ali works for NDEB Ltd, a small business that manufactures printed circuit boards. The company has a network of computers and peripheral equipment connected to a central server. Ali is an IT technician responsible for keeping everything working and for installing new pieces of equipment.

NDEB has just taken delivery of new computer-controlled machine and it is proving difficult to link this machine to the IT network. There are software and connector incompatibility problems – the machine refuses to 'see' the network.

The manufacturing director is very concerned and asks Ali to sort out the problem as a top priority.

Suppose you are Ali. How will you go about this task?

Assessment activity 2.2   P2 P3   BTEC

You only need to carry out **one** of the P2 tasks. Choose a task that relates to your area of interest.

P2 Find a relatively simple engineered component, such as pulley bracket or a toolmaker's clamp, and produce a freehand sketch of it.

P2 Produce a pneumatic circuit diagram comprising at least 10 different components to a standard that is acceptable to industry.

P2 Produce an electronic circuit diagram comprising at least 10 different components to a standard that is acceptable to industry.

P2 After new manufacturing machines have been installed into a work area, they are commissioned. Using network diagrams and test equipment, technicians carry out procedures to ensure that all the various machine and interface systems are functioning correctly. Construct your own example of a network diagram.

Your work – whether it is a sketch, a circuit diagram or a network diagram – should be presented using the correct BS standards, symbols and conventions.

P3 Identify the BS standards, symbols and conventions you have used by adding brief notes to a **hard copy** of what you have drawn.

Grading tips

P2 Your sketch or diagram must be sufficiently detailed so that it will effectively communicate technical information to a third party. It is good practice to use a drawing template so that you can include information such as your name and title and the date your produced the work.

P3 You need to demonstrate that you understand standards, symbols and conventions. Do this, by annotating your drawing.

Did you know?

The phrase 'a picture speaks a thousand words' is attributed to a Chinese emperor who lived about 4000 years ago. The saying is still relevant in the twenty-first century, but engineers are more likely to say 'a drawing is worth a thousand words'. This book contains many images: pick one of them at random and think how many words might be needed to describe it fully.

PLTS

Thinking about what you are going to sketch or draw requires creativity. It also is quite likely that you will have discussed and reviewed your ideas with your tutor. This will help you generate ideas and explore possibilities.

2.2 Be able to use verbal and written communication skills in engineering settings

2.2.1 Written work

The first contact that potential customers have with a business is usually through the written word. For example, a prospective customer might read the company website and its promotional literature, or might have been sent letters and emails. If this writing is badly presented or ambiguous, or if it contains spelling and grammatical errors, it will be difficult to read. It will certainly not impress any potential or existing customers, and they may decide to take their business elsewhere.

Much of the communication in an engineering business is by use of technical drawings and graphics, but if the accompanying documentation is poor it will cause confusion and doubt in the minds of people looking at it. CAD systems make it straightforward to produce 'perfect drawings', and design and simulation software packages can perform complex calculations, but writing good documentation cannot be automated, and it requires special skills on the part of the writer.

Note taking

When taking notes at a meeting it is important that you capture the key points being discussed so that you can follow up by writing a full report of the discussion (if required). You can take notes on paper, but many people prefer to use a laptop computer so that they can easily fill out headings and move blocks of text around. Making a list of key points is a simple way of getting information down on paper and could act as prompts when carrying out further research or follow-up activities.

When you are working on the design and project units on this engineering course, there will be times when you need to bounce ideas around between yourself and other people. Producing a mind map on a flip chart or interactive whiteboard is a good way to get started. You write down a central key word or idea, and then create a spider's web of thoughts, words or ideas around this idea. Mind maps encourage creative thinking, and sometimes an initial 'off the wall' idea which seems illogical may, in fact, be the one to develop. 'Thought showering' is another term that people use when thinking creatively or problem solving in a team.

At the end of a productive mind mapping session, it is usual to agree an action plan so that ideas can be taken forward. This could involve drawing up a flow chart which sets out the steps to be followed and the names of people responsible for specific actions.

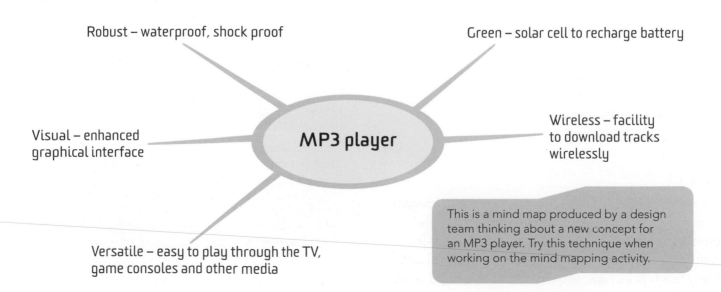

Robust – waterproof, shock proof

Green – solar cell to recharge battery

Visual – enhanced graphical interface

MP3 player

Wireless – facility to download tracks wirelessly

Versatile – easy to play through the TV, game consoles and other media

This is a mind map produced by a design team thinking about a new concept for an MP3 player. Try this technique when working on the mind mapping activity.

Writing styles

The writing styles used in engineering are varied, and they include different styles appropriate for letter and report writing, for memos (paper based and email) and for faxing information.

Letter writing ranges from a simple one line email or handwritten note to a formal letter presented on headed company notepaper and signed by hand. The degree of formality depends on the relationship between the people who are communicating. When writing to someone for the first time it is good practice to use a formal tone; you can always adopt a more familiar style as you get to know them.

For most types of written communication the key to success is to be succinct and to keep to the point. People in business do not have the time or patience to read long documents padded out with unnecessary words, so short paragraphs and bulleted headings make for simpler and more accurate reading.

Paper-based memos are rapidly being replaced by electronic forms of communication such as emails and texts. However, if you do write a memo, be sure to include this information:

- name of intended recipient
- name of sender
- subject
- date.

Writing a good technical report requires a fair degree of skill, and this is something you will practise and develop on this BTEC National programme. There is no 'one size fits all' rule for preparing reports, and many businesses have their own special requirements.

When preparing a report, it is worth checking to see if there is a **template** into which you can type or write.

When you are writing, keep in mind who will be reading your report. Suppose you are writing a report presenting a very detailed design proposal, which contains drawings, text, calculations, edited research material and proposals. A subject specialist, such as your tutor, will read the document right through and pick up on all you have written. A busy training manager or director at your place of work may be more interested in just getting an overview of what you are proposing. To help them, it's worth including a summary section at the start of the report with key facts, findings and recommendations.

Beware of using shorthand that may not be understood by everyone reading your work. When preparing documentation you should explain the meaning of any acronyms that you use. An acronym is a word formed by the initial letters of a name or phrase, such as sonar which is formed from the first letters of the words '**so**und **n**avigation **a**nd **r**anging'. Most people understand what BBC1 means when looking through the television listings, but the meanings of many other acronyms are much less well known. You will come across many acronyms related to education in your course. Make sure you know what PLTS, FS and BTEC stand for.

Proofreading and amending text

In a professional context, such as business and engineering, any written work that will be read by people other than the writer should be grammatically correct, contain no spelling mistakes and use proper punctuation. This can be difficult to achieve, even with the help of the spell and grammar checkers in a word-processing package. Many people who produce and write reports and books (including the publishers of this book) employ the help of proofreaders. In the past, a proofreader would mark up any mistakes on a paper copy of the text using a coloured pen; now many proofreaders mark up text electronically on screen using the highlighters available in computer programs.

You can also proofread your own work by sitting back and quietly working through the text. The problem here is that many people skim read, particularly when their writing has been worked on several times and they can almost remember it word for word.

When you ask someone to proofread a document or technical report, be careful to make sure that they do not change the meaning of a block of text when they make amendments. They may not have the in-depth technical knowledge that you have, even though their English writing skills may be excellent.

Written text can be quite difficult to follow if it is badly presented with, for example, an unclear typeface, long sentences and huge paragraphs. It is much better to break text down into manageable blocks and, where appropriate, to use bullets or paragraph numbers. This is particularly important for technical reports. You may have some experience of improving the presentation of reports: think about a report that you have written and which you have tidied up following discussion with your tutor.

When you amend text, think about the people who will be reading your work. You need to capture and keep their attention. It may be worth adding images or diagrams to lighten the appearance of the page, or perhaps think about adding some colour.

We are moving towards a paperless environment, with all documentation being written and worked on electronically. This is fine, but many people who write technical reports still prefer to print it out so that they can spread the document out and look over the pages. Errors are usually easier to spot, amendments can be highlighted with a marker pen and corrections can be made to the original document in one hit.

Amendments to word-processed documents can be tracked using the 'track changes' command. This is really helpful if several people are involved with writing a report over a period of time. It provides an **audit trail** of their amendments and a clue to their thoughts.

Key terms

Audit trail a series of records so that you can go back and track what occurred.

Activity: Proofreading

Work with a colleague on this activity. Each of you should select a document that you have prepared with a word-processor. Email your documents to each other and then proofread each other's document.

Return the amended documents and look over the changes. Discuss your findings.

Functional skills

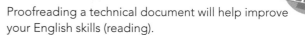

Proofreading a technical document will help improve your English skills (reading).

Presentation

This book uses a range of writing and graphic styles. The aim is to capture your attention and to make you want to read it from cover to cover.

It is interesting to see how these styles have changed over the years. A useful exercise is to find an engineering textbook written several years ago, and then compare the style of presentation between now and then. Ideally you should look for one covering the same level and type of course. You might find one tucked away at the back of a college teaching room. Start by picking a page from this book and one from the old one, and count up the number of words on each page. Then look at the font style and size. Which book is the more attractive to work with?

You need to ensure that any document you produce is pitched at the right level for the intended audience and is set out clearly.

Diaries and logbooks

Keeping a logbook or diary is a good way to maintain an up-to-date record of events as they take place. Many people keep electronic notebooks, but most of the great inventors and engineers wrote everything down by hand.

Using a diary is a good way to capture information that will help you plan and prioritise work schedules, but when you need to record something in more detail it is better to use a logbook. Logbooks are used to keep detailed records of what happened during a project. Your course logbooks should contain text, calculations, sketches, drawings and images, as well as feedback and comments from your tutor, mentor or supervisor at work.

Good personal organisational skills are needed if a diary or logbook is to be kept up to date. Discuss with your tutor an agreed format for a logbook that can be used to record the progress of an engineering project. Set up a time frame for how often it should be reviewed, and design a tracking sheet which can be signed off at each review meeting.

Graphics

Graphs, charts and diagrams form a significant part of the graphical communication used by engineers when they prepare reports and documents. It is very straightforward to insert them into a text-based document by cutting and pasting from a compatible software package. Most engineering businesses use Microsoft Office, and this allows easy import of files from digital cameras, scanners and other peripheral equipment.

Many files that you will be sent in engineering or which you download from the internet will be in 'pdf' format. This ensures that the layout of the document is not changed in any way when it is opened. This can happen when documents in other formats are opened in a different application or on a diifferent system to that on which they were created. Make sure you know how to save an electronic report created in doc (or docx) format in a pdf format.

Did you know?

The file extension jpeg was named after the Joint Photographic Experts Group. It is an agreed international standard for the compression of photographic images. The standard has been around for about 20 years and gives a compression ratio of about 10:1 for a typical camera or scanned image.

Functional skills

Writing about Beth's job role (see case study below) will help develop your skills in English (writing).

Case study: Beth helps produce electrical product guides

Beth works in the marketing department of a company that manufactures consumer electronics, such as digital radios and DVD recorders. Each time a new product is brought out, the company produces an operating guide. First drafts are written by the engineers who have designed the equipment.

It is Beth's job to make sure that the guides can be understood by the general public, some of whom will be technophobes. Beth will proofread and amend a draft without destroying the technical accuracy of what has been written and drawn. Her brief is to produce a user-friendly operating guide.

Suppose you are Beth.

1 How do you start the process of proofreading and amending a draft?

2 You are always given a copy of the full technical specification for the product as well as the draft operating guide. Why is this?

3 How will you track any changes which are made?

4 What notes will you write?

5 At what stages in your process will you involve the engineers?

6 Who should have responsibility for signing off the completed document?

2.2.2 Verbal methods

Effective verbal communication is a vital skill because it is important that everyone involved in a conversation has a clear understanding of what has been said and agreed. Unless a written record is kept, verbal communication can be an unreliable way of giving and receiving information. There are many situations where engineers speak and listen to each other, but these usually fall into one of two broad categories:

- informal discussions, such as face-to-face meetings or telephone calls, which are unrehearsed but are often based around lists of points to be covered

- formal presentations to a group of people all requiring the same information, usually supported by presentation graphics and handouts.

Engineers are usually very good at finding solutions to complex technical problems and turning ideas into products and services, but some are not so good at liaising with other people or presenting their work to a wider audience. The aim of this next section is to give you guidance on how to develop your listening and speaking skills so that hopefully you feel confident to converse at all levels within in an organisation.

Speaking

We do this all the time, and depending on who we are with we adjust our language between more formal and informal styles. The same rules apply when we are speaking as when we are writing to someone. Start by being formal and soften up as you get to know them better. It is important, and sometimes difficult, to strike the correct balance. If a customer rings up a company to complain, it will really make them angry if you call them 'mate' or use their first name. Listen, be polite and either address them formally – Mr Smith, Ms Smith etc – or don't use their name at all.

Think about what happened last time you were cold-called by a telesales person. From the start of the conversation did the salesperson assume that you were a friend and that it would be OK to be on first name terms? It's a technique designed to suck you into a conversation, so that you end up believing what they are telling you. They are not your friend, they just want to earn a commission by making a sale.

Engineers often have to be persuasive when talking to people so that they can get their message across. If you are going to be persuasive, then make sure you are fully prepared before you start to speak. Do you have the facts and figures in your head or on a prompt sheet? Are you able to take questions? What happens if you don't know the answer to a question? Do you look confident? Will people trust your judgement?

Listening

When someone talks to you, they can adopt one of two approaches. The first is to speak *at you* in a bombastic way, probably showering you with their opinions, facts and other information. Some teachers adopt this approach and very often their students take little notice of what they are saying.

The other approach is to speak *with you*. Even in a group situation, the conversation will appear to be personal with each listener being made to feel included. This is the preferred approach, but it does require effort from the listener as well as the speaker. It requires active listening. The best way to achieve active listening is to make eye contact with the speaker, raise questions at suitable points, allow the speaker to continue even if you disagree with what is being said, and generally be good mannered.

A successful business is one that has good products and employs staff who talk to each other. Because an engineering company relies on teamwork, you will find it really helpful to your career if you develop good speaking and listening skills.

Body language

Body language is an interesting topic. Think of someone you took either an instant liking or disliking to from the first time you met, perhaps before they even spoke a single word. Why was this? Was it their physical appearance, did they need to take a shower, or was it something in the way they behaved? Body language and personal chemistry are seemingly indefinable properties. Actors use these attributes to great advantage; in one film they might play the good guy and we all love them; in another film they are a horrible person who scares or revolts us.

When conversing with people be careful with your body language. Be too familiar, and people will be put off. Appear too cold and calculating, and most people won't like you. Striking the right balance requires great skill and can only be developed through practice.

Making a presentation

You will need to put all these skills into practice when making a presentation. As well as the written skills in preparing, for example, your PowerPoint slides to the required format and quality, you will need consider:

- making a good introduction
- delivering the main content
- finishing up
- answering questions
- engaging with the audience
- making a point
- maintaining eye contact
- ensuring clarity of speech
- demonstrating positive body language
- timing.

Think about the principles involved under each heading. For example, what's a good way to start a presentation? Should you stand on your head, cough loudly for a few minutes or introduce yourself?

Activity: Hearing, listening and communicating

Form a small group and discuss each of these statements.

I hear what you say, but I'm not listening.

There are ways to improve listening skills.

I agree to disagree with you.

We respect others' opinions.

Assessment activity 2.3

 BTEC

Choose a sport, hobby or other topic in which you are really interested and which you can use as the basis for a presentation to be made to other members of your group. You should plan to speak for about five minutes and have available a one- or two-page A4 leaflet which the audience can take away.

- Put together an outline of your presentation in note form and go through it with your tutor.
- Following this discussion, amend your notes.
- Prepare the leaflet. It should be around 250 to 300 words in length, and include at least one image, chart or diagram.
- Show your writing to a colleague and ask for feedback. Based on these comments, amend and refine your document.
- Now prepare what you are going to say. Think about different ways of giving your talk and select the one you think most appropriate. For example, you could make a formal presentation using PowerPoint slides, or run a question and answer session supported by images projected onto a screen, or deliver a semi-formal presentation using a flip chart.
- Make the presentation and take questions.

Grading tips

P4 You need to show that you can take notes and turn them into a piece of properly laid out text, which includes graphics. Your charts, diagrams or images should be linked to the text using figure numbers and titles.

P5 Evidence will be obtained through tutor observation records. These will record the discussion you had with your tutor and your presentation to the group. You need to demonstrate that your speaking, listening and body language skills complement each other and you are to communicate effectively.

M1 You can achieve this grade by developing your work. You need to review the content of your leaflet, come to a conclusion about its quality and identify ways in which it can be improved.

D1 You must fully justify your choice of the communication methods that you used and the reasons for rejecting the other option(s) that you considered. The key is to be able to reflect and evaluate.

2.3 Be able to obtain and use engineering information

Engineers use information sources when designing, manufacturing and testing products. It is very important to have an effective search strategy and to establish that data obtained from any information source is valid and correct. Much of the information used in engineering is in electronic form and it is very easy to fall into the trap of information overload. A strategy is required for identifying what material is really needed so that irrelevant or suspect data can be filtered out. This is particularly important when writing reports which include research data placed in an appendix.

2.3.1 Information sources

Information sources can be classified into groups, including:

- sales catalogues, used when purchasing components for incorporation into a product that is being designed
- published scientific data, such as the properties of materials, which is factual and presented in a variety of forms
- British and European standards
- company databases of reference material, built up over many years, which contain information such as the results of product performance tests and reliability data
- company drawing and documentation libraries.

Non-computer sources

Despite the increasing use of computers to store and distribute information, there are still many reference materials produced in hard copy format.

- Many engineering textbooks (like this one) and reference books are still published each year. If you are using a book, it is important to make sure that it is up to date, particularly where it makes reference to standards and legislation that may have changed since the book was published. Always check the dates of first publication and revised editions.

Activity: Finding information

Suppose you work for a company which manufactures electrical equipment for cars. You need to find this information:

- the results of performance tests carried out on alternators
- a customer design specification
- chemical analysis data relating to waste water produced during the manufacturing process
- hardness tests on aluminium stock delivered to the factory
- the results of safety tests carried out on electrical power tools used in the assembly department.

Where would you look for this information? The information is likely to be held by different departments in the company. Where could each piece of information be found in the company?

- Technical reports, either in-house or for general use, are often produced in hard copy.

In-house reports are like the ones you will prepare during this BTEC National programme or at your place of work. Only specific people are interested in reading them, and very often they will contain confidential information. For example, confidential reports might contain test results or design proposals, which would be of interest to business competitors if they were made generally available.

General use reports, such as *Which?* publications containing the results of product testing, are often available to buy. Published reports are usually covered by copyright, which means that material in them cannot be reproduced without the writer's permission. If you are going to use statements from an **open source** report, then it is good practice to acknowledge in your writing where they came from. A simple reference in the bibliography is all that is needed.

- Institute and trade journals are good sources of information because the material is often specific to a particular industry. You must usually buy an annual subscription to obtain a journal. Sometimes you can only buy a subscription if you work in the industry.

- Data sheets and test results data are concise ways of presenting information, and they remain very popular in places such as design offices and maintenance departments. The sheets can be filed in a ring folder, and it is quick and easy to refer to the information you need. Several pages of A4 can be laid out on a table and overviewed very easily.

- Manufacturers' catalogues are still a very popular way of presenting information, even though they may contain many pages and require regular updating. They are robust and can be used in places where IT equipment is not available or will not work.

Key terms

Open source freely available.

ISP an internet service provider.

Computer-based sources

There are many computer-based sources of information.

- An increasing amount of information is stored online. Online access is via the internet or a company intranet. Internet access is done using a fixed or mobile connection and linking through an **ISP**. Intranet access is internal to a business and works through the computer network linked to a database held on a company server.

- CD-ROMs are a useful resource because they can be built up into a catalogued library, but, as with paper-based sources, they need to be regularly updated. CD-ROMs are relatively robust and they can used in manufacturing environments where magnetic interference might corrupt data held on USB flash drive memory sticks. The type of data held on CD-ROM includes manufacturers' catalogues, service manuals, and specialised software. To access some types of data, for example test results, you may need an access code or password.

- Spreadsheets holding design calculations and test results are normally filed centrally in a company computer. Engineers and other people who have authorised access can log in to access the data.

- Databases holding information on a company's products are filed centrally in the business.

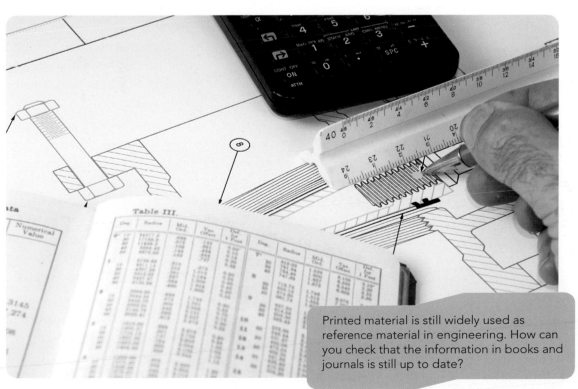

Printed material is still widely used as reference material in engineering. How can you check that the information in books and journals is still up to date?

Case study: Kalpa, sales engineer

Kalpa is a sales engineer working for Pycom Electronics plc. The company manufactures electrical connectors that are used in motor vehicles, computers and consumer electronics. There are two main product ranges:

- 12V, 24V, 120V and 240V power connectors

- data connectors, such as USB, parallel and serial connectors.

The company has a huge database of components, which can be accessed online or in printed catalogues.

A typical order from a Pyco customer might be for half a million units worth about £200,000, so it is important that the correct connector is ordered.

Kalpa's job is to prevent customers from ordering the wrong components.

1 What do you think is the significance of Kalpa's job role for both the customer and Pyco?

2 A new customer contacts Kalpa. What do you think happens next?

3 What specific details will Kalpa check after a sales order has been raised for the customer?

4 How much technical knowledge does Kalpa need to do her job?

Did you know?

The commercial use of the World Wide Web started in 1995. Before that date few people had heard of the term 'www'.

2.3.2 Use of information

Once you have picked up some information, what do you do with it? Are you able to confirm its accuracy? Is it primary or secondary data?

An example of primary data would be the results you collect when carrying out an experiment. Assuming you accurately read and recorded the experimental results, then this primary data will be correct. Suppose you give these results to someone else for processing, and this person carries out calculations, plots graphs and writes a report that does not include your original figures. If a third person now looks at the report, what they see is secondary data. They will either have to accept the figures in the report or, if they want to dispute anything, then they must refer back to your primary data.

When sourcing information from the internet, do try to ensure that the site is reputable and provides accurate information. Your tutor will give you guidance on the best sites to use to obtain specific information. If you enter 'health and safety at work' into the search box in Google, you will get over 100 million hits. Many of these hits will be to sites offering to sell information or providing their own interpretation of health and safety legislation. What you really want is some good primary data, and the place for that in the UK is the Health and Safety Executive's website.

Having found information, you will want to put it to use. For example, you might have conducted an information search because you wanted to solve an engineering problem such as calculating the dimensions and mass of a load-bearing component made from stainless steel. To do this, you will need information on the tensile strength and density of stainless steel, the factor of safety to be applied and the formulae for working out cross-sectional areas and stresses.

Worked example: How to use information

A design proposal involves fixing chromium-plated steel brackets onto an aluminium motor casing using titanium set screws. The assembly is to be part of a drive unit for a power boat.

We need to investigate the electrochemical corrosion problems that will occur. How should we go about this task?

First, we need to access the electrochemical (galvanic) series (see Table 2.1).

The next piece of information we require is about the corrosion properties of base and noble metals. Common knowledge tells us that base metals are more likely to corrode than noble ones when combined as a galvanic cell.

Sea water acts as an electrolyte – this fact can found by looking for information on the internet and checking in a materials textbook (such as *Materials for the Engineering Technician* by RA Higgins). These data sources also tell us that the bigger the difference in electrode potential, the higher the rate of galvanic corrosion.

Using all the data we have accessed, we can now come up with an answer. Titanium and aluminium are close together in Table 2.1, so there will be very little reaction between them. Chromium is higher up the table, and the potential difference between it and aluminium is 0.74 – 1.66 = 0.92 V. The aluminium will corrode in the vicinity of the bracket.

Table 2.1: The electrochemical (galvanic) series

	Metal	Electrode potential (volts)
Noble metals (cathodic)	Gold	+1.50
	Silver	+0.80
	Copper (Cu+)	+0.52
	Copper (Cu++)	+0.34
Reference	Hydrogen	0.00
	Iron (Fe+)	–0.50
	Lead	–0.13
	Tin	–0.14
	Nickel	–0.25
	Iron (Fe++)	–0.44
	Chromium	–0.74
	Zinc	–0.76
	Titanium	–1.63
	Aluminium	–1.66
	Magnesium	–2.37
Base metals (anodic)	Lithium	–3.04

Another important use for information is when you need to check that you have done something correctly. Here are some examples to think about.

- Your tutor asks you to carry out a maintenance procedure on a piece of equipment. You need a maintenance schedule and a sign-off document to prove that the task has been carried out correctly.

- You carry out an experiment in the science laboratory and process the results. Perhaps you measured the softening temperature of a polymer or found the surface hardness of a metal. How do you know if your answers are correct? You could ask your tutor, but it's more than likely the tutor will suggest you look them up in a reference source.

- You are in the workshop machining a component on a milling machine. The finished dimensions and accuracies are specified in a drawing. You need to check that your work is correct and get it signed off.

- You are building and testing an electronic circuit. You are given circuit and PCB layout diagrams, a test schedule and an inspection report pro forma. Once it is built, you must check the validity of your own work by completing the **test report**.

Key terms

Test report a report of a performance test conducted on a product to see if it conforms to its specification. If it does, then the product can be signed off as fit for purpose.

PLTS

If you use several different sources to find the same piece of information, it will be necessary to make a judgement on which one to accept. This will help you analyse and evaluate information, judging its relevance and value.

Functional skills

Using a variety of information sources to solve an engineering task will help you develop your skills in ICT.

Assessment activity 2.4

 P6 **M2** **BTEC**

PSL Ltd manufactures packaging machines and you have just moved into the design office. Before starting on the detail design of a new machine you need to source a variety of information so that you can carry out design calculations and costings.

This is the information required:

- tensile strength of mild steel

- maximum service temperature of polypropylene

- the contact details of a company that sells double-acting pneumatic cylinders

- a supplier part number for a 5 kW, 415 V electric motor

- the specification of a limit switch that can be used in the safety interlock circuit of a packaging machine

- health and safety data about noise levels for packaging machinery

- the price of 300 mm wide vacuum packing film

- the cost of vee belts that will handle 5 kW of power

- the dimensions of a deep groove ball bearing to fit a 12 mm shaft

- a manufacturer's order code and price for a bulk pack of 47 kΩ resistors

- a supplier part number for a sensor that will monitor the movement of cartons through a machine

- the limits of size on a 15 mm shaft for an H8F7 fit

- a COSHH data sheet for hydraulic fluid.

P6 Obtain the required information, and present both the data and the source of the information. You might find it useful to set this out in a table.

You must use both computer-based and non-computer-based sources to find the required information. You should provide proof of your sources in the form of screenshots and photocopies of pages taken from manuals. Use a highlighter pen to indicate collected data and be selective in how much evidence you present.

Grading tip

M2 To achieve the higher grade, you will need to present copies of all material accessed, suitably annotated in order to explain its value and why specific information has been used or rejected. If you have paged through lots of web pages to get to specific information, explain your methodology.

2.4 Be able to use information and communication technology (ICT) to present information in engineering settings

Getting accurate information to the right person at the correct time is crucial if an engineering business is to survive in the global marketplace. To maintain synergy between the various departments, the flow and control of information must be carefully structured when using ICT systems. All staff within an organisation will at some time be exposed to the use of software packages and hardware devices when communicating information. A business will have systems in place to protect its internal data and to prevent people being overloaded with unnecessary information.

The key consideration when setting up and using an ICT system is that it should complement the efficient running of a business. There are many occasions when writing on a piece of paper is a more efficient method of communication than using ICT, such as when noting down a phone message on a pad. Some people argue that if all data is entered into a computer system, nothing will be lost – this may be true, but the problem sometimes is finding where the data is stored on the system.

2.4.1 Software packages

There is a huge range of software packages in current use, but probably the most well-known is the Microsoft Office suite. It is popular because the programs in the suite are compatible, making it very easy to move data and files between applications. You will already be very familiar with many applications used regularly in business life, such as those which allow you to prepare documents, create spreadsheets, design presentations, set up databases, and send and receive emails. At an entry level, Office is very easy to use and most of the commands are intuitive in the way that they work.

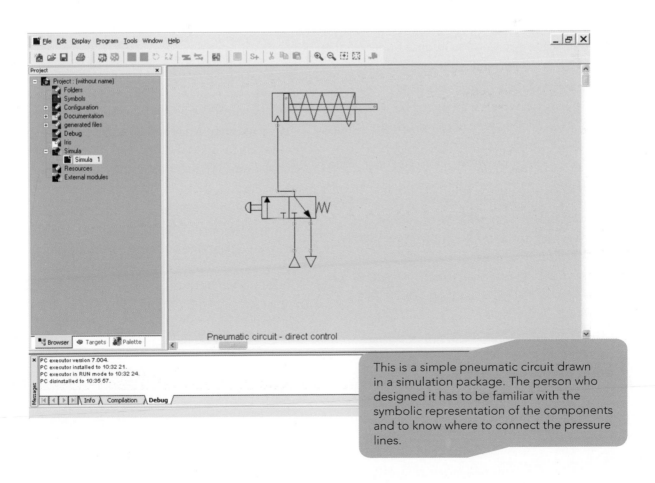

Pneumatic circuit - direct control

This is a simple pneumatic circuit drawn in a simulation package. The person who designed it has to be familiar with the symbolic representation of the components and to know where to connect the pressure lines.

There is a commonly held view in business that, in terms of functionality and price, Microsoft Office is a powerful package.

The other types of software that engineers use, such as simulation and graphics packages, tend to be relatively expensive because of their specialist nature. It is more difficult to teach yourself how to use these packages, and people using them for the first time require special training. The great thing about a simulation package is that it allows you to try out a design or process before committing to spending money on hardware or machining materials.

Computer-aided drawing (CAD) packages now feature in most engineering design departments and, in many cases, they are linked to manufacturing software that generates instructions for machine tools. Running a 3D simulation before actually cutting metal is a very cost-effective way of debugging a manufacturing process because it only involves paying for a person's time.

Simulation software is used when designing electronic and fluid power circuits, the layout of machinery in a manufacturing plant and processing systems. The trap that some people fall into is thinking that no subject knowledge is needed by the person using the software. In its simplest form simulation software just allows you to set up 'what if' scenarios, such as 'what happens to the performance of a circuit if I change this electronic component for a different one?'

Communication software and systems now allow people to work in ways which were not possible ten years ago. For example, a sales engineer might have a meeting with a customer and then go to her car for a technical discussion with someone back at base. Using a laptop computer and mobile internet connection, the engineer could send files, talk or video conference and agree delivery dates and prices. The engineer then goes back to the customer, and completes the deal and sends confirmation emails. Job done, the engineer drives on to the next customer, checking where to go by 'talking' to the car's speech recognition satellite navigation system.

2.4.2 Hardware devices

The first use of the term hardware was in the early days of computing when it applied to the actual computer. It meant a piece of electronic equipment, which

had in-built input, processing, storage and output systems. Now the term is used in a much wider context and covers any form of device that contains 'hard' components. Products which connect to a computer, such as a mouse, are called peripherals. You will be familiar with many types of hardware device. Indeed you may have used many of the following devices:

- desktop PC
- laptop (with Wi-Fi)
- modem/router
- USB pen drive
- external hard drive
- process controller
- scanner
- digital camera
- optical recognition device
- speech recognition device
- printer
- plotter
- interactive whiteboard.

Personal computers (PC) are now ubiquitous items in most homes and businesses, but this is not the end of the story. Most products or systems that need to be controlled will include a computer of some form. It may not be called a computer; microprocessor is the name you may be familiar with. For example, the engine management system in a car is effectively a computer – it inputs data from **sensors**, processes this data, makes decisions and then carries out adjustments to parameters such as the amount of fuel injected into the cylinders. All of this happens in microseconds.

The control of plant and manufacturing processes also requires the use of complex computer systems. An individual piece of equipment would be controlled by a programmable logic controller (PLC), with performance data sent back over a network to a master computer which monitors the system. This control computer might be many miles away and accessed remotely by a technician who is on call-out duty.

Key terms

Sensor a device which receives and responds to a signal/input.

2.4.3 Present information

Although there are many definitions of 'engineering', they all come down to one simple phrase: engineering is about turning ideas into reality through the appliance of knowledge, science, resources and effort.

People continually come up with ideas for making money, saving the planet, making life easier etc. It would be interesting to know how many ideas are generated throughout the world in a year. No one can put a figure on it. What we do know is that only a relatively small number actually make it to market.

To bring a product to market involves presenting information which will:

- convince investors to back the project
- motivate people working on the project
- allow the design of the product to be finalised
- set out how the product is to be made and tested
- drive forward marketing initiatives
- encourage customers to buy the product.

What we are really saying here is that engineers must be good at preparing and communicating information if they are to succeed in business. How is the information communicated? As you will have seen by working through this unit, it is by:

- writing – letters, reports, emails, memos
- tabulating – technical specifications, test data
- graphics – graphs, charts, images, diagrams, drawings
- speaking – telephone, face to face, presentations.

Some of these methods don't require the use of ICT, but most are much easier to carry out if you do.

Activity: Presenting information in writing

Some students from a local college are going to visit your company. Their tutor wants them to discover that there is more to engineering than just cutting metal, assembling parts or soldering components. You and a colleague work in the manufacturing department, and you have been asked by your manager to help out by preparing a document to show the students the writing skills required by engineers.

Working with your colleague, put together a 200-word technical mini-report. This should be word-processed and the report should include:

- original text
- an image from a digital camera and an image sourced from the internet
- an imported spreadsheet and chart
- text, cut and pasted from a different report
- a table with some shaded cells
- bullet points
- page numbers
- a title page and company logo.

Print off a hard copy of the report and save it on a computer in a folder, which should be part of a properly structured electronic filing system.

Suppose the teacher likes what you have shown and asks if you can email a copy of the report to the head of technology at the college. Now:

- write a covering letter as a formal email
- attach the report to the email and send it to a colleague
- check that it arrives, and that it can be downloaded and saved.

Activity: Visual presentation

Working with a colleague, select an engineering topic that interests you both. Then:

- plan a five-minute presentation about the topic
- put together a short set of PowerPoint slides, including text and images, with one slide containing a video clip and at least one slide with a pasted-in (pie, bar or scatter) chart
- set up an ICT system comprising a computer, multimedia projector, interactive whiteboard and printer
- run the presentation, pause at the chart, have a brief discussion about its content and mark-up some comments on the whiteboard using an electronic pen
- investigate how to save and print the marked-up slide.

Assessment activity 2.5

P7 Put together a portfolio of evidence which proves that during the time spent studying this unit (or other units on your course) you:

- correctly selected IT hardware and software packages for use in an engineering situation
- used a software package to word-process a document
- used a software package to produce a 2D drawing
- handled and processed data using software packages
- used a simulation software package
- communicated using e-systems
- used a computer system to present information in written, numerical and graphical forms
- prepared and made a visual presentation using a software package and multimedia facility.

M3 Select one of the software packages that you have used when preparing and presenting information. Then write a 250-word report of its effectiveness as a tool.

D2 Write a 500-word document, relating to your project, which evaluates your use of an ICT presentation method and identifies an alternative approach.

Grading tips

P7 You will have much of the evidence you need from previous assessment activities in this unit, and it should be just a case of pulling it all together. This is very much a tracking exercise, and you should discuss with your tutor whether it is necessary to print everything off again. What is important to realise is that when your evidence is verified, you must have a good tracking system in place so that evidence can be easily found.

M3 Take care with this report. You should evaluate the effectiveness of the software in terms of its use to support the preparation and presentation of information. You do not need to report on how well you performed in terms of the quality of your drawing, writing or speaking.

D2 You need to evaluate your use of an ICT presentation method and identify an alternative approach. This should be about the method of presentation and not the method of communication. You could, for example, base your evaluation on the leaflet you produced for assessment activity 2.3, which you probably produced in Microsoft Word. Would it have been easier and better produced, if you used desktop publishing (DTP) software such Adobe InDesign?

PLTS

This last assessment activity can only be successful if you plan it well and organise your time. As you are pulling together information and equipment resources you may well be multitasking.

Functional skills

Selecting and evaluating the use of ICT software packages and hardware devices to present engineering information will help develop your skills in ICT.

David Short
Design engineer

I am the team leader for a small group of people who work on the design and development of new products. My company produces portable hydraulic power packs for use on construction sites in the UK and mainland Europe. A power pack is constructed from three main parts: a four-stroke petrol engine, a hydraulic pump and a sump, filtration and valve control system.

The projects I work on usually start with me picking up an email from my technical director worded something like this: *Dave, To expand the product range, marketing want us to design a pack which has a 110 volt AC generator fitted so that it can be used to power electric hand tools. An electrical control unit containing a voltage regulator and overload circuit breaker will need to be fitted.*

I will then meet up with the chief designer to discuss ideas and firm up some design proposals with my team. I will arrange to meet with the manufacturing department and then get back to the technical director with finalised design proposals, including estimates of manufacturing costs. I will arrange a design review meeting at which we select the proposal to be taken forward for production.

How long does this take?

This first phase of the project usually takes a couple of weeks. My team have different specialist knowledge and we work with a CAD system so that it is very easy to pass ideas around.

The design review meeting is a major event and it has to be well organised, because as well as the engineers there will be people from the marketing, sales, logistics, finance and legal departments. I find these types of meeting quite challenging, but it's worth the effort when you see the new product rolling off the production line and being despatched.

Think about it!

1. What information will Dave take to the review meeting?
2. How will he present the design proposals?
3. Who will chair the meeting?
4. What type of graphics will Dave show the non-engineers?
5. Why do think Dave finds review meetings challenging?
6. Dave's job sounds interesting. Why do you think this is?

Just checking

1 Identify the three categories of information that might be presented in an engineering sketch, circuit diagram or network diagram.

2 Explain what is meant by 2D and 3D drawing techniques.

3 Why do engineers use British and International standards?

4 If you needed to find a particular standard, how would you start your search?

5 Why is it important to keep good notes when recording the progress of a project?

6 Explain how to plan the layout of a technical report.

7 What are 'active listening skills', and how can you improve them?

8 What is a reference source?

9 At the end of a report or document you may find a bibliography. What is its function?

10 Most electronic information sources contain vast amounts of data. Explain the steps you should take to ensure that an information search is efficient.

11 How can you be sure that an information source is accurate and up to date?

12 You need to send a personalised letter with the same main content to 50 customers. Explain how you will do this using Microsoft Office.

13 You have to deliver a 10-minute presentation on a technical subject to a small group. Explain the ICT equipment you will need to prepare and deliver your talk.

edexcel

Assignment tips

- You don't have to be a brilliant or super-confident speaker to be an effective communicator. Practice helps, and most of the activities in this unit are designed to be carried out in pairs or small groups so that all the time you are communicating.

- The evidence you need to produce for this unit will not always be in a written form. Make sure that your tutor obtains observation records or witness statements for any assessment activity which requires non-written evidence. This could be when you are speaking or presenting to an audience, amending a document on screen, or doing something in real time which needs reporting on.

- Ensure that all drawings and diagrams are produced to appropriate standards. Drawing standards can be large documents, and it can sometimes be difficult to find what you need. Ask your tutor for a cut-down printed version specific to your needs.

- Communication skills are generic, and much of what you have covered in this unit can be applied throughout your BTEC National programme. In particular, this unit has strong links with three other units, and some of the evidence you have collected could be used to help demonstrate that you have met some of the grading criteria for Unit 3: Engineering Project (P6, P9 and P10), Unit 8: Engineering Design (P6) and Unit 16: Engineering Drawing for Technicians (P1, P3 and P6).

3 Engineering project

All projects have three common elements: a starting point, a desired outcome and a procedure for getting to the outcome. But what is an engineering project? One definition is the application of technical knowledge to produce a specific outcome to a given problem through the application of planned and monitored activities.

In this unit you are going to manage and realise a personal engineering project. In doing so, you will integrate knowledge and skills gained in studying the other units on the course by applying them to a major piece of work that demonstrates your ability to work as an engineering technician.

You will be developing the ability to identify and plan a course of action, and to implement this plan to produce a viable outcome to an agreed specification and timescale. The end result might be an engineered product, a modification to an existing product, the design of a system or process, or the evaluation through testing of a product or service. You will need to demonstrate skills in keeping records, planning and following procedures, monitoring progress and presenting the outcome both in writing and to a small group of your colleagues.

Learning outcomes

After completing this unit you should:

1 be able to specify a project, agree procedures and choose a solution
2 be able to plan and monitor a project
3 be able to implement the project plan within agreed procedures
4 be able to present the project outcome.

Assessment and grading criteria

This table shows you what you must do in order to achieve a pass, merit or distinction grade, and where you can find activities in this book to help you produce the required evidence.

To achieve a **pass** grade the evidence must show that you are able to:	To achieve a **merit** grade the evidence must show that, in addition to the pass criteria, you are able to:	To achieve a **distinction** grade the evidence must show that, in addition to the pass and merit criteria, you are able to:
P1 prepare and maintain project records from initial concepts through to solutions that take account of changing situations **Assessment activities 3.1 page 74 and 3.6 page 102**	**M1** maintain detailed, concurrent records throughout the project that clearly show the progress made and difficulties experienced **Assessment activities 3.1 page 74 and 3.6 page 102**	**D1** independently manage the project development process, seeking guidance and support where necessary **Assessment activity 3.6 page 102**
P2 prepare a project specification **Assessment 3.2 page 85**	**M2** use a wide range of techniques and selection criteria to justify the chosen option **Assessment activity 3.2 page 85**	**D2** evaluate the whole project development process, making recommendations for improvements **Assessment activity 3.6 page 102**
P3 agree and prepare the procedures that will be followed when implementing the project **Assessment activity 3.2 page 85**	**M3** evaluate the project solution and suggest improvements **Assessment activity 3.4 page 95**	
P4 use appropriate techniques to evaluate three potential solutions and select the best option for development **Assessment activity 3.2 page 85**	**M4** present coherent and well-structured development records and final project report **Assessment activity 3.5 page 101**	
P5 outline the project solution and plan its implementation **Assessment activity 3.3 page 92**		
P6 monitor and record achievement over the lifecycle of the project **Assessment activities 3.3 page 92 and 3.6 page 102**		
P7 implement the plan and produce the project solution **Assessment activity 3.4 page 95**		
P8 check that the solution conforms to the project specification **Assessment activity 3.4 page 95**		
P9 prepare and deliver a presentation to a small group, outlining the project specification and proposed solution **Assessment activity 3.5 page 101**		
P10 present a written project report **Assessment activity 3.5 page 101**		

How you will be assessed

This unit will be assessed by internal assignments designed and marked by the staff at your centre. The type of evidence which you will be asked to present when you carry out an assignment could be in the form of:

- a portfolio containing written descriptions, progress charts, images, copies of emails, edited research material, sketches and formal drawings
- a logbook and planning documents
- observation records relating to practical and skills-based activities
- written records of discussions held with your tutor
- a hard copy of the slides and handouts used to support a formal verbal presentation.

Waleed, 27–year–old technical director

The company I work for manufactures portable power tools that are used on construction sites. Up to about two years ago most of our tools were mains powered, but now our main range is battery powered using a common interchangeable power module. Over an 18 month period I led the team that designed and developed the new product range.

We had a very strict timeline to follow because the marketing department had arranged a big launch and many promotional events for the new range – television and press advertising, demonstrations to buyers from the major DIY stores and on-site trials with large construction companies. This had to be planned well in advance, so we were under pressure to have the new tools operational and fully tested well before the launch.

The specialists in my team all worked really hard and we successfully completed the project on time, to specification and within budget. We did have a minor performance issue with a hammer drill, but the problem was easily resolved because I was able to refer back to my design notes and the specification. The new tools are now selling really well, and I have just been promoted to technical director.

I think one of the reasons for the total success of the project was that I appreciated the importance of planning and progress monitoring. I learnt this on both my BTEC National course and on my foundation degree. What I learned also helped me when making short presentations to the board of directors about technical issues and progress against completion targets. Had things not gone to plan, I don't think I would still be with the company.

3.1 Be able to keep records, specify a project, agree procedures and choose a solution

Start up

Sat navs

In a small group use the internet to review the portable satellite navigation systems (sat navs) currently on sale in the UK and which retail for about £100 (at 2010 prices). Look through a typical specification and identify the features that will interest car drivers as they use sat navs to guide them on a journey.

Suppose you and your colleagues work in the product development department of a company that makes sat navs. You have been asked to design a new model to go on sale in 18 months' time. The brief is to include innovative features that are not available in models currently on the market.

- How might you find out what new features should be added?
- How do you assess the size of the potential market?
- What factors will influence where the new model is manufactured?

After discussing these questions, present your findings as a **mind map**.

Now think about running the project. Plan out the project steps and present them as a flow chart.

- What technical expertise should each team member have?
- What records will be kept?
- How might the success or failure of the project be assessed?

When an engineering business develops a new product, it will usually adopt a project approach. The first thing to do is to put together a team of people led by a project manager. The members of the team will each have specific skills that will be needed to complete the project. The job of the project manager is to lead the team so that resources are used effectively, team members receive support and the finished product comes in on time, to specification and within budget. The word 'product' needs to be considered in the widest sense. Here are some examples of engineering-related products:

- hardware – microwave cooker, car engine, camera, DVD recorder, air conditioning system
- software – computer operating system, CAD package, iPhone app, video game
- procedure – quality assurance, maintenance, testing and evaluation, health and safety
- system – telecommunications, safety, business management, stock control, budgeting

Key terms

Mind map a spider's web of thoughts, words or ideas around a central key word or idea written on paper, a flip chart or interactive whiteboard.

Many products cross the classifications. For example, a digital camera is really both a hardware and a software product, because it has some of the parts of a traditional mechanical camera, such as the lens and body, combined with powerful software to make it operate.

The important thing to realise is that irrespective of its type, there is a requirement for any product to meet its design specification. Think about some of the products you may have bought recently, such as a mobile phone, an MP3 player or a broadband connection. Do they live up to the claims made in advertisements and by sales advisers? Recent consumer research suggests

Case study: The Airbus A380

The Airbus A380 airliner is good example of a highly complex engineering project. In about 1990 the Boeing Corporation had a monopoly on the production of wide-bodied, large capacity, long haul, passenger aircraft. European aircraft manufacturers wanted to break that monopoly. The specified solution to this problem was to produce a plane that would have lower operating costs (at least 20 per cent lower than the competition) and that could carry more passengers over longer distances without refuelling.

It took about 18 years to get the A380 into service. In addition to its design, manufacture, testing and approval by regulators, the infrastructure of many airports had to be changed so that the A380 could be refuelled, loaded and unloaded in the minimum amount of time. Every activity had to be planned. There were many thousands of engineers, technicians and other workers involved with the project.

1 Who had overall responsibility for the A380 project? Was it one person or a small team? Try researching the answer to this question.

2 Think about building the infrastructure for the London 2012 Olympics. This is a prestige project with an immovable end date. What would it be like having the top job on this construction project?

that some broadband connections may not meet their advertised speeds.

Specialists in a project team might be electrical and mechanical design engineers, manufacturing engineers, test engineers, quality standards and legislation advisers, IT and data communication engineers, production controllers, budget controllers and marketing specialists. The size of the team will depend on the complexity of the project. When developing a new passenger aircraft, there could be many teams based in many different countries, whereas to produce a hand-crafted piece of furniture the 'team' might be just one person carrying out all the tasks (producing a drawing, sourcing material, manufacturing, despatch and delivery to the customer). Project managers may not always have specialist technical knowledge – but what they do need are very good skills in getting the best out of people and a willingness to 'take ownership' of the project.

When you undertake your project, you will need to think about the team you will need. Suppose your chosen project involves a specialist machining or assembly process. You may have learned about this process in class and had a practice in the workshop, but if you are not too confident about your ability, it might be more sensible to enlist the help of a college technician. But how do you approach the technicians, what documentation will they expect to see, how busy are they, when is a good time to meet them and discuss your requirements, will they be happy working for you? If you are well organised, able to talk through what you are hoping to achieve and adopt a diplomatic approach, then you stand a good chance of getting their total support.

Irrespective of your team size or project complexity, it is crucial that you maintain a complete record of everything relating to the project. This should be properly recorded using industry-standard techniques. The starting point for recording data is the initial concept stage when ideas are brought to the table for consideration.

Many projects fail or go over budget because the initial specification is not properly worked out, market expectations are too ambitious, legislation changes, costs get out of hand or the project is just badly managed because nobody keeps proper track of what is going on and ensures that agreed procedures are followed. To critically review the outcome of any project (both those that succeed and those that fail), you must have access to records. These can be grouped as records that relate to technical functions and those that relate to management.

Activity: Success and failure

In 1985, the entrepreneur Sir Clive Sinclair launched a battery-powered electric vehicle. The Sinclair C5 was a three-wheeled vehicle, with a top speed of 15 mph. Only around 12,000 units were sold, and the project was a commercial failure.

In 2013 the Japanese car manufacturer Nissan plans to start production of a new electric car at its UK manufacturing plant in Sunderland. The UK government, the European Investment Bank and Nissan are jointly investing £420 million (as reported in early 2010) in the project.

Working with a colleague, research the answers to the questions below. A good starting point for information on the Nissan project is media articles from March 2010.

1   Why do most informed observers expect the Nissan project to be a success given that Sir Clive Sinclair's attempt in the 1980s at producing a mass market electric vehicle ended in failure?

2   What would be the consequences if the Nissan project were to fail?

3   Who put up the money to develop the C5? What were the consequences when the project failed?

This book is part of a publishing project aimed at supporting the new 2010 specification for the BTEC National in Engineering. The starting point was a meeting between the writers and the publisher, followed by the preparation of a project specification – what units to cover, chapter layout, format of the activity sheets and unit overviews, timescales. The project manager then worked out what resources would be needed once writers began to send in their chapters. This meant, for example, organising graphic artists, copy editors, proofreaders, reviewers and people to produce marketing materials. Many different activities had to be planned, monitored and paid for. Your choice of project will be less complex but should look to have the same end result – completion on time, to specification, within budget and with a traceable record of how time and money were used.

3.1.1 Project records

There are many ways of keeping a record of decisions and actions taken during an engineering project. A major reason for keeping records is that it allows people to refer back to design specifications, quality assurance data and development testing results should a problem arise with a product or system.

This has practical applications. Car manufacturers are able to recall specific vehicles for rectification because they have details on file and can contact owners direct. Lower priced, mass-produced electrical white goods, such as electric toasters and kettles, also often feature in manufacturer recalls. Advertisements are placed in newspapers asking customers to return products that have the listed serial or model numbers. Accountability and traceability can only work effectively if good records are kept. These are important issues in engineering; when things go wrong, people want to be able to apportion blame and, in today's litigious society, seek redress in the courts.

Traceability has always been a key aspect of the aerospace industry. This is one of the reasons why aircraft components are very expensive compared to those fitted to cars. For example, a simple bolt supplied to a mass production car factory may only cost a few pence, whereas a bolt with similar dimensions supplied to a manufacturer of aero engines will cost several pounds. Why is this? The main reason is the level of traceability – at every stage of the design and manufacture of aircraft engine bolts, records are kept so that, in the event of catastrophic failure, air accident investigators are able to do a full historical trace. For example, they will want answers to these questions:

• Who machined the bolt, and in which factory?

• Which company supplied the raw material?

• Who worked out the stresses produced in the bolt when under load?

• Who fitted the bolt, and when was it last checked?

When a Concorde crashed in July 2000 shortly after take-off from Charles de Gaulle Airport near Paris, investigators strength-tested samples from the aluminium frame of the crashed aircraft and compared the results not only with those recoded on file but also with ones taken from tests made on samples of material that had been locked away for over 30 years. The investigators were checking that the airframe material was as specified in the drawings.

The Concorde project ran for about 40 years and was incredibly heavily documented.

In the early 19th century, Isambard Kingdom Brunel designed and built the Clifton suspension bridge over the river Avon in Bristol. A full set of his calculations and drawings together with 18 other sets of documentation about the financing and construction of the bridge are now held in the Brunel Archive at Bristol University. Brunel died five years before the project was completed, but because everything was written down and well documented other engineers were able to successfully finish the bridge.

When it was opened to the public, the Burj Kahlifa in Dubai was the tallest structure in the world. Find out if there were any financial or technical problems encountered during its construction. Establish who managed the project.

Activity: Keeping records

In 2009 the Burj Kahlifa was completed in Dubai. Its height is 828 metres. When it opened to the public in January 2010, it was confirmed as the tallest free-standing structure ever built.

1 Use the web to review the reasons for building such a tall structure. In 2020 do think it will still be the tallest building in the word? Explain your answer.

2 Buildings such as the Burj Kahlifa have very complex internal systems to manage lifts, air conditioning, fire prevention measures and emergency evacuation procedures. What sort of data will be kept about these systems, how might it be recorded and who will need to have access to it?

3 When a large new commercial building is completed there is usually a handover ceremony marking the point that the construction company formally passes responsibility for the building to its new owners. Before this happens, the owners will want to confirm that the building has been constructed to specification. A consulting engineer, acting for the owners, will need access to records. What records will they expect to see?

Notes, sketches and drawings

Notes, sketches and drawings can be stored on paper or electronically. It is very important to plan how they are filed, because there must be a complete record of how a project has developed from conception to completion. It should be very straightforward for someone with no specific engineering knowledge to look through these records and to review the progress of the project. An expert might use the records for other reasons, such as challenging design decisions on the choice of materials and manufacturing processes.

Notes should be interpreted in the widest sense – it includes free writing, jottings, calculations, spreadsheets, charts and cross references to research materials. The same caveat applies to sketches and drawings – all types are acceptable provided that information is accurately conveyed. Remember, however, that you are aiming for quality not quantity when putting together notes, drawings and sketches.

Some important project data will be held on digital devices. Think about the best way of storing (and backing up) these records.

Plans

A project must be properly planned out before starting, otherwise it may fail for lack of time and/or money. The engineering industry is highly competitive and in most companies it is the accountants who have the final say on whether a project proceeds. A highly innovative product may seem like a good idea to a design engineer but if the business runs out of money during the development process, then it will never come to market and all will be lost.

Note also, that plans can be changed. There will be situations where plans have to be modified, such as when a change in legislation makes a design unrealistic or when the price of the specified raw materials becomes too expensive.

Setting and monitoring targets

If a project is to have a successful outcome, it is crucial to set achievable targets. There are two overall targets which must be set:

- the production of a solution that meets the requirements of the project's specification
- a schedule for achieving the solution within the given time frame.

Think about the project which you are going to work on for this unit. You will probably be given an overall time frame of about six months to complete this project. This may seem like a long time but this unit is intended to take just 120 guided learning hours to complete – that's about three weeks' full-time work in an engineering company. So you do not have very long, unless you decide to devote a lot more of your own time to the project.

Within the overall targets, there should be staging and review points so that you can monitor progress and make possible modifications to the project plan. For example, if manufacturing is running behind schedule, you might be able to get help from one of your centre's technicians.

To achieve a pass grade for this unit, you must meet ten grading criteria. These are sequential and can be set out against a timeline. You may find it difficult to decide how much time to allocate to each criterion, and this may be something which is better done in discussion with your tutor. Look back at the case study on the A380 aircraft – setting time targets for this project must have been a very complex task.

Project monitoring in industry can take two forms: internal monitoring by the project manager and project team, and external monitoring by someone else within, or external to, the organisation. In the case of the A380 project, external monitoring was done by the governments of the various European countries that gave financial backing to the project. On your project, you should monitor your progress on a regular basis – this is internal monitoring and you should use the planning techniques discussed later in the unit (see page 86) – and your tutor will provide the external monitoring.

Activity: A project timeline

Look at the ten pass grade criteria for this unit and set them out on a proposed timeline.

How does this fit with the other units on your course and the end date of the programme?

Does adding the merit and distinction criteria to the timeline complicate things?

Planning tools

The planning tools that you will use during the project have to be readily accessible. You need to decide how you are going to keep them readily to hand – are they to be paper based or is it better to go straight for an electronic approach? One of the tools you should consider using is a Gantt chart, and these are very easy to set up in a spreadsheet, or you can use a software package such as Microsoft Project.

Recording initial concepts

Once a project topic has been provisionally agreed, the next step is to make a record of initial concepts. This may involve 'thinking outside of the box' and will certainly involve discussing ideas with others. A design team should sit around a table and come up with initial concepts or ideas. These should all be recorded – even those which may seem totally unrealistic. As these meetings tend to be very interactive, with lots of discussion and argument, you need to have a means of capturing and recording all ideas and contributions so that they can be fleshed out at a later date and decisions taken about which to develop further. Rapid reporting can be done by making lists, notes, mind maps, flow diagrams and charts – all techniques that are considered in Unit 2: Communications for Engineering Technicians. An interactive whiteboard is very useful in these preliminary project meetings because everything that is written on the board can be saved to computer and printed off later. It provides an instant record of what has been going on. The whiteboard should be used with some caution, however, otherwise irrelevant notes may mask out the good material that is worth keeping.

A note on the unit project

The aim of the project that you will undertake as the basis for the assessment for this unit is to produce a product or system relevant to your area of study. The six assessment activities in this unit link together and are intended to help you develop skills in:

- specifying a project, agreeing procedures and selecting a method of solution
- planning and monitoring a project over its lifecycle
- implementing a project within agreed procedures and to specification
- presenting a project outcome to an audience.

Throughout the project you will also be developing the creative, management and communication skills that are needed when working in environments such as design, manufacture, research and development.

There are links to a number of other units within the BTEC Level 3 National in Engineering and you should discuss these with your tutor. There is particular synergy with Unit 2: Communications for Engineering Technicians, and the project can be used to produce evidence for some of the tasks in the assignments that you will be set for Unit 2.

There are 16 grading criteria associated with this unit. Most of them are linked to the processes used to manage and progress the project, so take care not to be over ambitious if manufacturing processes are involved.

On completion of the unit you must present a formal portfolio of evidence for assessment. This will be a personal project on a theme chosen by you and agreed with your tutor.

Assessment activity 3.1

P1 Choose a problem or task that can be solved within a realistic time frame and that is directly related to the engineering programme you are studying. Through discussion with your tutor, agree a project brief.

Design and set up a system to record all the activities that you will be carrying out as you progress your project from initial ideas through to the presentation of a final solution.

Set up a computer file structure for saving your electronic documents, drawings and spreadsheets and for logging data sources. Create a system for storing (unedited) research materials.

Grading tips

P1 Examples of the type of problem that you will be solving are designing and manufacturing a new product or system, modifying an existing product or system, or testing a product, system or service. You are looking for a problem or task to be solved, not for a finished item as a starting point.

Your reporting system should include a logbook, planning charts, a file for storing unedited research material, pro formas for transcripts of

discussions with your tutor and a photo archive. It can be a paper-based or an electronic system, or a combination of the two. The aim is to produce a system which can be regularly updated, reviewed and audited.

This activity will only produce part of the evidence you need for P1. Assessment activity 3.6 will help you generate the additional evidence needed to fully complete P1. You can also link this activity to *Unit 2: Communications for engineering technicians*, grading criterion P4: Communicate information effectively in written work.

M1 To achieve M1 your reporting system must allow for detailed records to be kept and for comments to be made about positive aspects and difficulties encountered as you progressed your project.

This activity will only produce part of the evidence you need for M1. Assessment activity 3.6 will help you generate the additional evidence needed to fully complete M1.

3.1.2 Initial concepts

There are several ways in which someone might generate an initial concept. An inventor might have a eureka moment, a product designer may be searching for a new design to beat the competition or an entrepreneur might identify a gap in the market. The BBC series *Dragons' Den* is worth watching. Some people present very flimsy ideas, which usually are quickly dismissed by the dragons; the concepts which attract the money have usually been developed into realistic ideas with proper specifications.

Did you know?

A Swiss engineer, George de Mestral, was walking his dog when he noticed that burdock seeds had stuck to his trousers. Looking under a microscope, he realised that tiny hooks on the seeds were attaching them to his trousers. This gave him an idea, which eventually became the product we know today as Velcro.

Setting limits

Before embarking on the development of an initial concept or idea into a product, there must be a realistic chance of success. This is because of the resource implications. Development will require the expenditure of time and money, and so before embarking on full-scale development it is usual to carry out a feasibility study. This involves reviewing the project against four main parameters.

- Time – how long will it take to achieve a viable solution? This is a particularly important consideration if the concept involves fast-developing technology. This applies especially to any microelectronic and telecommunication product.
- Cost – what will be the development costs?
- Feasibility – is the concept realistic or off the wall?
- Need – is there a perceived market need? For example, it is debatable whether it would be worth developing a low-cost digital camera given that most makes of mobile phone now have a camera function.

These parameters are referred to as limits. One of the catch phrases used on *Dragons' Den* is 'let's do the numbers' – engineers are very good at working with numbers and presenting numerical data when trying to prove a point – and it is usual to attach numerical values to these parameters wherever possible. It is relatively easy to quantify time and cost. Need could also be a numerical measure if market research has been carried out. The third parameter, feasibility, is more difficult to quantify, and this assessment requires a fair degree of subjectivity.

How does this relate to the concept that you will come up with when you start your project? The bottom line is that you must convince your tutor that your concept can be turned into something which is achievable within the limits set for the project and that it will also generate evidence covering all the grading criteria.

Activity: Assessing market needs

The Apple iPhone is a very successful product. What was the conceptual thinking behind the iPhone when Apple CEO Steve Jobs first put the idea to his designers at Apple Corporation?

Value and cost-benefit analysis

Coming at a project from a business angle, there is no point in developing a concept if it is not going to bring in revenues or add value to the business. However, sometimes a concept is developed purely for altruistic reasons and brings value in other ways. For example, Trevor Baylis developed a clockwork radio having seen a programme about the spread of Aids in Africa and the need for an educational tool which did not run on electricity. The big manufacturers were not convinced of the need for a wind-up radio and refused to back him, so Baylis went ahead using his own money.

There are various methods used to assess the benefits of a project against its costs. In industry, many decisions are made on the basis of return on investment. This is investigated in Unit 7: Business Operations in Engineering (see page 227). When you decide on which concept to develop for your project, it is important to work out how much it will cost to resource and who is going to meet this expense – you, your employer or the centre where you are studying?

Generating ideas

Not everyone finds generating ideas easy. It depends to some extent on whether a person is an innovator or an implementer. Innovators are people who come up with ideas, bounce them around and then quite often move on to other things, leaving others to pick up the pieces. Creativity is their strength but getting the job finished relies on implementers, people who have an eye for detail, are good at problem resolution and can carry a job through to the end. A project team will have innovators and implementers – you will need to be both as you push forward with your project.

There are many ways to develop ideas. The most popular are group discussion, thought showering (this is often called brainstorming) and mind mapping, which are all explored in Unit 2. It does not matter what method is used, provided that an end result is achieved in a reasonable time. At this stage, it is only concepts that are being investigated and there is no point wasting time going into fine detail or endlessly arguing a point. The time to focus on detail is when the project moves into the specification phase.

Research techniques

Once an initial concept has been identified, you need to research the chosen topic in some depth. The idea here is to draw together enough information to be able to make an informed decision about what should be written into the project's specification.

Suppose you come up with the concept of a solar-powered charger for notebook computers. This seems like a good idea, but there are several obvious questions that need to be addressed.

- What type of people use notebooks in situations where there is no electricity supply?
- What is the power consumption of a notebook?
- How much energy do voltaic panels generate?
- How would the power be stored and regulated?
- Is a clockwork (wind-up) device a better option?
- What are the marketing costs likely to be?

These questions need to be answered through directed and relevant research. Before starting on any type of research exercise, you must plan what you want to find out, otherwise you will just go around in circles. The internet is an incredibly powerful resource, but without care and discipline you may easily end up with a mountain of research data which is difficult to edit and **synthesise**. You need to consider the validity of the data that you collect from the internet. There are many free websites that hold unverified data – be careful with these. Some websites require a subscription before you can access information, such as the British Standards Institution (BSI) website, but they provide accurate and verified data.

Don't just rely on the internet. Asking someone with expert knowledge is a good research technique. Technical libraries are also good resources, allowing access to books, paper-based and electronic data sheets, and technical journals.

Data gathered through research should be pulled together and catalogued so that it can be easily referred to. For the purpose of assessing this project, a portfolio of primary research should be created so that reference can be made to it when the final written report is prepared.

Activity: **Research terms**

Make sure that you understand these terms:

- primary research
- secondary research
- edited data
- referencing.

Explain each term, using examples to illustrate your answers.

Lines of communication

Good communication is a key aspect of a successful project. In a business context, communication will be both internal and external to an engineering company. In industry, a project team will consist of a leader and people with specific knowledge in, for example, mechanical, manufacturing and electrical engineering. Lines of communication between the team members will be informal and, depending on the organisational structure of the company, there be links up, down and across the organisation. The team leader will report to a senior manager or director, and team members will communicate with staff in other departments, such as workshops, quality assurance and testing.

The lines of communication that you will follow when working on your project are quite specific. They will be

with your tutor as line manager (vertical communication up), colleagues who provide support (horizontal communication), support staff who help to progress the project (vertical communication down, but better if you go for horizontal), and, possibly, outsourcing of manufacturing (vertical communication down).

These simple protocols will help you communicate effectively:

- ensure clarity when writing or speaking
- respect other people's views
- negotiation is better than confrontation
- make written transcripts of any decisions that are agreed verbally.

Activity: **Initial concepts**

Work with a colleague to produce three sets of prompt cards that you could use when making a five-minute presentation on each of the following three issues.

1   Dyson – How did the concept of James Dyson's bag-less vacuum cleaner come about?

2   Sony – In the late 1970s, Akio Morita of the Sony Corporation had a concept that he asked his design engineers to develop into a marketable product. What was the product, where did the idea come from and which industry did it revolutionise?

3   Concept cars – What are the reasons for displaying concept cars at motor shows?

Key terms

Synthesise combining ideas, objects or data to produce a complex whole.

Specification a detailed description of the features and performance characteristics a product. This is normally presented in writing and with much numerical information.

3.1.3 Specification

Once a concept has been approved for further development, it will be developed into a design brief. The brief should contain sufficient information to put the concept into context, outline operational

Case study: Roger's chair

Roger Lewis, a college teacher, has passed this brief to a colleague who is responsible for teaching design, technology and projects.

The other day one of the students I was teaching starting rocking back and forwards on a chair. I think the student was either getting bored as it was near the end of the lesson or just simply messing about. I have bad memories about this type of action because when I was a student teacher someone in the class did the same thing but ended up tipping right back over and badly damaging their spine.

If you are looking for project ideas would one of your students be able to work up something from this brief?

- *A small device which clips onto the back of a stacking plastic chair*
- *Can only be removed by a member of staff using a key*
- *Emits an audible or vibratory warning when the chair back tilts more than a given angle*
- *Self-powered so that it does not restrict free movement of the chair*
- *Robust enough to withstand people and chairs knocking into it*

A problem has been identified and a concept has been thought up to solve the problem. But is the concept realistic? One immediate concern that the design teacher identified was that if an audible warning system is used, some students might deliberately keep rocking back on their chairs to trigger the alarm in order to disrupt the class.

However, the design teacher decides to develop the idea and asks a group of students to carry out some initial research to find information on:

- the number of reported cases of students injuring themselves by falling backwards from a chair
- the means of fixing and locking portable devices to flat and curved surfaces
- the shapes of school chair backs
- the angle to which a chair can be tipped back before it becomes unstable
- sensors which measure angular movement
- electronic circuits for producing warning tones and vibration
- batteries and power supplies.

requirements, and provide a launching point for development into a full-blown **specification**.

If following research it is decided to go ahead with a project, then the project brief will need to be converted into a full specification that contains sufficient information for someone to put together detailed design proposals. This specification will contain detailed information on operational requirements, conformance with standards, materials, physical dimensions, maximum and minimum operating temperatures etc. When a product has been manufactured and sold to a customer, it should function according to its specification. If it fails to function as specified, then many customers are likely to be unhappy and some may start dispute proceedings against the manufacturer.

But what happens if a customer decides to operate the product outside of its design specification envelope? Let's consider a recent example. In April 2010 the ash ejected into the atmosphere by a volcano in Iceland caused a total stoppage of aircraft flights over the

UK, Ireland and much of western Europe. Turbine engines are designed to run on the clean air that is normally found at high altitude, and the authorities stopped flights because it was considered too risky to operate them outside of specification. Because of the costs involved in grounding all passenger aircraft, manufacturers reviewed the specification relating to the volume of dust particles that an aero engine can tolerate. After testing and other investigative work, it was agreed that aero engines could tolerate higher levels of volcanic dust, and the flight ban was relaxed.

This issue highlights one of the problems often encountered by engineers when they embark on a project – deciding on an appropriate level of risk. They have to take into account commercial pressures, and balance the need to reduce risk to minimum levels against cost and inconvenience. They must be able to communicate effectively, as non-experts may not appreciate the technicalities of the problems that engineers are trying to resolve.

Type of project

Before you can draw up any specification, of course, you need to decide what type of project you intend to undertake for this unit. There is a wide choice. This list of different types of project may give you a few ideas when trying to choose a topic:

- designing or modifying a product – this could be a physical product or software
- testing an electrical, electronic or mechanical product or system
- designing or modifying a plant layout such as an assembly line
- producing a complex maintenance procedure for a product or system
- designing a production method for a product or system, such as automated assembly or CNC manufacturing
- auditing and making proposals relating to quality assurance or health and safety in an industrial situation
- making a business improvement proposal
- mathematical modelling an engineering function, such as undertaking a stress analysis or electronic circuit design.

In addition, you can do a project on anything that has an engineering context and that involves the application of expertise gained from other units on your BTEC National engineering programme.

When preparing a project proposal for a product or system that you are going to design, make or test, you must think about and present information on both the technical and the operational aspects of the project. The technical aspects involve considerations about the product's (or system's) parameters of performance, physical dimensions, mass, reliability and conformance with standards. Essentially you need to provide information that helps define the way that the product will be expected to perform in service. The operational aspects involve considerations about the procedures that will progress the project, such as access to human and physical resources, controlling the budget, progress monitoring and reporting, and schedules and timescales.

Now let's consider in more detail the information that should be included in the specification for a project.

Technical information

Technical information should be presented in writing. It will include much numerical information as well as drawings and diagrams. Depending on the specific project, information should be provided on:

- functionality
- reliability indicators
- operating conditions
- process capability
- scale of operation
- cost
- style
- ergonomics.

Let's consider each of the factors in turn. First, functionality. This concerns physical properties such as dimensions (size), mass, operating voltage or pressure, connection configurations – electrical connectors, screw threads etc. – software compatibility and materials. You will need to provide a detailed specification for all these properties.

Reliability indicators might require specifying the **mean time between failure** for the product or system. For example, an aircraft manufacturer will calculate and then specify the operating life of each major component in an undercarriage so that a maintenance schedule for replacing the components can be devised.

The conditions under which the product or system will operate include many environmental factors. It might be necessary to specify the conditions in which the product will function properly by, for example, placing limits on temperatures (maximum and minimum), humidity, interference by magnetic fields, and vibration.

When the design of a product has been finalised, thought must be given to how it will be manufactured. This might involve machining metal, assembling electronic components, assembling a telecommunications network, setting up a quality assurance system in a factory, or creating a customer services facility – in fact, any operation that processes

Key terms

Mean time between failure (MTBF) the average length of time a component or system can be expected to work before it fails. The higher the MTBF, the more reliable the product.

a product from design to a finished artefact or service. You need sufficient human and physical resources to carry out these operations – this is known as process capability.

The scale of operation for a manufactured product might be the quantity to be produced after a prototype has been built, tested and approved. The production quantity will help to determine which manufacturing processes are used. For example, large-scale production will involve the design of special tooling and the use of automated machinery, such as injection moulding machines and pick-and-place robots. If the production quantity is small, it may be more cost-effective to fabricate the product by, for example, welding together several separate components.

It is important to provide a reasonably detailed analysis of how much it will cost to progress a project from start to finish. The calculation should take account of physical and human resource requirements. For your project there will be no human resource costs unless you decide to pay someone to help you.

The style or external appearance of the product should reflect current fashion or ideally anticipate future trends. Consumer products, such as cars and mobile phones, sell into very competitive markets and, although technical features do have an impact on purchasing decisions, physical appearance and style is often the discriminator for the customer.

Ergonomics is the science of designing products and systems to interface well with humans. If it is a physical product, the specification should include information about features such as the size of touch buttons, design variations to take account of right-handed and left-handed people, and the font size of visual displays. If software is being produced, the specification should include details about the presentation of menus and intuitive command sequences.

Health and safety

There are two aspects to health and safety. First, a product must conform when it is in service to any relevant legal requirements. For example, motor vehicles must conform to regulations on exhaust emissions and crash protection; electrical products must conform to regulations on electromagnetic

compatibility (EMC). A current concern is the amount of background electromagnetic radiation produced by electronic devices that have wireless connectivity. Manufacturers of this type of equipment have to limit radiation to levels set by EU directives.

Second, businesses must protect the health and safety of workers employed to produce or deliver a product or service. This means that engineering companies must use manufacturing techniques and materials that meet workplace health and safety regulations. For example, companies in the electronics industry must use lead-free solder and minimise the number of components made from beryllium copper because this material poses a health hazard when machined.

Environmental and sustainabilty issues

When drawing up a specification for a new product, a business must be take into account its carbon footprint as well as end-of-life factors and other 'green' issues. Some products, such as laptop computers, mobile phones and low-energy light bulbs, contain materials that can be very detrimental to the environment, so they need special recycling and disposal procedures when they reach the end of their life.

It is not always easy to specify materials that are derived from sustainable sources, and product designers are always looking for ways to increase the amount of components in a product that can be recycled or refurbished. Softwoods are probably the only raw materials available to engineers which can be claimed to come from renewable sources. Even products that use biofuels have an environmental impact, as biofuel production usually involves deforestation and the loss of food-producing land.

The majority of design specifications must have statements explaining how the proposed product and its manufacturing procedures meet the current requirements of environmental and sustainability legislation.

Quality standards and consumer legislation

Consumer legislation is enacted to protect the interests of the customer. Customers expect a product to be fit for purpose – does it perform to specification and is it of the expected quality? One measure of quality is reliability, and customers may be able to use consumer legislation to seek redress if they consider that what they have bought is unreliable. Most domestic electronic appliances, such as television sets, are sold with a 12-month guarantee. After that period, the customer is expected to take responsibility if the product malfunctions. What happens if an expensive plasma television goes wrong after say 18 months? Assuming that it has not been physically abused – it has not, for example, been knocked over, had water spilled on it or been connected to an electricity supply with the wrong voltage – the purchaser may have a case under UK consumer legislation by claiming that the product is not fit for purpose. This is still very much a grey area, but consumers with legitimate claims are having more and more success in getting compensation (or replacement products) from retailers and manufacturers.

This issue may not apply to your project, but it is worth considering if perhaps you are designing and building a prototype product that may have possibilities for future development into a marketable product. The 2010 Brit Insurance Design Award was won by a young graduate who designed a folding 13 amp plug. He came up with the concept when he realised that the standard UK 13 amp plug is very bulky in relation to modern portable electronic equipment. He is now looking for a manufacturer with a high-volume production capability to back the project, so that his innovative design can be brought to market.

Timescales

Producing an end result within a given timescale is a key element for the success of a project. If the project is a one-off, such as the construction of the stadiums and athletes' village for the London 2012 Olympics, then failure to meet the deadline would result in huge national embarrassment and financial penalties for the contractors. The credibility of the UK to stage future major international sporting events would be severely damaged. Deadlines are equally important in less high profile projects. If a manufacturer of mobile phones or latest-generation televisions does not meet project timescales, then it could be overtaken by competitors and go out of business.

Setting achievable timescales is crucial. You must complete your project within a set timescale agreed with your tutor. Along the way there will be review points, also called staging posts. What happens if you discover that you are running out of time and are not going to finish on time? Bringing in more resources may help, but a more sensible approach is to have a review strategy worked out before you really get started. This involves identifying the risks that may prevent you completing part of the project on time and coming up with plans for overcoming the problems you have anticipated. For example, if you are designing and manufacturing a product, then break the production down into clearly identifiable steps which you can check off as you go along. If it is not possible to evaluate the whole solution against its specification, then at least you can evaluate the various stages. (Remember that most of the grading criteria for this unit are about the management and recording of the project.)

Timescales for individual elements of the project are best set by using planning tools, and these are explored later in this unit (see page 86). The problem you may face is actually deciding how long each part of your project will take. It is useful to be able to draw on previous experience, which is why it is important to discuss your timescales with your tutor and any other people who will be giving support to ensure that they are realistic. For example, if you are going to be ordering components from the RS catalogue, you need to know how long it will take for the order to be processed by your school or college before it actually reaches RS. Buying goods on line from sites such as eBay is very easy, but with a turn around time of just a few days, school and college buying arrangements tend to be much more convoluted even if you have been given an agreed budget.

Did you know?

The RS catalogue is produced by RS Components, a leading European distributor of electrical, electronic and industrial components. There are other suppliers such as Farnell, Rapid and Maplin. Web searches will throw up catalogues for other types of components useful for projects.

Physical and human resources

Physical resources are things such as materials, components, manufacturing equipment, test equipment and CAD/CAM software, in fact everything you need to progress the project. Human resources are the people working on the project and the application of their particular skills to a solution.

Engineering companies specialise in particular product lines and only decide to expand their product range if they are sure that they have adequate resources. Be sure to choose a project about a topic for which you have sufficient technical knowledge and practical ability. It may be that you decide to work with a colleague so that you can combine your skills base. This is what is done in industry, and this approach will work for you provided that you are able to review and record your individual input to the project.

Table 3.1 is an example of a specification. It relates to a portable hydraulic power pack that can be used on construction sites. An air-cooled petrol engine is coupled to a hydraulic pump and control system – and the power tools are connected to the pack by flexible hoses.

Table 3.1: Specification for a hydraulic power pack

Hydraulic power pack: AB 150	
Engine	
Engine capacity	250 cc
Engine power	5 kW
Engine fuel	95 unleaded
Engine fuel tank capacity	12 litres
Maximum noise output	60 dB
Footprint	200 x 300 mm
Height	300 mm
Total mass	25 kg
Pump and control system	
Operating pressure	150 bar (nominal) (+/– 5 bar)
Over-pressure relief valve	170 bar
Maximum flow rate	0.5 l/s
Sump capacity	4 litres
Hydraulic oil specification	ISO-L-HV
Operating temperature range	–10 to 40°C
Flow and return connections	M18 x 1.5
Torque setting for connections	40 Nm

Activity: Writing a specification

Revisit the case study on Roger's chair. The idea was to fit a tilt warning device to the backs of classroom chairs. Working with a colleague, develop the brief that was set out in the case study.

Your starting point should be to carry out a very simple experiment to see how far back a chair can be tilted before it tips backwards. This must be done safely. So for health and safety reasons, do not try this experiment with a real person sitting in the chair. Instead, build a very simple crash test dummy.

PLTS

Preparing a project specification is a complex process because many factors have to be considered such as technical requirements, timescale, resources and budget. You will develop many PLTS, including IE1 (identify questions to answer and problems to resolve), IE2 (plan and carry out research, appreciating the consequences of decisions), TW1 (collaborate with others to work towards common goals) and EP4 (identify improvements that would benefit others as well as themselves).

3.1.4 Procedures

Engineering is a competitive business, and when a company decides to develop and market a new product, it is important that it follows the correct procedures to manage the process. The responsibilities of the various people employed on the project must be clearly defined, particularly with respect to making decisions. It is relatively straightforward to come up with ideas, but turning them into viable products or services requires careful planning. It requires input from people with the experience and knowledge to say 'no' if the product is not viable or will never make money for a company. Making this type of decision can be difficult, particularly if a company is producing a product that features the latest technology and may become obsolete very rapidly as competitors come up with better innovations.

Roles and responsibilities

It is important that everyone involved with a project knows their roles exactly and what level of responsibility they are to assume. Unless it is an established team, the project leader or manager will prepare a brief job description for each person in the team.

In the 1970s Meredith Belbin and his team at the Henley Management Centre carried out a research project to determine the types of generic roles that would make for effective team working. Belbin theory is fairly complex, but in simplistic terms it says that a balance of talents is needed within a team. For example, you need individuals that are creative, those that can turn ideas into reality, and others who can complete tasks to the last detail. You also need people who are good at monitoring and evaluation,

at planning the way forward, and at investigating the opposition. As well as the generic role functions, there is also a requirement to have the correct level of technical knowledge within a team. This is a wide range of skills and talents, and this is why it is unusual to find just one person working on a project. Also, one person cannot share or delegate responsibility; they must bear total responsibility for the project. If a project turns out to be incredibly bad, only one person gets to take the blame; of course, if it is spectacularly brilliant, the one person gets all the credit.

If you are going to work alone on your project, you will have to assume a number of roles, responsibilities and technical competencies – this is quite a challenge.

PLTS

Implementing a project involves the use and management of resources, for example, the expertise of people, materials, equipment and money. Bringing them all together can be a complex process. This will enable you to demonstrate EP1 (discuss areas of concern, seeking resolution where needed).

Case study: The Gorgon project

Asher works for a large multinational company, which was one of the contractors involved with the construction of the largest natural gas project in Australia's history – the Gorgon project. Gas is piped from undersea fields situated 130 kilometres off the coast of Western Australia to a processing plant located on a small island. Here it is liquefied and loaded into ships for global distribution and fed into pipes for mainland distribution. The gas reserve is large enough to meet the needs of a city the size of London for about 60 years. Over 10,000 people were directly or indirectly involved in the design and construction of the project. The processing plant is located in an area classified as environmentally sensitive, and several endangered wild life species live on the island. Unfortunately, there is no other viable location for the processing plant.

Asher's company provides strategic project management support for the oil and gas industries, and planning Gorgon took several years. Her job as lead document controller was to lead the team that managed all the technical and commercial documents associated with the engineering aspects of the project, including drawings, technical

specifications, environmental assessment reports, planning permissions, health and safety procedures, risk assessments, incident management, timescale planning and monitoring.

1 Discuss three reasons why it is important to keep accurate records for the Gorgon project.

2 What sort of file structure will the team be using so that engineers can gain straightforward access to a particular document?

3 What types of documentation might outside agencies (third parties) want access to? Why would this be?

4 Who monitors projects of this size?

5 What challenges might Asher face as she carries out her job?

6 A project of this size would throw up many challenges. It is said that any problem can be solved if you throw enough money at it. Discuss whether this is a helpful attitude in project management.

Reporting methods

Before embarking on a project there should be clear strategy for recording and reporting what is going on. This is important for monitoring purposes and for providing an evidence base if an independent audit is needed after the project has been completed. The actual reporting mechanisms are discussed in detail later in this unit (see page 98); at this point it is just necessary to think about the mechanics of a reporting system – that is, how to make a report, on what, when (at what intervals), and for whose benefit?

Resource allocation

There must be sufficient physical and human resources allocated to a project if it is to be successful. For big projects resource allocation is a complex process and it is done using planning tools such as network analysis. This involves working out what resources are needed and then scheduling them so that that they are utilised in the most effective way. Suppose you have ordered some components and it is going to take a couple of weeks for them to arrive. Do you stop the project and sit around waiting, or do you do something else, perhaps starting to put together a report or tidying up design drawings and sketches? Adopting the latter approach is called parallel working: you have two (or more) activities taking place at the same time. On large projects there will be many activities taking place at the same time and it is the task of the project manager to shuffle people and other resources around to best effect. The key to resource allocation is not to waste anything.

3.1.5 Techniques

Before a project gets the go-ahead, decisions have to be made about whether the project proposal is viable and stands any chance of success. Even when a project is under way, its progress must be evaluated and decisions made about whether to continue. Sometimes changes in technology will make a good idea obsolete, rendering it unviable and not worthy of continued investment. In a team situation, these decisions can be difficult and can lead to many arguments. A design engineer may see technical value in what is being proposed but the company accountant and marketing team may doubt whether the project will make any money. Who wins the argument? To come to a reasoned conclusion requires proper analysis using well-accepted techniques.

Comparison methods

When the project development department of a company comes up with ideas for new products, these are judged to see whether they are feasible. Are the proposals technically and financially viable? How will they fit into the existing market? Part of this process involves looking at statistical data, such as predicted market share, competitors' like-for-like sales and consumer trends.

Once the project has been approved, the next step is to write a specification and to produce detailed and costed design proposals. The decision about which proposal to develop further will be influenced by the result of a comparison technique such as an evaluation matrix (see Figure 3.1 overleaf). Each possible solution is evaluated against a list of selection criteria and numerical scores, or a plus/minus scoring system, can be assigned to each criterion. Each design proposal ends up with an overall score and the one with the best score is chosen for development. The selection criteria will consider aspects such as:

- manufacturing process – for example, machining from solid versus fabrication
- resources – raw materials, components, labour, finance
- processing capability – for example, how many units of a manufactured product are required over a given timescale
- fitness for purpose – for example, will the finished product meet the requirements of the design brief?

Fitness for purpose is particularly important in meeting customer expectations. Sometimes businesses fail to deliver. For example in 2009, there was a huge increase in the sales of netbook computers and mobile broadband USB dongles. The generic design brief for all the major manufacturers and network suppliers was to produce equipment and systems that would provide fast mobile broadband coverage over the whole of the UK. However, many customers were dissatisfied with the access and the download speeds. The network suppliers argued in their defence that they had not anticipated the huge uptake and were therefore having trouble coping with demand.

Selection criterion \ Option	Fabricate from aluminium sheet	Press out from thin mild steel sheet	Injection mould in polypropylene (PP)	Vacuum form in high density polyethylene (HDPE)
Complexity of construction	Complex (–)	Simple (+)	Simple (+)	Simple (+)
Tooling cost	Low (+)	High (– –)	Very high (– – –)	High (–)
Finish/appearance	Low (–)	Medium (0)	Very high (++)	High (+)
Waste material generated	Low (+)	Medium (0)	Low (+)	Low (+)
Manufacturing skill level req'd	High (–)	Low (+)	Low (+)	Low (+)
Cost of material	Medium (0)	Low (+)	High (–)	Medium (0)
Score Σ	–	+	0	+ + +

Figure 3.1: An evaluation matrix

Analysis

Engineers are very good at identifying problems, coming up with a strategy for their solution and then implementing the solutions. This involves analysing the problem against set criteria. The problem could be anything – from designing a new product, coming up with a better way to carry out a maintenance procedure, designing a procedure to mechanically test a component without destroying it, to improving the performance of a software package. Any proposed solution to a problem should be subject to two tests.

First, it needs to be considered in cost–benefit terms. Will the solution generate revenues for the business that will cover the development costs within a given period of time and then add to the profitability of the business? Equally important, will customers who buy the product appreciate the cost–benefit?

For example, consumers may be prepared to pay a premium for a new design of car which uses less fuel, has cleaner emissions and is not subject to inner city congestion charges. Cost–benefit analysis involves mathematical modelling using similar techniques to those investigated in Unit 7.

Second, the solution needs to be feasible. It can be very difficult to carry out feasibility studies for some projects. For example, some bioengineering projects run over many years and must incorporate new and emerging technology. It is difficult to assess whether these projects will be a technical and financial success. Many engineering projects have more structure and shorter timescales, such as a project to develop a new digital camera; these are much easier to assess because the new design can be evaluated against current models.

Case study: An evaluation matrix

A manufacturer of electrical equipment is producing a batch of 100 prototypes of a new product. A number of established customers have agreed to evaluate the performance of the product by carrying out field trials, also known as 'beta testing'. Once the trials have been carried out, modifications will be made to the design so that it can be produced in large quantities.

The designer is at the point of selecting a manufacturing process and material for the casing which will hold the circuit boards and components. They are considering four options and have evaluated them using an evaluation matrix (see Figure 3.1).

On the basis of the evaluation matrix, the designer decides to use vacuum forming.

Activity: Analysing different options

Suppose you work for a company that makes heavy power tools for use in the body-pressing workshops of car manufacturers. You have been asked to investigate the design of the flywheels fitted to the machines. You are presented with three options for the flywheel:

- machine from solid steel
- fabricate by welding spokes to a machined hub and rim
- cast and finish machine.

Make a list of the information which you must look at before coming to a decision about which of the three methods is the most effective method of production.

PLTS

Engineering is a creative discipline, and to achieve success, people working in the industry must be innovative and able to 'think outside of the box'. In developing potential solutions for your project, you will demonstrate CT1 (generate ideas and explore possibilities).

Assessment activity 3.2

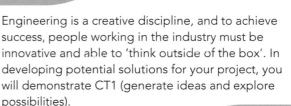 

P2 Write a specification for the product or system which is to be developed in your project.

P3 Prepare a set of procedures that you intend to follow as you progress your project to a satisfactory conclusion.

P4 Produce outlines for three potential solutions that meet the requirements of your specification. Evaluate each solution against the specification and select the best one for development.

M2 Use a range of techniques and selection criteria to fully justify your choice of which solution to develop.

Grading tips

P2 You need to research a suitable topic for your project, write a proposal and make a list of the resources you will need to carry it through to completion. Discuss the proposal with your tutor, agree a final outcome and decide on a title. Make the first entries in your project logbook, which should include written confirmation from your tutor that the project aims are realistic and achievable. The specification should contain quantifiable parameters against which you can accurately assess the finished product or system.

P3 It might be helpful to make reference to a flow chart and any other type of recognised planning aid. You must agree with your tutor the procedures that you will follow as you progress your project. You must also consider budgetary constraints and resource/time limitations.

P4 Present your ideas as three sets of detailed and annotated sketches, which can be discussed with colleagues, your tutor or a design engineer. Evaluate each proposal against the specification and select the best one for development. Think about and assess the availability of the resources that you may need, such as materials, technician support and access to workshops.

You could link this activity to grading criteria P2 and P5 of Unit 8: Engineering Design, and grading criterion P2 of Unit 2: Communications for Engineering Technicians.

M2 Assess your design proposals by using an evaluation matrix and two other formal comparison methods (statistical and graphical). Through discussion with your tutor and by written commentary, present a detailed justification for your chosen option.

3.2 Be able to plan and monitor a project

Many factors contribute to the cost of running a project, but the two biggest contributors are the cost of labour and materials (including their processing). It is important that people's time and skills are used in the most effective way and that materials are available when needed. To make this happen, businesses use scientific planning and monitoring techniques. These have been developed over many years. Originally worked out by hand, these techniques are now computer-based and come as standard options in integrated design and manufacturing software packages.

A project will have an aim and several objectives. Your overall aim at the moment is to achieve the BTEC National qualification. This should improve your career prospects. You may not be too sure of where you want to go in the future, but at this moment there is a definite aim in your life – to better yourself. An aim is a general statement of intent. In this case it might be: 'I want pass the course and improve my employment prospects.' To achieve this aim, you should be able to write down a set of objectives, also often referred to as goals. These are activities that have prescribed and measurable outcomes. One of these objectives might be to successfully complete the project that you must do for this unit. How you can do this is set out in the unit specification. Objectives are set out using specific and detailed statements.

Let's take a business example. Suppose the aim of a start-up electronics business is to capture 20 per cent of the available market share for a particular type of hand-held barcode scanner. Some of the company's objectives would be:

- a new model to be marketed within 9 months
- first year turnover to be £600,000
- a second model to be marketed 12 months after the first one
- product reliability to be better than 95 per cent
- return on investment to be achieved by year 4 of trading
- a 10 per cent market share by year 2 of trading, and 20 per cent by year 6.

Note that these are similar to the type of objectives that are regularly quoted when budding entrepreneurs make pitches on *Dragons' Den*.

Now let's return to how you might achieve success on the BTEC National. You should identify your objectives and put together a plan for how these might be achieved. Your programme manager will have already provided a timetable showing when the units are going to be delivered. This gives you a one- or two-year timescale to achieve your objectives. Your tutors will have identified some dates which will allow you to set specific objectives, such as points at which assignments are due or the dates when portfolios must be submitted for inspection. On a unit-by-unit basis, you can set yourself personal goals.

Once you have established aims and objectives for any project, you can then start the detailed planning.

3.2.1 Planning

How do you go about planning your project once you have decided on a topic? The first step is to identify the activities to be carried out over, say, the next six months, and to set them out as a list with approximate timings against each activity. Consider each activity as a goal or objective, think about the resources which will be needed, and come up with ways to monitor progress and the achievement of each goal.

You then need to think about what you expect to achieve by certain points of the project and to set milestones. This word derives from the stone markers that were placed by the sides of roads and indicated the mileage to a reference point such as the centre of town. Having identified your milestones – such as producing three design proposals – decide how and when you are going to monitor them. Time markers showing where your milestones occur should then be added to planning charts.

Long-term planning

This relates to the whole life of a project. You can use several techniques to provide a visual overview of the whole project, setting out the activities that need to be completed.

First, you can use a simple flow chart set out as a block diagram (see Figure 3.2). This has no timings attached to each activity. However, it is ideal for showing the various stages of a project in an easy-to-see format.

It is useful for presenting information about how your project is being set up.

Second, you can use a project planner such as a Gantt chart (see Figure 3.3). This is a very well-established method for showing the various activities which contribute to a project. These are set out against a timeline and will have review points.

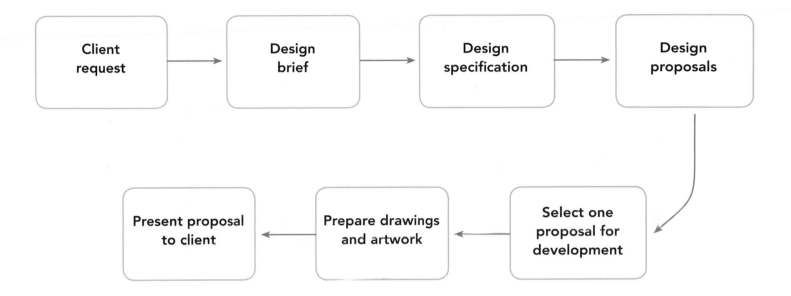

Figure 3.2: A project flow chart for preparing and presenting a design proposal

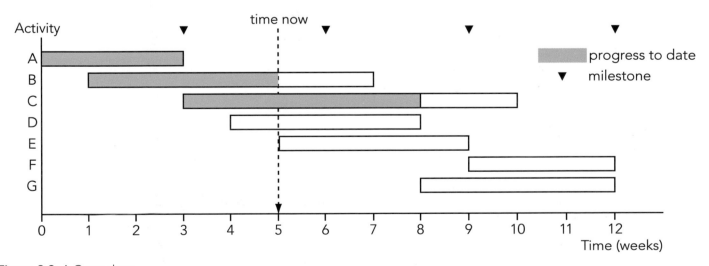

Figure 3.3: A Gantt chart

Figure 3.4: A network diagram with five events and four activities

Third, you can carry out network analysis by using techniques such as programme evaluation and review (PERT) and critical path method (CPM). A network diagram (see Figure 3.4) consists of a series of events, which form the **nodes** of the network. Events are linked by arrow-headed straight lines that denote activities (things that happen). The expected time for the activity is written alongside the line. The total time to complete all the activities in Figure 3.4 is 12 hours (5 + 2 + 4 + 1 = 12).

Now suppose some of the activities are carried out at the same time. The network diagram becomes more complicated because there may be more than one line linking the activity circles. Figure 3.5 shows a network for the manufacture of a engineering product. As you can see, some activities take place in tandem. For example, some elements of the product are being fabricated in the factory at the same time as other components are being requisitioned from suppliers and made by subcontractors.

Within a network diagram there will be the critical path. This is the path that links the activities that have the greatest expected time – in other words, it is the

> ### Key terms
>
> **Node** a junction or connection point.

longest route through the diagram. The critical path allows the project manager to identify those activities that have the greatest effect on the overall project time. By devoting extra resources to these activities so that they are completed more rapidly, a project manager would be able to reduce the overall time taken for the project.

There are some conventions that are used when drawing up network diagrams. When two events run in parallel and one finishes before the other, a dummy event is added to the diagram. This is shown in Figure 3.6.

In a complex network (such as that shown in Figure 3.5), some activities cannot start before others have finished. For example, the parts cannot be received until they have been requisitioned, and assembly cannot begin until parts have arrived. When constructing any network

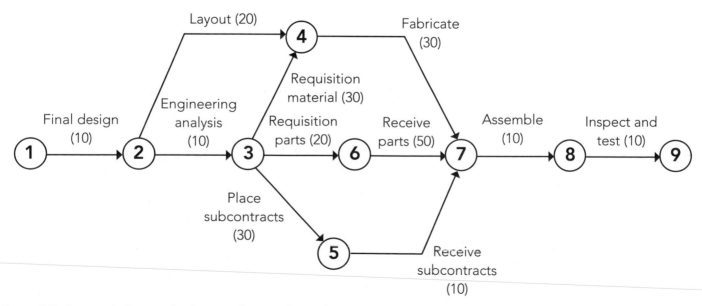

Figure 3.5: A network diagram for the manufacture of a product

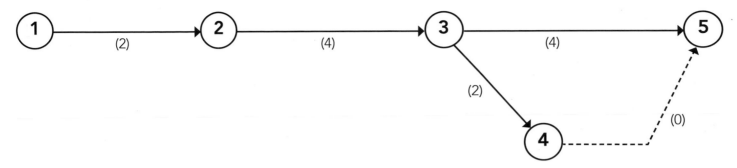

Figure 3.6: A network diagram with a dummy activity

diagram, you need to make sure that for each activity you take account of any activities on which it depends and, therefore, which need to have been completed first. These preceding dependent activities are called predecessors. One way to do this is to first list each activity in a table (see Table 3.2), noting the time that the activity takes and any predecessors that must be completed before the activity can begin. Then you can use the table to draw up the network diagram as shown in Figure 3.7. Remember to include dummy activities where appropriate.

Table 3.2: Activity list

Activity	Preceding activity	Time for the activity
A	none	5
B	none	4
C	A, B	2
D	A	1
E	B, C, D	4
F	A, B, C, D, E	1

Setting priorities

It is very important to prioritise project activities, identifying those which must be completed before others can start. If you are going to manufacture something in a workshop, there is no point in booking time on a machine unless you know that the materials you need have been ordered and will arrive in time. Your priorities when carrying out your project will be made quite clear to you by your tutor – one of them will be to achieve certain targets by agreed dates. As there will be a cut-off point for the submission of your portfolio and other assessment evidence, it may be worth working backwards from this date when you plan out how to progress the project.

Priorities may have to be adjusted in the light of changing circumstances, but with most projects the bottom line is that they must completed on time.

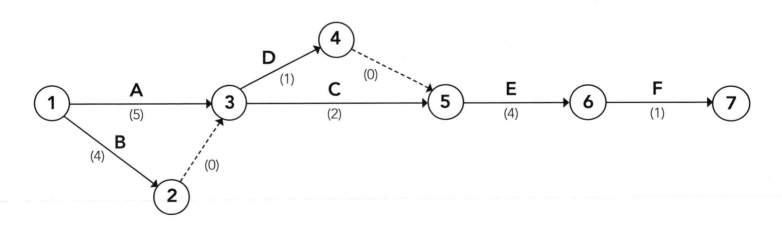

Figure 3.7: A network diagram with dummy activities and predecessors

Activity: Planning your project

Have a look at the assessment and grading criteria grid for this unit, which is presented on page 66. Now think about how the grading criteria align against the activities which you are carrying out for your project.

Using college weeks as a timeline, set out the activities relating to each grading criterion using a Gantt chart. You can do this using a spreadsheet or commercially available project management software. Add appropriate milestones to your chart. Discuss, amend and agree the plan with your tutor.

Now think about your priorities. Identify the activities that may be difficult to carry out or will require specialised resources, and the ones that will be critical and could delay the project if they are not completed sufficiently early in the work.

PLTS

It is important to set goals that are realistic and achievable within a given timescale. Project planning will help you develop this skill.

Resource infomation

Because progressing a project will require the deployment of human and physical resources, it is important to plan how much resource is likely to be required. Questions that need to be addressed during the planning phase are what type of resources are required, how much of each resource, and when each will be needed. This can only be done if information is known about the resources you intend to use. For example, suppose your project involves fabricating a component by welding and you do not have the necessary skills for this work. As project manager, you decide to outsource this task to a workshop technician. You'll need to find out whether there is a technician with the skill to do welding, whether your centre has a welding facility, and whether you need to give notice and, if so, how much.

If you are doing an electronic design project, you may need to get access to simulation software. You need to find out if your centre has the application package and, if not, whether there is a local company or a student on a higher level engineering course who might be able to help you. These types of question can only be answered by accessing information.

Earlier in this unit, we discussed Brunel's Clifton Suspension Bridge and the Airbus A380 project. How much information was needed about available resources when these two projects were being planned? Brunel had access to significantly less technical information about the properties of materials than the designers of the A380. He carried out mathematical modelling to determine the loads and stresses in the supporting chains and links of the bridge, but he relied heavily on his professional judgment when specifying the physical dimensions of components. There was no **finite element analysis** software available in the 19th century. The A380 was an infinitely more complex project but the engineers had access to a much greater range of useful resources. They were able to use these to devise ways to save weight and improve construction techniques, and they were able to select materials with improved mechanical and physical properties that would ensure long-term structural integrity.

Finding and using information in this way is another key feature of being able to deliver a successful project.

Activity: Planning terms

Make sure that you are familiar with common acronyms used in planning. What does SMART mean (in the context of target setting)? What about PERT and CPM (in the context of project planning)?

Key terms

Finite element analysis computerised numerical modelling of the stresses and deformations produced in components when subject to external loading.

3.2.2 Monitoring

Monitoring and recording achievement is done using a logbook and a diary. A logbook is a working document, and it should contain notes and records made at the time of doing something. This might be a note of a discussion between a designer and manufacturing engineer about revising a machining process or a comment about problems encountered when testing a component. A good principle to adopt when using a logbook is 'write it down so that you don't forget'. However, you need to be careful that you don't write too much and have so many notes that you get thoroughly confused.

A diary is used for recording important dates, names and addresses, telephone and email contacts, goals and milestones. Unless your tutor gives you specific instructions, it is up to you to decide whether to keep a separate diary and logbook or to combine these into a single record with two sections.

A logbook does not need to be a perfectly presented document, but it should be an effective tool to capture information in real time or shortly after an event or activity has taken place. A traditional paper-based logbook will contain text, calculations and sketches. An electronic logbook could include images downloaded from a mobile phone and short verbal comments.

When setting up a logbook, it is important to establish:

• its format

• how and when it will be reviewed

• who will do the reviewing.

What should you put in your logbook? You should certainly not place every piece of paper that you generate in the logbook, otherwise it will become a huge and unwieldy portfolio. However, it should contain enough essential detail to show the progress of your project and you should provide links to other documentation and drawings that relate to the project. For example, your initial design ideas might be sketched out in the logbook but the developed solution presented as CAD drawings.

Many people in industry now keep electronic notebooks, but most of the great inventors and engineers of the past wrote everything down by hand in bound volumes. A paper-based logbook does not necessarily need a hard binding. The problem is that unless you produce very neat records and know exactly what to write, then you are going to end up with some pages that look very untidy. A ring binder might be a better option, so long as you do not waste too much time rewriting or tidying up pages.

The main thing to be aware of is that there must be a complete record of any engineering project, which sets out what happened and provides important data including the specification, manufacturing data and test results. This provides a full audit trail.

Activity: Monitoring

With a colleague, monitor your progress on the course by looking over your assignment record.

• Are there some pass grading criteria that you have yet to achieve?

• What actions have been agreed with your tutor so that you can rework assignment evidence and achieve better results?

Case study: Satbir

Satbir is the technical manager of a small business that carries out independent testing of electrical and electronic equipment. The company is certificated to carry out electromagnetic compatibility (EMC) testing and other types of electrical safety evaluation. Satbir must keep up to date with the latest EU directives and international regulations and understand how they apply to manufactured products.

A typical day for Satbir starts by meeting with a customer who has a product that needs to be independently tested for CE (European conformity) and BEAB approval. The BEAB (British Electrotechnical Approvals Board) approved mark can provide a defence in law for a manufacturer against a product liability claim.

He will look at the manufacturer's specification for the product, and then identify the compliance requirements to be assessed and plan a test schedule. He will be thinking about test equipment needed,

how the results will be recorded and what advice he will give to the customer if the product fails any of the tests.

1   Why are products tested for compatibility?

2   What are the implications for a manufacturer if it tries to sell a product that does not conform to the standards?

3   Why does Satbir look at the customer's product specification?

4   If the product is found to comply, it will be signed off by Satbir's company and the test results will be logged. If the product goes into large-scale production, how will the compliance of products coming off the production line be monitored? What involvement will Satbir's company have in this process?

Assessment activity 3.3

 P5 P6   BTEC

P5 Write an outline of your chosen project solution and how you expect to achieve it.

Then refine or modify your specification, so that it contains at least ten statements against which the final outcome can be evaluated.

Prepare an implementation plan that you will follow as you progress your project to a solution.

P6 Update your logbook and other records with evidence to show that you have been monitoring your progress and are successfully moving forward with the project.

Grading tips

P5 You need to identify resource and regulatory issues that will impact on what you propose to design, manufacture or test.

You could link this activity to grading criteria P3 and P4 of Unit 8: Engineering Design, grading criterion P5 of Unit 7: Business Operations in Engineering, and the grading criteria that relate to learning outcomes 2 and 4 of Unit 9: Commercial Aspects of Engineering Organisations.

P6 Annotate your planning documentation to indicate changing situations and decisions made. Provide enough information so that someone repeating the project can 'learn from your mistakes'. You should ask your tutor for a witness statement confirming that you have been monitoring progress.

This activity will only produce part of the evidence you need for the P6. Assessment activity 3.6 will help you generate the additional evidence needed to fully complete P6.

3.3 Be able to implement the project plan within agreed procedures

Engineering projects are usually organised in several stages comprising, for example, specification formulation, conceptual design, detail design, manufacture, testing and evaluation on completion against specification. The successful implementation of a project requires the management and use of many different types of resource, including time, people, research sources, materials and processing equipment. Resources must be utilised effectively and progress must be monitored and evaluated against a plan. If things are not progressing as expected, it may be necessary to adapt the plan so that targets can be met or to make agreed changes to the technical specification and expected outcome.

3.3.1 Implement

Up to now, you have been studying the principles of managing and delivering a project. Now it is up to you to put into practice the principles that you have studied. Effectively, you are on you own – all we can do to help here is to give you some tips and advice.

You must come up with proposals for a project and discuss these with your tutor and decide which one to follow through. This first stage can be difficult and it may take a little time to come up with a theme and title for a project. If you can choose something that is related to one of the other units on your engineering course, then you should find the project more interesting.

To complete the project requires the use of many resources. Here is a checklist of the resources that you may need to use:

- equipment and tools found in the school or college, the company where you do work experience or are apprenticed, or at home
- raw materials, electrical and mechanical components
- money needed for buying materials
- people – your and other people's time and expertise
- techniques and methods for generating ideas and for planning
- a facility for keeping records so that you can look back and adapt ideas.

Activity: Organising resources

Suppose you need to manufacture some components for your project and this involves gaining access to a college workshop for about six hours. As you are running behind schedule, your tutor suggests that you put in some extra time over the next two weeks. The workshop is busy for most of the week and occupied by classes, but it does have some spare capacity when classes are small. Provided you are adequately supervised by a technician and follow health and safety procedures, you can take up this spare capacity for project work.

The workshop technician has offered to help, but does need to know in advance exactly what you expect to achieve in six hours.

- What information will the technician need?
- Who else will you need to talk to?
- What resources will you require?
- How will your tutor monitor your progress?

3.3.2 Checking solutions

It is important to carry out final checks to ensure that the outcome of the project fulfils the requirements of the specification. In an industrial situation if the outcome is not to specification, then a resolution action plan will be created. Managers might stipulate that extra time and resources are devoted to the project so that it can be completed or, in the worst-case scenario, they might cancel the project.

There are two questions to consider when checking the outcome of a project:

- project management – how well was it organised, were there any delivery issues, was best use made of available resources?
- technical competence – does the product or system that has been produced by the project function in accordance with its planned specification?

Solutions are checked using recognised evaluative and analytical techniques.

Evaluative and analytical techniques

The comparison methods introduced earlier in this unit (see page 83) should be applied at the relevant stages during the progress of your project to help you:

- select which idea from a range of proposals has the greatest chance of success
- choose which of your three proposed design solutions is most suitable for development
- monitor the progress of the project
- evaluate the outcome of the project in terms of project management and technical competence.

To assess these in an objective way, evaluative and analytical techniques are used.

Earlier in this unit you may have used evaluation matrices when selecting your project. Project time and resource management may have been done using a Gantt chart and/or a network analysis diagram, to provide an accurate audit trail. Project modifications should be recorded and all versions of the chart and diagram kept on file.

Controlling the budget of a project is crucial, particularly where large amounts of money are involved. At the planning stage, a budget will have been drawn up using a spreadsheet or software package. This should be updated at regular time intervals and progress reports generated. These reports are required as a concise record of the current project status. In large projects, financial reporting may include statistical analysis; for example, the percentages of budget spent on human resources and raw materials can be examined at a particular milestone.

The final outcome will be evaluated against the original specifications. Technical outcomes are evaluated by performance testing of the finished product and comparing the data with the specification values. Project management success can be evaluated by using the Gantt chart to compare planned progress at milestone points against actual progress. Another measure is to review financial reports for project budget spend.

Ideally, an individual project should progress at a uniform rate. So, if progress is plotted against a scale of time, a straight line will run from zero to 100 per cent completed. However, many individual projects are slow to start and slow to finish, with a surge of progress through the middle time period – effectively an 'S' shape superimposed on the straight line. If you can see potential slow areas in your project you could bring in more resources to get it back on track, such as guidance from your tutor or help from a technician.

Case study: Akiko

Akiko works in the business development division of Tromecy plc, a UK company that has three overseas manufacturing facilities. All design work and customer support, and some manufacturing, is done at the company headquarters in the south west of England. About 70 per cent of manufacturing is passed to plants in Bulgaria, India and China with finished products air-freighted back to the UK.

Akiko's division has responsibility for assessing conditions in the marketplace, evaluating competitors' products and working with the design department on the development of new products. Her current job role is to monitor the progress of product development projects and to provide support to the people who are managing them. A typical day starts with a review meeting between Akiko, a project manager, a design team leader, a manufacturing engineer and a logistics manager. This is done by telephone, or video conferencing if the manufacturing is being done at one of the overseas facilities. After the meeting Akiko produces a short report which she emails to the operations director.

1 What questions will she ask each of the other four people at the review meeting?

2 What figures and documentation will they present to her?

3 Against what criteria will she evaluate the information presented?

4 How will Akiko come to a decision about whether the project is being correctly implemented?

5 Suppose the project is over budget and behind schedule. What other information will she need to look at before making a recommendation to the operations director?

Activity: Checking solutions

Suppose you work in the development department of a company that manufactures modular electronic devices used in data communications systems. You have just completed the design, construction and testing of a prototype high-speed router and are to meet with the technical director to evaluate the new design.

- Prepare a checklist of the drawings and documentation that will be needed for the meeting.

- What is the 'big question' that the director will ask?

PLTS

As your project progresses you may have to revise targets and adapt what you are doing. For example, you may book a supervised slot in a workshop but the technician forgets to order your raw materials. This will help demonstrate that you can seek out challenges or new responsibilities and show flexibility when priorities change.

Assessment activity 3.4

P7 Prepare a resource plan which should include details of:

- materials and components to be bought or borrowed

- tools and test equipment

- specialised technical help that you may need

- access to IT equipment and software packages.

Then obtain the necessary resources and use them to produce the project solution, following any agreed procedures. Monitor, review and record progress through this work.

P8 Check that your developed solution conforms to its specification as detailed in assessment activity 3.3.

Review the procedures followed when implementing your plan to see if they conformed to the operational specification you produced for assessment activity 3.2.

M3 Evaluate the project solution against its specification and suggest improvements you would make if you had to repeat the project.

Grading tips

P7 Evidence relating to production activities should include annotated images and tutor observation records. Be careful not to spend too much time on 'practical' activities that may involve equipment and materials. If a substantial amount of manufacturing is involved, then subcontract the work, as would happen in industry, but be aware that you are responsible for managing the process.

You may wish to link this activity to: Unit 21: Engineering Secondary and Finishing Techniques and Unit 34: Electronic Circuit Manufacture.

P8 If the developed solution does not conform to its specification, make modifications (if time allows). Make reference to this in the written project report (assessment activity 3.5).

M3 Your project solution could take many forms. For example, you might produce a manufactured product (hardware), a detailed design proposal, a software package or write a quality assurance procedure. To achieve M3, you must produce a critical review of what you have produced and make suggestions for improvement even if everything appears to be 100 per cent correct. These improvements should add value to the project solution. Feedback from 'customers' is one way to come up with improvements, which may enhance the value of your solution. The 'customers' could be other members of your group or an engineer from a local company.

3.4 Be able to present the project outcome

Effective communication is a vital skill for anyone working in business and it can sometimes be overlooked, particularly when the technical aspects of a job seem more interesting than telling people about it. Engineers are usually very good at finding solutions to complex technical problems and turning ideas into products and services, but some are not so good at presenting the outcome of their efforts to a wider audience.

3.4.1 Presentations

In Unit 2, there is some advice about making presentations (see page 53). If you have not read this part of the book, then this is the time to do so. The section contains some activities designed to improve your presentation skills.

Delivering a presentation

Making a verbal presentation about a topic can be a daunting experience, particularly if you are giving a talk for the first time. Some people do get genuinely terrified when asked to stand up in front of a group to make a presentation, and even the most experienced speakers sometimes get nervous, but you must deliver a presentation to pass this unit. This verbal presentation must also involve the use of ICT. (It does not state this explicitly in the grading criteria, but this is made clear in the unit content range statements.)

A confident speaker will be happy to present to a large group, a less confident speaker will talk to a small group of colleagues and someone who gets totally nervous will present informally to one or two people such as sympathetic tutors. This is no different to what happens in industry, and often you will find that the quietest and most reserved people are the ones with the greatest knowledge and technical expertise.

It is important to appreciate that as far as your project is concerned, people will be on your side and wanting you to make a successful presentation. Your tutor will certainly hope for a good result and if you feel that your colleagues are trying to put you off, remember it may be their turn next. As you deliver your presentation give people time to take in what you are saying, look at them rather than your notes and try to pick up when they are not understanding what you are saying or are losing interest. If this occurs, you need a recovery strategy – ask your tutor for a few ideas.

You can do much to make this presentation a success. Practice and preparation are vital. If you adopt a very laid back approach and simply 'turn up and have a go', then you might have problems. If you are well prepared, then things will run much more smoothly.

Preparation techniques

The key to a successful presentation is being well prepared. Some people over prepare – they try to cram too much into their allocated time and present their audience with too much to take in. You may have heard the phrase 'death by PowerPoint'; it is difficult for anyone to take in a presentation comprising, say, 30 slides each containing eight lines of text and whizzed through in 25 minutes. This is far too ambitious.

Preparing a presentation about a technical subject requires proper planning. You need to consider the following questions.

- How long will you speak for?
- Do you need to allow time for questions?
- What is the make-up of your audience?
- Will the audience have any prior knowledge of the subject you are talking about?
- Will presentation graphics, such as PowerPoint slides, add value to the presentation?
- Should you read from a script or work off prompt cards?
- Will visual aids such as models, hardware or documents enhance the presentation?
- Is there any value in including a short video clip?
- Should the audience be given a handout or other documentation before you start?
- Do you have a recovery strategy, if it all goes wrong?

A pitfall to avoid is becoming too familiar with what you are going to present. Suppose you produce a script as a starting point, covering say a page of A4. How long does it take you to read and understand it? Most people tend to read text with which they are familiar much more rapidly than material they are seeing for the first time. The same applies if you prepare a script and then read it out to an audience. Unless you can control your speed of delivery, you will race through in no time at all and the audience will be totally lost. Some people tend to go even quicker if they are nervous or unsure of themselves.

When trying out what you are going to say to an audience, practise speaking at half your normal speed and try to pause for several seconds between each paragraph. This gives the audience time to take in and think about what you have just said. Try doing this in front of a video camera and then play it back.

Once you have rehearsed what you are going to say, go back to the script and mark up headings. Transfer these headings to a set of prompt cards or list them in order on a single sheet of paper. Without looking at your script, use the cards to deliver your talk to camera or to someone who can give guidance and feedback.

If you are happy with what you want to say, and think that a PowerPoint presentation will enhance your talk, then produce a small number of easy-to-read slides. They could contain basic information, such as the title of your talk, your name and the headings taken from the prompt cards. The important fact to grasp is that it is bad practice for a presenter to simply read from the slides – your audience is quite capable of doing this for themselves. Slides are there to support what you are saying. It is fine to put simple bullet point headings on the slides, which you can use for prompts as you speak.

Activity: Perfect preparation

Discuss with a colleague how you will plan the preparation and delivery of your end-of-project presentation.

Use the internet to investigate the various interpretations of the 5Ps checklist which some people use to help deliver good presentations. Select or adapt the version that you think is most appropriate for students on a BTEC National Engineering programme.

Visual aids

The thing to appreciate about visual aids is that they are there to support or enhance a presentation. Remember this when preparing your talk – the aim is to present technical information about your project effectively and not to show off your artistic prowess. Simple, easy-to-read PowerPoint slides are all you need when addressing grading criterion P9.

Your choice of visual aids will depend on your topic and the content you need to get across. In making this choice, apply a simple test – will the visual aid enhance the presentation? Most people tend to go straight for PowerPoint slides because they are easy to create. You can just cut and paste from a Word document, add in a couple of spreadsheet charts, add some clipart and away you go. But there are other visual aids which can be used. Here are some ideas.

- 'Old fashioned' hand-drawn overhead transparencies are useful as a quick way to present graphs produced from experimental results. You can also add notes or details to the transparencies as you speak.

- A very good way to explain the operation of an electronic circuit is to use simulation software, which can be run on a laptop computer and projected on a screen.

- Similarly, you can use 3D CAD software running on a laptop to show and rotate a solid model of component on a screen.

- Charts of experimental results can be hand produced on large sheets of paper and clipped up for the audience.

- Cardboard and polystyrene models can be passed around the audience. The problem here is that you may lose the attention of the audience as they look at what is being passed around.

- Video clips can usefully break up a lengthy presentation. If your presentation only lasts a few minutes, then keep the video content to an absolute minimum. Do not try to use video as a way to avoid speaking.

- If you wish to demonstrate a practical activity, you could enlist a trained helper to provide a demonstration while you explain what is happening.

Case study: Peter

Mitjulz Ltd manufactures taps, mixer showers, extractor fans, siphon tubes for toilets, and other bathroom fittings. Peter is a trainee sales executive working in the marketing department.

Mitjulz has developed a new line of stainless steel, hi-tech bathroom fittings. These new products are innovative and stylish, and Mitjulz is promoting them as the face of bathrooms for the 2010s. The company is hoping to set up a lucrative exclusivity deal with a DIY superstore, and Peter has been asked to make a presentation to the superstore's chief buyer.

Peter must deliver a polished and informative presentation to the buyer. This is the first time of going solo and although a reasonably confident speaker he is feeling apprehensive because a lot rests on the effectiveness of his presentation.

- What form will his presentation take?
- How long do you think it should last?
- What visual aids should he use?
- What questions should he expect from the buyer?
- Would it be useful to have the support of a technician?
- What documented data will the buyer want to take away?
- How can he rehearse for the event?
- How will Peter report back to the marketing manager?

Activity: Prepare and make a three-minute presentation

A college is holding an open day to showcase its courses to year 11 students from local schools. You have agreed to help out on the engineering stand, which will have photo displays, samples of portfolios, hands-on experiments and short rolling video presentations showing what goes on in laboratories and workshops.

Your brief is to produce a three-minute video that takes someone through an exciting practical activity which you have carried out in a science laboratory. Work with a colleague to:

- prepare a storyboard and voice-over commentary
- rehearse the presentation

- shoot the video using either a proper video camera or your phone
- save the video to a laptop computer
- evaluate the video with your tutor.

Note, a storyboard is a series of rough sketches arranged in sequence to map out a video or film.

There is no need to carry out complex editing or voice dubbing. Something in the style of a YouTube clip is perfectly adequate. It is the content which is important in this exercise.

PLTS

When you made your presentation were you confident or nervous? Think about how you controlled your emotions and kept the attention of the audience. This will help you demonstrate that you can manage your emotions, and build and maintain relationships.

3.4.2 Project report

The final stage of any project is to report back to the people and organisations that have an interest in the initiative. This interest might be because of a financial involvement – the backers of a project want to assess its outcome – or because someone has simply heard about the project, found it interesting and wishes to read the report.

Project reports usually take two forms: internal reports and reports written to go in the public domain. The internal report is written solely for the benefit of people working within the organisation in which the project team is based. The report may contain commercially sensitive information, so the people reading the report are bound by the rules of confidentiality set out by their employer. Anyone leaking any of the content to a competing business could face legal action. Reports in the public domain are sometimes called research papers. They will not contain commercially sensitive information, but will have information of interest to other researchers and the wider engineering industry. These reports can be published in scientific journals or made available on the internet (sometimes on websites where you have to pay a subscription to access the material).

When you write reports in industry, it is likely that they will be for internal use only because of the competitive nature of the engineering business.

Logbooks and project diaries

Logbooks and diaries are working documents that chart the progress of a project. On completion of a project, they are very useful reference sources, which should be used in preparing a detailed written report and putting together a verbal presentation. It is not necessary to rewrite parts of a logbook that appear untidy as long as you can understand what's on the page.

Written technical reports

Before starting to write a technical report it is important to plan its format and to decide on its style. In industry, reports are sometimes written with the help of a template. This is done so that if several reports are being produced over a period of time, they will all have the same 'feel' and appearance. You will need to make your own style choices. You will also need to consider the number of sections the report will contain and decide on a consistent method of numbering each section.

Try to mix text and graphics. Most engineering reports contain a lot of text, and it makes for easier reading if this is split up with relevant graphics. Relevant is the key word here – a technical report is a factual document; it should not look like a glossy marketing brochure. Sometimes it is better to provide engineering drawings and circuit diagrams in a separate folder and provide cross references in the text using a numbering system. Charts and graphs should be incorporated into the report. If these have been created using a spreadsheet, it should be very easy to cut and paste them into the report. They can be placed between blocks of text or grouped in a single section (or appendix) of the report and cross referenced to the text using a numbering system.

You need to think about how to present scientific equations and mathematical calculations. This can be difficult if you are using basic word-processing software. If a college project report requires many formulae, equations and mathematical calculations, it can sometimes be less time-consuming to write them out by hand and then insert them as referenced pages. In industry, specialised software is used to prepare mathematical content.

You will need to consider the readers. Who is going to have access to the project report? If it is highly technical and may be seen by non-specialists, it is important to provide a non-technical overview of how the project progressed and a summary of the final outcome. Finally, it is good practice to have the report proofread and checked before it is submitted.

Information and communication technology (ICT)

In Unit 2, there is a section on the use of ICT to present information in engineering settings (see page 53). If you have not read this part of the book, then this is the time to do so as it contains guidance as well as activities designed to improve your ICT skills. You will be expected to use ICT in putting together your written report. (Again, it does not state this explicitly in the grading criteria, but this is made clear in the unit content range statements.)

Activity: Prepare a written report

Following on from the college open day at which you presented a short video (see page 98), a teacher from a local school has been in contact with your programme manager. The teacher was very impressed with the video and has asked if you would be prepared to help out with the school's careers guidance programme. The school wants you to supply a technical report similar to those used in industry.

You agree to help and it has been decided that the report should have this format:

- organisation – in three sections comprising an overview, the main body of report and the references and bibliography

- length – 800 to 1000 words

- non-text features – to include an image, a simple imported spreadsheet, a table with some shaded cells

- style – bullets and/or numbering, page numbers, title page.

The report should be on a topic of your choice, but it must relate to engineering. You could use an existing report that you have written and adjust it to meet the required format.

Keep the report formal but remember that it will be read by year 11 students with limited knowledge of engineering and technical language.

Functional skills

Preparing a technical report will develop your writing and ICT skills.

Assessment activity 3.5

P9 Prepare and deliver a short verbal presentation to a small group of people outlining your project specification and proposed solution.

P10 Prepare a written project report.

M4 Present a portfolio that includes a set of well-structured development records and the report that you produced for task 2.

Grading tips

P9 You should consider linking this to Unit 2: Communications for Engineering Technicians, as there are close links with grading criterion P5 (communicate information effectively using verbal methods). Evidence presented in your portfolio should include hard copies of the presentation, such as handouts, slides and witness statements. Also put in observation records from your audience.

P10 Present your report to a standard that allows it to be put on display and read by a variety of people who work in industry. For the benefit of someone who is not an engineer, the report should contain an overview explaining in non-technical terms what you achieved. You should be able to use this task as a data source for grading criterion M3 of Unit 2: Communications for Engineering Technicians.

The report can be handwritten, but a much better option is to word-process the document so that you can easily drop in charts and images, and it is easy to revise and redraft paragraphs if required.

M4 In assessment activity 3.1 you set up a system to record all the events relating to your project, from selection of the topic to the final presentation. During the project, you should have built up this record in various ways, such as through handwritten notes in your logbook, jottings on bits of paper, sketches, drawings, observation records, research materials and first drafts of your final report.

To achieve M4, you must have carried out this process in an orderly manner. Assemble your material in a well-structured way so that someone looking through your work can easily see the developmental process taking place. Every step of the project should be recorded with all actions and decisions traceable.

Assessment activity 3.6

P1 P6 M1 D1 D2 · BTEC

P1 Complete the project records that you have been keeping and present them in an appropriate format. Show clearly how progress was made and identify any difficulties that had to be overcome.

P6 Complete the monitoring records that you have been keeping and present them in an appropriate format. Describe progress made and how you resolved any difficulties encountered along the way.

D1 Provide evidence to prove that you were able to manage the project development process independently, seeking support and guidance where necessary.

D2 Extend the report you produced for task 2, assessment activity 3.5, by adding an 800-word section that critically assesses your success in managing the project and evaluates how well the finished solution conformed to its specification.

Grading tips

P1 Make sure that your logbook is up to date and that you have a record of what was agreed in review meetings with your tutor. Correspondence, such as emails, notes and any other forms of communication, should be filed and indexed. Any industrial visits should be logged, and paste images of practical activities into your final report. Think about how your portfolio of evidence is going to be assessed – make it straightforward to track evidence against the grading criteria.

P6 You should check that your logbook includes full details of how you coped with changing situations during your project. Make sure that your logbook evidence is supported by tutor observation records and witness statements.

M1 Your records must be detailed and concurrent and clearly show the progress you made as the project developed. Make reference to any difficulties that you experienced and explain how you overcame them.

D1 You must demonstrate that, during the development of your project:

- you adopted the project management role with a degree of responsibility

- you regarded your tutor as you would a senior engineer in a company – there to offer strategic guidance but not to get involved at a detailed level

- you fully justified and documented the decisions you made

- you had a high level of self motivation and only requested help and guidance when absolutely necessary, such as checking with your tutor that a proposed workshop activity met health and safety requirements.

Witness statements and observation records are a form of evidence that you could use for D1.

D2 The purpose of this activity is to get you thinking about how you might do things differently next time around. To help you in this process, you might reflect on these questions.

- Did I manage my time effectively?

- How easy was it to access resources such as the workshop, technician help or IT equipment?

- Were delivery times for materials and components problematic?

- Was I over ambitious in what I was trying to achieve in the time allocated?

- Does the finished solution conform to specification within acceptable tolerances?

- If the finished solution is to specification, is there anything that could be done to make it even better?

- What other issues may have had an impact on the development process?

NorkSpace Matt Ryan
Manager, Hews Networking plc

I am the manager responsible for all UK and EU networking projects that are designed, installed and operated by Hews. Our head office is a new facility in Milton Keynes. I studied computing and electronics at college and university and have been with Hews for about ten years. My job can take me anywhere in UK and northern Europe for review meetings with my team of senior engineers, each of whom is responsible for individual projects. Where possible we try to audio or video conference, but there are many occasions when I need to work face-to-face with colleagues, such as when we are looking at systems diagrams and making alterations to computer program code.

This is a fairly typical project. I and a senior engineer had an initial meeting with representatives from a major retailer that wants to put in a new point-of-sale and a state-of-the-art stock control system. The retailer has branches in the UK, mainland Europe and the Far East. It wants all its shops to be linked back electronically to head office so that staff have real-time information about sales, customer card transactions at the tills and stock levels. The system should enable customer profiling and automated reordering of new stock from suppliers. It must be totally secure and have full back-up protection.

The next step is to assign a team to the project and to get them started on evaluating how much data is to be currently processed and producing estimates of the amount of data that the customer will wish to process in the future. We need to decide how data is to be stored and accessed, and we must specify the types of equipment to be located in each shop and at head office. Then we design the communications infrastructure (for example, carrying data over telephone networks and by other methods) and we build in remote monitoring of all hardware so that if anything fails there will be back-up systems ready to take over while a rapid response engineer is despatched to replace the faulty hardware or reset the software.

Once the initial design work has been done, the team and I meet with the technical people from the retailer and we present them with a fully costed proposal. After suitable discussion a specification is agreed and the project goes ahead. We then build, install and monitor the operation of the system for the customer. Monitoring is carried remotely with performance data being fed back to our office in Milton Keynes. We cannot actually access the data being moved around by the customer – our job is to monitor the effectiveness and reliability of the system as it operates.

Think about it!

1 Why does Matt need good management skills?
2 What specific technical skills are needed by the team?
3 Matt's job can be quite stressful at times – why do you think this is?

Just checking

1 Describe three processes used to keep project records.

2 Why is it important to keep good notes when recording the progress of a project?

3 Explain what is meant by the expression 'initial concept'. Give an example of an initial concept.

4 What information would you expect to see presented in the specification for a new product?

5 Describe three procedures that are carried out when running a project.

6 Describe one of the techniques used to evaluate design proposals and making a decision about which to develop.

7 Discuss why long-term planning is important.

8 Describe the principles of project monitoring.

9 Why is it important to properly use resources?

10 What are some of the techniques used to review the success of a project?

11 Describe the ICT equipment requirements for preparing and delivering a verbal presentation.

12 State two uses for a logbook.

13 Produce a checklist of the things to consider when planning the layout of a technical report.

14 At the end of a report or document you may find a bibliography. What is its function?

edexcel

Assignment tips

- Many of the skills that you need to demonstrate for this unit are ones that you will develop and use throughout the course. For example, managing time and resources are generic skills and much of what you have learned in the unit can be applied to others in the programme.

- Presentation skills will also be needed in other parts of the programme. You don't have to be a brilliant, super-confident writer or speaker to be able to communicate technical information effectively. But if you want to deliver a good presentation, you do need to prepare.

- Make sure that you get your tutor to complete observation records or witness statements for any assessment activity that generates non-written evidence. This could be when you are speaking or presenting to an audience, or doing something in real time that needs to be reported.

- This unit links with three others and some of the evidence you have collected can be used in assignments for Unit 2: Communications for Engineering Technicians (P2, P4, P5, P7), Unit 8: Engineering Design (P6) and Unit 16: Engineering Drawing for Technicians (P1, P3, P6).

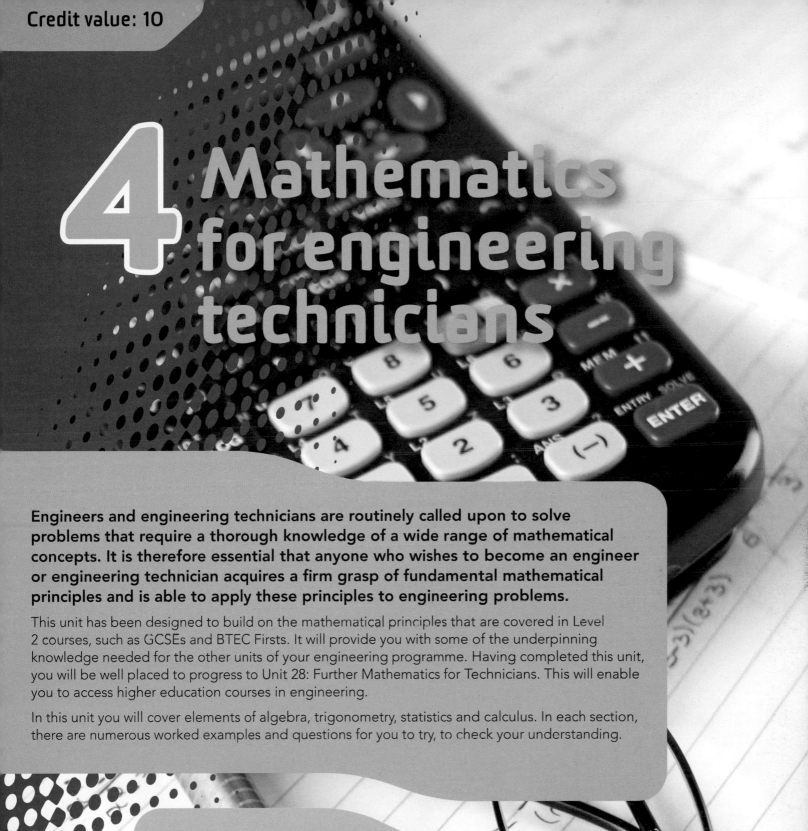

4 Mathematics for engineering technicians

Engineers and engineering technicians are routinely called upon to solve problems that require a thorough knowledge of a wide range of mathematical concepts. It is therefore essential that anyone who wishes to become an engineer or engineering technician acquires a firm grasp of fundamental mathematical principles and is able to apply these principles to engineering problems.

This unit has been designed to build on the mathematical principles that are covered in Level 2 courses, such as GCSEs and BTEC Firsts. It will provide you with some of the underpinning knowledge needed for the other units of your engineering programme. Having completed this unit, you will be well placed to progress to Unit 28: Further Mathematics for Technicians. This will enable you to access higher education courses in engineering.

In this unit you will cover elements of algebra, trigonometry, statistics and calculus. In each section, there are numerous worked examples and questions for you to try, to check your understanding.

Learning outcomes

After completing this unit you should:

1 be able to use algebraic methods
2 be able to use trigonometric methods and standard formula to determine areas
3 be able to use statistical methods to display data
4 be able to use elementary calculus techniques.

Assessment and grading criteria

This table shows you what you must do in order to achieve a pass, merit or distinction grade, and where you can find activities in this book to help you produce the required evidence.

To achieve a **pass** grade the evidence must show that you are able to:	To achieve a **merit** grade the evidence must show that, in addition to the pass criteria, you are able to:	To achieve a **distinction** grade the evidence must show that, in addition to the pass and merit criteria, you are able to:
P1 manipulate and simplify three algebraic expressions using the laws of indices and two using the laws of logarithms **Assessment activity 4.1 page 122**	**M1** solve a pair of simultaneous linear equations in two unknowns **Assessment activity 4.1 page 122**	**D1** apply graphical methods to the solution of two engineering problems involving exponential growth and decay, analysing the solutions using calculus **Assessment activity 4.4 page 144**
P2 solve a linear equation by plotting a straight-line graph using experimental data and use it to deduce the gradient, intercept and equation of the line **Assessment activity 4.1 page 122**	**M2** solve one quadratic equation by factorisation and one by the formula method **Assessment activity 4.1 page 122**	**D2** apply the rules for definite integration to two engineering problems that involve summation **Assessment activity 4.4 page 144**
P3 factorise by extraction and grouping of a common factor from expressions with two, three and four terms respectively **Assessment activity 4.1 page 122**		
P4 solve circular and triangular measurement problems involving the use of radian, sine, cosine and tangent functions **Assessment activity 4.2 page 130**		
P5 sketch each of the three trigonometric functions over a complete cycle **Assessment activity 4.2 page 130**		
P6 produce answers to two practical engineering problems involving the sine and cosine rule **Assessment activity 4.2 page 130**		
P7 use standard formulae to find surface areas and volumes of regular solids for three different examples **Assessment activity 4.2 page 130**		
P8 collect data and produce statistical diagrams, histograms and frequency curves [IE4] **Assessment activity 4.3 page 137**		

P9	determine the mean, median and mode for two statistical problems and explain the relevance of each average as a measure of central tendency **Assessment activity 4.3 page 137**		
P10	apply the basic rules of calculus arithmetic to solve three different types of function by differentiation and two different types of function by integration **Assessment activity 4.4 page 144**		

How you will be assessed

This unit will be assessed by assignments that will be designed and marked by the staff at your centre. The assignments are designed to allow you to show your understanding of the unit outcomes. These relate to what you should be able to do after completing this unit.

Your assessment could be in the form of:

- written assignments
- class tests
- case studies.

Tania, 21, prototype builder and rework operator

Working for an electronics company I was given the opportunity to develop my skills by enrolling on a BTEC National engineering course.

Initially I was unsure whether my maths ability was adequate for the course. So I took a short refresher course to develop my maths a little further to gain the foundation knowledge that enabled me to enrol.

The maths unit within the course was quite a challenge for me to face but with a great deal of determination, hard work and support from my tutor I came away with a distinction after my first year.

This achievement certainly gave me a new-found confidence, showing me that I could achieve my goals, and I look forward to the challenges ahead.

I have aspirations to become a test engineer and in this role I would be required to analyse tests carried out on prototype equipment. This will require me to understand sinusoidal and exponential functions. Both these topics are discussed at length as part of this unit. I am confident that this knowledge will help me to fulfil this role.

4.1 Be able to use algebraic methods

Using mathematics to solve engineering problems

Working in small groups think of an engineering problem that you could solve using the mathematical knowledge that you have acquired from your previous studies. Here are some examples to get you started:

- calculating the area that a dwelling covers
- calculating the cost of painting a room
- determining the volume of a specific product
- estimating the material cost for manufacturing a specific product
- finding the angle that a force is acting to a given reference plane
- using statistics to monitor production processes
- using calculus to predict the performance of engineering systems.

4.1.1 Indices and logarithms

Engineers often have to process numerical data and this means that they must be competent when dealing with numbers. In many applications, numbers are expressed using various forms of mathematical shorthand because they are easier to write down. In this part of the unit, we will look at numerical expressions using indices and logarithms.

Indices

Indices are a way of simplifying numerical expressions. For example, the quantity $2 \times 2 \times 2$ may be written as 2^3, where 2 is the **base** and 3 is the **index** or **power**.

The index gives the number of times the base has to be multiplied by itself. So, for example, you can write:

$$5 \times 5 \times 5 \times 5 = 5^4$$
$$125 \times 125 = 125^2$$

In algebra we use letters to represent numbers. For example:

$$a \times a \times a \times a \times a = a^5$$
$$x \times x \times x = x^3$$

Sometimes the index is unknown or may be variable in which case you can use a letter to represent the index. So, for example, you can write:

$$a^m$$
$$x^n$$

Consider, now what happens when you multiply numbers with the same base but different indices.

$$4^4 \times 4^2 = (4 \times 4 \times 4 \times 4) \times (4 \times 4)$$
$$= 4 \times 4 \times 4 \times 4 \times 4 \times 4$$
$$= 4^6$$

Note that you could have obtained the answer by adding the indices.

$$4^4 \times 4^2 = 4^{4+2}$$
$$= 4^6$$

When two or more numbers with the same base are multiplied, you add the indices. This can be written as a general rule:

$$a^m \times a^n = a^{m+n}$$

Key terms

Base the number or variable which is raised to a power.

Index (or **power**) the number or variable to which the base is raised.

Root the root of a number is the number which when multiplied by itself the number of times it is rooted, gives the original number. For example, the square root of 4 ($\sqrt{4}$) is 2, because 2 multiplied by itself twice is 4, i.e. $2 \times 2 = 4$. The cube root of 125 ($\sqrt[3]{125}$) is 5, because 5 multiplied by itself three time is 125, i.e. $5 \times 5 \times 5 = 125$.

Consider now what happens when we divide numbers with the same base.

$$\frac{4^5}{4^2} = \frac{4 \times 4 \times 4 \times 4 \times 4}{4 \times 4}$$
$$= 4^3$$

Note that you could have obtained the answer by subtracting the indices.

$$\frac{4^5}{4^2} = 4^{5-2}$$
$$= 4^3$$

When two or more numbers with the same base are divided, you subtract the indices. Again this can be expressed as a general rule:

$$\frac{a^m}{a^n} = a^{m-n}$$

Consider now what happens when we apply an index to a number that already has an index applied to it.

$$(4^3)^2 = (4 \times 4 \times 4) \times (4 \times 4 \times 4)$$
$$= 4 \times 4 \times 4 \times 4 \times 4 \times 4$$
$$= 4^6$$

Note that you could have obtained the answer by multiplying the indices.

$$(4^3)^2 = 4^{3 \times 2}$$
$$= 4^6$$

When numbers that have an index applied to them are raised to a further index, you multiply the indices. So, the rule is:

$$(a^m)^n = a^{m \times n}$$

Consider now what happens when the index of a number is a fraction.

$$4^{\frac{1}{3}} \times 4^{\frac{1}{3}} \times 4^{\frac{1}{3}} = 4^{\frac{1}{3} + \frac{1}{3} + \frac{1}{3}}$$
$$= 4$$

You also know that:

$$\sqrt[3]{4} \times \sqrt[3]{4} \times \sqrt[3]{4} = 4$$

It follows then that:

$$4^{\frac{1}{3}} = \sqrt[3]{4}$$

When the index of a number is a fraction, then the number may be written as a **root** where the denominator of the fraction in the index is the root. This can be written as:

$$a^{\frac{m}{n}} = \sqrt[n]{a^m}$$

Consider now what happens when the index of a number is zero.

$$\frac{4^3}{4^3} = 4^{3-3}$$
$$= 4^0$$
$$= 1$$

When the index of any number or variable is zero, its value is one. So:

$$a^0 = 1$$

Consider now what happens when the index of a number is negative.

$$4^{-2} = 4^{0-2}$$
$$= \frac{4^0}{4^2}$$
$$= \frac{1}{4^2}$$

A number with a negative index is the reciprocal of the number with the same positive base. So the rule is:

$$a^{-m} = \frac{1}{a^m}$$

These rules for manipulating numbers written in base and index form are summarised in Table 4.1.

Table 4.1: Laws of indices

Operation	Rule
Multiplication	$a^m \times a^n = a^{m+n}$
Division	$\dfrac{a^m}{a^n} = a^{m-n}$
Powers	$(a^m)^n = a^{m \times n}$
Roots	$\sqrt[n]{a^m} = a^{\frac{m}{n}}$
Reciprocals	$\dfrac{1}{a^m} = a^{-m}$
Zero index	$a^0 = 1$

Writing simple indices and roots

If the index of a number is 1, then it is assumed. For example, 7 to the power of 1 is written as 7 not 7^1. If you are asked your age, you might reply that you are (say) 16; you would not say that you are 16 to the power of one years old.

If a number is expressed using the root symbol but the symbol is not preceded by a number such as $\sqrt{16}$ then you assume that this refers to the square root of the number. In other words, you write $\sqrt{16}$ and not $\sqrt[2]{16}$.

Worked examples: Simplifying terms with indices

1 $a^3 \times a^4 \times a^7 = a^{3+4+7} = a^{14}$

2 $\dfrac{b^4 c^6}{b^2 c^9} = b^4 b^{-2} c^6 c^{-9} = b^{4-2} c^{6-9} = b^2 c^{-3} = \dfrac{b^2}{c^3}$

3 $\sqrt[3]{27 \times a^6} = \sqrt[3]{27} \times \sqrt[3]{a^6} = 3a^{\frac{6}{3}} = 3a^2$

4 $(2x^{-2})^{-3} = 2^{-3} x^6 = \dfrac{x^6}{2^3} = \dfrac{x^6}{8}$

5 $37^0 = 1$

Activity: Using indices

Here are some questions for you to try.

1 Determine the value of these expressions without the use of a calculator.

a) $2^{\frac{1}{2}} \times 2^{-\frac{1}{2}}$

b) 4^{-2}

c) $(3^{-2})^{-1}$

d) $25^{\frac{1}{2}}$

e) $27^{\frac{2}{3}}$

f) $16^{0.5}$

g) $8^{\frac{4}{3}}$

h) $\dfrac{4^3 \times 3^{\frac{1}{2}}}{4^2 \times 3^{-\frac{1}{2}}}$

i) $\dfrac{5^3 \times 5^{-2}}{5}$

j) $2^{\frac{1}{2}} \times 2^{\frac{1}{2}}$

k) $8^{\frac{2}{3}}$

l) $25^{-\frac{1}{2}}$

m) $125^{-\frac{2}{3}}$

n) $(0.25)^{-2.5}$

o) $16^{-0.25}$

2 Simplify these expressions:

a) $a \times a^5 \times a^{-2}$

b) $a^3 \times a^4 \div a^2$

c) $\dfrac{a^4 \times b^6}{a^2 \times b^3}$

d) $\sqrt[3]{a^6}$

e) $(a^3)^{-2}$

f) $(x^2)^3$

g) $(27x^3 y^{-6})^{\frac{1}{3}}$

h) $\dfrac{3^{-n} 9^{2n-1}}{3^{3n-1} 9^{-2}}$

i) $\dfrac{4^3 \times 3^{\frac{1}{2}}}{4^2 \times 3^{-\frac{1}{2}}}$

j) $\dfrac{(a^{-\frac{5}{3}} b^3 c^{-\frac{2}{3}})^{\frac{1}{2}}}{(a^{\frac{1}{2}} b^{\frac{9}{2}} c^{-1})^{\frac{1}{3}}}$

Logarithms

There are many engineering problems that require the use of logarithms as part of the solution. These include problems related to thermal expansion, changes in electrical resistance with a change in temperature,

belt tension, radioactive decay, current growth in a capacitive circuit and the discharge of a capacitor.

Logarithms are very closely related to indices. The logarithm (log) of a number is the power to which the base must be raised to give that number.

You can write a number in either the indicial form or its logarithmic form. The general forms of these expressions are given in Table 4.2.

Table 4.2: Indicial and logarithmic forms

Indicial form	Logarithmic form
$N = a^x$	$\log_a N = x$

If $\quad a = 10 \quad$ then $\quad N = 10^x$ and $\log_{10} N = x$

If $\quad 1 = 10^x \quad$ then $\quad x = 0$

If $\quad 10 = 10^x \quad$ then $\quad x = 1$

If $\quad 100 = 10^x \quad$ then $\quad x = 2$

Worked example: Logarithmic expressions

1 If $\log_a 9 = 2$ then $9 = a^2$ and $a = 3$

2 If $\log_2 16 = x$ then $16 = 2^x$ and $x = 4$

3 If $\log_3 N = 2$ then $N = 3^2$ and $N = 9$

4 If $\log_{10} N = 2$ then $N = 10^2$ and $N = 100$

5 If $\log_a 8 = 3$ then $8 = a^3$ and $a = 2$

Activity: Solving logarithmic expressions

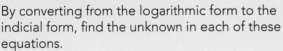

By converting from the logarithmic form to the indicial form, find the unknown in each of these equations.

1 $\log_a 81 = 4$

2 $\log_5 125 = x$

3 $\log_4 N = 3$

4 $\log_7 N = 0$

5 $\log_a 27 = 3$

By appropriate manipulation, we can use logarithms to convert multiplications to additions, divisions to subtractions and powers to multiplications problems. In order to do this, we need to develop the laws of logarithms.

If $\qquad N = a^x \qquad$ and $\qquad M = a^y$

Then $\qquad \log_a N = x \qquad$ and $\qquad \log_a M = y$

First, consider the case of multiplication:

$$NM = a^x a^y = a^{x+y}$$

Now take the logarithm of this number to get:

$$\log_a NM = x + y = \log_a N + \log_a M$$

This is our first law of logarithms. The log to any base of two numbers multiplied together is equal to the sum of the log of each number, to the same base.

Now consider the case of division:

$$\frac{N}{M} = \frac{a^x}{a^y} = a^{x-y}$$

Hence:

$$\log_a \frac{N}{M} = x - y = \log_a N - \log_a M$$

This is the second law. The log to any base of one number divided by another is equal to the difference between the log of the numerator and the log of the denominator to the same base.

Finally consider powers:

$$N^r = (a^x)^r = a^{xr}$$

Hence:

$$\log_a N^r = rx = r \log_a N$$

So the log to any base of a number raised to a power is equal to the log of the number, to the same base, multiplied by the power. This is the third law of logarithms.

For most purposes logarithms to the base ten (written $\log_{10}$ or $\lg_{10}$) are used. Sometimes, as you will see when we consider exponential growth (see page 112), we need to use logarithms to the base of the Euler constant (written $\log_e$ or $\lg_e$). Equations and expressions that use the Euler constant are discussed later in this unit (see page 113). Most scientific calculators have both of these functions. Logarithms to the base ten are called common logarithms. Logarithms to the base e are called natural or Naperian logarithms.

Using logarithms, use your calculator to check the answers to the three worked examples and then follow the same procedure to solve the questions in the activity by using natural logarithms.

Did you know?

On scientific calculators the logarithm key is denoted by the letters 'log' or sometimes 'lg'.

Worked example: Using logarithms

These examples show the use of logarithms to evaluate simple expressions and solve equations. Obviously the expressions in examples 1 and 2 can be calculated much more simply by multiplication and division, but these are useful exercises to get you used to the laws of logarithms and to using the logarithm keys on a calculator.

1 Evaluate 27.34×1.97 using the first law of logarithms to the base 10.

$$\log (27.34 \times 1.97) = \log 27.34 + \log 1.97$$
$$= 1.4368 + 0.2945$$
$$= 1.7313$$
$$27.34 \times 1.97 = anti\log 1.7313$$
$$= 53.86$$

2 Evaluate $3.59 \div 2.8$ using the second law of logarithms to the base 10.

$$\log\left(\frac{3.59}{2.8}\right) = \log 3.59 - \log 2.8$$
$$= 0.5551 - 0.4472$$
$$= 0.1079$$
$$\frac{3.59}{2.8} = anti\log 0.1079$$
$$= 1.282$$

3 Solve $3.714^{x+1} = 50$ using the third law of logarithms to the base 10.

$$\log (3.714^{x+1}) = \log 50$$
$$(x + 1)\log 3.714 = \log 50$$
$$(x + 1) = \frac{\log 50}{\log 3.714}$$
$$x = \frac{\log 50}{\log 3.714} - 1$$
$$= 1.98$$

Activity: Solving expressions and forumlae using logarithms

1 Evaluate these expressions using logarithms.

a) 5.75×0.038

b) $\dfrac{15.36}{1.83}$

c) $2.54^{1.36}$

d) $\sqrt[3]{16.397}$

2 Solve these equations for x.

a) $5.49^x = 70.62$

b) $1.54^{x+2} = 4.34$

c) $5.6^x = 175.6^{x-1}$

Exponential growth and decay

There are many situations in engineering where you may be interested in the growth or decay of some process. For example, you may want to know how the resistance in a circuit changes with temperature.

Growth and decay processes can be described by an equation of the form:

$$y = a^x$$

Where y and x are variables, and a is a constant (the base).

Table 4.3 shows some values of $y = a^x$ for different positive values of a. This data can be used to plot graphs for each of the functions. These are shown in Figure 4.1.

Table 4.3: Values of $y = a^x$ for different positive values of a

x	−2	−1	0	1	2	3
$y = 1^x$	1	1	1	1	1	1
$y = 1.5^x$	0.44	0.67	1	1.50	2.25	3.38
$y = 2^x$	0.25	0.50	1	2.00	4.00	8.00
$y = 3^x$	0.11	0.33	1	3.00	9.00	27.00

The growth or decay of many physical properties can be defined by a particular type of $y = a^x$ function, the **exponential function**. The basic exponential function is given by:

$$y = e^x$$

The base of this function is the Euler constant, $e \approx 2.718$. This is defined as the particular value of the base a where the graph has a slope of 1 at $x = 0$. Note also that if $y = e^x$, then the slope of a graph of y versus x is equal to e^x.

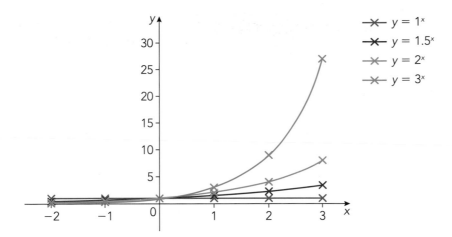

Figure 4.1: Graphs of $y = a^x$ for different positive values of a

Table 4.4 lists the respective equations that define six physical properties that are of interest in different branches of engineering. As you can see, each equation contains an exponential term.

Table 4.4: Physical properties defined by exponential functions

Property	Function
Thermal expansion	$l = l_0 e^{\alpha \theta}$
Change in resistance with temperature	$R = R_0 e^{\alpha \theta}$
Belt tension	$T = T_0 e^{\mu \alpha}$
Radioactive decay	$N = N_0 e^{-\lambda t}$
Current growth in a capacitive circuit	$i = I - Ie^{-\frac{t}{CR}}$
Discharge of a capacitor	$q = Q_0 e^{-\frac{t}{CR}}$

Key terms

Exponential function a mathematical function that inlcudes the Euler constant (e).

Did you know?

The Euler constant (e) can be determined from this convergent series:

$$e = 1 + \frac{1}{1!} + \frac{1^2}{2!} + \frac{1^3}{3!} + \frac{1^4}{4!} + \ldots \ldots \frac{1^r}{r!}$$

Where:

$1! = 1$
$2! = 1 \times 2$
$3! = 1 \times 2 \times 3$

etc.

Activity: Exponential functions

1 Plot graphs of these four equations on the same set of axes between the limits of $x = -2$ and $x = 3$.

   a) $y = e^x$

   b) $y = e^{-x}$

   c) $y = 2e^x$

   d) $y = 2e^{2x}$

2 The relationship in an inductive circuit between the instantaneous current (i) measured in amperes (A) and the time (t) in seconds is given by the equation:

   $$i = 2(1 - e^{-10t})$$

   Plot a graph of i against t for values of $t = 0$ to $t = 0.4$ s, and determine the time for the current to increase from 0 to 1.5 A.

4.1.2 Linear equations and straight-line graphs

Engineers may have to assess the effect of applying different loads to a structure, to determine the power requirement from a machine to fulfil a particular function, to ensure that a fluid flow system has sufficient capacity or to ensure that an electric circuit will produce the desired effect. To complete these tasks, an engineer will probably have to collect and process some data. This will involve the use of equations, and the drawing and interpretation of some graphs.

Linear equations

Linear equations contain only the first power of the unknown quantity. These are typical examples of linear equations:

$$3x + 4 = 10$$
$$6t - 11 = 4t + 1$$

In contrast, the two equations below are not linear equations. This is because they contain the terms x^2 and t^2 respectively, which are second powers of the unknown quantity

$$x^2 = 36$$
$$t^2 + 6t - 4 = 0$$

Linear equations are solved by **transposing** the equation to make the unknown quantity the subject of the equation. So, for example:

$$3x + 4 = 10$$
$$3x = 10 - 4$$
$$x = \frac{6}{3} = 2$$

Key terms

Transposing the mathematical process of changing the subject of an equation.

If the unknown quantity occurs more than once in the equation, you must collect all the terms of the unknown quantity together on one side of the equation and all other terms on the other side. So, for example:

$$6t - 11 = 4t + 1$$
$$6t - 4t = 11 + 1$$
$$2t = 12$$
$$t = \frac{12}{2} = 6$$

Transposing an equation

Always remember that when transposing an equation, whatever you do to the left-hand side, you must do the same to the right-hand side.

Activity: Solving linear equations

Solve these linear equations.

a) $7 - 3x = 2x + 5$

b) $2(x + 5) - 3(2x - 3) = -5$

c) $\frac{4x}{2} = 8$

d) $\frac{2x}{5} = \frac{7}{2}$

e) $\frac{2(x - 1)}{3} - \frac{(2x - 3)}{5} = \frac{3}{10}$

Straight-line graphs

Two-dimensional graphs have two axes at right angles to each other. One axis is usually horizontal and the other is vertical. These axes are sometimes referred to as Cartesian axes. The horizontal axis is called the abscissa and the vertical axis is called the ordinate.

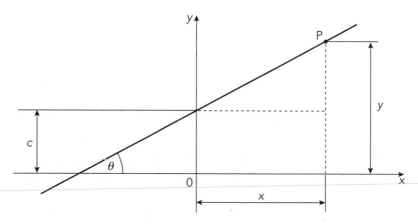

Figure 4.2: A straight line graph

An equation with two unknowns can be represented by a line drawn on a two-dimensional graph. Conventionally the horizontal axis is often referred to as the x-axis, while the vertical axis is referred to as the y-axis.

Figure 4.2 shows a straight line graph. The gradient (or slope) of the line is given by the tangent of the angle that the line makes with the x-axis. The intercept is given by the point where the line crosses the y-axis when the x value is zero.

From Figure 4.2, we can deduce that:

$$\tan \theta = \frac{y - c}{x}$$

Therefore:

$$y = \tan \theta \times x + c$$

$$y = mx + c$$

Where:

  m is the gradient of the line

  c is the intercept of the line on the y-axis when $x = 0$.

A straight line graph can be plotted using two points, but it is recommended that you plot at least three points. The third point acts as a check on the other two. For example, suppose you want to draw the graph of:

$$y = 3x + 2$$

and that you want to draw it from $x = -2$ to $x = 3$. So choose three points, one when $x = -2$, one when $x = 3$, and one at a point between these two, say when $x = 0$. Find the corresponding values of y for each of the three values of x by using the equation. So:

  when $x = -2$, $y = -4$

  when $x = 0$, $y = 2$

  when $x = 3$, $y = 11$

We can now use these points to plot the graph, as in Figure 4.3. You can check that the graph actually shows the correct equation by calculating the gradient and reading off the intercept of the line with the y-axis, and then substituting these values in the general equation for a straight line $y = mx + c$.

You should be able to calculate that the gradient of the line shown in Figure 4.3 is 3, and the intercept is 2, so the equation is $y = 3x + 2$. It has been drawn correctly.

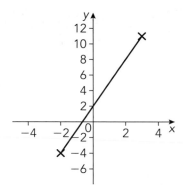

Figure 4.3: Graph of $y = 3x + 2$

Now consider another example. This time suppose you want to draw a graph between $x = 4$ and $x = 9$ of the equation:

$$y = -2x + 29$$

The graph of this equation is shown in Figure 4.4. This has been done by finding three points on the straight line defined by the equation. Again we can check that the graph shows the correct equation. The gradient of the line is -2. In this case we cannot read off the value for the intercept directly from the figure as the line doesn't extend to the y-axis. However, we can determine its value by substituting into the equation for a straight line the value for the gradient and the coordinates of a point on the line. We have:

  when $x = 4$, $y = 21$

So substitute these values and the value for the gradient ($m = -2$) into the general equation for a straight line $y = mx + c$. This gives:

  $21 = -2 \times 4 + c$

  $c = 21 + 8 = 29$

So the equation is $y = -2x + 29$ as before. Now, with the next case study, we can begin to apply this theory to a practical engineering situation.

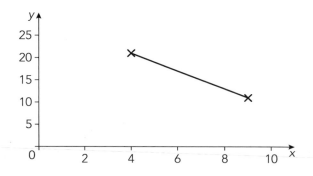

Figure 4.4: Graph of $y = -2x + 29$

Case study: Steve tests a lifting machine

Results obtained from laboratory or workshop experiments often have a linear relationship. Steve, an engineering technician, is testing a simple lifting machine to determine whether the effort and load have a linear relationship.

Table 4.5 shows the results of his tests, recording the effort (E) required to lift different loads (W). Steve then plots these values using a suitable scale, so that he can use the graph to determine the law of the machine.

Steve's graph is shown in Figure 4.5. You should note that not all the points recorded in these tests lie exactly on a straight line. This often happens in practical experiments as a result of experimental error. When you plot a set of points that look to be

roughly in a straight line, place a line on the graph so that all the points lie close to (or on) the line. This is sometimes known as the best straight line or line of best fit. The equation of this line is known as the law of the line of best fit.

This is the approach Steve has adopted in drawing the graph in Figure 4.5. He has drawn the best straight line through the plotted points and found the law of the line of best fit, which is the law of the machine. Having determined the law of the machine he can substitute into the equation a value for the load (W) in order to find the required effort (E) and vice versa.

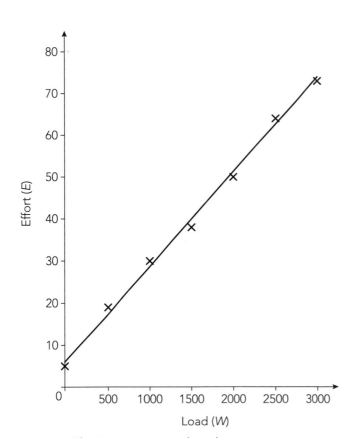

Figure 4.5: Plotting experimental results

Interpreting graphs

If the graph does not include the origin you may not be able to read off the intercept but you can always find the gradient and then calculate the intercept using the equation for the line.

When finding the gradient it is good practice to identify two convenient points on the line a reasonable distance apart to not compromise the accuracy.

Table 4.5: Test results

W (N)	0	500	1000	1500	2000	2500	3000
E (N)	5	19	30	38	50	64	73

Table 4.6: Results from four experiments

a)	V (V)	20	40	60	80	100	120
	I (A)	0.12	0.25	0.33	0.47	0.58	0.68
b)	W (N)	15	25	38	57	74	88
	E (N)	9	11	14	17	21	24
c)	TS (MN/m²)	450	515	550	600	665	710
	HB	125	140	154	168	183	199
d)	V (m³)	26.1	26.8	27.3	27.9	28.5	29.1
	T (°C)	10	20	30	40	50	60

Activity: Four experiments yielding linear relationships

1 Tests are carried out on a DC electric circuit to examine the relationship between the voltage (V) and the current (I). The results are given in the first set of figures (labelled a) in Table 4.6.

   a) By plotting a suitable graph show that this circuit complies with Ohm's law.

   b) Determine the resistance of the circuit.

2 An experiment is conducted with a set of pulley blocks to see if there is a linear relationship between the effort (E) and the load (W). It is thought that effort and load are connected by a law of the form $E = mW + c$. The results of the experiment are given in Table 4.6b.

   a) Show that the law $E = mW + c$ is valid for this data, by plotting a suitable graph.

   b) Determine the values of the constants m and c and hence determine the law of the line.

   c) Use the law of the line to calculate the effort when the load is 30 N.

   d) Use the law of the line to calculate the load when the effort is 20 N.

3 Tests are carried out on a metal to determine a relationship between the tensile strength (TS) and the Brinell hardness (HB) number. The results are shown in Table 4.6c.

   a) Plot these values with a base of tensile strength to show that they have a linear relationship.

   b) Determine the law connecting the two variables.

4 The volume of a gas V is measured at various temperatures T and the results are given in Table 4.6d.

   a) Show that the volume and temperature are connected by a law of the form $V = mT + c$ and determine the values of the constants m and c.

   b) Determine the volume of the gas when its temperature is 24°C.

   c) Determine the temperature of the gas when it occupies a volume of 27 m³.

Simultaneous equations

Sometimes engineers need to solve simultaneous equations (equations with more than one unknown quantity). In these cases you need to determine a value for each unknown that satisfies each equation. If there are two unknowns you will require two independent equations, three unknowns and you will require three equations, etc. Engineers use these techniques to calculate the current flowing in specific sections of an electric circuit, to determine certain characteristics of lifting machines and in many other practical contexts.

In this course you will only need to solve simultaneous equations with two unknowns. We will consider three methods of solving simultaneous equations with two unknowns:

• the substitution method

• the elimination method

• the graphical method.

Substitution method

In the substitution method, one equation is written in terms of one unknown and substituted into the other equation to deduce an equation with one unknown.

The value of this first unknown is then determined, and substituted back into either of the original equations to determine the second unknown.

This is easier to understand if you work through an example. Consider this pair of simultaneous equations:

$$2x + y = 10 \qquad\qquad (1)$$
$$3x + 2y = 17 \qquad\qquad (2)$$

Rearrange equation (1) to get:

$$y = 10 - 2x \qquad\qquad (3)$$

Substitute equation (3) in equation (2) to get:

$$3x + 2(10 - 2x) = 17$$

Solve for x:

$$3x + 20 - 4x = 17$$
$$4x - 3x = 20 - 17 = 3$$

Substitute $x = 3$ into equation (1):

$$2(3) + y = 10$$
$$y = 10 - 6 = 4$$

So, the solution is $x = 3$ and $y = 4$. We can check that this is correct by substituting the values obtained for x and y into each of the original equations. From equation (1) we have:

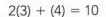
$2(3) + (4) = 10$

And from equation (2) we have:

$3(3) + 2(4) = 17$

Since both of the original equations are satisfied the solution is correct.

Elimination method

In the elimination method, the equations are manipulated until the subtraction or addition of the two equations results in the elimination of one of the unknowns. The other unknown can then be determined and, by substitution in one of the original equations, the second unknown can be determined. This method is generally used to solve equations where the unknown quantities are raised to the first power only.

To illustrate this method, consider the following pair of simultaneous equations:

$3x + 4y = 11$ (1)

$x + 7y = 15$ (2)

Multiply equation (2) by 3:

$3x + 21y = 45$ (3)

Subtract equation (1) from equation (3) to get:

$17y = 34$

$y = 2$

Substitute $y = 2$ into equation (1):

$3x + 4(2) = 11$

$3x = 11 - 8$

$x = 1$

So, the solution is $x = 1$ and $y = 2$. We can check that this is correct by substituting the values obtained for x and y into each of the original equations. From equation (1) we have:

$3(1) + 4(2) = 11$

And from equation (2) we have:

$(1) + 7(2) = 15$

Since both of the original equations are satisfied, the solution is correct.

PLTS

Trying out different ways to solve a mathematics problem will help develop your creative thinker skills.

Graphical method

The graphical method involves plotting a graph for each equation on the same axes. The solution is given by the coordinates of the point of intersection of the two graphs.

Consider this pair of simultaneous equations:

$2x + y = 7$ (1)

$x - 5y = 9$ (2)

Rearrange each equation into the form $y = mx + c$. This gives:

$y = -2x + 7$

$y = 0.2x - 1.8$

Now draw the corresponding straight lines by finding three points on each line. Table 4.7 shows three values of x and the corresponding values of y for each equation. These can be used to draw the lines shown in Figure 4.6.

Table 4.7: Points on $y = 22x + 7$ and $y = 0.2x - 1.8$

x	$y = 22x + 7$	x	$y = 0.2x - 1.8$
−4	15	−4	−2.8
0	7	0	−1.8
6	−5	6	−0.6

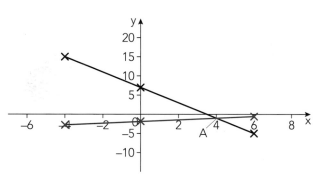

Figure 4.6: Solving simultaneous equations by the graphical method

At point A on Figure 4.6 the graphs intersect. Here each line has the same coordinates, which will therefore give the solution. This is $x = 4$ and $y = -1$. Again check by substituting the values obtained for x and y into each of the original equations. From equation (1) we have:

$2(4) + (-1) = 7$

And from equation (2) we have:

$(4) - 5(-1) = 9$

Since both of the original equations are satisfied, the solution is correct.

Activity: Solving simultaneous equations

1 Solve these simultaneous equations using the substitution method.

a) $3x + 2y = 14$
$2x + 5y = 24$

b) $5x + 2y = -9$
$3x - 5y = 7$

c) $4x - 2y = 22$
$-5x + 3y = -30$

2 Solve these simultaneous equations using the elimination method.

a) $x + 4y = 14$
$2x + 3y = 13$

b) $4x + 2y = 2$
$3x + y = 0$

c) $-3x - 2y = -16$
$2x + y = 9$

3 Solve these simultaneous equations using the graphical method.

a) $8x + 2y = -4$
$2x + 6y = 10$

b) $2x + 4y = -2$
$3x + 2y = 5$

4.1.3 Factorisation and quadratics

We now consider quadratic expressions and equations. In contrast to a linear expression or equation which has a variable raised to the power one, a quadratic expression or equation has a variable raised to the power two. Similarly while a linear equation has an equals sign and a variable raised to the power one, a quadratic equation has an equals and a variable raised to the power two.

Table 4.8: Examples of linear and quadratic expressions and equations

	Linear	Quadratic
Expression	$3x - 6$	$x^2 - 5x + 6$
Equation	$3x = 6$	$x^2 - 5x = -6$

Engineers may be required to solve quadratic equations. Equations for the calculation of areas and volumes of regular shapes and some mechanical and electrical science relationships have a quadratic form. We will consider two methods of solution: solving by factorising and solving by using a formula.

A quadratic equation will have two solutions (sometimes called roots). One method used to solve quadratic equations is factorisation. So before you attempt to solve quadratic equations, it is a good idea to practise factorising some expressions.

Factorisation

If an expression is multiplied by a number or another expression, then that number or expression is a factor of the resulting expression. For example, consider the expression $2x + 3$ and multiply it by 4. We could write this as:

$$4(2x + 3) = 8x + 12$$

In this case 4 and $2x + 3$ are factors of the expression $8x + 12$.

Factorising is the reverse process of multiplying out two expressions. Consider the expression:

$$6x^2 + 9x$$

In this case you can see that $3x$ is a common factor – you can divide each term in the expression by $3x$ and not obtain a fractional number. We could therefore write:

$$6x^2 + 9x = 3x(2x + 3)$$

Sometimes factorisation is used to simplify parts of an expression. Consider this expression:

$$36x^2 + 25y^3 + 18x - 10y^2$$

We can simplify this expression by grouping together the x and y terms, and then factorising each part of the rearranged expression as follows:

$$36x^2 + 25y^3 + 18x - 10y^2 = 36x^2 + 18x + 25y^3 - 10y^2$$
$$= 18x(2x + 1) + 5y^2(5y - 2)$$

Activity: Factorisation

Factorise these expressions.

a) $8x^4 + 16x^3 - 4x^2$

b) $25t^6 - 20t^4 + 10t^2$

c) $16a^5 b^3 + 8a^3 b^2 - 4a^4 b^3$

Now consider the expressions $x + 3$ and $x + 2$. If we multiply these expressions together, we get:

$$(x + 3)(x + 2) = x^2 + 2x + 3x + 6$$
$$= x^2 + 5x + 6$$

Note that when multiplying out expressions of this type, each term in the first expression multiplies each term in the second expression in turn.

Because we have done the multiplication, we know that $x + 3$ and $x + 2$ are factors of the quadratic expression $x^2 + 5x + 6$. However, if we are presented with a quadratic expression (an expression containing terms to the second power), it is a little more difficult to factorise. However, we can make the following observations:

- If the coefficient of the x^2 term is 1, then the coefficient of each of the x terms in the factors will also be 1.

- The product of the number terms of the factors is always equal to the number term in the expression.

- If the coefficient of the x^2 term is 1, then the middle term of the expression is equal to the sum or difference of the two number terms of the factors.

Consider the expression:

$$x^2 - 4x - 32$$

Note first that the coefficient of the x^2 term is 1. The first term of each factor will therefore be x. The number 32 has three sets of factors: (1 and 32); (2 and 16); and (4 and 8). The coefficient of the x term is 4, which is the difference between 4 and 8. Hence:

$$x^2 - 4x - 32 = (x + 4)(x - 8)$$

Worked example: Factorising quadratics

Factorise the expression $F^2 + 3F - 10$

The coefficient of F^2 is 1.

The factors of 10 are (1 and 10) or (2 and 5)

The difference between 2 and 5 is 3, hence this is the correct combination.

Therefore the factors are $(F + 5)$ and $(F - 2)$.

In other words, we can write:

$$F^2 + 3F - 10 = (F + 5)(F - 2)$$

Activity: Factorising quadratics

Factorise these quadratic expressions.

a) $x^2 - 16x + 64$

b) $t^2 - 5t - 50$

c) $x^2 + 3x - 40$

Solving quadratic equations

We will consider two ways to solve a quadratic equation:

- by factorisation

- by formula.

To solve a quadratic by factorisation, follow these steps.

1 Rearrange the equation (if necessary), to make one side of the equation zero.

2 Factorise the side of the equation that contains the unknowns.

3 Equate each of the factors in turn to zero to obtain the roots of the equation.

4 Check that each root satisfies the equation by substitution.

For example, to find the roots of the equation:

$$x^2 - 5x = -6$$

First, rearrange to get:

$$x^2 - 5x + 6 = 0$$

Then factorise, to get:

$$(x - 3)(x - 2) = 0$$

Then equate each of the factors to zero. In this case this gives $x - 3 = 0$, so $x = 3$ is one root; and $x - 2 = 0$, so $x = 2$ is the other root.

Finally check that each root satisfies the equation. When $x = 3$, we have:

$$(3)^2 - 5(3) + 6 = 0$$

When $x = 2$, we have:

$$(2)^2 - 5(2) + 6 = 0$$

In both cases, the equation is satisfied (it equals zero for these values of x), so we have found the roots of this quadratic.

Sometimes a quadratic equation cannot be factorised easily. Often the factors of a quadratic expression are not obvious. The solution of these types of equation will be greatly simplified if we can establish a formula that will solve all quadratics.

The standard form of a quadratic equation is:

$$ax^2 + bx + c = 0$$

Transposition of this formula to make x the subject will give you an equation to solve any quadratic. This transposition is not straightforward, but you will only be required to use the formula. The transposition produces a general form of the formula for solving quadratics:

$$x = \frac{-b \pm \sqrt{b^2 - 4ac}}{2a}$$

You can use this formula to solve a quadratic problem. For example, suppose you need to find the roots of the equation:

$$3x^2 + 7x = 5$$

Write this is the standard form:

$$3x^2 + 7x - 5 = 0$$

In this case, $a = 3$, $b = 7$ and $c = -5$. We can now apply the formula:

$$
\begin{aligned}
x &= \frac{-b \pm \sqrt{b^2 - 4ac}}{2a} \\
&= \frac{-(7) \pm \sqrt{(7)^2 - 4(3)(-5)}}{2(3)} \\
&= \frac{-7 \pm \sqrt{49 + 60}}{6} \\
&= \frac{-7 \pm \sqrt{109}}{6} \\
&= \frac{-7 \pm 10.44}{6} \\
&= \frac{3.44}{6} \ or \ \frac{-17.44}{6} \\
&= 0.57 \ or \ -2.91
\end{aligned}
$$

You can check these answers by substituting each value in turn into the original equation:

$$3(0.57)^2 + 7(0.57) = 5.04 \approx 5$$
$$3(-2.91)^2 + 7(-2.91) = 5.03 \approx 5$$

Activity: **Solving quadratic equations**

1 Solve these quadratic equations by factorising.

a) $x^2 - 7x = -12$

b) $t^2 + 28 = 11t$

c) $x^2 = 6x - 9$

2 Solve these quadratic equations by using the formula.

a) $2x^2 - 7x = 3$

b) $9x + 5 = 4x^2$

c) $t^2 + 20 = 2t(t - 3)$

3 A rectangle has a length which is 10 mm greater than its width. If the area of the rectangle is 4500 mm^2, determine the dimensions of the rectangle.

PLTS

Reviewing your progress when solving mathematics problems will help develop your reflective learner skills. If you work with a colleague to solve mathematics problems you will also develop your team worker skills.

Assessment activity 4.1

P1 Simplify these expressions:

a) $D^3 D^{2.6} D^{-1} D^{-3.4}$

b) $V^2 V^{-1.2} V^{1.5} V^2$

c) $\dfrac{(x^3)^{\frac{2}{3}} (y^{-2})^{\frac{1}{2}}}{(\sqrt{z})^{-4}}$

P1 Solve these equations:

a) $5^{x+2} = 8.5$

b) $6.5^x = 8.4^{(4x-10)}$

P2 The volume of a gas is measured at various temperatures. The results are shown in Table 4.9.

a) By drawing a suitable graph, show that the volume and temperature are connected by a law of the form $V = aT + b$.

b) Determine the value of the constants a and b.

c) Use the law of the line to determine the volume at a temperature of 27°C.

d) Use the law of the line to determine the temperature when the volume is 43 m³.

P3 Factorise these expressions:

a) $cd + 6ce$

b) $5x^4 - 3x^3 + 4x^2$

c) $10a^4 - 5b^3 + 12a^3 + 25b$

M1 Solve these simultaneous equations:

$13 = 2x + y$

$22 = 5x + y$

M2 Solve this quadratic equation by factorisation:

$a^2 + 10a - 24 = 0$

M2 Solve this quadratic equation by the formula method:

$5x^2 = -(10x + 2)$

Grading tips

P1 Always present your solutions to these and all other tasks in full so that an assessor can see your working. Check your solutions in each case.

P2 Make sure that your graph has an appropriate title and that the axes are properly labelled.

Table 4.9: Results of measuring volume of gas at different temperatures

Volume (m³)	26.10	26.75	27.25	27.90	28.53	29.10
Temperature (°C)	10	20	30	40	50	60

4.2 Be able to use trigonometric methods and standard formulae to determine areas and volumes

Many engineering structures are fabricated using circular and triangular sections. A working knowledge of the formulae associated with these shapes is essential when designing these structures. More complicated sections can often be simplified into a combination of circular and triangular shapes. The solution of mechanical and electrical science problems involving vector diagrams often requires knowledge of trigonometric methods.

Engineers need to know basic trigonometry in understanding the forces that can be borne by this type of structure.

4.2.1 Circular measure

Angles are often measured in degrees. One degree represents one 360th of a complete rotation. Hence in one complete rotation – or one revolution – there are 360 degrees. We can write this as:

1 rev = 360°

Although one degree is a relatively small angle, in modern engineering we often have to measure to angles to greater accuracies. Each degree is divided into 60 minutes. So:

1° = 60 min

Each minute is divided into 60 seconds. So:

1 min = 60 s

It follows then that:

1° = 60 min
= 60 × 60 = 3600 s.

Note that a dash is often used to represent a minute, and a double dash is used to represent a second (i.e. 1° = 60′ = 3600″).

Sometimes angles are written as decimal numbers rather than in degrees, minutes and seconds. You need to be able to convert from one notation to the other. For example, to express an angle of 10° 15 min 24 s (10° 15′ 24″) in degrees, you do this calculation:

$$10 + \frac{15}{60} + \frac{24}{3600} = 10 + 0.25 + 0.007$$
$$= 10.257°$$

In engineering, angles are also often specified in radians (rad). This can be advantageous since it is defined in terms of the arc of a circle and not an arbitrary fraction of a circle. One radian is the angle **subtended** at the centre of a circle of radius r by an arc of length r.

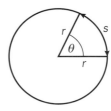

Figure 4.7: A sector of a circle

In one complete revolution, the angle turned through is 360° or 2π rad. We have then:

2π rad = 360°

So:

$$1 \text{ rad} = \frac{360}{2\pi} = 57.3°$$

$$1° = \frac{2\pi}{360} = 0.0175 \text{ rad}$$

Using the notation in Figure 4.7, we can make some more general statements about the relationship between an arc length (s), the radius of a circle (r) and the angle subtended in radians (θ). When θ is:

1 rad	then	$s = r$
2 rad	then	$s = 2r$
3 rad	then	$s = 3r$
θ rad	then	$s = \theta r$

The area of a circle is given by the formula:

$A = \pi r^2$.

A sector is a fraction of a circle, so by proportion the area of a sector is given by the formula:

$$A = \pi r^2 \times \frac{\theta}{2\pi} = \frac{1}{2}r^2\theta$$

In summary, if θ is measured in radians, we have these general formulae.

Arc length $= r\theta$

Area of a circle $= \pi r^2$

Area of a sector $= \frac{1}{2}r^2\theta$

Did you know?

When marking out angles in a workshop, technicians work in degrees, but when engineers are carrying out scientific calculations they usually work in radians. Check that you can set up a scientific calculator in degree and radian modes. You may also come across a key marked 'Gra'. Do you know what this means?

Worked example: Areas and arc lengths of circles

1 Calculate the cross-sectional area of a bar having a diameter of 30 mm.

$$A = \pi r^2 = \pi \left(\frac{30}{2}\right)^2 = \pi \times 15^2 = 707 \text{ mm}^2$$

2 Calculate the length of arc on the surface of a bar having a diameter of 30 mm and subtended by an angle of 40°.

$$s = r\theta = 15 \times 40 \times \frac{2\pi}{360} = 10.5 \text{ mm}$$

3 Calculate the area of a sector of a bar having a diameter of 30 mm and with an included angle of 60°.

$$A = \frac{1}{2}r^2\theta = \frac{15^2}{2} \times 60 \times \frac{2\pi}{360} = 118 \text{ mm}^2$$

Activity: Problems involving angles and areas in radians

1 Convert these angles to radians.

   a) 30° 43′

   b) 125° 27′ 54″

   c) 257.35°

2 Convert these angles to degrees, minutes and seconds.

   a) 0.237 rad

   b) 2.584 rad

   c) 1.5π rad

3 A circle has a diameter of 120 mm.

   a) Find the angle subtended by an arc length of 100 mm.

   b) Find the area of the minor and major sectors.

4.2.2 Triangular measurement

Similar triangles (see Figure 4.8) have equal angles and the ratios of the lengths of their corresponding sides are also equal.

Hence

$$\frac{A_1B_1}{A_1C_1} = \frac{A_2B_2}{A_2C_2}$$

$$\frac{B_1C_1}{A_1C_1} = \frac{B_2C_2}{A_2C_2}$$

$$\frac{A_1B_1}{B_1C_1} = \frac{A_2B_2}{B_2C_2}$$

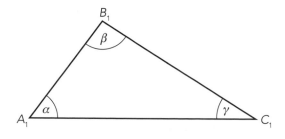

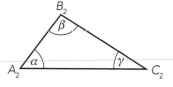

Figure 4.8: A pair of similar triangles

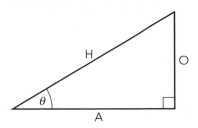

Figure 4.9: A right-angled triangle

For right-angled triangles (see Figure 4.9) these ratios are given names:

$$\sin \theta = \frac{O}{H}$$

$$\cos \theta = \frac{A}{H}$$

$$\tan \theta = \frac{O}{A}$$

Where sin is short for sine, cos is short for cosine, and tan is short for tangent. You may find it useful to use the acronym SOH CAH TOA to help you remember these ratios.

A further relationship can be deduced as follows:

$$\frac{\sin \theta}{\cos \theta} = \frac{O/H}{A/H} = \frac{O}{H} \times \frac{H}{A} = \frac{O}{A} = \tan \theta$$

You can use these relationships to find unknown lengths and angles in right-angled triangles. For example, we can use these ratios to find the side length BC, the hypotenuse AB and the angle at A in Figure 4.10.

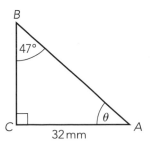

Figure 4.10: Right-angled triangle some unknown dimensions

To find BC, we can use the tangent ratio. We know that:

$$\tan 47 = \frac{32}{BC}$$

So:

$$BC = \frac{32}{\tan 47} = 29.84 \, \text{mm}$$

To find AB, use the sine ratio:

$$\sin 47 = \frac{32}{AB}$$

$$AB = \frac{32}{\sin 47} = 43.75 \, \text{mm}$$

Finally using the cosine ratio to find the angle at A:

$$\cos A = \frac{32}{43.75}$$

$$A = 43°$$

Activity: Using trigonometric ratios

1 Use your calculator to determine the value of:

   a) sin 30°

   b) cos 120°

   c) tan 60°

2 Use your calculator to determine each of the angles in a right-angled triangle where the sides are in the proportion 3 : 4 : 5.

3 Determine all unspecified angles and side lengths in the triangle ABC shown in Figure 4.11

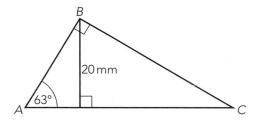

Figure 4.11: A right-angled triangle

Graphs of trigonometric functions

If you plot the values for sin θ or cos θ vertically against θ horizontally you will obtain a waveform. The second column of Table 4.10 shows values of sin θ for some values of θ. Figure 4.12 shows a plot of a graph of $y = \sin \theta$ for values of θ between 0° and 360°.

Values for cos θ and tan θ for some values of are given in the third and fourth columns of Table 4.10. The graphs of $y = \cos \theta$ and $y = \tan \theta$ for values of θ between 0° and 360° are shown in Figure 4.13 and 4.14.

Table 4.10: Values of sin θ, cos and tan

θ°	sin θ°	cos θ°	tan θ°
0	0	1.00	0
30	0.50	0.87	0.58
60	0.87	0.50	1.73
90	1.00	0	∞
120	0.87	−0.50	−1.73
150	0.50	−0.87	−0.58
180	0	−1.00	0
210	−0.50	−0.87	0.58
240	−0.87	−0.50	1.73
270	−0.50	0	∞
300	−0.87	0.50	−1.73
330	−0.50	0.87	−0.58
360	0	1.00	0

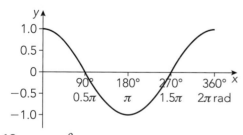

Figure 4.12: $y = \sin \theta$

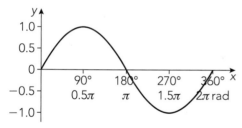

Figure 4.13: $y = \cos \theta$

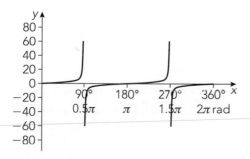

Figure 4.14: $y = \tan \theta$

You should see that both the sine and cosine functions are waveforms. Both have an **amplitude** of 1 and a **period** of 360° or 2π radians. The plot of the tan function does not yield a smooth waveform. This has an amplitude of infinity (∞) and a period of 180° or π radians.

Having plotted the graphs for sine, cosine and tangent relationships, you can now determine the value for the sine, cosine and tangent of any angle between 0° and 360° by reading its value off the graph. These graphs are cyclic, and if you plotted these functions for values of θ from 360° to 720° you would obtain identical shapes to those obtained from 0° to 360°.

From Figures 4.12, 4.13 and 4.14 you can see that by drawing a horizontal line for any value for sin θ, cos θ or tan θ in the range 0° to 360° there are two possible values for θ. Note also that each function has positive and negative phases.

- From 0° to 90° sine, cosine and tangent are all positive.
- From 90° to 180° sine is positive, cosine and tangent are negative.
- From 180° to 270° tangent is positive, sine and cosine are negative.
- From 270° to 360° cosine is positive, sine and tangent are negative.

Figure 4.15 shows the quadrants where the trigonometric functions are positive. Note that zero degrees is taken from the horizontal to the right of the origin and angles are measured positively in an anticlockwise direction from the horizontal to the right. You may find it useful if you use the acronym CAST to help you remember the position of each trigonometric function in this diagram.

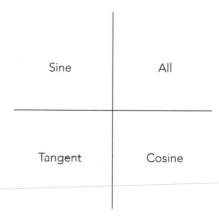

Figure 4.15: The quadrant where the trigonometric functions are positive

Key terms

Amplitude the maximum and minimum ordinate values.

Period the length of one cycle.

Sine and cosine rules

The basic trigonometric functions sine, cosine and tangent can only be applied to right-angled triangles, but the sine and cosine rules can be applied to any triangle.

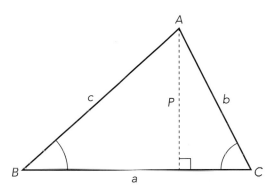

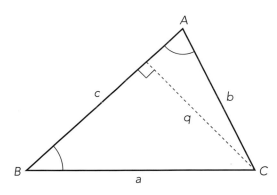

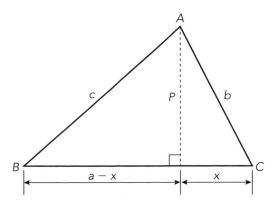

Figure 4.16: Deriving the sine and cosine rules

Consider the triangles shown in Figure 4.16. From the first triangle (triangle i), we can write:

$$\sin B = \frac{p}{c} \quad \text{and} \quad \sin C = \frac{p}{b}$$

Therefore:

$$p = c \sin B = b \sin C$$
$$\frac{b}{\sin B} = \frac{c}{\sin C}$$

From the second triangle (triangle ii), we can write:

$$\sin B = \frac{q}{a} \quad \text{and} \quad \sin A = \frac{q}{b}$$

Therefore:

$$q = a \sin B = b \sin A$$
$$\text{and} \quad \frac{a}{\sin A} = \frac{b}{\sin B}$$

Combining these findings gives the sine rule:

$$\frac{a}{\sin A} = \frac{b}{\sin B} = \frac{c}{\sin C}$$

Now consider the final triangle In Figure 4.16. Using Pythagoras' theorem, we know that:

$$b^2 = p^2 + x^2$$
$$\text{and } c^2 = p^2 + (a - x)^2$$
$$= p^2 + a^2 - 2ax + x^2$$

Rearrange the first equation so that p^2 is the subject, and substitute this in the second equation to obtain:

$$c^2 = a^2 + b^2 - 2ax$$

But:

$$x = b \cos C$$

Therefore:

$$c^2 = a^2 + b^2 - 2ab \cos C$$

This is the cosine rule, and we can similarly derive other formulations of this rule:

$$b^2 = a^2 + c^2 - 2ac \cos B$$
$$a^2 = b^2 + c^2 - 2bc \cos A$$

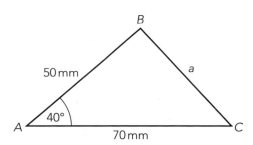

Figure 4.17: A triangle to solve using the sine and cosine rules

Worked example: Using the sine and cosine rules

If the lengths of two sides and the included angle of a triangle are 50 mm, 70 mm and 40° respectively determine the length of the third side and the other two internal angles. A sketch of the problem is shown in Figure 4.17.

First use the cosine rule:

$$a^2 = b^2 + c^2 - 2bc \cos A$$

This gives:

$$a^2 = 70^2 + 50^2 - 2 \times 70 \times 50 \cos 40$$

$$= 4900 + 2500 - 5362$$

$$= 2038$$

$$a = 45.1 \text{ mm}$$

Next use the sine rule:

$$\frac{a}{\sin A} = \frac{b}{\sin B} = \frac{c}{\sin C}$$

So we have:

$$\frac{45.1}{\sin 40} = \frac{70}{\sin B} = \frac{50}{\sin C}$$

Hence:

$$\sin C = \frac{50 \sin 40}{45.1} = 0.7126$$

$$\therefore \quad C = 45.4°$$

And:

$$\sin B = \frac{70 \sin 40}{45.1} = 0.9977$$

$$\therefore \quad B = 86.1°$$

Now if we are right the sum of the three internal angles should be 180° (or close to 180°). We have:

$$A + B + C = 40° + 86.1° + 45.4° = 171.5°$$

This is not an acceptable error! If you look now at the sine curve you will see that for any value of $\sin B$ there are two values of B between 0° and 360°. For $\sin B = 0.9977$, B could be 86.1° or 93.9° (90° ± 3.9°). The correct angle in this case is 93.9°. To check that this is right, now add all three angles:

$$A + B + C = 40° + 93.9° + 45.4° = 179.3°$$

Activity: Solving problems with the sine and cosine rules

1 Figure 4.18 shows a phase diagram for two currents where $I_1 = 6.5$ A and $I_2 = 5.0$ A. Calculate the resultant current, I_R, and its phase angle $\theta°$.

2 Calculate the resultant of the two forces shown in Figure 4.19.

3 If the lengths of each side of a triangle are 50 mm, 70 mm and 75 mm determine each of the internal angles.

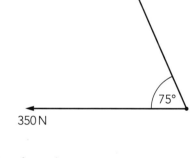

Figure 4.19: A force diagram

Functional skills

Using formulae to solve electrical and mechanical problems will help develop your skills in mathematics.

Figure 4.18: A phase diagram for two currents

4.2.3 Mensuration

We will now consider the surface area and the volume of three regular solids: cylinder, sphere and cone. These are shown in Figure 4.20 and the respective formulae for surface areas and volumes are given in Table 4.11.

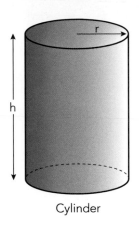

Cylinder

Sphere

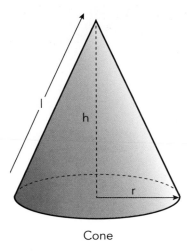

Cone

Figure 4.20: Regular solids

Table 4.11: Surface area and volume formulae for regular solids

Solid	Total surface area	Volume
Cylinder	$2\pi rh + 2\pi r^2$	$\pi r^2 h$
Sphere	$4\pi r^2$	$\frac{4}{3}\pi r^3$
Cone	$\pi rl + \pi r^2$	$\frac{1}{3}\pi r^2 h$

Often you can break down a complex shape into simpler, regular shapes, and then calculate the surface area and volume of each part using standard formulae. For example, if you want to calculate the total surface area and the volume of a plumb bob (see Figure 4.21), you can regard this object as cone (right-hand side diagram) attached to a cylinder.

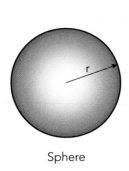

Did you know?

The symbol ∅ is used by engineers to indicate that the dimension that follows is the diameter of a circular section.

First we need to calculate the slant height of the cone.

$$l = \sqrt{20^2 + 12.5^2} = 23.6\,\text{mm}$$

Now considering the separate elements of the cylinder and the cone, but remembering that only one end of the cylinder and only the curved area of the cone form part of the surface area of this object, we can calculate the total surface area:

$$A = \pi r^2 + 2\pi rh + \pi rl$$
$$= \pi \times 12.5^2 + 2 \times \pi \times 12.5 \times 40 + \pi \times 12.5 \times 23.6$$
$$= 491 + 3142 + 927$$
$$= 4560\,\text{mm}^2$$

And the volume:

$$V = \pi r^2 h + \frac{1}{3}\pi r^2 h$$
$$= \pi \times 12.5^2 \times 40 + \frac{\pi \times 12.5^2 \times 20}{3}$$
$$= 19635 + 498$$
$$= 20133\,\text{mm}^3$$

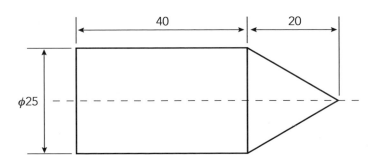

40   20

$\phi 25$

Figure 4.21: A plumb bob

Assessment activity 4.2

P4 P5 P6 P7 :BTEC

P4 A pin in part of a mechanism rotates with a radius of 150 mm and it is observed to turn through an angle of 0.6 rad in 5 s. Determine:

a) the distance travelled by the pin

b) the angular velocity of the pin in rad/s and rev/min

c) the linear tangential velocity of the pin in m/s.

P4 Figure 4.22 shows a triangle. Use trigonometry to determine the lengths of the unknown sides of this triangle.

P5 Sketch the following functions in good proportion in the range from 0° to 360°:

a) $y = 4 \cos 3\theta$

b) $y = 2 \sin \theta$

c) $y = 6 \tan \dfrac{\theta}{2}$

P6 Part of the framework of a glass roof is triangular in shape. The lengths of two sides of the roof and the included angle between them are 1900 mm, 2700 mm and 40° respectively. Calculate the length of the third side and the other two internal angles.

P6 You work in the design department of a company that produces fabricated steel structures. Figure 4.23 shows a sketch of a roof frame. The frame is symmetrical about the vertical axis through point A. Calculate the lengths of all the members and all the angles between the members.

P7 A swimming pool has these dimensions: length 30 m, width 12 m, depth at shallow end 1 m and depth at deep end 3 m. It is to be renovated. Assume that the floor of the pool slopes uniformly from one end to the other.

In order to estimate the costs of tiling, calculate the total surface area of the pool. Then calculate the volume of water in litres needed to fill the pool.

P7 Determine the total surface area and the volume of an object comprising a cylinder with a diameter of 200 mm and length 150 mm that has a cone at one end with a base diameter of 200 mm and a length of 300 mm.

P7 Plastic granules are fed into an injection moulding machine through a hopper. The dimensions are shown in Figure 4.24. Calculate the surface area of the outside of the hopper. Neglecting the thickness of the material, calculate the volume of the hopper.

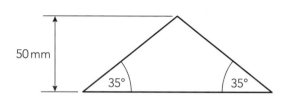

Figure 4.22: Triangle for second P4 question

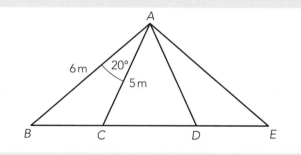

Figure 4.23: Triangle for second P6 question

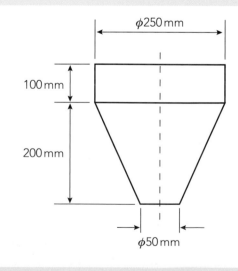

Figure 4.24: Hopper for third P7 question

4.3 Be able to use statistical methods to display data

Engineers need to be confident about handling numerical information and this requires some understanding of statistical methods. Statistics is concerned with the collection, sorting and analysis of numerical data, and with the presentation of the information gathered in the form of tables, charts and diagrams.

Did you know?

Manufacturing companies use statistical analysis to monitor the quality of their products. When mass producing machined components, samples are regularly checked after specific intervals to ensure that the products are within tolerance. Results for critical dimensions are then plotted on a chart to monitor variations in size. Statistical analysis is also used to ensure that a particular method of manufacture is cost effective by ensuring that scrap rates are within acceptable limits.

4.3.1 Data handling

In engineering, you need to able handle, organise and present data. Sometimes you will examine all the components of a data set, but more often you would take a sample. For example, you may examine every 100th component in a mass production process or perhaps take a measurement of some process every hour.

The measured quantities in a data set are called variables. You need to know the difference between discrete and continuous variables.

Discrete variables are measurements that can only have specific values although they are not necessarily whole numbers. For example, if the variable is people, the measurements will be whole numbers (you cannot have 0.25 of a person); but if the variable is shoe sizes, the measurements could include half sizes.

Continuous variables are measurements that can take any value in a range between set limits. For example, the size of metal bars turned on a lathe will be manufactured between given limits.

Having collected a set of data, it may appear that you are presented with a seemingly random list of numbers that is difficult to interpret. However, you can use statistical analysis techniques to present and interpret the information. Consider the data in Table 4.12, which records the diameters in millimetres of a sample of 100 turned bars. The bars have a nominal diameter of 50 mm according the specification for this type of bar. Do you think that a quality assurance engineer would be satisfied with this production run?

Frequency tables give a much clearer picture of the **scatter** associated with these results. Table 4.13 has been constructed from this basic data set by counting the occurrences of each number in the data set in Table 4.12.

Key terms

Scatter a measure (or picture) of how data is spread between the largest and smallest values.

Table 4.12: Measurements of the diameters (mm) of turned bars

49.8	49.9	50.0	49.9	50.0	49.7	50.1	49.9	49.9	49.7
50.2	50.1	50.0	49.9	50.0	49.9	50.1	50.3	50.0	50.0
50.1	50.1	50.1	50.0	49.9	50.0	49.8	49.9	50.3	50.0
50.0	49.6	49.9	50.0	50.1	50.2	50.0	49.9	50.3	50.0
50.0	50.0	50.0	49.7	50.1	50.2	49.8	49.8	50.4	49.9
50.3	49.9	50.1	50.1	49.9	49.9	50.1	50.2	49.8	49.8
49.9	50.0	50.1	50.0	50.0	50.0	50.1	49.6	50.0	50.3
49.8	50.2	50.2	50.4	49.8	50.1	50.1	50.3	49.9	49.9
49.9	50.2	49.9	50.2	50.1	50.3	50.1	49.9	49.9	50.1
49.8	50.1	50.3	49.8	50.0	50.0	50.2	49.7	50.0	50.1

Table 4.13: A frequency table of the data in Table 4.12

Diameter (mm)	Number	Frequency
49.6	II	2
49.7	IIII	4
49.8	IIIII IIIII	10
49.9	IIIII IIIII IIIII IIIII I	21
50.0	IIIII IIIII IIIII IIIII IIII	24
50.1	IIIII IIIII IIIII IIIII	20
50.2	IIIII IIII	9
50.3	IIIII III	8
50.4	II	2

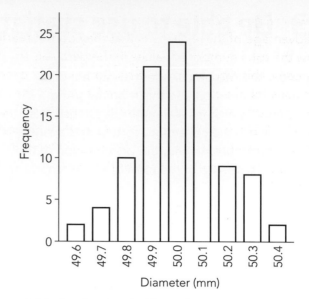

Figure 4.26: Bar chart (vertical format)

The diameter of a turned metal bar is a continuous variable. The measurements taken to produce the data set in Table 4.12 have been given to one decimal place. In practice, a bar recorded as having a diameter of 49.7 mm could have an actual diameter anywhere in range 49.7 ± 0.05 mm.

The upper and lower limits of each group of continuous variables are known as class boundaries. The class boundaries for the group of bars recorded as having a diameter of 49.7 mm are therefore 49.65 and 49.75. Class width represents the size between the upper and lower limits. In our data set, the class width is 0.1 mm. For any data set, the class width is usually a constant value.

Bar charts rely on the length (or area) of a bar to represent the data. The bar may be horizontal as

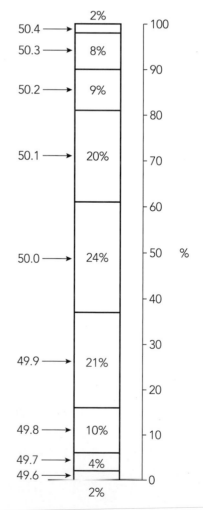

Figure 4.27: A proportional bar chart

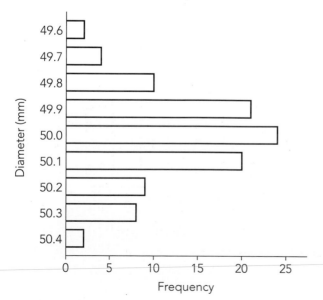

Figure 4.25: Bar chart (horizontal format)

shown in Figure 4.25 or vertical as shown in Figure 4.26. A disadvantage of these charts is that they do not readily show the total number of values in the data set. To overcome this, you could use a proportional bar chart. This consists of a single bar. The total length of the bar represents all the data in absolute or percentage terms. This bar is then divided into sections, with each section representing one class of the data. Figure 4.27 shows a proportional bar chart for the data in Table 4.12.

Pie charts are similar to proportional bar charts except that they display the proportions of the data represented by each class as angles or sectors. The complete circle represents the total sample, and the angle of each sector represents the fraction that each class has of the total sample. Table 4.14 shows how these angles are calculated for the data in Table 4.12. There are 100 measurements in the sample, so to get the angle for a given class you must divide the frequency that this class appears in the data (from Table 4.13) by 100, and multiply the answer by 360 to get a result in degrees. Figure 4.28 shows a pie chart for our data set constructed from the calculations in Table 4.14.

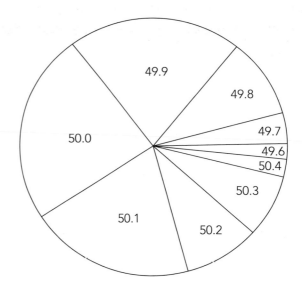

Figure 4.28: A pie chart

Histograms are similar to bar charts, but there are no gaps between the bars and the class widths are all equal. Figure 4.29 shows a histogram for the data in Table 4.12. Note that a frequency polygon has been drawn on Figure 4.29. This connects the midpoints of the class widths at the top of each bar. With many data sets, the smaller the class width the more a frequency polygon tends towards a smooth curve.

Table 4.14: Calculating the angles for each class in a pie chart

Class	Angle
49.6	$\theta_1 = \frac{2}{100} \times 360 = 7.2°$
49.7	$\theta_2 = \frac{4}{100} \times 360 = 14.4°$
49.8	$\theta_3 = \frac{10}{100} \times 360 = 36.0°$
49.9	$\theta_4 = \frac{21}{100} \times 360 = 75.6°$
50.0	$\theta_5 = \frac{24}{100} \times 360 = 86.4°$
50.1	$\theta_6 = \frac{20}{100} \times 360 = 72.0°$
50.2	$\theta_7 = \frac{9}{100} \times 360 = 32.4°$
50.3	$\theta_8 = \frac{8}{100} \times 360 = 28.8°$
50.4	$\theta_9 = \frac{2}{100} \times 360 = 7.2°$

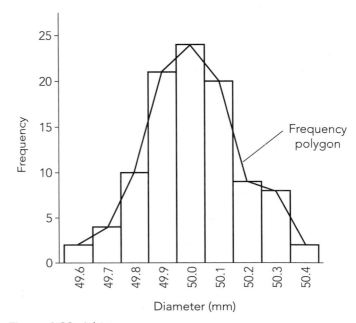

Figure 4.29: A histogram

Cumulative frequency curves (ogive diagrams) are produced by plotting the cumulative frequency against the class width. A cumulative frequency curve for the data in Table 4.12 is shown in Figure 4.30. Before this can be drawn, you must calculate the cumulative frequency for this data set. This is done by summing the frequencies in Table 4.13. The results are shown in Table 4.15.

Table 4.15: Calculating cumulative frequency

Diameter (mm)	Cumulative frequency
Not more than 49.65	2
Not more than 49.75	6
Not more than 49.85	16
Not more than 49.95	37
Not more than 50.05	61
Not more than 50.15	81
Not more than 50.25	90
Not more than 50.35	98
Not more than 50.45	100

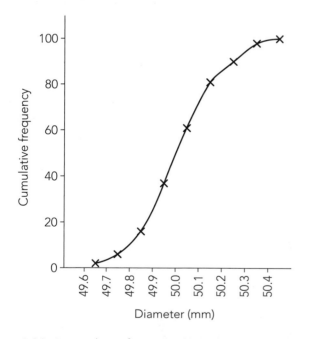

Figure 4.30: A cumulative frequency (ogive) curve

Did you know?

A spreadsheet program such as Excel is a very useful way to process statistical data if you know how to set up formulae and plot charts.

Table 4.16: Ambient temperature data

Temperature (°C)	16–18	18–20	20–22	22–24	24–26
Frequency	4	10	20	14	2

Activity: Presenting data

Table 4.16 shows the results of measurements of ambient temperatures recorded on 50 different occasions.

Use this data to draw:

- a pie chart
- a horizontal bar chart
- a proportional bar chart
- a histogram
- a cumulative frequency curve.

4.3.2 Statistical measurement

The **arithmetic mean** of a set of data is obtained by summing all the data items and dividing by the number of items. It is expressed mathematically by this formula:

$$\bar{x} = \frac{f_1 x_1 + f_2 x_2 + f_3 x_3 + \ldots f_n x_n}{f_1 + f_2 + f_3 + \ldots f_n} = \frac{\Sigma f x}{\Sigma f}$$

Where:

$\bar{x}$ = arithmetic mean

f = frequency

x = **variate**

Σ = the symbol used by mathematicians and engineers to mean summation.

To calculate the arithmetic mean of the data in Table 4.12, use the frequency data in Table 4.13. You would need to multiply each class by its frequency (49.6 × 2; 49.7 × 4; etc.), then add the results, and then divided by 100 (the total number of observations). A good way to do this if you have a large data set, is to place the data in a spreadsheet or table like Table 4.17.

Table 4.17: Preliminary calculations needed to work out the arithmetic mean

Diameter (mm) x	Frequency f	fx
49.6	2	99.2
49.7	4	198.8
49.8	10	498.0
49.9	21	1047.9
50.0	24	1200.0
50.1	20	1002.0
50.2	9	451.8
50.3	8	402.4
50.4	2	100.8
	$\Sigma f = 100$	$\Sigma fx = 5000.9$

We can now calculate the mean:

$$\bar{x} = \frac{\Sigma fx}{\Sigma f} = \frac{5000.9}{100} = 50.01 \text{ mm}$$

The **median** is the middle value in a data set when arranged in order of magnitude. If there is an even number of values the median is the average of the two middle values.

The median divides the histogram into two equal areas, and it is the value of the variate that corresponds to half the cumulative frequency on the ogive curve. To calculate the median from the histogram for the data set in Table 4.12, first draw and label the median line as in Figure 4.31.

Key terms

Arithmetic mean one measure of the average a set of data, calculated by summing all the data and dividing by the number of observations.

Variate a particular value of a variable.

Median the middle value in a data set when it is arranged in order of magnitude.

We know that $A_1 = A_2$, this is the definition of the median. So:

$$2 \times 0.1 + 4 \times 0.1 + 10 \times 0.1 + 21 \times 0.1 + 24 \times x$$
$$= 2 \times 0.1 + 8 \times 0.1 + 9 \times 0.1 + 20 \times 0.1$$
$$+ 24(0.1 - x)$$
$$0.1(2 + 4 + 10 + 21) + 24x$$
$$= 0.1(2 + 8 + 9 + 20 + 24) - 24x$$
$$3.7 + 24x = 6.3 - 24x$$
$$48x = 6.3 - 3.7$$
$$x = 0.054 \text{ (to three decimal places)}$$

So now we know x, we can calculate the median by simple arithmetic.

$$Median = 49.95 + 0.054 = 50.004 \text{ mm}$$

Due to plotting and reading errors, it is not possible to achieve the same degree of accuracy in finding the median by using the ogive curve. Reading from the ogive curve in Figure 4.32, we can see that the median would be given as 50 mm.

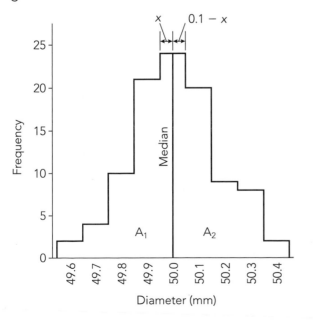

Figure 4.31: Finding the median from a histogram

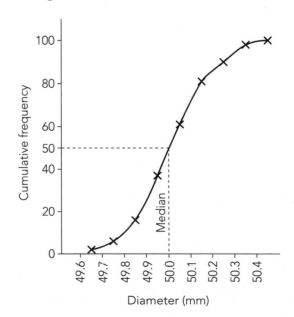

Figure 4.32: Finding the median from a cumulative frequency (ogive) curve

The **mode** is usually only determined for discrete data. It is the value that occurs the most frequently in a data set. It is possible to have more than one mode in a data set.

If the histogram of a data set is symmetrical, the data is said to have a normal distribution and the mean, median and mode will all have the same value, as shown in Figure 4.33. If the histogram is not symmetrical, the data is said to have a skewed distribution and the mean, median and mode will have different values, as shown in Figure 4.34.

Activity: Mean, median and mode

Using the data in Table 4.16 (see page 134), determine:

a) the mean

b) the median

c) the mode.

PLTS

Analysing and evaluating statistical data will help develop your independent enquirer skills.

Functional skills

Taking notes and presenting statistical data will develop your skills in English .

Key terms

Mode the value that occurs most frequently in a set of data.

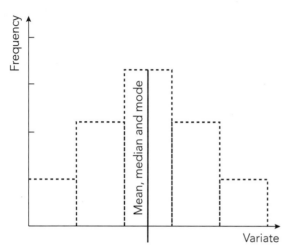

Figure 4.33: Normal distribution

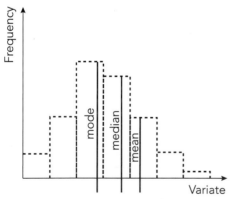 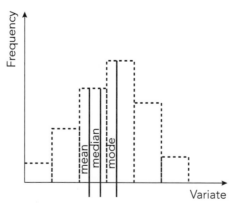

Figure 4.34: Skewed distributions

Assessment activity 4.3

P8 Select an appropriate variable and collect a data set of readings for this variable. Your data set should have at least 50 values. Represent this data using the following techniques:

a) a pie chart

b) a histogram

c) a cumulative frequency diagram.

P9 Table 4.18 shows the diameter of a sample of small manufactured wheels.

Table 4.18: Diameter of wheels

Diameter (mm)	Frequency
115	3
116	7
117	12
118	20
119	15
120	8
121	2

Use the results for the sample to find:

a) the mean

b) the median

c) the mode.

P9 A manufacturer of low-voltage power supplies has been experiencing problems with the life of a standby battery. The battery supplier claims that the battery should last for 200 hours under normal conditions. The supplier's tests show a mean life of 200 hours. The designer of the power supply is not convinced. A technician has tested 220 batteries for you and tabulated the results (see Table 4.19).

Table 4.19: Working life of tested standby batteries

Life (hours)	Number
190<192	46
192<194	15
194<196	26
196<198	25
198<200	28
200<202	27
202<204	24
204<206	12
206<208	8
208<210	5
210<212	4

The designer asks you to process this data and establish the battery's working life. Calculate the measures of central tendency (mean, mode and median) and feed back your thoughts to the designer.

Grading tips

P8 Check the presentation of your solutions. Make sure that the diagrams are annotated.

P9 Check that you have recorded the data correctly before starting the calculations for mean, median and mode.

4.4 Be able to use elementary calculus techniques

Calculus is used by engineers when carrying out a wide range of design calculations. Applications include vibration analysis, the interpretation of data supplied in graphical form, assessments of manufacturing efficiency (to ensure that products are manufactured by making the best use of the available material) and the determination of beam deflections.

4.4.1 Differentiation

The gradient of a curve can be found at a point on the curve by drawing a **tangent** to the line at this point and determining the gradient of the tangent. This method will not always give an accurate answer, because there is always an element of error in drawing a tangent by eye, but it will give a close approximation to the gradient. However, if you want to determine the exact gradient for any point on the curve without the need to plot the graph, you can find an equation for the gradient by differentiating the equation for the line.

Differentation from first principles

Consider the equation $y = 2x^2$. Figure 4.35 shows this curve between $x = 0$ and $x = 4$.

> **Key terms**
>
> **Tangent** a straight line that just touches the outside edge of a curve without cutting across it.

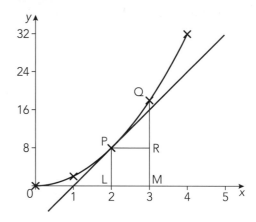

Figure 4.35: Graph of $y = 2x^2$

The gradient at point P is given by the gradient of the tangent to the curve at $P(2,8)$.

Rocket science is one example where calculus has to be considered by designers.

Now take point $Q(3,18)$ on the curve and join PQ. You can see that the gradient of PQ is steeper than the tangent at P, but we can determine its value. The gradient of chord PQ is:

$$\frac{QR}{PR} = \frac{18 - 8}{3 - 2} = 10$$

As Q approaches P, the gradient of PQ approaches the gradient of the tangent at P. If P and Q are coincident, the chord becomes a point and you cannot determine the slope of a point. You can bring Q close to P to obtain an approximation of the gradient at P by this method, but you will not obtain an exact answer.

However, we can develop this principle. Let P have the coordinates (x, y) and Q have coordinates $(x + \delta x, y + \delta y)$. The symbol δ is used by engineers to indicate a small change in a given quantity. Since both points P and Q lie on the curve, we know:

$$y = 2x^2 \tag{1}$$
$$y + \delta y = 2(x + \delta x)^2 \tag{2}$$

Subtracting equation (2) from equation (1) gives:

$$y + \delta y - y = 2(x + \delta x)^2 - 2x^2$$
$$\delta y = 2(x^2 + 2x\delta x + \delta x^2) - 2x^2$$
$$= 2x^2 + 4x\delta x + 2\delta x^2 - 2x^2$$
$$= 4x\delta x + 2\delta x^2$$

Dividing both sides by δx gives:

$$\frac{\delta y}{\delta x} = \frac{4x\delta x + 2\delta x^2}{\delta x}$$
$$= 4x + 2\delta x$$

This is the gradient of the chord PQ. So the gradient of the tangent at P is given by:

$$\frac{\delta y}{\delta x} \text{ as } \delta x \to 0$$

So the gradient of the tangent at P is $4x$. This is referred to as the limiting value (or derivative) of the expression:

$$\frac{\delta y}{\delta x}$$

The limiting value is written as:

$$\lim_{\delta x \to 0} \frac{\delta y}{\delta x} = \frac{dy}{dx} = 4x$$

Usually the first expression is not written down. So the gradient of the curve at $P(2, 8)$ is given by the formula:

$$\frac{dy}{dx} = 4x \tag{3}$$
$$= 4 \times 2 = 8$$

Equation (3) is the derivative of y with respect to x, and you can now use this formula to determine the gradient of the curve $y = 2x^2$ for any value of x.

Did you know?

The notation $\delta x \to 0$ is used extensively by engineers and mathematicians to indicate that the value of the small quantity δx tends to zero.

Differentiation by formula

By differentiating equations from first principles using the method outlined above, you could establish that when:

$$y = x \qquad \frac{dy}{dx} = 1$$
$$y = 3x^2 \qquad \frac{dy}{dx} = 6x$$
$$y = 4x^3 \qquad \frac{dy}{dx} = 12x^2$$
$$y = 5x^4 \qquad \frac{dy}{dx} = 20x^3$$

From these results, you can deduce a formula to differentiate y with respect to x. When:

$$y = ax^n \qquad \frac{dy}{dx} = nax^{n-1}$$

By using a similar technique you could deduce formulae to differentiate trigonometric, exponential and logarithmic functions. Table 4.20 shows these relationships for different types of functions.

Table 4.20: Rules for differentiating some common functions

Function type	General formula y	Derivative $\frac{dy}{dx}$
Power	ax^n	nax^{n-1}
Sine	$\sin ax$	$a \cos ax$
Cosine	$\cos ax$	$-a \sin ax$
Exponential	e^{ax}	ae^{ax}
Logarithmic	$\ln ax$	$\frac{1}{x}$

Often in engineering, you will come across expressions where the variable is not written as x. If you differentiate these expressions, you must use the appropriate notation in the solution. For example, engineers are often interested in the change of some property over time. The rate of change of some quantity represents the time taken for a change in the quantity to take place. Equations that represent rates of change are usually written in terms of time (t). Velocity (v) can be considered to be the rate of change of displacement (s) and acceleration can be considered to be the rate of change of velocity. An equation to represent displacement could be:

$$s = 4t + 3t^2$$

To determine an equation for velocity, you could differentiate the equation for displacement with respect to time. Hence:

$$v = \frac{ds}{dt} = 4 + 6t$$

To determine an equation for acceleration, you could differentiate the equation for velocity with respect to time. This gives:

$$a = \frac{dv}{dt} = 6$$

Worked example: Differentiation

1   Differentiate the following equation with respect to x:

$$y = x^3 + \frac{2}{x^2} - 4x + 6$$

This can be written:

$$y = 1x^3 + 5x^{-2} - 4x^1 + 6x^0$$

Differentiate using the standard rules:

$$\frac{dy}{dx} = 3 \times 1x^{3-1} + (-2) \times 5x^{-2-1} - 1 \times 4x^{1-1}$$
$$+ 0 \times 6x^{0-1}$$
$$= 3x^2 - 10x^{-3} - 4x^0 + 0$$
$$= 3x^2 - \frac{10}{x^3} - 4$$

2   Differentiate this equation with respect to x:

$$y = 2\sin x + 3\cos 2x$$
$$\frac{dy}{dx} = 1 \times 2\cos x - 2 \times 3\sin 2x$$

$$= 2\cos x - 6\sin 2x$$

3   Differentiate this equation with respect to x:

$$y = 4e^{2x} + 2\ln 3x$$
$$\frac{dy}{dx} = 2 \times 4e^{2x} + \frac{2}{x}$$
$$= 8e^{2x} + \frac{2}{x}$$

4   Find the gradient of the curve $y = 3x^2 - 4x + 5$ at $x = 2$.

$$\text{Gradient} = \frac{dy}{dx} = 6x - 4$$

At $x = 2$

$$\text{Gradient} = 6 \times (2) - 4 = 8$$

Activity: Differentiation

1   Select the appropriate formulae from Table 4.17 and differentiate the following expressions:

a) $4x^2 + \frac{1}{2x^3} - 3e^{2x} + 5\ln 2x$

b) $4\cos 2\theta + 3\sin 2\theta$

c) $5t^2 + 3t + 6$

2   Find the gradient of the curve $y = x^2 - 2x + 4$ at $x = 5$.

4.4.2 Integration

If you can differentiate an expression, it should be possible to obtain the expression from the differential coefficient of the expression by reversing the process. This is called integration.

We have established a formula for differentiating an algebraic expression. We know that:

$$\text{if } y = ax^n \text{ then } \frac{dy}{dx} = nax^{n-1}$$

Consider first the steps for carrying out differentiation:

• the power becomes a multiplier

• the power is decreased by one.

To indicate that an integration is to be performed we use the symbol $\int$. This is used in an expression of the form:

$$\int (\quad) dx$$

This means that the expression within the brackets is to be integrated treating x as the variable.

We can now write down the steps for integration:

- the power is increased by one
- the new power becomes a divisor.

Hence:

$$\int (ax^n)\, dx = \frac{ax^{n+1}}{n+1}$$

Now apply this rule to the expression $6x$. This gives:

$$\int (6x)\, dx = \frac{6x^{1+1}}{1+1} = \frac{6x^2}{2} = 3x^2$$

Check this by differentiating the resulting function $y = 3x^2$. We know that:

$$\text{if}\quad y = 3x^2 \quad \text{then}\quad \frac{dy}{dx} = 6x$$

It therefore appears that the equation we have obtained to carry out the process of integration is valid. But consider these two examples:

$$\text{if}\quad y = 3x^2 + 6 \quad \text{then}\quad \frac{dy}{dx} = 6x$$

$$\text{if}\quad y = 3x^2 - 10 \quad \text{then}\quad \frac{dy}{dx} = 6x$$

You can see that we have obtained the same differential equation, even though the original equations were different. This means that if you integrate to get back to the original equation, you will only obtain part of the solution.

To overcome this difficulty we introduce an arbitrary constant c, the value of which must be determined by some other means. Hence:

$$\int (ax^n)\, dx = \frac{ax^{n+1}}{n+1} + c$$

(Note that this equation is not valid when $n = -1$.)

So we can now restate our answer for the expression $6x$:

$$\int (6x)\, dx = \frac{6x^2}{2} + c = 3x^2 + c$$

The constant of integration c can be determined if a corresponding pair of values for x and y are known.

Formulae to integrate trigonometric, exponential and logarithmic functions can be found using similar techniques to the one we have used for algebraic functions. You do not need to know how to derive

Worked example: Integration

Find an equation for y given that:

$$\frac{dy}{dx} = 3x^2 + 4x \quad \text{and}$$

$$y = 2 \text{ when } x = 1$$

We find y as follows:

$$y = \int (3x^2 + 4x)\, dx = \frac{3x^{2+1}}{2+1} + \frac{4x^{1+1}}{1+1} + c$$

$$= x^3 + 2x^2 + c$$

But we know that when $y = 2$ then $x = 1$. So:

$$2 = (1)^3 + 2(1)^2 + c$$

$$\therefore\ c = -1$$

Therefore the equation is:

$$y = x^3 + 2x^2 - 1$$

Table 4.21: Rules for integrating some common functions

Function y	Integral $\int (\quad) dx$
ax^n	$\dfrac{ax^{n+1}}{n+1} + c$
$\sin ax$	$-\dfrac{1}{a}\cos ax + c$
$\cos ax$	$\dfrac{1}{a}\sin ax + c$
e^{ax}	$\dfrac{1}{a}e^{ax} + c$
$\dfrac{1}{x}$	$\ln x + c$

these proofs. However, the results are important and they are summarised in Table 4.21.

The integrals we have considered so far are referred to as indefinite integrals. This is because no limits have been assigned to the integrals.

When limits are assigned to the integral, the integral is known as a definite integral and the constant of integration will cancel out.

The expression below is a definite integral because limits have been assigned to the integral, indicated by numbers written above and below the integral symbol. The limit above the integral symbol is referred to as the top (or upper) limit and the limit below the integral symbol is referred to as the bottom (or lower) limit.

$$\int_1^2 (3x^2)\,dx$$

This can now be integrated in the usual way, but after integrating, the new expression is enclosed in square brackets and the limits are assigned to the right-hand bracket as shown here:

$$\int_1^2 (3x^2)\,dx = \left[\frac{3x^{2+1}}{2+1} + c\right]_1^2 = [x^3 + c]_1^2$$

The limits are then assigned to the integrated expression by substituting the top limit for x in the expression, and then substituting the bottom limit for x in the expression, and subtracting one from the other. This gives:

$$[x^3 + c] = (2^3 + c) - (1^3 + c)$$
$$= 7$$

At this point you can see that the constant of integration will always cancel out. For this reason, you would normally leave it out when dealing with definite integrals. So it would be acceptable to write:

$$\int_1^2 (3x^2)\,dx = \left[\frac{3x^{2+1}}{2+1}\right]_1^2 = [x^3]_1^2$$
$$= (2^3) - (1^3) = 7$$

Worked example: Definite integrals

Evaluate this definite integral:
$$\int_0^{\frac{\pi}{3}} (4 \sin 2\theta)\,d\theta$$

First perform the integration:

$$\int_0^{\frac{\pi}{3}} (4 \sin 2\theta)\,d\theta = \left[\frac{-4 \cos 2\theta}{2}\right]$$
$$= [-2 \cos 2\theta]_0^{\frac{\pi}{3}}$$

Then apply the limits:

$$= \left(-2 \cos \frac{2\pi}{3}\right) - (-2 \cos 0)$$
$$= (1) - (-2) = 3$$

Did you know?

If limits in an integral are specified in terms of π you can assume that the angles are in radians.

Activity: Practising integration

1   Select the appropriate formula and then integrate these equations:
    a) $y = x^2 + 2x - 3$
    b) $y = 4 \cos 2\theta - 3 \sin 2\theta$
    c) $y = 3e^t + \dfrac{1}{2x^2}$

2   Given that:
    $y = \int (4x + 2)\,dx$ find y when $x = 3$ if $y = 4$
    when $x = 2$.
    Find y when $x = 3$.

3   Evaluate these definite integrals:
    a) $\displaystyle\int_1^4 (t + 1)\,dt$
    b) $\displaystyle\int_0^{\pi} (4 + 2 \sin 3\theta)$
    c) $\displaystyle\int_1^2 \left(e^{2x} - \dfrac{1}{x}\right)dx$

Integral calculus can be used to determine the area under a graph. This has applications in engineering. Engineers sometimes do experiments that yield results that are plotted in graph form. The area under the graphs can provide useful information. For example, the area under a graph of the force exerted by a machine against displacement determines the work done by the machine, and the area under a graph of the velocity of an object plotted against time determines the distance travelled by the object.

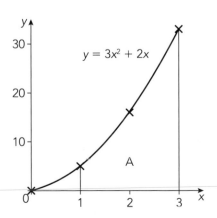

Figure 4.36: Graph of $y = 3x^2 + 2x$

Suppose you wanted to find area A in Figure 4.36. This is bounded by the curved line $y = 3x^2 + 2x$, the x-axis and the ordinates at $x = 1$ and $x = 3$.

The area is given by the definite integral of the equation for the line, with the limits set by the ordinate boundaries. Hence:

$$A = \int_1^3 (3x^2 + 2x)\, dx$$
$$= \left[\frac{3x^{2+1}}{2+1} + \frac{2x^{1+1}}{1+1} \right]_1^3$$
$$= \left[(x^3 + x^2) \right]_1^3$$
$$= ((3^3 + 3^2) - (1^3 + 1^2))$$
$$= 34$$

Activity: Finding the areas enclosed by curves

1 Find the area bounded by the curve, the x-axis and the given ordinates for these functions.

a) $y = x(3 - x)$ at $x = 0$ and $x = 3$

b) $y^2 = x$ at $x = 1$ and $x = 4$

c) $y = \sin 2\theta$ at $\theta = 0$ and $\theta = \pi$

2 Plot the graphs for the equations $y = x^2$ and $y = x + 6$ on the same axes in the range $-3 \leqslant x \leqslant 4$. Find the points of intersection and the area enclosed between the curves.

Assessment activity 4.4

P10 a) Differentiate this function with respect to x:

$$y = 6x^2 + 3x - 4$$

b) Differentiate this function with respect to t:

$$s = 4e^{3t} - e^{-2.5t}$$

c) Differentiate this function with respect to θ:

$$y = 4 \sin 2\theta - 3 \cos 4\theta$$

P10 Integrate these functions:

a) $\int (4 \sin 2t - e^{2t})\, dt$

b) $\int (2x^3 - 3x^2 + 5x - 2)\, dx$

D1 The voltage across the plates of a charging capacitor varies with time according to the formula: $v = 30(1 - e^{-0.25t})$, where t is the time in μs.

a) Draw a graph showing the change in the voltage in the first 15 μs.

b) Use the graph to estimate the rate at which the voltage is rising after 5 μs.

c) Use calculus to calculate the rate at which the voltage is rising after 5 μs.

D1 The discharging characteristic for a series capacitive circuit is given by this equation:

$$v = V\left(1 - e^{-\left(\frac{t}{T}\right)}\right)$$

where $T = CR$ and is called the time constant.

If $C = 100\,$nF, $R = 68\,$kΩ and $V = 12\,$V, investigate the discharging characteristic of the circuit and estimate the rate of change of voltage when $t = T$.

D2 Determine the area under the curve $s = 2 \cos \theta$ in the range $\theta = 0$ to $\frac{\pi}{2}$ rad.

D2 A sliding mechanism in a machine moves with a velocity given by the expression:

$$v = 7t + 0.8t \text{ mm/s}$$

Calculate the displacement that occurs between $t = 2$ and $t = 4$ seconds

Grading tips

P10 Check the presentation of your solutions, showing your working.

D1 Make sure that you annotate and title your graph. Give your answers with appropriate units.

D2 You may need to investigate the relationship between time, displacement and velocity to answer the second question. This is covered in Unit 5.

PLTS

When applying calculus techniques to the solution of problems you need to get organised so that you set out your work properly and use the correct notations. Doing this will help improve your self manager skills.

Judy Upson
Engineering technician

I work as a technician in a company that specialises in the manufacture, testing and calibration of measuring equipment. I do some of the testing, conduct experiments and do some analysis for the design engineers. We deal with a variety of equipment, so you are always learning and meeting new challenges. But it makes the job interesting.

I couldn't do my job without being good with figures and being able to work with precision. You soon learn that working accurately is much more important than working quickly. I also need to draw on my maths knowledge to produce the required results from the test data.

Yesterday, for example, a design engineer in the company asked me to test a spring that had been sourced from a new supplier. She wanted to know:

- the initial uncoiling load
- the spring stiffness
- the energy stored in the spring when the load is 12 N.

I started by carrying out some force and extension tests on the spring. This produced the data in the table below.

Load (N)	2	4	6	8	10	12	14	16
Deflection (mm)	0	4	12	19	27	34	42	50

I then plotted a graph of force against deflection and used this to help me determine the answers to the design engineer's questions.

Think about it!

1 Show how you could determine the energy stored in the spring using integral calculus.

2 Explain how you could use Judy's data to calculate the deflection for a load of 20 N. What assumption would you need to make when finding this value?

Just checking

1 State the six laws of indices and the three laws of logarithms.

2 Explain the meaning of the constants m and c in the equation for a straight line.

3 Explain the meaning of (a) an algebraic expression, (b) an algebraic equation, (c) a common factor in an algebraic expression, and (d) the letters a, b and c in the equation used to solve quadratic equations.

4 How many degrees are there in one radian?

5 State the acronym often used to remember the three basic trigonometric functions. What type of triangle can they be applied to?

6 How does a sine wave differ from a cosine wave?

7 State the sine and cosine rules. What type of triangle can they be applied to?

8 State the formulae used to calculate the surface area and volume for a cylinder, a sphere and a cone.

9 Give two examples of discrete variables and two examples of continuous variables.

10 Define (a) the arithmetic mean, (b) median and (c) mode.

11 State the formula to differentiate (a) a polynomial function, (b) an exponential function, and (c) a sinusoidal function.

12 State the formula to integrate (a) a polynomial function, (b) an exponential function, and (c) a sinusoidal function.

edexcel

Assignment tips

- Don't just provide the final line of the answer to mathematical problems. Always present your solutions in full, so that an assessor can see your working.

- Always check your solutions to problems that you might be set in assignments to ensure that they are realistic.

- Make sure that all graphs are given a title, and that the axes are properly labelled. Similarly, if you use any diagrams to support your answers, label these clearly so that an assessor can easily understand your work.

- When you are applying mathematical techniques to engineering problems make sure that you provide answers with appropriate units. You also need to ensure that your calculations use variables expressed in compatible units.

5 Mechanical principles and applications

Engineers are called upon to make judgements on a wide range of problems. For example, they might be asked to assess the load-carrying capacity of a structure, to determine the possible causes of failure of a component part, to ensure that a machine has sufficient power to fulfil a particular function, to calculate the flow rate of a fluid or to consider the effect of temperature on a component.

All these problems can be solved using a range of analytical techniques supported by experimentation. This unit will consider some of the important scientific principles required to solve problems related to static, dynamic, fluid and thermodynamic systems. It will build on the mathematical principles that are covered in GCSE and BTEC First courses.

There are worked examples and questions for you to try, to check your understanding.

Learning outcomes

After completing this unit you should:

1 be able to determine the effects of loading in static engineering systems
2 be able to determine work, power and energy transfer in dynamic engineering systems
3 be able to determine the parameters of fluid systems
4 be able to determine the effects of energy transfer in thermodynamic systems.

Assessment and grading criteria

This table shows you what you must do in order to achieve a pass, merit or distinction grade, and where you can find activities in this book to help you produce the required evidence.

To achieve a **pass** grade the evidence must show that you are able to:	To achieve a **merit** grade the evidence must show that, in addition to the pass criteria, you are able to:	To achieve a **distinction** grade the evidence must show that, in addition to the pass and merit criteria, you are able to:
P1 calculate the magnitude, direction and position of the line of action of the resultant and equilibrant of a non-concurrent coplanar force system containing a minimum of four forces acting in different directions **Assessment activity 5.1 page 163**	**M1** calculate the factor of safety in operation for a component subjected to combined direct and shear loading against given failure criteria **Assessment activity 5.1 page 163**	**D1** compare and contrast the use of D'Alembert's principle with the principle of conservation of energy to solve an engineering problem **Assessment activity 5.2 page 170**
P2 calculate the support reactions of a simply supported beam carrying at least two concentrated loads and a uniformly distributed load **Assessment activity 5.1 page 163**	**M2** determine the retarding force on a freely falling body when it impacts upon a stationary object and is brought to rest without rebound, in a given distance **Assessment activity 5.2 page 170**	**D2** evaluate the methods that might be used to determine the density of a solid material and the density of a liquid **Assessment activity 5.3 page 175**
P3 calculate the induced direct stress, strain and dimensional change in a component subjected to direct uniaxial loading and the shear stress and strain in a component subjected to shear loading **Assessment activity 5.1 page 163**	**M3** determine the thermal efficiency of a heat transfer process from given values of flow rate, temperature change and input power **Assessment activity 5.4 page 182**	
P4 solve three or more problems that require the application of kinetic and dynamic principles to determine unknown system parameters **Assessment activity 5.2 page 170**	**M4** determine the force induced in a rigidly held component that undergoes a change in temperature **Assessment activity 5.4 page 182**	
P5 calculate the resultant thrust and overturning moment on a vertical rectangular retaining surface with one edge in the free surface of a liquid **Assessment activity 5.3 page 175**		
P6 determine the upthrust on an immersed body **Assessment activity 5.3 page 175**		
P7 use the continuity of volume and mass flow for an incompressible fluid to determine the design characteristics of a gradually tapering pipe **Assessment activity 5.3 page 175**		

P8 calculate dimensional change when a solid material undergoes a change in temperature and the heat transfer that accompanies a change of temperature and phase **Assessment activity 5.4 page 182**		
P9 solve two or more problems that require the application of thermodynamic process equations for a perfect gas to determine unknown parameters of the problems **Assessment activity 5.4 page 182**		

How you will be assessed

This unit will be assessed by assignments designed and marked by the staff at your centre.

The type of evidence you will need to present when you carry out an assignment could be in the form of:

- written reports
- answers to classroom tests
- case studies.

John, 16-year-old engineering apprentice

I left school with a good range of qualifications including a grade C in GCSE maths, English, double science and IT. I started an apprenticeship with a local engineering firm and attended college on a day release National Certificate programme.

I found the mechanical principles unit interesting because my lecturer was able to explain how the content might be used in an engineering environment, and this made the learning process more meaningful. The tutorial questions we were given gave me plenty of opportunity to practise each topic and my problem solving skills improved very quickly.

The assignments were necessary to check that I understood each topic, but I enjoyed doing them because I felt confident that I had been well prepared.

5.1 Be able to determine the effects of loading in static engineering systems

Engineering calculations

Engineers and technicians may be called upon to devise a solution to a problem that requires the manufacture of a component or structure. These solutions may be intuitive but it will often be necessary to complete some calculations to ensure that the proposed solution will work. Working in small groups, consider the calculations that might be carried out in these scenarios:

- a winch to pull a trailer up an incline
- a pulley system to transfer raw material from a basement store to a first floor manufacturing area
- a floating platform in a leisure pool
- an irrigation ditch
- a receiver for an air compressor.

When designing or modifying a structure or mechanism, engineers have to ensure that it will be strong enough to safely sustain the loading that it will be subjected to in service throughout the expected life of the system. In this section, we introduce the graphical and analytical techniques that are used to determine the effect of a loading on an engineering systems.

5.1.1 Non-concurrent coplanar force systems

Mechanical systems often have components that will be pushing and pulling other components. To understand how these forces can be determined, you first need to know what is meant by the term force.

A force can be defined as that which changes, or tends to change, the state of rest of a body or of its uniform motion in a straight line. To describe a force completely it is necessary to know three things:

- magnitude – the physical size of the force (3 N, 10 kN etc.)
- direction – the **line of action** of the force (horizontal, at 30° to the horizontal etc.)
- sense – the way the force is acting on the line of action (upwards, leftwards etc.).

The three characteristics of a force may be represented graphically by a line known as a vector.

A space diagram shows the arrangement of the components that transfer the forces through the system, and a free body diagram shows the forces that are acting on the system or part of the system under consideration. These diagrams are often combined together.

Consider a mass suspended from a ceiling. The mass is pulling downward and the ceiling is pulling upward. At any point in the supporting cord you can consider the effect of the upward and downward forces. Figure 5.1 shows a space diagram and a free body diagram for this arrangement.

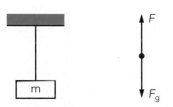

Figure 5.1: Space diagram (left) and free body diagram (right)

Now consider a mass suspended by two cords – Figure 5.2 shows the space and free body diagrams for the point where the cords intersect.

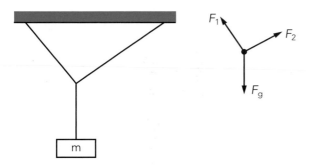

Figure 5.2: Space and free body diagrams at the intersection of two cords

Each force in the system can be represented by a vector which is a line where the magnitude is given by the length of the line, the direction is given by the angle of the line and the sense is given by the arrowhead. A vector diagram for a system of forces like the one shown in Figure 5.2 is produced by drawing the vectors for all the forces acting in the system consecutively. This is shown in Figure 5.3. It is important to note that the vectors can be drawn in any order.

Note the difference between a vector diagram and a free body diagram. In the vector diagram, the length of each vector represents the magnitude of that force. The vector diagram must be drawn to scale, but while it is desirable to draw the directions of the forces in the free body diagram accurately, no attempt should be made to represent the magnitude of the force by the length of the line in the free body diagram.

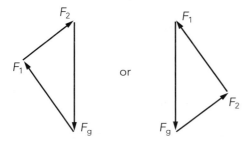

Figure 5.3: Force vector diagram

A system of forces acting on a component can be concurrent, where the lines of action of all the forces acting pass through a common point, or non

concurrent where the line of action of the forces do not pass through a common point (see Figure 5.4). The forces can be **coplanar**, in a single plane (that is, two dimensional), or in more than one plane (that is, three dimensional). You will only be asked to consider coplanar **force systems** when studying this unit.

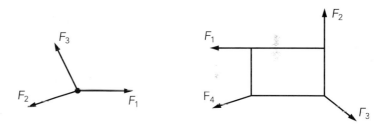

Figure 5.4: Concurrent (shown on the left) and non-concurrent (right) forces

Did you know?

The system of units used on all BTEC engineering programmes is the Systeme Internationalle d'unites (SI). In the SI unit system mass is measured in kilograms (kg) and weight is measured in newtons (N). The SI system recommends symbols to be used to specify scientific terms, such as F for force. To identify a specific force you can use a suffix, such as F_g for the force due to the effect of gravity.

When two or more forces act on a body and are arranged such that the body remains at rest, or moves at a constant speed in a straight line, the forces are said to be in equilibrium. If we now draw a vector that represents each force successively, the resulting diagram will end at the start point if the system is in equilibrium (as shown in Figure 5.3).

If the vector diagram does not end at the start point, the system will not be in equilibrium (it will be accelerating). The vector required to return to the start point will represent the extra force required to produce equilibrium. This force is called the **equilibrant** (F_E) (see Figure 5.5). Conversely, the **resultant** (F_R), is the vector is that represents the effect of a system that is not in equilibrium (see Figure 5.6). The resultant is equal in magnitude and direction but opposite in sense to the equilibrant.

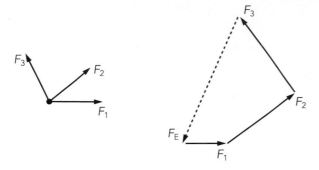

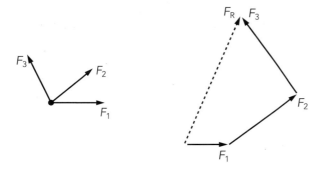

Figure 5.5: Vector diagram showing forces that are not in equilibrium

Figure 5.6: The resultant shows the effect of forces that are not in equilibrium

We can graphically determine the resultant (or the equilibrant) of simple coplanar force systems by plotting vectors representing each force in the system. You can then draw the resultant vector (or equilibrant if required), the magnitude of which is determined by measuring its length with a rule and scaling to determine the force in Newtons. Its direction is measured with a protractor. Figure 5.7 shows how this graphical method is used to find the resultant of a given concurrent coplanar force system.

Figure 5.8 uses a similar approach to determine the equilibrant of a non-concurrent coplanar force system acting on a plate. The equilibrant force (F_E) will put this force system into equilibrium only if it is applied at the correct position. To find this position, you will need to understand the principle of moments which we introduce later in this unit. We show how to make the necessary calculations in section 5.1.2 (page 154).

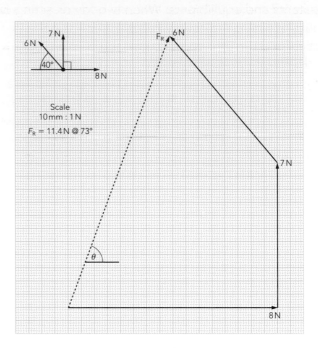

Figure 5.7: Using graphical methods to find the resultant of a concurrent coplanar force system

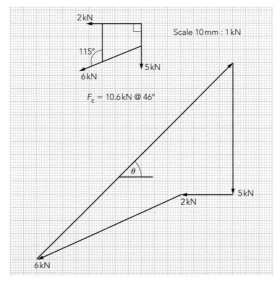

Figure 5.8: Using graphical methods to find the equilibrant of a non-concurrent coplanar force system

Key terms

Equilibrant the force that when applied to a system of forces will produce equilibrium.

Resultant the force that represents the combined effect of a force system.

Pythagora's theorem the square on the hypotenuse of a right-angled triangle is equal to the sum of the squares on the other two sides.

We can also use basic geometrical principles to find resultants and equilibrants. When two forces acting on a body are perpendicular to each other – say one is vertical and the other horizontal – the vector diagram for them will be a right-angled triangle. Similarly, any single vector inclined at some angle to the horizontal can be resolved into two components at right angles to each other (this is known as the resolution of forces). These perpendicular components are usually shown as a horizontal component and a vertical component (see Figure 5.9), although this does not necessarily need to be the case. You can use the basic trigonometric relationships and **Pythagoras's theorem** to calculate unknown quantities by resolving forces as shown in Figure 5.9:

$$\sin \theta = \frac{F_V}{F_R}$$

$$\cos \theta = \frac{F_H}{F_R}$$

$$\tan \theta = \frac{F_V}{F_H}$$

$$F_R^2 = F_V^2 + F_H^2$$

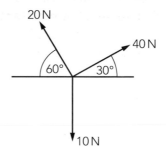

Figure 5.9: Resolving the force F_R into two perpendicular components, F_V and F_H

We can apply these principles to situations where several forces are acting on a body. Each force can be split into its vertical and horizontal components. The vertical components can be summed to give a single vertical force and the horizontal components can be summed to give a single horizontal force. This is usually done by taking upward forces as positive values, downward forces as negative values, rightward forces as positive values and leftward forces as negative values.

When the forces are in equilibrium, the sum of the vertical forces and the sum of the horizontal forces must equal zero. This can be simply expressed by these equations:

$$\Sigma F_V = 0$$

$$\Sigma F_H = 0$$

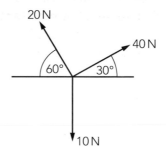

Figure 5.10: A concurrent coplanar force system

When the forces are not in equilibrium, we can use the basic trigonometric relationships and Pythagoras's theorem to calculate the resultant. Suppose we wish to determine analytically the resultant of the concurrent, coplanar force system shown in Figure 5.10. First split them into horizontal and vertical components. Note that there are two horizontal components – a positive (rightward) component of the 40 N force and a negative (leftward) component of the 20 N force. There are three vertical components – the 20 N and 40 N forces have positive (upward) vertical components, the 10 N force has a negative (downward) component. Summing these horizontal and vertical components we get:

$$\Sigma F_x = 40 \cos 30 - 20 \cos 60 = 15.8 \text{ N}$$

$$\Sigma F_y = 40 \sin 30 + 20 \sin 60 - 10 = 27.3 \text{ N}$$

Now combining these vertical and horizontal components into a single force (see Figure 5.11), we can use Pythagoras's theorem to calculate the magnitude of the resultant and one of the basic trigonometric relationships to calculate the direction of this force:

$$F_R = \sqrt{27.3^2 + 14.8^2} = 31 \text{ N}$$

$$\theta = \tan^{-1} \frac{27.3}{14.8} = 61.5°$$

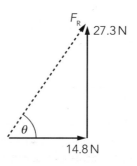

Figure 5.11: The resultant of the concurrent coplanar force system in Figure 5.10

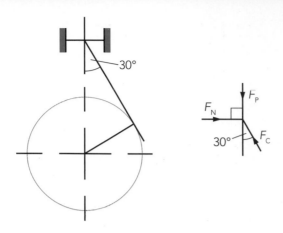

Figure 5.12: The force acting on a piston (F_p) in a small engine

Activity: Calculating forces

Figure 5.12 shows that the force F_p acting on the piston in a small engine is 2 kN.

1 Find (a) the **normal reaction** (F_N) between the cylinder wall and the piston, and (b) the force in the connecting rod (F_c) using a graphical method.

2 Check your answers to task 1 by using an analytical method to find the normal reaction (F_N) between the cylinder wall and the piston, and the force in the connecting rod (F_c).

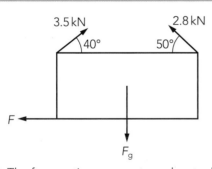

Figure 5.13: The force acting on a rectangular steel plate

Activity: Calculating forces acting on a rectangular steel plate

Figure 5.13 shows the forces acting on a rectangular steel plate, 2.5 m x 1.0 m, that is being moved by a crane across a factory floor.

1 Determine the horizontal force (F) required to move the plate across the factory floor.

2 Determine the mass of the plate.

Key terms

Normal reaction one where its direction is perpendicular to a given surface.

Moment the tendency of a force to rotate the object on which it acts.

5.1.2 Simply supported beams

Now we have a method to analyse the forces acting on an object, we can apply these techniques to some practical situations. In this section we will look at the forces acting on simply supported beams. But first, we need to revisit the concept of equilibrium.

If a body is in static equilibrium, there will be no out-of-balance force. If all the forces acting on the body are resolved into perpendicular components – say, vertical (y) and horizontal (x) components – then the sum of these forces will be zero. As you saw earlier in this unit, this can be summarised by these equations:

$$\Sigma F_x = 0$$
$$\Sigma F_y = 0$$

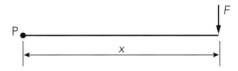

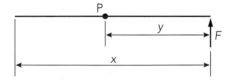

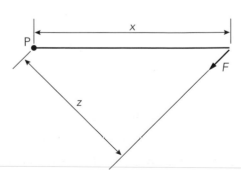

Figure 5.14: Moments of a force

In essence, this means that the body will not have any tendency to move vertically or horizontally. However, it could have a tendency to rotate. The tendency of a force to rotate a body about an axis is called the **moment** of the force about that axis. The magnitude of a moment is given by the product of the force and the perpendicular distance of the line of action of the force from the axis. When calculating moments, you must specify the axis you are considering. This can be done by labelling the axis and using this label as a suffix in the equation.

Consider the turning effect of the force (F) about the pivot point P in each of the three examples in Figure 5.14. Using the labelling convention, the turning effect (or moment) of the force about point P will be M_P.

In Figure 5.14a, the force (F) will have a clockwise turning effect about the pivot point P, and its magnitude will be given by:

$$M_P = F_x$$

In Figure 5.14b, the force (F) will have an anticlockwise turning effect about the pivot point P, and its magnitude will be given by:

$$M_P = F_y$$

In Figure 5.14c, the force (F) will have a clockwise turning effect about the pivot point P and its magnitude will be given by:

$$M_P = F_z$$

If a body is in equilibrium under the action of several forces the total clockwise moment of the forces about any axis will be equal to the total anticlockwise moments of the forces about the same axis. This can be summarised as:

$$\Sigma M = 0$$

We now have three conditions for equilibrium:

$$\Sigma F_x = 0$$
$$\Sigma F_y = 0$$
$$\Sigma M = 0$$

The following sign conventions (shown pictorially in Figure 5.15) are used with these equations:

- upward forces will be taken as positive
- rightward forces will be taken as positive
- clockwise moments will be taken as positive.

Now we can return to the example of a non-concurrent coplanar force system shown in Figure 5.8 (page 152).

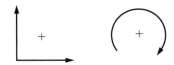

Figure 5.15: Direction of positive forces and moments

Two conditions for equilibrium will be satisfied by the force (F_E), that is $\Sigma F_y = 0$ and $\Sigma F_x = 0$.

But we must satisfy the third condition, that $\Sigma M = 0$, by finding the position at which the equilibrant must be applied to ensure that the plate does not spin. To do this you will need to know the dimensions of the plate and these are shown in Figure 5.16. By taking moments about the corner A you can determine the position of the equilibrant (F_E), to satisfy this third condition. Note that you could take moments about any point to determine the position of the equilibrant, but by choosing point A you effectively negate the effect of the moments due to the 6 kN and 5 kN forces since their moment arms are zero.

$$\Sigma M_A - (10.6 \times x) - (2 \times 53) + (6 \times 0) + (5 \times 0) = 0$$
$$10.6x = 106$$
$$x = 10 \text{ cm}$$

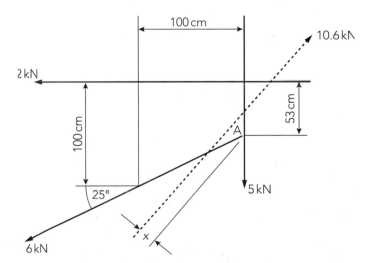

Figure 5.16: Determining the position of equilbrant for the system shown in Figure 5.8

Beams are used extensively in engineering to support a wide range of structures or component parts. We will now consider the equilibrium of simply supported beams under the influence of concentrated and uniformly distributed loads (udl). This analysis will be based on the three conditions for equilibrium. Note the implications of the third condition: $\Sigma M = 0$. This means that if a beam is in equilibrium, then the sum of the moments about any point, on or off the beam, will be equal to zero.

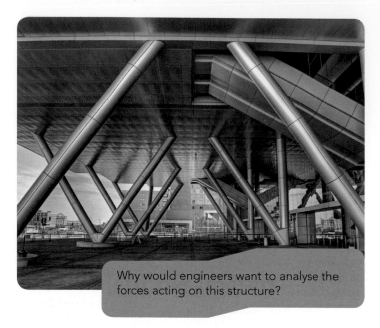

Why would engineers want to analyse the forces acting on this structure?

When a beam is subjected to a concentrated load the resulting force is assumed to act at a point on the beam, it is indicated by an arrow and its magnitude is usually given in N or kN. When a beam is subjected to a uniformly distributed load the resulting force is assumed to act over a length of the beam. The part of the beam over which the uniformly distributed load is acting is indicated by a wavy line, and its magnitude is usually given in N/m or kN/m. The wavy line can be drawn above or below the line representing the beam. If it is drawn above the beam the force acts downward, if it is drawn below, the force acts upward.

We are now going to consider a beam that is supported from below at two points, A and B. If the beam is in static equilibrium and we know the magnitude and positions of the loads acting on it, we can calculate the upward forces at the two support points. These forces are known as **support reactions**.

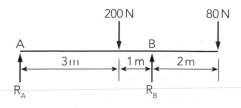

200 N   80 N

A   B

3 m   1 m   2 m

R_A R_B

Figure 5.17: Forces acting on a simply supported beam

Key terms

Support reactions the forces that are maintaining the equilibrium of a beam or structure.

The simply supported beam shown in Figure 5.17 is subject to two concentrated loads. To find the support reactions, first take moments about point A. Because the beam is in equilibrium, we know that these must sum to zero. Therefore:

$$\Sigma M_A = (200 \times 3) - (R_B \times 4) + (80 \times 6) = 0$$
$$R_B = \frac{600 + 480}{4} = 270 \, \text{N}$$

Note the sign convention – clockwise moments are positive, anticlockwise moments are negative. Now take moments about point B:

$$\Sigma M_B = (R_A \times 4) - (200 \times 1) + (80 \times 2) = 0$$
$$R_A = \frac{200 - 160}{4} = 10 \, \text{N}$$

You can now check these answers by resolving the vertical forces. If you add the vertical forces together, they should sum to zero, and it does:

$$\Sigma F_y = 10 - 200 + 270 - 80 = 0$$

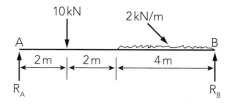

10 kN   2 kN/m

A   B

2 m   2 m   4 m

R_A R_B

Figure 5.18: Forces acting on a simply supported beam

The beam in Figure 5.18 is subject to a concentrated load and a uniformly distributed load. We can use the same approach, by first taking moments about point A. To do this, find the total load for the uniformly distributed load by multiplying the load per unit length by the length over which it acts, and calculate its moment by assuming that this total load acts at the centre of the length over which it acts. This gives:

$$\Sigma M_A = (10 \times 2) + (2 \times 4 \times 6) - (R_B \times 8) = 0$$
$$R_B = \frac{20 + 48}{8} = 8.5 \, \text{kN}$$

Now take moments about point B:

$$\Sigma M_B = (R_A \times 8) - (10 \times 6) - (2 \times 4 \times 2) = 0$$

$$R_A = \frac{60 + 16}{8} = 9.5\,\text{kN}$$

Again, check the answers:

$$\Sigma F_y = 9.5 - 10 - (2 \times 4) + 8.5 = 0$$

(a)

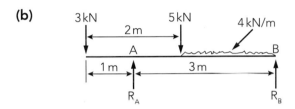

(b)

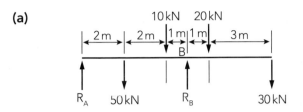

Figure 5.19: Forces acting on a simply supported beam (diagrams for the activity)

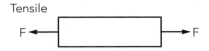

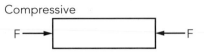

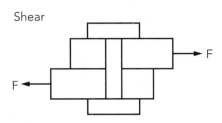

Figure 5.20: Types of force

Activity: Support reactions in simply supported beams

1 Find the support reactions for the simply supported beam subjected to concentrated loads shown in Figure 5.19a.

2 Find the support reactions for the simply supported beam subjected to a concentrated load and a uniformly distributed load as shown in Figure 5.19b.

When a bar of material is subjected to an externally applied force, a resisting force is set up within the material and the bar is said to be in a state of stress.

There are three states of stress, stemming from the three types of force. However, tensile and compressive stresses are usually grouped together for the purpose of calculations and are known as direct stresses.

Stress intensity is a measure of the load carried per unit area of the material. This can be expressed as an equation:

$$\text{Direct stress} = \frac{\text{Normal force}}{\text{Cross-sectional area}}$$

or

$$\sigma = \frac{F}{A}$$

$$\text{Shear stress} = \frac{\text{Shear force}}{\text{Shear area}}$$

or

$$\tau = \frac{F}{A}$$

When solving questions in mechanical science it is essential that due care is taken to ensure that the units of each term in an equation are compatible. Stress is given in units of newtons per metre squared (N/m^2) or pascals (Pa) ($1\,\text{N/m}^2 = 1\,\text{Pa}$). Note that the symbol used for direct stress is the Greek letter sigma (σ) and the symbol used for shear stress is the Greek letter tau (τ).

For direct stress the area resisting the normal force is perpendicular to the line of action of the applied force. For shear stress the area resisting the shearing force is in the same direction as the applied force

5.1.3 Loaded components

Forces may described in one of three ways:

- tensile forces – those which tend to pull the material apart

- compressive forces – those which tend to crush the material

- shear forces – those which cut across the material.

Worked examples: Stress calculations

1 A force applied to a rectangular bar with a cross-sectional area of 60 mm² generates a direct stress of 40 MPa. Determine the value of the force.

First, check that the units are compatible:

$\sigma = 40\,\text{MPa} = 40\,\text{MN/m}^2 = 40\,\text{N/mm}^2$

$A = 60\,\text{mm}^2$

Then apply the formula for direct stress:

$$\sigma = \frac{F}{A}$$

$$F = \sigma A$$
$$= 40 \times 60$$
$$= 2400\,\text{N}$$
$$= 2.4\,\text{kN}$$

2 A press tool is required to punch out discs of 40 mm diameter from brass plate 1.5 mm thick with a shear strength of 200 MPa.

a) Calculate the force in the punch.

b) Calculate the compressive stress in the punch.

Again, check that the units are compatible:

$d = 40\,\text{mm}$

$t = 1.5\,\text{mm}$

$\tau_{max} = 200\,\text{MPa} = 200\,\text{MN/m}^2 = 200\,\text{N/mm}^2$

To answer the first part of the question, you need to apply the formula for shear stress. To do this, you need to know the area of the plate that is subjected to the shear force. This will be the circumference of the brass disc multiplied by its thickness. Hence:

$$A_s = \pi d t$$
$$= \pi \times 40 \times 1.5$$
$$= 188.5\,\text{mm}^2$$

Now you can apply the formula for shear stress:

$$\tau = \frac{F}{A}$$

$$F_{max} = \tau_{max} A$$
$$= 200 \times 188.5$$
$$= 37.7 \times 10^3\,\text{N}$$
$$= 37.7\,\text{kN}$$

To answer the second part of the question, you need to apply the formula for direct force. To do this, you need to know the area of the plate that is subject to the direct force (the compressive action of the punch). This will be the area of the flat side of the brass disc:

$$A_d = \frac{\pi d^2}{4}$$
$$= \frac{\pi \times 40^2}{4}$$
$$= 1257\,\text{mm}^2$$

Now apply the formula for direct stress:

$$\sigma = \frac{F}{A}$$
$$= \frac{37.7 \times 10^3}{1257}$$
$$= 30\,\text{N/mm}^2$$

3 A bar with a length of 1 m extends by 0.05 mm. Determine the strain experienced by the bar.

Again, check that the units are compatible and then apply the appropriate formula, in this case the formula for direct strain.

$l = 1\,\text{m} = 1 \times 10^3\,\text{mm}$

$\delta l = 0.05\,\text{mm}$

Applying the formula for direct strain gives:

$$\varepsilon = \frac{\delta l}{l}$$
$$= \frac{0.05}{1 \times 10^3}$$
$$= 50 \times 10^{-6}$$

A material subjected to externally applied forces can change in shape, and the material is said to be strained. There are three types of strain (see Figure 5.21), which stem from the three types of stress. However, tensile strains and comprehensive strains are again grouped together and are known as direct strains.

Strain is the ratio of the deformation produced in the direction of the applied force to the original dimension. Hence:

$$\text{Direct strain} = \frac{\text{Change in length}}{\text{Original length}}$$

or $\qquad \varepsilon = \dfrac{\delta l}{l}$

$$\text{Shear strain} = \frac{\text{Change in length}}{\text{Original length}}$$

or $\qquad \gamma = \dfrac{\delta l}{l}$

Strain is a ratio of two lengths and therefore has no units. Note that the symbol used for direct strain is the Greek letter epsilon (ε), the symbol used for shear strain is the Greek letter gamma (γ) and the symbol used to represent a small change is the Greek letter delta (δ).

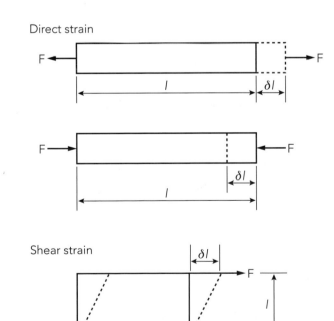

Direct strain

Shear strain

Figure 5.21: Types of strain

Activity: Stress calculations

1 A circular wire having a diameter of 3 mm and a length of 300 mm extends 0.04 mm when it is subjected to a tensile force of 100 N.

   a) Calculate the stress in the wire.

   b) Calculate the strain in the wire.

2 A rivet has a diameter of 20 mm and holds three metal plates together. Figure 5.22 shows the loads on the rivet. Find the shear stress that the rivet is subjected to.

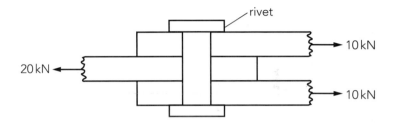

Figure 5.22: Loads on a rivet holding together three metal plates

One way that engineers examine the properties of metals is to test them to destruction. For example, you could apply an ever-increasing tensile force to a metal and measure the extension of the metal at each stage. Similar tests can be performed using compressive and shear forces. Figure 5.23 shows a typical graph of the force applied plotted against the extension observed for tests on **ferrous metals** and non-ferrous metals.

Key terms

Ferrous metal a metal that has iron as its major constituent.

Study the graphs in Figure 5.23. Note that at the end of the elastic range for ferrous metals, there is a clearly identifiable yield point. This is more pronounced in low carbon steels than in high carbon steels. This phenomenon is not observed with non-ferrous metals.

Specimens loaded within the elastic range will return to their original shape on removal of the load. However, specimens loaded within the plastic range will not return to their original shape on removal of the load. The elastic strain is recoverable, the plastic strain is not.

Ferrous metals

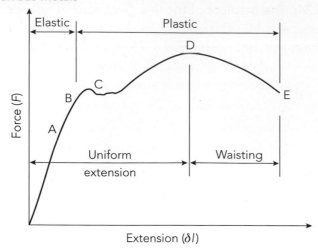

Non-ferrous metals

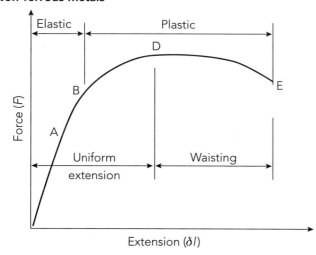

A – limit of proportionality
B – elastic limit
C – yield point
D – maximum load
E – fracture point

Figure 5.23: Typical force versus extension graphs

The following points should be noted with respect to this graph.

- Specimens loaded within the elastic range will return to their original shape on removal of the load.
- Specimens loaded within the plastic range will not return to their original shape on removal of the load – the elastic strain is recoverable, but the plastic strain is not.

- Up to the maximum load, the cross-sectional area of the specimen will not change significantly and is often assumed to be constant. The vertical axis of the graph could, therefore, be given in terms of stress (i.e. force divided by the original cross-sectional area).
- The original length is obviously a constant and the horizontal axis of the graph could therefore be given in terms of strain (i.e. the change in length divided by the original length).
- By working in terms of stress and strain rather than force and extension, the graphs are not affected by the dimensions of the test specimen.

Did you know?

If you bend a piece of metal, it may go into the plastic range and be subject to permanent deformation.

The mechanical properties of materials are important to design engineers when selecting a material for a particular application. The designers need to ensure that the chosen material will be strong enough to fulfil its function. The properties that you need to be familiar with are:

- Young's modulus of elasticity
- tensile strength
- factor of safety.

Figure 5.23 shows that within the elastic range, direct stress is directly proportional to direct strain. The slope of the stress versus strain graph for a particular material over this range gives Young's modulus (E) for that material. We can express this mathematically as follows:

Direct stress = Direct strain × Constant

$$\sigma = \varepsilon \times E$$

Therefore: $E = \dfrac{\sigma}{\varepsilon}$

Shear stress is also directly proportional to shear strain within the elastic range. The slope of the stress versus strain graph for a particular material over this range gives the shear modulus (G) for that material. (Note that the shear modulus is sometimes called the modulus of rigidity.)

Shear stress = Shear strain × Constant

$$\tau = \gamma \times G$$

$$G = \frac{\tau}{\gamma}$$

Tensile strength is defined as the maximum load attained divided by the original cross-sectional area. Hence:

$$\text{Tensile strength} = \frac{\text{Maximum load}}{\text{Original cross sectional area}}$$

$$TS = \frac{F_{max}}{A}$$

In order to build a 'margin for error' into these calculations, it is normal practice to include a safety factor. This could be set by the designer, by the customer or by custom and practice. The factor of safety is usually defined as the tensile strength divided by the operating or normal working stress. Hence:

$$\text{Factor of safety} = \frac{\text{Tensile strength}}{\text{Working stress}}$$

$$F \text{ of } S = \frac{TS}{\sigma_w}$$

Table 5.1 shows the results of a tensile test on an aluminium wire. The wire has an effective length of 20 mm and a diameter of 3 mm. Use this data to draw the force versus extension graph (see Figure 5.24) and determine Young's modulus for the material.

Table 5.1: Tensile test results for an aluminium wire

Force (kN)	40	60	80	100	120	140	160
Extension (mm)	0.9	1.9	2.5	3.5	4.4	5.1	5.9

We can substitute the formulae for direct stress and direct strain into the formula for Young's modulus to obtain:

$$E = \frac{\sigma}{\varepsilon} = \frac{F/A}{\delta l/l} = \frac{F}{A} \times \frac{l}{\delta l} = \frac{F}{\delta l} \times \frac{l}{A}$$

The first product can be found in the graph (Figure 5.24). The gradient of the line gives force (F) divided by extension (δl). The second product can be found using the given data – we know the length (l) of the wire and we can calculate the area (A) as follows:

$$A = \frac{\pi d^2}{4}$$

$$= \frac{\pi \times 3^2}{4}$$

$$= 7.07 \text{ mm}^2$$

Now we can substitute into the formula to get Young's modulus:

$$E = \frac{74 \times 10^3}{3} \times \frac{20}{7.07}$$

$$= 70 \times 10^3 \text{ N/mm}^2$$

$$= 70 \text{ GN/m}^2$$

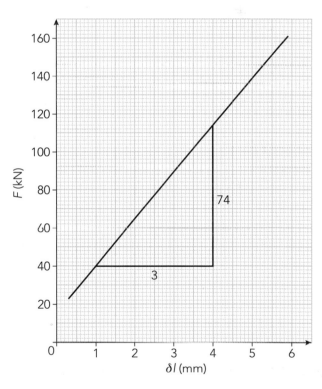

Figure 5.24: Force versus extension graph for a tensile test on a sample aluminium wire

Worked example: Calculating maximum loads

A steel tie rod has a tensile strength of 500 N/mm² and a cross-sectional area of 40 mm². If a factor of safety of 5 is to be used calculate:

a) the maximum load that the tie rod should be subjected to

b) the maximum permissible working stress.

To answer the first part of the question use the tensile strength formula.

$$TS = \frac{F_{max}}{A}$$

$$\therefore F_{max} = TS \times A$$

$$= 500 \times 40$$

$$= 20 \times 10^3$$

$$= 20\,kN$$

To answer the second part of the question use the factor of safety formula.

$$F \text{ of } S = \frac{TS}{\sigma_w}$$

$$\therefore \sigma_w = \frac{TS}{F \text{ of } S}$$

$$= \frac{500}{5}$$

$$= 100\,N/mm^2$$

Table 5.2: Tensile test results for a steel specimen

Force (kN)	8	14	19	24	29	36
Extension (μm)	15	28	38	47	58	72

Activity: Mechanical properties of metals

1 Table 5.2 shows the results of an experiment on a steel specimen with a gauge length of 40 mm and a cross-sectional area of 100 mm².

a) Plot a graph of force versus extension from the data in Table 5.2.

b) Determine Young's modulus for the specimen.

2 A brass bar 300 mm long with a diameter of 30 mm is subjected to a compressive force of 40 kN. Assuming Young's modulus for brass to be 100 GN/m² calculate the change in length of the bar.

(a)

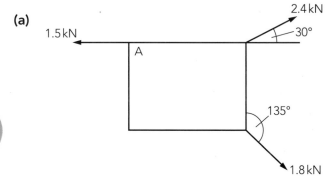

(b)

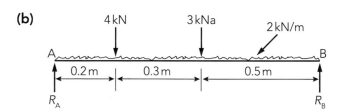

(c)

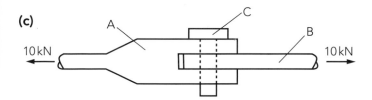

(d)

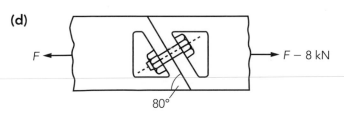

Figure 5.25: Diagrams for assessment activity 5.1

Assessment activity 5.1

P1 Figure 5.25a shows a uniform rectangular plate supported in a vertical plane by forces acting at three corners of the plate. The plate is 2 m × 1.5 m and has a mass of 200 kg.

a) Calculate the magnitude, direction and sense of the resultant force.

b) Specify the magnitude, direction and sense of the equilibrant force.

c) Calculate the position of the resultant force with respect to the corner A.

P2 Calculate the support reactions for the simply supported beam shown in Figure 5.25b.

P3 Figure 5.25c shows a shackle joint subjected to a tensile load. The connecting rods, A and B, are made from steel and the pin C is made from brass. Young's modulus is 210 GPa for steel and 100 GPa for brass. The shear modulus is 140 GPa for steel and 70 GPa for brass. The smallest diameter of the connecting rods A and B is 25 mm and the diameter of the pin C is 20 mm.

a) Calculate the maximum direct stress in the connecting rods.

b) Calculate the maximum direct strain in the connecting rods.

c) Calculate the change in length of a 500 mm length of the connecting rod.

d) Calculate the shear stress in the pin.

e) Calculate the shear strain in the pin.

M1 The diameter of the bolt shown for the angled joint in Figure 5.25d is 12 mm. It is made from a material with a tensile strength of 500 MPa and a shear strength of 300 MPa.

a) Determine the operational factor of safety in tension.

b) Determine the operational factor of safety in shear.

Grading tips

You must not simply provide numerical answers. You should demonstrate your method of working. An engineer should be able to interpret your calculations easily (if asked) to check for errors.

Ensure that your solutions are clearly presented, that your diagrams are neat and labelled, and that you specify appropriate units.

PLTS

When solving the tasks in the assessment activity, you will be given deadlines to meet. This will require you to organise time and resources, prioritising actions. Having submitted work, ask your tutor to give you feedback. When receiving feedback, you need to show that you can deal with it positively.

Functional skills

If you use an equation editor or spreadsheets to present solutions to the questions you will improve your skills in ICT. When solving questions you will improve your skills in mathematics and English.

5.2 Be able to determine work, power and energy transfer in dynamic engineering systems

In the first section of this unit, we considered the forces acting on static objects. Engineers are also interested in moving objects and in this next section we will introduce some of the basic principles and techniques that are used to understand dynamic systems.

Dynamic systems, by definition, are those that involve the relative movement of several component parts or the movement of a system as a whole. In this section, we will show how displacement, time, velocity and acceleration are related and how you can calculate the work done and the power required to overcome a resistance.

5.2.1 Kinetic parameters

The parameters that you will be considering in this section are time, displacement, initial velocity, final velocity, uniform linear acceleration and gravitational acceleration.

- Time (t) is the period over which you are considering the motion of a body.
- Displacement (s) is the distance travelled by a body in that period.
- Initial velocity (u) is the velocity that a body has at the start of the period over which you are considering its motion.
- Final velocity (v) is the velocity that a body has at the end of the period over which you are considering its motion.
- Uniform linear acceleration (a) is the constant acceleration that a body is subjected to. Note that this can be positive or negative. If a body is slowing down, it is subject to negative acceleration (which is called deceleration).
- Gravitational acceleration (g) is the acceleration that a body has when subjected to the effects of gravity.

5.2.2 Kinetic principles

Four equations are require to solve problems on uniform motion. These are developed from first principles here. The first equation is derived from the definition of the average velocity. This is simply the distance travelled divided by the time taken. If

the motion is uniform – that is, the system we are interested in is subject to constant acceleration – then the average velocity is equal to the sum of the initial velocity and the final velocity divided by two. We can express this mathematically as follows:

$$\text{Average velocity} = \frac{\text{Distance travelled}}{\text{Time taken}}$$

$$\frac{u+v}{2} = \frac{s}{t}$$

$$s = \left(\frac{u+v}{2}\right)t \qquad (1)$$

The second equation is derived from the definition of acceleration:

$$\text{Acceleration} = \frac{\text{Change of velocity}}{\text{Time taken}}$$

$$a = \frac{v-u}{t}$$

$$v = u + at \qquad (2)$$

Now substitute equation (2) in equation (1):

$$s = \left(\frac{u+u+at}{2}\right)t$$

$$s = \left(\frac{2u+at}{2}\right)t$$

$$s = \left(u+\frac{at}{2}\right)t$$

$$s = ut + \frac{at^2}{2} \qquad (3)$$

Now rewrite equation (2) as:

$$t = \frac{v-u}{a}$$

Substitute in equation (1):

$$s = \left(\frac{u+v}{2}\right)\left(\frac{v-u}{a}\right)$$

$$s = \frac{uv - u^2 + v^2 - uv}{2a}$$

$$s = \frac{v^2 - u^2}{2a}$$

$$2as = v^2 - u^2$$

$$v^2 = u^2 + 2as \qquad (4)$$

There are five variables in these equations: distance travelled, initial velocity, final velocity, acceleration and time. If you are given any three of these variables in a problem, you will be able to use one or more of the equations to determine the values of the other two variables.

Worked examples: Uniform motion problems

1 If a train accelerates at 1.5 m/s², calculate the time taken to increase its velocity from rest to 50 km/h and the distance travelled in this time.

First, express the known variables in mathematical notation:

$a = 1.5 \, \text{m/s}^2$

$u = 0 \, \text{m/s}$

$v = 50 \, \text{km/h}$

$t = ?$

$s = ?$

All variables must be in compatible units, so express the final velocity in m/s:

$v = 50\dfrac{\text{km}}{\text{h}}\left[\dfrac{1000\,\text{m}}{1\,\text{km}}\right]\left[\dfrac{1\,\text{h}}{3600\,\text{s}}\right] = 13.9 \, \text{m/s}$

To find the time taken (t) to accelerate to 50 km/h, you need an equation that has not got s in it. Use equation (2):

$v = u + at$

$t = \dfrac{v - u}{a}$

$= \dfrac{13.9 - 0}{1.5} = 9.3 \text{ seconds}$

To find the distance travelled (s), you need an equation that has not got t in it. Use equation (2):

$v^2 = u^2 + 2as$

$s = \dfrac{v^2 - u^2}{2a}$

$s = \dfrac{13.9^2 - 0^2}{2 \times 1.5} = 64.4 \, \text{m}$

2 A link in a mechanism is brought to rest with uniform deceleration from a velocity of 10 m/s over a distance of 400 mm. Calculate the deceleration and the time taken.

$v = 0 \, \text{m/s}$

$u = 10 \, \text{m/s}$

$s = 0.4 \, \text{m}$

To find a you need an equation that has not got t in it. Use equation (4):

$v^2 = u^2 + 2as$

$a = \dfrac{v^2 - u^2}{2s}$

$a = \dfrac{0^2 - 10^2}{2 \times 0.4} = -125 \, \text{m/s}^2$

To find t you need an equation that has not got a in it. Use equation (1):

$s = \left(\dfrac{u + v}{2}\right)$

$t = \dfrac{2s}{u + v}$

$t = \dfrac{2 \times 0.4}{10 + 0} = 0.08 \text{ seconds}$

Activity: Uniform motion problems

1 A car accelerates from rest with uniform acceleration to a velocity of 60 km/h in a distance of 40 m. Calculate the acceleration and the time taken.

2 A vehicle travels 80 m in 10 seconds whilst being accelerated at 0.6 m/s². Calculate its initial and final velocities.

Key terms

Inertia the resistance of a body that must be overcome in order to accelerate it. The accelerating force must overcome the inertia force.

5.2.3 Dynamic parameters

Now let's consider four other parameters of dynamic systems that are of interest to engineers. These are force, work, energy and power. A force is required to do work, energy is the capacity to do work and power is the rate of doing work.

Consider a vehicle which is moving along a road, the force acting between the wheels and the road that causes the motion is called the tractive effort (F). A braking force (F_b) may be applied to slow the vehicle down, and this acts in addition to any frictional resistances (F_f) that may be present. The **inertia** of the vehicle must be overcome if the vehicle is to accelerate (that is, to increase or decrease its velocity) and this will require an inertia force (F_I). (Remember that if a body is decelerating, for the purpose of calculation this is regarded as negative acceleration.) The weight of the vehicle (F_g) may also need to be considered, in which case you will need to take account of the acceleration due to the effect of gravity. Figure 5.26 represents these forces on a diagram.

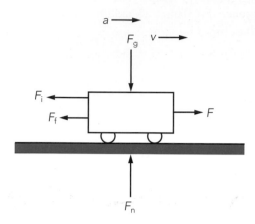

Figure 5.26: Forces acting on a moving vehicle

When the vehicle is moving it will have acquired **momentum** (mv), which is the product of its mass (m) and its velocity (v). If the mass remains constant, then a change in momentum can only occur if the vehicle accelerates.

If the vehicle travels with a constant velocity, then the work done (W) is given by the product of the force (F) causing the movement and the distance moved in the direction of the applied force (s). It is measured in joules (denoted by the symbol J).

$$W = Fs \text{ (J)}$$

The power (P) required is the rate of doing work (the work done divided by the time taken), and the instantaneous power is the product of force and velocity. Power is measured in watts (denoted by the symbol W).

$$P = \frac{W}{t} = \frac{Fs}{t} = Fv \text{ (W)}$$

The weight (F_g) of a body is given by the product of its mass (m) and the acceleration due to the effect of the gravitational field (g).

$$F_g = mg$$

The gravitational potential energy (E_p) is the energy possessed by a body by virtue of its position above a set reference point or datum. It is the product of its weight (F_g) and the vertical height (h) above the datum.

$$E_p = mgh = F_g h \text{ (J)}$$

Kinetic energy (E_k) is the energy possessed by a body by virtue of its velocity.

$$E_k = \tfrac{1}{2} mv^2 \text{ (J)}$$

Key terms

Momentum a measure of the impetus of a moving object. Its value is calculated by multiplying the mass of the object by its velocity.

5.2.4 Dynamic principles

Newton's laws of motion are three rules of physics that are extremely important for understanding dynamic systems. Developed by the eminent mathematician Sir Isaac Newton, these laws state that:

- a body continues in its present state of rest, or in uniform motion in a straight line, unless it is acted upon by an external force
- the rate of change of momentum of a body is directly proportional to the resultant force that is producing the change
- to every acting force there is an equal and opposite reacting force.

We can express Newton's second law – that the rate of change of momentum of a body is directly proportional to the resultant force producing the change – as an equation:

$$F = \left(\frac{mv_2 - mv_1}{t}\right)k$$

Where k is the constant of proportionality. We can express this equation in terms of acceleration:

$$F = m\left(\frac{v_2 - v_1}{t}\right)k$$

$$F = mak$$

In SI units, the constant k = 1. So:

$F = ma$

If a body is accelerating, it will be subjected to an out-of-balance force. By imposing a force equal in magnitude and direction but opposite in sense on the force system, you would in effect balance the forces enabling you to put the body in equilibrium. This is called d'Alembert's principle.

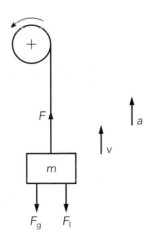

Figure 5.27: A body being raised by a pulley

Consider a body attached to a cord, which is in turn moving over a pulley causing the body to be raised (see Figure 5.27). If the body is moving with a constant velocity, then the weight (F_g) of the body would be equal to the force (F) in the cord. However, if the body is accelerating, the force in the cord would be greater than the weight of the body. The amount by which it would be greater is given by the inertia force (F_I), which is the product of the body's mass (m) and the acceleration (a). Hence:

$$F_g = mg$$
$$F_I = ma$$
$$F = F_g + F_I$$

The principle of the conservation of momentum is that the total amount of momentum in a system remains constant unless it is acted upon by an externally applied force. Consider two bodies moving in the same direction with different velocities which collide and then move together (see Figure 5.28).

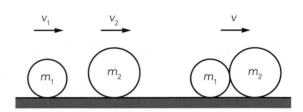

Figure 5.28: Illustrating the principle of the conservation of momentum

Since there are no externally applied forces, the momentum before the impact must be the same as the momentum after the impact. Hence:

$$m_1 v_1 + m_2 v_2 = (m_1 + m_2) v$$

Let's consider how these principles can be used to solve a practical problem. Suppose a car of mass 1.2 t is accelerated uniformly from rest to a speed of 60 km/h in 5 seconds on a level road. The total resistance to motion, which can be assumed to be constant, is 300 N. Calculate the tractive effort and the change in momentum of the car. Figure 5.29 shows this diagrammatically.

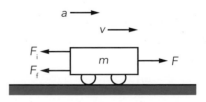

Figure 5.29: Forces acting on a car accelerating from rest

First, write down the variables that you know, remembering to convert all values into a compatible set of units.

$$m = 1.2 \times 10^3 \, \text{kg}$$

$$u = 0 \, \text{m/s}$$

$$v = 60 \, \frac{\text{km}}{\text{h}} \left[\frac{1000 \, \text{m}}{1 \, \text{km}}\right] \left[\frac{1 \, \text{h}}{3600 \, \text{s}}\right] = 16.7 \, \text{m/s}$$

$$t = 5 \, \text{s}$$

$$F_{\text{f}} = 300 \, \text{N}$$

To find F we need to calculate F_{I}. From Newton's second law of motion:

$$F_{\text{I}} = ma$$

So we must calculate a:

$$a = \frac{v - u}{t}$$

$$a = \frac{16.7 - 0}{5} = 3.34 \, \text{m/s}^2$$

Hence:

$$F_{\text{I}} = ma$$

$$F_{\text{I}} = 1.2 \times 10^3 \times 3.34 = 4.01 \times 10^3 \, \text{N}$$

$$F = F_{\text{f}} + F_{\text{I}}$$

$$F = 300 + 4010 = 4310 \, \text{N}$$

The change in momentum is a straightforward calculation:

$$\Delta mv = m(v - u)$$

$$\Delta mv = 1.2 \times 10^3 (16.7 - 0) = 20.04 \times 10^3 \, \text{kgm/s}$$

Note that you use the lower case Greek letter delta (δ) to represent a small-scale change in some quantity and the upper case delta (Δ) to represent a large-scale change in some quantity.

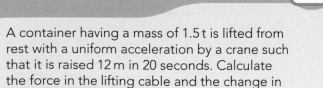

Activity: Momentum

A container having a mass of 1.5 t is lifted from rest with a uniform acceleration by a crane such that it is raised 12 m in 20 seconds. Calculate the force in the lifting cable and the change in momentum of the container.

First, a quick recap. Work is done on a body if it is moved through a distance by a force. The magnitude of the work done is given by the product of the force and the distance moved in the direction of the applied force. The unit of work is the joule (J) – this is defined as the work done by a force of one newton moving through a distance of one metre. In mathematical terms:

$$\text{Work} = \text{Force} \times \text{Distance}$$

$$W = Fs \, \text{(J)}$$

Energy is the capacity to do work and is measured in the same units as work (joules). There are many different forms of energy, such as chemical energy, electrical energy, thermal energy and nuclear energy. In this unit, we are concerned with two types of mechanical energy: gravitational potential energy (E_{p}) and kinetic energy (E_{k}).

The gravitational potential energy (E_{p}) of a body is the energy it posses by virtue of its height (h) above a set datum. If a body of mass (m) is lifted through a height (h), then work is done on it so that:

$$\text{Work} = \text{Force} \times \text{Distance}$$

$$W = Fs \, \text{(J)}$$

The work done is stored in the body in the form of gravitational potential energy, so that:

$$E_{\text{p}} = mgh \, \text{(J)}$$

The kinetic energy of a body is the energy it possesses by virtue of its motion. A body set in motion by a force doing work on it acquires kinetic energy, which enables it to do work against a resisting force before being brought to rest. Consider a body of mass (m) uniformly accelerated from rest to a velocity (v) over a distance (s).

$$\text{Work} = \text{Force} \times \text{Distance}$$

$$W = F_{\text{I}}s = mas$$

But we know from equation (4) (see page 164) that:

$$v^2 = u^2 + 2as$$

$$\therefore \quad a = \frac{v^2 - u^2}{2s}$$

And:

$$W = m\left(\frac{v^2 - u^2}{2s}\right)s$$

$$= \frac{m}{2}(v^2 - u^2)$$

This represents the change in the kinetic energy of the body, so that:

$$E_{\text{k}} = \frac{mv^2}{2}$$

The principle of the conservation of energy is that energy cannot be created or destroyed, but it can be changed from one form to another. Energy (E) can be used to do work (W). Power (P) is the rate of doing work (*W/t*), or the rate of change of energy (Δ*E/t*). The unit of power is the watt (W). Hence:

$$\text{Power} = \frac{\text{Work}}{\text{Time}} = \frac{\text{Force} \times \text{Distance}}{\text{Time}}$$

$$= \text{Force} \times \text{Velocity}$$

$$P = \frac{W}{t} = \frac{Fs}{t} = Fv \text{ (W)}$$

Another way of expressing power is:

$$\text{Power} = \frac{\text{Change of Energy}}{\text{Time}}$$

$$P = \frac{\Delta E}{t} \text{ (W)}$$

Activity: Dynamic systems

1 Calculate the constant braking force required to stop a car having a mass of 800 kg travelling at 90 km/h in a distance of 40 m.

2 Determine the distance that a car developing 20 kW will travel along a level road in 60 s if it has to overcome a total resistance of 500 N.

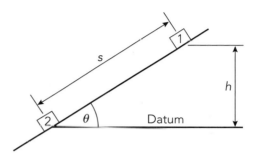

Figure 5.30: A crate on an incline

Worked examples: Dynamic systems

1 A crate with a mass of 100 kg is being hauled up an incline of 30° when the cable breaks. If there is a constant frictional resistance of 200 N between the crate and the plane, calculate the velocity of the crate after it has slipped 6 m down the incline.

It is useful to draw a diagram to illustrate this scenario (see Figure 5.30), and then to establish the known variables.

$m = 100 \text{ kg}$

$\theta = 30°$

$F_f = 200 \text{ N}$

$s = 6 \text{ m}$

Calculate *h* using basic trigonometry:

$$\sin\theta = \frac{h}{s}$$

$$h = s\sin\theta$$

$$= 6\sin 30 = 3 \text{ m}$$

Using the principle of conservation of energy, we have:

$$E_{p1} + E_{k1} = E_{p2} + E_{k2} + W_{f1-2}$$

But:

$$E_{k1} = F_{p2} = 0$$

So:

$$E_{p1} = E_{k2} + W_{f1-2}$$

$$mgh_1 = \frac{mv^2}{2} + F_{f1-2}\, s$$

$$v = \sqrt{\frac{2}{m}\left(mgh_1 - F_f s\right)}$$

$$= \sqrt{\frac{2}{100}(100 \times 9.81 \times 3 - 200 \times 6)}$$

$$= 5.9 \text{ m/s}$$

2 A pump is to raise 100 l of water a height of 12 m in 10 s. Calculate the power required assuming that 1 l of water has a mass of 1 kg.

$m = 100 \text{ kg}$

$h = 12 \text{ m}$

$t = 10 \text{ s}$

So:

$$P = \frac{Fs}{t}$$

$$= \frac{100 \times 9.81 \times 12}{10} = 1177 \text{ W}$$

Case study: Amanda

Amanda is a gap year engineering student who is working as a volunteer in a developing country. She has been asked to research and write a report for her sponsor on suitable pumps that could be used to raise water from a well in a village location.

Discuss the calculations that she would have to make when assessing the suitability of pumps for this project.

Assessment activity 5.2

P4 A railway wagon of mass 20 t is moving along a level track at 10 km/h when it collides and couples together with a second wagon of mass 25 t moving in the same direction at 5 km/h. If the two wagons couple together after the impact, what would be their common velocity?

P4 A crate having a mass of 500 kg is lifted from rest with a uniform acceleration by a crane such that after 5 s it has a velocity of 8 m/s. Calculate the tension in the lifting cable.

P4 A train of mass 250 t starts from rest and accelerates up an incline of 1 in 100 attaining a speed of 45 km/h after travelling 250 m. If the frictional resistance to motion is constant at 30 kN, calculate the work done by the train's engine using the principle of conservation of energy.

M2 A hammer of mass 100 kg falls 4 m on to a pile of mass 300 kg and drives it 80 mm into the ground.

a) Calculate the loss of energy on impact.

b) Calculate the work done by the resistance of the ground.

c) Calculate the average resistance to penetration.

D1 A motor vehicle having a mass of 0.8 t is at rest on an incline of 1 in 8 (sine) when the brakes are

released. The vehicle travels 30 m down the incline against a constant frictional resistance to motion of 100 N/t where it reaches the bottom of the slope.

a) Using the principle of conservation of energy, calculate the velocity of the vehicle at the bottom of the incline.

b) Using an alternative method that does not involve a consideration of energy, calculate the velocity of the vehicle at the bottom of the incline.

c) Discuss the merits of the two methods you have used for parts a) and b) of this question. Justify the use of an energy method for these types of problems.

Grading tips

You must not simply provide numerical answers. You should demonstrate your method of working. An engineer should be able to interpret your calculations easily (if asked) to check for errors.

Ensure that your solutions are clearly presented, that your diagrams are neat and labelled, and that you specify appropriate units.

PLTS

In solving the questions in your assignments, you will need to select the appropriate formulae and develop your solutions. This will show that you can identify questions to answer and problems to resolve. When completing these questions you will be evaluating the relevance and value of the given information. The final task for assessment activity 5.2 requires you to try out alternatives or new solutions and follow ideas through.

5.3 Be able to determine the parameters of fluid systems

There are many examples where engineers have been called upon to design a means of containing or transporting fluid materials. In this section we will show how the density of a fluid affects the force that it will exert on a plane surface. You will learn how to calculate the density of a fluid and how to determine whether an object immersed in the liquid will float or sink, and how to calculate the flow characteristics of a fluid being transported through pipes.

5.3.1 Thrust on a submerged surface

If you have ever dived down into a pool of water, you may have experienced the sensation that your hearing has changed. Our ears are very responsive to changes in pressure, and your ears are sensing an increase in pressure as you dive deeper.

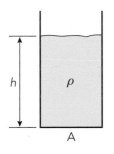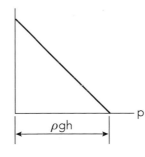

Figure 5.31: The pressure gradient in a column of liquid

Consider a column of liquid having a vertical height (h), cross-sectional area (A) and density (ρ) (Figure 5.31). We can determine equations for density and pressure from first principles.

$$\text{Density} = \frac{\text{Mass}}{\text{Volume}}$$

$$\rho = \frac{m}{V}$$

We can use this to obtain the force exerted by the liquid due to gravity:

$$m = \rho V = \rho Ah$$

$$\text{Weight} = \text{Mass} \times \text{Gravity}$$

$$F_g = mg = \rho Ahg$$

We can now obtain an equation for pressure:

$$\text{Pressure} = \frac{\text{Force}}{\text{Area}}$$

$$p = \frac{F_g}{A} = \frac{\rho Ahg}{A}$$

$$p = \rho gh$$

This is the hydrostatic pressure in the liquid. If the density of the liquid (ρ) and gravity (g) are constants, the hydrostatic pressure will be directly proportional to the depth of the liquid.

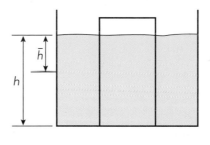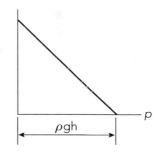

Figure 5.32: A rectangular plane surface immersed vertically in a liquid

Consider now the thrust on one side of a rectangular plane surface immersed vertically in a liquid (see Figure 5.32).

Since the pressure increases uniformly from zero at the free surface to ρgh at the lowest edge the average pressure (p_{av}) is half the maximum pressure. Hence:

$$p_{av} = \frac{\rho gh}{2} = \rho g\bar{h}$$

Where $\bar{h}$ is the vertical depth of the **centroid** of the wetted area below the free surface.

The hydrostatic thrust (F), acting on the plate, is therefore:

$$F = p_{av}A = \rho gA\bar{h}$$

The position at which the hydrostatic thrust (F) acts due to the pressure from the liquid is called the centre of pressure. For a rectangular plane surface immersed vertically in a fluid, the distance of the centre of pressure from the free surface is:

$\frac{2}{3}h$

Note that the free surface of a liquid is always the datum from which the depth is measured.

Activity: Hydrostatic thrust

A storage tank 2 m wide has a vertical partition across its width. One side of the partition is filled with oil with a density of 900 kg/m³ to a depth of 1.8 m, and the other is filled with oil with a density of 750 kg/m³ to a depth of 0.9 m. Find the resultant hydrostatic thrust on the partition.

Worked example: Hydrostatic thrust

An oil tank with vertical sides is 3 m wide and contains oil with a density of 800 kg/m³ to a depth of 1.8 m. Calculate the hydrostatic thrust on the side of the tank and its position above the bottom of the tank.

So we know:

$w = 3\,m$

$\rho = 800\,kg/m^3$

$h = 1.8\,m$

Apply the formula for hydrostatic pressure:

$F = \rho g A \bar{h} = \rho g w h \bar{h}$

$F = 800 \times 9.81 \times 3 \times 1.8 \times \frac{1.8}{2} = 38.1 \times 10^3\,N$

Let y equal the height above the bottom of the tank at which the hydrostatic thrust acts then:

$y = \frac{h}{3}$

$y = \frac{1.8}{3} = 0.6\,m$

5.3.2 Immersed bodies

Archimedes' principle states that a body totally or partially submerged in a **fluid** displaces a volume of fluid that weighs the same as the apparent loss in weight of the body.

Consider a body suspended by a cord immersed in two fluids (see Figure 5.33). In the case of the gas, the upward force exerted by the cord is balanced by the other forces acting on the body. Hence:

$F_1 = F_g = mg = (\rho V g)_{body}$

$F_2 = F_g - F_{up} = (\rho V g)_{body} - (\rho V g)_{fluid}$

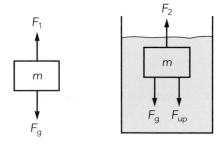

Figure 5.33: A body suspended by a cord immersed in a gas and a liquid

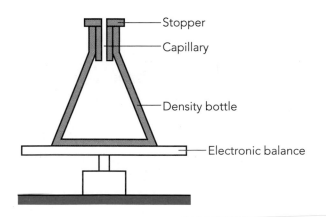

Figure 5.34: A relative density bottle

Key terms

Fluid any material in liquid or gas form.

The density of liquids can be found using a relative density (or specific gravity) bottle like the one shown in Figure 5.34. It can be used to determine the density of an oil. First, the mass of the bottle is determined by weighing it on an electronic balance. The bottle is now filled with pure water and its mass is determined by weighing the filled bottle on the electronic balance. The mass of the pure water can be easily calculated by subtraction. (Note that the mass of the pure water could be determined directly, if the electronic balance is set to zero with the empty bottle on the scales.) The bottle is now filled with the oil and its mass is determined in the same way.

Now, since the volume (V) is the same for the water and the oil, we know that:

$$\rho_{water} = \frac{m_{water}}{V}$$

$$\rho_{oil} = \frac{m_{oil}}{V}$$

So:

$$V = \frac{m_{water}}{\rho_{water}} = \frac{m_{oil}}{\rho_{oil}}$$

$$\rho_{oil} = \frac{\rho_{water}\, m_{oil}}{m_{water}}$$

The relative density (d) of a substance is defined as the density of the substance compared to the density of pure water. Hence, providing we have equal volumes of oil and water:

$$d_{oil} = \frac{\rho_{oil}}{\rho_{water}} = \frac{m_{oil}}{m_{water}}$$

Note that relative density is sometimes referred to as specific gravity, but relative density is the preferred term.

Worked example: Immersed bodies

A block of wood 1.8 m long, 300 mm wide and 200 mm thick floats in sea water. The sea water has a density of 1020 kg/m³, and 150 mm of the block of wood is below the free surface. Calculate the density and the mass of the wood.

We know by Archimedes' principle:

$$F_2 = F_g - F_{up} = (\rho V g)_{wood} - (\rho V g)_{sea\ water\ displaced}$$

But the block of wood is floating $F_2 = 0$, so:

$$F_g = F_{up}$$

$$(\rho V)_{wood} = (\rho V)_{sea\ water\ displaced}$$

So:

$$\rho_{wood} = \frac{(\rho V)_{sea\ water\ displaced}}{V_{wood}}$$

$$= \frac{1020 \times 1.8 \times 300 \times 10^{-3} \times 150 \times 10^{-3}}{1.8 \times 300 \times 10^{-3} \times 200 \times 10^{-3}}$$

$$= 765\ \text{kg/m}^3$$

$$m = (\rho V)_{sea\ water\ displaced}$$

$$= 1020 \times 1.8 \times 300 \times 10^{-3} \times 150 \times 10^{-3}$$

$$= 82.6\ \text{kg}$$

Case study: Tom

Tom works in a brewery. The specific gravity is an important characteristic of the beer and it must be monitored frequently. He has been asked to research different methods of determining the specific gravity of liquids. Discuss where he might look to find the required information. What method of determining the specific gravity would you recommend?

Activity: Immersed bodies

1 A submarine floats in sea water with a density of 1025 kg/m³. If its total volume is 2000 m³ and 80% of its volume is submerged, calculate the mass of the submarine.

2 Define the terms specific gravity/relative density. Explain how you would use a relative density bottle to determine the density of a liquid.

5.3.3 Flow characteristics of a gradually tapering pipe

Figure 5.35 shows the flow of a fluid through a gradually tapering pipe. For the purposes of investigating its flow characteristics, we shall assume that this is an incompressible fluid – that is, the volume of a fluid cannot be reduced by compression. For the continuity of flow of an incompressible fluid, the volumetric flow rate, the mass flow rate and the density of the fluid are assumed to be constant.

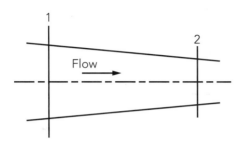

Figure 5.35: A tapering pipe

The rate of change of a quantity is defined as the change in the quantity divided by the time for the change to take place. In equations, this is often shown by placing a dot above the symbol for the quantity.

In our analysis of the tapering pipe, we are interested in the volumetric flow rate and the mass flow rate of the fluid. These are given by:

$$\text{Volumetric flow rate} = \frac{\text{Volume}}{\text{Time}}$$

$$\dot{V} = \frac{V}{t} \, (\text{m}^3/\text{s})$$

$$\text{Mass flow rate} = \frac{\text{Mass}}{\text{Time}}$$

$$\dot{m} = \frac{m}{t} \, (\text{kg/s})$$

The volumetric flow rate ($\dot{V}$) and the mass flow rate $\dot{m}$ can now be defined in terms of the velocity (v) of the fluid, the cross-sectional area (A) of the pipe and the density (ρ) of the flowing fluid:

$$\dot{V} = Av \, (\text{m}^3/\text{s})$$

$$\dot{m} = \rho\dot{V} = \rho Av \, (\text{kg/s})$$

Activity: Tapering pipes

Oil with a density of 800 kg/m³ flows through a horizontal pipe having a diameter of 120 mm with a velocity of 6 m/s. Calculate the volumetric flow rate, the mass flow rate and the pipe diameter required if the flow velocity is to be reduced to 3 m/s.

Worked example: Tapering pipes

Sea water with a density of 1020 kg/m³ flows through a horizontal pipe having a diameter of 0.4 m, with a velocity of 3.2 m/s. If the pipe is gradually reduced to a diameter of 0.25 m calculate the volumetric flow rate, the mass flow rate and the velocity of flow after the restriction.

We know:

ρ = 1020 kg/m³

d_1 = 0.4 m

v_1 = 3.2 m/s

d_2 = 0.25 m

First calculate the volumetric flow rate:

$$\dot{V} = A_1v_1 = \frac{\pi d_1^2}{4}v_1$$

$$\dot{V} = \frac{\pi \times 0.4^2 \times 3.2}{4} = 0.4 \, \text{m}^3/\text{s}$$

Then calculate the mass flow rate:

$$\dot{m} = \rho\dot{V}$$

$$\dot{m} = 1020 \times 0.4 = 408 \, \text{kg/s}$$

To calculate the velocity of flow after the restriction, use the fact that the volumetric flow rate is constant.

$$\dot{V} = A_1v_1 = A_2v_2$$

$$v_2 = \frac{\dot{V}}{A_2} = \frac{4\dot{V}}{\pi d_2^2}$$

$$= \frac{4 \times 0.4}{\pi \times 0.25^2} = 8.1 \, \text{m/s}$$

Assessment activity 5.3

P5 A vertical dock gate is 5 m wide and is hinged at 1 m from the base of the dock. The dock has sea water with a density of 1025 kg/m³ to a depth of 7.5 m on one side and fresh water to a depth of 3 m on the other side.

   a) Find the resultant horizontal force.

   b) Determine the overturning moment that the gate hinge has to withstand.

P6 A solid iron cylinder with a diameter of 150 mm, a height of 1 m and a density of 7860 kg/m³ is suspended in fresh water. Calculate the tension in the supporting cable when two-thirds of the volume of the cylinder is submerged.

P7 The diameter of a pipe changes gradually from 150 mm at a point A, 6 m above a datum, to 75 mm at B, 3 m above the datum. The pressure at point

A is 103 kN/m² and the velocity of flow is 3.6 m/s. Neglecting losses, determine the pressure at point B.

D2 Evaluate the methods of determining the density of a solid material and a liquid.

Grading tips

You must not simply provide numerical answers. You should demonstrate your method of working. An engineer should be able to interpret your calculations easily (if asked) to check for errors.

Ensure that your solutions are clearly presented, that your diagrams are neat and labelled, and that you specify appropriate units.

5.4 Be able to determine the effects of energy transfer in thermodynamic systems

The transfer of heat can have a significant affect on the operational characteristics of some engineered components. In this section, we will show how this can be assessed and how you can calculate the amount of heat energy required to complete certain processes. We also introduce the equations that will enable you to determine some properties of gases.

5.4.1 Heat transfer

Temperature is a measure of the kinetic energy of the vibration of the molecules that comprise a substance. It is measured in degrees Celsius (°C). If heat energy is transferred to a substance, this will result in an increase in the kinetic energy of the molecules and a rise in temperature, or a change in the state, of the substance.

A change in the temperature of a substance is associated with a change in the size of the substance. The change in size for a given change in temperature differs for different materials. The amount by which a material changes in length for each degree rise in temperature – known as linear expansivity – is given by the coefficient of linear expansion (α). The units for the coefficient of linear expansion are m/m°C or m/mK, which are shortened to /°C or /K, but these will be the same values since a change of 1°C is the same as a change of 1 K.

The change in length (δ) of a component with an original length (l) subject to a change in temperature (ΔT) is given by this relationship:

$$\delta l = \alpha l \Delta T \text{ (m)}$$

Worked example: The coefficient of linear expansion

A copper pipe 2 m long at 20°C is heated uniformly to 300°C. Calculate the length of the pipe after heating given that the coefficient of linear expansion for the pipe material is 17×10^{-6} /°C.

We are given:

$l = 2\,\text{m}$

$T_1 = 20°\text{C}$

$T_2 = 300°\text{C}$

$\alpha = 17 \times 10^{-6}$ /°C

$\delta l = \alpha l \Delta T$

$ = 17 \times 10^{-6} \times 2 \times (300 - 20) = 9.52 \times 10^{-3}\,\text{m}$

$\phantom{\delta l = 17 \times 10^{-6} \times 2 \times (300 - 20)} = 9.52\,\text{mm}$

Did you know?

When railway lines are joined mechanically, elongated holes are used in the plates to allow for the thermal expansion of the track.

Activity: The coefficient of linear expansion

If a steel rod measures 500 mm at 20°C and 500.48 mm at 100°C, calculate the coefficient of linear expansion for the steel.

Case study: Linda

Linda works in the development laboratory of a company that makes bimetallic strips. Most of the company's products are used in thermal overload trips fitted to domestic appliances such as electric kettles, fires and showers. The company is considering expanding its business and Linda has been asked to investigate other products that its expertise could support. Research other products where knowledge of the thermal expansion of a wide range of materials is important.

If a solid piece of metal is heated, its energy will be increased. This increase of energy will cause the temperature of the metal to rise until it begins to melt. The energy gained by the metal from the continued heating will now be used to change the state of the metal from solid to liquid, and there will be no further rise in temperature until the metal is completely liquid. This process will be repeated during the transformation from the liquid to the gaseous state. Figure 5.36 shows how the temperature (and state) of a substance changes over time with continued heating.

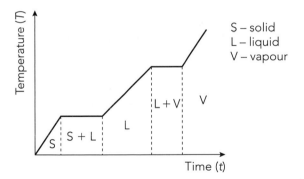

Figure 5.36: How the temperature of a substance changes over time with heating

The heat energy gained or lost by a substance which causes a change in temperature of that substance is called **sensible heat** (that is, it can be sensed by touch and measured with a thermometer). The amount of heat energy required to raise the temperature of a substance depends mainly on the mass and the type of material of which the substance is composed. It will also depend to a lesser extent on the temperature of the substance.

The specific heat capacity (c) of a substance is the amount of heat energy required to raise the temperature of unit mass of the substance by one degree. It is measured in units of J/kg°C or J/kgK. For a given material, the value for the specific heat capacity will be different for the solid, liquid and vapour **phases**.

To measure sensible heat transfer (Q) we use this relationship:

Heat flow = Mass × Specific heat capacity × Change in temperature

$$Q = mc\Delta T \text{ (J)}$$

When a change of state of a substance occurs without a change in temperature, the heat energy required is called **latent heat** (L) and it is measured in units of J/kg. For a given material, the latent heat of fusion, solid to liquid, will be different from the latent heat of vaporisation, liquid to gas.

To measure latent heat transfer (Q) we use this relationship:

Heat flow = Mass × Latent heat

$$Q = mL \text{ (J)}$$

Key terms

Sensible heat heat energy causing a change in temperature of a substance.

Phase the physically distinctive form of a substance – solid, liquid or vapour.

Latent heat heat energy causing a change of state of a substance without a change in temperature.

Worked example: Converting water to steam

Calculate the heat energy to convert 10 kg of water at 20°C to **superheated steam** at 150°C. Take the specific heats of water and steam to be 4.2 kJ/kg°C and 2.1 kJ/kg°C respectively, and the latent heat of vaporisation to be 2260 kJ/kg.

We know:

$$m = 10\,kg$$
$$\Delta T_{water} = 100 - 20 = 80°C$$
$$\Delta T_{steam} = 150 - 100 = 50°C$$
$$c_{water} = 4.2\,kJ/kg°C$$
$$c_{steam} = 2.1\,kJ/kg°C$$
$$L = 2260\,kJ/kg$$

Now apply the formulae. Note that you have to consider three phases: the heat energy to raise the water to boiling point, the heat energy required to change the water to steam, and the heat energy needed to superheat the steam.

$$Q = (mc\Delta T)_{water} + mL + (mc\Delta T)_{steam}$$
$$Q = (10 \times 4.2 \times 80) + (10 \times 2260) + (10 \times 2.1 \times 50)$$
$$= 27.01\,MJ$$

Activity: Calculating the energy required to melt aluminium

Calculate the heat energy to melt a 20 kg aluminium ingot from a temperature of 25°C. Given that the melting temperature of aluminium is 660°C, its specific heat capacity in the solid state is 0.9 kJ/kg°C and its latent heat of fusion is 390 kJ/kg.

Key terms

Superheated steam a colourless (dry) gas at a temperature above the boiling point of the water.

Energy value the amount of potential energy of a specified amount of fuel that is released as heat when the fuel is combusted. So when a fuel is used in a system such as a heat exchanger, the energy value is a measure of the input energy. It is also referred to as the calorific value of a fuel.

The efficiency of any process is the fraction of what you get out of the process divided by what you put in expressed as a percentage. Hence:

$$Efficiency = \frac{Power\ out}{Power\ in} \times 100$$
$$\eta_{th} = \frac{P_{out}}{P_{in}} \times 100$$

If the output and the input take place in the same time, then you can express the efficiency equation in terms of energy:

$$Efficiency = \frac{Energy\ out}{Energy\ in} \times 100$$
$$\eta_{th} = \frac{E_{out}}{E_{in}} \times 100$$

For a heat exchanger, you can express the efficiency equation in terms of heat energy:

$$\eta_{th} = \frac{Q_{out}}{Q_{in}} \times 100$$

Worked example: Heat exchangers

A gas-fired heat exchanger uses gas with an **energy value** of 40 MJ/m³ at a rate of 0.45 m³/h and produces 50 kg/h of water at a temperature of 70°C from feed water at 20°C. Given that 1 l of water has a mass of 1 kg and a specific heat capacity of 4.19 kJ/kg°C calculate the thermal efficiency of the heat exchanger.

We know that:

$$E_f = 40 \text{ MJ/m}^3$$
$$\dot{V}_f = 0.45 \text{ m}^3/\text{h}$$
$$\dot{m}_w = 50 \text{ kg/h}$$
$$T_2 = 70°C$$
$$T_1 = 20°C$$
$$c_w = 4.19 \text{ kJ/kg°C}$$

We can now use this data to calculate rate of energy used by the heat exchanger and the rate of energy output by the exchanger:

$$\dot{Q}_{in} = E_f \times \dot{V}_f$$

$$\dot{Q}_{in} = \frac{40 \times 10^6 \times 0.45}{3600} = 5 \times 10^3 \text{ J/s}$$

$$\dot{Q}_{out} = (\dot{m}c\Delta T)_w$$

$$\dot{Q}_{out} = \frac{50 \times 4.19 \times 10^3 \times (70 - 20)}{3600}$$

$$= 2.9 \times 10^3 \text{ J/s}$$

$$\eta_{th} = \frac{\dot{Q}_{out}}{\dot{Q}_{in}} \times 100$$

$$\eta_{th} = \frac{2.9 \times 10^3}{5.0 \times 10^3} \times 100 = 58\%$$

Activity: Heat exchangers

A gas-fired heat exchanger uses gas with an energy value of 38 MJ/m³, has an output rating of 2 kW and is 65% efficient. Given that 1 l of water has a mass of 1 kg and a specific heat capacity of 4.19 kJ/kg°C, calculate the time needed by the heat exchanger to raise the temperature of 120 l of water from 15°C to 68°C. Also calculate the volume of gas consumed in the process.

scale — or Kelvin scale — has the same increments as the Celsius scale but it starts at absolute zero. So, for example:

$$0 \text{ K} = -273°C$$
$$273 \text{ K} = 0°C$$
$$373 \text{ K} = 100°C$$

Did you know?

The Kelvin scale is named after the Scottish physicist and engineer William Thomson (1824–1907), who took the title Baron Kelvin of Largs when he was ennobled by Queen Victoria.

5.4.2 Thermodynamic process equations

We will now consider temperatures and pressures in more detail. If heat energy is transferred to a substance, this results in an increase in the kinetic energy of the molecules. This causes a rise in temperature, or a change in the state, of the substance (see Figure 5.36). It follows then that if heat energy is extracted from a substance, this will be associated with a fall in the kinetic energy of the molecules of that substance. If you could extract all the energy possessed by the molecules, the temperature of the substance would be absolute zero, which corresponds to approximately −273°C. The absolute temperature

As well as absolute temperature, there is also a concept of absolute pressure. The surface of the earth is covered by a layer of air that is commonly referred to as the earth's atmosphere. Air has mass and it therefore exerts a force on the earth's surface. This generates what is known as atmospheric pressure (p_{atmos}). When in section 5.3.1 we considered how pressure increases with depth in a liquid, we only considered the pressure exerted by the mass of the liquid. Our calculations ignored atmospheric pressure, and we produced a formula for what is called gauge pressure (p_{gauge}).

Absolute pressure (p_{abs}) is the sum of the atmospheric and the gauge pressures. Consider a column of liquid open to the atmosphere, having a vertical height (h), cross-sectional area (A) and density (ρ). From Figure 5.37, you can see that:

$$p_{abs} = p_{atmos} + p_{gauge}$$

Atmospheric pressure varies with height, temperature and the weather. It can affect the results of some types of thermodynamic experiments. In these situations, engineers must take account of atmospheric pressure. For many purposes, they use an average value, called standard atmospheric pressure, of 101 kN/m² or 1.01 b. Water boils at 100°C at standard atmospheric pressure. If the pressure on the free surface of the water is increased, the boiling temperature will also increase.

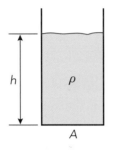
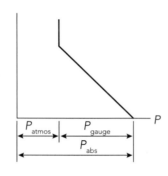

Figure 5.37: Absolute pressure

We will now consider the behaviour of gas when it is allowed to expand or is compressed. If the working temperature of a fluid is well above the temperature at which it vaporises, it is said to behave like a perfect gas. Although this is an ideal that cannot be realised in practice, gases like hydrogen and oxygen behave in a very similar manner to a perfect gas. There are two laws about the properties of a perfect gas that are of particular interest: Boyle's law and Charles' law.

Boyle's law states that provided the temperature of a perfect gas remains constant, then the volume of a given mass of the gas is inversely proportional to the pressure of the gas. We write this mathematically as:

$$p \propto \frac{1}{V}$$

$$\therefore \quad pV = c$$

Charles' law states that provided the pressure of a given mass of a perfect gas remains constant, then the volume of the gas will be directly proportional to the absolute temperature of the gas. Hence:

$$V \propto T$$

$$\frac{V}{T} = c$$

By combining Boyle's and Charles' laws it can be shown that:

$$\frac{pV}{T} = c$$

If the mass of gas involved in the process is constant, then we can write this equation as:

$$\frac{pV}{mT} = \frac{c}{m} = R$$

$$pV = mRT$$

This is known as the characteristic gas equation, where:

p = pressure (N/m²)

V = volume (m³)

m = mass (kg)

R = characteristic gas constant (J/kgK)

T = absolute temperature (K)

Worked example: Thermodynamic systems

1 A compressor with a compression ratio of 8 takes in air at an atmospheric pressure of 1 b and a temperature of 17°C. If the pressure after compression is 9 b, calculate the final temperature of the air.

Start as usual by expressing the provided information in mathematical terms, converting all values into the units used in the characteristic equation.

$$\frac{V_1}{V_2} = 8$$

$$p_1 = 100 \times 10^3 \text{ N/m}^2$$

$$T_1 = 17 + 273 = 290 \text{ K}$$

$$p_2 = 900 \times 10^3 \text{ N/m}^2$$

Applying the characteristic gas equation requires some basic algebra to get an equation for T_2, the parameter we need to find.

$$pV = mRT$$

$$\frac{pV}{T} = mR = c$$

Therefore:

$$\frac{p_1 V_1}{T_1} = \frac{p_2 V_2}{T_2}$$

$$T_2 = \frac{p_2 V_2 T_1}{p_1 V_1 T_2}$$

$$T_2 = \frac{900 \times 10^3 \times 290}{100 \times 10^3 \times 8} = 326 \text{ K} (= 53°C)$$

2 An air compressor receiver has a diameter of 1.5 m and a height of 2 m. The air is at a pressure of 3 b, a temperature of 20°C and the characteristic gas constant is 287 kJ/kgK. Determine the mass of air in the receiver.

We know:

$$p = 3 \times 10^5 \text{ N/m}^2$$

$$d = 1.5 \text{ m}$$

$$h = 2.0 \text{ m}$$

$$T = 273 + 20 = 293 \text{ K}$$

$$R = 287 \text{ kJ/kgK}$$

Applying the characteristic gas equation:

$$pV = mRT$$

$$m = \frac{pV}{RT}$$

$$m = \frac{3 \times 10^5 \times \pi \times 1.5^2 \times 2}{4 \times 287 \times 293} = 12.6 \text{ kg}$$

Activity: Thermodynamic systems

Air is drawn into a compressor at a pressure of 1.01 b with a temperature of 20°C. If the pressure of the air is increased to 12 b and the temperature rises to 115°C calculate the compression ratio of the compressor.

Assessment activity 5.4

P8 The stator of an electric motor winding is to be expansion fitted into its housing. If the diameter of the stator at 20°C is 150.1 mm and the diameter of the housing at 20°C is 150 mm, determine the temperature to which the housing must be raised to facilitate the assembly if the coefficient of linear expansion for the housing material is 12×10^{-6} /°C.

P8 Calculate the heat energy required to convert 5 l of fresh water at 20°C to superheated steam at 150°C. Take the specific heats of water and steam to be 4.19 kJ/kgK and 2.1 kJ/kgK respectively and the latent heat of vaporisation to be 2260 kJ/kg.

P9 Dry steam is compressed isothermally from a pressure of 1 b to 4 b. If the initial volume of the steam is 0.5 m³, calculate the volume of the steam after compression.

P9 The temperature of 1 m³ of air is 20°C and it is compressed to a volume of 0.8 m³ whilst maintaining a constant pressure of 1 b. Calculate the final temperature of the air.

P9 An air compressor operates with a compression ratio of 6 : 1. If the air is at a pressure of 1 b and a temperature of 20°C before compression and the temperature after compression is 200°C what will the final air pressure be.

M3 An oil engine uses fuel oil at the rate of 2.8 l/h and drives a generator with an output of 7.5 kW. If the fuel oil used has an energy value of 46 MJ/kg determine the thermal efficiency of the engine.

M4 A steel rod is heated to 200°C and is then rigidly clamped at both ends and allowed to cool. Determine the temperature at which the rod will break if the tensile strength, coefficient of linear thermal expansion and Young's modulus of elasticity of the steel are 150 MN/m², 12×10^{-6} /°C and 200 GN/m² respectively.

Grading tips

You must not simply provide numerical answers. You should demonstrate your method of working. An engineer should be able to interpret your calculations easily (if asked) to check for errors.

Ensure that your solutions are clearly presented, that your diagrams are neat and labelled, and that you specify appropriate units.

PLTS

In solving the questions, you will need to select the appropriate formulae and develop your solutions. When completing these questions you will be evaluating the relevance and value of the given information.

Mathew Miller

Engineering manager

The company that I work for manufactures valves for the aeronautical industry, and we are a wholly owned subsidiary of a US company. The five design engineers that I manage work in an open-plan office, but I have my own office adjacent to the main work area.

My main function is to ensure that the department operates efficiently. I oversee the distribution of work (and ensure that it is equitable), I chair design meetings, discuss design proposals with the engineers, and check design calculations. I also have to attend health and safety meetings and assist with the implementation of the company's health and safety policy.

I started with the company as an apprentice in 1974. On completion of my apprenticeship I had worked in most departments and achieved BTEC National and Higher Nationals in engineering with good grades. The company then sponsored me to attend university full time to complete an engineering degree. I worked in the design office for two years when I was given the opportunity to go to our US headquarters to train for a further year. On my return to the UK I worked in the design office for a further five years, before I was appointed to my current position of design engineering manager.

My daily routine involves liaising with customers and producing design solutions that will solve valve problems. We have a comprehensive manufacturing base, where the CAD system is linked to the CAM system, and we aim to convert a design problem into a design solution and manufactured sample product in four working days.

The design solutions that I and my team produce involve comprehensive flow calculations, stress calculations, material selection and manufacturing process considerations. I am fortunate in that I was taught basic engineering principles very thoroughly when studying for my BTEC National Certificate. This provided a firm foundation for further engineering studies that were challenging but that I found interesting and stimulating, and have helped me throughout my career.

Think about it!

Mathew has a good understanding of applied science and this has been a significant factor in the development of his career. Could you emulate Mathew's success?

Just checking

1 Describe the difference between a space diagram, a free body diagram and a vector diagram.

2 What three parameters need to be known to fully define a force?

3 Define a moment.

4 Make sure that you know how to apply the four equations for uniform motion.

5 What are the formulae for potential and kinetic energy?

6 What is Archimedes' principle?

7 State Boyle's and Charles' laws.

8 Explain when you might apply the heat transfer equations.

9 State appropriate symbols and units for these parameters: force, stress, moment, momentum, velocity, acceleration, energy, power, density, temperature, pressure, work and Young's modulus.

edexcel :::

Assignment tips

- When solving force system problems graphically, the free body and vector diagrams should be drawn on the same page. No attempt should be made on the free body diagram to represent the force magnitudes to scaled lengths: they should, however, be drawn at the correct angles. The scale for a vector diagram should be chosen to make the best use of the available space. It is often easier to project lines from a free body diagram using a set square and a rule rather than measuring each time with a protractor.

- Extract the given values in a question and tabulate them assigning appropriate symbols and units. Making a quick sketch will often help you to interpret a question correctly. Work in appropriate units and always give your answer in engineering form and state the units. Neat presentation of your work will make it easier for you to learn and for others to interpret.

- When drawing graphs it is good practice to include a title and avoid writing in the margins. Choose a scale that will make the best use of the available space to plot your values. Specify units for each axis if appropriate. Draw the best straight line through the plotted points if your graph has a linear relationship.

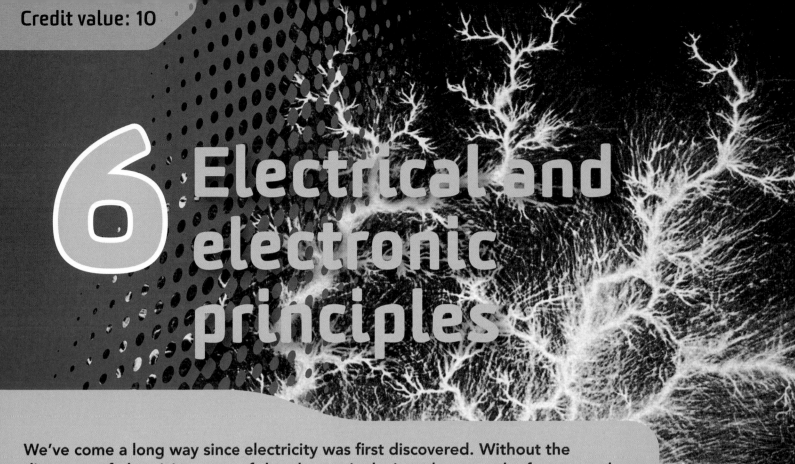

6 Electrical and electronic principles

We've come a long way since electricity was first discovered. Without the discovery of electricity, none of the electronic devices that we take for granted today would ever have been invented. But what is electricity and how does it work? A good understanding of electrical and electronic principles is vital to anyone considering a career in this field or intending further study of electrical and electronic applications. This unit provides you with the necessary underpinning knowledge.

Starting with simple direct current (DC) circuit theory, this unit will develop your understanding of the fundamental principles first discovered by early engineers fascinated by a relatively invisible energy. In fact, their names will probably never be forgotten as many of the terms you will learn bear the names of these pioneers in the electrical field, such as Michael Faraday, Heinrich Hertz and Georg Simon Ohm.

You will then study the concept of capacitance and the various properties and principles of magnetism and electromagnetic induction. The unit concludes by taking you through single-phase alternating current (AC) theory. You will also learn how to use an oscilloscope and multimeter to take DC and AC circuit measurements.

Learning outcomes

After completing this unit you should:

1 be able to use circuit theory to determine voltage, current and resistance in direct current (DC) circuits

2 understand the concepts of capacitance and determine capacitance values in DC circuits

3 know the principles and properties of magnetism

4 be able to use single-phase alternating current (AC) theory.

Assessment and grading criteria

This table shows you what you must do in order to achieve a pass, merit or distinction grade, and where you can find activities in this book to help you produce the required evidence.

To achieve a **pass** grade the evidence must show that you are able to:	To achieve a **merit** grade the evidence must show that, in addition to the pass criteria, you are able to:	To achieve a **distinction** grade the evidence must show that, in addition to the pass and merit criteria, you are able to:
P1 use DC circuit theory to calculate current, voltage and resistance in DC networks **Assessment activity 6.1 page 198**	**M1** use Kirchhoff's laws to determine the current in various parts of a network having four nodes and the power dissipated in a load resistor containing two voltage sources **Assessment activity 6.1 page 198**	**D1** analyse the operation and the effects of varying component parameters of a power supply circuit that includes a transformer, diodes and capacitors **Assessment activity 6.5 page 198**
P2 use a multimeter to carry out circuit measurements in a DC network **Assessment 6.2 page 198**	**M2** evaluate capacitance, charge, voltage and energy in a network containing a series/parallel combination of three capacitors **Assessment activity 6.3 page 207**	**D2** evaluate the performance of a motor and a generator by reference to electrical theory **Assessment activity 6.4 page 219**
P3 compare the forward and reverse characteristics of two different types of semiconductor diode **Assessment activity 6.2 page 198**	**M3** compare the results of adding and subtracting two sinusoidal AC waveforms graphically and by phasor diagram **Assessment activity 6.5 page 224**	
P4 describe the types and function of capacitors **Assessment activity 6.3 page 207**		
P5 carry out an experiment to determine the relationship between the voltage and current for a charging and discharging capacitor **Assessment activity 6.3 page 207**		
P6 calculate the charge, voltage and energy values in a DC network for both three capacitors in series and three capacitors in parallel **Assessment activity 6.3 page 207**		
P7 describe the characteristics of a magnetic field **Assessment activity 6.4 page 219**		
P8 describe the relationship between flux density (B) and field strength (H) **Assessment activity 6.4 page 219**		
P9 describe the principles and applications of electromagnetic induction **Assessment activity 6.4 page 219**		

P10 use single phase AC circuit theory to determine the characteristics of a sinusoidal AC waveform **Assessment activity 6.5 page 224**		
P11 use an oscilloscope to measure and determine the inputs and outputs of a single phase AC circuit **Assessment activity 6.5 page 224**		

How you will be assessed

This unit will be assessed by a variety of theoretical and practical assignments designed to allow you to show your understanding of the unit outcomes. Assignments may focus on the use of circuit theory to calculate current, voltage and resistance in DC networks plus the use of Kirchhoff's laws as well as demonstrating that you can use a multimeter to complete measurements in a DC circuit and compare the forward and reverse characteristics of two types of semiconductor diode.

Your tutor may use a mixed practical and theoretical assignment to test your understanding of capacitors, and a further assignment to assess your understanding of magnetism, the principles and concept of electromagnetic induction and allow you to evaluate the performance of a motor and a generator. A final practical assignment may allow you to demonstrate your understanding of single phase AC theory and your skills at making AC circuit measurements.

You will provide evidence through a combination of practical tasks, written reports and oral answers to questions.

Saj, 17-year-old electronics apprentice

I found this unit really interesting because it involved a lot of practical work as well as theory. I learned how to use a multimeter correctly, how to take measurements and what an oscilloscope is used for.

This unit helped me to understand what electricity is and how we use it. I quickly learned that there was much more to electricity than I had ever realised and although the theory and formulae seemed a bit strange at first, I soon found that it really wasn't that difficult once I'd put my mind to it. I also learned the difference between AC and DC.

Studying capacitors and magnetism was also interesting. We were shown how a capacitor can store a large charge of energy and how magnetism is used to generate electricity. It amazed me that we now understand so much about things you can't see such as electricity and magnetism, and I kept thinking how exciting it must have been for the early engineers when they were making their discoveries. We wouldn't have many of the electronic devices we now use every day if it hadn't been for them.

6.1 Be able to use circuit theory to determine voltage, current and resistance in direct current (DC) circuits

Start up

Conductors and insulators

Not all materials will conduct electricity. Some conduct electricity very well and are therefore called conductors, while others do not conduct any electricity, or hardly any electricity, and these materials are called insulators.

Draw up a list of the various materials you see around you in everyday life, such as different metals, plastics, rubber, glass and wood. There will be many different materials, so try to list as many as you can. For example, consider a light bulb – what is it made of? Try to work out what materials are used in a mains cable. Then look at other common objects, and so on.

Now divide your list into two groups: those materials you think will make good electrical conductors and those materials you think will make good electrical insulators. In small groups, compare and discuss your results. Has anyone listed a material you haven't got in your list?

Can you spot the types of materials that make good conductors and those that make good insulators?

6.1.1 DC circuit theory

In order to understand DC circuit theory, it is important to understand some basic concepts, such as voltage, electrical current and resistance. These concepts can appear difficult at first, because you cannot actually see some of the things you are studying, though you can detect their presence in an electrical circuit using equipment such as a **multimeter**. It is equally important to know something about the function and purpose of the electronic components and devices that are commonly used in circuits. For this unit, you also need to know the various formulae used in DC circuit calculations. Much of this material may be new to you, although you may have come across some aspects such as Ohm's law.

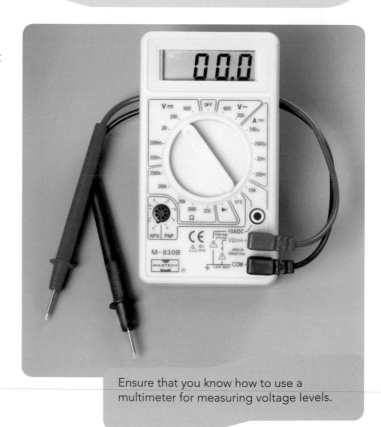

Ensure that you know how to use a multimeter for measuring voltage levels.

Voltage

The energy difference that exists between two points in an electrical or electronic circuit is known as the voltage. The correct name for this energy difference is **potential difference**, but most engineers simply call it voltage. In formulae, voltage is abbreviated to the letter V, and the unit of measurement is the volt. In a circuit, voltage is measured by placing a voltmeter in parallel across a component. In the laboratory or a workshop you would commonly use a multimeter that is set to the appropriate voltage range.

To see how a circuit works and to assess what effect voltage has, let's consider a simple example. Figure 6.1 shows a small electrical circuit consisting of a lamp, a cell (a DC power source) and a switch. The circuit is drawn using standard electrical symbols. For a list of commonly used electrical symbols, see Appendix 2 (page 378).

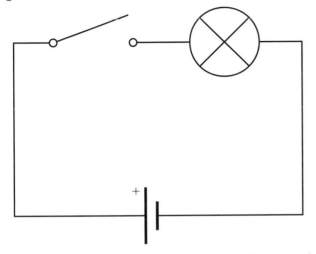

Figure 6.1: An electrical circuit consisting of a cell, lamp and switch

At the moment, nothing much is happening in the circuit in Figure 6.1. The lamp is not lit because no current can flow around the circuit. A complete path from one terminal of the cell to the other is needed for current to flow, but the open switch is breaking the circuit and preventing this from happening. If you were to measure the potential difference across the cell terminals, you would register a voltage. However,

Key terms

Multimeter an instrument that can measure electrical and electronic parameters in AC and DC circuits, such as voltage, current and resistance. Different settings can be selected to provide a range of readings on a single analogue or digital display.

Potential difference the difference in electrical energy (measured in volts) that exists between two points in a circuit. This is usually referred to as voltage.

the circuit is incomplete so the energy source – the cell in this case – is unable to produce a current flow. If the switch is now closed, completing the circuit, a current would now flow. The lamp would now be lit up because of the effect of the current flowing through the filament. By convention, the current is said to flow from the positive terminal of the cell (marked with a + sign) around the circuit to the negative terminal of the cell.

Current is the movement of electrons around a circuit. What actually causes electrons to move – and hence current to flow – is called the electromotive force, often shortened to just emf. The emf of an energy source, such as a cell, battery or generator, is measured in volts. This is because the electromotive force of an energy source is defined as the potential difference (hence voltage) between the terminals when no current is flowing. A voltmeter with a very high resistance must be used to measure emf. This is because when a power cell is connected to a circuit a load is put on it and if a voltmeter with a low resistance is used to measure the emf of the cell, this would have the effect of placing a load on the cell and current would flow, giving an inaccurate emf reading.

Did you know?

The term electromotive force is attributed to the inventor of the battery, Alessandro Volta. His name is immortalised in another term, the volt.

Before looking at DC theory, it is necessary to understand how and why electrons move. In simple terms, all materials consist of atoms, and these in turn consist of protons, neutrons and electrons (see Figure 10.1, page 266). The number of protons, neutrons and electrons that make up an atom varies from one material to another. A neutron has no electrical charge, a proton has a positive electrical charge and an electron has a negative electrical charge. There are equal numbers of protons and electrons in an atom. This means that their positive and negative charges cancel each other out, and the atom is said to be electrically balanced.

As Figure 10.1 shows, protons and neutrons are contained within the nucleus of the atom, while the electrons are arranged in small groups at various distances around the nucleus. The electrons are held in place around the nucleus by a powerful force, but this force gets less powerful as you get further away from the nucleus and it is possible for an atom to lose an electron and become electrically unbalanced. An atom that loses an electron is called an ion – it has become positively charged and is now able to attract an electron from another nearby atom. The electrons that move from one atom to another are called free electrons.

When a voltage is applied across a material, these free electrons all move in the same direction and it is this movement that constitutes a flow of electric current. Therefore, electric current can be defined as the rate of movement of electric charge. It is measured in amperes but identified by the symbol I.

Resistance

An electric current does not flow freely through a circuit but it is subject to an opposition, something that opposes that flow of current. This is called resistance. In formulae, resistance is abbreviated to the letter R. The resistance is a property of whatever is conducting the current. It is measured in ohms (usually abbreviated to the symbol Ω), where 1 ohm is defined as the resistance that will result in a current of 1 amp flowing through an element when a potential difference of 1 volt is connected across the element.

Materials can be divided into two general types – those that are good **conductors** and those that are good **insulators**. This classification is based according to how well they will pass an electric current, or how little resistance they provide to a current. Table 6.2 shows the resistivity for some common materials. Metals have a low resistivity and are usually good conductors; rubber and glass have a high resistivity and are good insulators. There is a third type of material, semiconductors, which have special properties that are exploited in electronic devices such as diodes and transistors. These are considered in Unit 35.

Conductors materials with atoms in which the electrons are loosely bound to the nucleus and can therefore easily move from one atom to another, resulting in good current flow.

Insulators materials with atoms in which the electrons are very firmly bound to the nucleus, resulting in little or no current flow.

Table 6.1: Classification of materials by their resistivity

Classification	Material	Resistivity (at 20°C)
Conductors	Aluminium	$2.82 \times 10^{-8}\,\Omega\,m$
	Brass	$8 \times 10^{-8}\,\Omega\,m$
	Copper	$1.72 \times 10^{-8}\,\Omega\,m$
	Gold	$2.44 \times 10^{-8}\,\Omega\,m$
	Mild steel	$15 \times 10^{-8}\,\Omega\,m$
	Nickel	$6.99 \times 10^{-8}\,\Omega\,m$
	Silver	$1.59 \times 10^{-8}\,\Omega\,m$
Insulators	Glass	$10^{10}\,\Omega\,m$ to $10^{14}\,\Omega\,m$
	Mica	$\geq 10^{11}\,\Omega\,m$
	Paraffin	$10^{17}\,\Omega\,m$
	PVC	$\geq 10^{13}\,\Omega\,m$
	Rubber	approx. $10^{13}\,\Omega\,m$

You will notice in Table 6.1 that the resistivity is given at 20°C. This is because the resistance of a material normally changes with temperature. As a general rule, most conductors increase in resistance as the temperature rises, while insulators tend to decrease in resistance as the temperature rises.

The temperature coefficient of resistance is a measure of the change of resistance as the temperature rises. For any material, it is defined as the increase in the resistance of a 1 Ω resistor made of that material when its temperature is raised by 1°C. For example, using data from Table 6.2, you can see that if you heat a piece of copper that has a resistance of 1 Ω by 1°C, then its resistance would increase by 0.0039 Ω to 1.0039 Ω. If you increase its temperature by 10°C,

Table 6.2: Typical temperature coefficients of resistivity at 0°C

Material	Temperature coefficients of resistivity at 0°C
Aluminium	0.0040 / °C
Copper	0.0039 / °C
Iron	0.0050 / °C
Lead	0.0040 / °C
Silver	0.0038 / °C
Gold	0.0034 / °C
Platinum	0.0039 / °C
Nickel	0.0062 / °C
Mild steel	0.0045 / °C
Tungsten	0.0045 / °C
Carbon	−0.0005 / °C
Silicon	−0.075 / °C
Germanium	−0.048 / °C

then its resistance would increase by ten times the temperature coefficient to 1.039 Ω.

If you know the resistance of a material at 0°C and its temperature coefficient of resistance at 0°C, then its resistance at any other temperature can be calculated using the formula:

$$R_T = R_0 (1 + \alpha_0 T)$$

where R_T is the resistance of the material at temperature T

 R_0 is the resistance of the material at 0°C

 α_0 is the temperature coefficient of resistance of the material at 0°C.

A negative value of temperature coefficient of resistivity means that the resistance of the material falls as the temperature increases. Carbon has this property as do and silicon and germanium, which are both semiconductor materials used in diodes and transistors.

> ### Did you know?
>
> Materials with a negative temperature coefficient have been used in floor heating for about 30 years. The property helps to avoid any excessive local heating and thus prevents damage to the floor or any floor covering such as a carpet.

Let's return to the circuit in Figure 6.1. If the switch is closed to complete the circuit, current will flow through the lamp and a load will also be put across the cell terminals. If a voltmeter is connected across the terminals, you would see that the voltage reading would drop slightly as a load is placed across the cell. This is due to the internal resistance of the cell – in effect, the material of the cell is trying to oppose the flow of current. This internal resistance acts as if it were connected in series with the load resistance.

With no load connected across the cell, and hence no current flowing in the circuit, then the potential difference (V) at the cell terminals is the same as the electromotive force or emf (E) of the cell. In mathematical terms:

$$V = E$$

A load connected across the cell terminals causes a current (I) to flow. By Ohm's law (which we will set out later in this section, see page 193), this produces a voltage drop across the cell terminals due to $I \times r$,

where r is the cell internal resistance. Therefore the potential difference at the cell terminals is:

$$V = E - Ir$$

By rearranging the formula for V, it is possible to calculate the internal resistance of the cell or battery:

$$r = \frac{E - V}{I}$$

Let's consider an example. If a car battery with an off-load emf of 14 volts and an internal resistance of 0.01Ω delivers a current of 100 A when a load is connected, the potential difference across its terminals will reduce to:

$$V = 14 - (100 \times 0.01)$$
$$= 14 - 1 = 13 \text{ volts}$$

This is why you should always use a high resistance voltmeter when measuring the voltage across a cell or battery. This avoids placing a load on the battery and getting a false reading.

> ### Did you know?
>
> In practice, a battery consists of more than one cell. For cells connected in series the total emf is the sum of all the emfs of the individual cells; for cells connected in parallel the total emf is the emf of one cell.

Circuit components

In studying DC circuit theory, you need to understand about some of the basic components that are commonly used in circuits. These include power sources, resistors and diodes.

Cells and batteries provide a simple DC power source. However, when carrying out practical experiments, it is more common to use a stabilised power supply. This is a mains-powered device that produces an accurately regulated DC output. It allows the user to select a range of voltages to suit specific requirements. The unit often has meters on the front panel to monitor both the voltage and the current being delivered, and there is usually some means of limiting the current in case of circuit malfunction.

Resistors are used to limit the current flowing through a circuit. They are available in a wide range of tolerances and values, from a fraction of an ohm to many megohms (10^6 Ω). There are several types of resistors, include wire wound, metal film and carbon

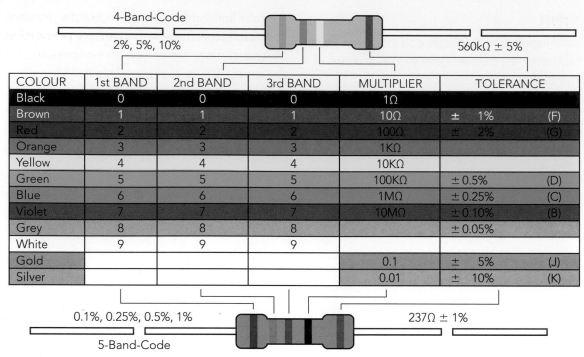

Figure 6.2: The four-band and five-band resistor colour codes

resistors. The choice of which resistor to use in a circuit depends on usage and power handling requirements.

Unlike some other electrical components, the values and tolerances of resistors are not always marked on their casings. This can be for two reasons – first, many resistors are very small and it would be difficult to read the print, and second, the print may burn off due to heat generated in the circuit. Instead, resistors are more commonly identified using a number of coloured bands to represent their ohmic value. Figure 6.2 shows the four-band and five-band resistor colour codes. For example, you should be able to see from the table that a four-band yellow-violet-orange-gold resistor identifies a 47 kΩ resistance with a tolerance of ±5%. A five-band orange-red-green-black-brown resistor identifies a 325 Ω resistance with a tolerance of ±1%.

Diodes are used in many electronic circuits. It is an electronic device that allows current to flow in one direction only. It acts rather like a one-way valve but has no physical moving parts. When diodes are shown in circuit diagrams, the current flows in the direction indicated by the arrow in the diode symbol (see Figure 35.1).

A diode is said to be forward biased when an external voltage is applied in such a way that a current flows through the diode. It is said to be reverse biased when an external voltage is applied the opposite way round so that no current flows through the diode. A full explanation of how diodes work and the different types of diodes used in circuits is given in Unit 35 (see section 35.1.1 on pages 350–353).

The key point to understand for this unit is that connecting a diode one way round in a circuit allows current to flow, while connecting it the other way round prevents current flow. This property is used in a circuit that transforms an AC current to a DC current. The diode (or diodes) only conduct on half cycles of the AC current, and the resulting waveform is then further smoothed using capacitors. The properties and use of capacitors is considered later in this unit.

Activity: Identifying resistors

Write down ten typical values and tolerances of resistors. Use colour pens to draw the five-band and four-band resistors that would have these values.

Now, working in pairs, swap your drawings with a partner and see if you can work out the values of your partner's selection.

Circuit layout

Resistors – and indeed many circuit components – can be connected in series, parallel or in a combination of series and parallel elements.

Figure 6.3 shows three resistors connected in series. Resistors in series are connected along a single path. The key point to note here is that the same current flows through each resistor. Figure 6.4 shows three resistors connected in parallel. Resistors in parallel are connected so that the same voltage is applied to each resistor.

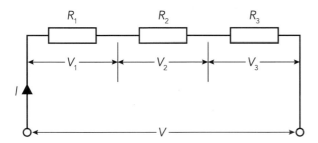

Figure 6.3: Resistors connected in series

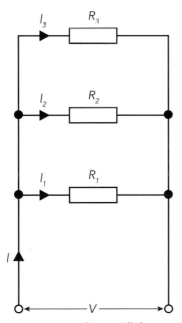

Figure 6.4: Resistors connected in parallel

Many DC circuits will have a combination of series and parallel elements. You will need to know how to determine the current, voltage and resistance in various parts of DC circuits. To do this, we need to introduce some fundamental laws.

Ohm's law, power and energy formulae

The relationship between resistance, voltage and current is called Ohm's law. This states that the current flowing in a circuit is directly proportional to the applied voltage and inversely proportional to the resistance, assuming the temperature remains constant. This is expressed by this formula:

$$I = \frac{V}{R}$$

This formula can easily be transposed to obtain two further equations for resistance and voltage respectively:

$$R = \frac{V}{I}$$

$$V = IR$$

Electrical power (P) is a product of the voltage and current. It is measured in watts (symbol W). Thus:

$$P = VI$$

Using Ohm's law and substituting V in the formula gives:

$$P = I \times R \times I = I^2R$$

Using Ohm's law and substituting I in the formula gives

$$P = V \times \frac{V}{R} = \frac{V^2}{R}$$

Ohm's law is suitable for simple circuits, but for more complex resistor networks Kirchhoff's laws would also be used. There are two laws, the current law and the voltage law.

Kirchhoff's current law states that at any junction of an electric circuit, the total current flowing towards the junction is equal to the total current flowing away from the junction. Therefore if five resistors are connected to a common point, with currents (I_1, I_2 and I_3) flowing through three of the resistors towards the junction and currents (I_4 and I_5) flowing through the other two resistors flowing away from the junction, then:

$$I_1 + I_2 + I_3 = I_4 + I_5$$

So:

$$I_1 + I_2 + I_3 = I_4 + I_5 = 0$$

Kirchhoff's voltage law states that in any closed loop network, the sum of the voltage drops measured around the loop is equal to the sum of the emfs acting in that loop.

6.1.2 DC networks

We can now use Ohm's law and Kirchhoff's laws to calculate the current, voltage and resistance in DC circuits.

Series

When resistors are connected in series, as shown in Figure 6.3, the current I flowing through each resistor is the same. The sum of the voltage across each resistor will be equal to the applied voltage V.

$$V = V_1 + V_2 + V_3$$

Using Ohm's law, we know that $V = IR$, so:

$$V_1 = IR_2, V_2 = IR_2 \text{ and } V_3 = IR_3$$

It follows that:

$$IR = IR_1 + IR_2 + IR_3$$

Dividing by I gives:

$$R = R_1 + R_2 + R_3$$

So for resistors connected in series, the total resistance is obtained by adding the values of the separate resistors together.

Parallel

When resistors are connected in parallel, as shown in Figure 6.4, the voltage V across each one is the same. The sum of the currents flowing through each resistor will be equal to the total circuit current I.

$$I = I_1 + I_2 + I_3$$

Because the voltage is the same across each of the resistors, from Ohm's law we know that:

$$I = \frac{V}{R}$$

So:

$$I_1 = \frac{V}{R_1}, I_2 = \frac{V}{R_2} \text{ and } I_3 = \frac{V}{R_3}$$

It therefore follows that:

$$\frac{V}{R} = \frac{V}{R_1} + \frac{V}{R_2} + \frac{V}{R_3}$$

Dividing by V gives:

$$\frac{1}{R} = \frac{1}{R_1} + \frac{1}{R_2} + \frac{1}{R_3}$$

where R is the total circuit resistance.

This is the formula to use when finding the total resistance of resistors connected in parallel. However, where only two resistors are connected in parallel we can use simple algebra to simplify the equation:

$$\frac{1}{R} = \frac{1}{R_1} + \frac{1}{R_2} = \frac{R_2 + R_1}{R_1 R_2}$$

Therefore:

$$R = \frac{R_1 R_2}{R_1 + R_2}$$

Series and parallel combinations

When resistors are connected in a combination of series and parallel elements, as in Figure 6.5, it is necessary to use a combination of the series and parallel formulae derived above to calculate the various current, voltage and resistor values.

The method is to split the combination network into smaller elements that are either series or parallel circuits, and then apply the appropriate formulae to produce an equivalent single resistor circuit. For example, Figure 6.5 is really a R_1 and R_2 parallel combination in series with a R_3 and R_4 parallel combination. The worked example below shows how you should proceed to calculate a value in this circuit given some parameters.

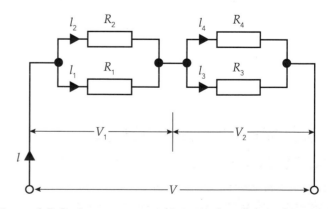

Figure 6.5: Resistors connected in series/parallel combination

Worked example: Resistors in series and parallel

Suppose that we know the value of some of the resistors in Figure 6.5: $R_1 = 5\,\Omega$, $R_2 = 20\,\Omega$, $R_4 = 24\,\Omega$ and the supply voltage (V) is 200 V. If the total power dissipated by the circuit is 2 kW, what is value of R_3?

To tackle this problem, first find the total current I. To do this, use the power formula:

$$P = I \times V$$

Hence:

$$2000 = I \times 200$$

$$I = 10\,A$$

Now find the total circuit resistance (R) using Ohm's law:

$$R = \frac{V}{I} = \frac{200}{10} = 20\,\Omega$$

Now just consider the R_1 and R_2 parallel network and find the equivalent total resistance. We can use the simplified formula for two resistors connected in parallel:

$$\frac{R_1 R_2}{R_1 + R_2} = \frac{5 \times 20}{5 + 20} = \frac{100}{25} = 4\,\Omega$$

Then find the equivalent total resistance of the R_3 and

R_4 parallel network. We can regard the two parallel networks – R_1 and R_2, and R_3 and R_4 – as being in series. We can use the series formula because we have calculated the total circuit resistance and the equivalent total resistance of the R_1 and R_2 parallel network. So the equivalent total resistance of the R_3 and R_4 parallel network is:

$$20 - 4 = 16\,\Omega$$

Finally we can use this value in the simplified formula for two resistors connected in parallel to find of R_3:

$$16 = \frac{R_3 \times 24}{R_3 + 24}$$

The rest is simple mathematics:

$$16(R_3 + 24) = 24R_3$$

$$16R_3 + 384 = 24R_3$$

$$384 = 24R_3 - 16R_3 = 8R_3$$

$$R_3 = 48\,\Omega$$

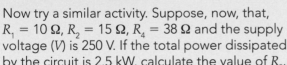

Activity: Resistors in series and parallel

Now try a similar activity. Suppose, now, that, $R_1 = 10\,\Omega$, $R_2 = 15\,\Omega$, $R_4 = 38\,\Omega$ and the supply voltage (V) is 250 V. If the total power dissipated by the circuit is 2.5 kW, calculate the value of R_3.

6.1.3 Measurements in DC circuits

Because the measurements of voltage, current and resistance are often related in electrical circuits, it is convenient to use one rather than three separate instruments for making measurements in DC circuits. A multimeter – its name being derived from its use as a multi-function and a multi-range meter – can measure voltage, current and resistance. Some multimeters also incorporate a facility for checking diodes, transistors and even capacitors.

There are two basic types of multimeter. Analogue meters display values using an indicator on a graduated marked scale, whereas digital multimeters, as the name suggests, use a numerical digital display. A digital multimeter is shown at the beginning of this unit on page 188.

Safe use of a multimeter

Because there may be high voltages present, it is always advisable to take great care when taking circuit measurements using a multimeter. You will be connecting directly on to power sources or points of high voltage. When you are measuring current, the multimeter is connected in line, and the full current will be passing through the equipment.

It is important, therefore, to always ensure that the test leads and probes are in good condition. Check that the insulation is not broken – if it is broken, you could come into direct contact with the current through the test leads or the wiring in the circuit itself.

Before using a multimeter, you must also ensure that the correct mode and range has been selected.

Typically, there is a single control for this purpose. Select one of the modes, which are usually labelled around this control, to determine the parameter you want to measure. For example, you can choose to measure:

- AC voltage
- AC current
- DC voltage
- DC current
- resistance
- transistor current gain.

You can also usually measure capacitance, check the condition of a battery and perform a continuity test by means of a buzzer.

The modes are subdivided into ranges, such as 20 V, 200 V etc. You must always make sure that you select the correct mode and range. An incorrect setting could possibly damage the circuit and the multimeter. Worse still, it could even harm you.

Measurements

The way the multimeter is used depends on the DC measurement that is required.

For voltage measurements, select the correct DC voltage range and connect the red and black test leads across the positive and negative terminals respectively of the component.

For current measurements, first select the correct current range. This is very important because the multimeter must be connected in line with the component. This allows the current flowing through

the component to be measured. Again, the red lead will go to the positive source. Switching to higher ranges selects an appropriate internal shunt resistor.

For resistance measurements, select the appropriate resistance range and then connect test leads across the resistor leads. The display will show the value of the resistor. If the reading is off the scale (analogue meter) or does not give a correct reading (digital display), the value may be beyond the set range. If so, try switching to a higher range.

To test the condition of battery – that is, how charged it is – select the correct battery voltage and connect the multimeter test leads to the battery terminals. In doing so, a small load is applied to simulate the effect of the battery being connected in circuit. This allows a true reading to be obtained. Without this load, a false (and higher) reading would be measured. Again, the red lead goes to the positive terminal and the black lead to the negative terminal of the battery.

To determine the polarity of a diode, select a very low resistance range and connect the test leads to either lead of the diode (see Figure 6.6). A low resistance reading indicates forward biased, while a high resistance reading indicates reverse bias. If the multimeter has a diode check setting in the resistance range, normally identified by the diode symbol, this can be used to actually check the forward voltage drop. To do this, connect the red lead to the anode and the black lead to the cathode of the diode.

You should take a look at any multimeter available in your laboratory or workshop. Make sure that you understand its measurement functions and know how to use the different ranges and settings.

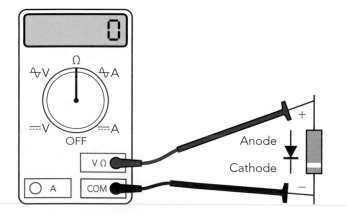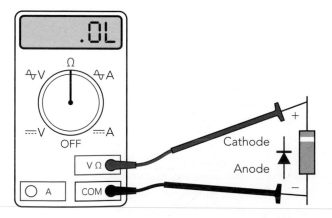

Figure 6.6: Determining forward bias (left) and reverse bias (right) of a diode

Activity: Using a multimeter

Suppose you are about to start work in the circuit testing laboratory of a small company that makes power supplies. You want to show your employer and fellow engineers that you are competent to work with circuit test equipment. You have decided to prepare notes that will help you when using a multimeter.

Produce notes on the safe use of a multimeter with regards to:

- health and safety
- handling
- settings.

Then explain how to use a multimeter to measure:

- DC voltage
- DC current
- resistance
- diode polarity.

The power consumption for this circuit is 12 W
Assume the open circuit voltage is 14.5 volts

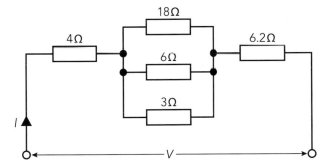

The power consumption for this circuit is 60 W
Assume the open circuit voltage is 32 volts

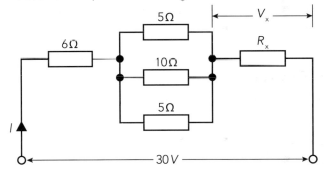

Assume the open circuit voltage is 35.5 volts

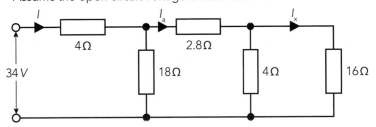

Figure 6.7: Circuit diagrams for P1 tasks of assessment activity 6.1

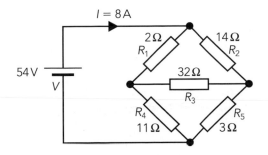

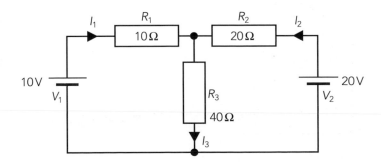

Figure 6.8: Circuit diagrams for M1 task of assessment activity 6.1

Assessment activity 6.1

 BTEC

You work as a trainee test engineer for a small but thriving electrical and electronic design company. Your team has been given the task of designing a bench power supply unit suitable for use in electronics workshops and that will go on sale later in the year.

Your responsibility is to calculate various circuit values of voltage, current and resistance from circuit diagrams and to design a specification prior to testing. These calculated values will later be used in a second assignment for comparison against measured values taken whilst you carry out tests on an initial prototype of the power supply to ensure that it meets the design specification.

The circuit diagrams in Figure 6.7 show networks containing one DC power source with two series resistors and three parallel resistors connected in a series/parallel arrangement. The known values of voltage, current, resistance and power requirements taken from the design specification are marked on the diagrams. Some components or circuit values are marked as unknown.

P1 Study the circuit diagrams in Figure 6.7 then, using appropriate formulae, calculate and record all the unknown values.

P1 For each circuit diagram in Figure 6.7, calculate the internal resistance of the DC power source from the stated open circuit and on-load voltages and load currents.

M1 Now study the second set of circuit diagrams (Figure 6.8), which consist of DC networks. Use Kirchhoff's laws to determine the current in each branch of the bridge network, and the power dissipated in R_3 in the circuit containing two power sources.

Grading tips

P1 You must show the formulae that you used in getting your answers. Set out the individual steps in all calculations so that your work can be checked. Make sure that all answers are clearly identified.

M1 As before, make sure that all formulae used, calculation steps and answers are clearly shown.

Assessment activity 6.2

 BTEC

This assignment continues the work started in assignment activity 6.1. Your responsibility now is to construct some of the circuits you studied in assignment activity 6.1, measure the various circuit values of voltage, current and resistance and compare them against the values you calculated in your first assignment.

P2 Build the circuits in Figures 6.7 and 6.8, selecting the correct resistors. Use a variable DC power supply to provide the power source for the circuits.

Use a multimeter to measure and record the associated currents, voltages, power consumption and resistances of the circuits, and compare them against your calculated values.

Use a multimeter to measure the open circuit voltage and the on-load terminal voltage plus supply current of the power supply. Calculate the internal resistance of the power supply, compare

the results against the previously calculated values.

P3 Using a variable DC power supply as a power source and a multimeter, measure and record the forward and reverse voltage and current values of two types of semiconductor diodes. Use the results to compare the characteristics of the two diodes.

Grading tips

P2 This is a practical task. However, you should write up your results. When you undertake your assessment for this task your tutor will observe you working in the laboratory to see whether you can use a multimeter to take circuit measurements.

6.2 Understand the concepts of capacitance and determine capacitance values in DC circuits

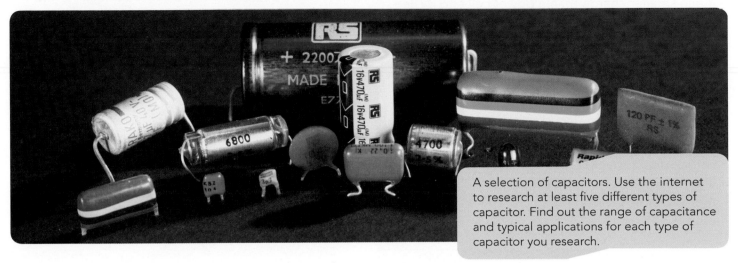

A selection of capacitors. Use the internet to research at least five different types of capacitor. Find out the range of capacitance and typical applications for each type of capacitor you research.

Capacitors are widely used components in electrical and electronic circuits. There are several different types, classified by how they are made, the materials used in the capacitor, whether they have a fixed or variable value, and so on. In this section, we are going to look at capacitors in some detail.

The electrostatic field

Figure 6.8 shows two metal plates placed with their surfaces in parallel to each other. Plate A is charged to a positive potential and plate B to a negative potential. Any negatively charged electrons between the plates will find themselves being pushed away from the negative plate B towards the positive plate A. Any positive charge between the plates would be pushed away from positive plate A towards negative plate B.

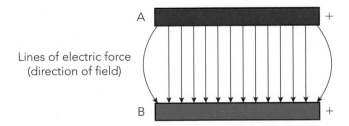

Figure 6.9: Electric field between two parallel plates

The area between the plates is called an **electrostatic field**. Its direction is defined as the direction in which a positive charge would move. The field can be represented by lines of force drawn between the two charged surfaces – the closer the lines, the

stronger the field. It is easy to calculate the strength of this **electric field**. Figure 6.10 shows two parallel conducting plates separated by air and connected to the opposite terminals of voltage source (V). There is a gap of d metres between the plates. An electric field exists in this space. Assuming the lines of force are parallel and equally spaced over the area of the plates, then the electric field strength (E), measured in volts/metre, is given by the formula:

$$E = \frac{V}{d}$$

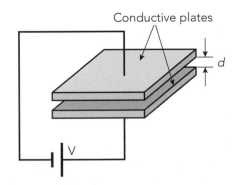

Figure 6.10: Two conducting plates separated by air

Key terms

Electrostatic field the field of energy that exists between two objects of opposite polarity.

Electric field the area surrounding electrically charged particles. The electric field strength is also called the potential gradient.

6.2.1 Capacitors

A capacitor is a device that stores electrical energy, rather like a cell or battery. However, a capacitor stores a much smaller charge than a power cell and it can be charged or discharged almost instantaneously. Capacitors have many uses.

- Small-value capacitors are used in tuned circuits and for coupling and decoupling radio frequency signals.
- Medium-value capacitors are similarly used for coupling and decoupling the various stages of audio frequency amplifiers.
- Large-value capacitors are used in power supplies, their ability to store more electrical energy making them suitable for smoothing out any ripple on the output of a rectifier.

Did you know?

The name capacitor is derived from the fact that it has the capacity to store energy. It was previously called a condenser, but this name is no longer in current usage.

The simplest form of capacitor is shown in Figure 6.11. It consists of two parallel plates separated by an insulating material called a dielectric. The distance between the plates is d. Most capacitors have a fixed value of **capacitance**, but some can have a capacitance value that can be varied. The dielectric can be simply air, in which case the capacitor is known as an air-spaced capacitor. Variable air-spaced capacitors are used in radio tuning circuits.

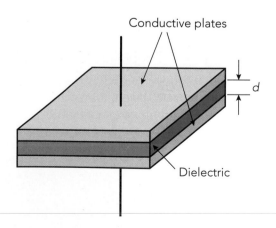

Figure 6.11: Construction of a simple capacitor.

Small-value capacitors are generally unpolarised, which means that they can be connected in a circuit either way round. Electrolytic capacitors are polarised, and they have a positive and a negative terminal. These must be connected the correct way round in a circuit. Table 6.3 shows the symbols for fixed, electrolytic and variable capacitors that are used in circuit diagrams.

Table 6.3: Capacitor symbols

Type	Circuit symbol
Fixed	
Electrolytic	
Variable	

Activity: Capacitor colour code table

Although many capacitors have their value printed on them, some are identified by using a colour code similar to that used for resistors (see Figure 6.2). Use the internet to research how the colour codes apply to capacitors. Draw a capacitor colour code table on a small piece of card that you can use during your practical sessions. Include three examples to help you use the table.

The charge (Q) stored in a capacitor is measured in coulombs. Charge is calculated using the formula:

$$Q = I \times t$$

where I is the current in amperes and t is the time in seconds.

Capacitance (C) is a measure of the amount of electrical charge Q that the capacitor can store between the plates for a given potential (voltage ç). It is calculated by:

$$C = \frac{Q}{V}$$

The farad (F) is the unit of capacitance. By definition, a farad is the capacitance when a potential difference of one volt appears across plates charged with one coulomb. One farad is quite a large value. In practice, capacitor values tend to be in the order of microfarads (which is 10^{-6} F, abbreviated by the symbol μF) or picofarads (10^{-12} F, symbol pF).

Flux density

A unit of flux is defined as the flux which emanates from a positive charge of 1 coulomb. Therefore electric flux (symbol ψ) is also measured in coulombs. So, for a charge of Q coulombs:

$$\psi = Q$$

Electric flux density (D) is defined as the amount of flux passing through a given area (A) that is perpendicular to the direction of the flux. It is measured in coulombs per square metre. It is given by:

$$D = \frac{Q}{A}$$

Charge density (symbol σ) is the alternative term for electric flux density.

> ### Did you know?
>
> The term flux comes from the Latin word *fluxus*, which means flow.

Permittivity

Permittivity relates to the measure of resistance encountered when an electric field is formed. In capacitor theory, it can also be seen as a measure of how an electric field affects, or is affected by, the dielectric. It is measured in farads per metre (F/m). It is given by the flux density divided by the electric field strength. For a field established in a vacuum, this is a constant (ε_0). Expressed as a formula:

$$\frac{D}{E} = \varepsilon_0$$

This constant is called the **permittivity of free space** and has a value of 8.85×10^{-12} F/m. When the dielectric (the material between the plates) is something other than a vacuum, such as paper, plastic, mica or ceramic, the **relative permittivity** (ε_r) of the dielectric has to be considered. The ratio becomes:

$$\frac{D}{E} = \varepsilon_0 \varepsilon_r$$

This ratio ($\varepsilon_0 \varepsilon_r$) is also called the absolute permittivity (ε), therefore $\varepsilon = \varepsilon_0 \varepsilon_r$. Table 6.4 gives typical values of

> ### Key terms
>
> **Capacitance** a measure of the amount of electrical charge that a capacitor can store between the plates for a given voltage.
>
> **Permittivity of free space** the ratio of D/E for a field established in a vacuum, also called the free space constant.
>
> **Relative permittivity** the insulating power of the dielectric compared with that of a vacuum.

relative permittivity for common materials. Note that the dielectric is considered to be an insulating material between the capacitor plates, and as such has a very high resistivity compared to, say, a conductor.

Table 6.4: Typical values of relative permittivity

Material	Relative permittivity (ε_r)
Air	1
Polythene	2.25
Polystyrene	2.4 to 2.7
Paper	3.5
Glass	3.7 to 10
Rubber	7
Water	80
Ceramics	6 to 1000

Variable capacitors

An air-spaced variable capacitor. A capacitor like this is used in the tuning circuit of a radio.

Capacitors can be fixed value or variable. A typical variable capacitor assembly consists of two sets of meshed multiple plates separated by air. One set of plates is fixed in position, while the other is moveable. As the moveable plates are swung in and out of mesh, the capacitance of the device alters between its maximum and minimum values. The photograph (on the previous page) shows a dual-gang capacitor. It has two variable capacitors sharing the same fixed mount and variable rotating spindle. Each section has an approximate minimum value of 16 pF when fully open and 390 pF when fully meshed.

Fixed capacitors

Most capacitors have fixed values. There are several different types of fixed capacitors, including the polarised electrolytic capacitor and its much smaller counterpart, the tantalum capacitor. Non-polarised types include mica, plastic, paper and ceramic capacitors. Table 6.5 lists different types of capacitor, with their capacitance range, **working voltage** and typical uses.

> ## Key terms
>
> **Working voltage** the voltage that can safely be applied to the capacitor without the insulating material (dielectric) breaking down.

Capacitors in parallel

A capacitor can be used in a circuit on its own or connected in parallel with other capacitors. Figure 6.12 shows three capacitors connected in parallel to a voltage (V).

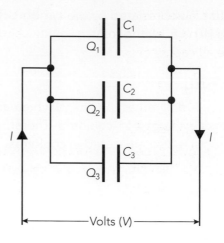

Figure 6.12: Capacitors connected in parallel

Some of the total current (I) flowing round the circuit will flow though each of the capacitors. This will cause a charge to be built up in each capacitor. The total charge will be the sum of the charges in each of the three capacitors:

$$Q_{total} = Q_1 + Q_2 + Q_3$$

However, since:

$$Q_{total} = CV$$

And:

$$Q_1 = C_1 V, \ Q_2 = C_2 V, \ Q_3 = C_3 V$$

Then:

$$CV = C_1 V + C_2 V + C_3 V$$

where C represents the total equivalent capacitance. Therefore:

$$C = C_1 + C_2 + C_3$$

Table 6.5: Types of capacitor

Type	Capacitance range	Typical working voltage	Usage
Electrolytic	1 µF to 1 F	3 to 600 V	Large capacitors. Power supplies and smoothing.
Tantalum	0.001 µF to 1000 µF	6 to 100 V	Small capacitors. Where space is restricted.
Mica	1 pF to 0.1 µF	100 to 600 V	Very stable. High frequency applications.
Ceramic	10 pF to 1 µF	50 to 1000 V	Popular and inexpensive. General usage.
Mylar	0.001 µF to 10 µF	50 to 600 V	Good performance. General usage.
Paper	500 pF to 50 µF	100,000 V	Rarely used now.
Polystyrene	10 pF to 10 µF	100 to 600 V	High quality and accuracy. Signal filters.
Oil	0.1 µF to 20 µF	200 V to 10 kV	Large, high voltage filters.

We can generalise this result. For n capacitors connected in parallel, the total capacitance will be the sum of the all capacitor values:

$$C = C_1 + C_2 + C_3 \ldots + C_n$$

Capacitors in series

Figure 6.13 shows three capacitors connected in series to a voltage (V). The voltage across each individual capacitor is V_1, V_2, and V_3.

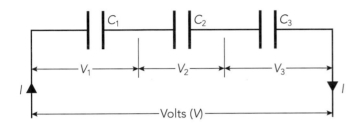

Figure 6.13: Capacitors connected in series

The charge on one plate of capacitor C_1 induces an equal but opposite charge on the other plate. This causes an equal but opposite charge to appear on the plate of C_2 that it is connected to, and so on. Therefore, for capacitors connected in series, the charge (Q) in each one is the same.

Now:

$$V = V_1 + V_2 + V_3$$

Using:

$$V = \frac{Q}{C},$$

Then:

$$\frac{Q}{C} = \frac{Q}{C_1} + \frac{Q}{C_2} + \frac{Q}{C_3},$$

where C represents the total equivalent capacitance. Therefore:

$$\frac{1}{C} = \frac{1}{C_1} + \frac{1}{C_2} + \frac{1}{C_3}$$

Again, we can generalise the result. For n capacitors connected in series, the total capacitance will be:

$$\frac{1}{C} = \frac{1}{C_1} + \frac{1}{C_2} + \frac{1}{C_3} \ldots \frac{1}{C_n}$$

When a circuit consists of several capacitors in a combination of both series and parallel configuration, you must consider the individual elements that are in series and that are in parallel. You calculate the value of one of these elements, then use that value in the next element, and the next, until you have reduced the complete circuit to a single value.

Dielectric strength and stored energy

Dielectric strength is defined as the maximum amount of field strength that a dielectric can withstand. Like electric field strength, dielectric strength is calculated by the formula:

$$E = \frac{V}{d}$$

The energy (W) stored in a capacitor is measured in joules. It is calculated by the formula:

$$W = \tfrac{1}{2} CV^2$$

Activity: Capacitors in series and parallel

To help you remember how to calculate the total capacitance where capacitors are connected in a combination of series and parallel configurations, write down the formula you would use for capacitors in series and for capacitors in parallel. Write a simple explanation of what each formula means, so that you can easily recall the formula each time it is needed. Then explain how you would tackle finding the total capacitance of a circuit where a number of capacitors are connected in both series and parallel.

6.2.2 Charging and discharging of a capacitor

Figure 6.14 shows a capacitor (C) and resistor (R) connected in series to a DC source, with a switch to open or close the circuit. When a DC voltage is applied to this circuit (that is, the switch is closed), a current will initially flow for a short period. The charge in the capacitor begins to build, until at some point the capacitor is fully charged and current no longer flows. During the time when the capacitor is changing from being fully discharged to fully charged, the voltages across the capacitor and the resistor, and the current flowing through the circuit are constantly changing. These value changes are called transients.

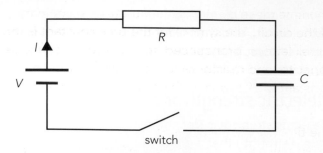

Figure 6.14: Capacitor and resistor in series

Charging a capacitor

Let's consider the circuit in Figure 6.14 further. Because the capacitor and resistor are connected in series, we know from Kirchhoff's voltage law that when the switch is closed, the total voltage V will be equal to the sum of the voltage across the capacitor and the voltage across the resistor. The charge in the capacitor is initially zero, but as the charge builds up, the voltage across the capacitor increases. The current through the resistor is decreasing, so the voltage across it falls. When the capacitor is fully charged and current no longer flows, the voltage across the capacity will be at its maximum, and equal to V, while the voltage across the resistor R will be zero. The point at which a capacitor reaches full charge and no current flows is called the steady state.

Measurements of voltages across the capacitor (V_C) and the resistor (V_R) and the current (I) flowing in the circuit can be taken at various points in time. Figures 6.15, 6.16 and 6.17 show typical graphs produced by plotting V_C, V_R and I respectively against time. The capacitor voltage transient graph is an **exponential growth curve**. This shows that the voltage across the capacitor initially increases rapidly because the current is large, before slowing down as the current decreases. The resistor voltage and current transient curves are **exponential decay curves**.

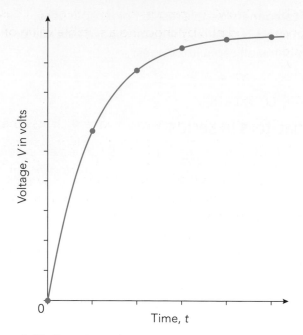

Figure 6.15: Capacitor voltage transient

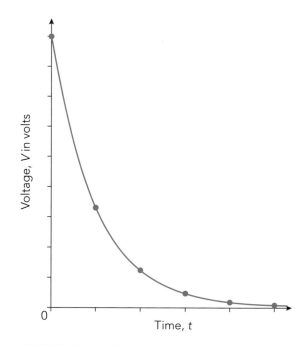

Figure 6.16: Resistor voltage transient

Key terms

Exponential growth curve a curve raising steeply, then flattening out as it reaches a maximum value.

Exponential decay curve a curve that shows a rapid fall then flattens out as it reaches the minimum or zero point.

The time taken for a capacitor to reach the fully charged state will normally be extremely short and difficult to measure in the laboratory. However, as the resistor in the circuit has an effect on current flow, it is

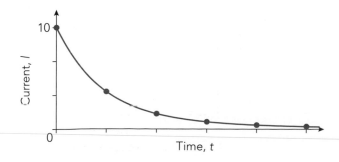

Figure 6.17: Current transient

possible to 'slow' the process down and make it easier to observe and plot by choosing a suitable value of resistor.

Time constant

Figure 6.15 shows the increase in voltage across the capacitor slowing down as it charges. Now suppose we replace the fixed voltage supply (V) by a variable voltage supply. If at the point that the curve begins to grow less steeply (t_1) the voltage is increased so that the current flowing through the circuit remains constant, then the curve will follow a tangent to its previous path until it reaches the final value of V at t_2. This is illustrated in Figure 6.18.

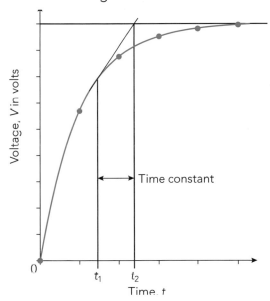

Figure 6.18: Time constant

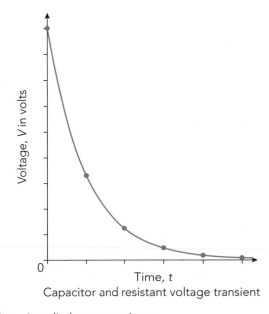

Capacitor and resistant voltage transient

Figure 6.19: Capacitor discharge transients

The time given by $t_2 - t_1$ is called the time constant of the circuit. The symbol for the time constant is the Greek letter τ, pronounced 'tor'. In a series-connected capacitor and resistor circuit, the value of the time constant is CR seconds. Expressed as a formula:

$$\tau = CR$$

The time constant can be defined as the time taken for a transient to reach its final value from the time when the initial rate of change is maintained.

Discharging a capacitor

To fully charge the capacitor in Figure 6.14, the switch will have been closed allowing current to flow from the DC voltage source. If the voltage source is now replaced by a short circuit, then the current will continues to flow for a short time as the capacitor starts to discharge. Again we can measure the changing current and voltage during this process. Figure 6.19 shows typical decaying current and voltage transients.

Note that when a capacitor is disconnected from a power source, it may retain its charge for a considerable length of time. It is good practice therefore to connect a high value resistor in the circuit across the capacitor terminals. This ensures that the capacitor is automatically discharged once the supply is switched off.

Activity: Charged capacitors

To show that you have understood how a capacitor retains a charge, write an explanation of why you should exercise care when handing capacitors with large values. Describe any precautions that should be incorporated into a circuit containing large value capacitors. Give examples of what are typically large values for capacitors and the type of capacitor that can hold a high charge.

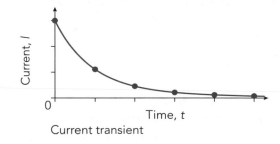

Current transient

6.2.3 DC network that includes a capacitor

Capacitors are used for smoothing the output of a DC power source. As Figure 6.20 shows, the diodes only conduct the AC input during half cycles. The output is rather poor DC. However, if two or three capacitors are connected in parallel as in Figure 6.21, the energy storing effect of the capacitors results in a more stable DC output.

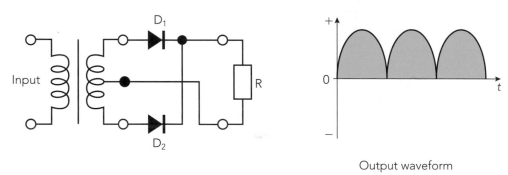

Figure 6.20: DC power source output without capacitors

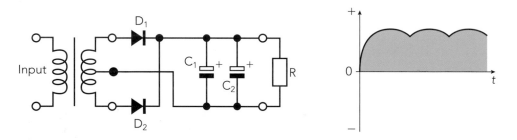

Figure 6.21: DC power source output with smoothing capacitors

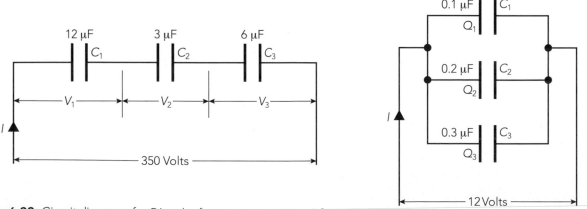

Figure 6.22: Circuit diagrams for P6 task of assessment activity 6.3

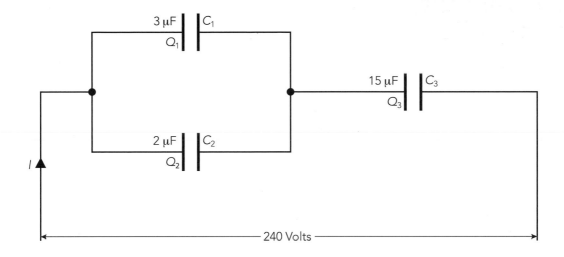

Figure 6.23: Circuit diagram for M2 task of assessment activity 6.3

Assessment activity 6.3

You work as a trainee test engineer for a small but thriving electrical and electronic design company. Your team has been given the task of designing a bench power supply unit suitable for use in electronics workshops and that will go on sale later in the year. Your latest responsibility is to assist with the design of the power supply by carrying out various tasks involving capacitors.

P4 Research different types of capacitors to evaluate their suitability for use in the new power supply design. Obtain data sheets for a selection of different capacitors, and use these to create a table listing each type of capacitor, its value, working voltage and typical use or application.

Write a short report identifying which of the capacitor types would be suitable for use in the power supply.

P5 Using one of the capacitor types you studied in the P4 task and a resistor and suitable test equipment, carry out a suitable test to determine the relationship between the voltage and current when charging and discharging this capacitor.

P6 Figure 6.22 shows three capacitors connected in series and three capacitors connected in parallel.

Calculate the charge, voltage and energy values in each capacitor using appropriate formulae.

M2 Figure 6.23 shows three capacitors connected in series/parallel combinations. Calculate the charge, voltage and energy values for each capacitor using appropriate formulae.

Grading tips

P5 Record the charging and discharging values of current and voltage in table form, then produce a suitable graph from the data. This is a practical task. When you undertake your assessment for this task your tutor will observe you working in the laboratory to assess whether you can use the test equipment properly.

P6 M2 You must show the formulae you used in getting your answers. Set out the individual steps in all calculations so that your work can be checked. Make sure all answers are clearly identified.

6.3 Know the principles and properties of magnetism

Inventors have been very good at discovering things that we cannot actually see. In the case of **magnetism**, early scientists knew that there was something to investigate because they noticed effects that they could not be explain. Driven by natural curiosity, they realised that there was a phenomenon to be researched and, indeed, to be discovered.

We are surrounded by magnetic fields. You will probably be familiar with the **earth's magnetic field**, but there are many others. Anything that uses a magnet generates a magnetic field. Many metals have a magnetic field. When you switch on a light or turn on the television, a magnetic field is generated. Sometimes the magnetic field is large and sometimes it is so small that it is hardly detectable.

Some people even wear a magnetic band, because they believe its effect helps to keep them in good health. It doesn't matter that you cannot see magnetism, since its discovery it has been put to many uses. There is a strong link between electricity and magnetic fields, so it's time to look at magnetism in more detail.

6.3.1 Magnetic field

A magnet is a piece of material that has a magnetic field. This field, which surrounds the material, is strong enough to influence other materials. Some materials do not have a strong magnetic field. Permanent magnets, as the name suggests, have a permanent magnetic field. A permanent magnet is typically a piece of **ferromagnetic material**, such as iron, in which the molecules are permanently aligned. Note that not all ferromagnetic materials are permanent; in some, the molecules only line up temporarily when the metal is brought into the magnetic field of a strong magnet. Some of these temporary magnets lose their magnetism quickly, some slowly.

If it is suspended freely, a permanent magnet will rotate until it positions itself in a direction that matches the earth's magnetic field. You can see this in a compass, where the permanent magnet is the pointer. The end pointing north is called the north pole (N) and the other end the south pole (S). Note, however, that if another strong magnetic field is close to the compass, this will have an influence on the pointer and provide an incorrect reading.

You can detect the effects of the magnetic force produced by the magnet within the area of a magnet's magnetic field. You cannot see or touch this field, but as Figure 6.24 shows, you can liken the magnetic field to lines of magnetic flux arcing from one pole of the magnet to the other.

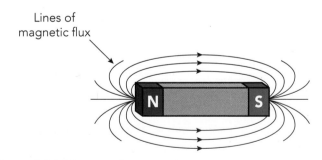

Lines of magnetic flux

Figure 6.24: Magnetic flux around a magnet

Magnetic field patterns

One way to 'see' magnetism is to perform a simple experiment. Place a piece of card over a bar magnet and then sprinkle iron filings onto the card. Gently tapping the card will cause the iron filings to move slightly and join up in lines that follow the magnetic field of the magnet underneath. Figure 6.25 shows a typical result. Note that this is very similar to the lines of flux depicted in Figure 6.24, proving that the theory is correct.

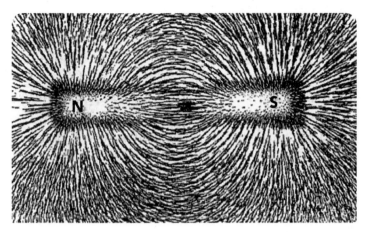

Figure 6.25: Iron filings showing lines of magnetic force around a magnet

The experiment demonstrates that a magnetic field exerts a force on iron filings and causes them to arrange into lines. The magnetic field surrounds the magnet in all directions. You could prove this if you could enclose the magnet in a sphere and repeat the experiment in three dimensions. The magnetic field is strongest close to the magnet, and decreases as you move away.

If you now take two bar magnets and place them with their ends facing each other the magnetic force becomes even more noticeable. Placing the two north poles facing each other causes the magnets to push each other away, because the lines of magnetic flux are acting against each other. If, however, you rearrange the bar magnets such that opposite poles are facing, the magnetic force acts to draw the two magnets towards each other.

These are the fundamental laws of magnetic attraction – opposite poles attract each other, like poles repel each other. This is easy to understand if you look at the arrows that show the direction of the lines of flux. Conventionally, the lines are depicted as flowing from the north pole, around the magnet and back into the magnet through the south pole. In Figure 6.26, the lines of flux are working against each other, pushing the poles apart. In Figure 6.27, the lines of flux are following the usual path, flowing out of a north pole and into a south pole, and pulling the poles towards each other.

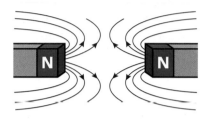

Figure 6.26: Like poles repel

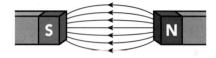

Figure 6.27: Opposite poles attract

Magnetic flux density

Let's now consider the amount of magnetic field produced by a magnetic source. This is called the **magnetic flux**. This abbreviated to the symbol Φ in equations – the Greek letter phi – and is measured in webers (abbreviated Wb). If you know the amount of magnetic flux and the size of the area (A) it is issuing from, you can calculate the **magnetic flux density**. This is given by the formula:

$$B = \frac{\Phi}{A}$$

Key terms

Magnetism the property of how a material responds when subjected to a magnetic field.

Earth's magnetic field the lines of magnetic force radiating from the polar areas surrounding the earth. The north magnetic pole is offset from the actual North Pole and moves gradually over time. Because of this, the earth's magnetic field is not symmetrical.

Ferromagnetic material a metal which has molecules that can be easily lined up to turn it into a magnet.

Magnetic flux the number of lines of force, or the amount of magnetic field, produced by a magnetic source.

Magnetic flux density the amount of magnetic flux per unit area of a magnetic material, measured in tesla.

where B is the symbol for magnetic flux density and A is the area in m^2.

The magnetic flux density is measured in tesla (T). One tesla equals one weber per metre squared ($1\ T = 1\ Wb/m^2$).

Magnetomotive force and field strength

We can now begin to establish a relationship between electricity and magnetism. Just as electric current flows around an electric circuit, when a current flows through a coil that is wound around a ferromagnetic core it creates a magnetic flux that flows around the core, too. This creates a magnetic circuit. Magnetomotive force (or mmf) is what causes there to be a presence of magnetic flux in the magnetic circuit:

mmf (or F_M) = NI

where N is the number of conductors or turns, I is the current in amperes, and F_M refers to force in magnetic terms.

The unit of mmf should be expressed as ampere-turns. However, if we are considering a simple straight conductor circuit rather than a coil, then there are no 'turns' and the correct unit is simply the ampere.

Magnetic field strength (known as H) is a measure of the magnetising force. If l is the mean length of the flux path in metres then:

$$H = \frac{NI}{l}$$

Activity: The compass

A compass works on the principle of magnetism. Write a detailed description of a compass, including a diagram with the parts accurately labelled and an explanation of how a compass works and is used. Remember to focus on the actual polarity of the needle, and detail the polarity of each end.

By rearranging this formula, you can see that:

$NI = Hl$

So the magnetomotive force (mmf) is Hl amperes.

Permeability

The term permeability relates to the degree to which a material magnetises in relation to the strength of magnetic field acting upon it. Permeability is calculated by dividing the produced magnetic flux density (B) by the magnetic field strength (H). It is measured in units of henry per metre (H/m). For air or any non-magnetic material or medium, B/H is a constant. This constant is known as the permeability of free space (μ_0) and is equal to $4\pi \times 10^{-7}$ H/m.

For all other material or media other than free space:

$$\frac{B}{H} = \mu_0 \mu_r$$

where μ_r is the relative permeability.

Relative permeability is defined as:

$$\mu_r = \frac{\text{flux density in the material}}{\text{flux density in a vacuum}}$$

Note that μ_r has different values for different types of magnetic material. Table 6.6 shows an approximate range of values of relative permeability for various magnetic materials. Relative permeability is defined as having a value of 1 in a vacuum. It has no unit because it is a ratio of flux densities.

Table 6.6: Relative permeability of some common magnetic materials

Magnetic material	Relative permeability (μ_r)
Ferrite (nickel zinc)	16 to 640
Cobalt	70 to 250
Cast iron	100 to 600
Nickel	100 to 600
Steel	100 to 800
Rhometal	1000 to 5000
Permalloy	2500 to 25,000
Mumetal	20,000 to 100,000

B/H curves and loops

A B/H curve shows the relationship between the flux density (B) generated by magnetic field strength (H) for a particular material. Figure 6.28 shows typical curves for three magnetic materials.

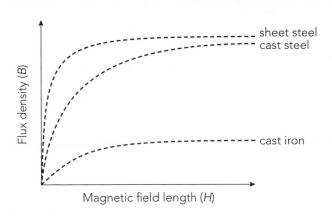

Figure 6.28: Typical B/H curves

If you want to learn more about the magnetic properties and characteristics of a magnetic material, then you need to produce its full B/H curve (or hysteresis loop as it is sometimes known). Figure 6.29 shows an example of a full B/H loop, which shows how the B/H curve behaves if H is also applied in one direction and then in the opposite direction. The closed loop shows the relationship between the induced magnetic flux density (B) and the magnetising force or magnetic field strength (H) in greater detail.

When the values of B and H are zero, the ferromagnetic material is completely demagnetised. The curve starts to rise from zero as H steadily increases (dotted line), until a point is reached where any further increase in H produces a negligible increase in B and the curve stops rising and levels out. This is called the saturation point because the material has reached magnetic saturation.

As H is then gradually reduced back to zero, notice that B also falls but the material retains some magnetic flux so that B does not fall to zero immediately. This is the level of residual magnetism retained by the material – the retained flux. As H continues to move in the opposite direction, a point is eventually reached where B becomes zero, meaning that all retained magnetism has now been lost. The force needed to remove all of the residual magnetism from the material is called the coercive force. This is also called the coercivity of the material.

As H continues to increase in the opposite direction, a second saturation point is reached. Applying H in the original direction now produces a similar effect as before, so that when the graph reaches the first saturation point again, a complete closed loop is produced.

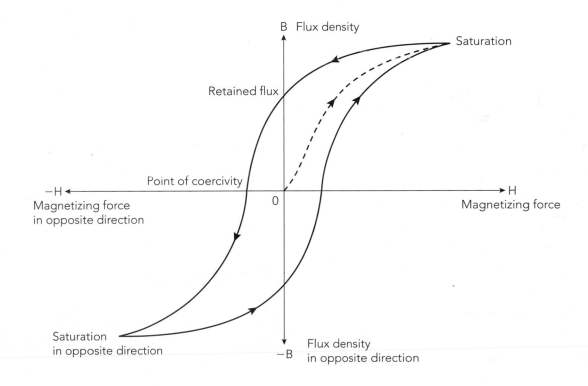

Figure 6.29: A typical B/H (hysteresis) loop

211

Reluctance and magnetic screening

In the same way that some metals readily accept a magnetic field and become magnets themselves (temporarily or otherwise), some metals have a resistance to the presence of a magnetic field. Reluctance (S) is a measure of this magnetic reluctance. It is sometimes abbreviated to R_M. The unit of reluctance is amperes per weber (A/Wb). It can be calculated as follows:

$$S = \frac{F_M}{\Phi} = \frac{NI}{\Phi} = \frac{Hl}{BA} = \frac{I}{(B/H)A} = \frac{l}{\mu_0 \mu_r A}$$

Sometimes it is necessary to screen a material or electronic circuit from a magnetic field to prevent it being affected. Ferromagnetic materials make very good magnetic screens because they have a low reluctance. The screen can be made by simply placing a strip of ferromagnetic material between the source of a magnetic field and the material or circuit that requires screening. You can also place the item that requires screening inside a container lined with ferromagnetic material.

Activity: Is it magnetic?

Try a little experiment. Just using a magnet, look around your workshop or laboratory. Identify whether materials you come across are magnetic or non-magnetic. Draw up a table of magnetic materials and non-magnetic materials. Include at least ten different materials in your table.

6.3.2 Electromagnetic induction

Electromagnetic induction describes the phenomenon in which electricity is produced in a **conductor** by a changing magnetic field. Put simply, if you move a conductor within a magnetic field, it becomes subjected to a force that causes an electric current to flow. The important thing to note is that the magnetic field must be changing in order for an electromotive force (emf) to be produced in the conductor – the faster the change in the magnetic field, the greater the electromotive force produced. This change is usually produced by moving the conductor in relation to a magnetic field, though it doesn't matter whether it is the conductor that is moving or the source of the magnetic field that moves.

The direction that the induced current flows in depends on the effective direction of the movement of the magnetic field. This phenomenon was first noticed by Michael Faraday and Joseph Henry in the 19th century. In this section we will introduce Heinrich Lenz's laws that explain the relationship between movement and current flow. First, you need to understand the principles of electromotive induction.

Key terms

Conductor a material whose electrons will easily move from one atom to another, such as a length of copper wire in this case.

Galvanometer a very sensitive ammeter used to measure tiny currents flowing through a circuit.

Specially formulated shielding tapes made of various combinations of polyester and copper are suitable for electromagnetic shielding. The tape is suitable for many magnetic screening applications, including transformers and induction loops.

Electromotive force

When an electromotive force (emf) is produced in the conductor, an electric current can be observed flowing if the conductor is part of a closed circuit. This emf – and, hence, the current – is induced in the conductor as it passes through the lines of flux while moving across a magnetic field. You can study this phenomenon quite simply using a coil of wire (the conductor), a magnet and a **galvanometer** with its zero point at the centre of the scale so that it can show in which direction the induced current is flowing.

Figure 6.30 shows a coil connected to the terminals of a galvanometer so that a circuit is completed. If a magnet is passed through the coil (the conductor) in one direction, you should notice a deflection on the galvanometer, starting at zero and rising to a maximum before returning to zero as the magnet passes through and eventually out of the coil. This deflection shows that a current has been produced in the coil.

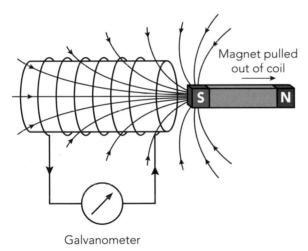

Figure 6.30: Current induced flows in one direction

If the magnet is now passed back through the coil in the opposite direction, you will note another deflection on the galvanometer but in the opposite direction. If at any time the magnet stops moving, then the galvanometer reading immediately returns to zero even if the magnet is still inside the coil. This demonstrates that movement is needed to induce an emf. Note that you would obtain the same results if you keep the magnet stationary and instead moved the coil over the magnet.

There are several ways in which you can increase the emf generated by electromagnetic induction. Remember, it is the effect of the relative movement of the coil and the magnetic flux that causes a current

to be induced in the coil. So you can increase the emf by increasing the speed at which the magnet is passed through the coil. If you double the speed you double the deflection on the galvanometer (the current is twice as strong). This relationship was noted by Faraday all those years ago and forms one of his laws. You can also increase the current by using a stronger magnet or by increasing the number of turns of wire in the coil

Did you know?

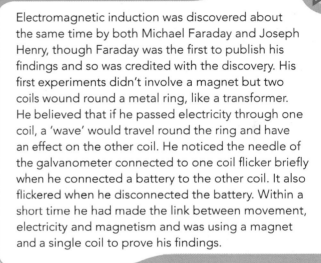

Electromagnetic induction was discovered about the same time by both Michael Faraday and Joseph Henry, though Faraday was the first to publish his findings and so was credited with the discovery. His first experiments didn't involve a magnet but two coils wound round a metal ring, like a transformer. He believed that if he passed electricity through one coil, a 'wave' would travel round the ring and have an effect on the other coil. He noticed the needle of the galvanometer connected to one coil flicker briefly when he connected a battery to the other coil. It also flickered when he disconnected the battery. Within a short time he had made the link between movement, electricity and magnetism and was using a magnet and a single coil to prove his findings.

Faraday's and Lenz's laws of electromagnetic induction

As Figure 6.30 shows, as the magnet travels through the coil, the lines of magnetic flux 'cut' through the coil. Remember that by convention these lines of force travel out of the magnet's north pole, round the magnet and into the south pole. The magnetic flux is therefore travelling in one direction at the north pole and in the opposite direction at the south pole. Because of this, the emf force or current generated as a south pole is pushed through the coil will be opposite to that generated when the north pole is pushed through the coil.

Following many simple experiments with magnets and coils, Faraday summarised the results in two laws.

- Whenever the magnetic field surrounding a coil changes, it will cause an emf to be induced in the coil.

- The amount of emf induced is directly related to the rate of change of magnetic flux through the circuit.

Lenz's investigations led him to propose a further law.

- The direction of an induced emf is always such that it opposes the force or change that is creating it.

There is an alternative to Lenz's law for determining the direction of the current produced by electromagnetic induction. It is called Fleming's right-hand rule and is demonstrated in Figure 6.31. To apply this rule, extend the thumb, first finger and second finger of your right hand so that they are all at right angles to each other. If you align your hand so that the first finger points in the direction of the magnetic field (north to south) and the thumb points in the direction of the motion of the conductor, then the second finger will be pointing in the direction of the induced current. Try to remember that the first finger represents the field, the thumb represents the motion, and the second finger shows the direction of current.

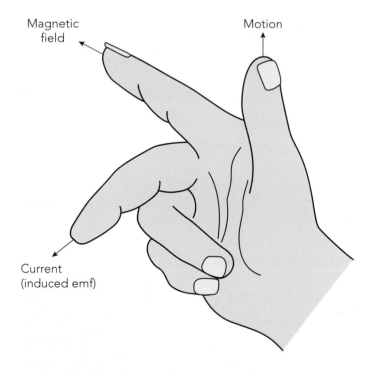

Figure 6.31: Fleming's right-hand rule

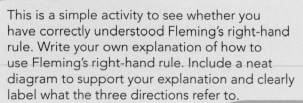

Activity: Fleming's right hand rule

This is a simple activity to see whether you have correctly understood Fleming's right-hand rule. Write your own explanation of how to use Fleming's right-hand rule. Include a neat diagram to support your explanation and clearly label what the three directions refer to.

Eddy currents

If we investigate further, we find that depending on the conductor something else is being generated. Some years after Faraday's work, it was discovered that when a solid conductor is exposed to a changing electric field, secondary currents, called **eddy currents**, can also be produced. These eddy currents are swirling currents (hence the name eddy) created in the body of the conductor in response to the changing magnetic field.

According to Lenz's law, the currents will swirl in a manner that creates a magnetic field opposing the changing magnetic field creating them, hence resulting in an opposing force. Because eddy currents oppose, it follows that they cause energy to be lost. More accurately, they convert some of the useful energy (the induced current) into heat. Some devices where eddy currents occur, such as transformers, have to carefully designed so that the energy loss is kept to a minimum and that they do not overheat.

Eddy currents do have their uses though. Some train brake systems make use of the eddy current effect. As the brakes are applied, eddy currents are generated in the wheels by means of an electromagnet exposing the metal wheels to a magnetic field. The opposing force of the eddy currents acts to slow the wheels down. The faster the wheels are turning, the greater the opposing force. As the wheels slow down, this force reduces and the train is brought to a smooth halt.

Key terms

Eddy currents swirls or whirlpools of current induced in the body of a solid conductor resulting in a force opposing the force creating them. These currents can be reduced by cutting slots in the solid conductor.

Self and mutual inductance

A change in the current through an electrical circuit produces an opposing electromotive force to the change in the electric current. This property is called inductance. If this emf is induced in the same circuit as that in which the current is changing, this is known as self inductance (symbol L). If the emf is induced in a circuit due to a change of current in an adjacent circuit, the inductance is called mutual inductance (symbol M). The unit of inductance is the henry (H), named after Joseph Henry.

A circuit is said to have an inductance of one henry when an emf of one volt is induced in it by a current that is changing at a rate of one ampere per second. This formula is used to calculate the induced emf in a coil:

$$E = -N\frac{d\Phi}{dt}$$

where N is the number of turns in the coil, $d\Phi$ is the change in flux in webers and dt is the time in seconds taken for the flux to change.

Similarly, the induced emf in a coil of inductance L is calculated by:

$$E = -L\frac{dI}{dt}$$

Where dI is the change in amperes in the current and dt is the time in seconds taken for the current to change.

In reference to Lenz's law, both of these equations contain a minus sign to indicate the direction. The results are given in volts.

Inductors

An inductor is used if an element of inductance is required in a circuit. These can take many forms. The simplest form is a coil of wire. This is called an air-cored inductor. The coil can be wound round an iron or ferrite core – this is called an iron-cored inductor and when used in AC circuits it is often referred to as a choke because it 'chokes' or limits the current flowing through the circuit.

The inductance of an inductor is governed by the number of turns of wire, the way they are arranged, the cross-sectional area of the wire and the presence of an iron core. If a current changing from 0 to I amperes causes a change of flux from 0 to Φ webers, it follows that $dI = I$ and $d\Phi = \Phi$. We can now use the two formulae above to calculate the induced emf:

$$E = \frac{N\Phi}{t} = \frac{LI}{t}$$

Therefore, the induction of the coil (in henrys) is:

$$L = \frac{N\Phi}{I}$$

Electromagnetic induction can be put to several uses. Three common devices that make use of the laws of electromagnetic induction are electric generators, motors and transformers. Let's consider each in turn.

A selection of inductors.

Electric generators

It is theoretically easy to generate electricity by moving a conductor through a magnetic field in a linear manner. However, finding a practical way of moving a wire at a constant speed through a fixed magnetic field poses problems, because the most common means of propulsion is in a rotary form. The answer is to shape the conductor into a loop which can then be rotated inside a permanent magnetic field, which is polarised north on one side and south on the other (see Figure 6.32). Each end of the loop is connected to a copper

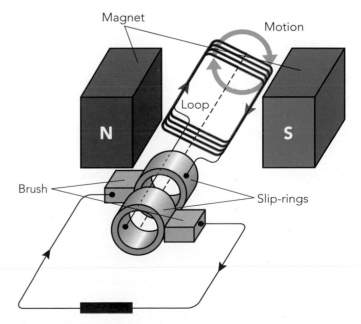

Figure 6.32: A simple electric generator

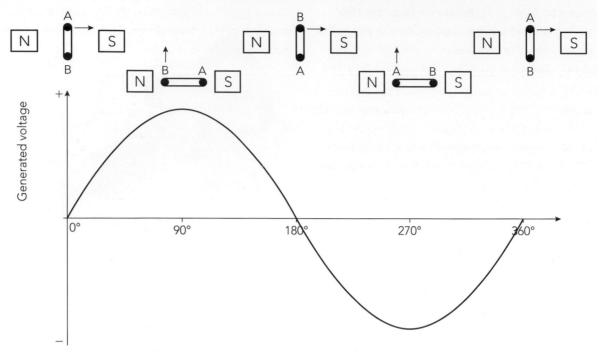

Figure 6.33: Voltage generated by rotating loop

slip ring, and carbon brushes are used to make contact with the slip rings. In practice, the loop would not be a single loop but a coil of wire wound on a non-magnetic former. By Faraday's laws, the emf generated will be directly proportional to the number of loops of wire. Other factors governing the voltage that would be generated include the speed of rotation and the strength of the magnetic field.

As the loop rotates inside the magnetic field, the generated emf rises to a peak, falls through zero to a peak in the opposite direction then back to zero for each complete turn of the loop. Thus an alternating voltage and current is generated. Figure 6.33 shows how the magnitude and direction of the voltage generated by the rotating loop varies depending on the alignment of the loop inside the magnetic field.

Electric motors

Electric motors and generators are machines. With a generator, the input is in the form of a mechanical

energy and the output is electrical energy. With an electric motor, the situation is reversed – the electrical input results in an output of mechanical energy.

In an electric motor, the conductor is made to rotate by being placed in a uniform magnetic field. Figure 6.34 shows a single loop conductor mounted between a north and a south permanent magnet. The loop is free to rotate. When a current is passed through the loop, the magnetic field generated acts against the magnetic field of the permanent magnets causing

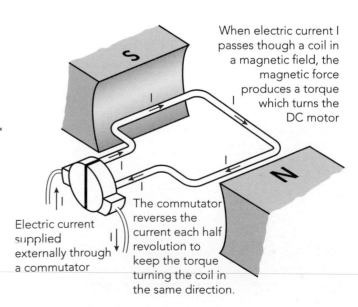

When electric current I passes though a coil in a magnetic field, the magnetic force produces a torque which turns the DC motor

Electric current supplied externally through a commutator

The commutator reverses the current each half revolution to keep the torque turning the coil in the same direction.

Figure 6.34: A basic electric motor

the loop to start rotating. As it rotates through 180° the force acting on it diminishes because the magnetic fields are no longer in opposition.

For the loop to continue rotating, it is necessary to reverse the current flow through the loop so that the magnetic fields are again in opposition. A **commutator** is used to achieve this current flow reversal. Instead of two slip rings, as in the generator, the commutator consists of a single ring split across the middle so that it is in two segments. Brushes again maintain electrical contact with the ring. When a voltage is first applied the current flows in one direction. As the conductor rotates, so does the commutator. When the rotation has gone through 180°, the split ring commutator has the effect of reversing the electrical connection to the loop – current now flows in the opposite direction restoring magnetic opposition of the fields and so the loop continues rotating. To make the process more efficient the commutator is normally split into not just two but many segments. Each sector has its own conducting loop.

In practice, a DC machine consists of:

- a stationary outer construction called the stator, consisting of a steel ring (the yoke) to which is attached the magnetic poles surrounded by a **field winding**
- a bearing-mounted rotating inner part called the armature consisting of a laminated iron or steel cylinder (the core) which is surrounded by the armature windings and the commutator.

There are a several ways in which field winding can be connected in a DC machine. Series winding means that the field winding is connected in series with the armature, as shown in Figure 6.35. When the field winding is connected in parallel with the armature as shown in Figure 6.36 it is said to be shunt wound.

Key terms

Commutator the part of the armature in an electric motor where the brushes make electrical contact. Its purpose is to switch the current flowing through the windings as the armature turns in such a manner that the magnetic force created always keeps the armature moving.

Field winding turns of a conductor wound around the pole core so that when a current is passed through this conductor an electromagnet is created, avoiding the need for a permanent magnet.

There is a third option involving a combination of series and shunt windings. This is called a compound wound machine.

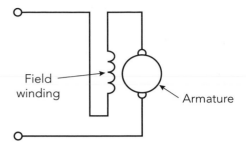

Figure 6.35: Series winding arrangement

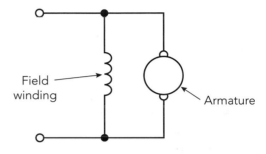

Figure 6.36: Shunt winding arrangement

Transformers

A transformer is a device that transforms an AC voltage/current into AC voltage/current with a different value. The term transforms isn't strictly correct, as what a transformer really does in simple terms is use the effect of mutual inductance to deliver a different value of voltage at its output to the value supplied as input. Transformers can raise or lower the value of the input voltage/current. Sometimes a transformer is used simply to isolate a circuit or item of electrical equipment from the main energy source, in which case no change may be necessary and the input and output values remain the same.

Well-designed transformers are extremely efficient electrical machines. Transformers are designed to minimise eddy currents, reducing the amount of heat that is generated and energy lost. With no moving parts, transformers have a long life span and are very reliable. Transformers play a key role in the energy distribution system. An AC voltage from a power station can be distributed easily and conveniently and then increased or decreased using transformers for different applications. The large power transformers used in mains electricity distribution systems are often oil filled to assist with cooling and insulation.

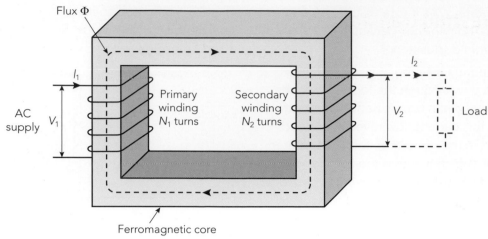

Figure 6.37: A transformer

Transformers come in all shapes and sizes, from miniature devices used in electronic circuits to large power transformers used in electricity generating plants, but the principle of operation is exactly the same in all devices. Figure 6.37 shows this basic principle.

Two coils are wound around a common ferromagnetic core. The coil connected to the AC electricity supply is called the primary winding and the other coil, to which an electrical load may be connected, is called the secondary winding. Assume for the moment that no load is connected to the secondary winding so that it is an open circuit. If you think about the laws of electromagnetic induction, the operation of a transformer will be easy to understand. When an alternating voltage (V_1) is applied to the primary winding, a small current flows that creates magnetic flux in the core. Because this magnetic flux flows around the core, it links the primary and secondary coils and induces an emf in each coil by mutual induction (of E_1 and E_2 respectively). If a coil has N turns, the emf induced in a coil is given by:

$$E = -N\left(\frac{d\Phi}{dt}\right)$$

where $\frac{d\Phi}{dt}$ is the rate of change of flux.

Assuming an ideal transformer, this rate of change of flux is the same for both the primary winding and the secondary winding. Therefore E_1/N_1 is equal to E_2/N_2 and the induced emf per turn in the coils is constant. Assuming that there are no losses, then $E_1 = V_1$ and $E_2 = V_2$, therefore:

$$\frac{V_1}{N_1} = \frac{V_2}{N_2} \text{ or } \frac{V_1}{V_2} = \frac{N_1}{N_2}$$

The relationship of V_1/V_2 is termed the voltage ratio, and N_1/N_2 is called the turns ratio. It follows that if N_2 is greater than N_1, then V_2 will be greater than V_1. This type of transformer is called a step-up transformer because the output voltage is greater than the input voltage. A step-down transformer is where N_2 is less than N_1, so V_2 will be less than V_1, giving a lower output voltage than input voltage.

Connecting a load across the secondary winding results in a current I_2. Because a transformer has very low energy losses, you can for practical purposes consider it to be 100% efficient – that is, the input power will equal the output power. The primary and secondary power can be considered as equal, so:

$$V_1 I_1 = V_2 I_2$$

Therefore:

$$\frac{V_1}{V_2} = \frac{I_2}{I_1}$$

So that:

$$\frac{V_1}{V_2} = \frac{N_1}{N_2} = \frac{I_2}{I_1}$$

The turns ratio is the relationship between the number of turns in the primary winding and the number of turns in the secondary winding. For example, a turns ratio of 2:5 means that for every two turns in the primary winding there will be five turns in the secondary winding. If a mains transformer connected to a 240 V AC supply has this turns ratio, it would produce a 600 V secondary voltage.

The rating of a transformer refers to the volt-amperes it can safely transform before starting to overheat, and it is usually expressed in terms of $V_1 I_1$ or $V_2 I_2$.

Activity: Testing transformers

Suppose you have recently started working for an electronics company and you will soon be required to work in a laboratory testing transformers. Write some notes that will help you prepare for this work.

- Accurately explain the concept of a transformer and describe how it works with reference to electromagnetic induction.

- Describe the effects of eddy currents in a transformer.

- Describe what is meant by the terms inductance and mutual inductance.

- Explain primary and secondary current and voltage ratios.

- Describe the relationship between the number of turns in the primary and secondary winding.

Assessment activity 6.4

You work as a trainee test engineer for a small but thriving electrical and electronic design company. Your team has been given the task of designing a bench power supply unit suitable for use in electronics workshops and that will go on sale later in the year. Your latest responsibility is to produce reports discussing the principles and properties of magnetism.

P7 Prepare a report describing the characteristics of a magnetic field.

P8 You must ensure that your report for the P7 task includes a detailed explanation of the relationship between flux density (B) and magnetic field strength (H). Using a graph of B/H curves show how the slope of the graph represents the permeability (μ) of a material.

P9 Now produce a similar report describing the principles and applications of electromagnetic induction. You must include an explanation of Faraday's and Lenz's laws and describe how they apply to a generator and transformer.

D2 With reference to electrical theory, produce a final report evaluating the performance of a motor and a generator. Include diagrams or graphs in your report where appropriate.

6.4 Be able to use single-phase alternating current (AC) theory

Electricity is produced by large generators at power stations and distributed via the National Grid to the end user. For industry, the supply is usually three-phase but for domestic use it is normally single phase. It is cheaper and easier to produce AC (alternating current) than DC (direct current) electricity and AC is easier to distribute.

6.4.1 Single-phase AC circuit theory

Electricity is generated by means of a coil rotating within a magnetic field. The magnitude and polarity of the generated voltage varies depending on the orientation of the coil to the north and south poles of the magnetic field. For one revolution of the generator, the resulting emf will alternate between a maximum positive and maximum negative value. Because it alternates, the generator is also called an alternator.

Waveform characteristics

When the value of the generated emf is plotted against time, the resulting image is called a waveform. Look back at Figure 6.33 (see page 216). This shows a waveform that alternates from a positive value, through zero to a negative value and back again. These waveforms are called alternating waveforms. In some cases, the generated emf changes with time but never actually has a negative value. This produces a waveform called a unidirectional waveform.

The waveform shown in Figure 6.33 is typical of that produced by an alternator. It is sinusoidal in shape, and is therefore called a sine wave. One complete series of values is called a cycle, and the time taken to complete one cycle is called the periodic time (*T*) of the waveform or period. The number of cycles completed in one second is referred to as the frequency (*f*) of the supply and is measured in hertz (Hz). The periodic time and frequency are simply related:

$$T = \frac{1}{f}$$

$$f = \frac{1}{T}$$

Figure 6.38 shows square, triangular and sawtooth waves, all examples of non-sinusoidal waveforms. These are not pure single frequency sine waves.

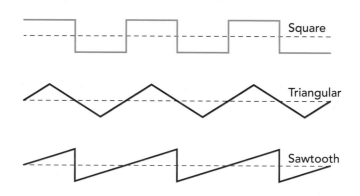

Figure 6.38: Examples of non-sinusoidal waveforms

> ## Did you know?
>
> Frequency used to be measured in cycles per second before this unit was changed to hertz in honour of Heinrich Hertz's important research into electromagnetism.

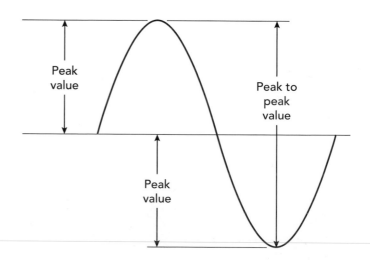

Figure 6.39: Peak and peak-to-peak values of an AC current

Table 6.7: Measures of AC

Value	Description
Peak	The maximum value reached in a positive or negative half cycle.
Peak-to-peak	The difference between the positive peak value and the negative peak value.
Root mean square (rms)	The value of a direct current that would produce the same heating effect as the alternating current. For a sine wave, rms value = 0.707 × maximum value.
Average	The average of all the instantaneous measurements in one half cycle. For a sine wave, average value = 0.637 × maximum value
Instantaneous	The value of voltage or current at a particular time instant. If measured at the instant that the cycle polarity is changing, then this value would be zero.
Form factor	The form factor is the rms value divided by the average value. For a sine wave, the form factor is 1.11.
Peak factor	The peak factor is the maximum value divided by the rms value. For a sine wave, the peak factor is 1.41.

Values of AC

Because the value of alternating voltage or current is always changing, it can be expressed in different ways, such as peak, peak-to-peak, root mean square (rms), average and instantaneous. It is important to understand these terms as each has a different meaning and produces different values. Table 6.7 defines the various different ways of measuring an AC current. Figure 6.39 shows the peak and the peak-to-peak values diagrammatically.

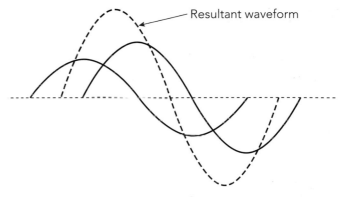

Figure 6.40: Graphical representation of adding two waveforms

Combining sinusoidal waveforms

The result of adding two sinusoidal voltages together can be determined in two ways, either graphically or by phasor representation. Figure 6.40 shows the graphical approach. It shows the result of combining the two alternating voltage waveforms of different amplitudes (shown with solid lines). Adding them

together produces the resulting waveform shown with a dotted line.

Figure 6.41 shows (on the left) the phasor diagram for two alternating voltages called V_1 and V_2 (which lags V_1 by 40 degrees) and (on the right) the phasor diagram showing the resultant voltage from the addition of the two waveforms.

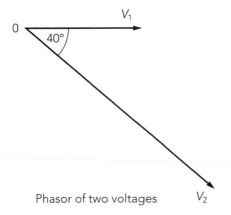

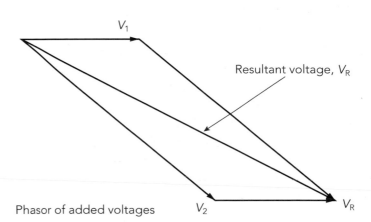

Figure 6.41: Phasor representation of two waveforms

Purely resistive, purely capacitive and purely inductive AC circuits

Where an AC circuit is purely resistive, the current and the voltage are in phase. This is shown in Figure 6.42.

In a purely capacitive circuit, the current leads the voltage by 90° (see Figure 6.43). The opposition to the flow of alternating current is called the capacitive reactance X_C. This is given by the formula:

$$X_C = \frac{V}{I}$$

In a purely inductive circuit the current lags the voltage by 90° (Figure 6.44). The opposition to the flow of alternating current is now called the inductive reactance X_L. This is given by the formula:

$$X_L = \frac{V}{I}$$

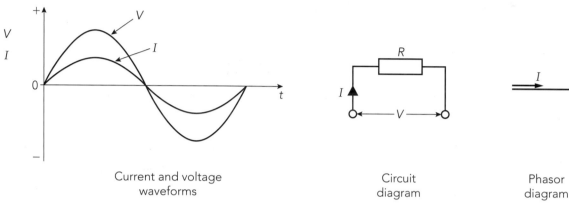

Current and voltage waveforms — Circuit diagram — Phasor diagram

Figure 6.42: Waveform and phasor diagram for a purely resistive circuit

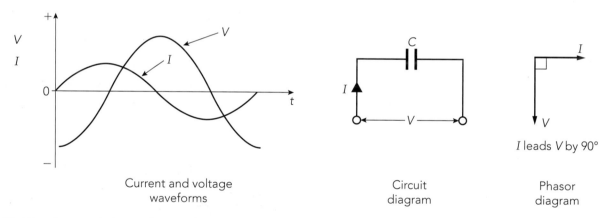

Current and voltage waveforms — Circuit diagram — Phasor diagram

I leads *V* by 90°

Figure 6.43: Waveform and phasor diagram for a purely capacitive circuit

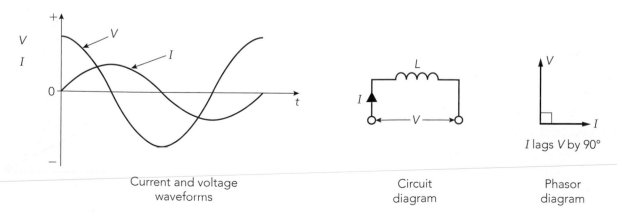

Current and voltage waveforms — Circuit diagram — Phasor diagram

I lags *V* by 90°

Figure 6.44: Waveform and phasor diagram for a purely inductive circuit

6.4.2 AC circuit measurements

Various measurements can be taken from AC circuits, including the frequency, amplitude and peak-to-peak value of the current, and so on. Some instruments can only measure one or two of these values, but others can measure most parameters. For example, a multimeter can measure AC voltage, resistance and capacitance, but unless it has a built-in frequency counter (in which case it would have to be a digital not an analogue multimeter) it cannot measure frequency.

There is some other equipment available for taking AC circuit measurements. A frequency counter allows you to measure frequency but not see the actual waveform. A more useful type of instrument would be one that allows you to actually observe and not just measure the waveform.

Oscilloscopes

One such instrument is the oscilloscope (often abbreviated to 'scope by engineers), which can be used for several applications. It is one of the most comprehensive and versatile items of test equipment. Its most distinctive feature is that allows the display of time-related voltage waveforms.

The display on an oscilloscope is traditionally a cathode ray tube. The typical screen area is approximately 8 cm by 10 cm. There is a ruled 1 cm grid (or graticule) on the display, with the major x-and y-axis in the centre. By applying a scaling factor, set using the appropriate front panel switches, very accurate time and voltage measurements can be taken. Because the oscilloscope allows you to 'see' the waveform, it is also possible to observe at a glance if the waveform is clean or whether there is any distortion, noise or irregularity such as **ringing** – something that a frequency counter would not be able to show.

The controls on an oscilloscope allow the user to adjust for the amplitude of the incoming signal, adjust the frequency rate using a timebase control, alter the position of the trace on the screen, and determine how the trace is triggered. Any adjustable front panel controls should be set to the calibrate position (if appropriate) before taking any measurements from the display, otherwise they may be inaccurate.

Care must be taken when using an oscilloscope. Because there may be high voltages present when probing points in a circuit, you should observe the same precautions as when using a multimeter. You will be connecting directly onto power sources or points of high voltage so always ensure that the leads and probes are in good condition. Again you should check that there is no broken insulation that would allow you to come into direct contact with the wiring in the leads of the probes or in the circuit itself.

Circuits

Rectifier circuits, where an AC power source is converted into a DC, provide an excellent opportunity for using an oscilloscope to make typical AC circuit measurements, such as frequency, amplitude and peak-to-peak. The oscilloscope also allows you to observe the input and output waveforms and hence the rectification action of a diode.

Key terms

Ringing the effect observed when the change of amplitude direction is not cleanly executed. This usually indicates that a circuit component is failing or not working to specification, possibly due to incorrect biasing. This is often most noticeable on the edges of a square waveform, where switching should be 'instant'.

Activity: Using an oscilloscope

Construct a simple half- or full-wave rectifier circuit from the diagrams shown in Table 6.8 (over the page) then, using an oscilloscope, carefully measure and calculate the periodic time, frequency, amplitude, peak, peak-to-peak, rms and average values of the input and output waveforms. Neatly record your work in a table, together with accurate diagrams of the waveforms.

Table 6.8: Simple rectifier circuits

Rectification	Circuit diagram	Input	Output
Half-wave (1 diode)	Input ... D ... R		
Full wave (2 diodes)	Input ... D$_1$ ... D$_2$ ... R		

Assessment activity 6.5

P10 P11 M3 D1   BTEC

You work as a trainee test engineer for a small but thriving electrical and electronic design company. Your team has been given the task of designing a bench power supply unit suitable for use in electronics workshops and that will go on sale later in the year. Your latest responsibility is to produce reports on AC theory and to demonstrate that you can correctly use an oscilloscope.

P10 Write a report detailing how a sinusoidal waveform is generated by electromagnetic induction – in other words, describe how an electrical generator works. Illustrate your explanation with suitable diagrams. Include a drawing of a sine wave in your report, and label it accurately to show its characteristics

P11 Measure the inputs and outputs of the single phase AC circuit that contains a resistor and capacitor (or inductor) using an oscilloscope. Observe and accurately record the voltages across the resistor and reactor. Explain your observations of any phase shift in the voltage waveforms.

M3 Study these mathematical equations for two sinusoidal AC waveforms.

$v_1 = 120 \sin \omega t$ volts

$v_2 = 180 \sin(\omega t - \pi/4)$ volts

Add and subtract these waveforms together graphically and by using a phasor diagram. Compare the results obtained from each of these methods.

D1 This is another practical task. You need to perform a set of tests on a power supply circuit that contains a transformer, diodes and capacitors. Analyse the operation of the circuit and record the effects of varying the component values in the circuit on the output waveform. Accurately record all your actions and observations, and write an evaluation of your findings.

Grading tips

P10 Your diagram of a sine wave should show amplitude, peak value, peak-to-peak value, average value, root mean square (rms) value and time period.

P11 This is a practical activity. When you are producing evidence for this grading criterion during an assignment, your tutor will observe your work to assess whether you can use an oscilloscope correctly.

Martin Peters
Electrical engineer

I work in the testing laboratory of a major electronics company with a team of four other engineers. The company produces, amongst other things, power supplies designed to a very precise specification for use in medical equipment.

I am responsible for testing prototypes of new units to ensure that they accurately meet the design specification. This involves writing test reports to feed back to the design engineers, suggesting changes or improvements to a design where needed, liaising directly with the design department when a prototype fails to meet design specification, designing a test procedure that can be used on production units and ensuring that all relevant paperwork is completed.

My typical day usually starts with a 30-minute meeting with the other members of my team to discuss progress on various jobs. We consider any problems that have recently been encountered and talk through how they could be resolved. We decide who will take responsibility for new prototypes due to arrive from the design department.

When the meeting is finished I spend some time checking my email, and reply to any that need answering immediately. I then read any replies I have received on my testing reports and contact the design department to discuss any issues that have arisen. With the morning paperwork out of the way, I then move on to the part of the job I enjoy the most, the practical bit. I resume testing the latest prototype power supply unit that I am responsible for, taking measurements, writing notes and producing graphs. I then check the measured results against the design specification and write up a report that goes back to the design department. I finish off with an informal meeting with various members of my team to discuss any issues arising from the day's work.

I really enjoy my work as it is both stimulating and challenging. The best part for me is when I am actually testing a prototype. I enjoy taking the measurements and readings, then producing graphs of the results. This is when you get to see how the prototype is working – if it is very close to its design specification or whether it needs some modification. If it does need modification, it is up to me to suggest how the design could be improved by referring to the results of my measurements. This gives me a great feeling of satisfaction, especially when the prototype comes back with the modifications I suggested and this time it correctly meets the design specification.

Think about it!

1 What topics in this unit provide you with the skills and background knowledge to become proficient at safely using a multimeter and an oscilloscope for making circuit measurements? Write a list.

2 What further skills might you need to develop? For example, you might need additional training on the use of simulation software for making DC circuit measurements before progressing to working with real components.

Just checking

1 Differentiate between potential difference and electromotive force.

2 Describe what is meant by the term temperature coefficient of resistance.

3 Describe what a diode could be used for in a circuit.

4 State the formulae for Ohm's law and the power law.

5 How would you calculate the total resistance of three resistors connected a) in parallel and b) in series?

6 Explain how you would use a multimeter to measure the current flowing through a resistor.

7 Describe the main parts of an air-spaced variable capacitor and explain how it works. State one application where such a capacitor would be used.

8 With the aid of a diagram, explain what is meant by a B/H curve and describe what it shows.

9 What are eddy currents and what effect can they cause in a transformer?

10 Describe a simple experiment that you can use to demonstrate the lines of force around a magnet.

11 Differentiate, with examples and diagrams, the difference between a sinusoidal and a non-sinusoidal waveform.

12 Describe how you would use an oscilloscope to measure frequency.

Assignment tips

- Familiarise yourself with the standard symbols for the components mentioned in this unit, such as diode, resistor, capacitor and transformer. This will come in useful and save time when building a circuit from its circuit diagram.

- To help you make accurate DC circuit measurements, practise using a multimeter. Become familiar with the range of selector settings, what they are used for and how to read the display, especially if it is an analogue multimeter.

- Make accurate and detailed notes of any practical work carried out. The notes can be used as proof that the work has been successfully completed. Before testing a circuit, note how you expect it to function and then compare the measured results against your predictions.

- Learn what the various controls and functions typically found on an oscilloscope are used for, such as timebase selector, trigger selector, input amplitude control, horizontal and vertical shift, channel selector, voltage calibrator. This will help you to take accurate AC circuit measurements quickly.

7 Business operations in engineering

Engineering companies operate in competitive business environments. Running a business is a complex operation requiring a whole range of skills. Suppose you and a colleague have a great idea for a new product, and you want to set up a small manufacturing company. You are likely to need to raise capital to buy machinery and raw materials and to pay yourselves during the development phase.

Your enterprise will need to comply with current regulations and other constraints that impact on the operation of engineering businesses. You should also be aware of the impact that changes in the economic environment might have on your business, such as interest rate changes and swings in consumer confidence.

You must have a good business plan, providing data about your costs and estimating how long it will take to get a return on the money invested in your fledgling business. You will need this plan when pitching to investors. They will undoubtedly ask about competitors in the marketplace and how you intend to structure your business as it grows.

Learning outcomes

After completing this unit you should:

1 know how an engineering company operates
2 understand how external factors and the economic environment can affect the operation of an engineering company
3 know how legislation, regulation and other constraints impact on the operation of engineering businesses
4 be able to apply costing techniques to determine the cost effectiveness of an engineering activity.

Assessment and grading criteria

This table shows you what you must do in order to achieve a pass, merit or distinction grade, and where you can find activities in this book to help you produce the required evidence.

To achieve a **pass** grade the evidence must show that you are able to:	To achieve a **merit** grade the evidence must show that, in addition to the pass criteria, you are able to:	To achieve a **distinction** grade the evidence must show that, in addition to the pass and merit criteria, you are able to:
P1 describe the different sectors in which engineering companies operate and the function that they carry out in that sector **Assessment activity 7.1 page 239**	**M1** explain how improvements in information flow could enhance the functional activities of an engineering company **Assessment activity 7.1 page 239**	**D1** evaluate the information flow through an engineering company in relation to an engineering activity **Assessment activity 7.1 page 239**
P2 describe the organisational types of three given engineering companies **Assessment activity 7.1 page 239**	**M2** explain the impact of legislation on a specific operation within a typical engineering company in terms of benefits and limitations **Assessment activity 7.2 page 251**	**D2** evaluate the importance and possible effect of the external factors that directly impact on an engineering company. **Assessment activity 7.2 page 251**
P3 outline how information flows through an engineering company in relation to an engineering activity **Assessment activity 7.1 page 239**	**M3** demonstrate how the cost effectiveness of an engineering activity could be improved. **Assessment activity 7.3 page 260**	
P4 explain how external factors and the economic environment affect the way in which an engineering company operates **Assessment activity 7.2 page 251**		
P5 identify the legislation and regulations that impact on the way an engineering business operates **Assessment activity 7.2 page 251**		
P6 describe the environmental and social constraints that impact on the way an engineering business operates **Assessment activity 7.2 page 251**		
P7 carry out costing techniques to determine the cost effectiveness of an engineering activity **Assessment activity 7.3 page 260**		
P8 carry out costing techniques to reach a make-or-buy decision for a given product **Assessment activity 7.3 page 260**		

How you will be assessed

This unit will be assessed by internal assignments designed and marked by the staff at your centre. The type of evidence which you will be asked to present when you carry out an assignment could be in the form of:

- a portfolio containing written descriptions and flow diagrams
- a summative test relating to a small group research activity
- a portfolio containing spreadsheets and written commentary
- a printout of a PowerPoint presentation.

John, 19-year-old full-time student

This unit has helped me to understand the organisational, financial, legal, social and environmental constraints that affect the way that engineering companies operate. It also helped me to realise how important it is for businesses to make profits so that they can invest in new products and remain sustainable.

Before starting on the unit I had planned to go to university to study mechanical engineering, with the aim of becoming a designer in the aerospace industry. I am now planning to do a course with much more business studies as I would really like to end up running a company – preferably my own. There is so much more to engineering than just designing and making things.

The research activities in the unit involved visiting a local engineering business and talking to the finance, technical and manufacturing directors. They gave me lots of good information and also introduced me to other people in the business who could help my research.

One thing that I did have to watch when taking this unit was not going into 'information overload'. I got help from my tutor on how to edit information when researching data and to just pick out the details that were really needed.

7.1 Know how an engineering company operates

Start up

The mobile phone market

Working in a group, compare your mobile phones. Note the different makes and brands that you own. Then briefly discuss the reasons why manufacturers bring out new models each year and why phone companies regularly change their tariff plans. You could create a mind map to stimulate your thoughts. (For more on the use of **mind maps**, see Unit 2, page 49.)

Now think about the production facilities (factories) which manufacture the mobile phones. How is a company like Nokia organised, what types of staff does it employ, how does it finance the development of new models, what's its game plan for survival in a competitive marketplace? Produce another mind map.

Finally focus on the organisation of a factory. What departments will it have, are the factory's operations regulated by statutes such as health and safety regulations, and what standards do mobile phones have to meet? Create a third mind map.

A modern engineering business is a complex undertaking. Investigate the structure of a large engineering business that has operations in your region.

To begin an investigation into business operations, let's start by focusing on how a modern business is organised.

7.1.1 Sectors

Engineering companies are involved with a wide range of business activities. These activities – and the companies that undertake them – can be classified into three broad sectors: primary, secondary and tertiary.

Primary sector

Companies working in the primary sector are involved in the gathering or extraction of raw materials or the growing of crops. These primary products can then be processed into a form that can be sold to manufacturing companies. Here are some examples of primary activities:

• extracting crude oil from underground deposits, and then distilling and processing the oil into polymers that can be used as the raw material for products like granules for the injection moulding industry and carbon fibre

• strip mining bauxite and processing into aluminium, which is then sold on as **ingots**

- extracting gas from under the North Sea – the gas is cleaned up, pressure regulated and pumped to factories where, for example, it can be used to heat metal-smelting furnaces
- growing crops, such as rapeseed, hemp, maize and sugar, which can be processed into biofuels.

Primary sector businesses are usually located where it is easy to source raw materials and where there is access to the energy supplies needed to process these materials. Many primary processes have heavy energy requirements. For example, it is extremely energy intensive to convert bauxite into aluminium, and aluminium smelters are usually in locations where there are abundant supplies of 'cheap' hydroelectric power.

Decisions on where to locate primary sector production facilities used to be taken purely on economic grounds, but today there are also carbon footprint issues. In the 21st century, businesses have to be much more responsible about the amounts of CO_2 they release into the atmosphere. As a result, there is ever-increasing pressure on primary sector businesses to develop processes that use less energy in extracting and processing raw materials.

Secondary sector

Secondary sector activities involve the manufacture of products, usually within a factory environment using the resources of materials, machinery, labour and energy. The secondary sector is huge, and it operates in a global business environment. Products might be designed in one country, manufactured on a different continent and then sold all around the world.

To be effective and profitable, businesses need sophisticated management and manufacturing systems to ensure that resources are used in the most efficient ways possible. It is crucial to monitor and control costs. At the end of this unit you will investigate how to calculate the cost of producing a product by estimating its four key cost components: materials, machinery, labour and energy.

The secondary sector is subdivided into many specialised industries. Here are a few of these subsectors with examples of the products each makes:

- chemical – medicines, paints, fuels, resins, carbon fibres
- manufacturing – domestic white goods, electronic equipment, composite materials
- automotive – commercial and domestic vehicles, replacement parts
- aerospace – civil and commercial aircraft, satellites, rockets
- marine – ships, underwater structures, light craft
- sports goods – hi-tech racquets and skis, timing devices, sports science body function monitoring equipment.

Tertiary sector

Companies in the tertiary sector provide services. Tertiary operations in engineering involve the setting up and operation of systems that use manufactured parts. For example, a company might be commissioned to construct a telecommunications network from equipment (hardware). This would be installed and maintained by skilled technicians. The hardware might be sourced from different manufacturers (in the secondary sector), and it is the job of a system designer to select the correct hardware. This may involve modelling the network with a computer software package so that the performance of the network can be analysed. Having set up the network, its operation is monitored by a computer which collects data from the various pieces of hardware. If the network develops a fault, a message is passed to a service technician.

The tertiary sector like the secondary sector is also subdivided into many specialised industries. Here are a few of these subsectors with examples of the services each provides:

- energy – distribution of gas and electricity by the UK national transmission system
- waste management – sewage, domestic rubbish, recycling (domestic and industrial)
- water – collection, storage, purification and distribution to commercial and private customers

Key terms

Mind map a spider's web of thoughts, words or ideas around a central key word or idea written on paper, a flipchart or an interactive whiteboard.

Ingot a block of metal cast into a shape which can be used for further processing.

- building services – environmental control in a building (heating, lighting and ventilation)
- health – scanning and X-ray services, data systems
- telecommunications – internet connections, mobile phones (transmission networks and phone services).

Now think about how you might get linked up to broadband. You might start by buying a laptop computer and router from an electronics retailer. These items will have been manufactured by a company in the secondary sector using raw materials sourced from the primary sector. You then would need to select an internet service provider, agree a contract and set up a direct debit with the bank.

A few days later a letter arrives confirming that your telephone connection is suitable for broadband and a first payment has been taken from your account. You connect up your equipment, follow the set-up procedure and wait for your computer to install and activate the web browser. Usually this works well, but suppose this message appears on the screen:

> *Cannot find server> error>check hardware connections> error code 1234> contact your ISP>.*

Is the problem being caused by your hardware, the telephone system or the internet provider? Resolving

the problem might be easy, perhaps by making a simple tick in a drop-down menu box, or it could involve lengthy phone calls to the internet service provider. Whatever the outcome, you are involved with products produced by companies operating in the secondary and tertiary sectors.

7.1.2 Engineering functions

When a product is manufactured by an engineering company for sale in the marketplace several interrelated functions must be carried out. In a large organisation these will be undertaken by teams of specialists, but in a very small business just one person may be responsible for completing all tasks.

It is very important that a business organises its engineering functions in ways that allow marketable products to be produced. If not, the business will not be sustainable. Let's consider the engineering functions that are required to bring a new product to the marketplace.

The first phase in the life of any product is research and development (R&D). This is a particularly important function in hi-tech industries. Companies invest to stay ahead of their competitors. This means that even as

---

Activity: Sectors

Try task 1 on your own and then discuss tasks 2–5 with a colleague making brief notes.

1. Identify the correct sector for each of these business activities:

- gas extraction
- mining bauxite
- producing flat-pack furniture
- producing particle board
- boat building
- instrument calibration services
- making yoghurt pots
- manufacture of electric cable

- offshore wind farming
- running the National Grid
- paint production
- sports equipment design
- nuclear waste reprocessing
- transmitting television programmes
- operating a mobile CAT scan unit
- diamond mining

2. What do you think influences the wholesale price of polymer granules?

3. Why are so many primary sector industries based in developing counties?

4. Overview a company which operates in more than one sector.

5. Many UK companies in the secondary sector outsource production to countries such as Poland and China. Why is this?

consumers are buying new high-definition television sets with their hard-earned cash, back at the factory engineers are developing even more sophisticated models which will eventually come into stores (often at lower retail prices). Pharmaceutical companies expend huge resources on R&D in the hope that their scientists and product developers will come up with revolutionary, money-making products.

Did you know?

James Dyson spent over ten years developing the operating principles for his first vacuum cleaner. Then the detail design work started.

Design is the next stage in the development of a new product. Design engineers take ideas developed through research and work them up into products which can be manufactured economically (and, importantly, profitably). Not all ideas become commercial products. Consider the concept cars that are often on display at motor shows. These will contain many great ideas and futuristic styling, but only some of the concepts will make it into mass-produced cars.

It often takes extensive R&D and design before a product reaches the manufacturing stage – turning raw materials and components into marketable products. Manufacturing engineers have to be good at turning low-value raw materials into higher value finished products.

This requires a materials supply and control function. It is important that raw materials and any bought-in components are of the required quality and that they are available when needed by the manufacturing teams. However, it is very expensive to hold large stocks of raw materials because you need space to store them and money to pay your suppliers. For this reason, the majority of engineering businesses operate just-in-time systems – materials arriving at the plant exactly as and when required. For this to work, there must be robust contracts in place with suppliers.

The production planning and control function is also important in the manufacturing phase. Businesses invest substantial **capital** in machine tools, and they need to be kept running to get a return on this investment. A production planning engineer will

organise the loading on a workshop so that machines and operators are kept as busy as possible and best use is made of resources.

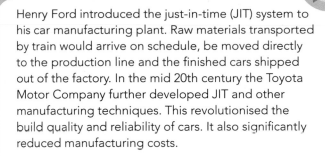

Did you know?

Henry Ford introduced the just-in-time (JIT) system to his car manufacturing plant. Raw materials transported by train would arrive on schedule, be moved directly to the production line and the finished cars shipped out of the factory. In the mid 20th century the Toyota Motor Company further developed JIT and other manufacturing techniques. This revolutionised the build quality and reliability of cars. It also significantly reduced manufacturing costs.

After products are manufactured, there are other important engineering functions that must be carried out. Engineers are involved in the installation and commissioning of a product, and checking that it is operating to specification after it has been delivered to a customer's premises. The manufacturer takes full responsibility for the performance of the product.

Maintenance can be on-site at a production facility or at a customer's premises. There are many types of maintenance procedure, including dealing with breakdowns, as well as routine servicing and planned replacement of consumable parts.

Most businesses also offer some degree of post-sale technical support. In other words, customers are given a continuing service by the seller. In its simplest form this would be merely a guarantee against faulty workmanship, but technical support goes well beyond this in many situations. If customers are having operational difficulties with a complex product, they need to be able to talk to someone with a proper technical background, such as the designer or a responsible technical person. There will be times when technical support involves an engineer or technician visiting a customer in order to work through why a product is not operating to specification.

Engineers can also be involved in the technical sales function. Often when a customer orders a product

Key terms

Capital money used to purchase equipment and which is effectively tied up in the business.

with a customised specification they will discus their requirements with a technical sales engineer. People working in technical sales must have good product knowledge combined with the ability to do pricing.

Finally, let's consider two key functions that impact on the whole process. The first of these is project planning and management. When a product or system is being developed it is important that the project remains within budget and is completed on time. Those responsible for the financial management of a business have to be convinced that any new project has been properly planned and costed. Only then will they release funds. There are various software tools that planners use (for more information see Unit 3, pages 86–89).

Second, and equally important, is **quality assurance**. Engineering is a very competitive business and if a company gains a reputation for poor quality, then it will lose market share. Quality assurance is much more than just simple dimensional and performance checks carried out on a product. It is a systematic holistic process, which provides confidence in a product's suitability for its purpose. Businesses can achieve the quality management standard ISO 9001 by going

through a rigorous accreditation procedure. The meaning of 'product' is taken in its widest sense, and would include all hardware and associated software, services, processes and systems.

7.1.3 Organisational types

Three parameters are commonly used to classify business organisations. These are size, legal status and structure.

Size

A common way of classifying businesses is in broad bands depending on the number of people that a business employs. Typically there are four bands ranging from micro (very small businesses with less than 10 employees) to large (250 or more employees). You might also find references to **SMEs** – this acronym stands for small and medium-sized enterprises and is used as a shorthand to describe any business that is not large.

When researching information about business classifications be aware that there is no agreed standard definition. Countries can assign different numerical ranges to each band and this can cause confusion. Member states of the European Union (EU) are reaching agreement over a standard definition for the size of a business.

Key terms

Quality assurance a management tool that provides confidence that quality requirements are being met. A quality assurance (QA) system consists of procedures to maintain (and sometimes improve) quality standards.

SMEs small and medium-sized enterprises – businesses employing less than 250 people (EU definition).

Functional skills

Describing the engineering functions that companies carry out will improve your skills in written English.

Activity: Engineering functions

Visit a local engineering business and identify the senior person responsible for each of the these functions.

Research and development	Production planning and control
Project planning and management	Design
Installation	Technical sales
Manufacture	Commissioning
Quality assurance	Materials supply and control
Maintenance	Technical support

Put your data together in the form of an organisational chart.

Status

This relates to the legal status and ownership of a business. Many businesses have a legal status as a company, but individuals working for themselves can operate as sole traders. Their only legal obligation is to file a tax return each year with HM Revenue & Customs, the UK's tax department. Sole traders often finance their businesses by taking a loan secured against private collateral, such as their home. If a sole trader's business fails, there is no legal protection against the debts incurred by the business. The sole trader may lose everything.

At the other end of the scale are public limited companies (plc). These are financed by shareholders. They are listed on the London Stock Exchange, and their shares can be freely brought and sold. Because shares in a plc can be openly traded, a whole business can be sold without the employees having any say in what happens. The accounts of a public limited company can be accessed by the general public. Annual accounts are filed with Companies House and they can usually be viewed on a company's own website.

The aim of all commercial businesses is to make a profit for its owner(s) – the people who set up the business or its shareholders. There are some charitable businesses – also called not-for-profit organisations – that aim to break even but operate for other reasons. For example, a small business might be set up with the primary purpose of employing people with disabilities. This could be run by a charitable (not-for-profit) organisation as a sheltered workshop.

Structure

Understanding how a company operates is made much easier if you are able to refer to a diagram which shows its internal structure. An organisational chart shows the links between the various business (and engineering) functions and often identifies the people responsible for particular functions. The simplest structure is a sole trader business, run by a single owner-manage. There is no chain of command and no links between different departments – the owner does everything in this business.

The most complex structure is hierarchical, and will involve several management layers – from directors and the chief executive, down to senior managers, divisional managers, managers, supervisors, skilled employees etc. – and link many different functions. This type of structure can have problems. The lower level employees (such as staff working on the shop floor) can feel remote from senior staff and it can take a long time for information to pass up and down the chain of command.

Many businesses have sought to address these problems by stripping away layers of middle management. They have become much more dynamic in the way that they operate because the resulting 'flatter' organisational structures gives much greater autonomy to individual workers. People are able to make decisions without having to refer back constantly to someone 'at the top'. Figure 7.1 shows a flat organisational structure. See

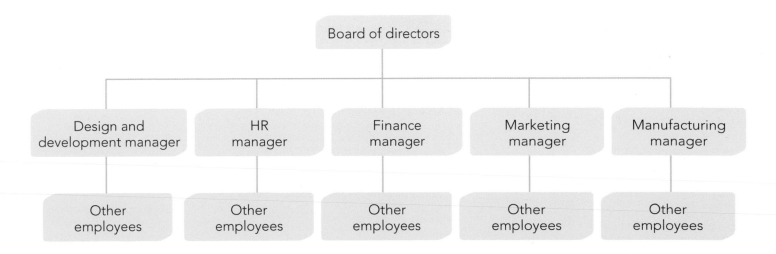

Figure 7.1: A flat organisational structure for an engineering company

if you can identify a local company that has this type of structure. Was it originally set up with a flat structure or has it evolved this structure from something more complex? Find out who in the company would be able to give you information about its structure.

Activity: Organisational types

1 Businesses can be classified as either micro, small, medium or large enterprises. Find out the European Union definition of these classifications in terms of the number of employees working for a company.

2 A business can be set up as a registered charity, sole trader, partnership, private limited company (Ltd) or public limited company (plc). Identity two key features of each status.

3 In the past, engineering companies tended to have hierarchical management structures, but state-of-the-art manufacturing systems demand a more flexible and responsive way of working. Management structures are usually now either flat or matrix. Research the differences between hierarchical structures, flat structures and matrix structures.

4 Some engineering companies have decided to strip away layers of middle management so that their structures become flat rather than hierarchical. Why have they made this change?

Functional skills

Researching data about companies will improve your skills in ICT. Describing the organisational structures of companies will improve your skills in written English.

7.1.4 Information flow

For any business to operate effectively, there must a robust and accurate flow of information between the various engineering and business functions. Communications will be both internal and external (see Table 7.1) – that is, to other staff within the business (internal) and to customers, suppliers and others outside the organisation (external). This information serves many different purposes, and covers content and formats as varied as drawings, production schedules, sales figures and personal data about employees.

Data must be accessed, moved and stored in a controlled way that conforms to ethical (and legal) standards. All businesses are covered by the Data Protection Act, which sets out how personal information on employees, customers and others should be stored, and it places limits on how this information can be used. Systems should be in place that only let individuals access data relevant to their particular job roles.

All employees of a business are involved with internal communications, but customers, suppliers of materials, and other people and organisations outside the business may only communicate with a limited number of staff. These employees have an important role. The way that a business interfaces with external parties is crucial, because its credibility very often depends on the impressions gained when someone rings up or speaks to a member of staff or looks at the company website. People usually remember bad experiences but forget the good ones. Successful businesses give staff involved with external relations the power to make proper decisions when speaking to customers, suppliers and other people.

Table 7.1: Internal and external communications

Internal communication	External communication
Booking time off for a holiday	Sending an invoice to a customer
Responding to a supervisor's email	Arranging a service call to a customer
Investigating the failure of a component under test	Disputing the accuracy of a supplier's invoice
Gathering and processing statistical data for quality monitoring purposes	Investigating the failure in service of a complex assembly sold to a customer who is threatening litigation

Case study: A problem at sea

Suppose you work as a senior technician in the quality assurance (QA) department of a business that manufactures vibration monitoring equipment. Because your company is an approved subcontractor for a major UK helicopter manufacturer, all products leaving the factory have to be tested and certificated. Components, down to the smallest nut and bolt, must have full traceability so that if a problem occurs in service, investigators are able to follow an audit trail.

Mike is the QA manager at your company and calls you to an urgent meeting. A helicopter has crashed into the North Sea and initial clues, including pilot voice recordings, seem to indicate a rotor head failure caused by excessive vibration. The Civil Aviation Authority (CAA) has grounded all helicopters fitted with the same type of rotor head and monitoring equipment.

An enquiry is under way and Mike has been advised that an investigator from the CAA wants to meet with people from your factory tomorrow. So that nothing is missed, he asks you to put together a checklist of the engineering functions to be represented, together with the necessary drawings and documentation.

1   Why is Mike treating the issue with such great seriousness?

2   Identify a job role within each of the company's engineering functions that will be represented at the meeting with the investigator.

3   What types of documentation will be on your checklist?

4   The investigator will want to see copies of all technical correspondence between your company and the aircraft manufacturer. In what form might this correspondence be?

5   Your technical director will be at the meeting. How will the confidential **minutes** of the meeting be communicated to the managing director who is overseas on company business?

Internal systems

Having good lines of communication between people in a company is important if information is to flow effectively. The lines can be verbal, written (hard copy) and electronic (such as email and specialised software). There should be controls in place to prevent information overload – a growing problem brought about by the proliferation of information on the internet and the overuse of text and emails. It is easy to copy emails to too many recipients, but this is not always necessary. Suppose you are a design engineer sending an email about a routine enquiry to someone in the production department: do you need to copy in your manager and the manufacturing director?

Key terms

Minutes a written summary of the words spoken and a record of any decisions taken at a meeting. They are usually annotated with action points that allocate tasks to specific people.

Activity: People and information

Discuss with a colleague the barriers to effective communication in an engineering organisation, and suggest some ways of overcoming them.

People at work often receive information through conversations and meetings. However, some information must be put in writing. Give some examples of information that should be in writing.

Types of information

Let's now review the different types of information needed to run an engineering business.

- Technical information – this would be needed by employees who are manufacturing a product or setting up a system. The information might be in the form of engineering drawings, circuit diagrams, flow charts, operations sheets, test schedules and inspection procedures.

- Production management data – this is needed by managers responsible for controlling production. They would need a range information, including data from progress records, stock levels, orders and deliveries of raw materials, and quality assurance reports.

- Marketing and sales figures – this would include sales (by turnover and by volume), customer orders and information about customer support services and customer feedback.

- Financial data and general management information – this would include sales projections, income and expenditure accounts, cash flow forecasts, share price movements (if a public company) and budgets for capital equipment.

Ethics

Much of the information flowing around a business will be confidential to some degree. When new staff are taken on they will be expected to sign up to a company policy on communication procedures, such as not passing data to competitors, showing respect for colleagues in written and verbal communication, avoiding unacceptable email content and accessing the internet. Some of the content of this ethical policy is required to ensure that the company complies with the Data Protection Act (see page 246) and the Employment Act (see page 245). Some provisions will be to protect the company's commercial interests (by not passing sensitive information to competitors) and some will be designed to maintain good working relationships.

In a successful organisation you tend to find mutual respect between personnel working at all levels of the business. There will be a culture of integrity in communications. There will be a focus on solving problems rather than generating conflict. For example, consider what happens if a manager is unhappy about the quality of work being produced by a shop floor worker. The manager might summon the worker into the office, threaten the person with dismissal and end up having a row. A better approach – and one likely to adopted in successful organisations – might be to talk through the quality issues and to find out what is causing the problem. Perhaps the worker requires more training or perhaps there are personal problems affecting their performance. A negotiated solution can then be found.

Assessment activity 7.1

P1 P2 P3 M1 D1 **BTEC**

P1
P2 Taking each of the three industry sectors in turn, identify one engineering company that operates in that sector. For each company, state the sector it operates in and its status (the type of business organisation), and describe the nature of its business, its range of products and/or services, and the engineering functions it carries out.

P3 With the help of someone in a local manufacturing company, draw up an organisational chart that shows the lines of command in that company. Then select a product that this company manufactures and describe, with the aid of a flow chart, how information is passed in an effective manner between the people responsible for its design, manufacture, sale and continued maintenance.

M1
D1 Suppose you work for an engineering company that has limited CAD facilities. There is no integration between the CAD systems and the CAM software being used by the manufacturing engineers to produce programmes for the workshop CNC machines. The company's IT facilities are limited and much communication is still by paper-based systems. When a customer phones in to check on the progress of an order, there is usually no up-to-date information available.

You have been asked by your manager to survey the various types of information being passed around the company and between its customers and raw materials suppliers.

(a) Write a detailed memo to your manager explaining how you think information flow and communications can be improved.

(b) Write an evaluation of how the information flow impacts on a specific activity in the company.

Grading tips

P1 P2 For each company, include a brief pen portrait and an image of its logo in your report. You should find useful information on each company's website.

P3 A good starting point here is company flow charts. They may be over complex, and what you should do, with help from an employee, is to simplify them so that just the key elements are presented. Then add written notes.

M1 You should write in a generic way about how information moves around the business and how improvements could enhance the functional activities of the business.

D1 Your evaluation should consider the key aspects of information flow based on evidence gathered for a specific engineering activity. You are evaluating not just how information flow impacts on a chosen activity but also on other functional activities within the business. You should describe problems that might arise from this information flow and suggest opportunities for improvement. The chosen activity should be complex, such as design and manufacture, product development and quality assurance, or commissioning and customer service.

PLTS

Organising a meeting with company manager can be difficult because they tend to be busy people. It may take several phone calls or emails to sort out exactly the information you want. This will help you demonstrate that you can work towards goals, showing initiative, commitment and perseverance.

When you are gathering information about how information flows through a company you will be working with a company manager and probably other employees. For your efforts to be effective you need to have good teamworking skills.

7.2 Understand how external factors and the economic environment can affect the operation of a company

The profitability of a business is influenced by interactions with the marketplace it sells into and the economic climate of the countries in which it is operating. These interactions are classed as external to a business, because they are factors over which it has little or no direct control.

7.2.1 External factors

Many external factors can affect the operation of an engineering company. However, some key questions concern the markets in which the company operates:

- the market conditions – how big is the market into which a company is selling and how much economic confidence is there in the marketplace?

- customers – are the company's products attractive to customers (these could be other businesses or consumers) and are they willing to part with their cash?

- the level of competition – how many other businesses are selling similar products in the market?

Note that strong competition is not necessarily a bad thing. Reacting positively to competition is a key strategy for most businesses. The positive effects of competition are that a business will try to improve its products while at the same time reducing its costs.

Any business that sells directly to consumers (the general public) needs to consider demographic and social trends. Demographics concerns the characteristics of a population, such as age profile, employment status and ethnic background. Currently the average life expectancy of people in the UK is increasing each year, and the manufacturers of products for older persons can take advantage of this expanding market.

An example of a social trend is increased environmental awareness. This is putting pressure on companies to reduce their carbon footprints and it is also influencing consumer choices. For example, it is

shaping the habits of car buyers, with more consumers opting for smaller, more fuel-efficient vehicles. Successful companies anticipate – and react very quickly to – social trends that impact on their markets.

Successful companies also make considerable efforts to maintain good relationships with their customers and clients. If customer relationships are excellent, this will inspire brand loyalty and also generate additional business through customer recommendation. This is a very effective form of free advertising. Some businesses seek to establish good relationships by adopting a 'cradle-to-grave' approach with their customers, by managing all aspects of the relationship from an initial enquiry to providing excellent after-sales support.

Innovation and technological change poses a challenge for engineering businesses. Today's successful product can quickly become obsolete through some technological innovation that transforms the market. This is always going to be an issue for companies that are involved with hi-tech products, such as consumer electronics. There is intense competition to offer 'more for less' and to develop the next generation of 'must have' items which can be sold at a premium price (before competitors catch up with rival products).

Engineering companies must also pay attention to their supply chain and ensure the availability of sustainable resources. When a manufacturing business negotiates contracts with the suppliers of raw materials, it will want assurances that they are able to maintain a continuous (sustainable) supply. Commodity and raw material markets can be volatile. The price of most metals, for example, is influenced by global demand. These are strategic resources, and many commodities and raw materials are sourced from countries that can be politically unstable, which, in a worst case scenario, could result in supplies being severely disrupted.

Activity: Company operations and external factors

Perfect Pots plc produces margarine tubs and containers for the food processing industry. It operates out of a factory with limited storage space. As soon as containers are moulded, they are freighted away by road to its customers' food processing sites across the European Union. The factory operates on a 24/7 basis.

Discuss the impact of each of these events on the operation of Perfect Pots.

- New research is published claiming that low fat spreads are bad for people.
- There is a major fire at a UK fuel storage depot.
- The Channel Tunnel freight service is disrupted.
- There is major damage to offshore oil production platforms.
- Wholesale energy prices increase.
- OPEC decides to increase crude oil production by 20 per cent.
- A new moulding process is invented that uses less material per shot.
- A new type of container has been developed that is made from paper and corn starch.
- The government introduces a green tax on the movement of goods by road.

7.2.2 Economic environment

The profitability of a company will be affected by the economic environment in which it operates. In times of growth and optimism customers have confidence about spending money, and investors are ready to back businesses. When there is a downturn in the economy people (and companies) become worried about racking up too much debt and they are more careful with their money. Consumers postpone or put off planned purchases and companies cut back on capital investment. This presents problems for manufacturers. Should they cut back on production, perhaps risking not having enough stock to meet demand when the economy picks up? Or should they maintain production and stockpile products ready for when demand picks up?

This is a particular problem for any business making mass-produced products. Manufacturing costs will be calculated on achieving an optimum throughput per unit timescale. If, for example, an assembly line is slowed down or stopped for a period of time, the business still has to meet its fixed costs but these now have to be apportioned over a smaller quantity of output. So its unit costs go up.

In a downturn, a business may cut its prices to stimulate demand for its products. If business and consumer confidence is low, there is a danger that customers may wait to see if prices are going to drop further before committing to a purchase, and the situation could become a deflationary spiral (prices exhibit a long-term downward trend). A business might facing rising unit costs (because it has been forced to cut production) and be forced to drop its prices – a recipe for making substantial losses.

Have any engineering companies recently been forced to close in your local area?

Measures

The economic health of a country can be assessed by several measures or indicators. Three measures are particularly useful:

- gross national product (GNP)
- gross domestic product (GDP)
- balance of payments.

Gross national product (GNP) is the monetary value of the total output of all businesses owned by UK citizens irrespective of where the output is produced. Factories that are located in the UK or overseas are counted in this measure (providing that they are UK owned), so while this is a useful measure for comparing the economic performance of different countries it does not give a really clear picture of what is happening in the UK.

Gross domestic product (GDP) is the monetary value of the total output of all businesses situated in the UK irrespective of ownership. This means that the output of businesses like the Japanese company Toyota (UK) and the US company Ford (UK) are included in the measure. It shows what is actually happening inside the UK. The year-on-year change in GDP, expressed as a percentage, is a good measure of economic wellbeing and an indicator of consumer confidence.

For a business or national economy to remain viable, its expenditure should not be greater than its income over the long term. If a country does spend more than it earns, then it is effectively borrowing money to stay afloat. The balance of payments is the difference between all the money coming into a country and all the money going out. Money coming in is generated from exports (of goods and services such as manufactured products and financial services) and money going out is that spent on imports (of products, raw materials, energy supplies etc.).

Services that are sold abroad, such as UK firms providing consultancy expertise to companies overseas, are called invisibles. This is because, unlike with the export of manufactured goods, they do not result in the transfer of a physical product. Countries like the UK that have moved many manufacturing facilities overseas to lower-wage economies usually have a negative balance of payments in visible trade. If invisibles are added into the equation, the trading balance looks much more favourable.

Location

Businesses generate income for the local economies in which they operate. This is for two reasons. First, businesses will often use local services, such as hiring contractors to maintain the building and buying in cleaning services and catering supplies. Second, many employees will live and spend money in the local area. Even employees who commute large distances will spend some money in shops and on local entertainment.

If a large business decides to relocate or close down, this will cause a severe knock-on effect for the local and, possibly, the regional economies. Multinational businesses that have manufacturing plants in different countries regularly review the profitability of each facility, and managers show little sentiment when deciding to a close a plant. This is why local and regional governments take active steps to encourage businesses to locate and remain in their areas. Regional development agencies (RDAs) help new businesses set up, and run campaigns to attract businesses to relocate to different regions within the UK. They are proactive in helping people to develop their skills and businesses to improve their performance. Many small and medium-sized enterprises have been successfully supported by the regional development agencies in the UK.

Economic variables

Businesses regularly borrow money from banks and other sources, so that they can pay for raw materials, acquire new equipment and machinery, and finance the development of new products. Unless a business can set up a deal where the rate of interest on a loan is fixed, the interest payments will be at a variable rate and the business may run into problems if interest rates go up. Commercial interest rates track the Bank of England base rate. This is set on a monthly basis, making it difficult for businesses to carry out long-term planning. When rates are low, it only takes an increase of just a few **percentage points** to effectively double the amount of interest being charged by a bank. For example, if the interest rates is 2 per cent and is increased by two percentage points, the new interest rate would be 4 per cent – it has doubled.

Exchange rates are another factor that a business has to consider when pricing products and paying for imports. Fluctuating currency exchange rates can have a big impact on a business's costs. Figure 7.2 shows the exchange rate of the pound against the US dollar for a 17 month period in 2008 and 2009. Over the period, on average a pound was worth $1.61, but this masks a considerable variation from a high of $2.01 (in July 2008) to a low of $1.35 in March 2009.

This volatility can have significant cost implications. Let's consider an example of a company that needs to buy oil on the wholesale market to fuel its operations. Oil is paid for in US dollars. If the company took bulk delivery of $50,000 of heavy oil in July 2008, this would cost approximately £25,000 at prevailing exchange rates. A year later, a similar bulk delivery of $50,000 of heavy oil would cost approximately £30,500 at the prevailing exchange rates – an increase of 22 per cent. If the unit price of oil remained unchanged over this period (the cost of a barrel of oil in US dollars), the company experienced a significant cost increase in its raw material supplies simply through a change in the exchange rate.

Key terms

Percentage points the difference between two percentages.

Activity: Running a business in uncertain economic environments

With a colleague discuss these scenarios and the questions that they raise.

1   A public limited company (plc) is doing badly and has large bank loans which it finds difficult to service. Last year it was unable to pay a dividend to its shareholders. However, it has now developed a new product with a huge market potential. Its directors are keeping a watchful eye on the company's share price. Why?

2   Many UK companies with markets in the European Union would much prefer the UK to adopt the euro (symbol €) as its currency. Why is this?

3   An engineering company that manufactures metal components using machine tools, presses and welding equipment cannot compete against cheaper imports from the Far East. The owners decide to change its product base, and make equipment from small plastic components and electronic assemblies using its existing labour force. What are the issues which will need to be addressed?

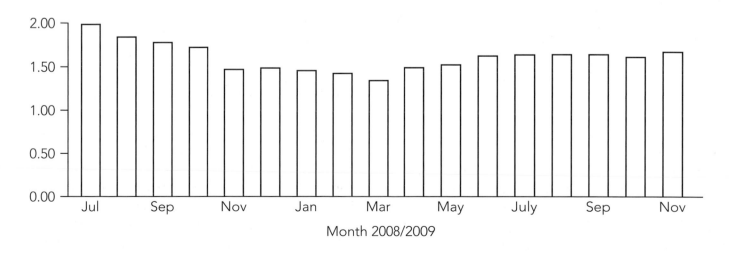

Month 2008/2009

Figure 7.2: US dollar/GB pound exchange rate from July 2008 to November 2009

Case study: A proposal to outsource production to China

Jenny is the marketing director of Powrtol Ltd, an SME that manufactures power tools for the building trade and do-it-yourself markets. Currently all its production is sold to large out-of-town multiple retailers. Due to fierce competition and uncertainty in the economy, the company is struggling to remain viable and must come up with a way to increase **turnover** and profits.

Two years ago the company set up a factory in China, and this has helped to significantly reduce the cost of making products. About 50 per cent of the company's production has been moved to the new factory, and the company's bankers have recommended that all manufacturing be transferred overseas. Under this proposal, Powrtol would operate solely as an importer, distributor and service agent to customers. If it sold its UK factory site to property developers, Powrtol could raise sufficient cash to pay off the company's **bank overdraft** which is increasing at the moment.

Jenny and several of the other directors do not like this idea as it will put a lot of the company's skilled people out of work. They are determined to fight the proposals and want to put together an action plan with some alternative suggestions. Initial thoughts include direct selling through a company website, development of a new product range, a rebranding and marketing campaign, and refinancing. They plan to take advice from the regional development agency (RDA).

You work for the RDA as a consultant and have a meeting planned with Jenny and her directors. To prepare for this meeting, you intend to write some briefing notes based on initial investigations. What information do you need, and where will you find it?

Key terms

Turnover all the income that a business generates in a year.

Bank overdraft a loan facility where a company's bank account is allowed to be 'in the red' up to an agreed maximum. This allows a business to borrow money to pay for raw materials and other expenses before it generates income from selling products.

Royal Assent the final procedure in enacting UK legislation. When proposed legislation (also called a bill) has completed all its parliamentary stages it receives Royal Assent from the monarch (Queen). This is the final stamp of approval.

Statutory instrument secondary legislation (law) produced by an executive authority under powers granted by the legislative authority (Parliament).

7.3 Know how legislation, regulation and other constraints impact on the operation of engineering businesses

Businesses have a duty of care towards their employees, visitors to their premises, customers and anyone else with whom they have a relationship. They also have a responsibility towards the environment. They must adopt recognised financial and accounting practices, and pay any due taxes to the HM Revenue & Customs and other government agencies. Businesses will have auditable systems in place to confirm compliance with UK and European Union legislation and regulations. Non-compliance is treated as a criminal offence and can result in large financial penalties. For cases of serious fraud or serious breaches of health and safety issues, directors can face possible custodial sentences. Non-compliance can also have knock-on effects, such as loss of customer confidence and a reduction in business activity.

The day-to-day operation of engineering businesses is regulated by Local Authorities (through planning control and other local rules) and national statutory controls. These are designed to enable companies to exist in harmony with their near neighbours and the rest of the world. Many UK companies coexist quite happily with their neighbours. They are seen as an asset, providing employment and generating income to support the local infrastructure and services.

Unfortunately, some companies flout local planning and environmental constraints, and do not fully abide by statutory controls governing employment protection and working conditions. This causes public concern, and it then falls on businesses who 'play by the rules' to allay these worries and to influence people's opinions about the contribution that engineering makes to local and national economies.

7.3.1 Legislation

Legislation, also called statutory law, is law that has been enacted by a legislature or other governing body. For example, the Health and Safety at Work Act is a United Kingdom Act of Parliament. This means that it has progressed through the parliamentary system and been given **Royal Assent**. Any person who does not comply with the act is breaking the law and renders themselves liable to prosecution. The European Parliament also legislates by passing directives that have to be implemented by each EU member state.

Several major pieces of legislation have an impact on the operations of every business.

Health and Safety at Work Act (HSAWA) 1974

This is the primary piece of legislation covering occupational health and safety in the UK. The Health and Safety Executive (HSE) is responsible for enforcing this and several other acts and **statutory instruments** that apply to the working environment. For further information about the responsibilities placed on employers and employees by the Health and Safety at Work Act and other safety regulations see the first section of Unit 1 (pages 4–14).

Employment Act 2002

The purpose of this act is to give employees greater protection from being unfairly exploited by employers. The key elements include providing statutory rights that help parents to balance work and family commitments, and it has provisions covering flexible working hours, employment tribunal procedures, workplace dispute resolution mechanisms, equal pay, employment rights for part-time employees, and redundancy payments.

Factories Act 1961

When this act was originally passed it brought together various pieces of legislation covering health, safety and welfare in factories producing manufactured products. It has been superseded by the Health and Safety at Work Act, which applies in all workplace environments.

Regulatory Reform (Fire Safety) Order

This order applies to any type of business premises where people are present. Its provisions are designed to protect people from fire risks.

Every business has to carry out a fire risk assessment of its premises. It then has to implement measures to prevent fires from breaking out and plan how to react to them if they do. This involves identifying the fire hazards, considering the people who may be at risk, evaluating the risk and acting on it, and planning and training staff on how to react if a fire does break out.

The risk assessment has to be regularly reviewed and, if the business employs more than four people, properly recorded.

Data Protection Act 1998

This act concerns the holding and processing of data relating to identifiable living people. It is very easy to collect information about people during many business operations. For example, details about your buying habits are logged every time you use a loyalty card in a shop. This data may then be used for marketing purposes – you might receive mailshots advertising products that might interest you, given your previous buying history.

The Data Protection Act covers the following aspects of handling personal data:

- data can only be used for the specific purpose for which it was collected
- personal data must not be disclosed to other parties without the consent of the individual unless there are legitimate reasons to share it (such as the prevention or detection of crime)
- individuals have a right of access to the information held about them subject to certain exceptions (such as when to disclose the information could interfere with the prevention or detection of crime)
- personal information must not be kept for longer than is necessary and must be kept up to date
- personal information cannot be sent outside the European Economic Area unless there is consent

from the individual, or systems are in place to protect it in the destination country
- businesses that process personal information must register with the Information Commissioner's Office
- businesses holding personal information must have security measures in place to prevent unauthorised access to it
- people have the right to correct factual errors in any information that is held about them.

The Information Commissioner's Office is an independent body set up to uphold information rights in the public interest. It promotes openness by UK public bodies and upholds data privacy rights for individuals.

Companies Act 2006

There have been companies acts on the statute book for around 150 years. They set the framework within which companies operate. The same rules apply to both private limited companies (Ltd) and public limited companies (plc). All companies have limited liability – this means that the owners (shareholders) of a company are not personally liable for all the debts of the business should it fail.

Before 2010, every company had **articles of association** and a **memorandum of association**. These provided information about the purpose and operation of the company. Since October 2009, the articles of association have become the primary document, subsuming the role of the memorandum of association.

Key terms

Articles of association regulations which govern the relationships between shareholders and directors of a company, including voting rights, issuing of shares, declaration of dividends.

Memorandum of association a document which governs the relationship between a business and the outside world. It details the purpose of the business and how it operates.

The Companies Act sets out key elements of company law and corporate governance. It sets out the legal framework within which companies are formed, operate and do business. It has provisions covering:

- a statement about the purpose of the company
- how a company should be formed
- valid company names
- shareholder arrangements and officers (management)
- how decisions should be made
- raising share capital
- accounting procedures and annual returns
- mergers and takeovers
- disqualification of directors
- transparency obligations, such as publishing accounts.

Did you know?

All limited companies in England, Wales, Northern Ireland and Scotland are registered at Companies House. There are more than two million limited companies registered in the UK, and more than 300,000 new companies are incorporated each year. Many companies fail, particularly new start-ups, and a substantial number of companies are also dissolved each year.

7.3.2 Regulations

Business are subject to many regulations that govern or constrain their operations. Many regulations derive from the implementation of European Union directives into UK law. These directives ensure 'harmonisation and fair trading' across all EU member states.

There is a whole raft of legislation that applies to working in engineering. Many of these regulations are designed to protect employees in the workplace. These have been considered in some detail in Unit 1. You should be aware of these regulations:

- Employment Equality (Age) Regulations 2006
- Management of Health and Safety at Work Regulations 1999
- Provision and Use of Work Equipment Regulations (PUWER) 1998

- Control of Substances Hazardous to Health (COSHH) Regulations 2002
- Lifting Operations and Lifting Equipment Regulations 1998
- Manual Handling Operations Regulations 1992
- Personal Protective Equipment at Work Regulations 1992
- Confined Spaces Regulations 1997
- Electricity at Work Regulations 1989
- Noise at Work Regulations 1989
- Reportable Injuries Diseases and Dangerous Occurrences Regulations 1998
- Working Time Regulations 1998
- Workplace (Health, Safety and Welfare) Regulations 1992
- Health and Safety (First Aid) Regulations 1981.

You do not need to have detailed knowledge of these regulations, but you should be aware of the broad areas that they cover and their main purpose. Read through pages 4–14 of Unit 1 to refresh your understanding.

The titles of the regulations that apply to engineering, and to the situations in which you may find yourself working, are usually self explanatory. It is very easy to access information about them from web searches. For example, there is useful information about legislation and regulations on the website of the Office of Public Sector Information (OPSI). You might also find printed copies of legislation at your place of work or at college. The specific content of any legislation can be very complex and sometimes difficult to understand. Businesses sometimes employ legal specialists who can provide advice on the precise obligations in law. Bodies such as the Health and Safety Executive publish guidance to the law, written in simple and clear language to help employers and workers understand their legal responsibilities.

It is worth exploring the consequences for a business if it disregards the legislation and regulations applicable to its industry. Investigate a company with which you are familiar and find out what administrative procedures it has in place to ensure regulatory compliance. If it exports to other EU member states or to the USA, find out if it needs to take additional steps to conform with the legislation in these countries.

7.3.3 Environmental constraints

An engineering business should operate in an ethical and responsible way. This means showing responsibility towards the environment and due care for its employees. There is increasing public concern both about how we treat the planet and about the treatment of workers, particularly in the context of outsourcing production to low-wage economies and transporting finished products over large distances. This concern can sometimes influence purchasing choices. So not only does a company have an ethical duty of care, it also makes business sense not to alienate customers. This helps a company maintain market share.

Several environmental issues have an impact on the operation of engineering businesses, including

• sustainability

• environmental impact of operations

• use of renewable energy resources

• reducing carbon footprints

• recycling and product end-of-life strategy.

Let's consider each of these in turn. Environmental sustainability is a key concept of the green movement.

There is increasing pressure to manufacture products from materials derived from renewable sources, such as using softwoods rather than hardwoods in wooden features and components. The problem in engineering is that many products are made from metals and polymers, which are derived from finite, diminishing resources of raw materials.

Engineering companies must consider the environmental impact of their operations on the environment in terms, for example, of noise, traffic movements, carbon emissions, generation of waste, and energy needs. Current environmental legislation is very tough. When a new factory is designed it has to conform to many regulations, including provisions covering thermal insulation, energy management and external light pollution.

Most factories use large amounts of power taken from the National Grid. Some companies are looking to cut their energy bills by using renewable energy resources generated on site and by better energy management. For example, fitting solar voltaic panels to a suitable roof can reduce electricity demand. These are successfully used in some office buildings to power IT systems. Other applications of using solar energy are improving natural lighting and installing thermal updraft ventilation.

Businesses, like individuals, need to consider their carbon footprint. This is a major issue for the 21st century. Businesses must react positively to legislation to meet CO_2 emission targets. They need to respond to pressure from consumers to produce products that have lower manufacturing and operating footprints.

In the past, companies have not been required to pay attention to what happens to their products at the end of their useful life. The problem now faced by society is that the principle of 'use it and chuck it' is no longer a viable option, and we all need to take responsibility for what we make and use. Engineering companies have always been good at recycling scrap materials, such as swarf, waste oils and cutting fluids, generated during the manufacturing process. They now need to consider an end-of-life strategy, which covers repair, refurbish and recycle or disposal. This is now a requirement when designing a new product. In the future, it is likely that legislation will be introduced making it illegal to sell products, such as cars and domestic appliances, without a proper end-of-life strategy. This process could be monitored by a standards agency.

Engineering businesses need to consider their carbon footprint. Can you suggest some ways that companies can reduce their energy costs?

Activity: A greener society?

Write a brief commentary to go with these statements.

Designers must take account of what will happen to a product when it reaches the end of its useful life.

Remanufacturing a product to extend its working life benefits the environment.

The general public can influence the design and manufacture of products in the global marketplace.

7.3.4 Social constraints

A business will operate more effectively if it has well-motivated, trained staff working at all levels throughout the enterprise. Some people, such as directors, will be making strategic decisions, others will largely be working under supervision, such as production line operatives. The key to success is for everyone to add value to the business through effective working. Everybody in a company needs to understand that they make a contribution. However, a problem that you may have when starting out in engineering is accepting the huge differences in salaries. Why is a senior manager earning perhaps six times the wage of a machine loader? Why do managers get the use of a company car and laptop? One answer is the different level of training and responsibility required for each role.

Senior managers will be expected to be on call from home if a major problem occurs at any time. At weekends, they may spend a few hours at home doing catch-up work. They have responsibility for the whole business. But what about the role of the machine loader? Loaders work set shifts, and if they don't carry out their job properly, the machines will stop, and production will be lost. So who has the more important job and whose contribution should be more valued by the shareholders? How senior managers and machine loaders perform at work can have the same consequences on the **bottom line** – make mistakes and the business suffers. Although not all equal in pay and status, if each employee respects the other's contribution the business will function much more effectively. Even more important is that everyone in the business has respect for their fellow workers.

Key terms

Bottom line the final line in a profit and loss account. In other words, how much profit a business makes.

To achieve the general aim of having a well-motivated and effective workforce, a business needs to take account of several issues.

Employment levels

The first thing a business needs to consider when setting up a new production facility or manufacturing plant is where to find staff. Key questions include:

- are there enough people with the required skills in the local area?
- will the recruitment process need to be national or international – that is, will it involve finding workers from other parts of the country or from Europe?

Workforce skills levels and training requirements

Across a business there will be a huge range of skill and expertise requirements. Matching the correct person to a particular job role requires great skill on the part of a company's human resources department. People work better if there is a degree of stretch or challenge in their jobs, but not to the point where the roles are so challenging that they become stressed and demotivated.

To understand this point, consider the course you are taking. You may find some of the units on the BTEC National programme easier to understand than others because you have a natural flair for them. You might get merits and distinctions for some units, but only a pass for others. This will help you recognise your strengths, and you can use this to advantage in the next stage of your studies.

The same principle applies to matching people to job roles. A company needs to assess employees' skill levels and aspirations, train them to what they are capable of achieving, periodically review their performance and, where appropriate, provide further training or updating.

Self improvement, progression and motivation

Some people are quite happy doing a routine job for many years, and will remain loyal committed company workers. Others like to be challenged and they will actively seek promotion through looking for training and being self-motivated to build on and improve their expertise. Progression opportunities are very often identified when a line manager reviews performance with a member of staff during an appraisal meeting. This information is then passed to the human resources department, where a company training and development plan is put together. This is usually done on an annual basis, with a review every six months.

Keeping people motivated is a key feature of successful businesses. Interestingly, several studies have shown that money is not always the main motivating factor at work. Job satisfaction seems to be a much bigger motivator. How do you motivate an assembly operative fitting one small component to a sub-assembly moving along a conveyor belt? One well-known national company improved staff motivation (and quality of work) by explaining to its operatives where the sub-assembly was going to be fitted and showing what the final product looked like. The operators could see the purpose and value of what they were doing – and they were being praised for their efforts. People like to be thanked, and it costs nothing to do it.

Outsourcing

To remain competitive, many UK companies have been forced to outsource their production to areas of the world where labour costs are lower than the UK. This raises all sorts of social and moral issues. There are concerns about the working conditions in low-wage economies. People question whether companies pay fair wages in these countries and whether there is too much exploitation of poor workers. There is growing consumer awareness and unease about the worst aspects of outsourcing production abroad, making it difficult for some businesses to strike a balance between economic viability and responsibility.

When production is transferred overseas it results in job losses in the UK, with a reduction in disposable income in the locality of the UK plant and a knock-on effect on shops and other businesses. The argument put forward by company shareholders and directors is that only by lowering manufacturing costs can the business survive. Fewer UK jobs, they argue, is better than no employment at all if the business is forced to fold. This debate will run and run. What do you think?

Case study: Finding a replacement for Kem

Kem is the health and safety officer for Ocla Engineering, a successful small business that produces fabrications from aluminium and stainless steel sheet. Its products include benching and fume extraction systems that are fitted in commercial kitchens. Each product is tailor made to the customer's specification, and the finished product installed and commissioned by Ocla technicians.

Fabrication processes include guillotining, stamping, bending and welding – all potentially hazardous activities unless the correct health and safety procedures are followed. To date, the business has an excellent safety record and enjoys good relations with the local community.

Kem is being promoted to general manager and has to find a replacement. He knows that you have completed a BTEC National and you are currently in the final stages of a NEBOSH qualification. (NEBOSH is the National Examination Board in Occupational Safety and Health.)

The job specification for the new health and safety officer will also include responsibility for ensuring that the company complies with the latest environmental legislation. The owner of the business and Kem arrange an informal interview.

1 How will you prepare for the interview?

2 What questions might you be asked?

3 Do you know where to look for information on the relevant regulations?

Assessment activity 7.2

P4 A UK manufacturing company supplies most of its product to the USA and has negotiated regular deliveries over a 10-year period. The contract was signed five years ago, with the product being priced in sterling (£) and with an agreed price uplift each year equivalent to the average of the USA and UK inflation rates. At the time the exchange rate was $1.5 to the pound. The US customer has asked for a price review. Explain why they want this and what effect it might have on the profitability on the UK business.

P4 In 2009, the Chinese economy had a positive balance of payments and was able to build up large reserves in the bank. To take advantage of the lower cost base, many UK companies relocated their manufacturing facilities to China while maintaining design and support services in the UK and EU.

Why is a Chinese engineering company able to produce manufactured parts more cheaply than in the West while still maintaining quality?

What external and economic factors might derail a Chinese engineering company's manufacturing success?

P5 A CNC technician is using a machining centre which has only recently been installed and commissioned by its manufacturers. While setting up the tooling, the machine starts up without warning and the technician suffers a serious injury to both hands. A nearby worker cuts power to the machine and summons a first-aider. The technician is taken to hospital and will be off work for several weeks.

You are the company's health and safety manager. With the aid of a flow chart, describe the steps you will take to investigate the accident and identify the legislation and regulations that are relevant to this case.

Due to the serious nature of the injury you can expect a visit from an HSE inspector. What documentation will the inspector expect to see, and who will the inspector want to interview?

Your company is currently tendering for a big contract and is bidding against a competitor based about 10 miles away. You are under strict instructions from your managing director not to talk anyone outside the factory about the accident. Why is this?

continues...

Assessment activity 7.2 continued...

P4 P5 P6 M2 D2 **BTEC**

P6 A factory built originally on a greenfield site is now ringed by housing estates. It employs about 200 people and is the largest business in the locality. Some people living nearby are trying to get it closed down because they are concerned about two of the manufacturing operations: metal stamping, which they claim is very noisy, and electroplating, which involves the use of cyanide and they see this as a deadly process.

The company is to make a presentation to the residents' association describing the environmental and social constraints that impact on its business, and explaining how it complies with legislation and has good 'green credentials', particularly in respect of discharging waste water from the onsite treatment plant into a nearby river. The company also wants to highlight the economic benefits it brings to the local community.

Your manager asks you and a colleague to prepare an outline script and a ten-slide PowerPoint presentation. Try it out on others in your group.

D2 Using the company where you work, or one which you have visited, evaluate the importance and possible effect of external factors on its operation. You are looking to consider the effects of factors such as Bank of England base rate changes, political conflict between countries, climate change and carbon footprint issues, prices of raw materials, and supply of strategic materials.

Grading tips

P4 For these tasks, you should get hold of current dollar/pound exchange rate data and overview what is meant by the terminology 'weak pound' and 'strong pound'.

P5 All businesses have to follow set procedures when dealing with the type of problem described in this task. Ask a manager in a local company or a technician at your college to talk you through the steps they must follow when accidents occur. Think about how to establish who is responsible for the accident, and the possibility of claims for compensation, and litigation.

P6 You need to identify generic constraints that impact on engineering businesses and then home in on two issues highlighted by the residents. You must make reference to relevant legislation.

M2 To develop your P6 answer for a merit grade, you should make a balanced argument that picks up on the possible tensions between making a profit and complying with legislation in a highly competitive marketplace.

D2 By using a real company, you will have access to published financial data (such as share price movements and trading figures) and other economic data. Also think about European and world market conditions, consumer confidence and political disputes between countries.

PLTS

To explain the impact of legislation on the operation of a business you will have gathered and reviewed data, decided whether it was sufficient for your needs and then processed it to produce a conclusion.

Key terms

Share issue the process of selling shares in a company on the stock market to raise capital for investment in the business.

7.4 Be able to apply costing techniques to determine the cost effectiveness of an engineering activity

Operating an engineering business is a complex operation because it involves the integration of a wide range of functions when products are being manufactured or a service is being provided to a customer. These functions include designing, machining and assembly, testing, marketing, sales, public relations, recruiting and managing staff, after-sales support, raising finance, financial planning, day-to-day management of finances, biding for new work, and ensuring compliance with relevant standards and legislation. To ensure that the functions all interlock correctly, a business will follow short-term and long-term plans. These plans are produced by managers, and they will be based on accurate data provided by others within the organisation.

The consequences for not accurately assessing the cost effectiveness of an engineering activity can be severe – these range from negative customer reactions if prices are too high to making losses, leading to making employees redundant and perhaps ultimately business failure. A company may have a great idea for a new product that should 'clean up' in the marketplace but see it fail because development proves too costly or because development is not sufficiently robust, resulting in a finished product that is not fit for purpose and customers demanding financial compensation.

7.4.1 Costing techniques

To maintain profitability, a business needs to have in place an effective costing system that accounts for the true cost of manufacturing, delivering and servicing its products. There are several costing techniques that can be used, ranging from simple costing based solely on material and labour inputs to much more sophisticated procedures which build in the costs of research, development, overheads and the purchase of new equipment.

Income and expenditure

If you spend more than you earn, you will have a problem unless you can borrow to keep afloat. An engineering business derives most of its income from selling manufactured products and providing services to its customers. It may have other income, such as the interest on earned on bank deposits, and it may raise additional finance through borrowing and **share issues**. In this part of the unit, however, we will focus solely on trading income, that generated from the sale of goods and services.

Profit and loss

Each year a company will expect to make a trading profit, also called a surplus, on its trading activities. Some of this profit will be used to meet the company's tax liabilities, and some will be used to make dividend payments to shareholders. This remainder can be ploughed back into the business to finance new projects. If a business has several products, it can afford to make losses on one or two individual products. For example, it would expect to make a loss during the development stage of a new product – after all, there is nothing to sell to generate income – but it would carry this loss providing the product has good potential future earnings.

Cost control

An engineering business will incur a range of costs during the financial year, including:

- business rates and property rental charges
- utility charges for energy (gas and electricity) and water
- insurance premiums
- purchase of raw materials, and bought-in components and sub-assemblies
- waste recycling charges

- purchase and maintenance of **capital equipment**
- tooling and consumables
- salaries and national insurance
- office costs such as IT leasing, telephone, postage, printing
- transport costs, such as cars, lorries and handling equipment.

When calculating **factory gate prices**, the various cost elements have to be identified and then apportioned accordingly. There are four basic categories or types of cost:

- direct costs
- indirect costs
- fixed costs
- variable costs.

Direct costs are those that can be attributed to a particular activity or a particular product line. The direct costs for a product include the costs of raw materials, components and labour involved in its production. This is easy to work out if you know, for example, the prices of materials and hourly wage rates.

Indirect are all the other costs incurred by the company. For example, the company has to pay business rates and insurance premiums but these cannot be *directly* apportioned to individual activities or products. It is more complex to take indirect costs into consideration when working out the costs of individual products. One method is to use apportionment. Suppose the total indirect cost for a factory is £10,000, and it makes just two products A and B in equal quantities. Product A has direct cost of £10 and product B a direct cost of £50. We assume that product B is more complex, using more material and labour, and so it might be reasonable to suppose it 'consumes' more of the indirect cost. Using the apportionment method, we apportion the indirect cost to each product in the same proportion as the direct costs. So the indirect costs incurred by product A is:

$$10,000 \times \frac{10}{(10 + 50)} = £1667$$

Similarly, for product B it is:

$$10,000 \times \frac{50}{(10 + 50)} = £8333$$

The indirect cost per unit is then found by dividing these figures by the quantity manufactured.

Key terms

Capital equipment the large (and often expensive) machinery, such as a machine tool, required for production. The value of capital equipment is shown in the company balance sheet, but reduced each year to allow for depreciation. Depending on the type of equipment, its value is written off after a given length of time when it is assumed that the equipment is obsolete.

Factory gate price the price of a product when bought direct from the manufacturer. The shop price will be much higher because it has to take account of distribution costs and retail overheads. Factory gate price = production cost + manufacturer's profit margin.

The direct costs plus the indirect costs are the total costs of the business. However, it is useful for managers to know which of these costs are fixed and which are variable. Fixed costs are those that must be paid regardless of the amount of production. They are costs which are fixed for a given period of time, such as the buildings insurance (which is an annual premium) or the salary of a design engineer.

By contrast, variable costs vary according to the quantity manufactured or the amount of service provided. For example, the cost of electricity to power a machining centre or of staff paid by the hour will depend on the level of production. If in one period, the company decides to cut production and produce fewer units, these energy and staff costs will correspondingly reduce.

The factory gate price is based on the total of all costs (the job cost) plus a contribution to revenues. This is an added percentage, sometimes called a margin or mark-up.

Did you know?

Businesses can offset some of the cost of purchasing capital equipment against tax. HM Revenue & Customs (HMRC) publishes information about how small and medium-sized businesses can claim capital allowances on their investment in plant and machinery.

Table 7.2 shows how the cost breakdown for producing a product can be set out using a spreadsheet. Revised figures can be entered as things change, for example if the price of raw materials goes up.

Unit 7 Business operations in engineering

Table 7.2: Hydraulic actuator cost calculation

Direct costs	Cost/time		Unit cost (£)
Body (1 off)			
Material	4.00	£	4.00
Machining time	5.00	minutes	3.75
End cap (closed end) (1 off)			
Material	1.50	£	1.50
Machining time	3.00	minutes	2.25
End cap (rod end) (1 off)			
Material	1.60	£	1.60
Machining time	4.00	minutes	3.00
Piston rod (1 off)			
Material	3.00	£	3.00
Machining time	5.00	minutes	3.75
Seals			
Piston head	0.50	£	0.50
Piston rod	1.00	£	1.00
End caps	0.50	£	0.50
Long studs and nuts (4 off)	1.00	£	4.00
Assemble and test	18.00	minutes	9.00
Package for dispatch	10.00	minutes	2.50
Indirect costs	20.00	£ per hour	15.00
Machining centre cost	45.00	£ per hour	55.35
Assembly and test	30.00	£ per hour	total £
Package	15.00	£ per hour	

- The costs of materials and components are shown as values in the unit cost column.
- The cost of a timed operation is based on the cost per hour and the time taken. For example, the cost of machining the end cap is based on a machining rate of £45 an hour and a time of 3 minutes, so the unit cost is $(3/60) \times 45 = £2.25$

Check through the table and see if you agree with the calculations for all the timed operations.

Marginal costing

Suppose a factory has installed a new production line, which can produce a given number of products during an eight hour shift. The product has been costed on the assumption that the machinery will be paid off over five years. The company now decides to increase production by running the line for an extra two hours each day. This will involve additional variable costs, in terms of the cost of the additional materials, energy and labour needed to run the line for two more hours each day. However, the company's fixed costs will not have changed.

In costing the additional output, the company can therefore ignore the fixed costs. This is because fixed costs such as the cost of purchasing and installing the production line have already been accounted for in the previous costing. Using this as a basis for calculation is called marginal costing. The additional products will have lower costs because fixed costs (direct and indirect) are ignored.

255

Case study: Andrea seeks investment for her business

Andrea's project on her BTEC National Engineering course involved the design and manufacture of an innovative new product. Her tutor was so impressed that he suggested she enter a national engineering competition for young people, but Andrea was concerned that someone else might steal her idea.

Her business operations tutor explained that she could apply for a **patent** but warned that this would be an expensive process. With financial help from her family, Andrea obtained a patent for her invention. She entered and won the competition, and she has now decided to set up her own business to manufacture and market her product.

Andrea is forming a partnership with two of her colleagues from college and they are now looking for an investor to put start-up capital into the new business. The three partners have identified a suitable factory building and know what machinery

and equipment they need to get started. On the strength of the publicity associated with winning the engineering competition, a large multiple retailer has placed an order for 20,000 units.

Suppose you are a potential investor and you have invited Andrea and her colleagues to present their business plan. First they tell you about the function of the product and its potential in the marketplace. You say, 'Yes, great idea, I like the product but what's in it for me? We need to do the numbers.'

1 What numbers are you talking about?

2 How will Andrea and her team try to convince you to say, 'Yes, I'm in.'

3 If you do say 'yes' what paperwork will you expect to see in order to confirm that the numbers are correct?

Key terms

Patent prevents competitors from copying the ideas and features that make something work. Patents are valid for a fixed period of time.

Fixed assets

Fixed assets are equipment, property, plant, trademarks and other tangible items which a company owns and which cannot be easily converted into cash. These major assets will be listed in the company balance sheet with a value subject to year-on-year depreciation or possible appreciation in the case of buildings and land. A company's fixed assets are revalued at the end each financial year.

For example, suppose a machining centre is purchased for £250,000 and has an asset life of 10 years. What is its residual asset value after four years? Let's assume straight line depreciation – that is, the asset depreciates at a constant rate each year. So we assume that it is worth £250,000 when it is bought and nothing at the end of 10 years and it depreciates by £25,000 (£250,000 divided by 10) a year. So, at the end of year 4:

$$\text{asset value} = 250 \times \frac{(10-4)}{10} = £150,000$$

Activity: Cost analysis

Table 7.3 presents the bill of materials for an electronic control panel. The panels are assembled in batches of 500, each batch requiring 100 hours of labour charged at £21 per hour. The overhead apportioned to the product is £160,000 per year and the company works on a profit margin (contribution) of 35%.

Calculate the factory gate price per unit.

Table 7.3: Cost of materials

Part	Cost per unit (£)	Quantity per panel
LCD panel (60 x 40 mm)	2.00	1
Printed circuit board	12.00	1
Touch pad	3.00	2
Back-up battery	6.00	1
Processor	19.50	1
Chassis	5.00	1
Case	19.00	1
Memory chips	12.50	3
Connectors	2.25	4
Switches	2.00	3

7.4.2 Make-or-buy decisions

There are situations where it is not economic to manufacture a product. For example, if a product has high tooling costs but only a small production run, it may not be possible to make sufficient profit to pay for the tooling costs. It may be more economic to outsource production to a subcontractor who is already tooled up and who will sell you a finished product. Instead of making, you are buying. The questions that have to be asked before coming to a make-or-buy decision are:

- can the item be made using existing on-site facilities?
- if it can be made by the existing facilities, is there enough capacity to handle the extra production?
- if it cannot be made by the existing facilities, how much direct cost and resource is involved in setting up a new production facility?

The starting point is to carry out a breakeven analysis. To illustrate this concept, let's consider a worked example. We need to calculate the break-even quantity for a component, given this data.

Fixed cost (tooling and overheads)	£120,000
Variable cost per unit (materials and labour)	£26
Selling price (factory gate)	£40

One method is to present this data as a break-even graph. To do this, plot two lines. One line shows the costs (C) against quantity manufactured (N) using the formula:

$$C = 120{,}000 + 26N$$

The second plots the revenue (S) against quantity (N) using the formula:

$$S = 40N$$

The data used to plot these lines is shown in Table 7.4 (although you only need two points, see Unit 4 page 114) and the graph is shown in Figure 7.3. The break-even quantity is where the lines intersect on the graph. In this case, it is 8500 units.

Now suppose that a sales forecast estimates that the market can only take 5000 units. If production goes ahead, the company will incur a loss – it needs to produce 8500 units before it breaks even and more than 8500 units before it shows a profit. It simply is not good business practice to produce only 5000 units. It will make more sense to outsource the production to somewhere with lower costs.

Table 7.4: Breakeven data

Quantity (N)	Manufacturing cost (C) £'000s	Sales revenue (S) £'000s	Margin (M) = (C – S) £'000s
0	120	0	−120
1000	146	40	−106
2000	172	80	−92
3000	198	120	−78
4000	224	160	−64
5000	250	200	−50
6000	276	240	−36
7000	302	280	−22
8000	328	320	−8
9000	354	360	6
10000	380	400	20
11000	406	440	34
12000	432	480	48
13000	458	520	62
14000	484	560	76

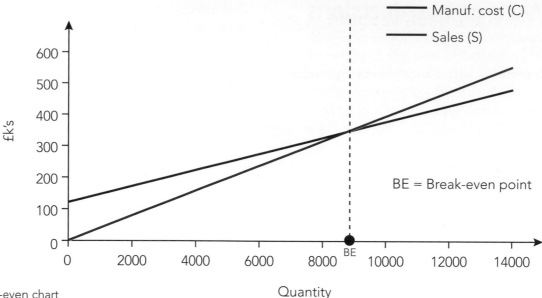

Figure 7.3: Break-even chart

Activity: Costing techniques

Calculate the break-even quantity for a component using a break-even graph. This is the cost and price information for the component:

Fixed cost	£94,000.00
Variable cost per unit	£17.50
Factory gate price per unit	£30.00

Investment appraisal and return on investment

Any business considering a new project must decide whether it is a worthwhile investment. A company might have a research and development department that generates many ideas, but how does it choose the ones which will give the best return on investment? Should it go for short production runs of highly profitable items which go out of fashion, or long continuous runs of products which produce regular but lower margins over a long period of time?

In general, the bottom line for any analysis of the return on investment is whether the likely profit that will be generated by the investment is greater than the interest that would be earned by leaving the money in an interest-bearing bank account. If you can make more than you could earn in interest, then the investment is potentially attractive.

Did you know?

Because newly purchased products lose a significant amount of their value in the first year of operation, some businesses prefer to buy second hand.

Pay-back time, financial risk and development costs

When money is invested in a new project, there is always an element of financial risk. Money is being tied up in development costs, materials, the costs of gaining of a patent, tools and equipment. When the product comes on stream and generates income, the profits will be used to pay back the initial investment. How long this takes depends on the requirements of the investors. These might be shareholders or simply the finance director committing funds from the company reserves. Long-term projects with high development costs carry the highest level of financial risk.

Activity: The Dyson vacuum cleaner

James Dyson used his own money to design and develop his first bag-less vacuum cleaner. Dyson offered his invention to major UK manufacturers, but they turned him down claiming that they were not interested in his new technology. He went to Japan, found investment, started manufacturing and launched the product. The rest is history.

Investigate the real reason why the major manufacturers of bagged vacuum cleaners were not interested in James Dyson's revolutionary design when he offered it to them.

Machining centre purchase price	£180,000	
Depreciation (straight line p/a)	18%	
Control valve		
Cost of material and parts	**Quantity**	**Cost per item (£)**
Aluminium casting	1	18.00
Connector	4	2.00
Spring	2	2.50
Piston	1	8.00
Solenoid actuator (includes seals and fixings)	1	32.00
Limit switch	2	6.40
Machining time per unit	0.50	
Machining centre cost per hour	£45.00	
Assembly time per unit	2.00 hours	
Labour cost per hour	£26.00	
Test and certification time per unit	0.60 hours	
Labour cost per hour	£28.00	
Variable overheads (% labour cost)	34.00%	
Fixed overhead (% variable cost)	25.00%	
Production quantity (p/a)	Variable	

Table 7.5: Hydraulic control valve cost details (see assessment activity 7.3 overleaf)

Assessment activity 7.3

P7 P8 Carry out a cost analysis for a product using this data:

Overheads	£20,000
Tooling	£2500
Variable cost per unit	£20
Production volume per month	100 to 1500.

If the factory gate price is to be £42, construct a break-even chart. Then investigate the effect on the break-even point if the selling price is increased to £48.

A wholesaler wants a trial order of 500 units but at the non-negotiable price of £35 per unit. Is this a viable proposition?

P7 P8 The body of a hydraulic control valve is machined from a bought-in casting. The machining centre currently in use is very old. It has stopped working and the manufacturing director is keen to replace it with a new one.

The finance director is not convinced that the machine should be replaced given the variable quantities of valves likely to be produced each year, particularly as the casting supplier has recently set up its own specialised machine shop. It has tendered to supply the valve body fully finished at a guaranteed fixed price of £80 a unit.

Produce a cost analysis for the valve by using the data in Table 7.5 and initially working on a figure of 1000 units per annum. Then carry out a what-if evaluation using production levels in the range 200 to 1600 units per annum.

Given that valve sales over the next 12 months may not be more than 600, what do you think is the best option – to purchase the machining centre and machine the body, or to buy in the body ready finished?

Fully justify your recommendations in a memo to the finance and production directors.

M3 Produce a 500-word report explaining some of the strategies that can be used to improve the cost-effectiveness of producing a manufactured a product. Explain how the make-or-buy decision could be amended or made more conclusive.

Grading tips

P7 P8 Present your findings for the cost analysis using a spreadsheet. You should investigate what is meant by 'marginal costing'. For the control valve problem, work on an initial quantity of 1000 units per annum, and set out the data in a spreadsheet. Use a chart to support your make-or-buy decision.

M3 Use either the valve detailed in the previous task or a product manufactured at your place of work as exemplars. Think about the cost and quality of raw materials, production quantities, labour content and overheads. Talk through your proposals with a manufacturing engineer before finalising your report.

PLTS

When you were reaching the make-or-buy decision for the given product this should have involved discussion with other people. You may well have used a bit of persuasion to get your case across. In completing this assessment activity you will also show that you able to process and evaluate information when carrying out investigations.

Functional skills

Carrying out costing calculations and techniques to inform make-or-buy decisions will develop your skills in mathematics (identify the situation or problem and the mathematical methods needed to tackle it).

Andrea Brown
Value engineer, Enneillag Ltd

My company has been in business for about 20 years and manufactures generic pharmaceuticals for two of the major high street chemists. Our factory operates on a 24/7 basis and has highly automated preparation, packaging and quality assurance systems.

The medicines and cosmetics business is highly competitive and our customers expect year-on-year reductions in unit prices. This can be very difficult to achieve because many of our products involve raw materials derived from oil, such as plastic bottles and vacuum packaging film. All the time we are looking for ways to reduce manufacturing costs by increasing the throughput of the machines and by developing new product lines.

I work with a colleague, and what we do is to look at how a product is made and see if we can come up with more cost-effective methods. Each production line has a supervisor and a several operatives who load up the packaging, change containers of bulk product and remove pallets of finished product.

An interesting part of my job is talking to the line operators, because they can sometimes come up with really good ideas about speeding up the production process. Last year we had a problem with a bath gel which is bottled in glass. The vibratory conveyor system feeding the bottles into the filling machine was shattering some of the bottles and also producing noise levels contravening the Noise at Work Regulations. Talking to one of the operators I discovered that the filling machine was a modified version of one originally designed for plastic bottles. The operator suggested that a solution might be to fit impact pads and guides to the sides of the conveyor and to run the machine a bit faster to prevent the bottles bunching up.

I said, 'It will mean fitting new electric motors and taking the machine out of commission for a couple of days – and there's the cost of adapting the machine and the lost production.' The operator, who was a second-year apprentice, said, 'I've worked out the cost of the modification – the pay-back time is only four weeks.' I talked to one of our production engineers and the modification went ahead.

Think about it!

1 What data would be needed to do the cost calculation?

2 Why does Andrea need to know about regulations?

3 The company receives an order that would involve hiring more staff and installing new production lines. Andrea joins a team to evaluate this proposal. List six items that the team should discuss at a first meeting.

Just checking

1 For each of the three main sectors of the economy, identify one engineering company operating in that sector. Describe the products and structure of each company.

2 Why is it important to have good lines of communication in a company?

3 Why do engineering businesses have to operate in accordance with enforceable legislation and regulations? What will be the economic consequences for a business if it fails to do this?

4 If you want to find information about a particular regulation, how would you start your search?

5 Businesses have systems in place to ensure that they keep up to speed with the latest legislation and regulations. Overview how they operate.

6 A company is reviewing its business plan in respect of external factors. What are external factors?

7 What effect do upturns and downturns in the UK and global economy have on a business's profits?

8 Why is it necessary to have a properly trained and motivated workforce?

9 An experienced shopfloor worker has applied for promotion to a management position in an engineering business. The human resources (HR) director is not sure if the worker is up to it. What specific concerns will the director have?

10 Why is it important for a business to have up-to-date information about its cash flow position?

11 What might be the consequences of not risk assessing the financial activities of a business?

12 How can a business ensure that it remains sustainable?

edexcel

Assignment tips

- Learning outcome 3 covers legislation and regulations. You are not expected to be an expert on all the regulations listed in the unit content. To achieve P5 you only need to identify the specific legislation and regulations that apply to a business scenario that your tutor will give you. For M2, you need to explain the impact of the legislation. Again it's not the fine detail that you are explaining – just the impact. For example, the COSHH regulations run to many pages, but what you are after is the overview and reasons for the regulations, which are given on the first page.

- Make sure that you get your tutor to complete observation records or witness statements for any assessment activity that has non-written evidence. This could be when you are speaking or presenting to an audience, or doing something in real time which needs reporting on.

- The distinction grading criteria require that you carry out evaluations. This means that you will be reviewing information and forming a conclusion based on the evidence that you have assembled. Because this evidence, or pointers to it, has to be presented in your portfolio, it is sensible to confirm with your tutor how much should be included.

- Where an assignment activity involves contacting an engineering company, you should acknowledge this in your written evidence by giving brief details of anyone you spoke to, such as their name, job role etc.

10 Properties and applications of engineering materials

An engineering material is, quite simply, any man-made or naturally occurring substance that can be used to build, construct or manufacture just about everything we see in the world today. Engineering materials are used to manufacture drinks cans, tools and machinery, cars, aeroplanes, ships, bridges, buildings etc. The list is endless, and so, almost, is the list of materials. There are some 22,000 materials available to use in engineering applications.

In order to gain an understanding of materials, we must understand, first and foremost, their structure. We need to know what a material is made from and what it looks like under close examination. Structure is important because it determines, to a large extent, the properties of the material. Properties dictate how a structure, component or product will react when it is subject to forces when it is put into service.

In studying this unit, you will develop a sound knowledge of materials. You will learn how they are 'put together' and how processing can change their behaviour. You will understand how engineers select materials for specific applications and also the ways in which materials can fail.

Learning outcomes

After completing this unit you should:

1 know the structure and classification of engineering materials

2 know material properties and the effects of processing on the structure and behaviour of engineering materials

3 be able to use information sources to select materials for engineering uses

4 know about the modes of failure of engineering materials.

Assessment and grading criteria

This table shows you what you must do in order to achieve a pass, merit or distinction grade, and where you can find activities in this book to help you produce the required evidence.

To achieve a **pass** grade the evidence must show that you are able to:	To achieve a **merit** grade the evidence must show that, in addition to the pass criteria, you are able to:	To achieve a **distinction** grade the evidence must show that, in addition to the pass and merit criteria, you are able to:
P1 describe the structure (including the atomic structure) associated with a given metal, polymer, ceramic, composite and smart material **Assessment activity 10.1 page 278**	**M1** explain how the properties and structure of different given engineering materials affect their behaviour in given engineering applications **Assessment activity 10.2 page 286**	**D1** justify your selection of an engineering material for one given application describing the reasons why the selection meets the criteria **Assessment activity 10.3 page 290**
P2 classify given engineering materials as either metals or non-metals according to their properties **Assessment activity 10.1 page 278**	**M2** explain how one destructive and one non-destructive test procedure produces useful results **Assessment activity 10.4 page 297**	**D2** evaluate the results of one test procedure **Assessment activity 10.4 page 297**
P3 describe mechanical, physical, thermal, electrical and magnetic properties and state one practical application of each property in an engineering context **Assessment activity 10.2 page 286**	**M3** explain how two given degradation processes affect the behaviour of engineering materials **Assessment activity 10.5 page 300**	
P4 describe the effects on the properties and behaviour of processing metals, polymers, ceramics and composites, and of post-production use of smart materials **Assessment activity 10.2 page 286**		
P5 use information sources to select a different material for two given applications, describing the criteria considered in the selection process **Assessment activity 10.3 page 290**		
P6 describe the principles of the modes of failure known as ductile/brittle fracture, fatigue and creep **Assessment activity 10.5 page 300**		

P7 perform and record the results of one destructive and one non-destructive test method using one metal and one non-metallic material **Assessment activity 10.4 page 297**			
P8 describe a different process of degradation associated with each of metals, polymers and ceramics **Assessment activity 10.5 page 300**			

How you will be assessed

This unit will be assessed by a series of assignments that are designed to allow you to achieve the necessary assessment criteria and to demonstrate your knowledge in terms of the learning outcomes.

The assessments themselves will be designed by your tutors at your place of study. They may take the form of:

- presentations
- case studies
- practical tasks
- time-constrained tests.

Steven, 17-year-old engineering apprentice

Studying materials science proved very difficult at first because some of the main concepts that you need to know in order to understand the structure and properties of materials were quite new and very challenging.

However, by studying hard I started to understand how materials behave, and how their structure and properties were key to understanding how they behave. I started to appreciate how engineers and designers select and use materials.

When I am at work, I now look at the metals that I work with in a different light. When I am working with a particular steel, I know what it is made from and what it looks like under a microscope. I know also, for example, that the greater the carbon content, the harder and stronger it will be.

Once you get to know materials in detail, the subject can be fascinating. I enjoyed carrying out all the practical tasks associated with this unit, because it made studying much more interesting. I got the opportunity to carry out tests on materials and investigate their properties in a very practical way.

10.1 Know the structure and classification engineering materials

**Starter stimulus:
Classifying materials**

Working in small groups, or with your tutor, think of as many engineering materials as you can and list them. See if you can fill a full side of A4 paper.

Next, see if you can group all of the materials in your list under a small number of main headings and, where necessary, subgroups. Finally, try to find examples of at least three materials in each group or subgroup.

To get you started, one of the main groups is metals, and these can be subdivided into ferrous alloys, non-ferrous metals and non-ferrous alloys. Now do the same with the others. Discuss your findings with each other and with your tutor.

It was the ancient Greeks who first had the idea that all matter was made up of tiny particles that we now know as **atoms**. They believed that an atom was what you ended up with if a piece of matter was divided in half repeatedly until it couldn't be divided any more. However, it was Niels Bohr, a Danish physicist, who first described the atom in a simple way. Figure 10.1 shows Bohr's model of the atom.

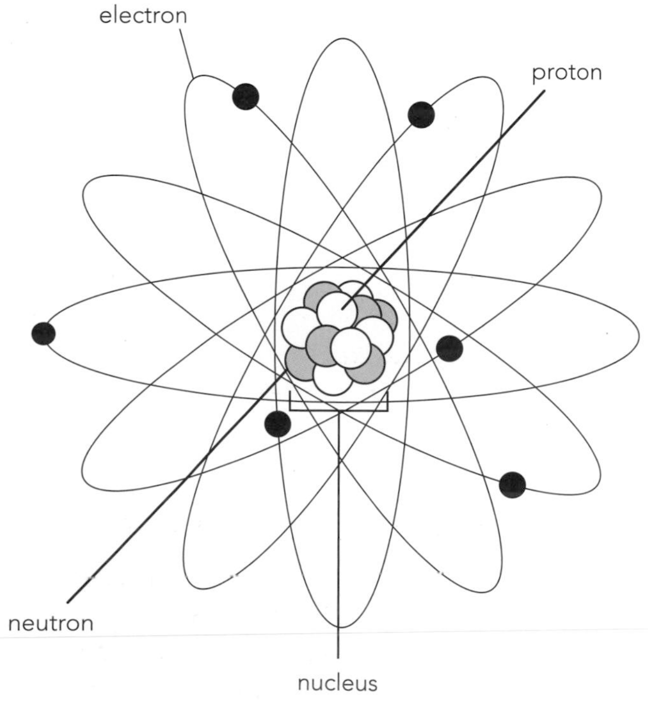

Did you know?

Niels Bohr (1885–1962) was one of the most important physicists of the twentieth century. He received the Nobel Prize in 1922 for his work on the atomic structure and quantum mechanics.

10.1.1 Atomic structure

There are three basic subatomic particles that make up an atom. These are protons, neutrons and electrons. Protons and neutrons bond together to form the central part of the atom, known as the nucleus. Protons have a positive charge. This means that they will repel each other in the same way as two like poles (north and north, or south and south) in magnets. Neutrons have zero electrical charge and they are able to hold protons together to form a stable nucleus. This is why neutrons are important. The atomic structure of any material needs a sufficient number of neutrons to hold the nucleus together.

Electrons – the third type of subatomic particle – orbit the nucleus. Electrons have a negative charge. They are tiny, and only have 1/1800 of the mass of a proton or neutron. In an atom, there are the same number of protons as electrons. This is to ensure that the atom remains electrically neutral – that is, the positive and negative charges are balanced.

electron

proton

neutron

nucleus

Figure 10.1: Bohr's model of the atom

Electrons orbit the nucleus in a series of 'shells'. The outermost shell of electrons of an atom is known as the valence shell, and the electrons in the valence shell are called **valence electrons**. Valence electrons are important because they characterise the atom. More importantly, valence electrons take part in atomic bonding and, therefore, chemical reactions.

Atoms bond together in order to form matter. Where atoms of the same type bond with each other, they produce what is known as an **element**. For example, the metallic element we know as iron is a collection of iron atoms bonded together. It is also possible for atoms of a different type to bond together. For example, two hydrogen atoms can bond with an oxygen atom to form H_2O (water). Where atoms of different types bond together the resulting particle is called a **molecule**. If a large number of molecules of the same type bond together, they form a **compound**.

Atoms bond together in different ways depending on whether they are metals or non-metals. Metals have either one, two or three valence electrons. Non-metals have five, six, seven or eight valence electrons. Atoms with four valence electrons – such as boron – can sometimes behave like a metal and sometimes like a non-metal, depending on circumstances.

The characteristics of valence electrons allow:

- metallic atoms to bond to non-metallic atoms
- non-metallic atoms to bond to other non-metallic atoms
- metallic atoms to bond to other metallic atoms.

Each case gives rise to a different type of atomic bond – the ionic bond, the covalent bond and the metallic bond. Let's take a closer look at each of these types of atomic bond in turn.

Key terms

Atom consists of a nucleus, made up of protons and neutrons, along with electrons which orbit the nucleus.

Valence electrons the electrons in the outermost shell (known as the valence shell) that orbit the nucleus.

Element a collection of atoms of the same type.

Molecule a particle formed when different types of atom bond together.

Compound a collection of molecules of the same type.

Ion an atom that has either a positive (cation) or negative (anion) electric charge through losing/gaining an electron.

The ionic bond: electron donors

Atoms are electrically neutral because they have the same number of protons and electrons. However, it is sometimes possible for atoms to gain or lose a valence electron. An atom that has gained or lost an electron is known as an **ion**. Losing an electron makes an atom positive because it effectively has an extra proton. Gaining an electron makes the atom negative because it has one more electron than protons. An ionic bond is one formed between two atoms, one a positive ion and the other a negative ion, and, since positives and negatives attract, the atoms bond with each other.

In order to understand the ionic bond, let's consider the atoms of sodium, a metal, and chlorine, a gas. The sodium atom has a single electron in its valence shell but has eight electrons in the next shell inwards towards the nucleus. Chlorine has seven valence electrons. Atoms need to be stable, and one of the ways that they can achieve stability is by having eight valence electrons (the most they can have in the valence shell). So let's review what happens when a sodium atom and a chlorine atom are brought together.

1 The sodium atom 'donates' its single valence electron to the chlorine atom. This effectively removes its existing valence shell. It is replaced by the next shell inwards, which has eight electrons and therefore a more stable structure.

2 The chlorine atom accepts the electron from the sodium atom, and adds it to its valence shell. It now has eight valence electrons, again a more stable structure.

3 The sodium atom, having lost an electron, has become a positive ion. The chlorine atom has become a negative ion because it has gained an electron. Since positive and negative charges attract, a bond is created between the two atoms.

4 This ionic bond between a metal and a non-metal creates the sodium chloride molecule (NaCl). This is the chemical compound we know as common salt.

The covalent bond: electron sharers

A covalent bond forms between two non-metals. Consider a situation in which the atoms of two elements both have seven electrons in their valence (outer) shells. In this case, an ionic bond will not form because if one atom was to 'donate' an electron it would only be left with six electrons in its valence shell (a weaker structure) although the other atom would have a full complement of eight outer electrons. However, if the two atoms 'shared' their seventh electron, then they would each effectively have eight valence electrons. To do this, the two atoms would need to be in close proximity to each other, and this resulting attachment is known as a covalent bond. The covalent bond can be seen in the molecule methane (CH_4). The single carbon atom has four valence electrons that it shares with four hydrogen atoms.

The metallic bond: electron losers

Because metals only have one to three valence electrons, the forces of attraction between the valence electrons and the atomic nucleus are relatively weak. This effectively means that valence electrons can become quite easily detached from the nucleus and they form a 'sea' of free electrons surrounding the atoms. The atoms become ionised as they lose electrons and, because they are all positively charged, they try to repel each other. However, they are held in check and balanced by the attractive forces of the free electrons. These forces of mutual attraction pull the whole structure into a regular pattern. It is for this reason that metals have a regular geometric structure.

Activity: Molecular bonding

We have described the bonding mechanisms between atoms. Molecules can also bond together. Find out more about molecular bonding by undertaking research on the internet or in a library. Describe a process by which molecules may be bonded.

10.1.2 Structure of metals

The metals and alloys used in engineering are produced by industrial processes. They are separated from the ore and mixed together in furnaces to form a molten mass. They are cooled and allowed to solidify.

To understand the structure of metals, we need to consider what takes place when a metal solidifies. Let's take as an example a mass of molten aluminium in a crucible. As the aluminium cools it eventually reaches its freezing temperature of 660°C. At this point, solidification takes place. Figure 10.2 shows the stages in this process, from nucleation, through dendritic growth and dendritic contact, to final solidification.

The first stage is nucleation (stage 1 in Figure 10.2). Atoms bond to form a tiny mass of solid metal.

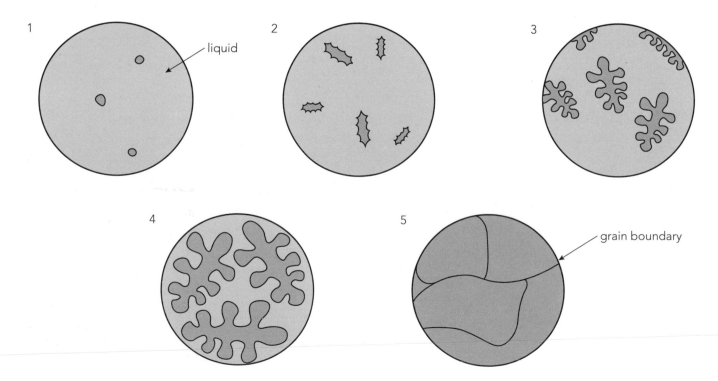

Figure 10.2: Solidification of a pure metal

These small clusters of atoms begin to grow larger (see stages 2 and 3 in Figure 10.2). However, they do not grow as uniform spheres. Instead, they develop a tree-like structure as more atoms join to the solid metal. This type of growth is known as dendritic growth, with each cluster eventually becoming a 'dendrite'. The word comes from the Greek *dendros* meaning 'tree'. The dendrites grow larger, developing more complex branched structures. This is because of the way that the atoms in the liquid bond with the atoms of solid metal. We will discuss this further when looking at metal crystal structures.

Eventually, the dendrites that formed from nuclei become so large that they will make contact with each other (stage 4 in Figure 10.2). It is important to note that when they do so, they do not become attached. Where a dendrite makes physical contact with another dendrite, any further growth will be stopped immediately. The metal will now consist of large dendrites of solidified aluminium with liquid aluminium in between the dendrite arms.

Eventually, the remaining liquid metal will solidify (stage 5 in Figure 10.2). The complex dendritic structure that existed before final solidification is replaced by one which consists of solid grains or 'crystals' of pure aluminium. The structure of the aluminium, and indeed all metals and alloys, is called 'polycrystalline' (that is, it comprises many crystals).

Activity: Solidification

Research the difference between the solidification of a pure metal and the solidification of an alloy that contains two metals. Why do you think the process differs?

Metal crystal structures

The structure of a material dictates its properties and behaviour, both during manufacture and when the material is subject to forces when it is being used in service. The structure influences material properties that are important in engineering, such as strength, hardness, toughness and ductility. These terms are

defined in section 10.2 (see page 279). We will return to and develop this theme – the relationship between a material's structure and its properties – throughout this unit.

The nature of the metallic bond is such that the atoms of metals are held together in a regular geometric pattern. This pattern is known as a crystal lattice structure (or, more commonly, a lattice structure). The smallest part of a crystal lattice that can be identified is known as a unit cell. The French metallurgist, Auguste Bravais, identified several different types of crystal lattice structure. Figure 10.3 shows three of the most commonly found crystal lattice structures:

- body-centred cubic (BCC)
- face-centred cubic (FCC)
- close-packed hexagonal (CPH).

The unit cell of a body-centred cubic structure is based on a simple cube. A metal atom occupies each corner of the cube and there is another atom that sits in the centre of the cube – hence the name 'body-centred cubic'. Metals with BCC structures are characterised as being relatively strong.

Face-centred cubic metals have a unit cell that, like the BCC structure, is based on a simple cube. Like BCC metals, FCC metals have an atom on each corner of the cube. They don't have an atom in the centre of the cube, but they do have an extra atom on each *face* of the cube. In total, FCC metals have 14 atoms: eight corner atoms plus six face atoms. Metals with FCC structures, such as copper and aluminium, are characterised as being tough and ductile, but relatively weak.

A CPH structure is more complex because it is based on a hexagon rather than a cube. Think of a regular two-dimensional hexagonal shape such as the head of a bolt. A CPH structure consists of two hexagons, one above the other. There is an atom on each corner of the hexagons (12 atoms in total: six on each hexagon), and a further three atoms arranged in the form of an equilateral triangle sitting in between the two hexagons. The triangle of atoms in the centre of the structure holds the two hexagonal components above and below in place. Metals with CPH structure are characterised as being relatively weak and brittle. Zinc, cadmium and pure titanium have CPH structures.

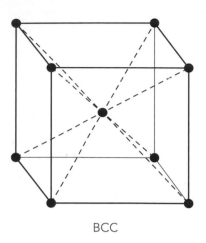

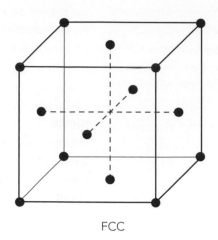

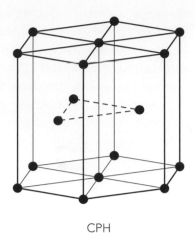

BCC   FCC   CPH

Figure 10.3: Three common crystal lattice structures

Activity: Crystal structures

We have featured three lattice structures. Bravais discovered several other types of lattice structure. Undertake some research so that you can identify some of the other structures described by Bravais.

We noted that the structure of a material governs its behaviour. So why does a crystal lattice structure dictate mechanical properties? When the shape or geometry of a piece of metal is changed, such as when a metal is formed, rolled, bent or squeezed during a manufacturing operation, vast numbers of atoms in every crystal must move. A metal's mechanical properties are directly related to the ease (or difficulty) of this atomic movement. In FCC metals, the movement of atoms is relatively easy. As a result, FCC metals are weaker but much more ductile. Atomic movement (also known as 'slip') in BCC metals is more difficult because the arrangement of atoms in the lattice structure. Consequently, BCC metals are stronger and also harder.

Metals with CPH structures behave in a slightly different way. The atoms in FCC and BCC metals can move in a several directions, which makes deformation easier, but the atoms in CPH metals are very constrained and can only move in a very limited number of directions. If the atoms cannot move by slip when a force is applied to the metal, then the atomic bonds fail and the metal breaks or fractures. This is why CPH metals tend to be weak and brittle.

Alloying

An alloy is a metallic material consisting of a mixture of two or more metals or a mixture of metals with a non-metallic element such as carbon. Table 10.1 lists some common alloys and gives their constituent elements.

Table 10.1: Common alloys

Alloy	Elements
Brass	Copper + Zinc
Bronze	Copper + Tin
Steel	Iron + Carbon
Stainless steel	Iron + Carbon + Chromium
Duralumin	Aluminium + (4–6%) Copper

Alloying is a very cost-effective way to improve the properties of a metal. Steel, which is made by the addition of carbon to iron, is far stronger than pure iron. Stainless steels, which contain at least 12% chromium, have exceptional corrosion resistance. Adding nickel to stainless steel produces a tougher and more ductile material, one that is easier to fabricate and that can be used for very low temperature applications where ordinary steels become brittle and prone to failure. In the vast majority of cases, the greater the content of the added element(s), the better the alloy.

Alloying works by impeding atomic movement. It is more difficult for atoms to move in the alloy, and this increases the strength of the material. When atoms of an additional element are integrated into the structure of the metal in which they are dissolved, they distort the crystal lattice because these atoms will be a different size (they could be smaller or larger) from that of the base metal. This creates what are known as strain fields. Because the crystal lattice structure is strained, extra energy is needed to cut, bend or shape the alloy in a machine, equating to greater strength.

This has practical consequences. For example, if the cutting capacity of a guillotine is 15 mm for mild steel plate, the same machine will have a lower capacity for stainless steel. It may only cut 12 mm thick stainless steel because the chromium atoms in the stainless steel cause lattice strain. So it requires more energy to cut a stainless steel plate than a mild steel plate of equal thicknesses. In order to avoid damaging the machine, a lower cutting capacity is set for stronger materials.

Solid solutions

All metals and alloys are made from some basic 'building blocks'. We have covered one of these building blocks – crystals of pure metal – above. However, alloying processes produce other forms of material. These are:

- solid solutions
- intermetallic compounds
- eutectics.

Let's first consider solid solutions. If we add salt (NaCl) to water, it will dissolve. The ionic bond between sodium and chlorine (sodium being the metallic and chlorine the non-metallic element) breaks, and the two atoms exist as positive sodium ions (Na+) and negative chlorine atoms (Cl-) in the water. This is known as a **solution**. The water in which the salt dissolved is called the **solvent** and the salt is called the **solute**.

Now consider when we melt two metals, say copper and nickel, together. In the molten state, this can be described as a solution – one metal is dissolved in the other in its liquid form. When this alloy solidifies, it forms a polycrystalline alloy with an FCC structure. This condition is known as a **solid solution**. If we could see the crystal lattice structure for this alloy, it would comprise copper and nickel atoms. The relative number of copper atoms and nickel atoms would vary with the amounts of each metal that were melted together. If equal amounts copper and nickel are used, then we would expect to see the same number of copper and nickel atoms. The two metals can still be regarded as being dissolved in each other, even though the alloy is solid.

There are several types of solid solution, but the main ones are substitutional solid solutions and interstitial solid solutions. In substitutional solid solutions, atoms of one element replace or 'substitute' atoms of another element in the crystal lattice structure. In interstitial solid solutions, the solute atoms (those which dissolve into the primary element) are small enough to take up residence in the spaces between the atoms of the solvent on the crystal lattice structure. The spaces between the atoms on a crystal lattice are known as **interstices**, hence the name interstitial solid solution.

Solid solutions are of interest to engineers because the elements used in these alloys – and the resulting structures – can produce a wide range of useful properties.

Intermetallic compounds

Solid solutions are formed when the atoms of the elements in the alloy have reasonably similar chemical and electrical properties. However, where the atoms of the elements are very dissimilar in nature, they will form compounds. The structure of a solid intermetallic compound – a compound with a metallic element – is very different from that of the bulk material in which the compound forms.

Intermetallic compounds are very hard and brittle. As a result, they have limited use in engineering alloys. Steel is, however, an exception. Iron carbide (Fe_3C), also known as cementite, is the intermetallic compound that gives steel its strength. Up to a certain point, you can make steel stronger by increasing its carbon content. However, too much carbide produces a negative effect and the steel will become brittle.

Key terms

Solution a mixture of two or more substances dissolved in each other.

Solvent a liquid, solid or gas that dissolves another liquid, solid or gaseous substance.

Solute a substance that is dissolved in another substance (or solvent).

Solid solution the solid-state of a solution that retains the crystal structure of the solvent.

Interstice a small intervening space between atoms.

Eutectic structures

There are only a few metals that will combine to form solid solutions. These include copper, nickel, gold and silver. However, while most metals are able to dissolve in each other in a liquid state, they cannot form a solution when the alloy solidifies. In these cases, a eutectic will form during solidification. The word 'eutectic' comes from the Greek word *eutectos*, which means easily melted.

An alloy that contains metallic elements that don't combine to form solid solutions will produce eutectic material along with crystals of pure metal. The amount of eutectic that forms within an alloy depends on the relative amounts of each metal in the material. The eutectic material has the effect of lowering the melting point of the alloy. You can adjust the alloy composition to find the combination that produces 100 per cent eutectic material. This material composition will give the alloy its lowest melting point, hence the term 'easily melted'.

Eutectics are easily identified in metallic alloys because they have a layered or laminated structure known as a lamellar. Eutectics are a beneficial constituent of alloys, especially where they consist of solid solutions.

10.1.3 Structure of polymeric materials

In the first decades of the last century, there were significant advances in material science. For example, Wallace Carothers, a chemist who worked for DuPont, invented nylon. This proved hugely successful when used to make women's stockings. Leo Baekeland, a Belgian chemist, invented a material that bears his name – Bakelite.

Both of these materials are polymers (known more commonly as plastics or plastics materials). There are three main types of polymer:

- thermoplastics, such as nylon
- thermosetting plastics (thermosets), such as Bakelite
- elastomers, such as rubber.

Thermoplastics are characterised by the fact that they soften on heating, and as a result they can be remoulded many times over. They are relatively weak and have poor properties at high temperatures. They are composed of long-chain molecules, which hold the

polymer together by a combination of entanglement and strong forces of molecular attraction.

There are some thermoplastic materials which do not gradually soften as temperature increases. These are rigid thermoplastics, which have associated with them the 'glass transition temperature' (abbreviated to Tg). The glass transition temperature is the temperature at which the plastic loses its rigidity and becomes soft. It is an important property because it can be used to specify the maximum service temperature of the polymer. For example, polycarbonate, which is widely used to manufacture television cabinets and computer casings, has a Tg of 150°C. It remains rigid up to that temperature, and then begins to soften, losing strength very quickly.

Thermosetting plastics undergo a clearly defined chemical change on heating. They are often referred to as condensation polymers, because water vapour is produced during their manufacture. The chemical change induced by heating results in a more rigid structure, and one that cannot be re-melted once formed. The structure of a thermosetting plastic is a solid network of molecules. This is why most thermosets are hard, rigid and quite strong.

Elastomers are based on either natural rubber (latex) or synthetic rubbers such as neoprene. They have high **elasticity**.

Key terms

Elasticity an elastic material is one that can return to its original shape after the removal of the forces that made it deform. Materials that display this property after relatively large forces are said to have high elasticity.

The process of polymerisation

The word polymer means 'many mers'. A mer (or monomer) is the smallest identifiable component of a molecule. (A monomer is similar to the unit cell in metals, the smallest part of a metal's crystal lattice structure that forms on solidification.) Polymerisation is the process by which monomers bond together to form polymer chains or, in the case of thermosets, networks of molecules.

We will use polyethylene, a very common plastic, to describe the polymerisation process. Ethylene is a gas with the chemical formula C_2H_4. It consists of

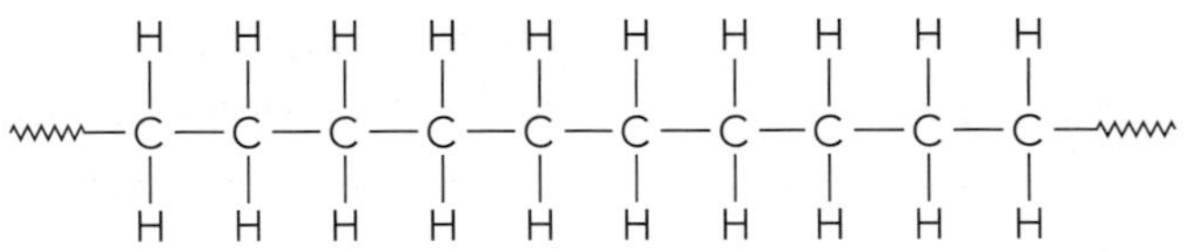

Figure 10.4: A polyethylene molecule

two carbon atoms sharing a double bond, with each carbon atom separately bonded to two hydrogen atoms. The carbon double bond is a point of instability, and this bond breaks under the action of heat and pressure in the presence of a catalyst. This leaves a single bond between the carbon atoms and frees up a valence electron, which then bonds covalently (shared electrons) with an adjacent carbon atom. As Figure 10.4 shows, this allows repeated carbon–carbon bonds to form a long-chain molecule.

Crystallinity in polymer materials

Polymers are generally amorphous, meaning that they have no regular structure. (Note, this is in direct contrast to the polycrystalline regular structures of metals.) However, some polymers exhibit structures in which there are areas where the chain molecules fold and align in precise regular patterns. Any type of regular arrangement of molecules in a polymer can be regarded as crystalline.

During the 1950s, polymer single crystals were first solidified. These crystals took the form of thin platelets, approximately 10 nm (nanometres) thick and with lateral dimensions as large as 0.01 mm. The most important discovery was that the chains were aligned at right angles to the flat surfaces. Since the length of an individual chain is up to a thousand times greater than the thickness of the platelet, the only conclusion that could be reached was that the chains were folded.

Many bulk polymers are crystallised to form spherulites. A spherulite consists of a number of ribbon-like chain-folded crystallites. A crystallite is a lamellar structure consisting of alternating bands of chain-folded and amorphous regions. In a spherulite, the crystallites radiate out from a common centre.

10.1.4 Structure of ceramics

Ceramic comes from the Greek words *keramikos*, which literally means 'dirty stuff', and *keramos*, the clay used by potters. Ceramics have a very varied chemistry,

and range from quite simple to extremely complex structures. Ceramics can be divided into two main categories – those that are covalently bonded and those that are ionically bonded. The more complex ceramics contain both covalent and ionic bonds.

Covalent ceramics may be further subdivided into two groups:

- simple covalent ceramics
- ceramics containing combinations of different atoms.

Simple covalent ceramics are made from a single element. Diamond, for example, is a simple covalent ceramic. It consists of carbon atoms bonded covalently in a specific way. The abrasive silicon carbide (SiC) has exactly the same structure as a diamond, but with silicon atoms replacing some of the carbon atoms.

The more complex covalent ceramics are silicates. Silica is formed when a silicon atom bonds with four oxygen atoms to form a tetrahedral structure – that is, a pyramid with an equilateral triangular base. This arrangement can be regarded as similar to the unit cells found in metallic structures. In this structure, the oxygen atoms can bond with other similar silicon tetrahedra or ionically bond with metal atoms. This produces a diversity of ceramic forms.

10.1.5 Structure of composites

A composite is a material made from two or more constituent materials, which retains the properties of each constituent material but has some superior overall properties through the combination of ingredients. The materials that make up a composite remain chemically inert. The concept of composites dates back several thousand years. For example, it has long been known that bricks made by mixing straw with clay are superior to bricks made from clay alone.

Composites are made from two separate structures or 'phases'. A phase is a material, or part of a structure, that has the same chemical make-up throughout. Water exists in three phases – liquid, vapour (steam) and ice. In steel, ferrite is a phase. In composites, the bulk material is known as the matrix phase or, more commonly, the matrix. The material that is added to the matrix, and which provides the superior properties of the composite, is known as the reinforcement phase. Let's look at an example. Glass-reinforced plastic (GRP), commonly known as fibre glass, consists of an epoxy polymer into which is mixed strands of glass fibre. In this composite, the polymer is the matrix phase, and the glass fibre is the reinforcement phase.

The matrix phase of a composite can be a polymer, a metal or a ceramic. The reinforcement phase may be fibres or particles. Examples of reinforcement used to produce composites include:

- glass
- silicon carbide
- ceramic materials
- carbon fibres
- boron fibres
- other metals.

The combination of the two materials in a composite generally produces a material that has high strength in relation to its weight. In other words, composite material usually has a high strength-to-weight ratio. Composites have many engineering applications, including:

- structural components such as boat hulls and train carriages
- machine components such as gears and cams
- advanced cutting tools.

Strength and loading conditions

The basic concept behind a composite material is that, in combination, the materials that make up the composite have superior properties to those of the individual ingredients. The matrix phase is designed to:

- hold the structure together as well as carrying the applied load over a large area
- transfer the load to the reinforcement, which can carry a greater load.

In addition to carrying the load, the reinforcement phase also makes the composite more rigid. It should be noted that in some composites the matrix acts as the main load carrier. Some other composites also share the load equally between the matrix and reinforcement phases.

Since it is the reinforcement phase that provides the main strengthening mechanism, it is convenient to classify composites according to the characteristics of the reinforcement phase. There are three main types:

- fibre reinforced – in this group, fibre is the main load-bearing component
- dispersion strengthened – in this group, the matrix (bulk) phase carries the major load
- particle reinforced – the load is shared between the matrix and the reinforcement phases.

The precise mechanical properties of a composite are governed by:

- the amount of fibre used in the reinforcement
- the ratio of the length to the diameter of the fibres – this determines how efficiently the load is transferred from the bulk material to the reinforcement
- the strength of the bond between the fibres and the matrix.

10.1.6 Structure of smart materials

A smart material is one that has a property (or properties) that can be radically altered by the application of an external stimulus, such as heat or an electrical current. Much research is currently being undertaken to develop these materials. The most common types of smart materials in use include piezoelectric materials, electro-rheostatic and magneto-rheostatic materials, and shape memory alloys.

Piezoelectric materials

Piezoelectric materials have two related properties. They produce a small electrical voltage when pressure is applied to them. Conversely, they can also change in volume (by up to 4 per cent in some cases) when an electric current is passed through them.

These materials are widely used in sensors that measure changes in fluid density or viscosity, or the force of an impact. For example, modern cars are fitted with piezoelectric crystal sensors to detect the force of a collision impact. A sufficiently large force causes the crystal to produce an electrical signal. This is transmitted through the firing circuit, causing the airbags to activate.

Electro-rheostatic and magneto-rheostatic materials

The main feature of these materials is that they undergo a radical change in their viscosity when subjected to either an electrical current or magnetic field. These materials are thick fluids (similar to motor oil) but they can become almost solid, sometimes within a millisecond, when a current or a magnetic field is applied. When the field is removed, they immediately revert back to their original form. These materials are used in shock absorbers, vibration damping equipment, prosthetic limbs, braking systems, clutches and valves.

Shape memory alloys

Shape memory alloys have two unique features: the 'shape memory' effect and 'pseudo-elasticity'. The most widely used shape memory metals are:

- nickel-titanium alloys
- copper-zinc-aluminium alloys
- copper-aluminium-nickel alloys.

The shape memory effect relies on a change in the crystalline structure of the alloy when a load is applied or the material is heated to some critical temperature. When a component is manufactured from a shape memory alloy, the material structure is initially austenitic – that is, it has a face-centred cubic structure. On cooling, the FCC structure transforms to a different crystal lattice structure known as martensite, after its discoverer, the metallurgist Adolf Martens. If a force is applied to the alloy that changes its shape in some way, the martensitic structure becomes deformed. However, if the alloy is then heated, the thermal energy supplied to the metal causes the deformed martensite to transform back to its original structure – FCC austenite. As a result, the alloy springs back to the shape it had prior to being deformed.

Pseudo-elastic shape memory alloys do not require the application of heat in order to achieve a change in shape. Instead, they rely on simple loading in order to achieve a change in structure and therefore shape. The case study on unbreakable glasses (see below) explains how these materials behave.

Typical applications of shape memory alloys include spectacle frames, medical equipment, dental implants and mobile phone antennae. They are biocompatible – they are non-toxic and don't cause unwanted side effects in medical applications – and they have good mechanical properties. However, they are very expensive to manufacture and they have poor fatigue properties compared to normal alloys. For example, a steel component can withstand 100 times more fatigue loading cycles than one made from a shape memory alloy.

Case study: Unbreakable glasses

Some brands of glasses are advertised as 'unbreakable'. They can be bent and twisted, but will spring back to their original shape. The frames of these glasses are made from a nickel-titanium alloy that has the property of pseudo-elasticity. When the frame is deformed by an applied force, then at some critical point the structure transforms from austenite to martensite. This transformation 'absorbs' the energy that is applied during the deformation process. Once the load is removed, there is an immediate reverse transformation from martensite to austenite – the original crystal structure that was present when the glasses frames were manufactured.

So, if you own such a pair of glasses and you accidentally sit on them, the frame does not become damaged beyond repair because of a metallurgical change in the structure of the alloy. As with all material properties, structure is the key.

1 Research some other applications of smart materials. Consider electro-rheostatic and magneto-rheostatic materials as well as shape memory alloys and piezoelectric materials.

2 Can you identify the relevance of smart materials to:

a) ultrasonic testing

b) braking systems in heavy goods vehicles

c) modern art (particularly sculpture).

10.1.7 Classification of metals

At the beginning of this unit, you were asked to group engineering materials together in some sort of order. This is known as classifying materials. There are several ways to classify materials. Some classifications are quite simple, such as grouping materials into metals and non-metals. Other material classifications are more complex as they take into consideration features such as structure, properties and behaviour. In this section, we will look at how we can classify materials in a simple and understandable manner. We will start by considering metals. Metallic materials can be subdivided into three main categories:

• ferrous alloys
• non-ferrous metals
• non-ferrous alloys.

Ferrous alloys

Ferrous alloys contain iron as the main alloying element. Wrought iron is the pure form of iron – there is no other element present. Iron, like all pure metals, is relatively weak but it can be greatly strengthened by alloying. This explains why pure iron has limited use in construction. Steel, however, is widely used. The addition of carbon to iron in order to make steel has been one of greatest breakthroughs in engineering.

Steels are classified according to their alloy content. Plain carbon steels – materials made of iron and carbon – are steels that contain carbon in progressively greater amounts. As the carbon content increases, so does the hardness and strength of the steel. However, there is also a corresponding reduction in toughness and ductility. Engineers need to choose a steel with the carbon content that provides an appropriate range of properties for a given application.

Manganese has been added to plain carbon steels for many years. Manganese improves the strength and toughness of a steel by acting as a grain refiner. It is also a deoxidising element, which is useful during the steel-making process.

Cast iron was used extensively by the Victorians because it was inexpensive, had very good compressive strength and high fluidity when molten, which made it ideal for casting. Many Victorian cast-iron structures are still in use today – just look at a Victorian railway station. Like steels, cast irons can be divided into subgroups. These include grey cast irons, white cast irons and malleable cast irons.

Table 10.2: Plain carbon steels and cast iron

Material	Carbon content
Low carbon steels	Up to 0.15%
Mild steel	Between 0.15% and 0.35%
Medium carbon steel	Between 0.35% and 0.6%
High carbon steels	Between 0.6% and 1.2%
Cast iron	Between 1.4% and 4%

Low alloy steels contain other alloying elements, such as chromium, nickel, vanadium, molybdenum, copper, boron and silicon, as well as carbon and manganese. The additional alloying elements are added in small amounts, ranging from a fraction of one per cent to a few per cent of the total content of the steel. These additional elements can improve the properties of the steel. Some steels, such as nickel-chromium-molybdenum steel, can be heat treated to produce very high levels of hardness and strength. These are used in the construction of steel structures that are subject to large loads and stresses, such as offshore installations.

Stainless steels

Harry Brierley, a metallurgist from Sheffield, discovered that if a steel contained at least 12 per cent chromium then it had excellent resistance to corrosion. It would, under normal circumstances, resist the rusting process encountered in any other type of steel. This type of ferrous alloy became known as 'stainless steel'. Over the years, a range of stainless steels have been developed for different applications. The main types are:

• ferritic stainless steel
• austenitic stainless steel
• duplex and super-duplex stainless steel
• martensitic stainless steel.

Ferritic stainless steels contain chromium as the principal alloying element. They have a BCC structure which makes them relatively strong.

Austenitic stainless steels contain nickel as well as chromium. The purpose of nickel is to stimulate production of a lattice structure that is face centred – that is, austenitic – rather than body centred (ferritic).

This is because an FCC structure produces a stainless steel that is tougher and more ductile than a BCC structure. This makes the steel easier to form, press and fabricate, and therefore more suited for many manufacturing applications. However, there is a drawback: austenitic stainless steel lacks the strength of a ferritic steel. Perhaps the most commonly used stainless steel alloys are the '18/8' stainless steels. These contain 18 per cent chromium and 8 per cent nickel. This is the lowest alloy content that produces an austenitic structure.

Duplex and super-duplex stainless steels have been developed for applications that require a better range of strength, hardness, toughness and ductility. By carefully controlling the relative amounts of chromium, nickel and other elements in the alloy, it is possible to produce a 'duplex' structure – one that is 50 per cent ferrite and 50 per cent austenite. These alloys combine the benefits of ferritic and austenitic stainless steels. Because there is a greater content of the main alloying elements in duplex alloys, these alloys display far greater corrosion resistance in so-called 'sour' chemical environments.

Martensitic stainless steels have relative high levels of carbon. This means that they can be heat treated to produce stainless steels with high hardness. These are ideal for surgical blades, medical equipment and surgical implants.

Non-ferrous metals and alloys

Pure non-ferrous metals, such as aluminium, copper, titanium and gold, are used in some engineering applications. For example, pure copper is used in domestic piping, and aluminium sheeting is used in several applications. However, in the vast majority of cases, non-ferrous metallic elements are alloyed. These materials are cost-effective to produce and have a greater range of mechanical properties.

With one or two exceptions, non-ferrous alloys are mixtures of two or more metallic elements. For general engineering applications, the important categories are:

- aluminium alloys
- cuprous alloys – brasses and bronzes
- titanium alloys
- nimonics – these are alloys where the predominant element is nickel.

10.1.8 Classification of non-metals (synthetic)

Synthetic non-metallic materials can be divided into three groups:

- polymers
- composites
- ceramics.

Polymers

Polymers are 'plastic' materials. We introduced the three main subclassifications of polymers when we considered the structure of these materials earlier in this unit. These are thermoplastics, thermosetting polymers (thermosets) and elastomers.

Thermoplastics can be re-melted and therefore recycled. They are relatively inexpensive to produce. They tend to be weaker than thermosetting polymers. Common thermoplastics include polyethylene (PE), polyvinyl chloride (PVC), nylon, polymethyl methacrylate (PMMA) – which is also known as Perspex, one of its trade names – and polystyrene.

Thermosets, unlike thermoplastics, cannot be re-melted once formed and cured. These polymers tend to be stronger than thermoplastics, and they do not soften in the same way as thermoplastics at high temperatures. Phenol formaldehyde, commonly known as Bakelite, is used in the manufacture of plugs, sockets and other electrical fittings because it is non-flammable. Other thermosets include urea formaldehyde and melamine formaldehyde.

Elastomers are rubbers, and they exhibit a high degree of elastic behaviour. Natural rubber is known as latex. Synthetic rubbers include neoprene, butadiene and nitrile.

Composite materials

Composites are classified with reference to the way in which the reinforcing material is present within the composite material. They may be:

- laminated
- fibre reinforced, such as glass-reinforced plastic (fibre glass)
- particle reinforced
- dispersion strengthened.

Ceramic materials

Ceramic materials can be classified into these categories:

- cements and concrete
- clay ceramics, such as brick and 'whiteware'
- refractory ceramics – these are able to withstand very high temperatures
- tool ceramics, such as cermets
- oxide and carbide abrasives.

10.1.9 Classification of non-metals (natural)

Finally, there are many natural non-metallic materials that are used in some engineering applications. These include natural rubber (latex), various woods and stone.

Assessment activity 10.1

P1 Describe the structure (including the atomic structure) of a metal, a polymer, a composite, a ceramic and a smart material.

P2 Produce a 'family tree' that groups a range of common engineering materials into categories according to their properties. The main division should be between metals and non-metals, but these broad categories should be further subdivided using the classifications considered in this unit.

Grading tips

P1 You will need to explain the atomic structure of your chosen materials.

P2 Your family tree should contain examples of materials in each category, including a ferrous material, non-ferrous material, non-ferrous alloy, thermoplastic polymer, thermosetting polymer, elastomer, ceramic, composite, smart material and natural material.

PLTS

By logically categorising and organising material types you will be demonstrating skills a creative thinker.

10.2 Know material properties and the effects of processing on the structure and behaviour of engineering materials

All materials can be defined or characterised by their properties (see, for example, Appendix 4 on page 381). Aluminium can be described as a light metal that is relatively weak in its pure form. It is silver grey in colour, non-magnetic, has excellent corrosion resistance and it melts at 660°C. These are some of the 'properties' of aluminium. Try describing steel and nylon in similar terms.

10.2.1 Mechanical properties

A mechanical property is one which is associated with how a material behaves when it is subject to a force. It is important to a sound understanding of the terms associated with forces – force, stress, strain and Young's modulus – in order to study the behaviour of materials.

A **force** is an effort that is applied to a material externally. There are four basic ways in which a force can be applied:

- tensile force – a 'pulling' force
- compressive force – a 'crushing' or 'squeezing' force
- torsional – a 'twisting' force
- shear – a 'cutting' force.

Materials, structures and components can experience several of these forces simultaneously. The unit for force is the newton (N).

As a result of the application of a force, **stress** is set up within a material. The actual value for stress is obtained by dividing the force by the area on which it is acting. In other words, stress is force per unit area. Since the unit of force is a newton and area may be expressed in mm^2 or m^2, then stress can be given as N/mm^2 or MN/m^2. (Note a meganewton, symbol MN, is 1,000,000 N.)

Strain is the physical movement or extension of a material (or a body) that results from an applied stress. Stress may be elastic, which means that when the applied force is removed, the material returns to its original dimensions. In this case, the strain is said to be elastic. However, the strain may lead to such a degree of extension that the material cannot return to its original dimensions. In this case, the strain is said to be plastic.

Strain is measured by the change in length divided by the original length. This means that strain does not have any dimensions – dividing length by length cancels out the units. However, strain is a useful value when carrying out design calculations involving force and stress.

Young's modulus gives a value for the 'stiffness' or 'rigidity' of a material. It is calculated by dividing stress by strain. However, Young's modulus is constant for any given type of material. For example, Young's modulus for steel is $200 \ N/mm^2$. It is perhaps more accurate to call this property Young's modulus of elasticity. It is denoted by the letter E.

It is essential to understand the forces, stresses and strains to which a material (or component or structure) might be subject. This knowledge is used to inform the design and selection of materials for a given application.

Did you know?

Young's modulus is related to the strength of the inter-atomic bonds in a material. Since these never change, Young's modulus for a material remains constant.
As an example, we can alter the strength of steel by adding more carbon, heat treatment or mechanical work, but the value of E will always be the same.

Key terms

Force the effort that is applied to a material externally.

Stress the amount of force exerted per unit area within the material.

Strain the physical movement or extension of a component as a result of an applied stress.

Young's modulus a measure of the 'stiffness' or 'rigidity' of a material.

Strength, hardness, toughness and ductility

Strength, hardness, toughness and ductility are the most important mechanical properties. Table 10.3 provides definitions for these terms. In each case, we might also add the words 'without failure'. This is why this is important.

- If a material is not strong enough, then it will fail in service because it cannot carry the imposed loads.
- If a material is not sufficiently hard, then it can become damaged prematurely which can cause failure.
- If a material is not tough enough, then when it experiences a shock load it will fail in service. Shock or impact loading is common in engineering. For example, a pipeline may suffer a shock load if a faulty pump overruns, causing a sharp increase in pressure.
- If a material is not sufficiently ductile, it may fail when subject to processes such as rolling, forming, folding and welding during manufacturing.

Table 10.3: Mechanical properties – key definitions

Property	Definition
Strength	The ability of a material to withstand an applied force or load
Hardness	The ability of a material to resist abrasion, indentation and wear
Toughness	The ability of a material to withstand sudden shock or impact loads
Ductility	The ability of a material to withstand plastic deformation

The properties listed in Table 10.3 are closely related. If a material is hard, it is also strong. Conversely if a material is tough, it is also quite ductile. More importantly, if a material is made stronger and harder by alloying or heat treatment, there will be a corresponding reduction in toughness and ductility. Engineers are able to use this knowledge to select materials that have the right combination of properties for a specific application. They can also modify the properties of materials in order to meet specific requirements.

Other mechanical properties

Other mechanical properties of a material are **malleability**, elasticity and brittleness. Brittleness, in particular, is an unusual and confusing property.

Consider two contrasting materials: tool steel and zinc. Tool steel is hard and therefore strong, but it is also brittle. The metal zinc is weak and brittle. Therefore, some metals (and metal alloys) are hard and brittle and some are weak and brittle.

To understand this, we need to consider what brittleness actually means. Brittleness means that the material breaks or shatters rather than deforming. Both tool steel and zinc, two very different metals, are brittle, so brittleness is *independent* of the material's strength, hardness, toughness and ductility.

10.2.2 Physical properties

Mechanical properties are of great importance, but materials have other properties that may be beneficial or of interest in some engineering applications. Important physical properties include a material's melting temperature and its density. The density of a material is given by its mass per unit volume.

10.2.3 Thermal properties

Engineers often want to know the effects of heat and temperature on a material. In other words, they are interested in a material's thermal properties. Important thermal properties of interest to engineers include:

- linear expansivity
- heat capacity
- thermal conductivity.

Linear expansivity is a measure of the amount by which a material changes dimension with each degree rise or fall in temperature. This property is important because it enables designers to allow for thermal expansion and contraction. If this was ignored significant changes in temperature could cause considerable damage to structures such as pipe systems and railway lines.

Heat capacity is the amount of thermal energy needed to raise the temperature of a substance by one kelvin. It is measured in units of joules per kelvin (J/K).

Thermal conductivity is a measure of the ability of a material to conduct heat. This is defined as the quantity of heat that will flow per unit area per second divided by the temperature gradient. This is an important consideration for materials that are used in equipment such as heat exchangers and boilers that need good thermal efficiency.

Key terms

Malleability the ability of a metal or other material to be hammered or beaten to shape (from the Latin word malleus meaning hammer).

Deep drawing a metal forming process in which sheet metal is drawn into a forming die by a mechanical punch.

10.2.4 Electrical and magnetic properties

- It is important to know if a material conducts electricity. Resistivity is a measure of the ability of a material to conduct electricity. We can categorise materials by their resistivity. Metals, by virtue of the metallic bond, are good-to-excellent conductors. Insulators, materials such as plastics and ceramics, cannot conduct electricity. Semiconductors, such as silicon and germanium, occupy the middle ground and conduct to a limited extent.

- There is a fuller discussion of the electrical properties of materials in Unit 35. See the section on the properties of materials used in electronic devices (page 351) and Table 35.1, which gives the resistivity (at 20°C) of many common materials.

Other electrical and magnetic properties of interest to engineers are dielectric strength, which is the maximum voltage an insulator may resist before breaking down, and permeability, the ease with which a material may be magnetised.

10.2.5 Effects of processing metals

A knowledge of the structure and properties of engineering materials is needed in order to understand how materials can be used and transformed through manufacturing processes. During a manufacturing process, a metal may be subject to mechanical working by rolling, drawing, pressing, cutting or punching. The aim is usually to achieve some form of plastic deformation – that is, to achieve some non-reversible change in the metal's shape.

When plastic deformation takes place, the individual crystals that make up the metal's structure also become permanently deformed. For example, bending a metal plate into a right angle causes the crystals on the outside of the bend to become stretched or elongated and the crystals on the inside of the bend to become crushed.

Cold rolling is a manufacturing process designed to increase the strength of a relatively weak metal, such as iron, aluminium or titanium, by squeezing it between a set of rollers. This causes the grains in the metal to deform and flatten, and this increases the strength of the material. In this case, plastic deformation increases the material's strength and hardness. However, there is a corresponding reduction in toughness and ductility.

The process of increasing the strength of a material by plastic deformation is known as 'work hardening' or 'strain hardening', since it is a natural reaction to plastic straining. The more rolling that a metal receives, the more plastic deformation takes place and the stronger it gets. For example, aluminium can be subject to repeated cold rolling, which enables manufacturers to produce aluminium alloys with the mechanical properties to suit a given application.

Work hardening can also cause problems. When manufacturing a product using **deep drawing** processes, there can be so much plastic deformation that the metal fully work hardens. When a metal is fully work hardened, it cannot deform any more without cracking. If an attempt is made to further deform the metal, it will eventually break. To continue working the metal without causing it to fail, you need to use a heat treatment process, which restores the original grain structure.

Recrystallisation

Above a certain temperature all plastically deformed metals begin to grow an entirely new grain structure that can partially or fully replace the existing structure. This process is known as 'recrystallisation'. The actual temperature at which recrystallisation begins is not fixed; it varies in any given metal with the amount of prior cold work it received.

Recrystallisation can be initiated through heat treatment. Depending upon the specific heat treatment process applied, the properties of a cold-worked metal can be refined, improved or totally altered. This has several advantages:

- it removes any residual stress within the metal

- it restores the original crystalline structure

- it allows further cold work by removing the effects of work hardening.

Recrystallisation can be regarded as replacing 'new grains for old'. New crystals with the material's original crystalline structure nucleate at grain boundaries within the metal in a similar way to those that form during solidification. However, there is no dendritic growth because there is no liquid metal present. Instead, the nuclei simply become larger until they meet and produce a new **equiaxed crystal** structure that completely replaces the old one.

Ideally, recrystallisation produces a uniform, fine and equiaxed crystal structure. An equiaxed grain is defined as one that if we measure its size in any three directions the values obtained are roughly equal. However, if the metal is kept at or above its recrystallisation temperature for a prolonged period, then the crystals become enlarged as they cannibalise the surrounding metal. This excessive grain growth weakens the metal and makes it more brittle. A fine-grained structure produces the optimum mechanical properties.

Hot working

Hot working involves the mechanical processing of a metal above its recrystallisation temperature. Cold working, by definition, takes place below the recrystallisation temperature. Note that this means that cold work can still take place when the metal is hot. As

long as the metal is being worked when it is below its recrystallisation temperature, it is still classed as cold working regardless of the actual temperature.

During hot working, the material remains above its recrystallisation temperature during the working process such as rolling. As with cold working, the grain structure undergoes plastic deformation. However, hot working allows recrystallisation after the forming process is complete – in contrast, cold rolling produces permanent deformation. Hot working is a closely controlled process. It is necessary to ensure that the metal is hot enough to recrystallise after working but not so hot that excessive grain growth occurs.

Alloying elements in steels

Steel at room temperature mainly has a ferrite structure (BCC iron) mixed with a small amount of eutectic material (pearlite). However, there are some additional elements that can be added to steel in order to modify its properties further. The most important and widely used alloying elements in steel are:

- manganese
- chromium
- nickel
- sulphur
- phosphorus
- silicon.

Manganese is useful when it comprises over 1 per cent of the steel content. It stimulates nucleation during solidification and this produces a finer crystalline structure. Fine grains in a metal produce greater strength and toughness. Manganese is also useful as a deoxidiser and de-sulphuriser during steel making. Oxygen and sulphur, when present in sufficiently large quantities, are detrimental to steel. Hadfield steels contain 12% manganese. They form a very hard surface when they are subject to abrasion, and this is why they are used in the manufacture of earth-moving tools and other heavy duty equipment.

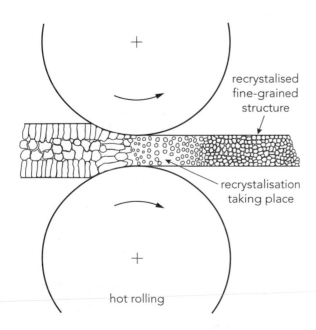

Figure 10.5: Hot rolling and recrystallisation

recrystalised fine-grained structure

recrystalisation taking place

hot rolling

Chromium reacts with the carbon in steel to produce chromium carbide. This is a very hard intermetallic compound that makes the steel resistant to abrasion and wear. Stainless steels, which have a chromium content of greater than 12 per cent, have excellent resistance to corrosion.

Nickel improves the toughness of steel and slightly increases its strength. Steels with 9 per cent nickel content are used for pipelines as they are less brittle at low temperatures. When the nickel content in stainless steel is greater than 8 per cent, the structure of the steel is face-centred cubic. In steel, the FCC structure is referred to as 'austenite' after its discoverer. This austenitic structure makes the steel very tough even at very low (cryogenic) temperatures. Austenitic stainless steel is the most commonly used stainless alloy in the fabrication and welding industry.

A metal machinist would tell you that sulphur and phosphorus are beneficial because they make it easier to machine steel. This is because these elements react with iron to make two intermetallic compounds – iron sulphide and iron phosphide. These particles act as 'chip breakers' during the cutting process. However, in the fabrication and welding industry, sulphur and phosphorus are regarded as impurities and they can cause severe cracking during the welding process.

Last but not least, silicon is useful because it acts as a deoxidiser during steel making.

10.2.6 Effects of processing thermoplastic polymers

Several methods can be used to process polymers. Many are suitable for both low volume and high volume production. Typical methods include:

- injection moulding
- extrusion
- blow moulding
- structural foam moulding
- thermoforming
- compression moulding
- casting.

Some polymer forms, such as plastic pipe and sheet, can also be fabricated, machined and even welded using solvents, ultrasonic waves and hot-joining processes such as hot gas welding.

In processing polymers, several key factors must be considered. Three of the most important of these factors are the processing temperature, the processing pressure and the cooling rate.

Processing temperature

Temperature affects the **viscosity** of a polymer. Viscosity is a measure of resistance of the molecules in a polymer chain to sliding over each other when they are subject to a stress. In addition to temperature, viscosity is also affected by the molecular chain structure of the material, the material's molecular weight and moulding pressure.

Viscosity is particularly important in processes that involve moulding. If the viscosity is too high, a polymer may not fill a mould cavity completely. This produces incomplete mouldings, and this can be a serious defect in complex parts and components.

Processing pressure

Processing pressure is important for similar reasons. As the moulding pressure is increased, the chain molecules in the polymer are forced closer together. This makes it harder for them to move past each other during the moulding process. In other words, the process increases the viscosity of the polymer. This, in turn, can result in defective mouldings.

Cooling rate

Some polymers show a degree of crystallinity that makes them harder, stronger, more rigid, more dense and more resistant to solvent attack. The degree of crystallinity depends on the cooling rate. The slower the cooling, the greater the degree of crystallinity, and vice versa. It is therefore possible to adjust the cooling rate to produce a range of polymers with different properties, in much the same way that engineers can produce steels with different properties by varying the carbon content or can refine the strength and toughness of a metal by fast cooling.

The degree of crystallinity that can be achieved also depends on the processing method. Some high-volume production processes, such as injection moulding, limit the amount of crystallinity because of the quick cycle times. This necessarily means that the polymers are subject to a fast cooling process.

10.2.7 Effects of processing thermosetting polymers

The manufacture of thermosetting plastics is usually a two-stage process. First, a raw, partially polymerised material is produced consisting of polymer chains. This raw material then undergoes final polymerisation during a high temperature and pressure moulding process. This 'cures' the polymer by forming cross links – the chemical bonds between the chains that effectively produce a continuous three-dimensional polymer. Thermosets are processed at much higher temperatures and pressures than thermoplastic polymers.

10.2.8 Effects of processing ceramics

Ceramic materials are manufactured by:

- crushing to produce fine particles – this process is also known as milling or comminution
- mixing the particles with additives such as binders, lubricants, wetting agents and plasticisers
- shaping using a variety of processes such as casting and pressing
- drying and firing to impart strength
- finishing to remove flaws and improve overall strength.

The shaping and pressing operation is important for ensuring the quality of a ceramic component. Friction between the mould walls and the ceramic particles can create large variations in the density of the material. This can lead to warping and deformation during the firing process, especially if the ratio of a component's length to its width or diameter is large. Consequently, a limit is placed on this size ratio. A limit of 2:1 is normally set. If this is impractical, an isostatic pressing process can be used that compresses the ceramic evenly in all directions. This creates a material with uniform density; however it is an expensive process.

Drying is a critical stage in the processing of ceramics because materials can warp and crack as their moisture content decreases. Complex parts that have a mix of comparatively thick and thin sections are particularly vulnerable. If warping and cracking is likely to occur, drying must be carried out in a humidity-controlled atmosphere. High humidity slows down the rate of evaporation of the moisture and it evens out the evaporation rate. This reduces the stresses in the material caused by shrinkage.

Another potential problem arises during the mixing stage if a large amount of water is added to the ceramic in order to produce a very fluid mixture (slurry), such as that used in slip casting processes. Particles of ceramic can settle, thereby producing a non-uniform mix. This is remedied by using a *deflocculant*, which changes the electric charge on the particles so that they repel rather than attract each other and, therefore, remain in suspension.

10.2.9 Effects of processing composites

The properties and behavioural characteristics of composite materials reflect the relationship between the reinforcement phase and the matrix phase of the composite. The matrix phase is the bulk material that holds the composite together. It gives the composite its overall shape and dimension, as well as transfers external forces to the reinforcement phase. The reinforcement phase, such as glass fibres, gives the composite its strength.

During the manufacturing process, careful control is exercised on the reinforcement phase because this governs the required properties of the composite. Typical parameters of interest in processing composites include:

- concentration of the reinforcement phase – this is usually 40–60% of the total volume
- size and shape of reinforcement phase, such as particles or fibres
- orientation of reinforcement phase – fibres can be aligned or randomly placed.

Where the fibres in the reinforcement phase are aligned – that is, the fibres are parallel to each other – the composite is strongest along the plane that lies in the same direction as the fibres. The material will be good at resisting an applied force that is parallel to the direction of the lie the fibres. However, if this composite experiences transverse loading – that is, a loading perpendicular to the direction of the fibres – its strength is comparatively very low and it is therefore prone to failure. Composite materials with randomly oriented fibres have similar strength properties in all directions.

Another critical factor in the production of composites is the strength of the bond between the matrix and reinforcement phases. This is because loads are transmitted to the reinforcement phase via the matrix phase. If the bond is weak, then under an applied stress these bonds may fail. This type of bond failure is known as delamination. Special surface treatments may be employed during composite manufacture to improve the strength of this bond. For example, in the manufacture of glass-reinforced plastic (GRP), the glass fibres are coated with silane to improve the bond between the fibres and the matrix phase.

As with other material processing methods, the key parameters – such as type, orientation, distribution and bonding of the reinforcement phase – are tailored to optimise the properties for a given application.

10.2.10 Effects of post-production use

Smart materials will significantly influence future technologies. Smart materials react to their environment and, more importantly, they change in a predetermined and measurable manner. For example, when a piezoelectric crystal is subject to a pressure it produces a voltage that varies in proportion to the strength of the applied force. This property allows piezoelectric crystals to be used as a key component in pressure sensors. In a similar way, electro-rheostatic and magneto-rheostatic materials respond to changes in electric and magnetic fields and the properties of shape memory alloys vary with changes in temperature.

Sophisticated control systems can be developed by coupling a smart material with an actuator, a device that carries out a physical action in response to a change sensed by the smart material.

Activity: ABS plastic

ABS is short for acrylonitrile butadiene-styrene. It is a dispersion-strengthened composite material. Research the structure and properties of ABS plastic in relation to its strength and toughness. How is the material tough?

Case study: Smart sensors in helicopter rotor blades

Helicopter cockpits can be very noisy because of the action of the rotor blades. However, a system has been developed to reduce the noise in cockpits. This uses piezo-electric sensors mounted into the rotor blades. These sensors react to the stresses in the blades in real time. They generate a voltage that varies with the level of stress, and this signal is sent to a computer-controlled device that produces antinoise, a sound wave that cancels out the noise from the rotor blades.

Functional skills

Researching a subject using a variety of information sources will help your ICT skills.

Assessment activity 10.2

P3 Describe the main mechanical, physical, thermal, electrical and magnetic properties that are used to characterise engineering materials.

P4 Describe how typical processing methods such as casting, hot and cold rolling affect the structure and behaviour of metals, polymers, composites, ceramics and smart materials.

Grading tips

P3 Your descriptions should state why engineers are interested in these properties and give an example of a practical application of each property. You could also produce simple diagrams to illustrate material properties. For example, you could illustrate toughness by showing a hammer blow to a piece of metal.

P4 You need to focus on how changes in a material's structure can alter its properties and affect the way in which it behaves.

M1 To develop your answers for a merit, you need to explain how the structure and properties of material affect the behaviour of materials in specific engineering applications.

10.3 Be able to use information sources to select materials for engineering uses

There are currently over 22,000 materials that can be used in engineering and manufacturing applications. Selecting the right material for a given application is vital. So, with so many materials available, how do designers even begin to select a material or materials for a given application?

The first and most obvious factor to consider is the environment in which a component must operate or a structure is to be placed. Is the environment corrosive? What are the loading conditions – static or alternating? Will the material have to withstand high temperatures?

When the operating conditions are known, then the selection process can proceed. A further series of questions then need to be addressed.

- What properties must the material possess?
- What design factors are involved?
- How will processing effect the properties and in-service behaviour of the material?
- Are the selected materials readily available in the required quantities?
- Are the material costs acceptable and within budget?
- Where can technical information be accessed about the material?

Activity: Designing a cheap and functional chair

This a very simple and inexpensive chair, similar to ones found in classrooms, doctor's surgeries and other public areas. It has metal legs and a simple injection-moulded seat.

Identify the criteria that the materials used in the manufacture of the chair need to meet in order to achieve a successful design.

Explain the reasons why this type of chair remains the most widely used design in the entire world.

10.3.1 Information sources

In order to specify and select materials for given applications, it is important to be able to access technical information. There are several sources available to engineers and designers that provide information on materials. One of the most important of these sources are standard specifications.

Standard specifications

A standard describes the methods by which a product should be manufactured or a service be provided. It focuses on aspects such as efficiency, quality and accuracy. It can also promote safe working practices, protect consumers and even enhance competitiveness of a manufacturing organisation.

A standard is set out in a technical document. Some provide specific and detailed information on materials. For example, there are standards governing the processing and composition of copper, titanium and its alloys, steel plate, sheet and strip, and polymers. Many separately cover the use of materials. For example, BS EN 1011-3:2000 provides recommendations for the arc welding of carbon-manganese steels. A welding engineer or designer would use this standard to ensure that a particular grade of stainless steel is welded correctly with a minimum of defects. In order to do this, the engineer must consider:

- the effect of alloying elements in the steel
- the thickness of the material
- the joint type – butt weld or fillet weld
- the effects of residual hydrogen
- the heat input and cooling rate.

This is done in order to determine what is known as *preheat*. This is a method of heating the joint to a predetermined temperature before welding commences. This is done to ensure that the weld does not cool down too quickly, because if it does it is likely to crack due to the formation of brittle phases within the weld.

The standard provides the technical information that allows an engineer to take all the factors in the bullet list above into consideration. For example, it gives a simple formula that is used to calculate the heat input, which must be kept to a specific level. Another formula allows calculation of the carbon equivalent – a measure of the overall alloy content. In this way, an engineer can use the standard to determine the amount of preheating required prior to welding so that the cooling rate is sufficiently slow to prevent cracking.

Standards are set and controlled by a variety of national and international bodies. The most important of these are:

- British Standards Institute (BSI)
- International Standards Organisation (ISO)
- German Industrial Standard (DIN or Deutsche Industrie Norm)
- American Society of Mechanical Engineers (ASME)

In recent years there has been a move to bring British standards into line with international standards. If you look at the standard for arc welding of stainless steels, you will notice that it has the prefix BS EN. This stands for British Standard European Number, and it signifies that the standard has been developed from previous standards to meet European norms.

Other data sources

There are several other data sources that can be consulted by engineers for specific and detailed information on materials.

- Data books – *The ASM Handbook* is a comprehensive source of materials information. Published in 22 volumes, it covers topics such as metal working, corrosion, welding, metallography, design and failure. Other useful books include the *ASM Metals Reference Book* and *Smithells Metals Reference Book*.
- Computer databases – A wealth of information on materials is now available online. Many online databases have search engines that allow rapid access to relevant data.
- Trade associations – Some trade bodies formed by groups of material manufacturers produce useful information. For example, the Titanium Information Group publishes technical data on the applications and properties of titanium and its alloys.
- Manufacturer data sheets – Data sheets on a specific material can be obtained from the manufacturer or from material suppliers.

- Test data – Many engineering organisations can draw on their own test data to obtain useful information, such as strength, hardness and toughness values, for specific materials.

Activity: Balloon diagrams

Research what is meant by the term balloon diagram. Explain how balloon diagrams can be useful in selecting appropriate materials for a particular application.

Functional skills

Your skills in English will be improved as you obtain information and read and understand texts.

10.3.2 Design criteria

Mechanical strength is perhaps the most important consideration when selecting materials. All things being equal, if a component or structure cannot withstand the forces that it will experience in service, then it will fail at some point. Engineers are therefore interested in the limiting factors for materials under particular conditions. In other words, they are interested in the point at which a material will fail. This allows them to select materials that will not fail in normal operating environments and to build in safety margins.

So, for example, engineers will want to know the yield stress of a material under simple loading conditions. If a component or structure is subject to fatigue loading, then the 'fatigue' or 'endurance limit' will be a more important consideration. The 'creep limit' needs to be considered if a component or structure is likely to be subject to high temperatures. The modes of failure of engineering materials – and an explanation of fatigue and creep – is covered later in this unit (see page 291).

Along with strength, a material's toughness will be an important factor if it is to be used in low temperature applications or situations where shock loads may be encountered, such as in an offshore structure that is pounded by waves. Ductility will also be an issue for metals used in any components that require mechanical work during processing, such as pressing, drawing, rolling or bending. If the metal does not have good ductility, it will fracture during manufacture.

It is important to take account of the fact that processing operations can have a far-reaching effect on a material's properties and subsequent behaviour. For example, casting processes produce unfavourable metallurgical structures, and a cast material may require further heat treatment before it can be used. In addition, it may also require several surfaces to be machined to meet fitting tolerances and surface finish.

10.3.3 Cost criteria

Cost considerations have to be taken into account when selecting materials. If there are several similar materials that have suitable properties for an application, the best choice may be the cheapest material. As long as the material can perform as required for the prerequisite length of time, this may be the sensible choice. Sometimes the most suitable material may have to be rejected – its cost may be prohibitive and it may not be available in the quantities required. In this case, suitable alternatives will need to be sourced.

Let's take a closer look at material costs. It is important to realise that engineering companies incur more expense than simply the cost of purchasing the raw material. Manufacturing costs and maintenance costs, sometimes referred to as the cost of ownership, need to be taken into account.

Raw materials costs are usually quoted on the basis of the price per unit length or price per unit volume. However, finished products may also be priced on a cost basis. Structural steelwork, for example, is often supplied for a fixed price per tonne. This price will reflect the material properties – high strength structural steelwork will be a higher price per tonne than lower strength steelwork.

Manufacturing costs are a function of the complexity of a product, the difficulty of working the materials used in the product, and associated labour cost. A manufacturer might face a large financial outlay (capital expenditure) simply to set up a line to produce a new component or product. For example, it might require investment in new injection moulding equipment or tooling for presswork. In general, a manufacturer would only consider substantial set-up costs for high volume production. Consider, for example, a company that manufactures injection moulded plastic model aircraft kits. The models have many individual parts that are moulded onto a series of 'sprues'. Each item on a sprue may incur a substantial set-up cost, and the model kit company can only drive down unit costs and profitably produce models at attractive prices for customers by high volumes of production.

The cost of maintaining a component or structure throughout its service life may be a significant factor in material selection. Steel structures, such as bridges, offshore installations and pipe systems, require regular painting and corrosion protection. However, the costs of maintenance may be lower than using non-corrosive but relatively expensive materials.

10.3.4 Availability criteria

A final set of considerations in selecting and sourcing engineering materials is availability. Materials can be hard to obtain because there is simply too much demand or because there is insufficient supply (the material is scarce). If many large-scale engineering projects are started within a short space of time, the increase in demand can lead to shortages of materials such as steel or titanium alloys. Of course the reverse can apply, and it is possible too for suppliers to over-produce some materials (see the case study on the Guggenheim Museum in Bilbao). The laws of supply and demand will impact on prices. When a particular material is scarce or in high demand, its price is likely to increase; where there is a glut or large surplus of a material, its price will come down.

Raw materials are usually supplied in standard shapes and forms. For example, metals come as sheets, plates, pipes, strips, bars, rods and structural sections. If materials are unavailable in the required form, the cost of manufacture can increase significantly and sometimes prohibitively. Many projects have had to be put on hold until the required materials become available in sufficient quantities and in the right forms. Sometimes, an engineering company will place large orders with manufacturers in order to ensure adequate materials supply. However, if a materials company switches all its resources to supply a particularly important customer or a massive project, its other customers may suffer.

Case study: The Guggenheim Musuem, Bilbao

Engineering materials are not always available in the required quantities. Large, complex engineering projects or high-volume manufacturing processes can be held up because raw materials are simply unavailable. Projects can even be at the mercy of (or stand to benefit from) global market forces.

The Guggenheim Museum (opposite) in Bilbao, Spain, has part of its structure clad in titanium. At the design stage, stainless steel, aluminium and titanium were all considered as cladding materials. Titanium was initially ruled out because it was the most expensive option. However, Russia then unexpectedly generated a large excess of titanium, and the price of the metal on the world market dropped significantly. The designers on the Guggenheim project saw this as a great opportunity. Although titanium remained the most expensive cladding option, it was now within budget. They immediately specified and purchased titanium for the project.

Titanium was the first choice for designers of the Guggenheim Museum because it is the most durable

and aesthetically pleasing material. Its use – and architect Frank Gehry's iconic design – has helped to create a world-famous landmark building.

1 Carry out research on recent large engineering projects. Find out if there were any problems sourcing materials for each project.

2 Describe how the cost and availability of materials may have influenced each project.

Assessment activity 10.3

P5 D1 **BTEC**

P5 Select two simple products or components. Use standard information sources to select appropriate materials for their manufacture.

D1 For one of these components or products, justify your selection of materials. Describe why they meet the selection criteria you set before making your choice.

Grading tips

P5 You need to select two materials for each product/component. Before you do this, you should outline the selection criteria that you intend to use. For example, you need to consider cost as well as material properties. If you are sourcing materials for a chair, you might consider

metals and plastics. The metal chair will be stronger but heavier. The plastic chair will be lighter and in all likelihood cheaper to produce.

D1 You must now justify (by providing good, well-researched reasons) why you made your choice of materials. Set out the materials you considered and describe why you favoured one material over the others. You need to consider the service environment and explain how your selected material meets the stated criteria. For example, if you are considering materials for a pipeline which is likely to be placed in a corrosive environment, then a stainless steel may be required. You can use a new example if you don't wish to use one of the examples you considered in the first task.

PLTS

You will demonstrate skills as an independent enquirer and creative thinker during assessment activity 10.3. You will also show that you can manage your time effectively.

10.4 Know the modes of failure of engineering materials

Nothing lasts forever. Unless they are withdrawn from service, all engineering materials will fail eventually. Structures and components are designed to have a useful service life. Depending on the application, an engineering structure or component may have a service life of a matter of hours or it may extend (often with maintenance) to several decades. If retained in service beyond its design life, a component may suffer material failure.

Some material failures can be spectacular. Think about the ways in which materials might fail. Don't just consider metals, think about the types of engineering material featured in this unit such as polymers, composites, ceramics and natural materials.

10.4.1 Principles of ductile and brittle failure

The forces applied to a metal structure may be tensile, compressive, shear or torsional. Usually a structure will experience several of these forces simultaneously. When these forces exceed the allowable stress of the material, then failure will occur by overloading. The actual mode of failure may be either ductile failure or brittle failure.

Ductile failure is characterised by a fracture surface that is torn or fibrous, and is usually dull in appearance. Ductile failure occurs above the yield point of the metal and, as a result, engineers have advanced warning that failure is imminent. This is important because it allows time for remedial action to be taken, such as repair, and an estimation to be made of the remaining useful life of the component or structure.

The mechanism of ductile failure is through microvoid coalescence. Microvoids are tiny cracks and other defects that are present in all metals. As the material is deformed, these voids open up and become gradually larger. Coalescence takes place when the voids merge into larger cavities. This reduces the load-bearing area of the metal and, at a critical value, the metal fails.

Brittle fracture surfaces are generally characterised as shiny, spangled or faceted. In metals that are extremely hard or that have a very fine grain structure, the brittle fracture surface is smooth and dull as seen, for example, in the fracture surface of a broken drill bit. Brittle failures occur below the yield point of the metal. This means that there is no prior plastic deformation and no advanced warning of failure. Brittle fracturing is extremely rapid, and cracks run through the metal at the speed of sound. There are two types of brittle fracture:

- intergranular fractures, which follow the grain boundaries of the metal
- transgranular fractures, which run through the grains themselves.

Did you know?

A crack running through a metal during brittle fracture is atomically sharp. This is because the mechanism of brittle fracture involves the breaking of the atomic bonds between atoms. There is, therefore, nothing sharper than the tip of a brittle fracture.

It is very unusual for metals to experience pure ductile or pure brittle failure. A typical fracture surface will be partially ductile and partially brittle. However, several factors influence whether the main mode of failure will be brittle or ductile fracture. These include temperature, the rate of loading and grain size.

Metals that experience low temperatures tend to become brittle. Even a low carbon steel, normally a very tough and ductile metal, becomes brittle below 0°C. Many metals have what is known as a ductile-to-brittle transition temperature. This is a rapid fall off in toughness over a narrow temperature range.

If the rate of loading is rapid, a normally ductile metal becomes more brittle. Slow loading has the opposite effect – the material becomes more and more ductile. Some titanium and aluminium alloys are known as super plastic, which means that when they undergo forming processes, such as deep drawing – they exhibit an elongation of several thousand per cent.

Fine-grained metals are tougher than coarse-grained ones. As a result, they tend to fail in a ductile manner.

10.4.2 Principles of fatigue

Fatigue failure occurs when structures and components undergo cyclical or alternating loading conditions. Think of a flag pole or lamp post swaying in the wind. At the base of the post where it is anchored to the ground, the forces acting on the post will be compressive as it moves one way, then tensile as it moves in the opposite direction. This is cyclic loading. **Fatigue** is by far the most common mode of failure. This is because the vast majority of structures and components do not experience static loading. Loading is almost always cyclical in nature.

There are two types of fatigue failure, one of which takes place below the yield point and one which takes place above it. Where fatigue failure occurs below the yield point it is known as high cycle, low strain fatigue and when it takes place above the yield point it is called low cycle, high strain rate fatigue.

High cycle, low strain fatigue is the most common form of fatigue failure. In order to understand how this occurs, you need to understand the concept of stress raisers or stress concentrations. When a material experiences a force, 'lines' of force run through the material in a uniform manner. However if a defect is placed in the way of these force lines, then it impedes their progress, causing them to gather or bunch around the extremities of the defect. This has the effect of concentrating the force at the edges of the defect. For example, a spherical defect within a material, such as a pore, actually doubles the stress within its vicinity.

Typically, stress concentrations occur as a result of:

- cracks and voids within the material
- surface defects, such as machining marks and centre punch marks
- hard zones caused by operations such as drilling and punching
- cracks, porosity and inclusions from welding and material manufacture.

Failure occurs as a result of the propagation of cracks caused by these stress concentrations. The actual mechanism is quite complex because it relies on slip theory.

In low cycle, high strain rate fatigue, the yield point is exceeded. As a result, work hardening takes place which eventually leads to brittle fracture.

Characteristics of fatigue fracture surfaces

A fatigue fracture surface consists of three essential elements:

- a point of initial failure
- a fatigue fracture surface – the surface takes on a 'burnished' appearance (see below)
- a zone where final fracture (brittle and ductile) takes place – this occurs because the remaining load-bearing area can no longer withstand the applied load.

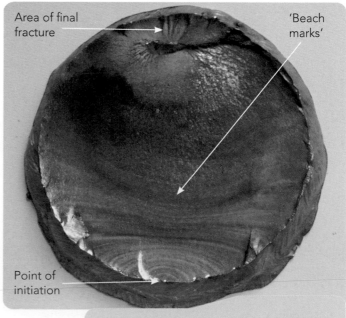

Area of final fracture

'Beach marks'

Point of initiation

The beach marks typically seen on a fatigue fracture surface

10.4.3 Principles of creep

Under certain conditions a material can slowly deform until it fails. This tendency is known as **creep**. To suffer failure by creep, a material has to be subject to high temperatures (usually in excess of 40 per cent of the melting temperature of the material in absolute terms) and to constant loading over a prolonged period.

Typical structures that fail by creep include:

• steam plant including pipelines and boilers

• steam and gas turbines

• furnace equipment

• chemical plant.

Creep takes place in three distinct stages (see Figure 10.6):

• primary creep, sometimes referred to as transient creep

• secondary creep, also known as steady state creep

• tertiary creep or final creep.

Key terms

Fatigue structural damage that occurs as the result of cyclical loading.

Creep the tendency of a material to slowly deform under the influence of stress, time and elevated temperature.

Initially, the component is loaded and stressed to its service conditions. This is why the creep curve shown in Figure 10.6 does not start at zero but at some point on the y-axis of the graph. In time, secondary creep takes over. This is a two-part mechanism that involves:

• straining of the material that produces measurable plastic extension

• relaxation of the stresses as a result of the previous strain.

This continuous and alternating stress-relax cycle of steady-state creep is shown by a straight line on this section of the graph. Notice that the line slopes

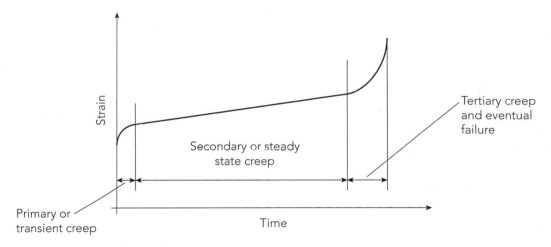

Figure 10.6: A typical creep curve

Case study: Creep failure – two extremes

In the jet engines of the Eurofighter aircraft, some of the turbine blades actually operate at temperatures that are higher than the melting point of the alloy from which they are made. In order to stop them melting, they have been designed to create turbulence around them as they spin, which carries away excess heat. This process is known as forced draught cooling. However, the temperatures is sufficiently high that the blades have a very short creep life, and they need to be replaced approximately every 20 hours.

At the other extreme, it may be many years before the effects of creep become evident in a reaction vessel in a chemical plant that is operating at or just above the temperature at which creep is a problem. Checks are made by taking measurements of the vessel diameter periodically. Over time, the extension that comes with creep will show itself as an increase in the diameter of the vessel.

upwards, indicating that higher levels of stress are required for the process to continue. Steady-state creep is the longest stage in creep failure. In some components steady-state creep can last for years; in others, particularly those subject to high temperature and stress levels, it may only last a few hours.

Eventually, the level of stress experienced by the component becomes excessive. When this occurs, tertiary creep brings about final failure. During tertiary creep, tearing takes place at grain boundaries. As grain boundary tearing continues, the load-bearing area of the component is reduced to the point where it cannot carry the applied loads, at which point failure occurs.

Activity: Creep in polymers

Research the process of creep in a polymer material. Compare this process with creep in metals.

10.4.4 Testing materials

Testing is an important aspect of materials science and engineering. Testing is carried out in order to determine the suitability of a material for a given application. It may involve either destructive testing or non-destructive testing.

Destructive testing

As the name implies, destructive testing involves loading a material until it fails. Different tests are applied to obtain specific parameters. We will consider:

- tensile tests
- impact testing
- hardness testing
- fatigue testing
- creep testing.

Tensile tests

Tensile testing is carried out by gripping the ends of the test piece in the jaws of the machine and applying a steady tensile force. A strain gauge measures the force that is being applied to the sample, and the

machine measures the amount by which the test piece extends. The test is continued until the piece fractures.

The results are usually plotted on a graph to produce the tensile curve. This is obtained by plotting the applied load against the extension of the sample material (or stress against strain). The tensile curve can be used to determine:

- the yield point of the material
- its ultimate tensile strength
- Young's modulus – by calculating the slope of the elastic portion of the graph.

If the broken test piece is reassembled, then special measuring equipment can be used to calculate the percentage elongation (the amount by which the specimen extended compared to its original size) and its percentage reduction in area (the change in cross-sectional area compared to the original). These measurements will give an indication of the material's ductility.

The area under the tensile curve will give an indication of the relative toughness of the material. A large area indicates a tough material whilst brittle materials show considerably less.

A tensile testing machine showing a sample placed in the jaws of the machine.

Impact testing

Toughness is a measure of the ability of a material to withstand shock loading. It can also be defined as the amount of energy a material can absorb before failure. If a material can absorb a large amount of energy, then it has high toughness. If only a small amount of energy is absorbed, then it has low toughness.

In order to assess toughness we need to simulate the conditions that are encountered in actual engineering situations. In particular, we need to take into account that most engineering structures and components contain areas that concentrate stress in a small area. These areas are known as notches or stress raisers. Examples of notches include:

- any sharp change in section of a component
- machining marks
- metallurgical defects such as porosity, cracks and impurities (inclusions)
- welded joints.

To allow engineers to assess the impact toughness of the material, it is important to consider the affect of a sudden loading where a stress raiser or notch is present. The Charpy and Izod tests have been devised for this purpose. Both use a weighted pendulum to apply a shock load to test specimens. The specimens should be a standard size and shape, and each should be machined to include a notch.

The impact test is conducted by placing each specimen into the testing machine. The pendulum is released and it strikes the test piece. At the point of impact, the stress is increased locally at the root of the notch and the specimen breaks. However, in so doing, it absorbs some of the energy contained within the swinging pendulum, slowing it down. If the sample absorbs a large amount of energy, the pendulum will only swing a small distance past the sample, indicating good toughness. If the pendulum carries on for a greater distance, little energy has been absorbed by the specimen, and the material can be regarded as brittle.

Readings of absorbed energy can be taken from the testing machine. This is because as the pendulum swings throughout the test, it pushes a pointer around a graduated scale and this provides a measure of absorbed energy.

Hardness testing

An assessment of hardness is taken by making an indentation in a test material. This is accomplished by pushing either a hardened steel ball or a pyramid-shaped diamond into the surface of the material under a specified load, and then carefully measuring the size of the indentation. The larger the indentation, the softer the material, and vice versa.

The Brinell test uses a hardened steel ball as an indenter, while the Vickers and Knoop micro-hardness tests use a diamond pyramid. The Rockwell test may be carried out using either a steel ball or a cone-shaped diamond pyramid depending on the type of test material and its potential application.

Fatigue testing

Fatigue testing involves applying a large number of stress cycles to the sample material in a reasonable time. One popular method is the Wohler test (see Figure 10.7). The sample is placed in a chuck and a known sustained load is applied to the end of the test piece. The chuck then rotates at high speed until the test material fails. A single revolution counts as one stress cycle. A counter records the number of revolutions to failure.

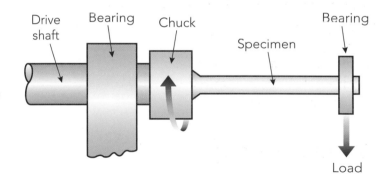

Figure 10.7: The Wohler fatigue test

The Wohler test is repeated for a range of loading conditions and this in turn is used to plot the S-N curve for the material (see Figure 10.8). This is a graph of the applied stress against the number of cycles to failure. This fatigue limit for this material and the endurance limit for a given level of stress can be easily read from this graph. The fatigue limit is the stress level below which the component can endure infinite cyclical loading. The endurance limit is the number of cycles to failure at a given level of stress. Note that another way of looking at the endurance limit is that is gives the maximum stress that a material can withstand over a specified lifetime (measured in loading cycles).

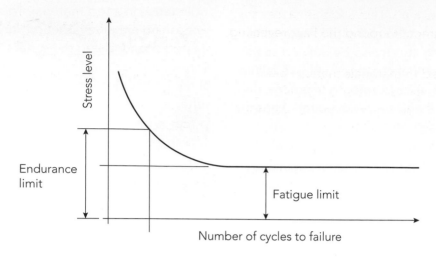

Figure 10.8: A typical fatigue curve

Creep testing

Creep testing involves placing the test specimen under a constant load or stress level while maintaining a constant temperature. The extension or strain is measured at regular intervals and plotted against elapsed time.

Non-destructive testing

Engineers often want to assess the condition of engineering structures or components that are in current use. For example, if an engineer wants to assess the possibility that a metal bridge might fail, it is not practical to use a destructive test. The bridge's structure must be examined using non-destructive testing (NDT). The methods briefly described below are in widespread use.

Liquid penetrant inspection

This is a simple test that uses a dye – usually a deep red dye – that has very low viscosity. The dye is applied to the material being tested, where it finds its way into any surface-breaking defects such as cracks. The dye can penetrate very fine cracks which might not be detected by a visual inspection. The process is carried out in stages.

- The surface is degreased using a solvent. This is important because surface contaminants can prevent the dye from entering any flaws that may be present.
- The penetrant dye is applied to the surface by spraying or painting. If the component is relatively small, it could be dipped into the dye.

- The dye is left for a predetermined time so that it can penetrate any flaws.
- The excess dye is wiped from the surface. This is done without using a solvent, which may wash the dye from a defect.
- A white chalky substance called a developer is then applied to the surface. This draws out the dye, thereby revealing the presence of any defects.

Liquid penetrant inspection (LPI for short) is a relatively quick test and it can be applied to finished components and welded joints. However, the test is limited in that it can only detect surface-breaking defects.

Magnetic particle inspection

Magnetic particle inspection (MPI) makes use of a magnetic field to reveal defects that are either break the surface or which lie just below the surface (subcutaneous). This test is also carried out in stages.

- The metal surface is degreased and a white developer, similar to that used in liquid penetrant inspection, is sprayed onto the surface and allowed to dry.
- A suspension of iron powder in a suitable carrier fluid such as paraffin is sprayed onto the surface.
- The area is then magnetised. This can be done with a powerful magnet or by passing an electrical current through the area between two probes, which creates a magnetic field.
- The iron particles align themselves in the direction of the magnetic field. However, if a flaw is present,

north and south poles are set up and this causes the iron powder to congregate around the flaw, revealing its presence.

MPI can only be applied to materials that can be magnetised, such as steels and nickel alloys. Non-ferrous alloys, such as aluminium and copper, cannot be tested in this manner.

Activity: Non-destructive testing

Radiography is another non-destructive testing method. Undertake some research to find out how this procedure is carried out to test welded components.

Assessment activity 10.4

P7 **M2** **D2**    ::BTEC

P7 Carry out a destructive test such as a tensile test or a Charpy impact test and record appropriate test data for a non-metallic material.

P7 Carry out a non-destructive test, such as liquid penetrant or magnetic particle inspection, and record appropriate test data for a metal. Take a photographic record of the results.

Grading tips

P7 A welded joint is an ideal specimen to use for the non-destructive tests because defects such as cracks are easily revealed.

M2 To develop this work for a merit grade, you should provide a written explanation of both of the test procedures you carried out, and explain why each test produces useful results.

D2 For a distinction, you must evaluate the results for one of your tests. Explain them in relation to the structure and properties of the test materials. For example, if you tested a range of steel samples with varying carbon content, evaluate how the properties of the test materials vary as a function of their carbon and pearlite content.

PLTS

If you carry out the practical tests in activity 10.4 in small groups you will be demonstrating skills as an effective participator and a team worker.

10.4.5 Degradation processes

As well as being subject to specific failure modes, such as brittle and ductile fracture, creep and fatigue, materials also experience a more generalised form of failure through the gradual 'worsening' of their properties, structure or surface appearance. This is known as degradation and is found, to a greater or lesser extent in metals, polymers, ceramics, composites and natural materials. In this section, we will consider some common degradation processes.

Metals

Metals degrade through a combination of oxidation, erosion and stress-assisted corrosion. Let's consider each of these processes in turn.

Oxidation is the chemical reaction between the metal surface and atmospheric oxygen. Some metals oxidise more easily than others. Steels require relatively high temperatures, such as those that they are subject to during hot rolling. The oxide has a grey-blue appearance. Copper, in contrast, produces a blue-green oxide, known as a patina, which is similar in colour to malachite, the ore from which copper is extracted. Noble metals such as gold do not readily oxidise.

Erosion is the general abrasion or scouring of the metal surface. It commonly occurs in fluid pipe systems that carry entrained solid particles. This scouring results in the pipe getting thinner, especially at changes in direction such as elbows and tees.

Stress corrosion is a specialised form of failure that results from the action of a specific chemical environment on a metal. For example, stress corrosion occurs in steel from the action of caustic solutions (such as sodium hydroxide), in stainless steel from the action of chloride ions, and in brass from the action of ammonia. The metal also needs to be subject to a constant and specific level of stress. Failure takes place gradually as the corrosive medium attacks surface-breaking cracks. The tensile stress keeps the cracks open, allowing further corrosion to occur. At some point, the remaining unaffected area becomes unable to withstand the applied load and eventually failure occurs, usually in a brittle manner.

Polymers

Polymers can suffer mechanical failure. Thermoplastics are relatively soft and ductile, and they lack the strength of thermosets. As a result, they fail in a ductile manner under normal circumstances. However,

The highly degraded metal hull of a ship.

thermoplastics can suffer brittle failure if subject to high strain rates and/or low temperatures, and where there is a degree of crystallinity or the presence of a notch. Thermosets, by their nature, fail in a brittle manner.

Polymers can also be subject to *swelling* and *dissolution*. Many polymers are *hygroscopic*, which means that they are able to absorb liquids such as water and oil. As a polymer absorbs fluid, the material begins to swell as molecules move between the polymer chains. This forces them further apart and weakens the attractive forces (van der Waals forces) that hold polymer chains together. This results in a loss in mechanical strength, making the polymer softer and weaker. Nylon is a good example of a hygroscopic polymer, and its susceptibility to swelling and dissolution means that any nylon bearing should never be lubricated.

The mechanical strength of a polymer depends largely on the length of the polymer chains within the material. Long polymer chains give the polymer high molecular weight and mechanical strength. Polymer chains can be made weaker if some mechanism shortens the polymer chains by breaking them. This is known as scission or bond rupture. Radiation (ultraviolet, x-rays and gamma rays) may penetrate the polymer and cause scission by breaking the covalent bonds. Chemical attack and high temperatures can also lead to bond rupture.

Ceramics

Typically hard and brittle, ceramics experience almost no plastic deformation when a force is applied to them at room temperature. Consequently, ceramics fail in a brittle manner through the initiation and propagation of cracks.

Ceramics can fail through mechanical and thermal shock. Mechanical shock equates to a high strain rate, which is one of prerequisites for brittle fracture. Rapid

increases in temperature produce excessive internal stresses. Since, in both cases, the plastic deformation that alleviates stress cannot take place, failure results.

Ceramics are almost immune to corrosion and degradation. If they are subject to corrosion, then direct chemical dissolution usually occurs. For example, glass is resistant to most chemicals, which is why glass containers are so commonplace. However, a substance such as hydrofluoric acid is so aggressive that it will dissolve glass.

The resilient properties of ceramics account for their use in some extreme environments. For example, ceramic bricks are used for the internal lining of a steel-making furnace. However, the bricks degrade over time at high temperature and become incorporated into the iron. Eventually, they need to be replaced by relining the inside of the furnace.

Composites

Composites are manufactured from a wide variety of materials, and their resistance to failure can vary from being extremely poor to excellent.

If the matrix phase of a composite is a polymer, the composite will exhibit the same degradation effects found in other polymers. The reinforcement phase in the composite, such as glass, will remain largely unaffected. Metal reinforced ceramic composites, while showing similar failure effects through thermal and mechanical shock as pure ceramics, will have some of the negative effect alleviated by the presence of the metal.

Remember that composites are developed so that their combined properties are superior to those of their individual constituents. So, in general, the negative properties of one material in the composite are often reduced through the properties and behaviour of the material in the other phase.

Assessment activity 10.5

P6 Describe the principles of how metals may fail by simple brittle/ductile fracture, fatigue and creep.

P8 Describe the different mechanisms of degradation seen in metals, polymers and ceramics.

M3 Select two given degradation processes and explain how they affect the behaviour of engineering materials when they are in use. For example, you might choose the corrosion of metals as one of the two degradation processes for this exercise.

David Alexander
Works metallurgist

I work as a metallurgist for a company that produces alloys of different types. Our customers are manufacturers who use the alloys to produce castings, forgings or machined components.

Starting at 16 years old as a shopfloor worker in the foundry, I have gradually worked my way up in the company. I've had the opportunity to get training in the laboratory where the alloys we produce are prepared and examined. In the laboratory we carry out metallographic analysis as well as a range of mechanical tests to assess hardness and tensile strength. I thoroughly enjoyed this part of the job and asked if I could be trained as a metallurgist.

When, a few years later, an opportunity came by, I was sponsored by my company to go to college. Initially, I studied at BTEC National and Higher National level on a day-release basis, and after that I studied metallurgy at degree level. I graduated two years ago and was given the job of works metallurgist when the previous one retired. I am now 27 and, as well as my day-to-day duties, I am about to embark on a Masters degree in materials science.

I can remember, as part of my earlier training, being given a problem to solve that is a good test of anyone's materials knowledge. The problem is this: what would be the most suitable alloy, that contains only two metals, which could be used to manufacture soft solder used by plumbers?

Think about it!

1 Which is the most popular alloy used for soft soldering?

2 Soldering is classed as a liquid-to-solid diffusion process. What do you suppose this means?

3 What properties or features would be required of the alloy?

4 What should be the composition of the alloy? How would you find this out?

5 If you examined the alloy under a metallurgical microscope, what would its structure be?

Just checking

1 Describe the stages in solidification of a pure metal.

2 Explain what is meant by the shape memory effect.

3 Explain how the properties of strength, hardness, toughness and ductility are interrelated.

4 Explain the degradation process of 'scission' as seen in polymer materials.

5 Outline the main differences between fatigue failure and creep failure.

6 State the main sources of data on materials that can be used for the selection of materials.

7 State four non-destructive tests that may be used to check cast components for external and internal defects such as cracks and voids. State why one of these tests would not be suitable for detecting internal defects.

8 Explain how the process of vulcanisation (that is, the addition of sulphur to rubber) creates a stronger and more rigid polymer.

9 Briefly explain the difference between an element, a compound and a molecule.

10 Explain the differences between these types of stainless steel: (a) ferritic; (b) austenitic; (c) martensitic.

edexcel

Assignment tips

• Keep a diary of your research into engineering materials science. This is a vast subject area and you will need to do a lot of background reading. It will help you develop in-depth knowledge which you can draw on in your assignments. This will allow you to write with authority.

• Visits to local engineering companies are always beneficial and good preparation for some assignments. You will see materials being used in manufacture and you may have the opportunity to see at first hand how materials testing is carried out. You will also gain first-hand knowledge from experts.

• Check out the engineering and laboratory facilities in your own school or college. Find out from those in charge how the machinery and equipment is used. If there are the right facilities, carry out supervised mechanical testing or metallurgical examination.

• The internet is a vast learning resource, but don't forget that books and periodicals are equally useful. Don't become internet lazy – aim for a 50:50 balance between internet and paper-based resources. Also, don't just cut-and-paste material – you will learn nothing this way. Read several articles on a subject and make your own notes. This will help you learn how to answer assignment questions and to solve problems in your own way.

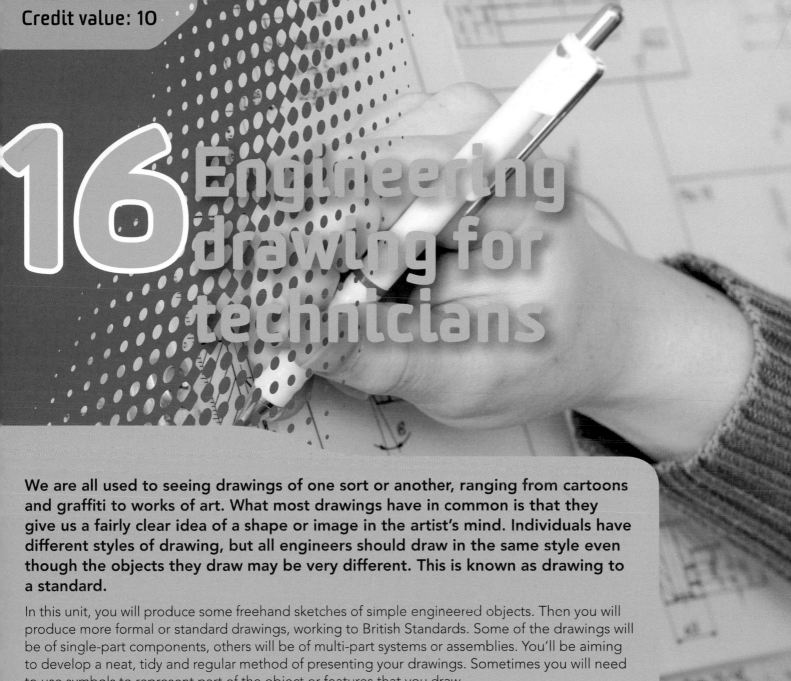

16 Engineering drawing for technicians

We are all used to seeing drawings of one sort or another, ranging from cartoons and graffiti to works of art. What most drawings have in common is that they give us a fairly clear idea of a shape or image in the artist's mind. Individuals have different styles of drawing, but all engineers should draw in the same style even though the objects they draw may be very different. This is known as drawing to a standard.

In this unit, you will produce some freehand sketches of simple engineered objects. Then you will produce more formal or standard drawings, working to British Standards. Some of the drawings will be of single-part components, others will be of multi-part systems or assemblies. You'll be aiming to develop a neat, tidy and regular method of presenting your drawings. Sometimes you will need to use symbols to represent part of the object or features that you draw.

You will also need to produce drawings with the aid of a computer, and this will help you make comparisons between the different techniques that you've used in the unit.

Learning outcomes

After completing this unit you should:

1   be able to sketch engineering components
2   be able to interpret engineering drawings that comply with drawing standards
3   be able to produce engineering drawings
4   be able to produce engineering drawings using a computer aided drafting (CAD) system.

Assessment and grading criteria

This table shows you what you must do in order to achieve a pass, merit or distinction grade, and where you can find activities in this book to help you produce the required evidence.

To achieve a **pass** grade the evidence must show that you are able to:	To achieve a **merit** grade the evidence must show that, in addition to the pass criteria, you are able to:	To achieve a **distinction** grade the evidence must show that, in addition to the pass and merit criteria, you are able to:
P1 create sketches of engineering components using a range of techniques **Assessment activity 16.1 page 314**	**M1** explain the importance of working to recognised standards when producing engineering drawings **Assessment activity 16.2 page 331**	**D1** evaluate the use of different methods of producing engineering drawings including manual and computer aided methods **Assessment activity 16.6 page 344**
P2 describe the benefits and limitations of using pictorial techniques to represent a given engineering component **Assessment activity 16.1 page 314**	**M2** explain how a given engineering drawing would be used and the reasons it is suitable for its intended audience **Assessment activity 16.6 page 344**	
P3 interpret the main features of a given engineering drawing which complies with drawing standards **Assessment activity 16.2 page 331**		
P4 produce detail drawings of three given single-piece components **Assessment activity 16.3 page 336**		
P5 produce an assembly drawing of a product containing three parts **Assessment activity 16.3 page 336**		
P6 produce a circuit diagram with at least five different components which uses standard symbols **Assessment activity 16.4 page 336**		
P7 prepare a template drawing of a standardised A3 sheet using a CAD system and save to file **Assessment activity 16.5 page 343**		
P8 produce, store and present 2D CAD drawings of a given single-piece component and an assembly drawing of a product containing three parts **Assessment activity 16.5 page 343**		

How you will be assessed

This unit will be assessed by a series of assignments designed and marked by the staff at your centre. Some of the assignments will require you to produce sketches, some will require more formal drawings; others will require you to use a computer to produce drawings. If you want to achieve a merit or a distinction grade, you'll need to produce some written work comparing the various methods of drawings that you've used.

The assignments are designed to give you practice in using a variety of techniques to produce engineering sketches and drawings. The evidence you need to present will comprise:

- freehand sketches
- hand-drawn formal drawings
- computer-aided drawings
- written work.

Jo, 17–year–old who wants to gain a modern apprenticeship

Before I studied this unit, I didn't realise that engineering drawings contained as much information as they do and that they needed to be a certain way so that other people can understand what they were about.

I think I enjoyed the sketching assignment most as I like drawing using a pencil and paper. I'd seen isometric paper before, but not used it much. The idea of the first and third angle seemed strange to me – I wondered at first what had happened to the second and fourth angles, but I now know the difference. I also know who uses first angle and who uses third angle drawings.

Using the drawing board and drawing instruments has been interesting. I had to be careful, so that simple things like the compass slipping when drawing a small circle didn't spoil my work. And the work we have done on CAD systems will definitely be of benefit. It should appeal to employers because I will not have to be trained from scratch.

I now know that engineering is all about getting things right. Nearly right isn't good enough. Nobody would travel on a plane or go over a bridge if these were only 'nearly right'. One of the main ways that engineers pass on information is to use drawings, so the only way they can get things right – rather than nearly right – is by having drawings that are properly made and easy to understand.

Of course, they're only easy to understand if you know the engineering drawing language. This is not a written language, but a language of symbols, lines, numbers and, sometimes, patterns. This unit helped me learn and practise the language of drawings, and I now feel confident handling and using drawings in the workshop.

16.1 Be able to sketch engineering components

Start up

What do we mean by sketching?

Sketches can be done in many ways. They can take many forms and be made for many different purposes. However, there are usually a couple of reasons that drive the need to produce a sketch.

One reason is that a person wants to put an idea on paper as quickly as possible before it gets forgotten and in a form that many people can understand. Another reason is that a well-produced illustration is an excellent way of communicating information. Just think how much information we receive in the form of illustrations or signs in shops on roads in schools and in colleges.

List or describe examples of four different types of sketch with which you are familiar or that you have done yourself.

Then in small groups, discuss why engineering drawings differ from these and other forms of drawn art. Suggest reasons why engineering drawings need to be accurately drawn.

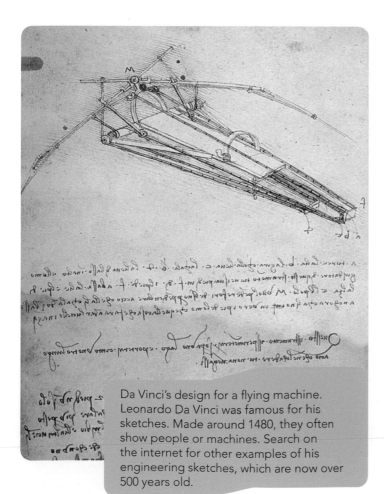

Da Vinci's design for a flying machine. Leonardo Da Vinci was famous for his sketches. Made around 1480, they often show people or machines. Search on the internet for other examples of his engineering sketches, which are now over 500 years old.

Try describing a new gadget, such as the latest version of a mobile phone, an MP3 player, a games console or a handheld computer, to a friend without naming the object. You can only use words to describe the object and you only have a minute to do this – no sketches or even hand gestures are allowed, and you cannot answer any questions your friend may have. Ask your friend to sketch the object, working only from your verbal description. Then check how closely the sketch matches the gadget. This simple exercise highlights the difficulties that can arise when trying to communicate ideas about shapes or everyday objects using words only. This is why engineers make sketches and produce drawings.

In this unit, we consider both formal (drawn to a standard) and non-formal (mainly pictorial) drawing techniques. We show how these can be combined to produce drawings that convey precise information. The use of non-formal techniques, without the application of standards, is often referred to as sketching. Even here, as we shall see in the first part of this unit, engineers use various conventions in depicting objects.

16.1.1 Sketches

Engineering technicians need to be able to produce sketches of what are known as regular solids. It is probably easier in some cases to relate the regular solids encountered in engineering to the regular solids that you will be familiar with from everyday life. Perhaps the simplest regular solid is the cube. Examples of cubes in everyday life are the dice used in board games and stock cubes used in cooking. In engineering applications, cubes may be used simply as packing pieces to support other objects or structures, or companies may receive cubes of raw material from which to manufacture other products.

A rectangular block is another regular solid – just imagine the shape of a cereal box or pizza box but made from solid material. As long as the corners are square and the sides flat, and it is not hollow, then you've got a rectangular block. It is a type of regular solid you'll need to sketch. In engineering applications, regular solids with these shapes would be made from solid steel, brass, aluminium etc. For example, material is often supplied in bulk in the form of flat bar, which we can think of as a rectangular block with one very long edge.

Let's now consider a different type of shape, the 90° angle bracket. You probably won't find many things around the home with this shape, because the angled edges could be a hazard. However, if you travel by bus, there is a good chance you'll have seen some 90° angle brackets in the bus shelter. Have a look at the ceiling of a bus shelter, and you may find angle brackets holding up the roof. Many lightweight buildings use L-shaped (or angle) sections of material in their construction, which are often produced from aluminium or even plastic.

Some objects that you will need to sketch are hollow, such as circular tubes and square tubes. These are usually a bit more difficult to sketch. Imagine a tin of beans or soup with both ends cut off or a cereal box with its top and bottom ends removed.

Typical examples of regular solids and hollow objects found in an engineering workshop include:

- solid round bar
- solid square section
- angle section
- rectangular hollow section
- circular hollow section.

You will also have to sketch standard components, such as:

- nuts, objects with a hexagonal or square shape with internal thread
- bolts and screws, objects with hexagonal or round heads and a threaded shank
- a pulley, a wheel-like device that may be flat or grooved, which is designed to change the direction of a driving belt or similar power transmission medium.

You also need to be able to sketch more complicated (from a drawing point of view) engineering components, such as:

- a pulley support bracket
- a machine vice, for holding a piece of wood or metal.

You are likely to find examples of these engineering components and standard components in school or college workshops and most engineering workplaces.

You have to be able to sketch standard components like this pulley.

Activity: Three simple sketches

Before we consider sketching techniques, try sketching some objects. Using plain A4 paper and a 2H pencil, produce simple sketches of:

- a compact disc (CD)
- an empty plastic case for a CD
- a cardboard box that would hold five CDs.

16.1.2 Sketching techniques

Suppose you have been asked to produce two sketches of the tower unit of a personal computer (PC). In one sketch, you have been asked to show the general shape of the unit. The second sketch should concentrate just on the features on the front of the unit. For this task, the chances are that you would use different techniques for the two sketches.

Computer tower units come in many different shapes and sizes, but they are usually based on a rectangular block shape. Your first sketch could show three faces (front, side and top) of the unit, similar to the view shown in Figure 16.1. This can be thought of as viewing the unit from above and slightly to one side. The advantage of this viewpoint is that it gives a good impression of the general shape of the unit.

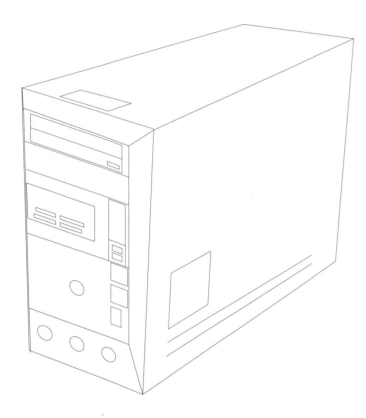

Figure 16.1: A perspective sketch of a tower unit

In your sketch of the front view of the tower however, you would probably produce a drawing similar to Figure 16.2. This is a view of the tower face on, as you might see it if you were inserting a disc into the CD/DVD drive. This view only shows the main features on the front, but, as you can see, this view provides no idea whatsoever as to the tower's depth.

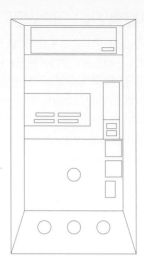

Figure 16.2: An orthographic sketch of the front face of a tower unit

The first sketch (in Figure 16.1) is an **isometric projection** or sketch (looking from the side and above) and the second (in Figure 16.2) is an **orthographic projection**. Think about the differences in these approaches. The isometric sketch gives an easy-to-understand representation of the tower unit provided it is drawn in good proportions, but it may not be that easy to produce. The orthographic sketch of the single face is easier to draw, but it doesn't give any indication of what the other faces look like.

Of course, you could combine two or more orthographic sketches together, say one showing the front of the tower unit and another showing the side. This way we'd be able to show the depth of the unit. This method of sketching is known as linked views. You've probably worked out by now that if you wanted to show important details of say the top, bottom or back of the unit – perhaps to show the cooling fan slots or the points where the printer cables and other accessories connect – you'd need to add more views showing these details.

Key terms

Isometric projection a pictorial method in which the receding lines are drawn at an angle of 30° to the horizontal to give an impression of depth.

Orthographic projection a pictorial method that utilises two or more views of the object. Each of the selected views shows a true face. The number of views required will depend on the complexity of the object being drawn. No illusion of depth is given in orthographic projection.

Producing isometric drawings

When you need to produce a drawing without the aid of isometric paper, it will be necessary to use a drawing board and drawing equipment. You will also need access to various drawing instruments, including:

- 300 mm plastic rule
- mechanical (propelling) pencil with 0.3 or 0.5 mm lead
- 2H pencil
- HB pencil
- 45°–45° set square
- 60°–30° set square
- protractor
- French curve
- circle template

The French curve is useful if you need to draw ellipses or sweeping curves. The circle template is useful when drawing small circles – you may find the circle template easier to use than a compass set to a small radius

When positioning your paper on the drawing board make sure that you align the bottom edge of the paper with the parallel rule (or T-square if you are using one) on your drawing board. Use board clips or a suitable alternative to secure your drawing paper to the drawing board. Make sure that the support mechanism of the drawing board you are using is properly engaged.

The receding lines in an isometric projection are always drawn at 30° to the horizontal. To produce an isometric sketch without using isometric paper, you therefore need a method of drawing the 30° angles required for the sketch. Figure 16.3 shows how this is done using a 60°–30° set square and a T-square or parallel motion square. The bold lines of the box shown in isometric projection in Figure 16.3 have been drawn using the bold edge of the 60°–30° set square. Note that the lower edge of the paper aligns with the T-square or parallel motion square.

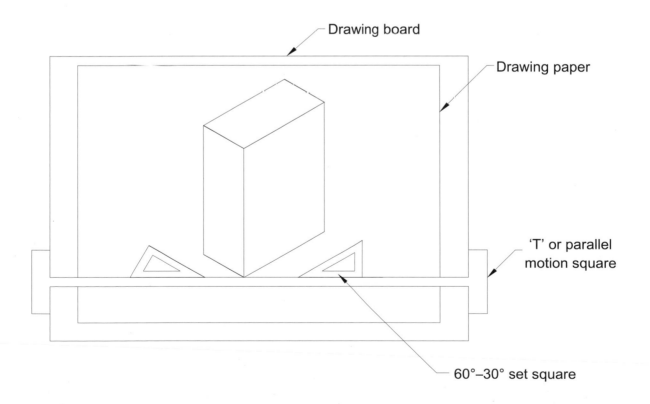

Figure 16.3: Producing an isometric drawing of a rectangular block

Activity: Isometric drawing

Now try to put these ideas into practice by making two isometric drawings of the angle bracket shown in Figure 16.4. The first should be drawn without using isometric paper, but use isometric paper for the second sketch.

For the first sketch, attach a piece of plain A3 paper (420 × 297 mm) to your drawing board. Reproduce the shape shown below in isometric projection to the dimensions (in mm) given in Figure 16.4. Be sure to consider where you start to draw to make sure that the shape fits onto the drawing sheet.

For the second sketch, use a sheet of A4 isometric paper to reproduce the drawing at half scale. This means that although the measurements shown in Figure 16.4 are 100 × 200 × 120 × 30 mm thick, you should draw the object to these dimensions 50 × 100 × 60 × 15 mm.

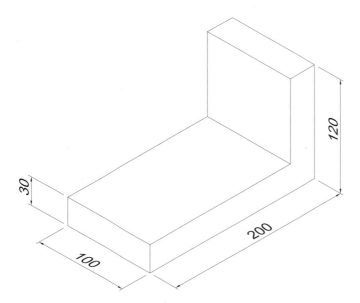

Figure 16.4: A test shape to practise isometric drawings

Let's now look at the angles we've actually drawn. On the orthographic sketch (Figure 16.2), they're more or less the true angles (90°) of the front of the unit, but if you measure the angles drawn on the isometric tower unit and the angle bracket (Figures 16.1 and 16.4), you will find that although we interpret the angles as being 90°, they are not so on the actual paper. Use a protractor to check the angles in both the isometric and orthographic illustrations throughout this unit.

Oblique projections

The **oblique projection** is another drawing technique. It is not much used today in finished technical drawings, but it can useful for uncomplicated shapes or simply to catch an idea quickly and easily. There are two methods of oblique projection, as we will consider later.

To show what oblique sketches look like, we're going to start with an isometric drawing (Figure 16.5) showing two views of the same machined block. The reason for showing two isometric views are that it is easier to get an idea of the general shape of the block because you cannot see all the details of the block in the lower (left-hand) drawing – in this drawing, the missing part of the second step is hidden from view.

Both of the oblique methods we are going to use employ the same basic principles. Draw the front face of the object and then project the lines backwards from it. The angles of these lines should be 45° to the horizontal. To produce the lines angled at 45° required for oblique sketches or drawings, you will need to use the 45°–45° set square and a T-square to keep the base of the set square horizontal.

If the object you're drawing has circular features, such as holes or bosses, make sure that the face with these features is used as the front face. Drawing circular features on either the side face or top faces of the oblique drawing, or indeed on any of the three faces of the isometric drawing, requires drawing ellipses. It is an advanced and difficult technique to construct and draw an ellipse manually.

The problem with the block shown in Figure 16.5 is which is the front face? By front, we usually mean the side that has most of the important details. The issue here is which face to choose as the front. Figure 16.6 looks at some options. If we produce front on views in the direction of arrows 1, 2, 3 and 4 we'd get the views shown in Figure 16.7.

If we then produced oblique projections of each of the four faces, we'd get the drawings shown in Figure 16.8.

Key terms

Oblique projection a method that uses a selected true face of an object to draw the width and height, and then projects lines backwards from the object's principal points at an angle of 45° to give the impression of depth or a third dimension.

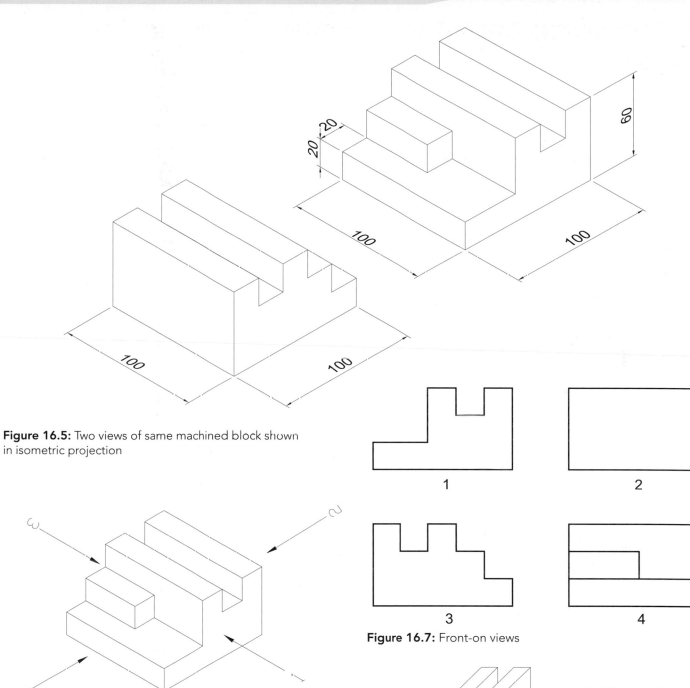

Figure 16.5: Two views of same machined block shown in isometric projection

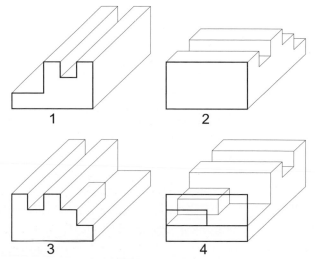

Figure 16.7: Front-on views

1

2

3

4

Figure 16.6: Four options for a front face

In each example the true front face is shown in bold lines. Note that in examples 1 and 2 part of the short block cannot be seen, and so some detail is missing from the drawing. Only examples 3 and 4 are therefore suitable for oblique projection.

From the isometric drawing (Figure 16.5), we can see that the base measurements indicate that the base is square. Now look carefully at the four oblique drawings in Figure 16.8. Does the block seem to change shape

Figure 16.8: Oblique projections

or distort as the views change? Remember that the base area should be a square. In each view, measure the length of the bold horizontal line at the base of the drawing and the length of the line at 45° to this line. Are the lengths you measured the same? Do they appear to be the same in the sketches?

Let's think about the approach we have taken here. An oblique drawing starts life as an orthographic sketch. It initially appears 'flat' on the paper, because it just has a horizontal x-axis and a vertical y-axis. We then have to decide which is the best face of the object to use as our front face. To give this flat object an impression of depth, or make it look 3D, we draw (or project) lines from the corners on the front face backwards at an angle of 45° to the right of the object.

How far back should we take these lines? Well, in the case of the four examples in Figure 16.8, the lines are drawn back so that they are the same length as in the original block. You should notice, however, that the lines that are drawn backwards at 45° appear to distort the shape of the block. They seem to be

too long when compared to the front face. Why is this? This is because Figure 16.8 uses a method of oblique projection known as **cavalier projection**, and this distorted view is an unavoidable feature of this method.

The other method of oblique projection is known as **cabinet projection**. This is named because it was used to illustrate items of furniture such as cabinets. Let's draw a standard double wall cupboard with these dimensions: 1000 × 720 × 300 mm (width × height × depth). To produce a cupboard in oblique projection, start by using the same reasoning and technique adopted for the cavalier projection. Select the best front face to draw, in this case the front of the cupboard is the obvious choice. Then draw the lines back at 45°, but for this projection draw them to half their true length. Figure 16.9 shows linked orthographic views and cavalier and cabinet projections for the double wall cupboard. As you can see, the cavalier projection looks a bit odd – the side is too deep. The cabinet projection is a much better representation.

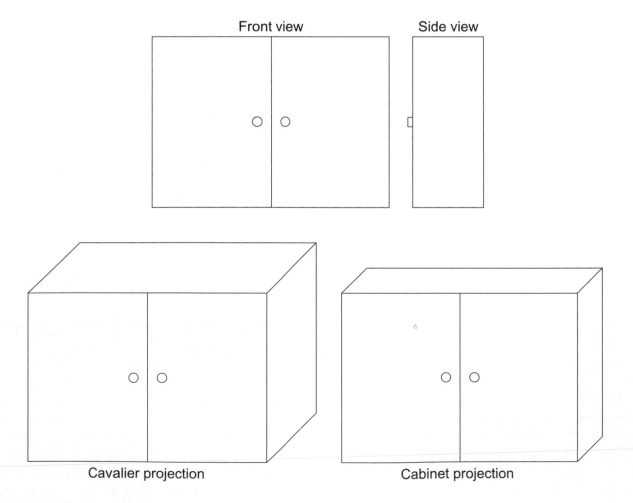

Front view Side view

Cavalier projection Cabinet projection

Figure 16.9: Different projections of a double wall cupboard

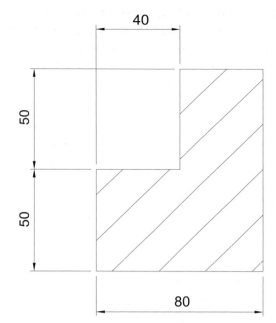

Figure 16.10: Applying linear dimensions to a drawn object

Dimensions

A good quality sketch is a valuable tool for quickly and accurately showing the shape of an object. However, even if the sketch is good and accurate, it won't be much use to anyone else unless you indicate the actual size of the object you've drawn. This is why the technique of applying **dimensions** to a sketch or drawing is important

Some of the drawings earlier in this unit have had dimensions. For example, Figure 16.5 shows how dimensions are applied to isometric drawings. Figures 16.10 and 16.11 show how linear dimensions should be applied to orthographic and oblique drawings. There are many points to remember about dimensioning, and we'll look at this topic in more detail later in section 16.2.

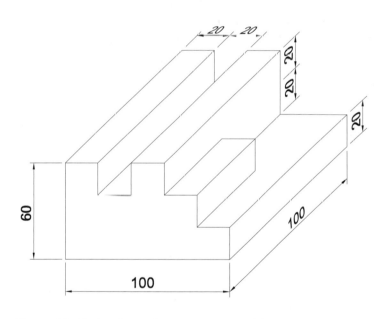

Figure 16.11: Applying dimensions to an oblique projection

16.1.3 Benefits and limitations of using pictorial techniques

By now you will have some idea of the sketching techniques that are used in engineering. Do you find it easier to produce drawings using one method rather than another? Does one technique make it easier to visualise or understand what is shown in the sketch? Which technique produces a true representation of the shape of a component. Are the sketches made to any particular standard?

The drawing methods we have covered in this section are often referred to as pictorial methods. (If you do some research into isometric and oblique drawing techniques, you may well find them referred to as axonometric projections, but we will use the terms isometric and oblique in this book.) These methods produce what appear to be three-dimensional (3D) images, although in reality they are only two-dimensional (2D) representations as the drawing medium only has breadth and height. The depth perceived in the drawing is an illusion.

Isometric sketches and drawings can be difficult to produce especially where circles, arcs or curved surfaces are involved. Oblique projections are easier to draw, but they don't contain as much detail as perhaps we'd like and the cavalier projection tends to distort the appearance of the object.

Figure 16.8 highlights one of the problems with oblique projections. Depending on which views we choose to illustrate the object, there is the possibility that some vital feature of the object may be obscured. Look again at views 1 and 2 in Figure 16.8, and you can see that the small step is not visible. It would be very easy to misinterpret this drawing if these were the only views presented of this object. This, in turn, could lead to unnecessary costs, particularly if it leads to a component being scrapped because it has been manufactured incorrectly.

Look again at Figure 16.11. Note that the 100 and 60 dimensions are relatively easy to read, as the numerals are perpendicular to the object's front face. However, the other dimensions, although appearing to be perpendicular to relevant faces, are in fact angled and inclined. To achieve this effect, the text, extension lines and arrow heads all need to be drawn at an oblique angle to make them appear to be perpendicular to the faces. This is quite difficult to achieve and it is time consuming to draw. This is another drawback of oblique projections.

Assessment activity 16.1

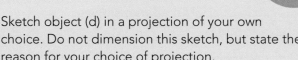

For this activity, you'll need some sheets of plain, isometric and graph A4 paper (210 × 297 mm) to create sketches of engineering components using a range of techniques.

P1 Produce pictorial sketches (isometric, oblique cavalier and oblique cabinet) of these engineering shapes.

  a) a regular solid, such as a dice

  b) a cylindrical solid, such as a bean tin with both ends still on

  c) a regular rectangular hollow, such as cereal box without its ends

  d) a workshop vice.

  You should produce both isometric and oblique sketches of objects (a), (b) and (c). Add dimensions to one of each of type of sketches.

Sketch object (d) in a projection of your own choice. Do not dimension this sketch, but state the reason for your choice of projection.

P2 On a separate sheet, describe what you think are the benefits and limitations of the techniques you used for the P1 task. You should also describe the benefits and limitations of using pictorial techniques for showing engineered products.

Grading tips

P1 P2 All sketches should include your name, the projection that has been used to create the drawing and the name of the object that has been sketched.

16.2 Be able to interpret engineering drawings that comply with standards

Information is only useful if it can be understood by the person who needs that information. You may have direct experience of some of the problems of understanding information if you stop and ask for directions to a place and find that the person you ask speaks in a different language (or accent) to your own. You may be getting valid instructions, but the problem is that you may not be able to get the full meaning of the information. As result, you may misunderstand what is being said and head off in the wrong direction.

In engineering, 'getting lost' or making mistakes can be very costly. So it is crucial that engineering drawings can be understood by everybody that works in the profession. For this reason, engineering drawings are produced to standards. This simply means that every engineering drawing is produced using similar features and conventions, even though the objects they depict might be very different.

Standards are applied in many areas of life. For example, all numeric keypads on a phone or a cash machine have the same basic layout: the numeral 0 is at the bottom of the display. Imagine the problems that might arise if a manufacturer introduced a non-standard keypad that commenced with the 0 at the top. It is bound to cause confusion. So it is with drawings – if drawings produced by different organisations use different symbols or conventions to represent the same thing, then there's bound to be confusion, and with confusion come mistakes.

16.2.1 Interpret

The *Oxford English Dictionary* defines the word 'interpret' as 'explain, make out or bring out meaning of'. You will need to develop the skills that will enable you to look at an engineering drawing and understand what it's all about. In a way it'll be like learning a new language, a language that doesn't make too much use of the written word.

We will consider in turn some of the main parts or features of this language. These are:

• dimensions

• tolerances

• surface finish

• manufacturing detail

• assembly instructions

• parts list

• circuit operation.

Dimensions

We have already briefly discussed dimensions in the previous section. Now we shall consider the topic in more detail. It is important that whenever you dimension an object, you clearly indicate exactly what you mean when you produce the drawing. So let's start off by looking at a few important terms that relate to dimensioning, and then we will review some things you must do and some practices that should be avoided.

Figure 16.12 shows some of the terms we will use when discussing what is good practice when adding dimensions to drawings. Refer to this when considering the drawings in Figures 16.13 and 16.14.

Figure 16.13 is an example of good practice. The dimensions can all be read by viewing the drawing from only two positions: from the bottom and from right-hand edge of the drawing. The numbers 90 and 50 on the left-hand side of the drawing are aligned and matching. The dimension text (that is, the numbers) are always placed above the dimension line. The arrow heads are in good proportion. There is a clear gap between the projection line and the object being dimensioned. The projection lines extend to just above the arrow heads. There are no unnecessary dimensions.

Any engineering drawing with dimensions as in Figure 16.14 would unacceptable for many reasons. To read the dimensions you need to turn the page to view it from its bottom, top, right- and left-hand edges. The numbers (dimensions) are poorly sized and positioned, and some split the dimension line. The 40s are upside down and of unequal size. The arrow heads are of mixed shape and size. There are no gaps between some of the projection lines and the object being dimensioned. There are large gaps between some of the projection lines and the object being dimensioned. Some of the arrow heads touch the ends

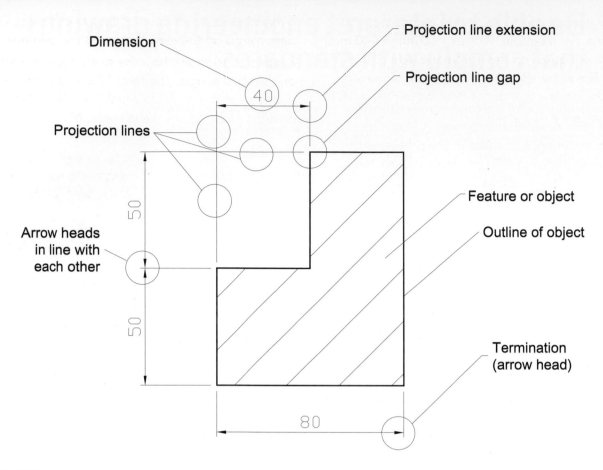

Figure 16.12: Terms used in dimensioning

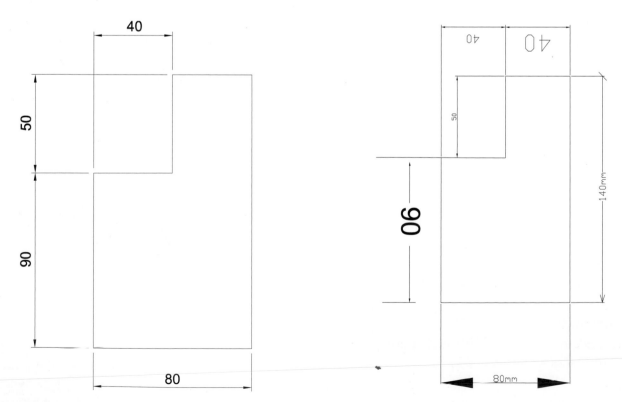

Figure 16.13: An acceptable standard for adding dimensions to a drawing

Figure 16.14: An unacceptable method of adding dimensions to a drawing

of the projection lines. There are also unnecessary dimensions. For example, 90 mm + 50 mm = 140 mm, so why state it again on the right-hand side of the drawing. The same applies to the 80 mm dimension given at the lower edge of the drawing in Figure 16.14.

Other faults are that the numbers 90 and 50 are misaligned and mismatched. Some of the dimensions have mm behind the number. It is difficult in some cases to tell which lines are the projection lines and which lines represent the object being dimensioned. The 50 dimension at the top left-hand corner is positioned within the boundaries of the object. This should be avoided if possible.

Figure 16.15 shows the methods used for placing dimensions on circles.

- Top left: centre lines. Note that they cross at the centre and extend slightly beyond the circumference of the circle.
- Top right: leader. Note that the arrow points towards centre of circle and that the text is horizontal.
- Centre: diameter. The text is placed off-centre to avoid conflict with centre lines
- Bottom left: this is an acceptable method of dimensioning diameter but note that the Ø symbol must be included.
- Bottom right: placing the arrows outside the projection lines is also acceptable.

An important factor in deciding which of the methods shown in Figure 16.15 to use would be the size of the diameter of the circle that you are drawing. When

dimensioning any diameter, you should place your dimensions on the view that gives the greatest clarity. Figures 16.16 shows how the diameters are identified on the steel flange. The term PCD indicates the diameter of the circle on which the **pitch** of the holes is centred. The pitch of the circles is 60°.

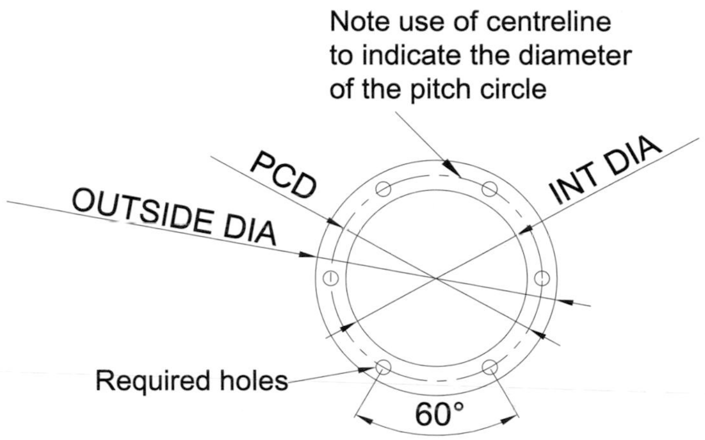

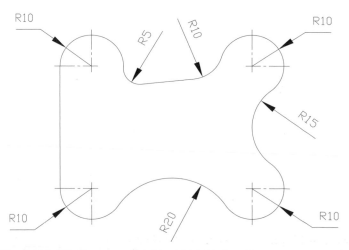

Figure 16.16: Steel flange showing how diameters are identified

Key terms

Pitch in engineering, pitch is a measure relating to distance. For example, the distance between drilled holes in a machined component would be described as the pitch.

In some engineering drawings, you also need to add dimensions to radii. Figure 16.17 shows how this is done. The R5 method of dimensioning is used where the centre of the radius need not have its centre located. The R10 method, at the four corner radii, is used where the centre of the radius needs to be located.

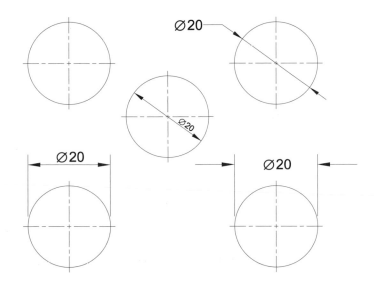

Figure 16.15: Placing dimensions on circles

Figure 16.17: Showing the dimensions of radii

Tolerances

Tolerance is the allowable variation in weight or measurement of an object. The idea of tolerance is important in engineering because when something is being manufactured it is not always possible to produce everything exactly to the specified measurements.

Let's consider three different products:

- a wheelbarrow body
- a soft drinks can
- an aircraft jet engine.

A wheelbarrow body is a fairly straightforward steel pressing. The dimensions for the body will be stated on the production drawings. The variation in manufacturing may allow for the body to be as much as 2 mm over or under the stated size. In production terms, this means that as the pressing tool wears or even moves slightly, the bodies that are produced will still be of a useable size for the finished product and they will not end up as scrap.

A soft drinks can is usually made from aluminium with a wall thickness of 0.01 mm (one hundredth of 1 mm). Although a can is a disposable product – it has no value as such (the value is in the drink it contains) and it probably becomes a piece of scrap within 15 minutes of being purchased – the can must be made to a very high degree of accuracy. This is because if the metal is too thin, the can could burst during transit or it might be difficult to open because the ring pull would break off. Conversely, if the material is too thick, you also may not be able to open the can because you wouldn't have the strength in your finger to tear the opening flap that is attached to the ring pull.

Another reason for making cans to a high degree of accuracy is that manufacturers make so many of them: millions of canned soft drinks are sold each year. So, if the can manufacturer is able to save even a small amount (less than a penny say) on each can by keeping the dimensions and the amount of metal used in the process to precise limits, there are big savings to be made overall.

Jet engines pose a different challenge. Because of the conditions under which they operate, failure is not an option. It wouldn't be acceptable for a component inside the jet engine to foul the engine's casing. You would expect that the tolerances set for engine components would be very small indeed. In other words, they are made to very high quality standards.

Key terms

Nominal the stated size of some dimension. In reality, parts cannot be manufactured to a given nominal measurement, so they are produced within some specified tolerance.

So let's look at how tolerances would be applied to a block and angular measurements. Suppose a simple rectangular block has **nominal** dimensions of 300 × 150 mm, but it is acceptable for the manufactured item to be up to 1 mm over or 2 mm below the nominal size. This can be shown in two ways on an engineering drawing (see Figure 16.18). The first method (top of Figure 16.18) shows how much the measurement can deviate from the nominal dimension

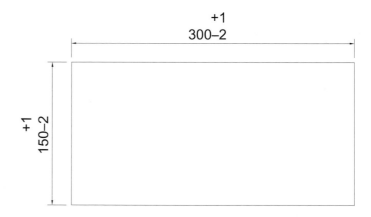

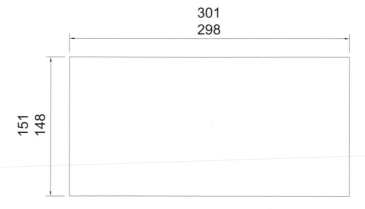

Figure 16.18: Marking tolerances on linear measurements

(between plus 1 mm and minus 2 mm). The alternative way of indicating these tolerances is to specify the limits directly on the component, and this is the approach adopted in the second drawing in Figure 16.18.

Figure 16.19 shows how tolerances are indicated on an angular measurement. The angle shown in Figure 16.19 is nominally 35°, but the drawing indicates that it is allowable for it to be up to 1° over or 2° under the nominal size.

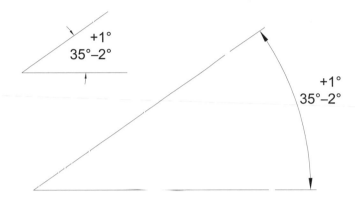

Figure 16.19: Marking tolerances on angles

Surface finish

Think about a cast iron engine block that may be used in the manufacture of a diesel engine. The outer surface of the casting could well have a slightly grainy feel owing to the casting process. On the other hand, the bore of the cylinder block into which the cylinder liner fits will need to be a lot smoother. There will be two different surface textures on a single component. So how does a designer tell the manufacturer of the casting what are the finished surface requirements?

We often talk of smoothness in relation to something else. When compared to a cobbled street, a tarmac road is smooth, but if you compare a tarmac road to a sheet of glass, the glass is smooth and the tarmac road becomes rough. The term smooth here is subjective: in other words it hasn't been quantified or measured. However, engineers like to work in specific quantities, and smoothness or surface texture needs to be measurable and indicated on drawings.

Figure 16.20 shows how surface texture is indicated on engineering drawings. The actual value has been stated in micrometres alongside the symbol. In this

illustration, a surface texture of 3 micrometres is required on all surfaces of the component (indicated by the words 'all over').

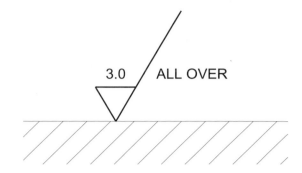

Figure 16.20: Surface texture symbol with 'all over' machining note

Manufacturing detail

A drawing will show us what the component looks like. For example, look at the drawing of the hydraulic cylinder on page 326 (Figure 16.30). This is a clear view of the cylinder, but the drawing doesn't tell us whether the cylinder is to be made from aluminium, brass, steel or another material. This drawing also does not show how the fittings are attached to the body of the cylinder. Are they to be welded on, shrunk fit or attached by a screw thread? Does the cylinder need to be heat-treated at some stage of the manufacturing process, and if so, when? These are some of the manufacturing details that the designer will need to pass on to the manufacturer to ensure that the end product matches the designer's specifications. If this information cannot easily be conveyed on the drawing using symbols, written notes may be added near to the feature to which they apply.

Assembly instructions

If you have tried to put together any self-assembly product, such as flat-pack furniture, you will be familiar with assembly instructions. Self-assembly units produced by furniture retailers such as Ikea are usually provided in picture form to overcome language difficulties. Engineering component assembly instructions can be much more complicated, depending on the nature of the assembly. This information would normally be provided on an assembly drawing. We will consider assembly drawings later in this unit.

Parts list

Everyone concerned in the manufacture and assembly of a component should know how many parts there are in the finished product. This is particularly important because some engineered components are assembled on site, and many are large and complex in nature For this reason, a parts list will be included on the assembly. The assembly drawing may indicate the individual parts by a number. This number may then be given a description and then the required quantity of the item will be noted.

Circuit operation

Electrical, pneumatic and hydraulic circuits are a feature of most engineered products. The function of these circuits will need to be indicated on the relevant drawing.

16.2.2 Drawing standards

An engineering drawing is one that has been prepared to scale and that conforms to accepted standards. This type of illustration conveys technical information in graphical form for the purpose of manufacturing an end product. A technical drawing must conform to standards that relate to symbols, lines, terminology, scale and other features.

As technology changes, it's not surprising that the standards that relate to a particular technology will also need to change. In recent years, the British Standards that relate to engineering drawing have gone through a process of updating. Some of the older standards have been revised or replaced.

Many years ago, *BS308: Engineering Drawing Practice for Schools and Colleges* was the standard reference to be used when studying engineering at your level. This was replaced by *PP7308: Engineering Drawing Practice for Schools and Colleges*. In addition, *PP7307:1989 Graphical symbols for use in schools and colleges* detailed of a range of symbols to be used in drawings.

These references have now been replaced by BS8888, which itself has undergone a number of revisions. (Note that if you have access to PP7307 and PP7308, although now out of date, they do contain information that will be very useful. Both publications should, for the majority of applications, be more than sufficient for your needs.)

The latest version of BS8888 (at the time of writing), was issued in 2008. This is: *BS8888:2008 Technical product specification*. The main function of BS8888 is to bring together all the international standards that engineers and designers need to prepare technical documents.

You may also find two other drawing standards useful:

- BS3939: Part 12:1991, IEC 60617-12:1991 Graphical symbols for electrical power, telecommunications and electronics diagrams
- BS2917-1:1993, ISO 1219-1:1991 Graphic symbols and circuit diagrams for fluid power systems and components. Specification for graphic symbols.

The topics covered in BS8888 that are relevant for this unit are:

- terms and definitions
- scales
- dimensioning
- tolerancing and geometrical tolerancing
- surface texture indication
- lines, arrows and lettering
- projections and views
- symbols and abbreviations
- representation of features and components.

We have covered dimensioning, tolerances and surface texture earlier in the unit. Let's now look at some of the other aspects of engineering drawing covered by British Standards in a little more detail.

Terms and definitions

The terms used in technical documents need precise meanings to avoid misunderstanding. BS8888 defines some of the terminology used in engineering drawing. For example, it defines pictorial representation as *parallel or central projection on a single projection plane giving a three-dimensional image of an object*. We have discussed these ideas already, though not in these terms. To translate:

- parallel projection means oblique projection
- central projection means isometric projection
- three-dimensional image means a drawing produced using oblique or isometric projections
- a single projection plane means a flat sheet of paper.

Table 16.1: Glossary of drawing terms

Term	Definition
Assembly drawing	A drawing that shows the relative positions of the items that form a complete assembly.
Component drawing	A drawing showing a single component that includes all the information required to accurately define the component.
Detail	A drawing showing an area of an item or assembly.
Detail drawing	This usually consists of a small area of a large drawing that has been purposely enlarged. The enlarged section allows easier detailing of items such as dimensions and shape of the object by the draughtsperson. In addition, detailed drawings enable easier interpretation of important design details by the reader of the drawing.
Diagram	A system drawing in which symbols are used to indicate the function of the components and how they are connected together.
Elevation	A view that shows a vertical plane of the object. For example, if you were to stand facing a house at ground level you would see either a front, back or side elevation
Item list	Sometimes referred to as a parts list. Found on assembly drawings, they are a complete list of the items that make up an assembly or sub-assembly
Part drawing	A drawing that shows a single unit of an assembly. The single unit should not be capable of being broken down into smaller parts. The part drawing should contain information necessary for its production.
Plan	Often referred to as a plan view. It is a representation of an object when viewed from a position directly above the object.
Production drawing	A drawing containing sufficient information for the successful production of the item depicted.
Sectional view	A view of a section of a component showing how it would appear if cut along an imaginary line.
Sketch	A freehand (not necessarily to scale) drawing of an object
View	Orthogonal projection that shows the visible parts of an object. Where necessary, details that are hidden from view are also indicated on the view, usually by means of dashed lines.

Table 16.1 contains a glossary of terms related to engineering drawings.

Scales

Not everything we want to draw will fit conveniently on a standard-sized drawing sheet. Look at a piece of A4 paper. It is 210 × 297 mm in portrait orientation and 297 × 210 mm in landscape orientation. You could probably draw one view of a CD case on an A4 sheet because a CD case measures approximately 140 × 120 mm. You could draw the case at full size – that is, at a scale of 1:1.

It is important to choose a suitable scale. If you wanted to draw a wristwatch face on A4 paper, you could draw it to a scale of 1:1, but you would have difficulty drawing and seeing some of the fine details. It would

be better to draw the watch at, say, five times its actual size. This means that every measurement on the watch is multiplied up five times; so, for example, 2 mm on the watch becomes 10 mm on the drawing. Or, to put it more simply, the watch is drawn to a scale of 5:1 (see Figure 16.21 overleaf). When making small objects larger in a drawing, it is a convention to use one of these scaling factors: 2:1, 5:1, 10:1, 20:1 and 50:1.

In many cases, you will have to scale down an object to draw it on an A3 sheet of drawing paper. Consider, for example, the wall cabinet shown in Figure 16.9. The cupboard would be too big to draw at full size on a sheet of A3 paper. It would need to be scaled down. When making objects smaller in a drawing it is a convention to use of these scaling factors: 1:2, 1:5, 1:10, 1:20, 1:50, 1:100, 1:200, 1:500 and 1:1000.

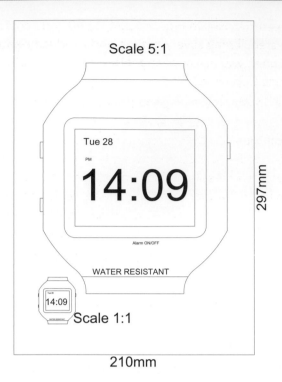

Scale 5:1

Tue 28

PM

14:09

Alarm ON/OFF

WATER RESISTANT

297mm

14:09

Scale 1:1

210mm

Figure 16.21: Scaling a wristwatch to show it in portrait orientation on A4 paper

You also need to consider the orientation of the paper and you should leave room for a border. Drawings laid out to British Standards should contain the drawing area and title block within a frame border (Figure 16.24). If you were to draw the wristwatch shown in Figure 16.21 at a scale of 5:1 in landscape

orientation, you would find that the edges of the scaled-up watch would be too near the edges of the paper and this would not leave enough space to draw a border around the edge of the drawing paper.

Geometrical tolerancing

The tolerance of an object or product indicates the permitted maximum and minimum sizes of key dimensions. However, it is possible that although dimensionally accurate and within tolerance, the object's geometric features such as flatness, **concentricity** may need further definition. Figure 6.22 (top image) shows the side view of a component whose perfect flatness is indicated by the dashed line. In reality though the actual shape may be more like that shown by the solid blue line. For this reason, geometric tolerances may be applied to specify how much variance is allowed. This is identified by the uppermost line. The lower image in Figure 16.22 shows how it would be shown on a drawing. Figure 16.23 shows other geometric tolerancing symbols.

Key terms

Concentricity if two (or more) circular features share a common centre point, they are said to be concentric.

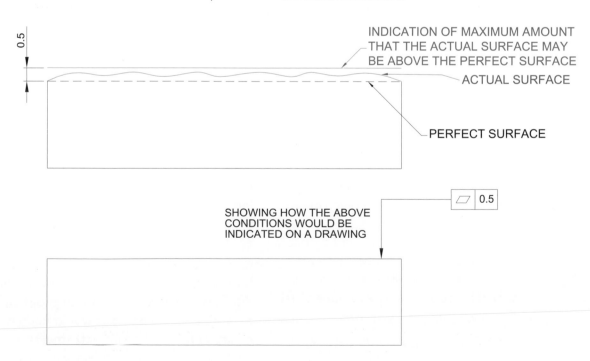

0.5

INDICATION OF MAXIMUM AMOUNT
THAT THE ACTUAL SURFACE MAY
BE ABOVE THE PERFECT SURFACE

ACTUAL SURFACE

PERFECT SURFACE

☐ 0.5

SHOWING HOW THE ABOVE
CONDITIONS WOULD BE
INDICATED ON A DRAWING

Figure 16.22: Showing a geometrical tolerance

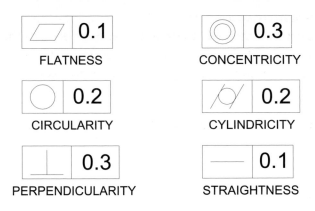

Figure 16.23: Geometric tolerancing symbols with tolerance shown left and value shown right

Lettering and lines

Lettering on drawings must be neat and uniform, with particular emphasis on spacing and style. All lettering should have a minimum height of 3 mm, and titles on drawings should normally be larger. If notes are required on the drawing, related groups of notes should be positioned together but not too near the feature to which they relate so as to crowd the view.

British Standards recommends that, in general, capital (upper case) letters should be used on drawings. A simple sans serif typeface should be used for computer-generated work. If you are writing on manually produced drawings, avoid the use of elaborate or personal styles of lettering. Instead, adopt a simple uncluttered style such as that shown in the

completed boxes in Figure 16.24, 16.40 and 16.41. A letter stencil may save you time and produce neater work when you are applying lettering to manually produced drawings.

Figure 16.24 shows a typical standardised layout used for engineering drawings. These are very useful, as they prompt you to include on all work the drawing number, title and issue number, date and the name of the person responsible for producing the drawing. When using standard drawing sheets (which come in A4, A3, A2, A1 or A0 sizes), the drawing should include a border and a title block. The title block should detail:

• name of the person producing the drawing
• date the drawing was produced
• projection symbol (see page 326)
• title
• drawing number.

There is a range of line styles or types specified by British Standards. Each type of line has a special function in that it represents a certain feature of the drawing. Interpreting the type of line and what it represents is part of the skill of understanding the non-verbal language of drawings. Figure 16.25 shows some of the line types used in engineering drawings. Table 16.2 gives the accepted applications of each type of line used in engineering drawings. As you work through this unit, look to see where the various line types have been used in the illustrations.

Figure 16.24: A standardised drawing layout using simple styles of letters and numbers

Table 16.2: Accepted applications for each type of line used in an engineering drawing

Description	Application
Continuous thick line	Visible outlines and edges
Continuous thin line	Dimension, projection and leader lines, short centre lines, outlines of revolved sections, hatching (example E, Figure 16.25), imaginary intersections
Continuous thin irregular lines (example D, Figure 16.25) or thin straight lines with zigzags	Limits of partial or interrupted views and sections, if the limit is not an axis
Dashed thin line (example B, Figure 16.25)	Hidden outlines and edges
Chain thin line (example A, Figure 16.25)	Centre lines of symmetry, trajectories and loci, pitch lines and pitch circles
Chain thin line, but thick at ends and changes of direction (example F, Figure 16.25)	Cutting planes
Doubled dashed chain thin line (example C, Figure 16.25)	Outlines and edges of adjacent parts, outlines and edges of alternative and extreme positions of moveable parts, initial outlines prior to forming, bend lines on developed blanks or patterns

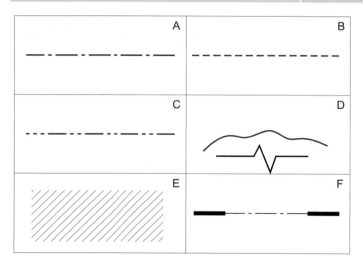

Figure 16.25: Examples of line types used in engineering drawings

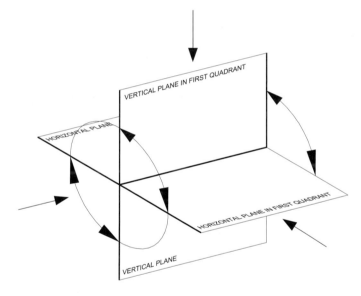

Figure 16.26: The four quadrants

First- and third-angle projections

We've already looked at several projections – isometric, oblique, orthographic and linked orthographic projections. We are now going to concentrate on two methods of displaying or arranging linked orthographic projections. These are first angle and third angle.

These are concepts that many people find difficult to grasp at first. Start by considering Figure 16.26. This shows two planes, one horizontal and one vertical. This gives us four quadrants or quarters. The section with arrows at both ends is the first quadrant (or first angle if you like). The quadrant diagonally opposite is the third quadrant (or third angle). The blue arrows indicate the

viewing positions we will be using when we create both the first and third angle orthographic drawing layouts.

Now let's focus on the first quadrant. Figure 16.27 shows a solid in the first quadrant. It may help you to think of the block as being drawn inside a three-sided box. The solid is positioned above the horizontal plane defining the quadrant and away from the vertical plane.

If you are looking directly at side A of the block, its image could be projected to the vertical plane directly behind it. If you are looking directly at side B, its image could be drawn on the newly included vertical plane to the right. If you are looking at the block from directly above, you could project the image you would see on to the horizontal plane below the block.

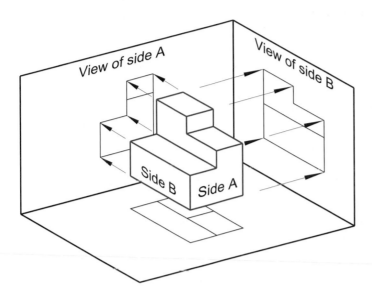

Figure 16.27: Working in the first quadrant

Now here's the important thing to remember. What you see from the three viewing positions is drawn or projected on to the surface *behind* the block. This is the key point: in first-angle projections whatever features we see on the object on any of the faces are *always projected behind*, or away from us, to a plane that is *behind the object*.

In third-angle projections, something different happens: whatever features we see on the object on any of the faces are always projected *forward*, or towards us, on to a plane that is *in front the object*.

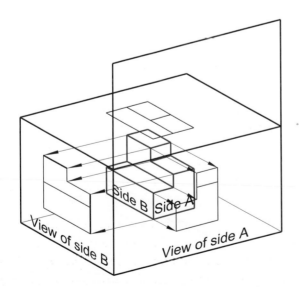

Figure 16.28: The block in the third quadrant or third angle

Figure 16.28 shows the block in the third quadrant or third angle – part of the first-angle quadrant has been removed for clarity. An extra vertical plane has been added at the left-hand side, the side from which you'll be viewing the block. Remember that the block is positioned below the horizontal face of the quadrant and also away from the vertical face of the quadrant.

As we look directly at the face of side A, what we see is projected forwards towards us on to the vertical plane. As we look directly at side B, what we see is also projected forward towards us on to the newly added vertical plane. If we look directly at the top of the block, what we see will be projected towards us, upwards on to the horizontal plane.

The important point about first- and third-angle projections is that they are ways of linking orthographic projections on a single drawing to provide clear information about the object being drawn. To produce a drawing in first-angle projection the views will need to be arranged as follows. Working from the front or principal view of the object:

- the view from above will be placed underneath (at the bottom of the drawing)
- the view from below (if it is required) will be placed above
- the view from the left will be placed on the right of the drawing
- the view from the right is placed on the left.

Note, that in many drawings only three views are required. It is therefore important to select the views that show the most useful detail.

To produce a drawing in third-angle projection the views will need to be arranged as follows. Working from the front or principal view of the object:

- the view from above will be placed above (at the top of the drawing)
- the view from below will be placed underneath
- the view from the left will be placed on the left
- the view from the right will be placed on the right.

You are likely to encounter both first- and third-angle drawings. Engineers tend to use third-angle views, but architectural drawings often use first-angle views. But how do we know when we are looking at linked orthographic projections whether we are looking at first-angle or third-angle views? And how do we indicate, if we are producing the drawing, which projection we are using? Engineers use two small but simple drawings as symbols to indicate first- or third-angle projections. These symbols (Figure 16.29) consist of two views of the same object – the frustum of a cone (a cone with the top cut off). Both symbols use two views of the cone, one looking directly at the cone from the side and one looking directly at the cone from the top.

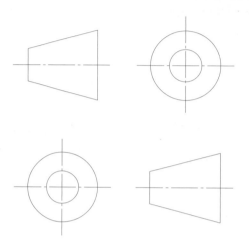

Figure 16.29: The symbols for first-angle projection (top) and third-angle projection (bottom)

Sections

A section view is one in which a component, usually complex in shape, has effectively been cut at some convenient point along an imaginary cutting plane to show detail that may be difficult to interpret from a standard orthographic view.

To get an idea of what a section view look likes, we'll look at a cylindrical shape such as would be used on a hydraulic lifting arm. Figure 16.30 shows the cylinder

in isometric projection so that its general shape and proportions can be easily understood. Notice that in the isometric projection, there is an arrow and a bold line. The arrow represents a viewpoint from which an orthographic view could be made. The bold line represents the imaginary cutting line from which a section view could be made.

Figure 16.31 shows an orthographic view of the same cylinder showing its general outline and some hidden detail. The hidden detail shows the thickness of the cylinder wall. Notice the different manufacturing methods used to locate the three bosses. Which of the bosses fit into the cylinder and which bosses fit on to the cylinder? The dashed lines represent details that we can't see in the isometric view shown in Figure 16.30.

Figure 16.31: Orthographic view of the cylinder

Figure 16.32 shows an isometric projection of the cylinder sectioned (cut) along the bold line. Figure 16.33 shows a sectioned orthographic view of the cylinder looking along the line of the arrow in Figure 16.30. This view uses hatching to highlight the different components of the cylinder and how they are assembled. Note how much easier it is to see in this view how the small bosses connect to the main body of the cylinder. This arrangement would be considered a poor design and is only used to illustrate the technique of sectioning and hatching.

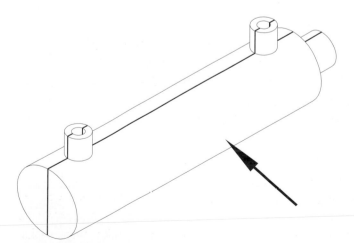

Figure 16.30: Hydraulic cylinder in isometric projection with the section line shown in bold

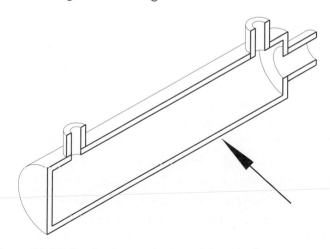

Figure 16.32: Section isometric view of the cylinder

Figure 16.33: Orthographic sectioned view of the cylinder with hatching

The orthographic view provides a view looking in the direction of the arrow showing hidden detail. In this case, the hidden detail is the thickness of the cylinder wall and the thickness of the three fittings. This view shows how one of the smaller cylindrical bosses fits *into* the cylinder and the other smaller one fits on to the top of the cylinder.

In Figure 16.33, notice how the sloping lines, known as hatching, have been applied to show that we are looking at a section. Notice that the hatching changes direction where there are two adjacent parts. Hatch lines should be drawn at 45° in each direction and should be equally spaced at not less than 4 mm apart unless on very small items.

A final note on these orthographic views. Note that we would not know from Figures 16.31 and 16.33 that the object is a cylinder without seeing the isometric view. Without the benefit of the isometric view, we would need a second orthographic view of the cylinder – this time viewing the cylinder from its end and showing it to be a circular component.

Interrupted views

You'll see that most of the useful detail in the orthographic view is contained at the ends of the cylinder. This means that we could easily remove a large part of the mid-portion of this drawing without losing any vital information. This can be achieved by using an interrupted view. We can save space by drawing the two ends close together but at the same time indicating that something is missing. Figure 16.34 shows an interrupted view of the cylinder. This shows the method of indicating break lines. Note the inclusion of a centre line.

Figure 16.35 shows the interrupted view of a solid shaft or bar. Look carefully at the centre lines in the right-hand end view. You'll see that they cross neatly at the middle and overlap the circumference equally on all four sides.

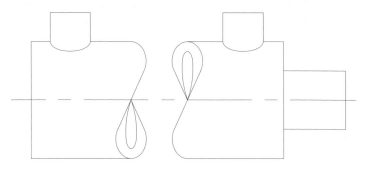

Figure 16.34: Interrupted view of a cylinder

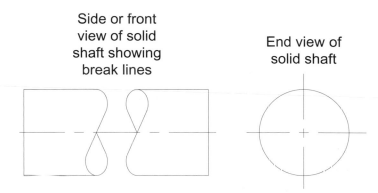

Side or front view of solid shaft showing break lines

End view of solid shaft

Figure 16.35: Orthographic view of the cylinder with hatching

Auxiliary views

Auxiliary projections are, in a way, a variant of orthographic projections. They show a view of the object from a viewing position other than from looking directly at the front, end or plan view of the object.

To illustrate this, we'll take an orthographic view of a block with a semicircular opening cut into it. Our viewpoint will be from a position 30° to the right of the front view. The auxiliary view will be shown above and to the left of the two orthographic views. Figure 16.36 shows how you construct this view. Construction lines are drawn at 30° from front view of orthographic projection. The construction lines drawn in bold (Figure 16.37) give the required auxiliary view.

Auxiliary views are used where the true representation of features is necessary, but they cannot be shown by only using orthographic views. Sometimes, for example, if we only have the side and plan view of an object, it would be difficult to dimension and interpret its true shape. An auxiliary view can make these tasks much easier.

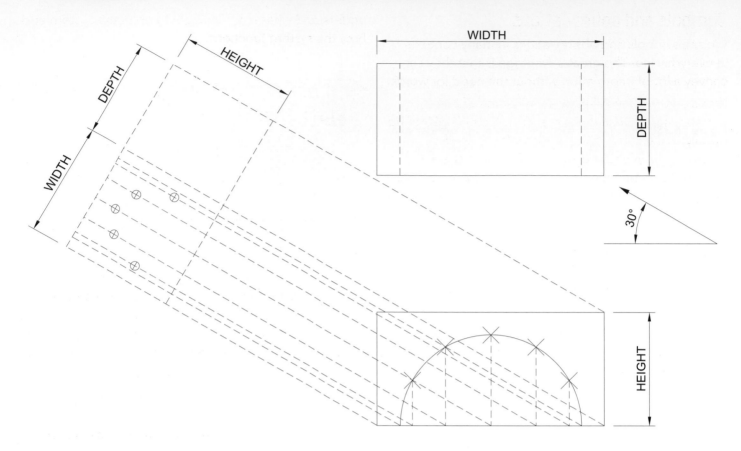

Figure 16.36: Constructing an auxiliary view of the block with opening

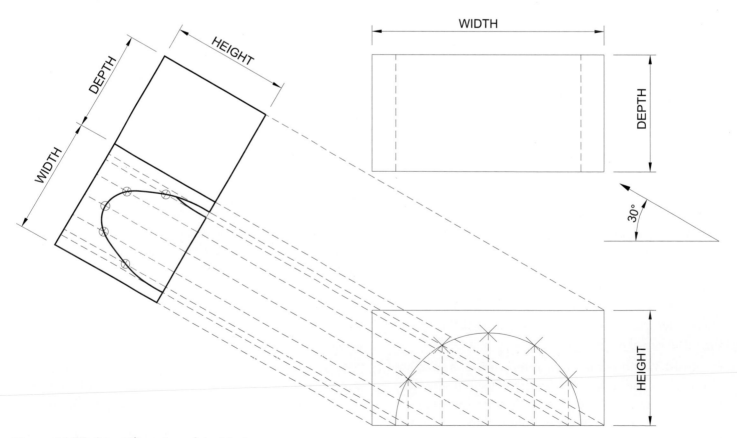

Figure 16.37: An auxiliary view of the block

Symbols and abbreviations

We see symbols and abbreviations in many contexts in everyday life. The great advantage is that they can convey a lot of information without the need for words.

In this unit, we have already shown some of the symbols and abbreviations that are used in engineering drawings. One area in which symbols are used extensively is in circuit diagrams. There are special symbols to denote the features in electrical, electronic, hydraulic and pneumatic circuits and systems. There are many examples of the symbols used in circuit diagrams in Unit 6. Two appendices in this book (see page 378 onwards) show some of the most commonly used symbols in electrical and electronic circuits (Appendix 2) and in hydraulic and pneumatic circuits (Appendix 3).

A full list of symbols used in engineering drawings is available from the published standards. The graphical symbols used in electrical and electronic standards are published in IEC 60617 *Graphical Symbols for Diagrams* (previously BS3939). The graphical symbols that are used in hydraulic and pneumatic circuits are published in BS2917 *Graphic symbols and circuit diagrams for fluid power systems and components: specification for graphic symbols*. Your study centre may have a copy *PP7307:1989 Graphical symbols for use in schools and colleges*. This standard has now been withdrawn, but it remains a good reference source.

Note that circuits represented by both hydraulic and pneumatic system diagrams will be similar in function and operation – the difference is simply that the medium used for transmitting the mechanical force is a liquid in a hydraulic system and a gas in a pneumatic system. The symbols make it much easier for us to understand what is actually going on in the system and how the system functions.

Activity: Symbols in electrical circuits

Can you identify the symbols used in Figure 16.38?

Representation of features and components

It would be extremely time-consuming to represent an item such as a screw thread on a drawing accurately, and it would not be very beneficial – one pitch of a bolt thread will look identical to the rest. Similar arguments apply to other engineering components with repeated features that may appear on drawings. These include:

- gears – these may be spur, bevel or worm wheel types
- bearings – these may be ball, roller or taper roller types
- splines – a series of raised flat-topped, saw-tooth shaped protrusions arranged axially around the end of a driveshaft
- springs – these may be cylindrical helical compression, cylindrical helical tension or cylindrical helical torsion
- serrations – a series of raised, saw-toothed shaped protrusions arranged axially around the end of a driveshaft.

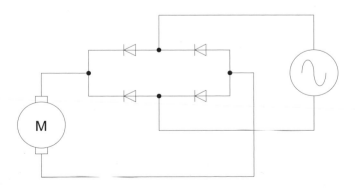

Figure 16.38: A simple circuit for a rectifier

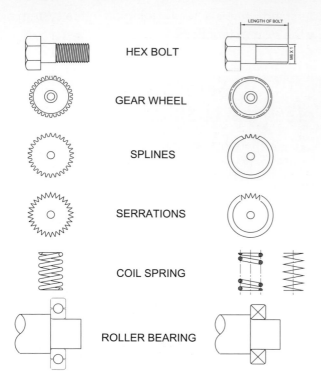

Figure 16.39 shows the conventions for representing some common engineering components. A simplified method of drawing the components is shown on the right.

HEX BOLT

GEAR WHEEL

SPLINES

SERRATIONS

COIL SPRING

ROLLER BEARING

Figure 16.39: Conventions for representing standard engineering components

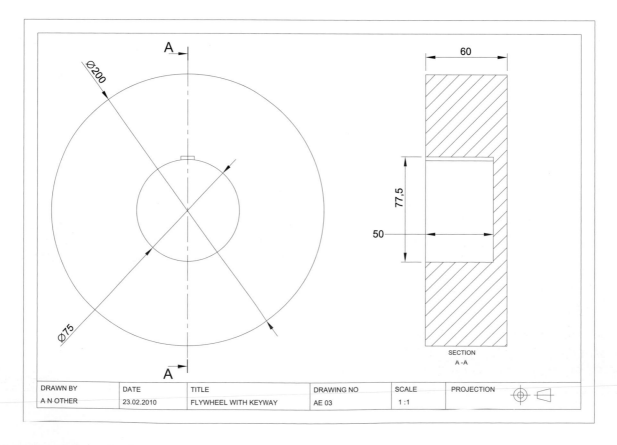

Figure 16.40: Detailed drawing for assessment activity 16.2

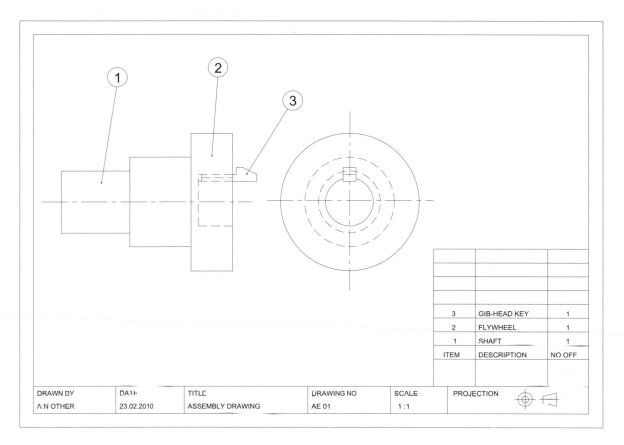

3	GIB-HEAD KEY	1
2	FLYWHEEL	1
1	SHAFT	1
ITEM	DESCRIPTION	NO OFF

DRAWN BY	DATE	TITLE	DRAWING NO	SCALE	PROJECTION
A N OTHER	23.02.2010	ASSEMBLY DRAWING	AE 01	1 : 1	

Figure 16.41: Assembly drawing for assessment activity 16.2

Assessment activity 16.2

P3 Extract information from Figures 16.40, 16.41 and 16.43 to show that you are capable of 'reading' the drawing. Examples of the items of information you should be able to interpret are:

- symbols – diameter, radius
- measurements – angular and linear
- projection symbol – first or third
- hatching
- section parts on drawings
- hidden detail.

M1 Now write a short report explaining the importance of working to recognised standards when producing engineering drawings.

Grading tips

P3 In addition to correctly produced examples of the requested types of information, you should contrast them with incorrectly produced examples that you have encountered.

M1 Your report should focus on the various additional costs that could result from drawings that do not conform to recognised standards.

16.3 Be able to produce engineering drawings

In this section, you now need to think about producing your own engineering drawings. This will require building on what we have covered so far in this unit, by combining sketching techniques with an understanding of drawing standards to produce engineering drawings to the right standard. You need to be able to produce drawings of components, as well as assembly drawings and circuit diagrams.

16.3.1 Detail drawings of single-piece engineering drawings

To get a better idea of component drawings, it may be worthwhile thinking about some everyday products that should be familiar to you, such as a motor car, bicycle, vacuum cleaner and an electric toothbrush. In each case, we'll look at a small part – a single component – of each product and not necessarily the whole finished item, and then think about how we could produce detail drawings of that component.

Detail drawings describe a component to be manufactured. They may consist of one or more drawings on a single drawing sheet. The drawing may provide information on:

• the size (dimensions) of the component

• the material from which it is to be made

• the acceptable tolerances to which the product must be made

• the surface finish

• details of any heat treatment process required during or after manufacture.

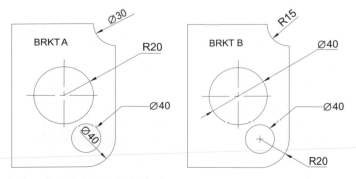

Figure 16.42: Two dimensioning styles – one is unacceptable, one uses the correct standards

This information should be provided using the accepted standards and conventions that we discussed in the previous section of this unit. In your assignment for this part of the unit, you will need to produce drawings using the correct standards. For example, one of the drawings in Figure 16.42 uses an acceptable dimensioning technique, and one is unacceptable. Make sure that you know which is the correct style, and that you adopt correct standards in all drawings you produce.

To go back to our four everyday products, a detailed drawing:

• could show the piston of a motor car

• the front chain-wheel of a bicycle

• the plastic cylinder for holding the dust on vacuum cleaner

• the recharging stand unit for an electric toothbrush.

Activity: Detail drawings

The detail drawing of a motor car piston would indicate the piston's:

• diameter

• length

• material from which it is made

• the manufacturing tolerance.

Write down four pieces of information that a detailed drawing should show about:

• the bicycle's front chain-wheel

• the plastic cylinder on a vacuum cleaner

• the recharging stand unit for an electric rechargeable toothbrush.

Choose one component from an everyday product or from an object that you can access in your workshop. Produce detail drawings of that component.

Figure 16.43 shows detail drawings of one of the components shown in Figure 16.41 (see page 331). Does this drawing contain sufficient information to

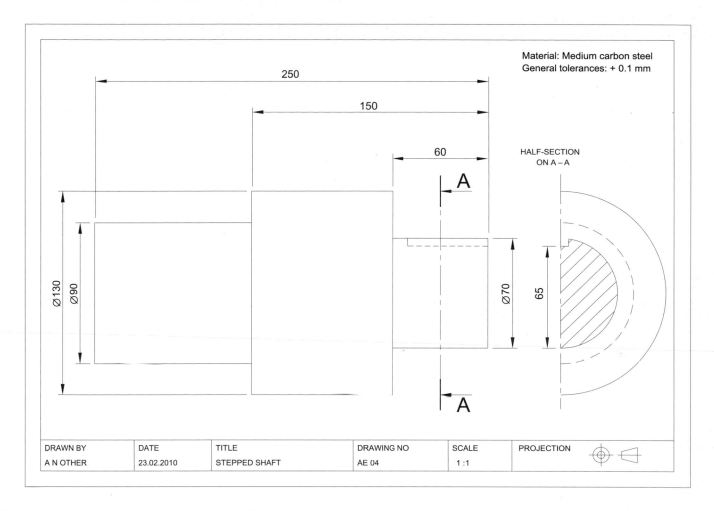

Figure 16.43: Detail drawing of a stepped shaft for assessment activity 16.2

allow this component to be manufactured? What other information would you expect to be provided on or with the drawing?

16.3.2 Assembly drawings

Assembly drawings show only a small part of a larger more complex structure. In some ways, engineering assembly drawings are similar to the assembly drawings that come with flat-pack furniture. These drawings show you how to put together a flat-pack kitchen wall cupboard, for example, but this shows only a small part of the whole assembly (your new fitted kitchen). Similarly, engineering assembly drawings may only show a small part of a more complex structure.

So, let's relate the assembly drawing to our four products again.

- On a motor car, an assembly drawing may show the order in which the three piston rings are fitted to the piston, and how the gudgeon pin fits inside the small end of the piston.

- On a cycle, an assembly drawing could show how the chain passes around the derailleur and over the rear sprocket wheel.

- On a vacuum cleaner, an assembly drawing could show how the dust filter and retaining clip are fitted into the filter housing.

- On an electric toothbrush, an assembly drawing could show the items that make up the oscillating brush head and how the various components fit together.

Figure 16.44 shows an assembly of a pulley. It consists of two views in orthographic projection. The reason that two views have been provided in the drawing is that if only the bottom view had been provided, we wouldn't know that the outer edge of the pulley is dished so that it will accept a rope. The second projection (the top drawing) indicates the dished shape. Other useful information can also be extracted from this second projection. For example, it shows that shaft passes through the full width of the assembly, as indicated by the dashed lines that show hidden detail. When producing an assembly drawing in your assignment for this unit, you should include sufficient views to show how the components that make up the assembly fit together.

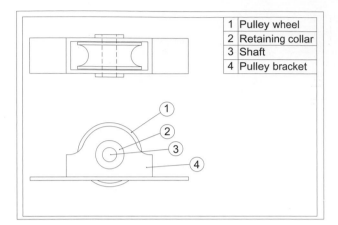

1	Pulley wheel
2	Retaining collar
3	Shaft
4	Pulley bracket

Figure 16.44: Assembly drawing a pulley

The assembly drawing in Figure 16.44 shows two orthographic views. Assembly drawings can use other projections. Figure 16.45 shows an assembly drawing of a flywheel. This is drawn in isometric projection. Contrast this with an assembly drawing of this flywheel using orthographic projections (see Figure 16.41). Note also that Figure 16.40 and 16.43 show detailed drawings of two of the components of this flywheel.

You might find the isometric projections in Figure 16.45 easier to interpret than the orthographic projections in 16.41. However, note that it is much more difficult to produce isometric drawings by hand, especially if they contain circular features (which become ellipses in isometric projections). For your assignment work, it is suggested that you produce assembly drawings using orthographic views.

Activity: Information provided on assembly drawings

Figure 16.45 shows a flywheel assembly. Look carefully at the drawing and answer these questions to check your understanding of engineering drawings.

- What do the sloping diagonal lines represent?
- What function do you think the gib head key performs?
- Which drawing (A or B) gives the clearer indication of the overall shape of the assembly?
- Which drawing (A or B) gives the clearer indication of how the parts interact?
- What vital information does the drawing *not* contain?

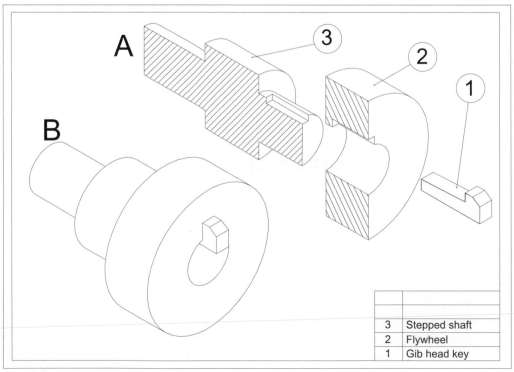

3	Stepped shaft
2	Flywheel
1	Gib head key

Figure 16.45: A flywheel assembly

16.3.3 Circuit diagams

You will also need to produce a circuit diagram in an assignment covering this part of the unit. This could be an electrical, electronic, hydraulic or pneumatic circuit.

Let's consider a worked example. Consider a simple mechanical digger arm. In this system, a lever is moved one way and the arm goes up. Move the lever back to its starting position and the arm goes down. Look at Figure 16.46 to see how it works. Figure 16.47 shows the symbols we shall need to represent parts of the system. (Further hydraulic symbols are given in Appendix 3.) Figure 16.48 shows how symbols are used to represent the function of the mechanical digger hydraulic ram. The diagram shows the stroke of the piston in both directions, but in practice only one of these drawings would be made – the illustration on the right would not be used.

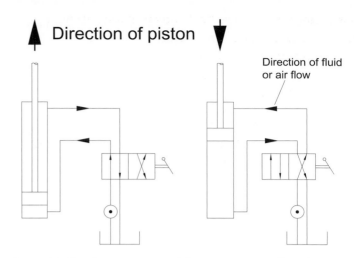

Direction of piston

Direction of fluid or air flow

Figure 16.48: The operation of the piston controlling the hydraulic lifting arm

In assessment activities 16.3 and 16.4, you are required to produce three sets of engineering drawings by hand. These should be drawn to the correct standards. If you've had experience using a CAD program, you may want to consider completing the first part of assessment activity 16.5 (see page 343), before undertaking these activities. You could use printouts on A3 paper of the template you produce for assessment activity 16.5 as a drawing sheet to use in the work for assessment activities 16.3 and 16.4. The template will contain space for some of the standard details you need to provide with each drawing.

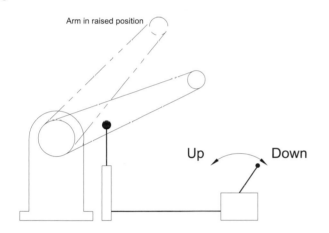

Arm in raised position

Up   Down

Figure 16.46: Simple hydraulic lifting arm

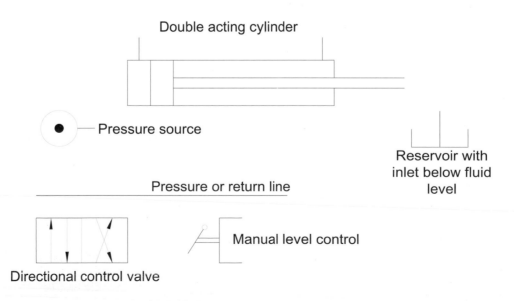

Double acting cylinder

Pressure source

Reservoir with inlet below fluid level

Pressure or return line

Directional control valve

Manual level control

Figure 16.47: Selection of hydraulic symbols (not to scale)

Assessment activity 16.3

In this activity you will produce detail drawings of three individual components that will go together to make a single assembly, and you will then produce an assembly drawing showing how these three components fit together.

You will need to choose a suitable object. For example, you could choose a pulley and produce detail drawings of:

- the pulley wheel
- the pin that passes through the centre of the pulley wheel
- the casting designed to hold the wheel and the pin.

P4 Produce detail drawings of three individual components. Your drawings should be drawn manually (you cannot use CAD for this activity).

P5 Produce a single drawing showing how the three components you drew in the P4 task fit together.

You should produce your drawings on A3 size drawing paper. You'll need to think about the actual size of the objects you are going to draw. It may be necessary to scale your drawings up or down depending on the components you have selected for the activity.

All drawings should contain neatly printed information giving your name (both printed and then signed as being your own work), the name of the object you have drawn, the date on which you produced the drawing, the scale at which the drawing was produced (for example, 2:1 if the drawing is twice the size of the original item) and a note stating the projection in which the drawing was produced.

Grading tips

P4 **P5** For both tasks, you need to apply similar skills and considerations. Before you put pencil to paper, check that where you plan to start each drawing will give you sufficient room to fit the whole of the object, at the scale that you are using, on to the drawing sheet. A few moments thought at this stage can save frustration later. You will be able to avoid the need to restart your drawing, or to make it untidy by having to erase lines drawn in error.

Don't attempt anything too complex: a simple drawing that is well executed is better than a complex piece that is drawn badly. Review your finished work with others to see if your drawing makes sense. Ask yourself, could I make this component from the information given in this drawing?

Assessment activity 16.4

Produce a circuit diagram on a single drawing sheet. The circuit diagram must contain *at least* five different components.

You can choose the type of circuit you draw. It could be:

- electrical
- electronic
- hydraulic
- pneumatic.

If you are involved in a project involving the use of one of these circuits, you could draw the circuit (or part of the circuit) for this activity.

Grading tips

P6 Your diagram should contain neatly printed information giving your name (both printed and then signed as being your own work), the type of circuit you have drawn (electronic, pneumatic etc.) and the date on which you produced the drawing.

16.4 Be able to produce engineering drawings using a computer aided drafting (CAD) system

Computers have changed the way that office work is carried out. No longer do large organisations have rows of typists using manual typewriters that need paper to be loaded manually to produce individual letters, and documents that need to be manually filed in a filing cabinet. They have been replaced by secretaries and administrators using word-processors that produce, file and often send electronic documents that are very simple to edit or change.

In a similar manner, drawing offices now require fewer people to produce drawings, and in many organisations the drawing equipment used by the draughtsperson has changed from the drawing board, pencil, ruler, set square, protractor and eraser to the computer keyboard, screen and mouse or tracker ball.

The great thing about computers is their accuracy. For example, if you draw a 100 mm line with a pencil, it may be a bit longer or shorter than 100 mm, depending on how carefully you use your pencil or even how sharp your pencil is. Drawing a 100 mm line on a computer-aided drafting (CAD) package will produce a line of exactly 100 mm, no more, no less. Remember though, that it'll be your job to tell the computer that the line needs to be 100 mm and that'll be just one of the many skills you'll need to learn and practise.

16.4.1 Prepare a template

Many CAD systems are supplied with standard drawing templates already loaded. These can vary widely and may conform to different international standards. For example, you may find drawing templates in your CAD package to ANSI (American), DIN (German) and JIS (Japanese) standards. You may also find that these templates use different drawing area sizes and may be in landscape or portrait orientation. The actual size of the paper that the CAD drawing will be printed on would be a factor in deciding which template should be used.

You need to be able to produce a template drawing in CAD. The template you draw will conform to certain standards. It must:

• be of A3 (420 × 297 landscape orientation)

• have a border

• have a title block.

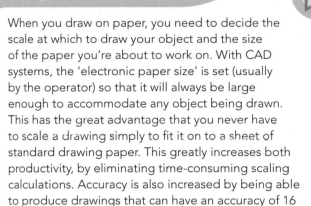

Did you know?

When you draw on paper, you need to decide the scale at which to draw your object and the size of the paper you're about to work on. With CAD systems, the 'electronic paper size' is set (usually by the operator) so that it will always be large enough to accommodate any object being drawn. This has the great advantage that you never have to scale a drawing simply to fit it on to a sheet of standard drawing paper. This greatly increases both productivity, by eliminating time-consuming scaling calculations. Accuracy is also increased by being able to produce drawings that can have an accuracy of 16 decimal places (depending on operator skill).

Let's look at these one by one. Why use A3 paper? Reason, there's probably a good supply of A3 paper in your school, college or workplace. Some CAD programs also have default extents or limits of 420 × 297 mm for their drawing area. Using an A3 size drawing template should make printing your hard copies easier.

The border is simply a line around the edges of the drawing sheet. Typically it would be drawn 10 mm in from the edges.

The purpose of the title block is to give information to the user. The title block should contain details such as:

• name of person that produced the drawing

• date on which the drawing was produced

• projection symbol to indicate if the drawing is first or third angle

• scale, to indicate at what scale the drawing is printed

• title, to indicates what it is that the drawing is showing

• drawing number.

You'll note that all this information is contained in the template shown in Figure 16.24 (page 323). In industry, the template would also have a company logo simply to make clear the owner and producer of the drawing.

The template should be saved to file. If the drawing template is saved to file, it is a simple matter to recall the drawing file, rename it giving it the name of the component you about to draw and then resaving it under its new name.

16.4.2 CAD systems

CAD systems have many advantages. When compared to the standard drawing boards used by professional draughting personnel, they take up virtually no space, since the programs can be run on desktop computers or laptops, which are already present in all offices. They make storage of drawings much easier – a library of drawings can be stored or transported on a memory stick that may be carried in your pocket. It is easier to make copies of drawings, simply send the electronic file to a printer or flatbed plotter from which any number of prints or plots can be made.

The real benefits of CAD are to be found in professional practice. An engineering company can have personnel working on many sites. CAD systems make it much easier for users to access drawings quickly. Even if users are based far from the office that produced the drawings, CAD drawings can be sent through electronically. The electronic nature of the drawings makes them easy to amend, giving designers the ability to respond quickly to any changes that need to be made to the production drawings.

CAD packages usually link up to computer-aided manufacturing (CAM) systems, allowing the electronic drawing to be used directly to set parameters in the programs that direct computer numerically controlled (CNC) machinery such as lathes, milling machines, plasma cutters and press brakes. This helps to increase productivity and lower costs, and it underpins modern multinational engineering operations. For example, a large and complex drawing might be produced in one part of the world where a company's design team is based. By the end of the day, the drawing could be electronically transmitted around the world for the start of the working day at an overseas production plant. In addition, with easily transferable electronic drawings, the production unit could outsource the machining process to yet another country where manufacturing costs may be lower.

CAD systems are initially expensive to purchase, and operators need to be trained to become effective users of particular systems. However, once they are skilled in the use of CAD, the major benefits of speed, flexibility and accuracy more than compensate for the set-up costs.

There are a range of computer-aided design (CAD) packages commercially available. These are some of the CAD packages that you're likely to encounter.

- AutoCAD is perhaps the best-known software package for 2D and 3D design. It is widely used in architecture, engineering, building construction and manufacturing. AutoCAD dates from the early 1980s, and was one of the first CAD programs that could be run on personal computers (before that you needed a mainframe computer to produce computer-aided drawings). This made CAD accessible to many more engineering companies.

- CATIA, which stands for computer-aided three-dimensional interactive application, was developed in France by the aviation manufacturer Dassault. It is widely used throughout the engineering industry, especially in the automotive, aerospace and US shipbuilding sectors. It has been used in the design of aircraft (by Boeing and Airbus), motor vehicles (by, for example, BMW, Renault and Ford) and naval ships.

- Solidworks was also developed by a subsidiary of Dassault. It is a 2D and 3D computer-aided design package that runs on Microsoft Windows. It is used widely in industry, and it is also used as a training package in many schools and colleges.

- MicroStation is a 2D and 3D design and drafting application. It is used in the design, engineering, building and operating of construction projects such as roadways, railways, bridges, buildings and utility networks.

- Pro/Engineer is an integrated CAD/CAM program. It enables mechanical engineers to draw and model solid objects and assemblies.

You will note that many commercial packages have 3D drawing capability. For the purposes of this unit, however, you are only required to produce CAD drawings in two dimensions (2D).

16.4.3 Produce engineering drawings

It is difficult to give specific operating instructions, as each software packages has different ways of achieving the end objective of producing drawings. Each system will have its supporters and its dissenters.

There are, however, certain features that all systems have in common and, as an outline, we'll group them into three categories:

• set-up commands

• drawing commands

• editing commands.

Set-up commands

Examples of set-up commands are the extents, grid, snap and layer functions.

Extents

Extents (or limits) of the drawing: this is an indication of the drawing area being worked on and is set by the operator. The choice of area is governed by the size of the object being drawn. If we attempted to draw the kitchen wall units we considered earlier (see page 312) on A3 (420 × 297 mm) limits, most of the wall unit would be drawn outside the extents or limits of the drawing. This could result in any subsequent print or plot of the drawing only showing what was actually drawn within the extents or limits. The good news is that if you start off with the wrong size extents or limits, it is a simple task to change them at any stage of the drawing.

Grid

Grid is a system of dots on the drawing area that can be turned on and off if required. The spacing of the dots can be changed and the X (horizontal) spacing and Y (vertical) spacing need not be the same. If you are required to produce an isometric drawing, it is often possible to set an isometric grid so that you can draw the required lines at 30° with ease.

Snap

Snap is another function that can be turned on and off as required. It usually causes the cross hairs on the screen to jump to the grid points. It is usual to set the grid and snap to the same numeric value. Snap can, however, be set independently of the grid settings if required.

Cross hairs are controlled by the movement of the mouse. The cross hairs may be, as the name implies, a small cross, or it may take the form of two continuous lines at right angles to each other that extend across the screen in the X and Y directions. The operator can,

by moving the mouse, indicate on screen where, for example, a line should commence or terminate.

Another very useful feature of CAD programs is the object snap (OSNAP) facility. Use of this causes the cross hairs to jump to existing features of the drawing entities, such as the midpoints of lines, end points of lines or centres of circles.

Layer

These can be thought of as transparent acetate overlays. Consider an illustration showing the outline of the human body. Over this you could lay a transparent acetate sheet showing the bones that make up the skeleton. On top of this on a separate transparency (layer) could be added showing the major internal organs. I think you've probably got the idea by now.

Well, so it is with layers in CAD drawings, the difference being that the outline could be our hydraulic cylinder and we could have layers showing hidden detail, surface finish, dimensions, text etc.

As our layers are electronic and not acetate, they have the advantage that should you draw something on the wrong layer, it can easily be transferred to the correct layer. Layers can be turned on and off at will and can have colours and names assigned to them by the operator for ease of working.

Drawing commands

Standard drawing commands are:

• coordinate entry

• line

• arc

• circle

• polygon

• hatch

• text

• dimension.

Coordinate entry

There are occasions when it is more convenient to input coordinates directly into the CAD program rather that indicating the desired position by moving the cross hairs via the mouse. This is known as coordinate entry.

This position of any point on the drawing could be said to be X units of measurement across and Y units of measurement up. It may be expressed as coordinates, say, (25, 35) – indicating 25 across and 30 up. Both measurements are usually taken from the origin of the drawing, normally at the bottom left-hand corner of the drawing area. The origin normally has the X and Y coordinates of (0,0). The numeric values are often referred to as Cartesian coordinates.

Activity: CAD coordinates

Figure 16.49 shows a dimensioned rectangle whose lower left-hand Cartesian coordinate is (70,50). The position of the circle's centre is half way along the X-axis of the rectangle and half way up the Y-axis of the rectangle.

What are the Cartesian coordinates of (a) the upper right-hand corner of the rectangle and (b) the centre of the circle?

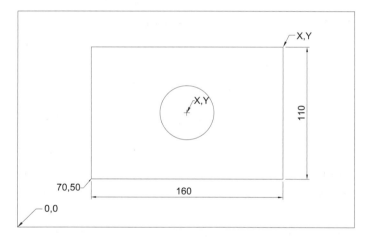

Figure 16.49: Cartesian coordinates

Line

When drawing lines, you'll need to specify the start and end positions. This can be achieved by using the mouse to pick a start and end point. On other occasions the length of a line can be specified by coordinate entry. It's worth remembering that there are a range of lines available in CAD programs; the choice of line will be governed by the purpose that the line serves.

Lines are available in a number of formats. They include:

- centre
- hidden
- dashed
- polyline.

To pick a start and end point involves positioning the mouse at the desired start point, picking that point, usually with the left button on the mouse, moving the mouse to the desired end position and again using the mouse to pick the new point. Sometimes it may be necessary to use the return or right-hand mouse button to terminate the line (or other) commands.

Arc

The arc command normally allows you to draw a curved line between two points. Typically you will have to state (input into the program) the arc's centre point, its end point and its radius. There are, however, other options for inputting the data that may include the arc's angle, length, direction or radius. A further option may be to specify the arc by picking three separate points on the drawing area.

Circle

These are usually specified in terms of their centre point coupled with a radius or a diameter. Other options include specifying a two- or three-point circle or drawing a circle that is tangential to other objects or entities.

Why use a three-point circle? Imagine that you had a drawing showing three separate circles of different sizes in front of you and you had the task of drawing a fourth circle that just touched them all. This would present a problem owing to the fact that you wouldn't know where the centre of the joining circle would be, nor would you know its radius/diameter. The three point option would therefore allow you to specify that the joining circle would be **tangential** to one point on each of the three circles

Polygon

A square is a four-sided polygon whose sides and internal angles are all the same length. A regular polygon that finds many uses in engineering applications is the hexagon. Bolt heads are a typical example of a hexagon. Polygons may be inscribed or circumscribed and can be drawn in terms of the number of sides they contain, the centre point of the polygon or the length of one side.

The circumscribed or inscribed feature refers to the fact that, for any circle, you could draw a polygon that fitted around the outside of the circle (circumscribed), or you could draw a polygon that fitted inside the circle (inscribed).

Hatch

The means of drawing hatching in CAD programs is simplified by the fact that hatch patterns of various sorts are embedded in the program. Standard hatching used on engineering drawings consists of lines sloping at 45°. Patterns of hatching to indicate different materials are also included in the library of patterns. Some CAD programs contain civil engineering (construction) hatching patterns as well. The program you're using will probably allow you to change the scale and angle of the hatch pattern.

Placing different hatches on different layers with different layer colours will produce hatch patterns of different colours.

You may need to take great care with the accuracy of your drawing to make sure the hatch pattern doesn't 'leach' beyond the hatch boundary lines. Problems can occur when lines in the drawing don't quite join together.

Text

Adding text to a drawing is a simple matter, but getting the height, font and position of the text may require a little more practice. Fortunately, like many other features of CAD programs, if you make an error in your drawing it isn't always necessary to erase what you've produced and start all over again.

Quite often, the properties of the object can be changed very much in the way that the style of text in a word-processing package can be changed using the format command. This allows you to adjust features such as:

- font
- height
- spacing
- justification
- bold

- italic
- oblique angle of the text.

Dimension

The methods of dimensioning your drawing will very much depend on the program that you're using. However, in some ways the dimensioning features of CAD programs are similar to the points noted earlier in discussing dimensions (see page 313), that is to say, there is scope to adjust the features of the dimension even after it has been applied to the drawing. You can adjust the size of the arrow heads (terminations), the dimension text and all the other features shown Figure 16.12.

Editing commands

Standard editing commands are:

- copy
- move
- erase
- rotate
- mirror.

- trim
- extend
- chamfer
- fillet

Copy

Most engineering drawings that you encounter will have features (lines, circles, arcs etc.) that are repeated throughout the drawing. Look again at the activity on page 310 (the drawing board and the L-shaped isometric bracket): many of the lines are repeated, and with practice you could produce this drawing with only a small number of lines, the remainder being produced by using the copy command. Copying usually involves selecting an **entity**, selecting a base point and then specifying where the new base point will be. The entity will be copied to the new base point and the original entity will be left in place.

Key terms

Tangential a line or arc that touches the circumference of a circle at one point only is said to be tangential to (or a tangent of) the circle. The line or arc does not pass through the circumference.

Entity a discrete part of a drawing. It could consist of a single line, arc, piece of text, a dimension or the whole drawing itself.

Move

This involves the repositioning of an entity to a new position within the drawing extents or limits. It sometimes happens though, that lack of practice can cause the entity to be moved to a position not intended by the CAD operator. The technique of moving objects or entities is similar to that employed in copy, the difference being that a blank space will be left where the original entity was.

Erase

This 'does what it says on the tin': it removes entities from the drawing. What is perhaps important about this command is the way that objects can be selected. Objects may be selected individually by 'picking' them. They may also be selected by putting a window around them or they may be selected by using a crossing box. If that's not enough, all three methods may be used together if desired and the complexity of the drawing warrants it.

Did you know?

Selecting a large number of entities for an operation (such as deleting) can be time consuming, and so a CAD operator would use a 'window'. This is done by placing the cross hairs above and usually to the left of the objects you want to select. Pick this point and then move the mouse down and to the right. You should see a box appear on the screen. This is the window. Stop moving the mouse when the window has surrounded the entities you want and then pick that point. All the objects within the window will be selected. Any entities that the window crosses or does not completely surround will not be selected.

A crossing box works in almost the same way, with two differences. The first is that we'd normally start below and to the right of the entities we're interested in and terminate the box at the top left-hand side. The second difference is that any entity that the box crosses will be selected. You may find, depending on the program you're using, that the window and the crossing boxes have a different appearance on the screen.

Windows and crossing boxes can be used to select entities for editing operations in the erase, copying, moving, rotating, mirroring and trimming commands.

Rotate

This command allows you to turn an entity or complete object through any desired angle clockwise or anticlockwise. The sequence of events involved in the rotate command is usually: first, select the item; second, specify a base point around which the entity or object will be rotated; third, input the rotation angle – this may be done by either specifying the angle by moving via the mouse or by direct entry via the keyboard.

Mirror

This produces a mirror image of the entities that have been selected. The operator has the option of retaining the original entity or removing it on completion of the operation. If the mirrored image contains text, there is an option to mirror the object and text but have the mirrored text remain in a readable orientation on the mirrored entity or object.

Trim

Lines or other features on CAD drawings will often overlap other features. The trim command allows removal of the overlapping parts. The trim command normally requires two entities to overlap or cross. A single line cannot usually be trimmed unless it is crossed by another line: this other line will form a trimming boundary.

Extend

This is a very useful option used to extend a line that doesn't quite, but should, reach another one. There is sometimes a temptation to fill the gap left between the two lines by drawing a short length of line thereby filling the gap. This is not a good practice as the short piece of line will be treated as an entity in its own right and, as such, will have its own end points, midpoints etc. It is much better to use the extend command as the extension becomes part of the original (too short) line.

Chamfer

If the chamfer command is used on two lines that are at 90° to each other, the two lines would then be joined by a straight, angled line. The length and angle of this joining line can be set by the operator.

Fillet

If the fillet command is used on two lines that are at 90° to each other, the two lines would then be joined by an arc or curve. The radius of this arc can be set by the operator.

16.4.4 Store and present engineering drawings

When you have produced your template drawing, you will need to save it to file. It is a good idea to set up some folders for your CAD work to help you keep a track of where your drawings are. You could use folder names such as XYZUnit 16 and, for your subfolders, XYZassigns and XYZdrawings, where XYZ are your initials.

Presenting the drawing involves producing a hard copy. Quite often, printer paper is wasted simply because people don't bother to use the 'print preview' facility that is always available in CAD and other software programs. Using this can save both paper and time.

When you've successfully produced your hard copy, you should sign it as being your own work before submission for marking.

Managing your files

You may be very keen to get on with your CAD drawings and that's a good thing. Don't forget though that a bit of thought as to how and where you're going to save and order your files will save you a lot of time later on. Avoid using the default file names as provided by the program, such as Drawing 1, Drawing 2 etc., and give your files meaningful names. Make sure there is a logical order to your filing system.

Assessment activity 16.5

This activity is in three parts.

P7 Prepare a template drawing of a standardised A3 sheet using a CAD system and save to file. Your drawing template should conform to British Standards in that it should contain these features:

- a border
- a title block (with room for date, name, title, drawing number, projection)
- a college or company logo

You will need to save this template file. Save your template drawing as XYZtemplate where XYZ are your initials. To show that you have saved the file, produce a detailed screen print showing the structure of your folders and assessment drawing files.

P8 Using this template, produce a 2D CAD drawing of the component. You can produce CAD drawings of one of the components you manually drew in assessment activity 16.3 or choose another component.

P8 Now produce a 2D CAD assembly of a product containing three parts. You can choose to produce CAD drawings of the assembly you drew manually in assessment activity 16.3 or choose another assembly.

Grading tips

P8 Save your work for under different filenames from the one you used for the template. Do this as soon as you start work on each new drawing. This means that you should have three separate electronic files containing your work for each task. For example, you could call your files XYZSPC (for the single piece component) and XYZTPP (for the three part product), where XYZ are your initials or a short from of your name.

As with the manual drawing task (assessment activity 16.4), make sure that your component and three-part drawings will fit within the drawing area inside the drawing border.

Assessment activity 16.6

Write a report explaining and evaluating topics concerned with the production and use of engineering drawings. This should be in two parts.

M2 Choose an engineering drawing and explain how it might be used and give the reasons why it is suitable for its intended audience (user). You may want to expand on how, for example, the drawing communicates information effectively.

D1 Evaluate the use of different methods of producing engineering drawings including manual and computer-aided methods.

You may want to consider writing your report in the form of a case study.

Grading tips

M2 You need to provide a good analysis of an engineering drawing.

D1 For this section of your report, you may also wish to consider CAD systems used by local industry, perhaps giving reasons for one company's choice of a particular CAD program. You may also wish to consider any negative points of the various methods. Your written text must be reflective and supported by good arguments. Avoid statements like 'it's fast' or 'the drawings are easy to read' without qualifying the statement you're making.

Steven Wu
Technician, NJT Engineering

NJT Engineering is a small engineering company that employs six people in a small purpose-built industrial unit. Its undertakes small one-off contracts for the local commercial sector and community. Some customers call in to describe to the owner what they want, but most produce a simple sketch of the product they require.

When a medium-sized company transferred its production base overseas, NJT saw an opportunity to expand its business by filling this gap.

However, NJT's owner realised that new customers would require more than just a simple sketch on a rough piece of paper. They would want a formal drawing showing what they had ordered from NJT.

NJT doesn't have a drawing office and doesn't employ a draughtsperson. The company had not produced formal drawings before and it looked as if the chance to expand might be lost. Fortunately, one of the staff, Steven Wu, is a confident CAD user so the owner decided to invest in a standalone CAD system and A3 laser printer.

Steven has now added the role of draughtsperson to his varied list of duties at NJT and he finds the opportunity to spend some of his time in the office a welcome change.

Last week, the owner asked Steven if it would be possible to find a local company that could print off A0 size drawings as the latest job NJT has tendered for requires scaled drawing on large format paper. At the moment, Steven is still working on it.

Think about it!

1 Why might customers want formal drawings rather than simple sketches?

2 What would NJT's options have been if Steven had not had good CAD skills?

3 Would any of these options have had an impact on the local economy?

Just checking

1 Why are sketches sometimes used in preference to professionally produced technical drawings?

2 How do drawings of the same object produced in cavalier and cabinet projections differ?

3 Which type of drawing uses construction lines that are angled at 30° to horizontal?

4 What does the prefix 'ortho-' refer to?

5 List five pieces of information that should appear in the title block of a drawing.

6 Which paper size has the larger area – A4 or A3? Give the size in millimetres of both sizes of paper.

7 How many millimetres in from the edges of your drawing paper should you draw your border?

8 Which two of the these combinations of orthographic projections should you use: (a) fourth and first; (b) third and first; (c) second and first; (d) third and fourth; (e) fourth and second?

9 In a CAD drawing, what is the effect of turning the snap option on or off?

10 With respect to polygons and the circles used in their construction, what is the difference between a circumscribed and an inscribed polygon?

11 When modifying a CAD drawing, how does a chamfer differ from a fillet?

12 How does a sketch differ from a technical drawing?

13 Which of these scaling factors should *not* be used (a) 1:2; (b) 1:5; (c) 1:2.5; (d) 2:1; (e) 5:1; (f) 5.2:1?

edexcel ▦

Assignment tips

- Learning outcome 1 requires you to produce a series of sketches and explain their benefits and limitations. As well as giving an accurate impression of the object you are sketching, make sure that the sketch is a good size. Don't produce a sketch the size of a postage stamp in the middle of a sheet of A4 paper. When discussing benefits and limitations, avoid phrases such as 'It's quick' or 'It's easy'. If you find a particular method easy, you need to explain why.

- Learning outcomes 3 and 4 require you to produce engineering drawings using both traditional (drawing board) and CAD methods. You may have limited time in your centre's drawing room or CAD suite. You should plan ahead to avoid wasting time and to reduce the amount of rework needed to correct errors. Where possible, decide well in advance what it is you are to draw and carry out some preliminary work outside the taught drawing sessions. Decide where to position the starting point(s) for your drawings, so that when you commence your actual assignment you can be sure that the drawing will fit the paper.

- The only assignments requiring written answers are those for P2, M1, M2 and D1. The tasks you will be set for M1 and M2 give you the opportunity to explain what you have learned about engineering drawing. D1 gives you the opportunity to express your opinions by evaluating the various methods of producing engineering drawings.

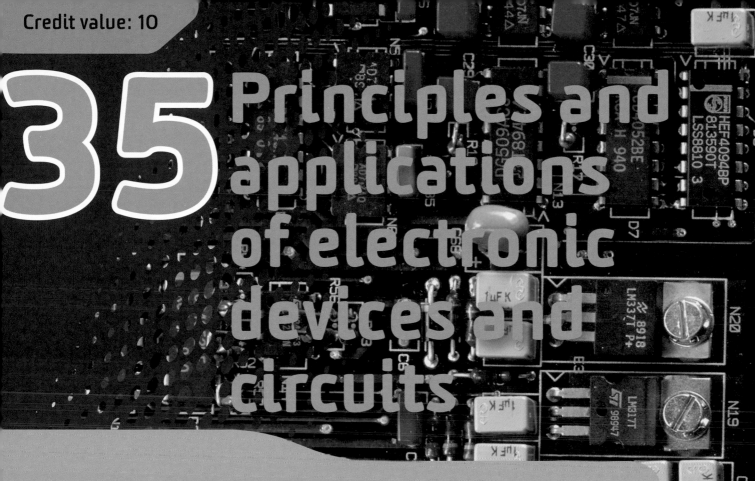

35 Principles and applications of electronic devices and circuits

Electronic devices play a major part in our everyday lives. The use of electronics continues to grow at an ever-increasing rate, from applications in popular consumer goods, such as cameras, mobile phones and music players, to the automated welding machines used in industry. A good understanding of analogue and digital electronic principles is vital to anyone considering a career in this field.

This unit provides a practical introduction to basic electronic principles as well as offering you the opportunity to investigate the characteristics and operation of two of the most important building blocks in electronic circuits – diodes and transistors. You will progress to building and testing circuits that make use of these devices and cover the operation of common integrated circuits such as operational amplifiers. You will also learn about logic gates and flip-flops, investigating them both through practical work and through the use of simple electronic principles such as truth tables.

The unit then introduces computer-based circuit design and simulation software packages that allow you to design, build and test analogue and digital circuits. Focusing on prototyping, constructing and measuring, you learn to construct and test a variety of simple electronic circuits.

Learning outcomes

After completing this unit you should:

1   understand the function and operation of diodes, transistors and logic gates
2   be able to build and test operational amplifier-based analogue circuits
3   be able to build and test combinational and sequential logic circuits
4   be able to use computer-based simulation software packages to construct and test the operation of analogue and digital circuits.

Assessment and grading criteria

This table shows you what you must do in order to achieve a pass, merit or distinction grade, and where you can find activities in this book to help you produce the required evidence.

To achieve a pass grade the evidence must show that you are able to:	To achieve a merit grade the evidence must show that, in addition to the pass criteria, you are able to:	To achieve a distinction grade the evidence must show that, in addition to the pass and merit criteria, you are able to:
P1 explain the purpose of two different types of diode, each in a different electronic circuit application **Assessment activity 35.1 page 364**	**M1** modify an existing analogue circuit to achieve a given revised specification by selecting and changing the value of one of the components **Assessment activity 35.1 page 364**	**D1** using a simulation package, analyse the effects of changing the values of circuit parameters on the performance of an analogue circuit containing an operational amplifier or transistors **Assessment activity 35.3 page 373**
P2 explain the operation of two different types of transistor, one in an analogue and one in a digital circuit **Assessment activity 35.1 page 364**	**M2** modify a digital circuit to achieve a given revised specification by selecting and changing up to two logic gates **Assessment activity 35.2 page 371**	**D2** compare and contrast two different types of logic family with reference to five characteristics **Assessment activity 35.2 page 371**
P3 explain the operation of three different logic gates with appropriate gate symbols, truth tables and Boolean expressions **Assessment activity 35.2 page 371**	**M3** evaluate and minimise a three-input combinational logic circuit containing three gates **Assessment activity 35.2 page 371**	
P4 build and test two different types of analogue circuit using operational amplifiers **Assessment activity 35.1 page 364**		
P5 build and test a combinational logic circuit that has three input variables **Assessment activity 35.2 page 371**		
P6 build and test a sequential circuit using integrated circuit(s) **Assessment activity 35.2 page 371**		
P7 use a computer software package to simulate the construction and testing of an analogue circuit with three different types of components **Assessment activity 35.3 page 373**		

P8 use a computer software package to simulate the construction and testing of a digital logic circuit with three gates
Assessment activity 35.3
page 373

How you will be assessed

This unit will be assessed by a series of assignments designed to allow you to show your understanding of the unit outcomes. One assignment may focus on analogue circuits and logic circuits, where you may construct, test and modify a variety of circuits. You may be required to explain the purpose and operation of the components in these circuits, and compare and contrast different types of components. You may also demonstrate your skills in using simulation software to construct and test both analogue and digital circuits, and to analyse the effect of changing circuit parameter values.

Overall, your assessment will be in the form of:

• practical tasks
• written assignments
• oral questioning.

Jack, 17–year–old electrical apprentice

Working through this unit made me understand that there is a lot more to electronic devices than I had ever realised. It also made me think more about the electronic gadgets I use every day.

I really enjoyed studying this unit because it involved practical work. It is exciting designing and then building an electronic circuit, and getting it to work, especially as you can't see electricity! Learning theory and using simulation software is interesting too, but being able to build a circuit and show that it really does what it is supposed to do gave me a great sense of achievement. It was especially satisfying to change some of the components and see the circuit perform exactly how I predicted it would. This is the bit I enjoyed most.

Learning how the digital gates and circuits worked was quite strange at first, because I had to learn to think in a different way. However, once I'd begun to understand it everything just seemed so obvious. I guess that's why it's called logic.

35.1 Understand the function and operation of diodes, transistors and logic gates

Start up

Analogue or digital?

Think about the various electrical and electronic gadgets you see around you in your home. Focus on the devices you use every day. Write down the names of the six gadgets that you use most frequently.

Divide your list into two groups; those gadgets that you think use analogue circuits and those that you think use digital circuits. Alongside each device, explain why you think it should be in the analogue or digital list as appropriate.

A circuit can be described as being either analogue or digital. In an analogue circuit, the signal voltage and current levels vary continuously, as in an audio amplifier, but in a digital circuit the signal levels are usually only two-state, that is they are either fully on or fully off, as in a computer. In this unit, you are going study the electronic devices used to build and control both analogue and digital circuits. These devices must have appropriate performance characteristics. The devices used in an analogue circuit must be capable of handling gradual changes in signal level. The devices used in a digital circuit must be able to switch from one state to the other extremely quickly.

35.1.1 Diodes

A diode is a common device that is used in many **electronic circuits**. Very simply, it is an electronic device that only allows current to flow in one direction. It is rather like a one-way valve, but with no physical moving parts. In a circuit diagram, a diode is represented by a symbol that incorporates an arrow (see Figure 35.1). The current flows in the direction indicated by the arrow – no current can flow through the diode in the opposite direction.

Key terms

Electronic circuit a collection of electronic components, such as transistors, diodes, resistors and capacitors, connected together to provide a particular function, such as amplifying a signal.

Semiconductor diode

Anode (+)   Cathode (–)

Zener diode

Anode (+)   Cathode (–)

Light-emitting diode (LED)

Anode (+)   Cathode (–)

Figure 35.1: Diode symbols

There are various types of diodes designed to do specific jobs. You will be familiar with light-emitting diodes (LEDs). These are commonly used for the on/standby indicator light on TVs, DVD players etc. Unlike a miniature light bulb, which a diode replaces in these applications, an LED has no filament. LEDs only use a very small amount of electrical power to generate light and they are much cheaper to produce than bulbs. They are also available in different colours and sizes.

Diodes are also used in most remote control handsets. The diode uses invisible light to send signals to the appliance that is being controlled by the handset.

Another use for diodes is in a mains adapter, where they rectify alternating current (AC) to produce direct current (DC). Yet another type of diode is used for voltage stabilising: the Zener diode.

Before we look at diodes in some detail, you need to know about the properties of the materials used in their manufacture. This will also be of use when we come to consider transistors later in the unit.

Table 35.1: Classification of materials by their resistivity

Classification	Material	Resistivity (at 20°C)
Conductors	Aluminium	$2.82 \times 10^{-8} \, \Omega \, m$
	Brass	$8 \times 10^{-8} \, \Omega \, m$
	Copper	$1.72 \times 10^{-8} \, \Omega \, m$
	Gold	$2.44 \times 10^{-8} \, \Omega \, m$
	Mild steel	$15 \times 10^{-8} \, \Omega \, m$
	Nickel	$6.99 \times 10^{-8} \, \Omega \, m$
	Silver	$1.59 \times 10^{-8} \, \Omega \, m$
Semiconductors	Germanium	$4.60 \times 10^{-1} \, \Omega \, m$
	Silicon	$6.4 \times 10^{2} \, \Omega \, m$
Insulators	Glass	$10^{10} \, \Omega \, m$ to $10^{14} \, \Omega \, m$
	Mica	$\geq 10^{11} \, \Omega \, m$
	Paraffin	$10^{17} \, \Omega \, m$
	PVC	$\geq 10^{13} \, \Omega \, m$
	Rubber	approx. $10^{13} \, \Omega \, m$

Here is a selection of semi-conductors. Can you spot which are the light-emitting diodes?

Properties of materials used in electronic devices

Materials can be classified as conductors, semiconductors or insulators according to their electrical resistivity. Metals are usually seen as good conductors – that is, they have low electrical resistivity. Table 35.1 lists value of resistivity of some common materials used as conductors, semiconductors or insulators.

Germanium and silicon are the most common materials found in the semiconductors used in electronics. Their resistivity reduces as temperature rises, until at a sufficiently high temperature they basically become conductors. Conversely, at very low temperatures (well below room temperature) their resistivity increases to the point at which they become insulators.

A pure semiconductor contains no free electrons. Heating the semiconductor releases a few electrons,

allowing for a small current flow. However, a much better way of increasing current flow is to add an impurity to the semiconductor. The process of taking a pure semiconductor and adding tiny amounts of impurities (a few parts per million) is called doping.

Atoms in a semiconductor are normally rigidly bonded together by a four-electron structure. Adding an impurity with a five electron structure causes a free electron to be left over – this electron has nothing to bond to. This is shown in Figure 35.2. An impurity that increases the number of free electrons is called n-type. Arsenic and phosphorus are n-type impurities. A semiconductor doped with an n-type impurity is called an n-type material.

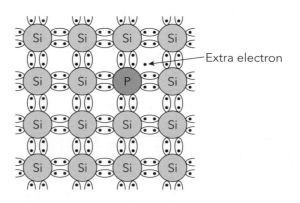

Figure 35.2: Silicon doped with phosphorus (n-type impurity)

Adding an impurity with a three-electron structure, means one semiconductor electron has nothing to bond to. This deficiency is called a hole and is shown in Figure 35.3. A material that creates holes is called a p-type impurity. Aluminium, boron and indium are p-type impurities. When a small amount of these impurities is added to a semiconductor, p-type material is formed.

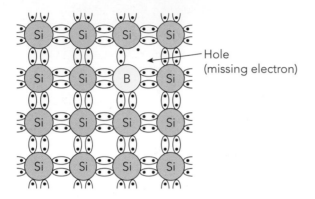

Figure 35.3: Silicon doped with boron (p-type impurity)

Did you know?

When doping introduces spare electrons, the atoms in the impurity are known as pentavalent atoms, meaning they have five valence electrons. The spare electrons are called majority carriers in the n-type material. Trivalent atoms have three valence electrons and create holes called the majority carriers in the p-type material.

The p-n junction

When a piece of p-type semiconductor material is joined to a piece of n-type semiconductor material, a p-n junction is created. If you think of a hole as a positive charge and an electron as a negative charge, it follows that they will be drawn towards each other and will bond together at the junction of the p-type and n-type materials. This forms a stable area called the **depletion layer**. Eventually the movement of holes and electrons stops due to the potential difference that exists across the junction. This is called the **contact potential**.

A diode consists of a sandwich of p-type and n-type material, inside either a glass or moulded container,

Key terms

Depletion layer the area at the junction of p-type and n-type material that contains no free electrons or holes because they have all joined together.

Contact potential the voltage that builds up at the p-n junction that stops the movement of electrons and holes across it.

with connecting leads. In other words a diode is made from a p-n junction, so the simple diode is also known as the p-n junction diode or semiconductor diode. We can see how a diode works by considering what happens when a voltage is applied across a p-n junction.

When you apply an external voltage that makes the p-type material positive with respect to the n-type material, the depletion layer is forced closer together and becomes thinner, allowing the holes and electrons to move through the junction again with the result that a current flows. This is shown in Figure 35.4, and this is known as forward bias.

For silicon, approximately 0.7 V forward bias is required to narrow the depletion layer sufficiently to allow current to flow. For germanium, approximately 0.4 V forward bias is required. Increasing the forward bias further results in a rapid rise in current flow and the material becomes a good conductor.

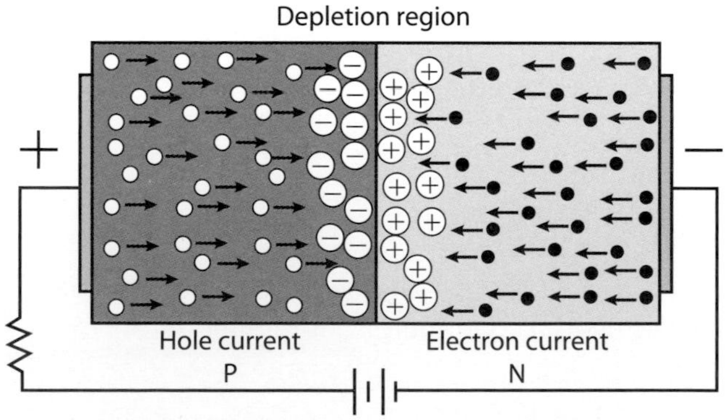

Depletion region

Hole current
P

Electron current
N

Figure 35.4: Forward bias results in hole and electron movement

When a p-n junction is reverse biased, the external voltage is applied the opposite way round so that the p-type material becomes more negative with respect to the n-type material. This strengthens the depletion layer and no current will flow. This is shown in Figure 35.5.

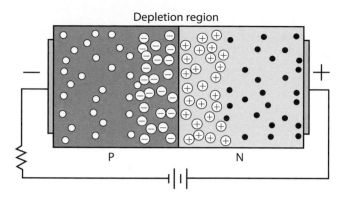

Figure 35.5: Reverse bias widens the depletion region and prevents hole and electron movement

Did you know?

Early radio receivers used a type of crystal diode called the 'cat's whisker' to detect radio signals. It rectified the received signal to provide a DC voltage that could power headphones. The diode was quite big and needed careful adjustment to make it work properly.

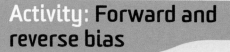

Activity: Forward and reverse bias

In pairs or small groups, discuss your understanding of what happens when you apply an external voltage across a p-n junction diode.

With the aid of diagrams, explain in your own words the effect on the depletion layer of applying the external voltage so that:

a) the p-n junction is forward biased

b) the p-n junction is reverse biased.

Discuss how forward and reverse biasing affects how a diode works when it is connected into an electronic circuit.

The diode as a rectifier

You should now have an understanding of how a diode works and why it only allows current to flow in one direction. This property is particularly useful when you want to convert alternating current and voltage

Table 35.2: Simple rectifier circuits

Rectification	Circuit diagram	Input	Output
Half wave (1 diode)			
Full wave (2 diodes)			
Bridge (4 diodes)			

into direct current and voltage. This is the function of a mains adapter. For example, you will have been supplied with a mains adapter for your mobile phone. This is used to charge the battery in the phone. It takes the AC mains supply and changes it to DC supply suitable for charging the battery. This process is called rectification. Table 35.2 shows three simple circuits for achieving different types of rectification, which use one, two and four diodes respectively.

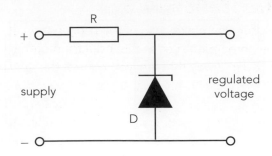

Figure 35.6: A Zener diode used with a resistor as a simple voltage regulator

Activity: Rectification

Working in pairs, consider the various reasons why engineers would want to rectify an AC input. List occasions or situations in which an AC input would be rectified. Draw up a table to record your ideas. This should have three columns: one column headed 'usage', one headed 'type of device' and one headed 'example'. List each situation you identify, such as 'to charge batteries', in the usage column, and then specify the type of device that would achieve that purpose and an example of that type of device in the other columns.

Zener diodes

A Zener diode is manufactured in such a way that when the reverse bias voltage is increased, at some point the diode will begin to conduct. The voltage at which a Zener diode begins to conduct when reverse biased depends on the amount of semiconductor doping. Increasing the doping, causes the **breakdown voltage** to drop. By precisely controlling the doping, it is possible to specify the breakdown voltage for a particular diode accurately.

Zener diodes are available with breakdown voltages ranging from 2.7 V to over 150 V. When used in conjunction with a resistor (see Figure 35.6), a Zener diode can be used to provide voltage regulation, helping to maintain a specific voltage output as the current being drawn changes.

Key terms

Breakdown voltage the reverse bias voltage at which a diode begins to conduct. This feature is called the Zener effect, hence the name Zener diode.

Light-emitting diodes

A light-emitting diode (LED) consists of a p-n junction formed from a semiconductor material that releases particles of light energy called photons when electrons recombine with holes across the depletion layer. They are available in red, orange, amber, yellow, green, blue and white. Blue and white LEDs are much more expensive than the other colours.

Light-emitting diodes are produced in a variety of shapes and sizes. The colour of the plastic body is often the same colour as the light emitted by the diode. A purple plastic is usually used for infrared LEDs and a clear plastic used for blue LEDs. Remember, though, that the colour of an LED is determined by the semiconductor material not by the colouring of the plastic body in which the diode is housed.

LED technology has advanced greatly in the last few years. Light-emitting diodes are now used for many different applications, such as in traffic lights and on cars.

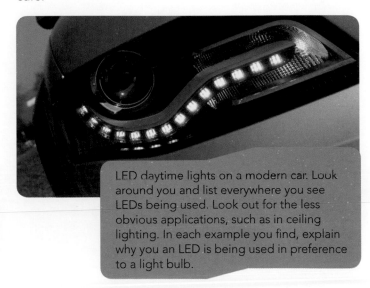

LED daytime lights on a modern car. Look around you and list everywhere you see LEDs being used. Look out for the less obvious applications, such as in ceiling lighting. In each example you find, explain why you an LED is being used in preference to a light bulb.

35.1.2 Transistors

A transistor also makes use of the p-n junction. It is simply three pieces of semiconductor material connected in a way that lets you control the flow of current. The very first bipolar transistor was made at Bell Laboratories in the USA by John Bardeen and Walter Brattain in 1947. Three years later William Shockley produced a much improved bipolar junction transistor. The transistor quickly started replacing valves in electronic circuits. It proved such an important invention that John Bardeen, Walter Brattain and William Shockley were awarded the Nobel Prize for physics in 1956.

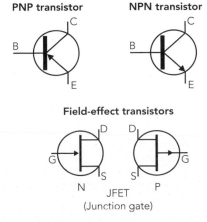

This is a replica of the first transistor. Can you imagine this being used in an electronic circuit today?

PNP transistor **NPN transistor**

Field-effect transistors

JFET
(Junction gate)

Figure 35.7: Transistor symbols

There are three common types of transistor: PNP transistors, NPN transistors and field-effect transistors (FETs). The symbols for each of these devices are shown in Figure 35.7.

PNP transistors

In a PNP transistor a thin layer of n-type material is sandwiched between two pieces of p-type material. The transistor has three connections – the connections to the two p-type pieces of material are called the emitter (E) and collector (C), and the connection to the n-type material is called the base (B).

By connecting the transistor to an electrical source in such a way that the base-emitter junction is forward biased and the base-collector junction is reverse biased it is possible to control the output from the collector (see Figure 35.8).

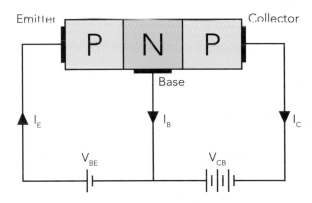

Figure 35.8: PNP transistor configuration

NPN transistors

As the name suggests, an NPN transistor consists of a thin layer of p-type material sandwiched between two pieces of n-type material. This transistor also has three connections, the emitter and collector connected to the n-type material and the base connected to the p-type material.

By connecting an electrical source so that the n-p base-emitter junction is forward biased and the p-n base-collector junction is reverse biased – this means connecting it to an electrical source in the opposite way to that of a PNP transistor – it is again possible to control the collector output.

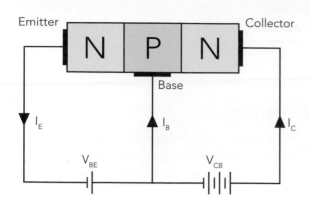

Figure 35.9: NPN transistor configuration

The PNP and NPN transistors are called bipolar transistors. Each bipolar transistor is a three-layer device constructed from two semiconductor diode junctions joined back to back, one forward biased and one reverse biased. The amount of collector output current is controlled by the amount of current flowing into the base connection. A bipolar transistor is therefore a current-operated device. An NPN transistor requires the base to be more positive than the emitter, while a PNP type requires the emitter has to be more positive than the base.

Field-effect transistors

The third type of transistor, the field-effect transistor (FET), is a voltage-operated rather than current-operated device. It uses the voltage applied to the input to control the output current. It works by means of the electric field generated by the input voltage, hence the term field-effect.

Unlike the bipolar transistor, the basic FET has no junctions. Instead it has a narrow channel of either

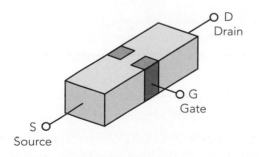

Figure 35.10: Field-effect transistor configuration

p-type or n-type silicon with connections at either end called the source (S) and the drain (D). By adding a third connection of n-type or p-type material to the channel, called the gate (G), you get the junction field-effect transistor (JFET).

Typical uses of transistors

Transistors are used in numerous applications. Their function depends both on how a transistor is connected in a particular circuit and how it is biased.

When choosing a transistor for use in a circuit that you are building, you need to consider how it functions as circuit voltages and currents are varied. You can obtain data sheets that explain the characteristics of each transistor. These data sheets contain graphs that show the characteristics of the transistor. For example, you will find that some transistors work in a linear manner. In other words, the graphs show a consistently varying current/voltage relationship across the operating range of the transistor. This type of transistor would be suitable for use in an amplifier or oscillator circuit.

Other transistor types can be heavily biased, such that in one state they don't conduct but then in another state they fully conduct. A transistor with these characteristics would work well in a circuit where its function is to operate as a switch. A device of this type is called a switching transistor, and it has many uses in different circuits. It can be used to directly switch a circuit or to control a relay that does the actual switching.

The most typical circuit configurations for a transistor are common-base and common-emitter configurations. In a common-base configuration the base terminal is connected to ground, and it is therefore common to both the emitter and the collector terminals. In a common-emitter configuration the base terminal of the transistor is the input, the collector terminal is the output and the emitter terminal is connected to ground and thus common to both, hence the name. Common-emitter configurations have been used for many years in circuits where the transistor is used as an amplifier.

Transistors can be used in both analogue and digital circuits. For example, they can be used to build a single-stage amplifier in analogue circuits (single-stage amplifier) or used within comparators and switches in digital circuits.

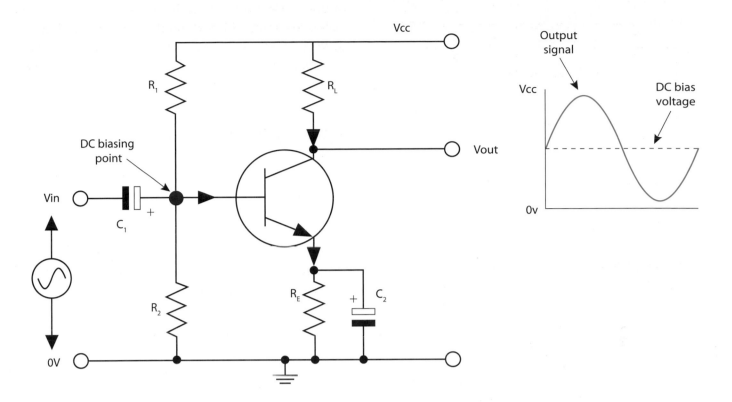

Figure 35.11: A single-stage amplifier circuit

Figure 35.11 shows a single-stage common-emitter transistor amplifier circuit. A small signal is applied to the base input and appears across the load resistance connected between the collector and the supply rail. Resistors R1 and R2 hold the base at a set voltage, called the bias point. The voltage developed across the load can be many times larger than the input voltage. The output signal is identical to the input signal but larger, hence the term amplifier.

A transistor with the right characteristics can be directly used as a small current switch. However, it is not advisable to force a transistor to switch large voltages or currents in case the transistor fails because it overheats or exceeds its maximum rating. You may also want to switch a number of circuits from just one transistor. It is common, therefore, to have the transistor operate a relay, which in turn does the actual switching. The relay contacts can easily switch any high power levels that might cause the transistor to fail. A relay can also be constructed with more than one set of contacts and so more than one circuit can be switched using a single transistor.

Figure 35.12 shows a simple transistor switch controlling a changeover relay. This transistor is used

to operate a relay whose contacts then perform a switching function. Using a relay in this way allows a large current to be switched using a low current input. The diode is included to protect the transistor.

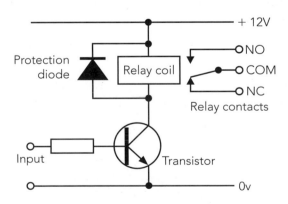

Figure 35.12: A simple switch circuit

When a transistor is used as a switch, it must be either 'off' or fully 'on'. In the fully on state the voltage across the collector and emitter is almost zero, so the transistor is said to be saturated because it cannot pass any more collector current.

Activity: Using transistors

The circuits in Figures 35.11 and 35.12 show a transistor being used for completely different functions. Both, however, involve a form of switching. Study these circuits carefully, and write down the term that identifies the type of switching that takes place in each circuit. As a hint, think back to the starter stimulus at the beginning of this chapter.

Discuss and write down why you think a diode is needed to protect the transistor in Figure 35.12. Now draw up a list of everyday applications where you might find a circuit such as that in Figure 35.12 being used.

Table 35.3: Standard logic gate symbols

Logic gate	ANSI/MIL	IEC	BS 3939
Buffer	▷	1	1
NOT	▷○	1	1○
AND	D	&	&
NAND	D○	&	&○
OR	D	≥1	≥1
NOR	D○	≥1	≥1○
XOR	D	=1	=1
XNOR	D○	=1	=1○

35.1.3 Logic gates

A **logic gate** is the term given to a circuit that performs a basic logic function. Logic gates are used extensively in computers. Table 35.3 lists the most common functions performed by logic gates. The table also gives the standard symbols used to denote logic gates in circuit diagrams. Three symbol conventions are shown American National Standards Institute (ANSI), International Electrotechnical Commission (IEC) and British Standards (BS 3939), and you might come across examples of all three symbols, because you may be using integrated circuits that have been produced in different parts of the world.

Key terms

Logic gates circuits designed to perform the basic logic functions, such as AND, OR and NOT, that are used in digital circuits and computers.

The signals used in logic gates are either off or on, hence the terms logic 0 or logic 1. This means that the inputs and output can only ever represent one of two states – a 0 (also known as a low state) or a 1 (known as a high state).

All the gates shown in the Table 35.3 provide logic functions except for the buffer. It always gives the same state on output as that on input. For example, a 1 on the input results in a 1 on the output. The buffer is often used to boost the current output of other gates.

The NOT gate (also called an inverter) and the buffer only have one input, while the basic AND, OR, NAND and NOR gates are available with up to eight inputs. The XOR and XNOR gates have two inputs.

Truth tables

An easy way of showing the function of a logic gate or circuit is to use a truth table. You simply list all the possible input combinations in the table (with one row for each combination), and note the resulting output state in the final column of the table. If you have a circuit consisting of several logic gates connected together, then you also show the output of each gate in your truth table to help you work out the eventual output result.

The AND gate

Let's look at the AND gate first. It only produces a logic 1 output when all its inputs are at a logic 1. Think of this in terms of needing a logic 1 on the first input AND a logic 1 on the second input, and so on, to get a logic 1 at the output – hence the name AND gate. This can be shown as a truth table (see Table 35.4).

Table 35.4: Truth table for a two-input AND gate

Input A	Input B	Output
0	0	0
0	1	0
1	0	0
1	1	1

The NAND gate

If you add a NOT function to the output of a gate, you simply get the opposite result. Instead of logic 0 you get a logic 1 output, and instead of a logic 1 you now get a logic 0 output. For example, the NAND gate, which we see in the 7400 logic chip below, performs the logic function NOT AND. In other words, it gives the opposite result for any input to that which would be obtained by the AND function. Table 35.5 shows its truth table.

Table 35.5: Truth table for a two-input NAND gate

Input A	Input B	Output
0	0	1
0	1	1
1	0	1
1	1	0

The OR gate

The OR gate is so called because you get a logic 1 output when you have a logic 1 on the first input OR a logic 1 on the second input OR a logic 1 on both inputs – hence the name OR gate. Table 35.6 shows the truth table for a two-input OR gate.

Table 35.6: Truth table for a two-input OR gate

Input A	Input B	Output
0	0	0
0	1	1
1	0	1
1	1	1

The exclusive OR gate

The exclusive OR gates – shortened to the XOR gate – is very similar to the OR gate. As long as one of the inputs is at a logic 1 and the other is at a logic 0, the output is always logic 1. However, when both inputs have the same logic state – that is, they are both at logic 1 or a logic 0 – the output is a logic 0. In other words, to produce a logic 1 output, only one of the two inputs has to be exclusively a logic 1 (see Table 35.7).

Table 35.7: Truth table for an XOR gate

Input A	Input B	Output
0	0	0
0	1	1
1	0	1
1	1	0

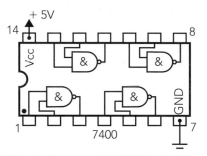

Figure 35.13: Circuit diagram of a 7400 logic chip

Case study: A 7400 logic chip

There are many different types of integrated circuits (ICs) used for processing digital signals. The simplest ones contain the basic logic gates we are exploring here. Because these simple gates have relatively few connections, it is possible to fit more than one of these gates into a single IC package.

The 7400 chip, shown here, contains four totally independent two-input NAND gates. The circuit diagram for this chip is shown in Figure 35.13. When designing a circuit using this chip, you can make use of all four gates or just one if that is all you need. You can even use one of the NAND gates to function as a

NOT gate by connecting its two inputs together. This is useful when you just need one NOT gate and only have a spare NAND gate available. In fact, you can make NOT, AND, OR and NOR functions using only NAND gates.

Look at the truth table for a NAND gate (see Table 35.5) and see if you can work out why it works as a NOT gate when its inputs are connected together.

Boolean expressions

You can write down the logic functions performed by logic gates. You do this using Boolean algebra. This is not as complex as it sounds because there are only three symbols to remember (see Table 35.8).

Boolean expressions and truth tables are simply mathematical descriptions of logic functions. It is possible to write out complex logic using Boolean algebra, though take care with your NOT symbols or you could end up with an expression that is more complex than it needs to be. Remember that if you NOT NOT an input called A, this is exactly the same as just writing A – in this case, two wrongs do make a right.

Table 35.8: Boolean functions

Symbol	Logical function	Examples	Meaning	Logic gate
·	AND	$A \cdot B$ $A \cdot B \cdot C$	A AND B A AND B AND C	two-input AND three-input AND
+	OR	$A + B$	A OR B	two-input OR
—	NOT	$\overline{A}$	NOT A	the output of a NOT gate
		$\overline{A \cdot B}$	A NAND B	two-input NAND
		$\overline{A + B + C}$	NOT (A OR B OR C)	three-input NOR

Did you know?

The inventor of Boolean algebra was called George Boole. He was the son of a shoemaker, and born in 1815 long before logic circuits were created. He wanted to show that true or false could be expressed as a formula.

Activity: Truth tables and Boolean algebra

1 See if you can work out some inverted output truth tables for yourselves. Produce truth tables for the NOR and XNOR two-input gates.

2 Now consider a gate that has more than two inputs. Produce truth tables for a four-input NAND gate and a four-input NOR gate.

3 Now write out the Boolean expressions for all these gates: two-input NOR, two-input XNOR, four-input NAND and four-input NOR.

35.2 Be able to build and test operational amplifier based analogue circuits

You will probably have seen electronic circuits built on printed circuit boards. The component positions are laid out in a neat manner and the connecting wires are already in place and etched from copper. Mounting holes are pre-drilled so that the components can simply be inserted into the board and soldered in place. The board may only have connections on one side, or you may come across more complex circuit boards with connections on both sides or even built into the board in different layers.

Circuit boards look neat and tidy. However, they are usually only produced after a circuit has been tested and passed for production. During its development, the circuit will have been built in a very simple and often untidy manner. Designers will often change their minds about the best approach, and they will want the flexibility to modify the circuit as it develops.

35.2.1 Building analogue circuits

There are several ways of building electronic circuits. Table 35.9 lists three common circuit construction methods. If you are at the early stages of designing a circuit, you will use a fairly simple method that allows you to easily change the circuit if it doesn't work properly. When the design is complete, you will probably want to build it using a printed circuit board.

When you first design a circuit, you should probably build and test it using the **breadboard** method to see if it works as expected. If it doesn't, you will want to change some of the wiring, and perhaps substitute components or even add extra components to the circuit. A printed circuit board is not suitable for this type of circuit development.

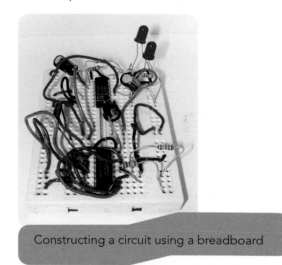

Constructing a circuit using a breadboard

Key terms

Breadboard construction a method that allows components and wiring to be easily changed if the circuit needs modifying. It is easy to access parts of the circuit with test probes. Used in the early stages of circuit design, breadboard construction is not suitable for permanent use or for large circuits with many components.

Table 35.9: Circuit construction methods

Method	Use	Advantages	Disadvantages
Breadboard	Suitable for the initial building and testing of circuits, before being built in a more permanent form	Changes can be easily and quickly made Components can be reused	Not suitable for permanent use Not suitable for circuits having more than about six active devices
Stripboard	Suitable for building circuits at the prototype stage	Cheaper and more permanent than breadboard as components are soldered in place Board can be reused a number of times	Copper tracks on the reverse of the board need to be cut with a knife Care is needed to avoid short circuits while soldering
Printed circuit board	Suitable for permanent circuit construction	All the connecting wires are etched onto the board, no loose wires Can be assembled by machine for mass production	Difficult to modify if changes are made to the circuit Difficult to change failed components, quicker to replace the complete board

Types of circuits

A circuit is a collection of electronic components connected together to perform a specific function. Some circuits only perform one function, others may perform several functions depending on their complexity. However, there are some basic circuits that form the individual electronic building blocks for circuit design. These are typical types of circuits that you will regularly come across in circuit design (their functions should be obvious from their names):

- oscillators
- filters
- comparators
- inverting/non-inverting amplifiers.

You can design a circuit by selecting individual components that are ideal for a specific application, such as a high frequency oscillator. Figure 35.14 shows a radio frequency oscillator circuit. You could build this from individual components, but most common basic circuits are now available as a single chip device. The device contains the complete circuit, except for the components that determine how it will operate. This device is called an integrated circuit. All you need to do is work out the values of the external components from the manufacturer's data sheets and you have a very stable and accurate circuit.

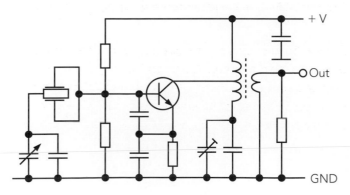

Figure 35.14: A radio frequency oscillator circuit

There are many different designs for each main type of circuit – oscillators, filters, comparators and amplifiers. Individual designs are tailored for specific applications. Some are named after their inventor, such as the Hartley and Colpitts oscillators. Some are designed using individual components while others are available as a single chip and use few external components.

Activity: Types of circuits

Working in pairs, use the internet to research oscillator, filter, comparator and amplifier circuits. Familiarise yourself with their properties, function and uses.

For each type of circuit, list at least three applications where you would expect to find such a circuit being used. For example, you would find an oscillator in a radio circuit. Now find other uses for an oscillator.

When you have researched all four types of circuits, compare your results with other groups to see how many different uses have been found for these basic circuit types.

PLTS

Building and testing circuits will help you develop your creative thinking skills.

35.2.2 Testing analogue circuits

Once you have designed a circuit, you need to build a prototype using breadboard or stripboard construction so that it can be tested. This is to ensure that the circuit does exactly what it is supposed to do. If it doesn't pass testing, then you modify the design, incorporate the changes into the prototype and test the circuit again. This process is repeated until your results prove that the circuit is working exactly as you intended.

Design requirements

Initially, a list of requirements will have been set out for a new circuit. When drawing up the circuit diagram, you will choose active components that are suitable for the circuit. If working on an oscillator for a radio receiver, you would choose small signal transistors designed to work at radio frequency. If designing a music amplifier, you would choose power transistors that work best at audio frequencies.

Formulae can be used to determine the correct values of other components, such as resistors and capacitors, to ensure that the circuit is correctly biased, that the input and/or output signals are at the correct level, and that no component burns out because it has too low a power rating. Most manufacturers issue data sheets for their devices. For a transistor, the data sheet will include a circuit showing how to use the device, with many of the component values already calculated for you. You can use this information to help design your own circuit.

When you have finished the design, you now have a circuit that should work in theory. Now you need to prove this by building and testing the circuit.

Did you know?

When a component gets warm its electrical characteristics could change, possibly affecting the operation of the circuit. Fortunately, this is no longer as big a problem as it once was, because manufacturers now 'burn in' components at the testing stage.

Testing performance

Testing the circuit doesn't mean just injecting a signal at the input and checking that there is a signal at the output. You need to measure the actual voltage levels at different parts of the circuit to ensure that the bias voltages are correct, that a component isn't taking too much current and that, above all, the circuit is stable and continues to work correctly after it has been powered up for a long time.

For example, a music amplifier may work perfectly well when it is first switched on, but it may start giving distorted sound after it has been on for an hour or so. Even though the voltage levels all measure correctly, one of the devices may be taking a bit too much current, getting warm and starting to distort the signal. This may not always be a problem with the circuit; you may just have a faulty component, but it still needs accurate testing.

Testing includes:

- recording voltages at different parts of the circuit and producing a data table or plotting a graph of the results
- measuring the **resonant frequency** and/or the **cut-off frequency** of a circuit, and comparing these with the design specification
- varying and recording the bias levels in a circuit to determine the point at which the circuit switches
- plotting the gain of a circuit by measuring input and output signal levels
- measuring frequency response to plot the **bandwidth** of a circuit.

Key terms

Resonant frequency the 'natural' frequency of a circuit. Circuit design often incorporates a means of slightly varying the resonant frequency to bring the circuit 'in-tune'.

Cut-off frequency the frequency at which the efficiency of a circuit drops off rapidly. There is often a lower and an upper cut-off point

Bandwidth a measure of the range of frequencies that a circuit can operate at or pass. This is the range between the lower and upper cut-off points.

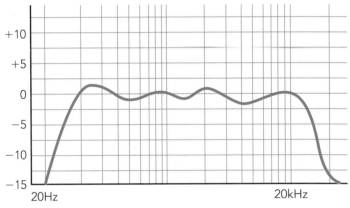

Figure 35.15: A frequency response graph produced during circuit testing

Figure 35.15 shows the frequency response measured during testing a circuit. Can you identify the lower and upper cut-off points of this circuit? What is the maximum frequency at which the circuit will work efficiently?

Assessment activity 35.1

P4 Study Circuits A and B. Choosing suitable components build and test the circuits and ensure that they work correctly. Carefully record your observations.

P1
P2 Record the type of diode used in both circuits, then produce a detailed explanation of the purpose of each diode. Record the type of transistor used and explain its operation in the circuit in Circuit B.

P2 Study the digital circuit diagram shown in Circuit C. Make a note of the type of transistor used and explain its operation in the circuit.

M1 Measure the minimum and maximum values for darkness and bright light of the light-dependent resistor (LDR) in Circuit B. Modify the circuit by selecting and changing just one of the components so that it can be made to operate over a different range of light levels.

Grading tips

P1 **P2** There are many basic circuits that use diodes and transistors where, simply put, the function of the device depends on how it is biased or connected into the circuit. By carefully studying the circuits you should be quickly able to identify what they do and the function of the diodes or transistor.

M1 Because a transistor requires few resistors to establish the bias point, it should be possible to alter when it begins to conduct by only altering the value of one component. Can you identify which one?

Circuit A

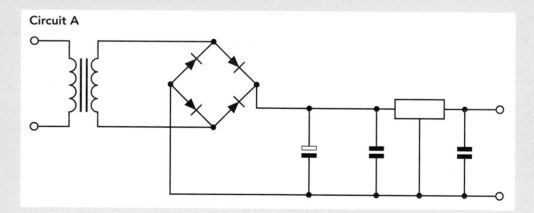

Circuit B

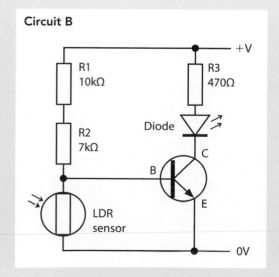

Circuit C

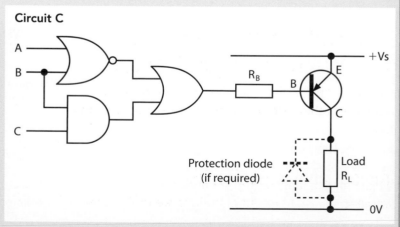

35.3 Be able to build and test combinational and sequential logic circuits

So far in this unit we have considered basic logic gates. There are many other types of logic gates and logic circuits – more complex than the simple ones we have covered so far – each having its own specific function. In this section we will look at the function and characteristics of some other types of logic circuits.

Logic circuits fall into two categories – **combinational logic** and **sequential logic**. In combinational logic circuits, the output is always a result of a particular set of input conditions. If one of those input conditions changes, then the output may or may not change, depending on the gate functions of the rest of the circuit.

It is easy to represent how a combinational logic circuit works using a truth table. Each possible input condition is shown in the table together with all of the other signal conditions as you work through the circuit. This is very useful when you are testing a circuit because you know exactly what signal should appear where.

Producing a truth table for sequential logic circuits is more difficult. These circuits can give an output state that is dependent both on the state of the inputs and on the state of any previous output condition. In other words, an output may be fed back and used as an input at an earlier point in the circuit. This makes sequential logic circuits suitable for use as data registers and counters, for example.

35.3.1 Building combinational and sequential logic circuits

Having become familiar with the simple logic gates, we can use this knowledge to put together actual logic circuits.

Combinational logic circuits

A simple logic circuit might contain three logic gates and three input variables. You show what output the circuit will give by working out its truth table.

Look at the circuit in Figure 35.16. The output of each individual gate is labelled and shown in the truth

> **Key terms**
>
> **Combinational logic** a logic circuit where the output is directly dependent on the state of the inputs. Used for circuits where you know the output you require for known input conditions.
>
> **Sequential logic** a logic circuit where the output is not only dependent on the state of the current inputs but also on previous input states. In other words, the circuit has a memory.

table in Table 35.10. See if you can follow this truth table. Note that this works out the expected output for the appropriate input condition for *each* gate. The completed table shows the expected output for all possible circuit input conditions.

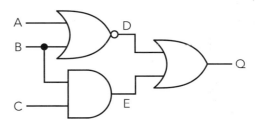

Figure 35.16: A three-input logic circuit

Table 35.10: Truth table for the circuit in Figure 35.16

A	B	C	D	E	Q
0	0	0	1	0	1
0	0	1	1	0	1
0	1	0	0	0	0
0	1	1	0	1	1
1	0	0	0	0	0
1	0	1	0	0	0
1	1	0	0	0	0
1	1	1	0	1	1

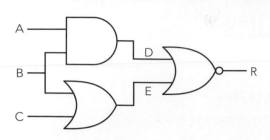

Figure 35.17: A simple logic circuit

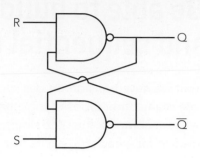

Figure 35.18: An R-S bistable circuit

Activity: Constructing a truth table

Now try one on your own. Study the logic circuit in Figure 3.17, identify each of the gates used in the circuit, and then produce a truth table for the circuit.

Compare your results with someone else's and see if you have worked everything out correctly.

Sequential logic circuits

Sequential logic circuits can be found in most electronic devices you have around the home. There are four common types of sequential logic circuits:

- R-S bistable
- JK bistable
- three-stage counter
- three-stage shift register.

An R-S bistable circuit has two stable outputs (hence the name bistable), which are almost always the opposite of each other, each feeding back to inputs. It

has two external inputs called reset (R) and set (S). An R-S bistable circuit is shown in Figure 35.18.

An R-S bistable is sometimes called a flip-flop because it flip-flops from one stable state to the other. Although the outputs are usually the opposite of each other, there is one unwanted condition where they could both be the same.

A JK bistable circuit is a modified version of the R-S bistable, which ensures that the two outputs are always the opposite of each other. The inputs are called J and K, plus there is a clock input to latch the output states.

A three-stage counter circuit is made up of three JK bistable circuits connected one after the other, the output from the first feeding the input of the second, and the output from the second feeding the third. They share a common clock signal so that an input signal eventually ripples through to the output after a certain number of clock pulses, hence the name counter.

A three-stage shift register (see Figure 35.19) is very similar to a three-stage counter. In operation, the circuit temporarily stores three bits of data and delays it by three clock periods from input to output. It is also called a serial-in/serial-out shift register.

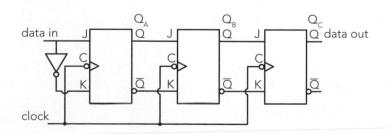

Figure 35.19: A 3-stage serial in/serial out shift-register

Logic families

Logic circuits belong to 'families' depending on the technology used to construct them. Early logic integrated circuits were the equivalent of circuits made from resistors, capacitors, transistors etc. This technology is called transistor-transistor logic (TTL). The circuits switched states very quickly, but consumed quite a bit of power in doing so.

Next came complementary metal oxide semiconductor (CMOS) technology, which uses considerably less power but with much slower switching speeds. Apart from the low power requirement, the other main advantage of CMOS devices is that they can work within a 3–15 volt supply range. In comparison, TTL technology requires a 5 volt power source.

Today's logic families have the low power characteristics of CMOS while being able to switch much faster than the early TTL devices. Logic integrated circuits (ICs), which process digital signals, can be split into two main groups (or families) according to their pin layout – the 74 series and the 4000 series. The main differences between the two are power requirements and operating frequency. The 74HC family will be the best choice for your projects. Table 35.11 lists some logic families in use today and gives a comparison of their characteristics.

Did you know?

There is a wide range of integrated circuits available, including logic gates, flip-flops, counters, registers and even display drivers. Care should be taken when handling the 4000 CMOS series as static electricity could damage the circuitry inside the circuit.

35.3.2 Testing of logic circuits

When you design and build a new logic circuit, you need to test that it functions as expected. These tests should be designed to establish that the circuit both satisfies the truth table and gives stable results.

Although it is in the order of nanoseconds, a logic circuit takes time to switch from one state to the other. Because digital signals are switching at high speeds, you must make sure that signals arrive at the input of a gate at the correct time and stay there for long enough for the output to switch to the appropriate state before the inputs change again, otherwise the output could switch back to (or remain in) its previous state.

Table 35.11: Comparison of logic families

Property	74LS series	74HC series	74HCT series	4000 series
Type	TTL low-power Schottky	High-speed CMOS	TTL-compatible high-speed CMOS	CMOS
Supply (+Vs)	5 V	2 V to 6 V	5 V	3 V to 15 V
Inputs	Pull up to logic 1 if unused	Very high impedance Connect unused inputs to 0 or 1 as appropriate	As 74HC but compatible with 74LS outputs	Very high impedance Connect unused inputs to 0 or 1 as appropriate
Outputs	Low current Use a transistor to switch higher currents	As 74LS but higher current, can source and sink 20 mA	As 74LS but higher current, can source and sink 20 mA	Very low current, can source and sink about 5 mA
Fan-out (per one output)	Can drive up to ten 74LS or fifty 74HCT inputs	Can drive up to fifty CMOS, 74HC and 74HCT or ten 74LS inputs	Can drive up to fifty CMOS, 74HC and 74HCT or ten 74LS inputs	Can drive up to fifty CMOS, 74HC and 74HCT or one 74LS inputs
Maximum frequency	35 MHz	25 MHz	25 MHz	1 MHz
Power usage	mW	µW	µW	µW

Transition time

The time it takes for the output of a gate to stabilise to the appropriate state for a given set of input conditions is called the transition time. If an input changes state in a shorter time than the transition time for that gate, then the gate cannot be relied upon to accurately function in accordance with its truth table. When testing a logic circuit that does not appear to function as the truth table says it should, use a logic analyser to follow the signals through the circuit and check that transition times are being observed.

Transition times become even more important when constructing and testing sequential logic circuits. Remember that in these types of circuits the output is often dependent on a previous output state. You must therefore always allow sufficient time for an output to stabilise *and* give it time to work its way through any gates and back into the circuit as an input before allowing it to switch again.

One method of recording a signal at a specific time is to use a clock signal to 'lock' or latch the signal at the input of a circuit. Once latched, the input can change states but it will not be registered until the next occurrence of a clock signal.

Digital test equipment

Switching, as the change from one state to the other is called, happens extremely quickly so it is not really possible to test or fault find digital circuits with test equipment that you would use for analogue circuits. A multimeter or an oscilloscope would not be much use because they are not capable of operating at digital switching speeds. Instead, you should use a logic probe, a logic analyser or a signature analyser.

A logic analyser is similar to an oscilloscope, but works much faster. It lets you compare many signals on the screen at the same time, and allows you to see what the circuit is doing and if an input or output is not switching correctly. You use a logic probe to test the logic state at the various gate inputs or outputs. A signature analyser is more sophisticated and can help you pinpoint which component is at fault.

In summary, the testing of logic circuits is accomplished through recording performance against design requirements, comparing the input and output states with the truth table, and through the use of suitable test equipment.

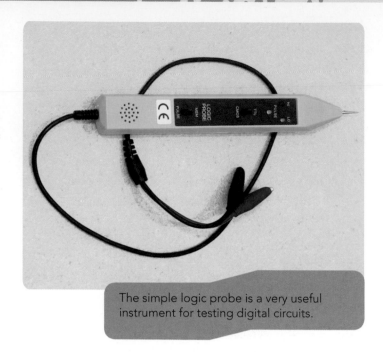

The simple logic probe is a very useful instrument for testing digital circuits.

35.3.3 Minimisation of logic circuits

Once you have designed a logic circuit, it is often possible to reduce the number of gates in the circuit and still get the same truth table result. This is called circuit minimisation, and it can be achieved using Boolean algebra, De Morgan's laws and Karnaugh maps.

Boolean algebra

There are several Boolean formulae or laws, but not all reduce the number of gates needed in a circuit. Some simply allow you to write the expression in an easier-to-understand way. However, you can use the distributive law to simplify a circuit as the examples below demonstrate.

For example, this logic expression uses three gates (two AND plus one OR):

$$(A \cdot B) + (A \cdot C)$$

This can be simplified using the distributive law to:

$$A \cdot (B + C)$$

This only uses two gates (one AND plus one OR).

Similarly this logic expression also uses three gates (two OR plus one AND):

$$(A + B) \cdot (A + C)$$

Again it can be simplified using the distributive law to:

A + (B · C)

This again allows the expression to be written using two gates (one OR plus one AND).

De Morgan's laws

These laws let you make similar simplifications. The first law can be written as:

$$\overline{A \cdot B} = \overline{A} + \overline{B}$$

Note that the left-hand side of this equation uses three gates (two NOT plus one AND), but the right-hand side uses just one NOR gate.

A second De Morgan law can be written as:

$$\overline{A + B} = \overline{A} \cdot \overline{B}$$

Again the left-hand side of this equation uses three gates (two NOT plus one OR), but the right-hand side uses just one NAND gate.

Activity: Circuit minimising

Study each expression that has been simplified using Boolean algebra and De Morgan's laws. For each expression, draw the logic circuit before minimising and the logic circuit after minimising to show that each results in fewer gates. Now produce truth tables for each circuit to prove that, in each case, the circuits before and after minimising give the same result.

Karnaugh maps

You can also use a Karnaugh map to simplify a circuit. A Karnaugh map is a pictorial way of grouping together expressions from a truth table with common factors. By doing this, you end up eliminating or discounting any unwanted variables. You can think of a Karnaugh map as just another way of drawing a truth table.

To show the relationship between a truth table and a Karnaugh map, let's consider an example. Table 35.12 shows a truth table for a simple two-input gate. The squares in a Karnaugh map are completed from the output values in the truth table, so for every row in the truth table, there will be one square in its corresponding Karnaugh map (see Figure 35.20).

The values of the two inputs are marked around the edge of the map, with A along the top and B down the left-hand side. The map is completed by filling in the squares – each square has the output value that is generated by the input states specified by the position of the square in grid. So, for example, the bottom right-hand square takes the output value when input A is 1 and input B is 1.

Table 35.12: Truth table for a two-input gate

Input A	Input B	Output
0	0	a
0	1	b
1	0	c
1	1	d

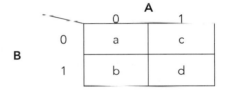

Figure 35.20: Karnaugh map for a two-input gate

We can use patterns in a Karnaugh map to help find simplified expressions for a logic function. To show how this is done, let's consider a very simple example. Figure 35.21 shows the Karnaugh map for the function OR (see Table 35.6 for the truth table for this function). Look for and circle adjacent pairs of 1s. There are two in this table: the horizontal loop represents the B and the vertical loop the expression A. So the resulting expression is:

A + B

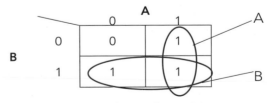

Figure 35.21: Karnaugh map for an OR gate

Now let's consider a more complicated example. Consider how you would produce a Karnaugh map for the truth table shown in Table 35.13.

Table 35.13: Truth table for a 3-input gate

A	B	C	Output
0	0	0	0
0	0	1	0
0	1	0	0
0	1	1	0
1	0	0	0
1	0	1	1
1	1	0	1
1	1	1	1

This has three inputs. So we need to do something slightly different to produce a Karnaugh map for this table. The approach that is taken to represent three inputs on a two-dimensional map is to group two of the inputs. As Figure 35.22 shows, the inputs A and B have been grouped together along the top of the map. Notice that the map still represents all possible combinations of inputs. There are eight rows in the truth table and eight squares in the map. Again look for adjacent pairs of 1s and write down the expression that these represent. Link the expressions together to produce an expression for the logic function represented by the truth table. In this case it is:

(A · B) + (A · C)

In practice you might actually use a combination of Boolean algebra, De Morgan's laws and Karnaugh maps to minimise a circuit. Because of their complexity, Karnaugh maps only tend to be used for reducing two-, three- and four-input circuits.

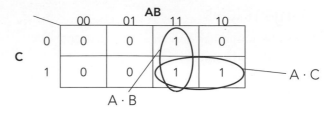

Figure 35.22: Karnaugh map for the truth table shown in Table 35.13

Activity: Testing logic circuits

Explain why it is necessary to use a truth table when testing a logic circuit, and demonstrate how you would use a logic probe to check a circuit against its truth table.

Assessment activity 35.2

The electronics company you work for designs logic circuits. Your employer has asked you to produce some material for new apprentices, which includes showing how to build and test some logic circuits to meet a new design requirement.

P3 Using the appropriate gate symbols, truth tables and Boolean expressions, explain the operation of:

a) a NAND gate

b) a NOR gate

c) an XOR gate.

P5 Work out the truth table for the circuit shown in Figure 35.23. Then build and test the circuit.

M2 Now modify the circuit so that its output matches the truth table shown in Table 35.14.

M3 Draw the logic diagram and truth table for this Boolean expression:

$$(A + B) \cdot (A + C)$$

Then minimise the expression, and produce the new logic diagram and truth table to prove your work.

P6 Build and test a simple three-stage shift register using integrated circuits.

D2 Compare and contrast the 74HC series and 4000 series logic families with reference to at least five characteristics.

Grading tips

M3 The laws of Boolean algebra will help you design and minimise logic circuits. Check your results by producing a new truth table for the minimised circuit and comparing it with the original circuit's truth table.

PLTS

Building and testing logic circuits will help you develop your creative thinking and self-management skills.

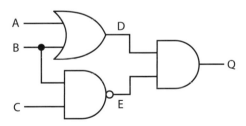

Figure 35.23: Circuit for the P5 task of assessment activity 35.2

Table 35.14: Truth table for the M2 task of assessment activity 35.2

Inputs			Outputs		
A	B	C	D	E	Q
0	0	0	0	1	1
0	0	1	0	1	1
0	1	0	1	1	0
0	1	1	1	0	1
1	0	0	1	1	0
1	0	1	1	1	0
1	1	0	1	1	0
1	1	1	1	0	1

35.4 Be able to use computer-based simulation software packages to construct and test the operation of analogue and digital circuits

It is very handy to be able to check if a circuit you are designing will work as intended before you actually build it. You can do this using simulation software on a computer. The program lets you build a virtual circuit and then test how it works when different input signals are applied. You can easily modify the circuit and see the effect of changing component values, supply voltages and other parameters.

Simulation software is available for both analogue and digital circuit design. Why do you think we need separate programs for developing digital and analogue circuits? You might find it useful to use the internet to research some of the main features of analogue and digital circuit simulation software.

35.4.1 Simulation of analogue circuits

Because there are so many things to consider when designing analogue circuits, it is a really good idea to use a simulation package to develop and test the design. There are many analogue circuit simulators available. Some can be downloaded free of charge from the internet, while the more sophisticated packages have to be purchased.

Using simulation software

Any simulation software package will have some similar features. It should have a library containing the symbols and function of all the common electronic components, such as resistors, capacitors, diodes and transistors. All you need to do is select the appropriate device, place it in the drawing area and allocate it a value. Some components, such as diodes and transistors, may already be pre-programmed with their working characteristics. Having placed all of your components on the drawing area, including any power source, you can connect the components together.

Once you have constructed your virtual circuit, you are ready to simulate the workings of the circuit. The simulator can be used to trace graphs from any part of the circuit, from which you can see how the circuit is working. If you want, you can add components or change component values to see how this affects the circuit. In this way, you can develop a circuit that works exactly how you intend without having to use a single real component. This saves both time and money.

You can use simulation software to draw complete circuits such as amplifiers, op-amps, rectifiers and even active filters. By changing signal source characteristics, you can see how the circuit will function under different conditions. You can check its gain or frequency response, test how hard you can drive it before distortion takes place, and so on. All of this can be done without ever picking up a soldering iron or handling an actual component.

A useful feature of most simulation software is that it can warn you if you have made a mistake in the design. For example, you could have accidentally connected two outputs together or forgotten to complete all of the connections to a component.

One of the most common general-purpose analogue simulation programs is called Spice, which stands for simulation program with integrated circuit emphasis. You can use it to check the design of your circuit and to predict how it will behave by tracing a graph of the signal at any point you choose in the circuit.

Did you know?

SPICE was developed at the Electronics Research Laboratory of the University of California. It is widely distributed and used. It has been continuously developed over the years, and there are now several different versions of the program.

35.4.2 Simulation of a digital circuit

There are also many popular computer-based simulation software packages available for designing and testing digital circuits. Most are simple to use. You simulate your circuit using the basic logic gates (such as NOT, AND, OR, NAND and NOR), sequential logic circuits (such as R-S and JK flip-flops) and the built-in range of digital integrated circuits (ICs).

You select the devices you require from the library, lay them out on the screen and add the connections. Because the software has been programmed with how the various gates and ICs work, you can easily simulate the circuit and see if it performs the function you require.

Signal traces

Digital simulation software is particularly useful, because it allows you to develop and test circuits for faults without using expensive analyser equipment. A simulator software package will draw traces of all the relevant signal paths so that, for example, you can check out the all-important transition times and confirm that, in theory at least, outputs and inputs have stabilised before being clocked into a gate.

The traces can also be used to analyse if an input stabilises too late, that the circuit is performing according to the original design requirements and whether any interference or 'noise spikes' are inadvertently triggering a gate and affecting how the circuit functions.

Assessment activity 35.3

You have been asked by your employer to demonstrate the potential of analogue and digital circuit simulation software to them. Use suitable simulation software to undertake these three tasks.

P7 Demonstrate the simulation of the construction and testing of an analogue circuit using at least three different types of components.

P8 Demonstrate the simulation of the construction and testing of a digital logic circuit containing at least three gates.

D1 Demonstrate the construction and testing of a simple amplifier circuit containing an operational amplifier. Now change the values of components that affect the gain of the circuit. Demonstrate and explain the revised performance of the circuit.

Grading tips

D1 Although simulation software is very useful, there are times when the simulated results do not exactly match the actual results. Did you consider this, especially when demonstrating the effects of changing the values of circuit parameters that affect the gain of a circuit?

PLTS

Using a simulator program will help you develop your creative thinking, self-management and ICT skills.

Did you know?

You can find screenshots of analogue and digital simulation software online – either do your own search or visit this book's Hotlinks (www.pearsonhotlinks. co.uk – see page ii).

WorkSpace

Susie Brown
Electronics engineer

I work for a well-known electronics company. Its product development division is involved in the design of both analogue and digital circuits. My team consists of five engineers, each with their own specialist skills in a different area of electronics.

I am responsible for contributing to the design specification. I design the digital part of the circuit, as logic and logic gates is my specialist field. However, I also organise the test schedules and supervise computer simulation tests of all circuits to ensure that they will perform as required.

There is also a management aspect to my job. I must ensure that circuit design, building and testing goes to schedule and is completed on time. I must then arrange for the circuit to go into production, once it has passed testing, and ensure that all the relevant paperwork is completed.

My typical day usually starts with a short meeting with the rest of the team to discuss progress on the current projects. We look at any problems that have cropped up and how to best deal with them. It might be that a part of a circuit doesn't work or is failing its test routine, or it could be a problem with putting a design into production.

I then move on to working on specific circuit design issues. I usually spend at least four hours a day using computer-based simulation software, ensuring that the circuit under design works as it should and feeding the results back to other members of the team. From this, I work out if any modifications are needed and then produce a test specification. The day is usually rounded off with a short progress report for my head of department.

The best thing about the job? I enjoy being able to come up with an idea and then turn it into a circuit that actually does something. I get a real buzz when I power up a design for the first time and it works. Mind you, sometimes it doesn't and then I have to go back over the design to see why. When I find the reason I feel pleased, because I now know it will work properly and it gives me a big sense of achievement. I like working with my team because we share our ideas and help each other if someone has a difficult problem.

Think about it!

1 What topics have you covered in this unit that provide you with the skills and background knowledge to become a good electronic circuit designer?

2 Think about what further skills might you need to develop. For example, you might need additional training on the use of simulation software in order to make your work more efficient.

Just checking

1   Define 'logic gate' and explain what a 0 and a 1 state equate to.
2   Describe these three basic methods of circuit construction: (a) breadboard, (b) stripboard and (c) printed circuit board.
3   Describe two methods that can be used to minimise a logic circuit.
4   What is a truth table?
5   What is the term for introducing a small impurity into a semiconductor?
6   Where would you use a Zener diode?
7   Draw a circuit diagram suitable for achieving half-wave rectification and one for full wave rectification.
8   Describe how an LED works.
9   What does R and S stand for in the term 'R-S bistable?'
10 How many connections does a transistor have?
11 Why is it important to handle the 4000 series CMOS family of integrated circuits with care?
12 Describe what happens at the depletion layer in a p-n junction when a forward biased voltage is applied.
13 Why is a multimeter an unsuitable instrument for use on a digital circuit?

edexcel

Assignment tips

• You may sometimes research a topic that appears to become too technical as you delve into it. Don't be put off; just keep looking for alternative sources and you will soon find a source that gives easier-to-follow information.

• Make sure that you familiarise yourself with the standard symbols for both analogue and digital components. This will come in useful and save time when building a circuit from its circuit diagram.

• Make accurate and detailed notes of any practical work carried out. The notes can contribute towards evidence that the work has been completed successfully. You can also record how you expect a circuit to function before simulating it, and then compare the simulation results with the results you predicted. Remember to also record the results of the simulation.

• There are many interactive tutorials on the internet that you can use to test your understanding of how logic gates work and how to simplify logic circuits and expressions. Check out how well you can use a Karnaugh map, for example, to minimise a logic circuit.

Appendix

Appendix 1: Abbreviations

2D – Two-dimensional

3D – Three-dimensional

AC – Alternating current

A/C – Across corners

A/F – Across flats

Alum – Aluminium

ASSY – Assembly

BDMS – Bright drawn mild steel

BH – Brinell hardness number

BS – British Standard

BSI – British Standards Institution

CAD – Computer aided design

CBORE – Counterbore

CHAM – Chamfer

CI – Cast iron

CIM – Computer integrated manufacturing

CL – Centreline

CNC – Computer numerical control

CRMS – Cold rolled mild steel

CRS – Centres

CSK – Countersunk

Dural – Duralumin

DTI – Dial test indicator

EMF – Electromotive force

FSH – Full service history

GPR – Glass-reinforced plastic

HDMI – High definition multimedia interface

HEX HD – Hexagon head

I/D – Inside diameter

ISO – International Organisation for Standardisation

LED – Light emitting diode

LDR – Light dependent resistor

MDF – Medium density fibreboard

MB – Megabyte

Ø – Diameter (preceding a dimension)

O/D – Outside diameter

PAT – Portable appliance testing equipment

PCB – Printed circuit board

Phos Bronze – Phosphor-bronze

PPE – Personal protective equipment

PVC – Polyvinylchloride

PTFE – Polytetrofluoroethylene

PE – Potential energy

PCD – Pitch circle diameter

R – Radius (preceding a dimension, capital only)

SG Iron – Spherodial graphite cast iron

SS – Stainless steel

SMT – Surface-mount technology

SWG – Standard wire gauge

THK – Thick

TIG – Tungsten inert gas welding

TYP – Typical or typically

USB – Universal serial bus

VA – Volt-amperes

VPN – Vickers pyramid hardness number

Appendix 2: Common symbols used in electrical and electronic circuit diagrams

Connected wires

Unconnected wires

Cell

Battery or cells

Earth

Fuse

Transformer

DC supply

AC supply

Lamp

Resistor

Variable resistor

Variable capacitor

Capacitor with pre-set adjustment

Voltmeter

Ammeter

Switch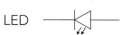

Capacitor

Capacitor (polarised)

LED

Diode

Amplifier

Bell

Buzzer

Transistor

Appendix 3: Common symbols used in hydraulic and pneumatic circuit diagrams

Basic symbols

Pump or motor

Measuring device

One square-pressure – control;

two or three adjacent squares – directional control

Conditioning apparatus such as a filter, heat exchanger, separator or lubricator

Spring

Restriction (affected by viscosity)

Restriction unaffected by viscosity

Direction of hydraulic fluid

Direction of pneumatic flow or exhaust to atmosphere

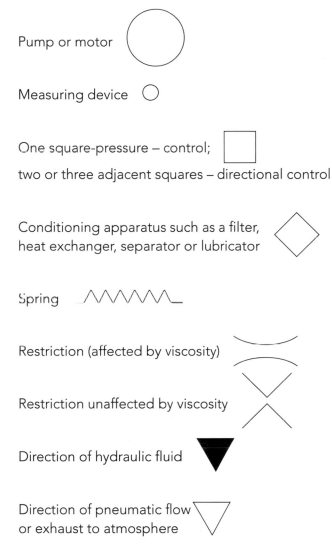

Energy conversion

Fixed capacity hydraulic pumps (convert hydraulic or pneumatic energy into rotary mechanical energy)

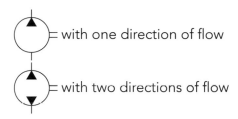

with one direction of flow

with two directions of flow

Motors (convert hydraulic or pneumatic energy into rotary mechanical energy)

Fixed capacity hydraulic motor with one direction of flow

Oscilliating motor with two directions of flow

Directional control valves (provide full or restricted flow by opening or closing of one or more flow paths)

Flow paths:

One flow path

Two closed ports

Two flow paths

Two flow paths and one closed port

Two flow paths with cross connection

One flow path in a by-pass position, two closed ports

Reservoirs

Reservoir open to atmosphere

 with inlet pipe above fluid level

 with inlet pipe below fluid level

with a header line

Pressurised reservoir

Filter or strainer

Non-return valve:

free (opens if the inlet pressure is higher than the outlet pressure)

spring loaded (opens if the inlet pressure is greater than the outlet pressure)

Sources of energy

Pressure source

Electric motor

Heat engine

Control methods

Muscular control:

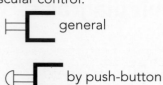 general

 by push-button

 by lever

controlled by pedal

Mechanical control:

 by plunger or tracer

 by spring

 by roller

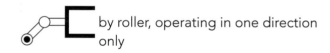 by roller, operating in one direction only

Appendix 4: Information on selected engineering materials

Ferrous metals

Material	Carbon content and other elements	Properties	Applications
Mild steel	0.1–0.3% carbon	Strong, fairly malleable and ductile	Wire, rivets, nuts and bolts, pressings, girders; general workshop material
Medium carbon steel	0.3–0.8% carbon	Strong and tough, can be hardened by heat treatment	Hammer heads, cold chisels, gears, couplings; impact-resistant components
High carbon steel	0.8–1.4% carbon	Strong, tough, and can be made very hard by heat treatment	Knives, springs, screw-cutting taps and dies; sharp-edged tools
Grey cast iron	3.2–3.5% carbon	Weak in tension but strong and tough in compression; very fluid when molten	Lathe beds, brake drums, engine cylinder blocks and cylinder heads, valve bodies
Stainless steel	Up to 1.0% carbon Up to 27% chromium Up to 0.8% manganese	Corrosion resistant, strong, tough	Food processing and kitchen equipment, surgical equipment, decorative items

Non–ferrous metals

Material	Composition	Properties	Applications
Copper	Almost pure	Very ductile and malleable; good conductor of heat and electricity; corrosion resistant	Electrical wire and cable, water pipes, soldering iron bits, alloying to make brasses and bronzes
Zinc	Almost pure	Soft, rather brittle, good fluidity when molten; corrosion resistant	Protective coating; alloying to make brasses
Tin	Almost pure	Very soft and malleable; highly corrosion resistant	Protective coating; alloying to make solders
Lead	Almost pure	Extremely soft, heavy and malleable; highly corrosion resistant	Roofs, lining of tanks; alloying to make solders
Aluminium	Almost pure	Soft, light and malleable; corrosion resistant	Wide range of domestic products and containers; wide range of alloys
Brasses	Up to 70% copper Up to 40% zinc Up to 1% tin	Very ductile with high copper content; very strong, tough, and fluid when molten with high zinc content	Tubes, pressings, forgings and castings for a wide range of engineering and marine components

Non-ferrous metals continued...

Material	Composition	Properties	Applications
Tin-bronzes	Up to 96% copper Up to 22% tin Up to 2% zinc Up to 0.5% phosphorus	Very malleable and ductile with high copper content; very strong, tough and fluid when molten with high tin content	Springs, electrical contacts, bearings, gears, valve and pump components
Aluminium alloys	Up to 97% aluminium Up to 5% silicon Up to 3% copper Up to 0.8% magnesium Up to 0.8% manganese	Ductile, malleable with good strength, and good fluidity when molten	Electrical power lines, ladders, aircraft and motor vehicle components, light sand and die castings

Common thermoplastic materials

Common name	Properties	Applications and uses
Low-density polythene (LDPE)	Tough, flexible, solvent resistant: degrades if exposed to light or ultraviolet radiation	Flexible squeeze containers, packaging, piping, cable and wire insulation
High-density polythene (HDPE)	Harder and stiffer than low-density polythene, with higher tensile strength	Food containers, pipes, mouldings, tubs, crates, kitchen utensils, medical equipment
Polypropene (PP)	High tensile strength and a high melting point; can be produced as a fibre	Tubes, pipes, fibres, ropes, electronic components, kitchen utensils, items of medical equipment
PVC	Can be made tough and hard or soft and flexible; solvent resistant; soft form tends to harden with time	When hard, window frames, piping and guttering; when soft, cable and wire insulation, upholstery
Polystyrene	Tough, hard, rigid but somewhat brittle; can be produced as a light cellular foam; liable to be attacked by petrol-based solvents	Foam mouldings used for packaging and disposable drinks cups; solid mouldings. Used for refrigerator mouldings and other appliances in its solid form
Perspex	Strong, rigid, transparent, but easily scratched; easily softened and moulded; can be attacked by petrol-based solvents	Lenses, corrugated sheets for roof lights, protective shields on machinery, aircraft windows, light fittings
PTFE	Tough, flexible, heat-resistant, highly solvent resistant; has a waxy, low-friction surface	Bearings, seals, gaskets, non-stick coatings for kitchen utensils, tape
Nylon	Tough, flexible and very strong; good solvent resistance, but does absorb water, and deteriorates with outdoor exposure	Bearings, gears, cams, bristles for brushes, textiles
Terylene	Strong, flexible and solvent resistant; can be made as a fibre, tape or sheet	Reinforcement in rubber belts and tyres, textile fibres, recording tape, electrical insulation tape

Common thermosetting plastics

Common name	Properties	Applications and uses
Bakelite	Hard; resistant to heat and solvents; good electrical insulator and machinable, colours limited to brown and black.	Electrical fittings and components, vehicle distributor caps, heat resistant handles
Formica	Similar properties to bakelite but naturally transparent, and can be produced in a variety of colours	Electrical fittings, bathroom fittings, kitchenware, trays, laminates.
Melamine	As above, but harder, and with better resistance to heat; very smooth surface finish when moulded or machined	Electrical equipment, tableware, control knobs, handles, laminates
Epoxy resins	Strong, tough, good chemical and thermal stability; good electrical insulator, good adhesive	Glass and carbon fibre reinforced panels for vehicles, flooring material, laminates, adhesives
Polyester resins	Strong, tough; good wear resistance, and resistance to heat and water. Good electrical insulator	Boat hulls, motor panels, aircraft parts, fishing rods, skis, laminates

Appendix 5: SI unit prefixes and symbols

Multiple	Prefix	Symbol
10^{12}	tera	T
10^{9}	giga	G
10^{6}	mega	M
10^{3}	kilo	k
10^{2}	hecto	h
10^{1}	deka	da
10^{-1}	deci	d
10^{-2}	centi	c
10^{-3}	milli	m
10^{-6}	micro	μ
10^{-9}	nano	n
10^{-12}	pico	p
10^{-15}	femto	f
10^{-18}	atto	a

Appendix 6: SI base and derived units

SI base units

Base quantity	Name	Symbol
length	metre	m
mass	kilogram	kg
time	second	s
electric current	ampere	A
temperature	kelvin	K
amount of substance	mole	mol
luminous intensity	candela	Cd

SI derived units

Physical quanity	Name	Symbol
Electric charge	coulomb	C
Electric capacitance	farad	F
Electrical inductance	henry	H
Frequency	hertz	Hz
Energy, work, amount of heat	joule	J
Illuminance	lux	Lx
Force, weight	newton	N
Electric resistance	ohm	Ω
Pressure, stress	pascal	Pa
Electric conductance	siemens	S
Magnetic flux density	tesla	T
Electromotive force	volt	V
Power, radiant flux	watt	W
Induction magnetic flux	weber	Wb

Appendix 7: Greek alphabet

Alpha	A	α
Beta	B	β
Gamma	Γ	γ
Delta	Δ	δ
Epsilon	E	ε
Zeta	Z	ζ
Eta	H	η
Theta	Θ	θ
Iota	I	ι
Kappa	K	κ
Lambda	Λ	λ
Mu	M	μ
Nu	N	ν
Xi	Ξ	ξ
Omicron	O	o
Pi	Π	π
Rho	P	ρ
Sigma	Σ	σ
Tau	T	τ
Upsilon	Y	υ
Phi	Φ	φ
Chi	X	χ
Psi	Ψ	ψ
Omega	Ω	ω

Glossary

2D two dimensions; two dimensional

3D three dimensions; three dimensional

Amplitude the maximum and minimum ordinate values

Annotations written notes and numerical information added to a drawing

Arithmetic mean one measure of the average a set of data, calculated by summing all the data and dividing by the number of observations

Articles of association regulations which govern the relationships between shareholders and directors of a company, including voting rights, issuing of shares, declaration of dividends

Atom consists of a nucleus, made up of protons and neutrons, along with electrons which orbit the nucleus

Audit trail a series of records so that you can go back and track what occurred

Balance of probability a less robust standard of proof than in criminal law, where cases must be proved beyond reasonable doubt

Bandwidth a measure of the range of frequencies that a circuit can operate at or pass. This is the range between the lower and upper cut-off points

Bank overdraft a loan facility where a company's bank account is allowed to be 'in the red' up to an agreed maximum. This allows a business to borrow money to pay for raw materials and other expenses before it generates income from selling products

Base the number or variable which is raised to a power

Bottom line the final line in a profit and loss account. In other words, how much profit a business makes

Breadboard construction a method that allows components and wiring to be easily changed if the circuit needs modifying. It is easy to access parts of the circuit with test probes. Used in the early stages of circuit design, breadboard construction is not suitable for permanent use or for large circuits with many components

Breakdown voltage the reverse bias voltage at which a diode begins to conduct. This feature is called the Zener effect, hence the name Zener diode

Cabinet projection a method in which one true face is drawn and the receding lines are drawn half their true length at an angle of 45° to horizontal

Capacitance a measure of the amount of electrical charge that a capacitor can store between the plates for a given voltage

Capital money used to purchase equipment and which is effectively tied up in the business

Capital equipment the large (and often expensive) machinery, such as a machine tool, required for production. The value of capital equipment is shown in the company balance sheet, but reduced each year to allow for depreciation. Depending on the type of equipment, its value is written off after a given length of time when it is assumed that the equipment is obsolete

Cavalier projection a pictorial method in which one true face is drawn and the receding lines are drawn their true length at an angle of 45° to horizontal to give an impression of depth

Centroid the centre of area of a plane shape. The position of the centroids of regular shapes can be found in reference texts

Combinational logic a logic circuit where the output is directly dependent on the state of the inputs. Used for circuits where you know the output you require for known input conditions

Common law based on the judgements made in past cases, called precedents

Commutator the part of the armature in an electric motor where the brushes make electrical contact. Its purpose is to switch the current flowing through the windings as the armature turns in such a manner that the magnetic force created always keeps the armature moving

Compensation an amount of money paid to an injured person by an employer (or the employer's insurance company) in the event that the accident resulted from the employer's negligence

Compound a collection of molecules of the same type

Concentricity if two (or more) circular features share a common centre point, they are said to be concentric

Conductors materials with atoms in which the electrons are loosely bound to the nucleus and can therefore easily move from one atom to another, resulting in good current flow

Contact potential the voltage that builds up at the p-n junction that stops the movement of electrons and holes across it

Conventions accepted ways of representing the features of an engineering component in a drawing

Coplanar lying in one plane. Coplanar forces can therefore be represented in two dimensions

Creep the tendency of a material to slowly deform under the influence of stress, time and elevated temperature

Cut-off frequency the frequency at which the efficiency of a circuit drops off rapidly. There is often a lower and an upper cut-off point

Deep drawing a metal forming process in which sheet metal is drawn into a forming die by a mechanical punch

Depletion layer the area at the junction of p-type and n-type material that contains no free electrons or holes because they have all joined together

Dimensions the actual measurements (usually in mm) of the object or feature being drawn

Drawing standards a publication that specifies how an engineering drawing should be produced so that there is no ambiguity in its presentation

Duty of care acting towards others in a manner that a reasonable person would adopt

Earth's magnetic field the lines of magnetic force radiating from the polar areas surrounding the earth. The north magnetic pole is offset from the actual North Pole and moves gradually over time. Because of this, the earth's magnetic field is not symmetrical

Eddy currents swirls or whirlpools of current induced in the body of a solid conductor resulting in a force opposing the force creating them. These currents can be reduced by cutting slots in the solid conductor

Elasticity an elastic material is one that can return to its original shape after the removal of the forces that made it deform. Materials that display this property after relatively large forces are said to have high elasticity

Electric field the area surrounding electrically charged particles. The electric field strength is also called the potential gradient

Electronic circuit a collection of electronic components, such as transistors, diodes, resistors and capacitors, connected together to provide a particular function, such as amplifying a signal

Electrostatic field the field of energy that exists between two objects of opposite polarity

Element a collection of atoms of the same type

Emergency lighting illuminated green and white signs indicating emergency evacuation routes

Energy value the amount of potential energy of a specified amount of fuel that is released as heat when the fuel is combusted. So when a fuel is used in a system such as a heat exchanger, the energy value is a measure of the input energy. It is also referred to as the calorific value of a fuel.

Entity a discrete part of a drawing. It could consist of a single line, arc, piece of text, a dimension or the whole drawing itself

Equiaxed crystals crystals that have axes of approximately similar length

Equilibrant the force that when applied to a system of forces will produce equilibrium

Exponential function a mathematical function that includes the Euler constant (e)

Expert knowledge specialist knowledge about a subject gained through education and training

Extent of risk the product of the number of persons likely to be affected by the hazard and the severity of the damage

Factory gate price the price of a product when bought direct from the manufacturer. The shop price will be much higher because it has to take account of distribution costs and retail overheads. Factory gate price = production cost + manufacturer's profit margin

Fatigue structural damage that occurs as the result of cyclical loading

Ferromagnetic material a metal which has molecules that can be easily lined up to turn it into a magnet

Ferrous metal a metal that has iron as its major constituent

Field winding turns of a conductor wound around the pole core so that when a current is passed through this conductor an electromagnet is created, avoiding the need for a permanent magnet

Finite element analysis computerised numerical modelling of the stresses and deformations produced in components when subject to external loading

First aid treatment for preserving life and minimising consequence of injury or illness until medical help arrives and treatment for minor injuries that do not require professional medical attention

Fixtures and fittings items like electrical wiring, lighting, doors, ventilation systems, windows, carpets etc

Fluid any material in liquid or gas form

Force the effort that is applied to a material externally

Force system the forces acting on a body

Galvanometer a very sensitive ammeter used to measure tiny currents flowing through a circuit

Hard copy a physical (not electronic) version of a document

Hazard something with the potential to cause harm, such as machinery being used by an untrained person

Heat treatment a process that changes the mechanical properties of a metal by using controlled heating and cooling

Hydraulic a system that operates using compressed oil

Index see *Power*

Induction programme introductory sessions and training that are provided to employees in the first few days of starting at a new place of work

Inertia the resistance of a body that must be overcome in order to accelerate it. The accelerating force must overcome the inertia force

Ingot a block of metal cast into a shape which can be used for further processing

Insulators materials with atoms in which the electrons are very firmly bound to the nucleus, resulting in little or no current flow

Interstice a small intervening space between atoms

Ion an atom that has either a positive (cation) or negative (anion) electric charge through losing/gaining an electron

Isometric projection a pictorial method in which the receding lines are drawn at an angle of 30° to the horizontal to give an impression of depth

ISP an internet service provider

Latent heat heat energy causing a change of state of a substance without a change in temperature

Line of action the direction in which a force is acting.

Logic gates circuits designed to perform the basic logic functions, such as AND, OR and NOT, that are used in digital circuits and computers

Magnetic flux the number of lines of force, or the amount of magnetic field, produced by a magnetic source

Magnetic flux density the amount of magnetic flux per unit area of a magnetic material, measured in tesla

Magnetism the property of how a material responds when subjected to a magnetic field

Malleability the ability of a metal or other material to be hammered or beaten to shape (from the Latin word *malleus* meaning hammer)

Manual handling the process of transporting or supporting a load (including lifting, putting down, pushing, pulling, carrying, or moving) by hand or by bodily force

Mean time between failure (MTBF) the average length of time a component or system can be expected to work before it fails. The higher the MTBF, the more reliable the product

Median the middle value in a data set when it is arranged in order of magnitude

Memorandum of association a document which governs the relationship between a business and the outside world. It details the purpose of the business and how it operates

Mind map a spider's web of thoughts, words or ideas around a central key word or idea written on paper, a flipchart or an interactive whiteboard

Minutes a written summary of the words spoken and a record of any decisions taken at a meeting. They are usually annotated with action points that allocate tasks to specific people

Mode the value that occurs most frequently in a set of data

Molecule a particle formed when different types of atom bond together

Moment the tendency of a force to rotate the object on which it acts

Momentum a measure of the impetus of a moving object. Its value is calculated by multiplying the mass of the object by its velocity

Multimeter an instrument that can measure electrical and electronic parameters in AC and DC circuits, such as voltage, current and resistance. Different settings can be selected to provide a range of readings on a single analogue or digital display

Negligence tort, or wrong doing, of one person (or organisation) against another

Node a junction or connection point

Nominal the stated size of some dimension. In reality, parts cannot be manufactured to a given nominal measurement, so they are produced within some specified tolerance

Normal reaction one where its direction is perpendicular to a given surface

Oblique projection a method that uses a selected true face of an object to draw the width and height and then projects lines backwards from the object's principal points at an angle of 45° to give the impression of depth or a third dimension

Open source freely available

Orthographic projection a pictorial method that utilises two or more views of the object. Each of the selected views shows a true face. The number of views required will depend on the complexity of the object being drawn. No illusion of depth is given in orthographic projection

Patent prevents competitors from copying the ideas and features that make something work. Patents are valid for a fixed period of time

Percentage points the difference between two percentages

Period the length of one cycle

Permit to work a document issued to control entry into confined spaces. These are usually issued by a senior engineer for a single activity to a competent engineer, who carries out the work

Permittivity of free space the ratio of D/E for a field established in a vacuum, also called the free space constant

Phase the physically distinctive form of a substance – solid, liquid or vapour

Pitch in engineering, pitch is a measure relating to distance. For example, the distance between drilled holes in a machined component would be described as the pitch

Pneumatic a system that operates using compressed air

Potential difference the difference in electrical energy (measured in volts) that exists between two points in a circuit. This is usually referred to as voltage

Power the number or variable to which the base is raised

Profile a short review which contains key facts about a person, object or process

Pythagora's theorem the square on the hypotenuse of a right-angled triangle is equal to the sum of the squares on the other two sides

Quality assurance a management tool that provides confidence that quality requirements are being met. A quality assurance (QA) system consists of procedures to maintain (and sometimes improve) quality standards

Relative permittivity the insulating power of the dielectric compared with that of a vacuum

Resonant frequency the 'natural' frequency of a circuit. Circuit design often incorporates a means of slightly varying the resonant frequency to bring the circuit 'in-tune'

Resultant the force that represents the combined effect of a force system

Ringing the effect observed when the change of amplitude direction is not cleanly executed. This usually indicates that a circuit component is failing or not working to specification, possibly due to incorrect biasing. This is often most noticeable on the edges of a square waveform, where switching should be 'instant'

Risk the combination of the likelihood that the hazard will cause damage or harm and the severity of the resulting injury

Root the root of a number is the number which when multiplied by itself the number of times it is rooted, gives the original number. For example, the square root of 4 ($\sqrt{4}$) is 2, because 2 multiplied by itself twice is 4, i.e. $2 \times 2 = 4$. The cube root of 125 ($\sqrt[3]{125}$) is 5, because 5 multiplied by itself three time is 125, i.e. $5 \times 5 \times 5 = 125$

Royal Assent the final procedure in enacting UK legislation. When proposed legislation (also called a bill) has completed all its parliamentary stages it receives Royal Assent from the monarch (Queen). This is the final stamp of approval.

Scatter a measure (or picture) of how data is spread between the largest and smallest values

Schematic a representation of a component using a graphic symbol

Sensible heat heat energy causing a change in temperature of a substance

Sensor a device which receives and responds to a signal/input

Sequential logic a logic circuit where the output is not only dependent on the state of the current inputs but also on previous input states. In other words, the circuit has a memory

Share issue the process of selling shares in a company on the stock market to raise capital for investment in the business

SMEs small and medium-sized enterprises – businesses employing less than 250 people (EU definition)

Solid solution the solid-state of a solution that retains the crystal structure of the solvent

Solute a substance that is dissolved in another substance (or solvent)

Solution a mixture of two or more substances dissolved in each other

Solvent a liquid, solid or gas that dissolves another liquid, solid or gaseous substance

Specification technical requirements that a product or service must conform to

Statutory instrument secondary legislation (law) produced by an executive authority under powers granted by the legislative authority (Parliament)

Strain the physical movement or extension of a component as a result of an applied stress

Stress the amount of force exerted per unit area within the material

Subtended the angle between two radii

Superheated steam a colourless (dry) gas at a temperature above the boiling point of the water

Support reactions the forces that are maintaining the equilibrium of a beam or structure

Surface coating substances applied to a surface after it has been machined, such as paint or chromium plating

Surface finish the roughness and waviness of a surface; also referred to as surface texture

Symbol something used to represent something else by association; for example ω represents angular velocity, © means copyright

Synthesise combining ideas, objects or data to produce a complex whole

Tangent a straight line that just touches the outside edge of a curve without cutting across it

Tangential a line or arc that touches the circumference of a circle at one point only is said to be tangential to (or a tangent of) the circle. The line or arc does not pass through the circumference

Template a document that has topic headings and page layouts already set up

Test report a report of a performance test conducted on a product to see if it conforms to its specification. If it does, then the product can be signed off as fit for purpose

Tolerance an allowable deviation from the desired size (no size can be achieved exactly)

Transposing the mathematical process of changing the subject of an equation

Turnover all the income that a business generates in a year

Valence electrons the electrons in the outermost shell (known as the valence shell) that orbit the nucleus

Variate a particular value of a variable

Viscosity a measure of the resistance of a fluid to a shear stress

Working voltage the voltage that can safely be applied to the capacitor without the insulating material (dielectric) breaking down

Young's modulus a measure of the 'stiffness' or 'rigidity' of a material

Index